CONGRESS RECONSIDERED

CONGRESS RECONSIDERED

Seventh Edition

Edited by

LAWRENCE C. DODD
University of Florida

BRUCE I. OPPENHEIMER
Vanderbilt University

A Division of Congressional Quarterly Inc.
Washington, D.C.

CQ Press
A Division of Congressional Quarterly Inc.
1414 22nd St. N.W.
Washington, DC 20037
(202) 822–1475; (800) 638–1710

www.cqpress.com

♾ The paper used in this publication meets the minimum requirements of the American National Standard for Information Sciences–Permanence of Paper for Printed Library Materials, ANSI Z39.48-1992.

Printed in the United States of America

04 03 02 01 00   5 4 3 2 1

Library of Congress Cataloging-in-Publication Data

In process.

ISBN 1-56802-487-8

Contents

✧ ✧ ✧

Tables, Figures, and Boxes   vii
Contributors   xi
Preface   xv

Part I Patterns and Dynamics of Congressional Change

1. The New World of U.S. Senators   1
   Barbara Sinclair

2. A House Divided: The Struggle for Partisan Control,
   1994–2000   21
   Lawrence C. Dodd and Bruce I. Oppenheimer

3. What the American Public Wants Congress to Be   45
   John R. Hibbing and James T. Smith

Part II Elections and Constituencies

4. Voters, Candidates, and Issues in Congressional Elections   67
   Robert S. Erikson and Gerald C. Wright

5. The Money Maze: Financing Congressional Elections   97
   Paul S. Herrnson

6. The Gender Gap in the House of Representatives   125
   Rosalyn Cooperman and Bruce I. Oppenheimer

7. *Keystone* Reconsidered   141
   Morris P. Fiorina

Part III Committee Politics and Institutional Change

8. The Evolution of the Committee System in Congress   163
   David T. Canon and Charles Stewart III

9. Committee Theories Reconsidered   191
   Tim Groseclose and David C. King

10. Committees, Leaders, and Message Politics   217
    C. Lawrence Evans

Part IV Congressional Leadership and Party Politics

11. The Dynamics of Party Government in Congress   245
    Steven S. Smith and Gerald Gamm

12. The Logic of Conditional Party Government: Revisiting the
    Electoral Connection   269
    John H. Aldrich and David W. Rohde

Part V Congress, the Executive, and Public Policy

13. Congress, the Executive, and the Production of
    Public Policy: United We Govern?   293
    Sarah A. Binder

14. Congress and Foreign Policy at Century's End:
    Requiem on Cooperation?   315
    I. M. Destler

Part VI Congress and Political Change

15. The Twentieth-Century Congress   335
    Joseph Cooper

16. Congress and the Emerging Order: Assessing the
    2000 Elections   367
    Lawrence C. Dodd and Bruce I. Oppenheimer

17. Re-Envisioning Congress: Theoretical Perspectives
    on Congressional Change   389
    Lawrence C. Dodd

Suggested Readings   415
Index   429

Tables, Figures, and Boxes

✧ ✧ ✧

Tables

1-1   The Increase in Filibusters and Cloture Votes, 1951–1998   6

1-2   The Increasing Frequency of Extended Debate–Related Problems   9

1-3   Where Major Measures Failed   14

3-1   Approval of Congress by Various Demographic Groups, 1998   60

3-2   Causes of Approval of Congress, 1998   62

4-1   Incumbents Facing Quality Challengers in the 1998 House Elections   80

4-2   Regression of 1998 Democratic Vote on 1998 Candidate Ideology, 1996 District Presidential Vote, and 1998 Candidate Spending, for Incumbent Races   84

4-3   Voter Perceptions of the Ideology of Their House Representatives   89

5-1   PAC Contributions in the 1998 Congressional Elections   111

5-2   The Allocation of PAC Contributions to House Candidates in the 1998 Elections   112

5-3   The Allocation of PAC Contributions to Senate Candidates in the 1998 Elections   113

5-4   The Allocation of Party Money in the 1998 Congressional Elections   114

6-1   Women in the House of Representatives by Party, 97th–106th Congresses (1981–2001)   126

6-2   Women Candidates by Party and Seat Status, 1982–1998   128

6-3   Women Candidates as a Percentage of Total Party Candidates,
       1982–1998   129

6-4   District Partisanship Averages, 1982–1998   131

6-5   Votes Received by Democrats in Contested House Elections,
       1982–1998   133

8-1   House Committees Appointed with More Than One Member
       from a Single State, 1st–45th Congresses (1789–1879)   178

8-A   Creation of House Standing Committees, 1st–45th Congresses
       (1789–1879)   183

8-B   Creation of Senate Standing Committees, 1st–45th Congresses
       (1789–1879)   185

9-1   Committee Institutions and Their Agreement with the
       Theories   198

10-1   Relevance of Major House Bills to Party Messages, 1999   225

12-1   Policy Opinions of Voters and Major Party
       Activists, 1996   278

13-1   Size of the Policy Agenda, 80th–104th Congresses
       (1947–1997)   296

13-2   Determinants of Policy Gridlock, 1951–1996   307

15-1   Indicators of Party Strength   336

15-2   Indicators of Presidential Leadership   337

15-3   Indicators of Societal Change   347

15-4   Indicators of Political Change   348

16-1   Distribution of Senate Seats, 1994–2000, and
       Seats to Be Contested in 2002 (by Party and Region)   374

16-2   Distribution of House Seats, 1994–2000
       (by Party and Region)   375

Figures

2-1   Ebb and Flow Patterns in House Membership, 83d–106th
       Congresses   33

3-1   Approval of Congress, 1975–1999   47

3-2   Approval of the Federal Government and Its Parts, 1998   50

3-3   Confidence in Political Institutions, 1966–2000   51

3-4   Evaluations of Congressional Referents, 1992   54

3-5   Evaluations of the Parties in Congress, 1994–1999   56

4-1   Democratic House Seats and Vote Share, 1952–1998   69

4-2   Partisanship and House Seat Shares, 1952–1998   70

4-3   Spending Preferences for Democratic and Republican
        Presidential Candidates, 1998   74

4-4   Party Differences among House Candidates on Selected
        Issues, 1998   75

4-5   Distributions of Candidate Ideology by Party, 1998   76

4-6   The Incumbency Advantage in the House, 1998   79

4-7   Republican and Democratic 1998 Candidate Ideology
        (by District Presidential Vote in 1996)   83

4-8   Ideology and the House Vote, 1998   86

4-9   Winner's Ideology by District Presidential Vote   88

7-1   Decomposition of Midterm House Elections (Contested and
        Uncontested Seats)   147

7-2   Decomposition of Presidential-Year House Elections (Contested
        and Uncontested Seats)   148

7-3   Personal Staffs of Representatives and Senators   150

7-4   Mail Franked by Representatives and Senators,
        1955–1993   151

7-5   House Incumbent Campaign Spending Average   152

8-1   House and Senate Select Committees Appointed Each
        Congress, 1st–45th Congresses (1789–1879)   172

8-2   Senate and House Select Committees Created to Consider a
        Specific Bill, 1st–14th Congresses   174

8-3   Raw Membership Turnover in House and Senate Standing
        Committee Assignments, 1st–45th Congresses   176

8-4   Net Membership Turnover in House and Senate Standing
        Committee Assignments, 1st–45th Congresses   177

8-5   Average Life Spans of House and Senate Select Committees,
        1st–45th Congresses (1789–1879)   180

10-1   Issue Advantages by Party, 1993–2000   223

11-1   The Conditional Party Government Thesis   247

11-2   Differences between the Parties in Median Liberal–Conservative Scores in the House, 1857–1998   250

11-3   Dispersions in the Parties' Liberal–Conservative Scores in the House, 1857–1998   251

11-4   Differences between the Parties in Median Liberal–Conservative Scores in the Senate, 1857–1998   254

11-5   Dispersions in the Parties' Liberal–Conservative Scores in the Senate, 1857– 1998   255

12-1   DW-NOMINATE Scores (91st and 105th Congresses)   281

13-1   Level of Policy Gridlock, 1947–1997   297

15-1   Models of Presidential–Congressional Relations   354

Box

5-1   Contribution Limits in Congressional Elections   101

Contributors

✧ ✧ ✧

John H. Aldrich is Pfizer-Pratt University Professor at Duke University. He received his Ph.D. from the University of Rochester in 1975. He taught at Michigan State University and the University of Minnesota before joining the Department of Political Science at Duke, where he served as chair. Aldrich has received or been corecipient of Kammerer, Eulau, Pi Sigma Alpha, and CQ Press awards for his research in American politics, positive theory, and methodology. He is currently working on projects that include the role of political parties in the U.S. Congress, the impact of economic globalization on political preferences, the emergence of electoral competition in the U.S. South, and strategic voting in Israel.

Sarah A. Binder is assistant professor of political science at George Washington University and fellow in governmental studies at the Brookings Institution. She received her Ph.D. from the University of Minnesota in 1995. She is author of *Minority Rights, Majority Rule: Partisanship and the Development of Congress* and coauthor of *Politics or Principle? Filibustering in the United States Senate.* Her work on legislative politics has also appeared in the *American Political Science Review,* the *Journal of Politics,* and elsewhere.

David T. Canon is professor of political science at the University of Wisconsin–Madison. He received his Ph.D. from the University of Minnesota in 1987. His teaching and research interests include American political institutions, especially Congress. He is the author of *Actors, Athletes, and Astronauts: Political Amateurs in the U.S. Congress* (1990); *Race, Redistricting, and Representation* (1999), which won the Richard F. Fenno award for the best book on legislative politics; *The Dysfunctional Congress? The Individual Roots of an Institutional Dilemma* (1999), with Ken Mayer; and various articles and book chapters. He also has edited several books and is involved in the Relational Database on Historical Congressional Statistics Project.

Joseph Cooper is professor of political science at Johns Hopkins University. He has served as Autrey Professor of Social Sciences and dean of social sciences at Rice University; staff director of the U.S. House Commission on Administrative Review, Obey Commission; and provost at Johns Hopkins University. He is currently a member of the U.S. Advisory Committee on the Records of Congress. His publications include several books and articles on the development of congressional structures and processes, party voting in Congress, presidential power, changing patterns of congressional leadership, and the decline of trust in Congress.

Rosalyn Cooperman is a Ph.D. candidate in political science at Vanderbilt University. Her research interests include representation in legislative institutions, congressional elections, and political parties.

I. M. Destler is professor at the School of Public Affairs, University of Maryland, and visiting fellow at the Institute for International Economics. He received his Ph.D. from Princeton University. His book *American Trade Politics,* 3d ed. (1995), won the APSA Gladys M. Kammerer Award for best book on U.S. national policy. Destler's most recent books, both coauthored, are *Misreading the Public: The Myth of a New Isolationism* and *The New Politics of American Trade.*

Lawrence C. Dodd holds the Manning J. Dauer Eminent Scholar Chair in Political Science at the University of Florida. He received his Ph.D. from the University of Minnesota in 1972. His books include *Coalitions in Parliamentary Government* (1976), *Congress and the Administrative State* (1979), *Congress and Policy Change* (1986), and *New Perspectives on American Politics* (1994). He has served as a Congressional Fellow (1974–1975), Hoover National Fellow (1984–1985), and University Fellow (1993–1994), and was the campuswide recipient of the 1997–1998 Superior Faculty Service Award for his leadership and program-building efforts at the University of Florida. A student of comparative politics as well as the U.S. Congress, Dodd is completing a coauthored book, *Learning Democracy,* which examines the advent of presidential elections in Nicaragua.

Robert S. Erikson is professor of political science at Columbia University. He received his Ph.D. from the University of Illinois. He has written numerous articles on congressional elections and is coauthor of *Statehouse Democracy: Public Opinion and Policy in the American States* (1993); *The Macro Polity* (2001); and *American Public Opinion,* 6th ed. (2001). He is former editor of the *American Journal of Political Science.*

C. Lawrence Evans is professor of government at the College of William and Mary. A former APSA Congressional Fellow, he is author of *Leadership in Committee, Congress Under Fire,* and numerous articles about legislative politics. He served as an associate staff member for Chairman Lee H. Hamilton on the Joint Committee on the Organization of Congress from 1992 to 1993.

Morris P. Fiorina is professor of political science and a senior fellow of the Hoover Institution at Stanford University. He earned his Ph.D. from the University of Rochester in 1972. Fiorina has written widely on American government and politics, with special emphasis on representation and elections. His eight books include *Congress—Keystone of the Washington Establishment; Retrospective Voting in American National Elections; The Personal Vote: Constituency Service and Electoral Independence,* coauthored with Bruce Cain and John Ferejohn; *Home Style and Washington Work,* coedited with David Rohde; and *Civic Engagement in American Democracy,* coedited with Theda Skocpol. Fiorina has served on the editorial boards of a dozen journals in the fields of political science, economics, law, and public policy and served as chairman of the Board of Overseers of the American National Election Studies from 1986 to 1990. He is a member of the American Academy of Arts and Sciences and the National Academy of Sciences.

Gerald Gamm is department chair and associate professor of political science at the University of Rochester. He received his Ph.D. from Harvard University. He is the author of *The Making of New Deal Democrats* (1989) and *Urban Exodus: Why the Jews Left Boston and the Catholics Stayed* (1999).

Tim Groseclose is associate professor of political economy at the Graduate School of Business, Stanford University. His research specialties include applying mathematical models of politics to legislatures, mostly Congress. Recent publications include "The Value of Committee Seats in the United States Senate, 1947–91," with Charles Stewart (*American Journal of Political Science*, 1999), and "Estimating Party Influence on Congressional Roll-Call Voting," with Jim Snyder (*American Journal of Political Science*, 2000).

Paul S. Herrnson is professor of government and politics at the University of Maryland. He received his Ph.D. from the University of Wisconsin–Madison in 1986. He is the author of *Party Campaigning in the 1980s* (1988) and *Congressional Elections: Campaigning at Home and in Washington*, 3d ed. (2000). He is coeditor of several books, including *After the Revolution: PACs, Lobbies, and the Republican Congress* (1998) and *The Clinton Presidency: The First Term* (1998). He has written numerous articles on Congress, campaign finance, political parties, and elections and has served as an American Political Science Association Congressional Fellow. Herrnson has received several teaching awards, including the Excellence in Teaching award from the College of Behavioral and Social Sciences at the University of Maryland.

John R. Hibbing is professor of political science at the University of Nebraska–Lincoln. He received his Ph.D. from the University of Iowa in 1981. His books include *Congressional Careers* (1991) and *Congress as Public Enemy* (1995). The latter, coauthored with Elizabeth Theiss-Morse, received the 1996 Richard F. Fenno Prize for best book on legislative politics. Hibbing and Theiss-Morse recently completed *Stealth Democracy: Americans' Beliefs about How Government Should Work* (forthcoming), continuing their interest in public attitudes toward democratic processes in the United States.

David King is associate professor of public policy at Harvard University, where he lectures on legislatures, political parties, and interest groups. His books include *Turf Wars: How Congressional Committees Claim Jurisdiction* and *Why People Don't Trust Government*, edited with Joseph Nye and Philip Zelikow.

Bruce I. Oppenheimer is professor of political science at Vanderbilt University. He received his Ph.D. from the University of Wisconsin. Oppenheimer was a Brookings Fellow in Governmental Studies from 1970 to 1971 and an APSA Congressional Fellow from 1974 to 1975. His latest book, *Sizing Up the Senate: The Unequal Consequences of Equal Representation* (1999), coauthored with Frances Lee, was awarded the D. B. Hardeman Prize.

David W. Rohde is University Distinguished Professor of Political Science at Michigan State University. He received his Ph.D. from the University of Rochester in 1971. Rohde has served as chair of the Michigan State political science department, editor of the *American Journal of Political Science*, and chair of the Legislative Studies Section of the American Political Science Association. He is the author of books and articles on various aspects of American national politics, including *Parties and Leaders in the Postreform House.*

Barbara Sinclair is Marvin Hoffenberg Professor of American Politics at the University of California–Los Angeles. She received her Ph.D. from the University of Rochester. She has written a number of articles and books on the U.S. Congress, including *Majority Leadership in the U.S. House* (1983); *Legislators, Leaders, and Lawmaking: The U.S. House of Representatives in the Postreform Era* (1995); and *Unorthodox Lawmaking: New Legislative Processes in the U.S. Congress* (1997, 2000). *The Transformation of the U.S. Senate* (1989) won the Richard F. Fenno Prize for outstanding book published in 1989 on legislative studies, awarded by the Legislative Studies Section of the American Political Science Association, and the D. B. Hardeman Prize for outstanding book on the U.S. Congress published in 1989–1990, awarded by the L.B.J. Foundation.

James T. Smith is senior graduate student in political science at the University of Nebraska–Lincoln. He received his B.A. from the University of California–San Diego in 1994 and his M.A. from San Diego State University in 1996. His interests primarily include American politics, political behavior, public opinion, and public policy. He is completing his dissertation on the causes and consequences of political scandals in the United States.

Steven S. Smith is Kate M. Gregg Professor of Social Sciences and director of the Murray Weidenbaum Center on the Economy, Government, and Public Policy at Washington University. He received his Ph.D. from the University of Minnesota. Smith is the author of *Call to Order: Floor Politics in the House and Senate* (1989) and *The American Congress* (1999). He is the coauthor of *Committees in Congress* (1984, 1990, 1995); *Managing Uncertainty in the U.S. House of Representatives* (1988); *Politics or Principle? Filibustering in the Senate* (1997); and *The Politics of Institutional Choice: The Formation of the Russian State Duma* (2000).

Charles Stewart III is professor of political science at the Massachusetts Institute of Technology. He received his Ph.D. from Stanford University in 1985. His books include *Budget Reform Politics* (1989) and *Analyzing Congress* (2001). He is conducting research on party competition in the United States and contests for the House Speakership throughout American history.

Gerald C. Wright is professor of political science at Indiana University and was formerly the political science program director at the National Science Foundation. He received his Ph.D. from the University of North Carolina at Chapel Hill. His publications include *Electoral Choice in America* (1974) and numerous articles in professional journals. He is coeditor of *Congress and Policy Change* (1986) and coauthor of *Statehouse Democracy: Public Opinion and Policy in the American States* (1993) and *Keeping the Republic: Power and Citizenship in America* (2000).

Preface

✧ ✧ ✧

The 2000 elections have been truly historic. For the first time since the 1920s, the Republicans have won control of the House in four consecutive elections. For the first time since the beginning of an elective Senate, the Democrats and Republicans are tied in the number of seats they control. And for the first time since the Hayes-Tilden election of 1876, the presidential outcome was seriously in doubt following the election, and the result was contested in the courts.

Although the outcome of the presidential election is still uncertain as we go to press, we have again worked to provide the readers of *Congress Reconsidered* with a thoughtful and accurate analysis of the congressional elections, a discussion of their implications for governing in the 107th Congress, and a glance ahead to the 2002 midterm elections. As with past editions, we are proud to produce not only the first analysis of the elections but also interpretations that students of Congress will value.

In the weeks following the November 7 elections, the deadlines for determining the outcome of Florida's presidential contest, for counting the electoral college vote, and for inaugurating a new president were not the only deadlines on our minds. We were concerned with the deadlines for the seventh edition of *Congress Reconsidered* as well. If the book was to be ready in time for spring 2000 courses, as promised, we and our editors at CQ Press had deadlines to meet, even if it meant going to press without knowing who had won the White House or what the precise makeup of the 107th Congress would be. But unlike the Gore campaign, which challenged the deadlines set by Florida's secretary of state, we had no court to which we could appeal the discretion of the printer's schedule or complain about the uncertainties of the tumultuous 2000 elections.

What we can say is that we have done the best we could under the circumstances. We hope our readers will make allowances for the necessary ambiguities and assumptions in our postelection chapter. We are satisfied that the major points we wanted to make will be clear and provide the proper focus for understanding the impact of the 2000 elections for the new Congress, even if every observation is not at the level of specificity that we would prefer. Readers are entitled to make whatever recounts and adjustments to the totals that they deem appropriate either by machine or by hand.

On a more positive note, we have again been privileged to work with a superb group of contributors who have made our job as editors a pleasure. As with contributors to past editions, the authors of this collection represent the best of current congressional scholarship. Together, their efforts present up-to-date analysis for understanding how Congress operates as an institution and how it continues to develop. Some of the writers add to our reconsideration of Congress by examining the contemporary Congress and the way it is functioning in the aftermath of six consecutive years of Republican control. Others want to ensure that we have a broader historical perspective on Congress and ask us to look back a century or more in its evolution. They also offer and at times test a variety of competing theoretical approaches for explaining and predicting the workings of the House, the Senate, and their members. As with the previous editions of *Congress Reconsidered*, the seventh avoids a "one size fits all" view of scholarship. The pluralist nature of the congressional research community has always been one of the book's great strengths, and it is one we hope this volume continues to foster.

True to the book's tradition, the overwhelming majority of the chapters are completely new, and the few that are not have undergone substantial revisions. The contributors prepared their chapters for this volume; they are not reprints from other sources.

What has not changed is the overall organization: again we divide the book into six parts that we think fit the way one might logically organize the teaching of Congress and that represent substantive divisions in research. The first part, "Patterns and Dynamics of Congressional Change," includes two overview pieces, one on the contemporary Senate and the other on the contemporary House, as well as a chapter that examines public expectations about Congress. Part II deals with issues of congressional elections and representation. It contains essays on the linkages between voters' opinions and candidates' issue positions in congressional elections, the changing nature of congressional campaign financing, and the gender gap between the parties in the House. It concludes with an essay by Morris Fiorina in which he revisits his argument from *Congress—Keystone of the Washington Establishment*, first published in 1977, and assesses new developments in American politics likely to shape congressional elections in the twenty-first century.

The third and fourth sections of the book focus on the internal workings of Congress. Part III deals with committees and the committee system: the three chapters address the historical development of committees, competing theories about the rationale for them, and contemporary message politics. Part IV features two related pieces. One compares the differences in the development and exercise of party leadership in the House and the Senate, and the other makes the case that the model of conditional party government is consistent with theories based on the electoral motivations of members.

The relationships between Congress and the executive branch are examined in Part V. One chapter addresses issues related to gridlock (its causes and consequences) and the thwarted efforts of the president and the two houses of Congress to resolve major public policy issues during the past half-century. The other raises questions about whether the level of cooperation between Congress and the president over foreign policy has undergone significant change since the mid-1990s.

In addition to our postelection chapter, the final section of the book includes two broad overviews. The first offers perspectives on the Congress of the twentieth century as a vehicle for raising important questions about the future of the institution. The final chapter examines the Republican Revolution of the past six years and its significance for how we think about Congress and explain congressional change.

As with previous editions, the quality of *Congress Reconsidered* is attributable to a goodly number of people. We have already mentioned our debt to those who wrote such fine chapters. In addition, the people with whom we have worked at CQ Press are a stellar group. For the third consecutive edition, we have had the good luck to work with Brenda Carter. Her concern, patience, and good humor have been constants upon which we have come to count. Gwenda Larsen made valuable suggestions at every step of the process, from proposing content changes to ensuring that things were completed in a timely fashion. Joanne Ainsworth, Ann Davies, and Tom Roche were incredibly professional and cooperative in the editing and production aspects of the book. We appreciate that it is no easy task to create a consistent whole when faced with manuscripts by so many contributors. Julie Rovesti and Amy Briggs did a marvelous job of ensuring a successful promotion of the book to its potential audience.

We are fortunate to enjoy backing for our research from our respective home institutions, the University of Florida and Vanderbilt University. We are also grateful to our departmental colleagues, who are regular sources of stimulation and ideas. Because we have day-to-day interactions with them, we tend to take their contributions for granted and fail to thank them as often as we should.

Naturally, the support and tolerance of our respective families is the magic ingredient in our ability to produce this book. Leslie still pulls Larry away from CNN to go out "two-steppin'" on Friday nights. And Susan and Anne ensure that Bruce has much to smile about. After working together for more than twenty-five years and through seven editions of this book, we still maintain the proper balance of professional respect and personal friendship that allows space for our individuality in both arenas. Dodd may prefer to view the world from atop a horse, while Oppenheimer opts for vehicles with four wheels rather than four hooves. Thankfully, however, doing this book every four years gives us a chance to "sit a spell" and talk.

CONGRESS
RECONSIDERED

Part I
Patterns and Dynamics of Congressional Change

1. The New World of U.S. Senators

Barbara Sinclair

- A courtly older gentleman—probably a conservative southern Democrat, perhaps even white haired and clad in a white linen suit—working in committee behind closed doors
- A policy entrepreneur—Democrat or Republican, liberal or conservative—pursuing his cause singly or with a few allies on the Senate floor, aggressively using nongermane amendments and extended debate as his weapons
- A partisan warrior, acting as a member of a party team, dueling with his opposing party counterparts in the public arena and on the floor, using all the procedural and PR tools available

These three images capture the differences among the Senates of the 1950s, the 1970s, and the 1990s. To be sure, they are simplifications, and some elements of the 1950s Senate and many of the 1970s Senate still persist. Yet the Senate at the beginning of the twenty-first century is very different from the 1950s Senate, which fictional and some journalistic accounts still often depict as current, and appreciably different from the 1970s Senate.

The U.S. Senate has the most permissive rules of any legislature in the world.[1] Extended debate allows senators to hold the floor as long as they wish unless cloture is invoked, which requires a supermajority of sixty votes. The Senate's amending rules enable senators to offer any and as many amendments as they please to almost any bill, and those amendments need not even be germane. The extent to which senators make full use of their prerogatives under the rules has varied over time. The Senate as it enters the twenty-first century is characterized by fairly cohesive party contingents that aggressively exploit Senate rules to pursue partisan advantage, but also by the persistence of the Senate individualism that developed in the 1960s and 1970s.

In this chapter, I briefly examine how and why the Senate changed from the 1950s to the present. I then analyze the impact of individualism and intensified partisanship on how the contemporary Senate functions and on legislative outcomes.

Development of the Individualist, Partisan Senate

The Senate of the 1950s was a clubby, inward-looking body governed by constraining norms; influence was relatively unequally distributed and centered in strong committees and their senior leaders, who were most often conservatives, frequently southern Democrats.[2] The typical senator of the 1950s was a specialist who concentrated on the issues that came before his committees. His legislative activities were largely confined to the committee room; he was seldom active on the Senate floor, was highly restrained in his exercise of the prerogatives the Senate rules gave him, and made little use of the media.

The Senate's institutional structure and the political environment rewarded such behavior.[3] The lack of staff made it hard for new senators to participate intelligently right away, so serving an apprenticeship helped prevent a new member from making a fool of himself early in his career. Meager staff resources also made specialization the only really feasible course for attaining influence. Restraint in exploiting extended debate was encouraged by the lack of time pressures, which would later make extended debate such a formidable weapon; when floor time is plentiful, the leverage senators derive from extended debate is much less.[4] The majority of senators, especially the southern Democrats, faced no imminent reelection peril so long as they were free to reflect their constituents' views in their votes and capable of providing the projects their constituents desired. The system of reciprocity, which dictated that senators do constituency-related favors for one another whenever possible, served them well. The seniority system, bolstered by norms of apprenticeship, specialization, and intercommittee reciprocity, assured members of considerable independent influence in their area of jurisdiction if they stayed in the Senate long enough and did not make that influence dependent on their voting behavior. For the moderate to conservative Senate membership, the parochial and limited legislation such a system produced was quite satisfactory. The Senate of the 1950s was an institution well designed for its generally conservative and electorally secure members to further their goals.

Membership turnover and a transformation of the political environment altered the costs and benefits of such behavior and induced members to change the institution; over time, norms, practices, and rules were altered.[5] The 1958 elections brought into the Senate a big class of new senators with different policy goals and reelection needs. Mostly northern Democrats, they were activist liberals, and most had been elected in highly competitive contests, in many cases having defeated incumbents. Both their policy goals and their reelection needs dictated a more activist style; these senators simply could not afford to wait to make their mark. Subsequent elections brought in more and more such members and, in the 1960s, the political environment began a transformation. A host of new issues rose to prominence, politics became more highly charged, the interest group community exploded in size and became more diverse, and the media—especially television—became a much bigger player in politics.

This new environment offered tempting new opportunities to senators.[6] The myriad interest groups needed champions and spokesmen, and the media needed credible sources to represent issue positions and for commentary. Because of the small size and prestige of the Senate, senators fit the bill. The opportunity for senators to become significant players on a broader stage with possible policy, power, reelection, or higher-office payoffs was there, but to take advantage of the opportunity senators needed to change their behavior and their institution.

From the mid-1960s through the mid-1970s, senators did just that. The number of positions on good committees and the number of subcommittee leadership positions were expanded and distributed much more broadly. Staff too was greatly expanded and made available to junior as well as senior senators. Senators were able to involve themselves in a much broader range of issues, and they did so. Senators also became much more active on the Senate floor, offering more amendments and to a wider range of bills. Senators exploited extended debate to a much greater extent and the frequency of filibusters shot up.[7] The media became an increasingly important arena for participation and a significant resource for senators in the pursuit of their policy, power, and reelection goals.

By the mid-1970s the individualist Senate had emerged. The Senate had become a body in which every member regardless of seniority considered himself entitled to participate on any issue that interested him for either constituency or policy reasons. Senators took for granted that they—and their colleagues— would regularly exploit the powers the Senate rules gave them. Senators became increasingly outward-directed, focusing on their links with interest groups, policy communities, and the media more than on their ties to one another.

The 1980 elections made Ronald Reagan president and, to almost everyone's surprise, brought a Republican majority to the Senate. As president, Reagan was more conservative and confrontational than his Republican predecessors of the post–World War II era, and his election signaled an intensification of ideological conflict that came to fall increasingly along partisan lines.

Realignment in the South, the Proposition 13 tax-cutting fever, the rise of the Christian Right, and the development of the property rights movement were changing the political parties. In 1961 not a single senator from the eleven states of the old Confederacy was a Republican; by 1973, seven were, and by 1980 that number had risen to ten. In 2000 the number stood at fourteen, which represented 64 percent of the senators from the once solidly Democratic old South. As conservative southern Democrats were replaced by even more conservative southern Republicans, the congressional Democratic Party became more homogeneously liberal and the Republican Party more conservative. Outside the South as well, Republican candidates and activists were becoming more ideologically conservative.

Voting on the Senate floor became increasingly partisan. In the late 1960s and early 1970s, a majority of Democrats opposed a majority of Republicans on only about a third of Senate roll-call votes. By the 1990s from half to two-thirds of roll calls were such party votes. The frequency with which senators voted with their partisan colleagues on party votes increased significantly as well. By the 1990s a typical party vote saw well over 80 percent of Democrats voting together on one side and well over 80 percent of Republicans on the other.

Partisan polarization has made participation through their parties more attractive to senators than it was when the parties were more heterogeneous and the ideological distance between them less. Recent Senate party leaders have sought to provide more channels for members to participate in and through the party.[8] Increasingly, senators of the same party are acting as a party team and are exploiting Senate prerogatives to gain partisan advantage.

Over this same time period, the Senate membership has become more diverse. Although most senators are still white men, the 106th Congress (1999–2000) did include nine women, one Japanese American, one of Hawaiian and Chinese descent, and one Native American. By contrast, in the 85th Congress (1957–1958), every senator was white and only one was female. This greater diversity influences how the Senate operates, but its impact cannot compete with that of individualism and intense partisanship.

The Legislative Process in the Contemporary Senate

What effect has the combination of individualism and partisanship had on the legislative process in the Senate? Individualism changed how Senate committees work and altered even more floor-related legislative routines, complicating the Senate majority leader's job of floor scheduling and coordination. Intensified partisanship exacerbated the problems the majority leader faces in keeping the Senate functioning as a legislative body.

Senate Committees

Senators hold multiple committee assignments and usually at least one and often more subcommittee leadership positions. In the 106th Congress, senators averaged 3.2 standing committee assignments and 6.8 subcommittee assignments each; majority party members averaged 1.6 chairmanships.[9] Thus senators are stretched very thin; they treat their committees not as work groups in which to participate on a continuous basis but as arenas in which they pick and choose whether to participate depending upon their interest in the issues being considered. Senators rely heavily on staff for committee work. Committee decisions on many issues are made by the "interesteds," who make up considerably less than the full committee membership.[10] A major tax bill will elicit active participation from all the members of the relevant committee; a rewrite of copyright law, important but narrower and more technical legislation, may be left to a handful of senators.

Because of senators' workloads and the large number of subcommittees, subcommittees are usually "starring" vehicles for their chairs. The chairs can use their subcommittees to publicize problems and policy solutions, to cater to allied interest groups, to promote themselves, or to do all three. Under most circumstances, other senators, even the committee chair, are too busy to interfere.

The marking up of bills, however, most frequently takes place in full committee.[11] Paradoxically, Senate committees remain more centralized than House committees in this respect. However, the reason most Senate committees actually write legislation in full committee rather than marking it up in subcommittee first is not deference to full committee leaders but, again, the enormous workload of senators and the desire of all committee members to have the opportunity to participate in decision making should they so desire. Those senators on the subcommittee do not have time to go through two mark-ups and they know that any interested committee member not on the subcommittee would insist on having a say at the full committee level.

Committee decision making must be sensitive to the policy preferences of interested senators who are not members of the committee. Because any senator can cause problems for the legislation on the floor and may in fact be able to block it from getting to the floor, committee proponents of the legislation have considerable incentive to try to anticipate other senators' views and to bargain with those with intense feelings before the committee reports the bill. Senate committees are perforce highly permeable.

Majority Leadership and the Senate Floor

In the contemporary Senate, floor scheduling is of necessity an exercise in broad and bipartisan accommodation.[12] Although he is not the Senate's presiding officer and lacks many of the powers the House Speaker commands, the Senate majority leader is as close to a central leader as the chamber has and he is charged with the scheduling of legislation for floor consideration. To bring legislation to the floor, the majority leader uses his right of first recognition, a prerogative he has had under Senate precedents since the 1930s. The majority leader can move that a bill be taken off the calendar and considered, but the motion to proceed is a debatable — and thus filibusterable — motion. Or he can ask unanimous consent that the bill be taken off the calendar and considered, a request that can be blocked by any senator's objection. Clearly, any senator can cause problems for the majority leader.

How Senators Cause Trouble: The Strategic Use of Senate Rules. Understanding the problems of legislative scheduling in the Senate and the routines that have developed requires a look at the strategic use of Senate rules by the individualistic and now also increasingly partisan Senate membership.

The filibuster, the use of extended debate to prevent a vote on a motion or measure unless a supermajority can be mustered, is certainly the best-known strategic use of Senate rules. With the development of the individualist Senate, the use of extended debate and of cloture to try to cut it off increased enormously (see Table 1-1). To be sure, the data must be regarded with some caution.[13] When lengthy debate becomes a filibuster is, in part, a matter of judgment. Furthermore,

Table 1-1   The Increase in Filibusters and Cloture Votes, 1951–1998

Years	Congresses	Filibusters (per Congress)	Cloture Votes (per Congress)	Successful Cloture Votes (per Congress)
1951–1960	82d–86th	1.0	.4	0
1961–1970	87th–91st	4.6	5.2	.8
1971–1980	92d–96th	11.2	22.4	8.6
1981–1986	97th–99th	16.7	23.0	10.0
1987–1992	100th–102d	26.7	39.0	15.3
1993–1998	103d–105th	28.0	48.3	13.7

Sources: Data for 82d–102d Congresses: column 3, Congressional Research Service, comp., "A Look at the Senate Filibuster," in *Democratic Studies Group Special Report,* June 13, 1994, app. B; columns 4–5, Norman Ornstein, Thomas Mann, and Michael Malbin, *Vital Statistics on Congress 1993–1994* (Washington, D.C.: CQ Press, 1994), 162. Data for 103d Congress: Richard S. Beth, "Cloture in the Senate, 103d Congress," memorandum, Congressional Research Service, June 23, 1995. Data for 104th–105th Congresses: *Congressional Quarterly Almanac* for the years 1995–1998 (Washington, D.C.: Congressional Quarterly).

as I show below, filibusters have changed their form in recent years and threats to filibuster have become much more frequent than actual talkathons on the floor. As a consequence, cloture is sometimes sought before any overt evidence of a filibuster manifests itself on the floor. Nevertheless, experts and participants agree that the frequency of obstructionism has increased. In the 1950s filibusters were rare; they increased during the 1960s and again during the 1970s. By the late 1980s and the 1990s they had become routine, occurring at a rate of more than one a month—considerably more, if only the time the Senate is in session is counted. Cloture votes have increased in tandem and more than one cloture vote per issue is now the norm. Cloture votes are, however, increasingly less likely to be successful; in the early to middle 1980s, 43 percent of cloture votes got the requisite sixty votes to cut off debate; in the late 1980s and early 1990s, 39 percent did; in the period 1993–1998, only 28 percent did.

As filibusters became more frequent, the character of the filibusterers and of the targeted legislation broadened. By the 1970s liberals as well as conservatives frequently used this weapon, and senators used it on all sorts of legislation, parochial as well as momentous. For example, as Congress was rushing to adjourn in October 1992, Sen. Alfonse D'Amato, R-N.Y., held the floor for fifteen hours and fifteen minutes to protest the removal from an urban-aid tax bill of a provision he said could have restored jobs at a New York typewriter plant.[14]

Senators use actual or threatened filibusters for a variety of purposes. Their aim may be to kill legislation, but it may also be to extract substantive concessions on a bill. Sometimes senators' use of extended debate is a form of position taking; the senator may know he cannot kill or weaken the legislation but wants to make a strong statement about his position and its intensity. Targeting one measure in order to extract concessions on another, sometimes known as hostage taking, has become an increasingly frequent use of extended debate. In 1995, for example, Jesse Helms, R-N.C., chairman of the Senate Foreign Relations Committee, sponsored a State Department reorganization bill that the Clinton administration and many Democrats opposed. Helms brought the legislation to the floor, but after two attempts at imposing cloture failed, Majority Leader Robert Dole, R-Kan., stopped floor consideration. Frustrated, Helms began bottling up ambassador nominations, the START II treaty, and the Chemical Weapons Convention. Democrats responded by blocking action on a flag desecration constitutional amendment and a Cuba sanctions bill, both priorities of Helms. Negotiations and concessions eventually unstuck the impasse, although only the Cuba sanctions bill actually became law.

Nominations as well as legislation can be filibustered. Senators use their powers to block nominations they oppose, even if a Senate majority clearly supports the nomination. Cloture votes showed a sizable majority for the confirmation of Henry Foster as surgeon general, but lacking the sixty votes to cut off debate the nomination died. Increasingly often, senators block nominees they do not oppose in order to gain a bargaining chip for use with the administration. The nomination of William Holbrook as ambassador to the United Nations in 1999 was held up for months over matters having nothing to do with him. Sen. Charles Grassley, R-Iowa, wanted the administration to respond to his concerns about the treatment of a State Department whistleblower; Sens. Mitch McConnell, R-Ky., and Trent Lott, R-Miss., hoped to extract from the president a promise to appoint their candidate to the Federal Elections Commission.

The offering of large numbers of not necessarily germane amendments on the floor is a signature characteristic of the individualist Senate. When major bills are considered, dozens of amendments are routinely offered. More than forty amendments were offered and pushed to a recorded vote on the budget resolutions of 1993, 1995, and 1997; in 1999, juvenile justice legislation considered in the aftermath of the Columbine High School shootings in Colorado was subject to thirty-one amendments that were pushed to a roll call. Most amendments are germane and the sponsor's aim is to influence the substance of the bill. Individual senators do use nongermane amendments to pursue their personal agendas and to bring to the floor issues the leadership might like to avoid. Thus, since he was first elected in the 1970s, Senator Helms has forced innumerable votes in every Congress on hot-button issues such as abortion, pornography, and school prayer.

With the growth of partisan polarization, the minorities making use of Senate prerogatives are more often organized partisan ones. In the 103d Congress the minority Republicans used actual and threatened filibusters to deprive President Bill Clinton and the majority Democrats of numerous policy successes. Clinton's economic stimulus package, campaign finance and lobbying reform bills, and bills revamping the Superfund program, revising clean drinking water regulations, overhauling outdated telecommunications law, and applying federal labor laws to Congress were among the casualties. In the 104th and 105th Congresses, minority Democrats used extended debate to kill many Republican priorities, including ambitious regulatory overhaul legislation and far-reaching property rights bills. In the 103d Congress, Republicans extracted concessions on many major Democratic bills—voter registration legislation ("motor voter") and the national service program, for example. Then, in the 104th Congress, Democrats used the same strategy to force concessions on product liability legislation, the Freedom to Farm bill, and telecommunications legislation, among others.

In the 1990s exploiting Senate prerogatives to attempt to seize agenda control from the majority party became a key minority party strategy. The lack of a germaneness requirement for amendments to most bills severely weakens the majority party's ability to control the floor agenda. If the majority leader refuses to bring a bill to the floor, its supporters can offer it as an amendment to most legislation the leader does bring to the floor. The majority leader can make a motion to table the amendment, which is nondebatable. That does, however, require his members to vote on the issue, albeit in a procedural guise, and the leader may want to avoid that. Furthermore, even after the minority's amendment has been tabled, the minority can continue to offer other amendments, including even individual parts of the original amendment, and can block a vote on the underlying bill the majority party wants to pass. The leader can, of course, file a cloture petition and try to shut off debate, but he needs sixty votes to do so. The minority party can use this strategy to bring its agenda to the floor and, if accompanied by a sophisticated public relations campaign (which the Senate parties are increasingly capable of orchestrating), can gain favorable publicity and sometimes pressure enough majority party members into supporting the bill to pass it. In 1996, Senate Democrats used this strategy to enact a minimum wage increase, and since then, they have forced highly visible floor debate on tobacco regulation, campaign finance reform, gun control, and managed care reform, all issues the majority party would have preferred to avoid.

Getting Legislation to the Senate Floor. Given the extent to which senators as individuals and as party teams now exploit their prerogatives, how does the Senate manage to legislate at all? As shown in Table 1-2, major legislation is now very frequently subject to some sort of extended-debate–related problem discernible from the public record.[15] In the 103d, 104th, and 105th Congresses (1993–1998), about half of the major legislation that was vulnerable to a filibuster actually encountered some sort of filibuster-related problem. If measures protected by rules from filibusters (budget resolution and reconciliation bills) are included, the proportion decreases only marginally.

Since the 1950s the Senate has done most of its work through unanimous consent agreements (UCAs). By unanimous consent, senators agree to bring a bill to the floor, perhaps to place some limits on the amendments that may be offered or on the length of debate on specific amendments and then maybe to set a time for the final vote. Some UCAs are highly elaborate and govern the entire floor consideration of a bill, but a series of partial agreements is more frequent than one comprehensive agreement.[16] As a highly knowledgeable participant

Table 1-2 The Increasing Frequency of Extended-
Debate–Related Problems

Congress	Years	Measures Affected (in percentage)[a]
91st	1969–1970	10
95th	1977–1978	22
97th	1981–1982	24
101st	1989–1990	30
103d	1993–1994	51
104th	1995–1996	52
105th	1997–1998	53

Source: Author's calculations.

[a]Figures represent percentage of "filibusterable" major measures that were subject to extended-debate–related problems.

explained: "Usually you have a UCA only to bring something to the floor, and then maybe you have another one that will deal with a couple of important amendments, and then perhaps a little later, one that will start limiting amendments to some extent, and then perhaps one that specifies when a vote will take place. So it's done through a series of steps, each of which sort of leaves less and less leeway."

Ordinarily, Senate floor consideration of legislation begins with the majority leader asking and receiving unanimous consent to take a bill off the calendar and proceed to consider it. This seemingly simple and easy process for getting legislation to the floor has been preceded by an elaborate consultation process to ensure that unanimous consent is forthcoming. The party leaders oversee the negotiation of unanimous consent agreements and are deeply involved in the more contentious cases. The majority and the minority party secretaries of the Senate now are the most important staffers involved; they serve as clearing houses and as points of continuous contact between the parties and often do much of the negotiating. When the majority leader, after consultation with the relevant committee chairman, decides he wants to schedule a bill, he may leave the negotiation of the agreement to the committee chairman or he may take the lead role himself. The more complex the political situation and the more important to the party the legislation at issue is, the more likely the majority leader is to take the lead. In either case the majority party secretary will be involved; he or she keeps the list of those senators who have requested that they be consulted before the bill is scheduled. If a fellow party member has expressed opposition to the bill being brought to the floor, negotiations may be necessary to take care of his or her concerns. When the majority has an agreement it can support, the majority party's secretary will convey it to the minority party's secretary in writing, who will give it to the minority leader and the relevant ranking minority member. The minority secretary will also call any senators on the minority side who have asked to be notified and find out their concerns. Eventually, the minority will respond with a written counteroffer and convey it to the majority through the secretaries. This process may go through several rounds. If and when the leaders reach a tentative agreement, both parties put out a recorded message on their "hot line" to all Senate offices. The message lays out the terms of the agreement and asks senators who have objections to call their leader within a specified period of time. If there are objections, they have to be taken care of. When every senator is prepared to assent to the unanimous consent agreement, the majority leader takes it to the floor and makes the request.

When a senator informs his leader directly or through the party secretary that he wishes to be consulted before a measure is scheduled, the senator may just want to be sure he is not otherwise committed; that he is prepared for floor debate or ready to offer an amendment. Often, however, such a notification is a *hold*. "A hold," as a knowledgeable participant explained, "is a letter to your leader telling him which of the many powers that you have as a senator you intend to use on a given issue." A typical such letter, addressed to Majority Leader Trent Lott and copied to the majority secretary, reads, "Dear Trent: I will object to any time agreement or unanimous consent request with respect to consideration of any legislation or amendment that involves ———, as I wish to be accorded my full rights as a Member of the Senate to offer amendments, debate and consider such legislation or amendment. Many thanks and kindest personal regards." Most holds, then, are threats to object to a unanimous consent agreement and, in a body that conducts most of its business through UCAs that is, in effect, as a leadership staffer said, "a threat to filibuster."

The party secretaries confer every morning and tell each other what new holds there are on legislation or nominations. They do not, however, reveal the names of their members that have placed the holds.

Visible filibusters are now just the tip of the iceberg. The Senate's permissive rules have much more effect on the legislative process through filibuster threats than through actual filibusters. (See Table 1-2; remember that holds and filibuster threats as well as actual filibusters are reflected in those figures.) "Classic" filibusters with the Senate in session all night, senators sleeping on cots off the Senate floor, and filibusterers making interminable speeches on the floor no longer occur. Holds are the "lazy man's filibuster," a staffer complained. Sometimes placed by staff on their own initiative, sometimes at the instigation of lobbyists, holds require little effort on the part of senators, the staffer continued, and yet they enormously complicate the legislative process and not infrequently kill or severely weaken worthy legislation. Many other participants and observers make similar complaints.

Since holds are nowhere specified in Senate rules, why do Senate leaders condone and, in fact, maintain the hold system? "It's to the majority leader's advantage to have holds because it gives him information," a knowledgeable observer explained. "He's always trying to negotiate unanimous consent agreements, and he needs to know if there are pockets of problems, and holds do that." An expert concluded succinctly, "The only way you could get rid of holds would be to change the rules of the Senate drastically."

Critics often argue that leaders should be tougher and call the bluff of members more often. The threat to filibuster supposedly inherent in holds would, in many cases, prove to be empty rhetoric if put to the test, such critics claim. In fact, holds are not automatic vetoes. A hold cannot kill *must-pass* legislation such as appropriations bills, and in deciding how seriously to take a hold on less vital legislation, the leader weighs the reputation of the senator placing the hold; "some people are taken more seriously because it's just assumed they're willing to back it up," a leadership aide explained. When senators place holds that their leader cannot honor, he will attempt to at least provide a face-saving way out for his member. Thus when President Clinton named James Hormel ambassador to Luxembourg by recess appointment, Sen. James M. Inhofe, R-Okla., one of the Republican senators most opposed to the appointment, very publicly put a hold on all administration nominations. This was an untenable hold, most participants and observers agreed, because "there will be people who will want appointments because it covers everything supposedly. So people will start pressuring him." Before he brought up any nominations, Lott extracted a letter from the administration essentially reiterating current policy on recess appointments but providing Inhofe with cover. Inhofe declared victory in a press release and lifted his blanket hold.

Although holds are certainly not absolute, the time pressure under which the Senate operates gives them considerable bite. As a staffer explained, "Holds are effective because the majority leader has a finite amount of time. If there are going to be cloture votes and the like, it can take days to ram something through this place. You can't do it on every bill. You can only do it on a selected few bills." Senators want floor time used productively. In making a choice of which bills to bring to the floor, the majority leader must consider how much time the bill will take and what the likelihood of successful passage is. As a result, senators who want their bills to receive floor consideration are under tremendous pressure to negotiate with those who have holds on them. "Things that aren't a top priority for the majority leader, he wants you to work it out," a senior staffer explained. "If you go to him and say you want something brought to the floor, he'll say, 'you work it out. You find out who has holds on it. You work out whatever problems they have, and I'll schedule it when you've worked it out.'" Thus, often simply to get to the floor, a measure must command a substantial majority. When time is especially tight—before a recess and at the end of a session—a single objection can kill legislation.

Majority and Minority, Cooperation and Conflict

Keeping the Senate functioning as a legislature requires broad accommodation; it dictates satisfying every senator to some extent. A reasonably cohesive majority party can run the House without consulting the minority. The Senate only runs smoothly when the majority leader and the minority leader cooperate and not always then. Majority Leader Lott and Minority Leader Tom Daschle, D-S.D., consult on a daily basis. "The two leaders talk extensively to each other during the day," a knowledgeable participant explained. "You see it during votes. We'll have two or three votes a day at least, usually, and that's one of the times when they confer. But they have to talk to each other; if they don't, that's when things break down."

The leaders often work together to get unanimous consent agreements and to get essential legislative business done. For example, just before—and blocking—adjournment in late 1999, the senators from Wisconsin and Minnesota, three Democrats and one Republican, were holding up approval of the conference report containing the final appropriations bills because it contained milk-pricing provisions that they believed put their dairy farmers at a disadvantage. Daschle cajoled and bargained with the Democrats and, together with Lott, came up with the assurances necessary to get the recalcitrants to yield. Getting the necessary cooperation from the minority and its leader requires that the majority leader accommodate the minority party to some considerable extent.

Yet the Senate leaders are party leaders, elected by their party members in the chamber, and are expected by those members to pursue partisan advantage. With the increase in partisan polarization, the narrow margins and the shifts in partisan control of the chamber, senators' expectations that their leader promote their collective partisan interests have intensified. With the change in the character of politics and the role of the media in political life, those expectations have also changed in form. Over the course of the second half of the twentieth century, the role of the media in American politics increased enormously; national politics have come to be played out much more on the public stage than they used to be, often with audience reactions determining who wins and who loses. In the 1990s, policy battles increasingly came to be fought out in public through public relations, or PR, wars.[17] Whether in the majority or in the minority, senators now expect their party leader to promote their collective partisan interests through outside-directed message strategies as well as by internal procedural and legislative strategies.

This creates a dilemma for the leaders, especially for the majority leader. Republican senators expect Lott to promote the Republican agenda by passing legislation and publicizing Republican positions and successes; they also expect him to keep off the floor the Democrats' agenda, which consists of issues on which Democrats and the public agree and thus puts Republicans in a tough position. Yet, in the Senate, unlike the House, a majority is not sufficient to act; to keep the Senate functioning requires supermajorities and this almost always requires that the majority leader accommodate the minority to some extent.

Senate Democrats use nongermane amendments and unlimited debate to bring their issues to the floor and force a full public debate. They employ the PR capabilities that both parties now command (everything from highly skilled press aides to television studios with satellite hookups to Internet sites) to make that debate as visible and newsworthy as possible.[18]

Under pressure from Republican senators, especially from the more junior conservatives, many of whom were schooled in the House under Newt Gingrich, Majority Leader Lott often responds with hardball procedural tactics. He files for cloture on a bill immediately, then pulls the bill from the floor until the cloture vote is due. If cloture succeeds, he has barred all nongermane amendments, since Senate rules require that all amendments after cloture is invoked be germane. If cloture fails, he does not bring up the bill. Lott has sometimes used the tactic of "filling the amendment tree," that is, he has used the majority leader's prerogative of first recognition to offer amendments in all the parliamentarily permissible slots, thus preventing Democrats from offering their amendments.

Democrats have reacted with outrage, charging that the majority Republicans were attempting to stifle debate on all controversial issues. They have also reacted by maintaining high cohesion on cloture votes, thus denying the majority the sixty votes it needs to make the tactics work. Consequently, when the majority employs these tactics, the result is most often gridlock, with no legislative work accomplished on the Senate floor until an accommodation is reached. As the Republican Policy Committee chairman, Larry Craig, explained, "Inevitably, anybody who wants to get a vote on the floor of the United States Senate will get it if they're persistent."[19]

At the same time that Senate leaders have to deal with sometimes unmeetable expectations from their members for the aggressive pursuit of partisan advantage, they also must handle the individualism within their own party that can derail partisan and bipartisan strategies alike. After President Clinton and congressional leaders had reached an agreement to balance the budget in 1997, Sens. Orrin Hatch, R-Utah, and Ted Kennedy, D-Mass., both usually party stalwarts, jointly sponsored a "deal breaker" amendment to raise the tax on cigarettes by 43 cents a pack and use the money to provide additional health insurance for uninsured children and to reduce the deficit. Sen. John McCain, R-Ariz., made his name by bucking the Republican Party establishment on tobacco taxes and campaign finance reform.

Individualism, Partisanship, and Legislative Outcomes

How does the combination of individualism and intense partisanship that characterizes the contemporary Senate affect legislative outcomes? As shown in Table 1-3 the likelihood of a major measure becoming law is less in recent Congresses than in earlier ones; in the three 1990s Congresses that saw about half of the major measures subject to some sort of filibuster problem, 45 percent of the major measures failed enactment; by contrast, in three earlier Congresses, characterized by lower filibuster activity, 27 percent of the major measures failed. Of course there are many steps in the legislative process and these figures by themselves do not prove that the Senate is responsible for the increase in legislative

Table 1-3 Where Major Measures Failed

	Number of Failed Measures	
What Happened?	91st, 95th, and 97th Congresses	103d, 104th, and 105th Congresses
Passed by neither House nor Senate	16	21
Passed by House but not by Senate	12	24
Passed by Senate but not by House	8	2
Passed by House and Senate	6	19
Total number of failed measures	42 (of 156 measures)	68 (of 150 measures)
Percentage of total measures that failed	27 percent	45 percent

Source: Author's calculations.

failures. However, as also shown in Table 1-3, for the latter three Congresses, legislation was much more likely to pass the House but fail in the Senate than the reverse; in the earlier Congresses, the difference was not very great.

Does the increasing frequency with which measures encounter extended-debate–related problems in the Senate explain this pattern? Filibuster problems do, in fact, depress a measure's chances of surviving the legislative process; of those measures that did not encounter such a problem, either because senators chose not to use their prerogatives or because the measure enjoyed statutory protection, 74 percent were enacted; only 54 percent of those that did experience a filibuster problem became law.[20] Since filibusters and filibuster threats are by no means always intended to kill legislation, those figures suggest a considerable effect. Filibuster problems are more likely to occur on partisan legislation, and when a measure is both partisan at the committee level and encounters a filibuster problem, its chances of enactment are significantly decreased. Less than half (46 percent) of such measures were successfully enacted, in contrast to 80 percent of the measures that were not partisan and did not experience an extended-debate-related problem and 57 percent that had one but not both of these characteristics.

Thus, the combination of individualism and intense partisanship that characterizes the contemporary Senate does depress the likelihood of legislation successfully surviving the legislative process. Yet, given the character of Senate rules and the ways in which senators currently exploit them, it is perhaps more surprising that the Senate manages to legislate at all. The Senate does pass a lot of legislation, both must-pass measures like appropriations bills and other major bills. To be sure, some measures—budget resolutions and reconciliation bills, most importantly—are protected from filibusters and nongermane amendments by law and this has been vital to the passage of some of the most important legislation of the last decade.[21] But much legislation without such protection gets through the Senate as well.

Dodging Legislative Breakdown

Clearly, the Senate could not function if senators maximally exploited their prerogatives, if, for example, every senator objected to every unanimous consent agreement on any matter he or she did not completely support. What, then, keeps senators as individuals and as party teams from pushing their prerogatives over the limit and miring the Senate in gridlock?

Asked that question, senators, staff, and informed observers uniformly responded that almost all senators want to "get something done" and that they are aware that many senators' exploiting their prerogatives to the limit would make that impossible. As one knowledgeable insider phrased it, "I like to think of the Senate as a bunch of armed nuclear nations. Each senator knows he can blow the place up, but most of them came here to do something, and if he does blow things up, if he does use his powers that way, then he won't be able to do anything." Using one's prerogatives aggressively entails concrete short-run costs, most argued. "If you do object [to a unanimous consent request], it's going to hurt someone and maybe more than one person," a senior staffer explained, "so the next time you want something, it may very well happen to you." Senators do not put holds on every bill or nomination they oppose, another experienced aide said, "because people will put a hold on their stuff then." In the Senate, individuals can exact retribution swiftly and often quite easily on those they believe have harmed them. Because of that, a junior senator and former House member reported, "in the Senate, you don't go out of your way to hack people off." In the House there is less such concern, he explained. The likelihood that some retaliation will be forthcoming forces the wise senator to be selective in the employment of his prerogatives.

The importance of guarding their reputations also constrains senators. Placing a hold or objecting to a unanimous consent request costs little senator or staff time; following through and actually employing delaying tactics on the floor costs a great deal of time. "Threats are taken seriously in the Senate," a senior staff aide said, "but they depend on a perception that you'll carry out your threat, so you need to do it selectively." A senator's reputation influences the leadership's reaction to a senator's threat. As a leadership aide explained, "When you get a letter [putting on a hold], you ask what is his track record in order to judge how seriously you need to take it."

Similar considerations restrain senators as party teams and especially their leaders. The leaders are very much aware that as much as senators want to gain partisan advantage on the big issues, they also want, for both reelection and policy reasons, to pass bills. As the earlier discussion of the interactions between the party leaders indicated, the leaders are instrumental in maintaining the cooperation necessary to keep the Senate functioning. They do so by working together closely, by adeptly employing both procedural and peer pressure to encourage the recalcitrant to deal, and by accommodating to some extent all senators with problems.[22] Although the procedural resources and the favors the leaders command

are fairly meager, they do have one persuasive argument for inducing cooperation. As a knowledgeable insider put it, "[Senators] can use the powers they have
to create chaos and confusion on the floor, in which case senators don't have a
life . . . where the floor debate goes on to all hours without any knowledge of
when anything will happen, or they can defer to their leaders to create a structure with some predictability, and then they do have a life. And that's the bargain
they have made."

Leaders also need to concern themselves with guarding the party's reputation within the chamber and with the public. The minority party's influence in
particular depends upon its being able to block cloture and that depends upon
using obstructionism selectively. The reputation with the public of both parties,
but especially that of the majority party, suffers if the Senate seems incapable of
legislating.

In its everyday functioning, the contemporary Senate exhibits a peculiar
combination of conflict and cooperation, of aggressive exploitation of rules and
of accommodation. The hottest partisan legislative battles are studded with
unanimous consent agreements. And the more intense the partisan fight, the
more frequently the majority and minority leaders confer. On bills not at the center of partisan conflict, senators routinely cooperate across the partisan divide. As
a senior aide expressed the consensus, "If you really want to move stuff, if it's not
a big partisan matter, a big ideological issue, and you really want to move it, then
you really have to be bipartisan. You've got to work out the difficulties, and you've
got to work across the aisle." Bipartisanship is especially important on legislation
of secondary importance because the majority leader requires that the problems
be resolved before he attempts to bring such bills to the floor. Senators as individuals do put holds on each other's bills, but they also often attempt to accommodate each other on an individual basis in ways that extend far beyond what
occurs in the House. A senior aide to a Democratic senator who had previously
served in the House illustrated this point:

> [The senator] was a senior member of the [House] Energy and Commerce
> Committee, and we would call [committee chairman John] Dingell's [D-
> Mich.] staff director and say X or Y is *really, really* important to [us]. And
> . . . the staff director would say no, we can't do that and sort of explain why,
> and then we'd spend three weeks trying to figure out a way of getting him
> to change his mind. And this, remember, is a senior member of the chair-
> man's party. Here, in the Senate, I call a Republican staffer on a commit-
> tee that [the senator] doesn't serve on and explain the same sort of thing —
> that we've got a problem, and 60, 70, 80 percent of the time it will get
> done. It will get taken care of.

The staffer explained such responsiveness not by norms of civility and reciprocity but by the facts of life in the contemporary Senate. It is "because they need to
accommodate you to move something," the aide continued. "They want to get

something done. They want to get legislation, and to do that you have to take care of people's problems."

Thus senators' acute awareness of the weapons all senators command can work to produce cooperation and some restraint. Everyone knows that legislative breakdown is a very real possibility and this seems to have a sobering effect. Yet, in an era of intensified partisanship combined with the continuing individualism that has characterized the Senate since the 1970s, the Senate legislative process is fragile. Senate party leaders are under considerable pressure from their members to pursue partisan advantage aggressively, and partisan battles aimed at electoral gain are zero-sum. The rewards of Senate individualism can be great, as John McCain's presidential candidacy demonstrated. Most of the time, the Senate manages to maintain the minimum restraint and cooperation necessary to avoid total gridlock, yet the chamber regularly seems to teeter on the precipice of legislative breakdown.

A Less Effective Senate?

Have individualism and partisanship and their impact on the legislative process made the Senate of today less effective than the Senate of the 1950s? Does the Senate play a less important role in our political life than it used to?

The contemporary Senate performs certain important functions well. It provides senators with an excellent forum for agenda setting, debate framing, and policy incubation.[23] Using their prerogatives under Senate rules and their access to the media, senators as individuals and now as party teams publicize problems, promote solutions, speak for a wide variety of claimant groups, and provide a visible and legitimate opposition view—and increasingly an alternative agenda— to the president's. Even were the Senate to have less impact on the details of legislation, so long as it significantly influenced the national agenda, one would have to conclude that it continues to play an important role in national politics.

Furthermore, some scholars and journalists argue that Senate rules and how they are currently used actually gives the Senate a bargaining advantage over other political actors. In particular, when Senate and House meet in conference committee to resolve their differences over a bill, Senate conferees can and do use the fact that Senate approval effectively requires a supermajority to their advantage; if the conferees move the bill too far from the Senate version, a filibuster will block the bill in the Senate, they argue. Certainly, House members complain bitterly about such Senate "blackmail."

Finally, legislative productivity, especially the enactment of nonincremental policy changes, seems considerably more a function of the external political environment than of the institutional structure within the legislative chambers.[24] For example, in 1995–1996, Democrats and some moderate Republicans, using Senate rules, blocked much of Newt Gingrich's Contract with America that the House had passed. On the one hand, Senate rules were instrumental, but on the other, it is most unlikely that, had there been strong public support for the bills in question, senators would have been willing to incur the public's wrath and kill the legislation.

So the question "Is the Senate of today a less effective legislative body?" has no simple answer. The Senate's nonmajoritarian rules as currently used greatly exacerbate the problems of building winning coalitions and so the contemporary Senate is always at risk of legislative breakdown. If a legislature cannot respond to the problems that concern the people it represents, it loses legitimacy. That has not happened to the Senate yet, but the possibility is not farfetched.

Notes

The definitive work on the Senate in the 1950s is Donald Matthews's *U.S. Senators and Their World* (New York: Vintage Books, 1960). The title of this chapter is intended as a tribute to Don and his classic, but should he consider an apology more appropriate, I offer that too. All unattributed quotations in the main text of this chapter are from interviews conducted by the author.

1. Barbara Sinclair, *Unorthodox Lawmaking* (Washington, D.C.: CQ Press, 1997; 2d ed., 2000); Sarah Binder and Steven S. Smith, *Politics or Principle? Filibustering in the United States Senate* (Washington, D.C.: Brookings Institution, 1997).
2. Matthews, *U.S. Senators and Their World.*
3. Barbara Sinclair, *The Transformation of the U.S. Senate* (Baltimore: Johns Hopkins University Press, 1989); Ralph Huitt, "The Internal Distribution of Influence: The Senate," in *The Congress and America's Future,* ed. David Truman (New York: Prentice Hall, 1965).
4. Bruce Oppenheimer, "Changing Time Constraints on Congress: Historical Perspectives on the Use of Cloture," in *Congress Reconsidered,* ed. Lawrence C. Dodd and Bruce I. Oppenheimer, 3d ed. (Washington, D.C.: CQ Press, 1985).
5. Sinclair, *Transformation of the U.S. Senate;* Michael Foley, *The New Senate* (New Haven: Yale University Press, 1980); David Rohde, Norman Ornstein, and Robert Peabody, "Political Change and Legislative Norms in the U.S. Senate, 1957–1974," in *Studies of Congress,* ed. Glenn Parker (Washington, D.C.: Congressional Quarterly, 1985).
6. See also Burdett Loomis, *The New American Politician* (New York: Basic Books, 1988).
7. Binder and Smith, *Politics or Principle?*
8. Patrick J. Sellers, "Leaders and Followers in the U.S. Senate" (paper presented at the Conference on Senate Exceptionalism, Vanderbilt University, Nashville, Tenn., October 21–23, 1999); Donald Baumer, "Senate Democratic Leadership in the 100th Congress," in *The Atomistic Congress,* ed. Ronald Peters and Allen Herzke (Armonk, N.Y.: M. E. Sharpe, 1992); Steven S. Smith, "Forces of Change in Senate Party Leadership and Organization," in *Congress Reconsidered,* ed. Lawrence C. Dodd and Bruce I. Oppenheimer, 5th ed. (Washington, D.C.: CQ Press, 1993); Mary Jacoby, "Waiting in Wings, a Kinder, Gentler Lott?" *Roll Call,* March 9, 1995, 22.
9. *CQ Weekly,* March 3, 1999, 630.
10. Richard Hall, *Participation in Congress* (New Haven: Yale University Press, 1996).
11. Christopher J. Deering and Steven S. Smith, *Committees in Congress* (CQ Press, 1997).
12. Roger H. Davidson, "Senate Leaders: Janitors for an Untidy Chamber?" in *Congress Reconsidered,* ed. Lawrence C. Dodd and Bruce I. Oppenheimer, 3d ed. (Washington, D.C.: CQ Press, 1985); Sinclair, *Transformation;* Smith, "Forces of Change."

13. See Richard Beth, "What We Don't Know about Filibusters" (paper presented at the annual meeting of the Western Political Science Association, Portland, Ore., March 15–18); also Sinclair, *Unorthodox Lawmaking,* 1st ed., 47–49. Sources for the data are given in the note to Table 1-1. The House Democratic Study Group publication relies on data supplied by Congressional Research Service experts; these experts' judgments about what constitutes a filibuster are not limited to instances in which cloture was sought. For the 103d through the 105th Congresses, instances in which cloture was sought are used as the basis of the "filibuster" estimate. One can argue that this over-estimates because in some cases cloture was sought for reasons other than a fear of extended debate (a test vote or to impose germaneness); however, one can also argue that it underestimates because those cases in which cloture was not sought—perhaps because it was known to be out of reach—are not counted. For an estimate based on a different methodology, see Table 1-2.

14. Phil Kuntz, "Drawn-Out Denouement Mirrors Character of 102nd Congress," *Congressional Quarterly Weekly Report,* October 10, 1992, 3128.

15. Holds and threats to filibuster, as well as actual extended-debate–related delay on the floor, were coded as filibuster problems (see below). The definition of major legislation used here—those measures in lists of major legislation published in CQ almanacs and the *CQ Weekly* plus those measures on which key votes occurred, again according to Congressional Quarterly—yields forty to sixty measures per Congress. Thus, although truly minor legislation is excluded, the listing is not restricted to only the most contentious and highly salient issues.

16. C. Lawrence Evans and Walter Oleszek, "The Procedural Context of Senate Deliberation" (paper presented at the Robert J. Dole Institute's Conference on Civility and Deliberation in the United States Senate, Washington, D.C., July 1999).

17. See Sellers, "Leaders and Followers"; Barbara Sinclair, "The Plot Thickens: Congress and the President," in *Great Theatre: The American Congress in Action,* ed. Herbert Weisberg and Samuel Patterson (Cambridge: Cambridge University Press, 1998); C. Lawrence Evans and Walter Oleszek, "Message Politics and Agenda Control in the U.S. Senate" (paper presented at the conference "The Myth of Cool Judgment?: Partisanship and Ideology in the Contemporary Senate," Florida International University, Miami, January 22, 2000).

18. See Sellers, "Leaders and Followers," and the managed care case study in Sinclair, *Unorthodox Lawmaking,* 2d ed.

19. *Roll Call,* July 5, 1999.

20. Measures that did not get far enough to encounter the prospects of a filibuster problem are coded as missing data on the filibuster variable.

21. See the case studies of the 1993, 1995, and 1997 reconciliation (that is, budget) bills in Sinclair, *Unorthodox Lawmaking,* 2d ed.

22. Barbara Sinclair, "The Senate Leadership Dilemma: Passing Bills and Pursuing Partisan Advantage in a Non-Majoritarian Chamber" (paper presented at the conference "The Myth of Cool Judgment? Partisanship and Ideology in the Contemporary Senate," Florida International University, Miami, January 22, 2000).

23. Nelson Polsby, "Good-by to the Senate's Inner Club," in *Congress in Change,* ed. Norman Ornstein (New York: Praeger, 1975).

24. David Mayhew, *Divided We Govern* (New Haven: Yale University Press, 1991); Barbara Sinclair, *Congressional Realignment* (Austin: University of Texas Press, 1982).

2. A House Divided:
The Struggle for Partisan Control, 1994–2000

Lawrence C. Dodd and Bruce I. Oppenheimer

The House of Representatives entered the twenty-first century as a divided chamber, preoccupied by partisan conflict and by a protracted struggle for institutional control. In 1994 an energized Republican Party had ended decades of Democratic majorities in the House and then for two subsequent elections retained its majority, albeit by decreasing seat margins. These years of Republican rule witnessed dramatic reforms of House politics (including imposition of term limits on committee chairs and the Speaker), historic changes in the nation's welfare policies, and the impeachment of the Democratic president, Bill Clinton, by House Republicans. Yet the Republicans' capacity to enact their most far-reaching proposals, such as across-the-board tax cuts and continued reduction in the size and role of the national government, was hampered by their narrow majority, a somewhat more moderate yet divided Republican Senate, the Democratic president, and the continuing opposition of House Democrats.

The question facing the nation in 2000 was whether and when the electorate would break the partisan standoff and point the House in a clearer and more definitive governing direction. Our purpose here is to present in greater detail the historical developments that gave rise to this momentous question and to highlight the political and electoral dynamics shaping the struggle for House control. We begin with a discussion of the decades of Democratic control that set the stage for Republican resurgence and the contentious partisan struggle of the 1990s.

The Era of Democratic Control

Long-term Democratic control of the House began with the Great Depression and the election of a Democratic majority to the Seventy-second Congress, which took office in 1931.[1] With the subsequent election of President Franklin D. Roosevelt and a Democratic Senate in 1932, the party unified control of government and enacted the New Deal legislation that laid the foundations of the modern social service state. The Democratic activists' response to the Great Depression created broad popular support that sustained the party's dominance in the House for sixty of sixty-four years, losing its majority only in the 1946 postwar elections and in the 1952 Eisenhower landslide.

When the Democrats came to power in 1931, they inherited an organizational structure based on committee government.[2] In the late nineteenth century both parties had moved to solidify an activist committee system under the control of strong House Speakers such as Thomas B. Reed and Charles F. Crisp. As a result, the Speaker oversaw the appointment of committee members and committee chairs, dominated the Rules Committee, and exercised extensive authority over floor proceedings. The office grew so powerful that in the early 1900s Speaker "Uncle Joe" Cannon could seriously challenge the policy leadership of Theodore Roosevelt, his party's president. This era of strong Speakers came to an end in 1910, when deep disagreements over policy and the distribution of power within the Republican Party led GOP progressives to turn against "Czar Cannon" and his conservative allies and unite with House Democrats, stripping the Speakership of its prerogatives and shifting power to committees. The Democrats during the presidency of Woodrow Wilson and the Republicans during the roaring twenties solidified committee control of the House and regularized the role of seniority in committee chair selections, thereby creating a complex and decentralized structure of House policymaking. This structure fostered policy expertise and stabilized policymaking processes, but it also hindered rapid, coordinated policy activism by the majority party.

The history of Democratic control of the House over much of the subsequent six decades was in many ways a continuing effort to use the policymaking expertise of the standing committees while overcoming the obstacles to party government created by committee seniority. During the first four to six years of Franklin Roosevelt's presidency, the House Democratic leadership used the extensive public support for the New Deal, enormous House majorities, and the resources of the presidency to generate committee and floor support among Democratic members. But in the late 1930s public support for the New Deal ebbed, and conservative Democrats, particularly southern Democrats, began to unite with Republicans to oppose New Deal legislation in committees and on the House floor.

When allied with Republicans in the so-called conservative coalition, southern Democrats were a substantial force in the House from the late 1930s into the 1960s. Their power flowed not just from the fact that they often constituted a House majority when combined with Republicans in the conservative coalition, but because they represented safe seats and easily accrued seniority. Accordingly, southerners came to dominate committee chairmanships. These southern committee chairs could use their power to block liberal Democratic legislation and push conservative policies to passage by the House. As a result, one cannot equate Democratic control of the House from the late 1930s to the 1960s with liberal Democratic Party dominance of congressional policymaking. Those years, rather, were characterized by coalitional politics, conservative policies, and strong committee government.

Only with the liberal successes in the 1958 elections, and the election of President John Kennedy in 1960, did the House Democrats begin a sixteen-year reform process that would constrain the conservative coalition. Liberal dominance of House policymaking begun under President Kennedy briefly surged forward with Lyndon Johnson's presidential landslide of 1964 and the subsequent Great Society legislation of the Eighty-ninth Congress (1965–1967). Not until the 1970s, however, was moderate-to-liberal control of the House Democratic

Party solidified with reforms that restricted the power of seniority, weakened committee government, and brought greater authority to party leaders. The passage of these reforms particularly benefited from the presence in the Ninety-fourth Congress (1975–1977) of a large number of "reform-minded" Democratic freshmen, who were elected in the Watergate elections of November 1974. These freshmen, winning office in the aftermath of the impeachment proceedings and resignation of Richard Nixon, also helped to increase and solidify the margin of Democratic control of the House and to magnify the party's more liberal policy stance.

The conservative coalition declined by the 1970s, in part because the congressional reforms undercut the procedural basis of its power, in part because of the growing numbers of moderate-to-liberal northern legislators in the Democratic Party, and in part because of the changes in southern Democratic representation in Congress resulting from the 1965 Voting Rights Act. With the registration of large numbers of black voters, and with party leaders in the House who pushed for stronger support for party legislation from House party members, Democratic candidates in the South moderated their views on social policy. The Republican Party then became more competitive in many southern districts by attracting conservative white voters. The distinction between southern and northern congressional Democrats waned, and interparty differences increased. Over the long run these shifts laid the foundation for growing Republican representation in the South. In the short run they increased the unhappiness among Republicans over their isolation in the House and their lack of a strong institutional role. Only episodically could they exercise considerable "hidden" power in the House through the conservative coalition.

Republican frustration over the isolation from power mounted when the Reagan landslides of 1980 and 1984 failed to produce Republican control of the House, despite growing success in winning some conservative southern House districts previously controlled by Democrats. House Republicans then began to consider a more aggressive assault on Democratic dominance. The impetus for this attack came from the younger and more conservative Republicans and was led by Newt Gingrich of Georgia. Their goal was to end Democratic control of the House and to institute Republican rule. By combining the growing number of southern Republicans with the pre-existing group of House Republicans, they would replace the conservative coalition with a conservative Republican governing party in control of the House.

The Republican Challenge

In the Ninety-eighth Congress (1983–1985), Gingrich and other junior Republicans organized the Conservative Opportunity Society and began to challenge the House Democrats on procedural, policy, and political grounds.[3] They pushed issues such as the balanced budget amendment, reform of House rules, the line-item veto, and social issues such as the repeal of laws concerning abortion and school prayer. Many of their concerns would form the basis of the Contract with America a decade later. They used televised coverage of House debates so effectively that they provoked Speaker Tip O'Neill, D-Mass., into an outburst against them in 1984, which led the House to take the extraordinary step of striking a Speaker's words from the House record. Over the next decade, Gingrich and his supporters mounted a direct assault on Speaker Jim Wright, D-Texas, who eventually resigned under an ethics investigation of his conduct. They pushed for an examination of the House Bank, which exposed a highly damaging public scandal over bank overdrafts that particularly discredited the governing Democrats. They continuously called for reform and reorganization of the House rules. In addition, when the term limits movement began to gain momentum in the late 1980s and early 1990s, many House Republicans began to embrace the idea as a way of ending Democratic dominance of Congress. Assuming the permanence of their majority status, House Democrats and their leaders failed to respond sufficiently to internal abuses, thus fueling Republican charges.

Gingrich increasingly became a visible force in his party and in the House Republican Conference. In 1988 he became head of GOPAC, a Republican political action committee, and began to use it to recruit conservative Republicans to run for state and local office. He focused on recruiting conservative ideologues who would be committed to implementing an aggressive party agenda and who would work passionately in behalf of the "party cause." In so doing he was creating a "farm team" of experienced politicians who could run for the House in the 1990s. Although he achieved considerable success around the country, his greatest inroads came in the South and Southwest, where GOPAC helped reinforce the growing Republican strength. In March 1989, House Republicans elected Gingrich as their minority whip over a more moderate candidate, positioning him as successor to their long-term minority leader, Bob Michel of Illinois.

As minority whip and prospective party leader, Gingrich pushed the House Republicans closer to confrontation with the majority party Democrats. This confrontation came to a head when the 1992 election of President Bill Clinton yielded Democratic control of both Congress and the White House. With united control of government for the first time since 1980, Republicans could hold the Democrats accountable for the nation's ills.

Gingrich and the House Republicans built their 1994 campaign around a common national agenda, the Contract with America, which constituted a direct attack on the "liberal" agenda of the Democratic Party. The Contract was dedicated to extensive reform of the House and the implementation of conservative policies. United behind the Contract, Republicans relied on a mix of strong, experienced candidates and antigovernment amateurs, and on extensive campaign funding strategies that the party had built over the previous decade. They focused their strong campaign on winning many open seats previously controlled by Democrats, on defeating freshmen Democrats elected in 1994, and on challenging a few key Democratic leaders, such as Speaker Tom Foley, who represented

competitive constituencies. The result was the first election of a Republican majority in the House since 1952. In winning control of the House, the Republicans
made a net gain of 52 seats, the largest partisan swing since 1948. They defeated
34 Democratic incumbents, including Speaker Foley, and picked up 18 seats in
open-seat contests. The party proved particularly successful in the South, picking
up 19 House seats in Dixie and turning a 54–83 southern deficit into a 73–64
advantage. Republicans emerged with a 230–204 House majority. The "Republican Revolution," as it became dubbed in the press, was clearly a testament to the
hard work that Gingrich and others had done over the previous decade to prepare
the groundwork for a serious challenge to Democratic dominance.

The pressing political concern was whether the Republicans could use this
victory to end the era of Democratic dominance and consolidate a new period of
long-term Republican rule in Congress. Would the 1994 victory result only in a
short pause in Democratic control that then would be followed by Democratic
resurgence in 1996 or soon thereafter, just as Republican victories in 1946 and
1952 had been followed two years later by renewed Democratic control? Or was
it now the Republicans' turn at long-term House dominance? The answer to
these questions appeared to lie in how well the Republicans used their moment
of opportunity, and particularly in the effectiveness of Newt Gingrich as the
Speaker of the House.

The Speakership of Newt Gingrich

Following the 1994 elections and through much of the 104th Congress
(1995–1997), it appeared that czar leadership, akin to that of the 1889–1910 era,
had returned to the House. In keeping with Reed, Crisp, and Cannon, Speaker
Newt Gingrich sought a level of control of the House and its committees that
had not been seen since the revolt against Cannon.[4] House Republicans, many of
them Gingrich recruits and followers of an agenda he set for the 1994 elections,
credited him with transforming their party from its accepted position as a permanent House minority into being the majority party. Appreciative of his leadership skills, they allowed him to assume powers that had been stripped from the
Speakership in 1910.[5] Gingrich's personal choices were appointed to chair committees, even when it meant bypassing more senior members. Republican committee chairs were limited to three terms in the leadership of a specific committee, depriving them of the ability to establish independent long-term bases of
power with which to challenge the power of the Speaker. The new Speaker
assumed considerable influence in the appointment of members to key committees slots, thereby increasing his power within the committee system. And
although Gingrich did not assume the chairmanship of the Rules Committee, as
Cannon had, he was allied with Republican members of the committee, whom
he knew would assist in providing him control over the agenda and the scheduling of House legislation. Admittedly, Gingrich himself was subjected to a new
restraint that previous Speakers had not faced, with the new House Republican

majority voting to impose a four-term limit on their Speakers. Nevertheless, Gingrich's overall authority looked unassailable as the 104th Congress began.

The 104th Congress

Relying on a kind of Speaker's cabinet to set policy direction for the House, and prepared to make use of Majority Leader Dick Armey and Majority Whip Tom DeLay in running that House and whipping party members into line, Gingrich presented the House Republicans as an aggressive, cohesive, and irresistible force that could not fail to create a new Republican era in Congress. Working with his cabinet he set forth the legislative agenda. He then used party leadership resources to ensure cooperation from the standing committees, often having committees do little more than rubber stamp legislation the party leadership had drafted. And once legislation came to the floor he was prepared to push for united Republican support. For a while it even appeared that Gingrich, exercising such strong leadership powers, could compete with, and perhaps surpass, the president in terms of legislative policy leadership, much as Speaker Cannon had done eighty years earlier.

The high point of Gingrich's effectiveness came during the first hundred days of the 104th Congress, from January through early April 1995, when House Republicans acted on the major promises of the Contract with America and propelled Gingrich into a role as policy leader on a par with the president. Following the first hundred days, Gingrich and his leadership team used their power to push numerous policy initiatives intended to dismantle the Democrats' liberal policy legacy. Drafting and negotiation of major legislation were carried on by the party leadership and selected members outside the confines of the standing committees, and committee hearings were occasionally dispensed with altogether. Legislation was presented for approval to the appropriate committees, which were given limited opportunity to consider alternatives. A Republican majority on the Rules Committee would then craft terms for debate that ensured Republican dominance in floor consideration and helped sustain Republican control of the policy process. Using these processes, complex legislation like welfare reform, tax cuts, regulatory overhaul, a budget resolution, and environmental legislation all passed the House as products of party leadership negotiations rather than committee deliberations. This success then encouraged Gingrich to use his authority to seek a level of legislative control and policy impact beyond that ever envisioned by previous Speakers and to put his Speakership at risk in a high-stakes confrontation with President Bill Clinton.

The low point of Gingrich's Speakership during the 104th Congress came during December 1995 and January 1996 as a conflict between the president and Congress over the national budget resulted in two lengthy and unpopular government shutdowns. Gingrich and House Republicans had sought to use the budget struggle to gain political dominance over a sitting Democratic president, ensure their control over national policymaking, and lay the foundations for Republican victories in the 1996 elections. Never before had a Speaker, even in Cannon's era, pursued such a concerted effort to dominate national policymaking. Clinton's refusal to accept the Republicans' budget, which they presented to the president weeks after the end of the fiscal year because of their slowness in passing appropriations legislation, left the national government with no budget at all and produced two government shutdowns. Polls indicated that the public blamed the shutdowns on the Republicans, which undermined rather than strengthened their political situation. Conservative junior Republicans, whom Gingrich had recruited and helped elect, nevertheless refused to support his efforts to compromise with the president. By the time they were forced to relent in late January, the momentum of the Republican Revolution had been broken and Gingrich's weakness both within the House and in the nation had been exposed. The crisis served to demonstrate the inability of a Speaker to mandate support from independently elected party members who disagree with him on policy matters and political strategy, a lesson analogous to the one Cannon learned in 1910.

Renewed Republican activism came during the spring and summer of 1996, when a more conciliatory and cooperative Gingrich began to work with President Clinton to enact major legislation, such as the minimum wage, and skillfully maneuvered Clinton into signing welfare reform into law. Gingrich also began to work more closely with House committees and Republican committee chairs. The party never fully recovered its momentum after the budget "train wreck," however, and the loss was attributed to the mistakes made by Gingrich. In particular, fellow Republicans blamed Gingrich and his leadership team for mis-estimating the power of the Speakership and his personal control of the Republican caucus, for failing to work effectively with the House Appropriations Committee in ways that might have avoided the government shutdowns and given the party more leverage over Clinton, and for giving the Democratic president an opportunity to use his communication skills and the resources of the presidency to turn the public against the House Republican Party.

The divisions within the Republican Party became magnified by increased unity among House Democrats and by their concentrated effort to regain control of the House in the 1996 elections. In the end the Democrats fell short of a House majority, making a net gain of ten House seats in 1996. For the first time since the coming of Democratic dominance in the 1930s, the Republicans had maintained control of the House for two consecutive elections. But their narrow twenty-seat majority gave them little opportunity for great legislative accomplishment and threw into doubt whether the party would consolidate long-term dominance of the House.

The 105th Congress

As the 105th Congress (1997–1999) opened, the most central issue was whether Speaker Gingrich could lead House Republicans in a unified manner while ensuring the effective operation of the House and its committees. His efforts to compromise with Clinton during the government shutdown, and his need to compromise over policy at the end of the 104th Congress in order to preserve a Republican majority in the 1996 elections, had alienated the conservative elements in his party. His ethics problems and other personal shortcomings continued to distract attention from the Republican policy agenda and to undermine support for him among moderate Republicans. His combative and controlling inclinations raised doubts as to whether he could work with committees and their chairs, who were increasingly acting in an independent fashion. Finally, in the midst of another confrontation with Clinton in the spring of 1997, he personally threatened and thus alienated many junior Republican members who had previously been his strongest supporters. The broad disaffection with Gingrich came to a head midway through 1997 when a group of House Republicans plotted unsuccessfully to oust Gingrich from the Speakership.[6] The coup efforts, although amateurish, demonstrated his vulnerability and the need for him to reorient his governing strategy.

Lacking a policy agenda that could unite the House Republicans now that the Contract with America had passed the House and popular items such as welfare reform were law, Gingrich came increasingly to rely on the prospect that the Lewinsky scandal engulfing President Clinton would provide the basis for uniting House Republicans and lead them to success in the 1998 elections.[7] Just as the Watergate scandal and impeachment proceedings surrounding Richard Nixon had helped solidify the Democratic majority in the 1974 elections, so too might the investigation and findings of Kenneth Starr produce the collapse of the Clinton administration and the consolidation of Republican rule. Propelled by this perception, Gingrich built the House Republicans' campaign strategy for the 1998 elections around impeachment, believing that Clinton's difficulties would energize the Republican base, demoralize Democrats, and produce the strong Republican gains needed to consolidate party control and his Speakership.

Ironically, the public stood with Clinton rather than Gingrich and the Republicans, disapproving of the president's behavior but hostile toward the impeachment efforts against him. The Republicans did maintain control of the House for a third straight election but with a reduced seat margin. The election was, however, interpreted as a major defeat for House Republicans, beyond what the small seat loss would suggest. For the first time since 1934 the president's party actually gained House seats in a midterm election and did so with their president facing impeachment charges. Faced with political calamity, and informed by friend and foe alike of his collapsing support among House Republicans, Gingrich felt compelled to step down as Speaker and to resign from the House.

By the time of Gingrich's departure, any lingering thoughts of a czar-like Speakership had already been abandoned. One of the attractions of Gingrich's presumed replacement, the Appropriations Committee chair Bob Livingston, R-La., was thought to be his preference for a more committee-oriented Speakership. But at a time when the Republicans were prosecuting their impeachment case against the president because of the Lewinsky affair the revelation of Livingston's own marital infidelity led him too to leave the House. Republicans then settled on Dennis Hastert of Illinois as Speaker. Although well respected for his hard work among House Republicans, Hastert had neither the prior public visibility of Gingrich nor the media presence of Livingston. Rather than being a czar in the 106th Congress, Hastert was expected to forsake the kind of centralized leadership strategy that characterized Gingrich when he assumed the Speakership. As in 1910, power in the House was once again expected to become dispersed. Moreover, there was considerable reason to believe that the House Republicans wanted it that way.

Assessing Gingrich's Fall

Despite the existence of the most cohesive congressional parties since the days of the Reed Speakership at the end of the nineteenth century, Gingrich's vision of a return to czar rule in the House a hundred years later had been misplaced, if not delusional. Gingrich, unlike the Speakers of the 1889–1910 period, had been forced to accept the position with a limit of four congressional terms. This limit meant that Gingrich could rapidly be seen as a "lame duck" Speaker whose authority would wane even if he succeeded in consolidating his party's majority control of the House. Moreover, precisely insofar as he was seen as a successful but term-limited Speaker, and an ambitious politician still in his fifties, he could be touted as a potential presidential candidate and drawn into presidential campaign politics in ways that diverted his attention from the House. Such a situation would provide opportunities for ambitious party members to challenge his authority and maneuver for the Speakership. With committee chairs limited to three terms of service, many members would have incentive to seek the Speakership and to do so before the end of Gingrich's four-term limit. In fact, this was precisely what began to happen in Gingrich's second term. Even his ally, Appropriations chair Bill Livingston, assuming that Gingrich would run for president in 2000, actively campaigned for the Speakership well before the 1998 elections and Gingrich's fall. The four-term limit on the Speakership thus created a procedural restraint on the Speakership that almost inherently constrained Gingrich's ability to resurrect czar-like control of the House. The four-term limit, however, was not the only structural factor undermining Gingrich.

As David Brady and Joseph Cooper have so clearly elucidated, the leadership that Speakers provide and the power that they exercise is clearly constrained by organizational context.[8] However tempting it may be to conjure up a vision of a modern House run in the smooth and effective manner associated with the strong Speakers of a century ago, in truth the House itself has changed in ways that make such an effort difficult if not impossible. For example, the job of the Speaker was simply a far less taxing one a century earlier. The number and range of policy issues facing the Congress were fewer. The overall workload was less. Sessions were shorter. Fewer bills were considered. Few votes were taken. Most critically, the range of responsibilities that the Speakership entailed was narrower.

Speakers were not as actively involved in recruiting House candidates, raising campaign funds, and campaigning for others. They did not have to spend time dealing with the media and presenting a party message. Instead they could focus their attention on the management of the House—organizing its committees, scheduling legislation, and mobilizing majorities. While in the minority, Gingrich as a leader of the Conservative Opportunity Society and then as minority whip had little responsibility for the management of the House. He could afford to devote his efforts to campaign and media activities designed to build a Republican majority. Once in the Speakership, however, the full range of tasks seemed to overwhelm him. As his Speakership progressed he first handed over much of the day-to-day management of the House to Majority Leader Dick Armey. Following the coup attempt, however, Gingrich placed his primary focus on running the House and being accessible to the rank and file of Republican House members.[9] Even with his unusual energies, Gingrich found it difficult to manage the competing roles available to him as Speaker.

Finally, and perhaps most critically, Gingrich was seeking to consolidate Republican control of the House at a moment when the increase in seats necessary to ensure a working majority in the House was a difficult and perhaps unachievable goal. Although certainly the growing tilt of the South toward the Republicans created an opportunity for a long-term Republican majority, the mid- to late-1990s were not a propitious period in which to consolidate such a majority in the House. The reasons for this have to do less with national or regional electoral dynamics and more with the ways in which the politics of House careerism, incumbent advantage, and member retirements shape House elections and affect the opportunity for short-term partisan swings. To understand how such factors constrained Gingrich, and their subsequent significance for both parties' efforts to gain decisive control of the House in the 2000 general elections, let us examine the 1996 and 1998 elections in a broader historical context.

The 1996 and 1998 House Elections

Nothing did more to deflate the efforts of Gingrich and House Republicans to establish a governing majority than the outcomes of the 1996 and 1998 elections. The loss of nine seats in the 1996 elections might reasonably have been expected.[10] Some of the Republicans elected in 1994 had won in districts that had not been traditionally safe for their party and therefore were potentially vulnerable incumbents. Conversely, 1994 cleared the House of vulnerable Democratic incumbents. Having survived the partisan swing of 1994, remaining Democrats were not easy targets in 1996. With Democrats taking credit for a robust economy, and with the Republican presidential candidate never given more than an outside chance of winning, House Republicans probably felt fortunate to keep their losses in single digits. Compromising with Democrats on a minimum wage increase and on other issues late in 1996 may have helped Republicans preserve their House majority.

Although the party had to govern with fewer House seats than in the 104th Congress, the prospect for the 1998 elections offered reason for optimism. Since 1934, the party of the president had lost seats in every midterm election and those losses tended to be larger six years into a president's service rather than at the two-year point. Further, the data on midterms might encourage strong Republican candidates to run for the House, whereas their Democratic counterparts might strategically decide to pass until conditions became more favorable.[11] And although the economy continued to prosper in 1997 and 1998 and the president's job approval rating remained high, the feeling among many was that Democrats would be held accountable for the scandal surrounding the president's denials in the Lewinsky affair.

Accordingly, the four-seat Democratic gain in 1998 came as a shock. With a healthy economy, the fact that over 98 percent of the 401 incumbents running in the general election were reelected was not unexpected. Despite Republican efforts to link marginal Democrats to the president's personal problems, only a single Democratic House member was defeated. And unlike the 1994 elections, when Republicans made a net gain of eighteen seats in fifty-two open-seat contests, in 1998 they made only a one-seat gain in the thirty-four open-seat races.

Whether the failure of Republicans to do better in the 1998 midterm elections resulted from too much willingness to compromise with the Clinton administration over the budget as conservatives claimed, an unwillingness to appear less extreme as moderates argued, or a mistaken campaign strategy of focusing on Clinton's personal shortcomings is not crucial for our analysis. What is important is that the party lost the opportunity to turn a tenuous House majority into a working House majority. Instead of having a comfortable cushion that could tolerate the defection of moderates on key House roll-call votes, House Republican leaders were faced with a situation in which the loss of as few as six or seven votes to a united Democratic Party in the House meant defeat rather than victory.

A critical reason for the Republican failure, we suggest, has less to do with strategy than the low number of House retirements in the mid- to late-1990s and the effect that low retirement had on reducing the Republicans' opportunity to gain additional seats. The total of 41 new members elected to the 106th Congress was the second lowest in three decades (surpassed only by the 1988 elections, which produced only 33 new members). After having the three preceding elections produce 110, 86, and 79 new members, the 1998 elections looked more like the congressional elections of the 1984–1990 period. As in that earlier period, there were few House retirements, relatively few open seats, and few vulnerable incumbents, so the 1998 elections offered the Republicans little opportunity to greatly increase its House majority. This lack of open seats and vulnerable incumbents stemmed from the wave of retirements and the defeats of weak incumbents in both parties in 1992, 1994, and 1996, which left little potential for turnover immediately thereafter. Of course, these same features limited the Democrats' chance to regain a House majority.

These ebbs and flows in the influx of new members and the opposed changes in the number of very senior House members is not a new phenomenon. As shown in Figure 2-1, the recent decline in junior members (those serving three or fewer terms) and the increase in careerists (those serving in their tenth or greater term) have occurred in a fairly patterned fashion. Thus, although the large number of new members who entered the House in the early 1990s may have been viewed as unusual, it actually was not. During the late 1940s and early 1950s, the number of new members grew, but then membership turnover dropped, and careerism increased. At the start of the Eighty-third Congress in 1953 there were 193 (44 percent) junior House members and only 42 (10 percent) careerists. Despite some fluctuation along the way, by 1971, junior members had declined to 150 (34 percent) and careerists had increased to 87 (20 percent). A new wave of membership turnover in the 1970s brought the number of junior members above 200 for four consecutive Congresses (95th–98th), and the number of careerists reached a low of 50 (11 percent) at the start of the Ninety-seventh Congress in 1981. This was followed by another cycle of low turnover. From 1984 to 1990 few members either retired or were defeated. The House was ripe for the turnover of the early 1990s. And we are again in that part of the cycle in which membership turnover is extremely low. And careerists, who continued to decline in number through the 105th Congress, have again begun to increase.

Clearly, House turnover does not have to occur in fairly regular waves. In much of the nineteenth century, it was consistently high. But there may be contextual conditions of the post–World War II era that have resulted in these ebbs and flows. First, for most of the period, continuing membership was rewarded. Except during the early years of subcommittee government in the mid-1970s and the start of the 104th Congress, when Speaker Gingrich bypassed some more senior members in selecting committee chairs, most members have recognized that the institution extends power and perks to those who stay. This has been the case since the Reorganization Act of 1946 reduced the number of committees, making committee chair positions more valuable. Second, a large number of House seats are considered safe by both parties. With the exception of the increased use of the House as a stepping-stone to other offices, there have been few incentives to leave the institution, and reelection rates for incumbents have again returned to very high levels after a drop to "only" around 90 percent in 1992 and 1994. From this it is reasonable to expect a certain level of membership stability. Only the Republicans' limiting of committee chairs to three terms may undercut the value of long service, removing the incentive of those who exhaust their terms as chairs to stay in the House. Of course, the Democrats have indicated that they will not place term limits on chairs should they win back control of the House.

Rewarding seniority and safe seats are ingredients that would seem to suggest that one might expect a steady level of junior members and careerists in the House. Instead we find that members tend to enter and leave the House in waves. Some of this movement results from elections that produce large partisan swings such as those of 1948, 1964, 1974, 1980, and 1994. And often the losing

Figure 2-1   Ebb and Flow Patterns in House Membership, 83d–106th Congresses

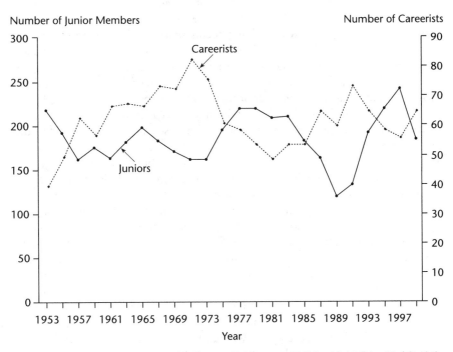

Source: Data from Norman J. Ornstein, Thomas E. Mann, and Michael J. Malbin, *Vital Statistics on Congress, 1999–2000* (Washington, D.C.: American Enterprise Institute Press, 2000), 16–17.

party recoups a sizable number of seats two years later. In addition, the ten-year cycles of reapportionment and redistricting result in spurts of voluntary and involuntary departures from the House. Between 1952 and 1998 the number of first-term House members was more than a third higher in the five Congresses that followed reapportionments than in the nineteen other Congresses. The reasons for this are fairly obvious. States gaining new districts elect new House members. New district lines may make some incumbents more vulnerable. Some incumbents may retire or be defeated, especially those senior members who may not want to reenter what Richard F. Fenno Jr. describes as an "expansionist" home style phase.[12] Finally, many of those entering the House will be between forty and fifty years of age. Having come in waves, those who stay will tend to reach careerist status in clusters and may also exit in clusters.

Taken together, these factors have led to ebbs and flows in the seniority mix in the House. The elections of 1992–1996 brought large numbers of new members to the House, ending four consecutive elections in which turnover averaged less than 10 percent. Having emptied the House of members prone to retirement, and also weeded out some vulnerable freshmen, those election periods created a

set of incumbents prepared to run effectively in the 1996 and 1998 elections, limiting the capacity of either party, particularly the Republican Party, to make great
gains. The 2000 elections, similarly, seemed likely also to see low turnover as in
the past two elections. With only thirty-one open seats and few incumbents
viewed as vulnerable, the 107th House seems poised to have even fewer new
members than the 106th. Only with reapportionment and redistricting for 2002
are we likely to see an upswing in retirements, some previously safe incumbents
defeated because of changes in the partisan composition of their districts, and the
resulting influx of a sizable number of first-term members.

The thrust of these observations is to suggest that the opportunities for
great swings in the partisan composition of House seats is heavily shaped in the
contemporary House by cycles of generational turnover. For three or four elections, few members tend to be so advanced in their House careers or in age that
they choose to leave; these low points in retirement then are followed by three or
four elections when growing numbers of members tend to retire, and then by a
swing back toward fewer retirements. Quite aside from immediate national or
regional electoral considerations, two simple factors produced by these generational waves can create an opportunity for one party or group significantly to
increase its House members: a large number of open seats due to retirements in
the opposing party, and a large number of freshmen legislators in the opposing
party who are running for reelection after winning such open seats. Because legislators tend to retire in generational waves or cycles, and because such waves may
be composed more of one party's members owing to its electoral successes in a
previous historical period, each party will have points in the cycle of generational
turnover at which they are vulnerable, particularly if short-term issue debates or
political circumstances favor the other party.

The early 1990s, and specifically the 1994 elections, provided the Republicans with an opportunity they were able to exploit. Democratic retirements in
1994 and redistricting created a large number of open seats, and first-term Democratic incumbents elected in marginal seats with Bill Clinton's victory in 1992
were potentially vulnerable. (Many of these districts, especially in the South, had
been voting for Republicans in presidential elections but had continued to reelect
Democratic incumbents. Previously, many of these seats had become open in
elections when the partisan forces favored the Democrats—1974, 1976, and
1982—allowing a new generation of Democrats to replace an old one.) In addition, the defeat of the administration's controversial health care proposals and the
enactment of its economic programs, including some tax increases, placed
Democrats on the defensive in the campaign. For the first time since the 1980
elections the short-term forces favored the Republicans, and the Democrats
were forced to defend a large number of open and insecure seats. In 1994 Gingrich and his allies targeted such seats, recruited effective challengers, and concentrated resources on the most promising contests.

By 1996, and certainly by 1998, the Republicans' advantage had passed. It
was the Republicans who had vulnerable freshmen up for reelection in 1996. And

by 1998 neither party had many open seats or freshmen seats at stake, since the wave of generational retirements of the early 1990s had passed, so that a substantial swing toward either party was unlikely. Only some strong contentious issue that might serve to undercut public support for "safe" incumbents of one party or the other was likely to produce a significant shift in party margins in 1998. Targeted districts, good challengers, massive spending, coordinated partisan attacks on the opposition—none of these factors that had proven so successful for the Republicans in 1994 was likely to work in 1998 without such a visible "crisis." With a prosperous U.S. economy, Republicans had to rely on the Lewinsky scandal and Clinton's pending impeachment as a campaign issue. Once this strategy backfired on them, their chance of winning a major victory analogous to the Democratic success in the 1974 Watergate elections was lost. In fact, their strategy served primarily to mobilize elements of the Democratic base so that what little change occurred in 1998 benefited the Democrats and allowed the president's party to increase House seats for the first time since 1934.

It was Newt Gingrich's good fortune to mount a coordinated Republican attack on Democratic dominance in 1994, at a time when generational turnover and short-term partisan forces made the Democratic Party particularly vulnerable to defeat. In 1996 and 1998, however, when Gingrich needed to expand the party's House majority and consolidate his control, he lacked the conditions which made 1994 a success. The wave of Democratic retirements had passed and the prosperous economy limited the vulnerability of House incumbents of the president's party. It thus was not simply Gingrich's mistakes that cost him his Speakership, nor organizational constraints operating on him, but electoral dynamics and retirement patterns largely beyond his control. It was his failed effort to gain control over these dynamics by fostering or inflaming crises that might benefit his party—the government shutdowns in 1995–1996 and the impeachment of Clinton in 1998—that ensured the dramatic nature of his fall.

As Gingrich left office, just over the horizon loomed the 2000 elections, and yet another moment when one party or the other might conceivably break loose and win a great victory. Yet from the perspective of generational turnover, the 2000 elections likewise seemed to present little decisive advantage to either party. With a five-seat margin between the two parties, shifts in only a few seats would alter party control of the House; the 2000 elections therefore posed substantial partisan opportunity for the Democrats and substantial risks for the Republicans. Thus, maneuvering for the 2000 elections became the dominant concern of congressional leaders as soon as the 106th Congress opened. But in the background of such concerns was the awareness that whichever party emerged with majority control in 2000, the elections were not likely to provide it with a large margin of control. The battle for partisan dominance of the House thus was likely to continue into the 2002 elections and beyond as redistricting and a new wave of generational retirements created new opportunities for larger partisan swings. Moreover, given the disaster experienced by the Republicans and Gingrich as he tried to use government shutdowns and impeachment to manufacture political opportunity in 1996 and 1998, few leaders of either party were touting dramatic plans for new "political train wrecks" that might help induce a partisan advantage. As both parties looked toward the 2000 elections after the experience of Newt Gingrich, caution and patience was the name of the game. It was into this political reality that members of the House stepped as they began service in the 106th Congress (1999–2001).

The "Do-Little" 106th Congress

As the 106th Congress opened in January 1999, the House members—whether seasoned veterans or newly elected novices—were virtually in shock. In the previous two months they had witnessed the resignation of the Speaker of the House and of his heir apparent, and then they had proceeded to vote two impeachment charges against the president of the United States, despite public opinion polls showing popular support for the president. On the other side of Capitol Hill the Senate was gearing up to hear the House managers present the impeachment case and to deliberate and vote on whether to convict the president. As they grappled with these extraordinary developments and prepared for the new legislative year, members confronted a more evenly divided House than any since the 72d Congress (1931–1933).

The First Session: 1999

Normally the first two months of a new Congress are a relatively quiet time. Party leaders and committee chairs plan their legislative agenda and organize the two houses. That was not to be the case for the 106th Congress. For seven weeks the conviction proceedings in the Senate preoccupied both chambers and their leaders. During this period virtually no discussion about the future legislative agenda took place between Senate majority leader Trent Lott and Speaker Dennis Hastert, and little significant movement occurred in the introduction of House bills or in committee planning. All eyes were on the Senate as the House managers made the case for the impeachment of Clinton and the senators grappled with the final decision. Only after the Senate completed the impeachment trial and Congress took an already scheduled recess did the House finally begin to focus on its legislative responsibilities and return to a semblance of normalcy.

Also contributing to the slow start of the House was the newness of the Republican Speaker, J. Dennis Hastert, and the difficult circumstances he faced.[13] Largely unknown to the public or the press corps when House Republicans promoted him from deputy whip to the Speakership, Hastert benefited from an "anti-Gingrich" persona—a quiet, deliberate, understated, and measured manner—that appeared to signal a new and more moderate approach to House politics. Yet the Gingrich years had left him a highly fractious, if ideologically conservative, Republican Conference, a demoralized membership, and a razor-thin majority with which to work. The term limits passed in the 104th Congress meant that twelve of his committee leaders in the 106th Congress were in their last term as chair and likely to be preoccupied with concerns beyond immediate committee legislation, with one chair, John Kasich of Ohio, already running for president.[14] It also meant that, as committee leaders faced the end of their terms, their committees could be distracted by competitive tensions among members seeking to replace the term-limited chair. Clinton's survival left in the presidency a skillful adversary with little love for House Republicans. And the 1998 election had left House Democrats believing that they could win control in the 2000 elections and thus seeking to find ways to foster their electoral advantage, even if that meant direct confrontation with the Republicans.

Hastert's overriding goal, clearly, was to position the House Republicans to maintain and expand their majority in the 2000 elections.[15] To do so, he and other Republicans believed that the party faced three critical tasks. First, House Republicans needed to "do no harm" during the 106th Congress; in other words, they needed to avoid the sort of political train wrecks that had hurt them with the public and cost them support in the 1996 and 1998 elections. In particular, Hastert and other Republicans believed that they needed to avoid any chance at government shutdowns and thus needed to make sure that the House had passed appropriations bills successfully in September and October so as to avoid closing the government down in ways that could boomerang on the party. Second, the party needed some significant legislative accomplishments to which it could point as demonstrating its capacity to govern and in order to avoid the "Do-Nothing" epitaph that President Harry Truman had used so effectively in the 1948 elections as he sought to persuade voters to throw the Republican majority out of the House. Third, the party needed to limit the number of retirements, which were likely to be fueled by term limits on committee chairs, and to recruit effective new candidates for office. Movement toward these goals was complicated by the reluctance of many House Republicans to work in concert with Clinton on legislative matters, by their desire to stress conservative legislative agenda, particularly tax cuts and the use of appropriations to serve ideological goals, and by the overall Republican demoralization.

Seeking to stabilize and unify the House Republicans, Hastert kept in place the leadership team—Majority Leader Dick Armey and Majority Whip Tom DeLay—installed by Speaker Gingrich in 1994 and proceeded to craft a "mainstream" Republican agenda focused particularly on a huge across-the-board tax cut. He reassured committee chairs of his willingness to work with them and then proceeded to rely heavily on committees for the review and crafting of Republican legislation. Concerned to create some opportunity for legislative success, Hastert also signaled a willingness to work with Clinton on common areas of legislative concern and did so even before the Senate held its final conviction votes.

Hastert's efforts were complicated in February 1999 when the Democrats' experienced minority leader, Richard Gephardt, made official his decision not to run for president and instead to focus his energies and skills on gaining House control for the Democrats. Gephardt, too, faced considerable challenges.[16]

Although fellow House Democrats had held together surprisingly well in the face of the Clinton scandals and impeachment proceedings and had won a moral victory in the 1998 elections, the Republicans still controlled the House and dominated the legislative process. It thus would be difficult to get their legislative priorities considered on the floor. Second, the ability to attract strong Democratic challengers for the 2000 elections was complicated by fears in the party that Vice President Al Gore would be a poor party standard-bearer, leaving the Democrats' without presidential coattails, and by concerns that the Clinton scandals would overshadow the 2000 elections. Finally, Gephardt and House Democrats worried about the role that President Clinton would play in the 106th Congress. They were particularly apprehensive that Clinton's concern with leaving a legacy after impeachment would lead him to seek legislative accomplishments through political alliances with Republicans on key pieces of legislation.

During 1999 it was in fact the legacies of the Gingrich era—term limits on chairs, the government shutdowns, and the impeachment—that shaped the decision of key actors and determined the flow of House politics. Term limits on chairs generated considerable debate, early in the Congress, as House leaders considered whether to backpedal on term limits, possibly creating exceptions for visible and important chairs.[17] While such debate went forward, various members who intended to contend for chairmanships made it clear that they would oppose such exceptions. Simultaneously, committees with term-limited chairs, such as the Commerce Committee, were engulfed in tension and conflict as subcommittee chairs began as early as February 1999 to mount campaigns for selection as committee chair in 2001.[18] In the face of support for chair term limits, Hastert made no move to alter the rule or to support exceptions and focused his energy on managing committee conflicts.

The fear of new train wrecks likewise generated great care on Hastert's part to ensure that House politics proceeded in an effective manner; it thus limited his willingness to risk and experiment in ways that might induce enthusiasm from his rank and file. The Speaker focused special attention on the appropriations process, encouraged the House Appropriations Committee to take a very workmanlike and sensible approach to appropriations legislation, and worked to ensure that the House passed appropriations bills that could gain the president's signature. Hastert and fellow Republicans also took care to pass an across-the-board tax cut, so as to create a visible legislative record, but they failed to win President Clinton's support or to override his veto. In fact, Republicans largely failed throughout 1999 to form any working alliance with Clinton or other Democrats, whereas Clinton did cooperate with House Democrats to highlight legislation on issues such as health care and education that helped position them and Al Gore for the 2000 election season.

In the end, the first session of the 106th Congress proved to be one of the most partisan, divided, and unproductive such periods in recent congressional history. The *National Journal* reported that during 1999, in key legislative areas, the members of each party voted together as blocs, and against each other, at the highest level in modern times.[19] Such divisiveness, when combined with the failure of the House to generate truly visible new laws, created a severe problem for the Republicans, suggesting an inability on their part to build bipartisan coalitions and govern effectively. Such problems were then reinforced by polls demonstrating strong public support for various health and education issues pushed by House Democrats, issues that Republicans might have stressed and used to generate bipartisan legislation and a record of accomplishment.

The Second Session: 2000

Faced with such developments, Hastert and fellow Republicans switched strategies early in 2000 and began to focus on ways to build a legislative record by working more explicitly with Clinton and elements of the House Democratic Party.[20] Rather than focus on Republican Party dominance of the policy process, they shifted toward a form of "constructive partisanship" designed to build a record of legislative accomplishment that would demonstrate their capacity to govern effectively.[21] In doing so, they gave up on across-the-board tax cuts as their central legislative agenda and focused instead on targeted tax cuts (to revoke the marriage penalty, for example), on popular social programs dealing with health and education that were supported by Democrats, and also on an alliance with Clinton to pass legislation normalizing trade relations with China. In response, Democratic leaders emphasized the conservative tilt of the Republicans' new taxing and social programs, pushed for more inclusive programs on topics such as prescription drugs, and held close to their union base on the China trade issue, opposing its passage. In the end, the House passed the China trade bill and a bill removing earning caps for Social Security recipients, as did the Senate, and they became law. The House also passed legislation to end the marriage tax penalty and to repeal estate taxes, which the president successfully vetoed following Senate approval. And the two houses passed different versions of such popular legislation as government funding for prescription drugs for seniors, which remained stuck in conference committee as the end of the 106th Congress approached.

The expanded activism of House Republicans in 2000 served to generate legislative accomplishments that were sufficiently visible to offset a do-nothing image, but they also came at a price. First, some of the most visible bills lingered in conference committee as Congress approached its end, highlighting the problems of the Republicans in moving legislation forward and raising issues about their sincerity in supporting such legislation. Second, diverted by the expanded legislative workload and preoccupied by the Republican and Democratic Conventions, the House moved slowly on appropriations legislation; moreover, ideological fervor among Republicans led to renewed efforts to use the appropriations process to implement a conservative agenda in areas such as environmental politics, a strategy virtually guaranteed to bring Clinton's veto.[22] To greatly delay the enactment of appropriations legislation risked reminding voters of the Gingrich era when such tactics helped generate the government shutdowns.

As the House returned in September 2000, following national conventions and Labor Day recess, suddenly the Republican leadership faced the prospect that it would not meet its October 6 deadline that it had set for adjournment.[23] Keeping members in Washington beyond this point was only likely to increase frustrations and tensions within the House, restricting members' ability to campaign for the November 7 elections, and increase national focus on the governing problems of the congressional Republicans. Yet compromising with the president, particularly on appropriations, threatened to create a spending spree that would undermine support for House Republicans among their conservative base. The difficulties of the Republicans, however, did not necessarily redound to the Democrats' benefit, as they, too, needed time to campaign. Moreover, the Republicans' activism in 2000 had muddied the differences between the parties on various political issues such as prescription drug benefits for seniors so that the Democrats' initial advantage on such issue terrain began to decline.

The tensions surrounding the completion of the 106th Congress left both House parties frustrated, neither party buoyed by a sense of reliable momentum, and both confronted with polls that seemed to foreshadow another close House election. The House parties appeared to be as deadlocked in their contest for public support as did their parties' presidential candidates. Neither party appeared to have great natural advantage that might break their razor-thin standoff. Democrats had experienced fewer retirements and thus had fewer open seats to defend. But there were only a modest number of Republicans seats that truly looked vulnerable. The Republicans had succeeded in recruiting a sufficient number of good candidates that to have a reasonable chance of holding their own open seats. Yet the Republicans likewise faced a dilemma, as they needed not just to hold their majority but to expand it, and only a few Democratic incumbents or open seats seemed sufficiently vulnerable to provide such an opportunity.

The election stalemate between the House parties during the fall of 2000, in combination with developments in the presidential and senatorial races, created the closest race for control of the national government—across the House, Senate, and the presidency—of modern times, rivaling not just the 1960 race highlighted by John Kennedy and Richard Nixon but also the 1948 race in which Harry Truman ran against the famous Do-Nothing Congress. The closeness of the race meant that any adverse developments in the last weeks of the campaign—a national crisis, developments in the presidential race, or last-minute activities of Congress—could have enormous consequences for control of the national government and the future development of the House of Representatives. These developments focused great attention on the capacities of the Republicans to find a way to end the 106th Congress that would not open them to charges of legislative ineffectiveness or irresponsibility and would allow their members to campaign effectively for reelection. Conflict between the House Republicans and the president finally exploded in the closing days of October, as the Republicans sent Clinton appropriations legislation he strongly opposed, and he responded with a veto. Just as another historic battle appeared likely to engulf them, possibly including a government shutdown days before the election, House Republicans and the president backed away from a "train wreck" and agreed on November 4 to a bill that kept federal agencies running until November 14. The House immediately recessed. In doing so, it put off a number of hard decisions until a "lame duck" session of the 106th Congress, following the November 7 elections, and members returned to their home districts to campaign for three final days and await the election outcome.

The House and its leadership thus approached the end of the 106th Congress, and the 2000 elections, in much the same manner as it had opened in the winter of 1999 — preoccupied by external events and internal divisions, uncertain about the future, hobbled by the past, awaiting developments largely beyond their control, and certain only of their ability to make matters worse through misstep and miscalculation. The great success of Republicans in the 106th Congress lay in Hastert's ability to move his party beyond the calamity of the 1998 elections and the impeachment period and to accomplish enough — particularly the China trade agreement — so that Clinton and the Democrats could not easily campaign against the "Do-Nothing Congress." In the auspicious phrase of Richard Cohen and Eliza Carney, the 106th was more nearly a "Do-Little Congress."[24] The issue was whether "little" had been good enough to neutralize the Democrats' issue assault and maintain Republican control. The great success of the Democrats came in the fact that, without control of the House, they had managed to push forward issues on health and education that had come to dominate the 2000 election, issues that the public seemed to embrace and historically had identified with the Democratic Party. The concern for Democrats was whether sufficient congressional races would be close enough, and the political environment of early November favorable enough to Democrats, to allow such issues to aid their capture of the House.

The dilemma for both parties was that, despite extensive efforts over the previous two years, control of the House appeared to rest in a relatively small number of truly competitive races — about forty — that would be affected as much or more by local concerns and candidates, and by presidential coattails, as by anything the House parties might do to aggressively gain partisan advantage. A train wreck in the last week could conceivably have doomed whichever congressional party was held responsible. But a party's success depended heavily on mistakes by the other party, sudden national crises that favored it, and ultimately by the ability of its candidates to win the support of the American public, district by district.

Conclusion

As the national campaign entered the last week prior to November 7, national polls showed the Republican and Democratic presidential candidates running neck and neck and the public essentially tied in whether it preferred a Republican or Democratic Congress. The Senate, which had for two years seemed certain to stay in Republican hands, now appeared too close to call. Control of the House appeared to be a toss-up, as it had since the election of 1998. American politics truly seemed to be at a historic crossroads wherein the November elections could send the country down starkly different paths, toward united government led by Republicans or Democrats, or divided government in which one party controlled the House, the Senate, or both, and the other party controlled the presidency. In no small measure, this moment of choice was testament to the Republican Revolution of 1994 and the success of Newt Gingrich in breaking the Democrats' historic dominance of the House and thereby breaking open the historic partisan structure of American national politics.

The special circumstances confronting the House parties as they contested for power in 2000 likewise demonstrated the continuing legacy of Newt Gingrich and the Republican Revolution. On the one hand it was the Republicans who held majority control of the House and Senate and were in position to call the shots at the end of the 106th Congress in ways that might serve their party. It was Gingrich's leadership in the late 1980s and early 1990s that had made this possible. On the other hand a critical issue was whether the Republican Party was an effective legislative party capable of running Congress—a question highlighted by the experience of the Gingrich years.

In the end, the decision by Speaker Hastert and the House Republicans early in 2000 to strike a somewhat moderate pose, avoid the kind of protracted crises that had characterized the Republican Revolution in earlier years, and create a constructive legislative record served them well. Although they lost seats for a third straight election, they managed to hold on to a slim majority in the House despite an aggressive assault by House Democrats in the 2000 elections. The electorate had failed to break the standoff between the two parties, and in fact had produced an even more closely divided House. But the power to organize the House, name committee chairs, and oversee rules and procedures remained in Republican hands.

As the Republicans took control of the House for a fourth straight Congress, their governing tasks were greatly complicated by the developments of the previous six years and the electoral realities looming on the horizon. The experience of the Republicans in the mid- to late-1990s suggested that term limits on the Speaker and committee chairs had greatly destabilized the majority party. A new Republican majority would need to consider ways to address this problem, or it would face continuing difficulties. The contentiousness of the parties in the House over the previous decade, the narrow margin of Republican control of the House after the 2000 elections, and the protracted struggle for control of the Senate and the presidency that emerged in the aftermath of the 2000 elections meant that the Republicans confronted a difficult environment within which they would have to manage the House and enact their agenda during the 107th Congress. And the 2002 elections promised to preoccupy and upend the political strategems during the new Congress and generate a range of new challenges. The redistricting of House seats by state legislatures following the 2000 census, and a likely surge of House retirements in 2002 and 2004, meant that a new wave of open seats and vulnerable freshmen could provide one party or the other an opportunity to pursue a strong working majority, consolidate House control, and end the close partisan division of the House set in motion by the Republican Revolution of 1994. Extensive maneuvering for partisan control of the House thus was likely to preoccupy the House during the 107th Congress, to limit its legislative accomplishments, and to set the stage for a new period of electoral upheaval and organizational change in 2002 and 2004.

Notes

1. For a more extensive discussion of the era of Democratic dominance, and the subsequent takeover by Republicans in the 104th Congress, and for relevant reading, see Lawrence C. Dodd and Bruce I. Oppenheimer, "Revolution in the House: Testing the Limits of Party Government," in *Congress Reconsidered,* ed. Lawrence C. Dodd and Bruce I. Oppenheimer, 6th ed. (Washington, D.C.: CQ Press, 1997). See also David W. Rohde, *Parties and Leaders in the Postreform House* (Chicago: University of Chicago Press, 1991); Gary W. Cox and Mathew D. McCubbins, *Legislative Leviathan: Party Government in the House* (Berkeley: University of California Press, 1993); Barbara Sinclair, *Legislators, Leaders, and Lawmaking: The U.S. House of Representatives in the Postreform Era* (Baltimore: Johns Hopkins University Press, 1995).
2. For a helpful discussion of the development of the committee system and its contemporary role, see Christopher J. Deering and Steven S. Smith, *Committees in Congress,* 3d ed. (Washington, D.C.: CQ Press, 1997).
3. Douglas L. Koopman, *Hostile Takeover: The House Republican Party, 1980–1995* (Lanham, Md.: Rowman and Littlefield, 1996); William F. Connelly Jr. and John J. Pitney Jr., *Congress' Permanent Minority? Republicans in the U.S. House* (Lanham, Md.: Rowman and Littlefield, 1994).
4. An excellent discussion of the development of the Speakership is Ronald M. Peters Jr., *The American Speakership* (Baltimore: Johns Hopkins University Press, 1990). For a helpful analysis of the Gingrich Speakership, see Peters's essay, "The Republican Speakership" (paper presented at the annual meeting of the American Political Science Association, San Francisco, August 29–Sept 1, 1996).
5. C. Lawrence Evans and Walter J. Oleszek, *Congress Under Fire: Reform Politics and the Republican Majority* (Boston: Houghton Mifflin, 1997).
6. The dissidents planned to use a motion to "vacate the chair" as a means of unseating Gingrich and then replacing him with a candidate of their choosing. To do so, however, would have required that the Democratic House members cooperate in those efforts. And the rebels seemed to assume that this would occur. It may well have required them to agree to vote for a Democrat as Speaker. See Jackie Koszczuk, "Coup Attempt Throws GOP Off Legislative Track," *Congressional Quarterly Weekly Report,* July 19, 1997, 1671–1674.
7. Richard E. Cohen, "The Rise and Fall of Newt," *National Journal* 31 (March 6, 1999): 598.
8. Joseph Cooper and David W. Brady, "Institutional Context and Leadership Style: The House from Cannon to Rayburn," *American Political Science Review* 75 (1981): 411–25.
9. Jackie Koszczuk, "Concerned GOP Urges Gingrich: Settle Down to Housekeeping," *Congressional Quarterly Weekly Report,* August 30, 1997, 2030–33.

10. Between the 1994 and 1996 elections, the Republicans gained a net of six seats as a result of switched party affiliations and the outcomes of special elections to fill vacancies. The nine-seat loss in 1996 is measured against the number of seats the Republicans held at the end of the 104th Congress and not the number they won in the 1994 election.

11. Gary C. Jacobson and Samuel Kernell, *Strategy and Choice in Congressional Elections* (New Haven: Yale University Press, 1983).

12. Richard F. Fenno Jr., *Home Style: House Members in Their Districts* (Boston: Little, Brown, 1978).

13. Jennifer G. Hickey, "Dennis Hastert at the Helm," *National Journal* 31 (April 5, 1999): 16.

14. By the end of the 106th Congress it also became clear that two other committee chair positions, Science and Small Business, would be open. The chair of the former, James Sensenbrenner of Wisconsin, is likely to move to chair the Judiciary Committee, and the chair of the latter, James Talent of Missouri, is leaving the House. In addition, seven Appropriations Committee subcommittee chairs will have served three terms.

15. Richard E. Cohen, "It's Campaign 2000, Stupid," *National Journal* 31 (September 25, 1999): 2714.

16. Alexis Simendinger, "Democrats: Divided They Stand," *National Journal* 31 (September 25, 1999): 2710.

17. Kirk Victor, "Gaveling Down the Chairmen," *National Journal* 31 (March 6, 1999): 620.

18. Brody Mullins, "A Scandal Fanned by a Chairmanship Battle," *National Journal* 31 (July 31, 1999): 2228.

19. Richard E. Cohen, "A Congress Divided," *National Journal* 32 (February 5, 2000): 382.

20. David Baumann, "A Republican Resurgence," *National Journal* 32 (May 6, 2000): 1414.

21. On the strategy of constructive partisanship and its potential advantages to House Republicans, see Lawrence C. Dodd and Bruce I. Oppenheimer, "Congress and the Emerging Order: Conditional Party Government or Constructive Partisanship?" in Dodd and Oppenheimer, *Congress Reconsidered*, 6th ed., 410–12.

22. David Baumann, "Full Steam Ahead to Derailment," *National Journal* 32 (May 20, 2000): 1608; Margaret Kriz, "Riding a Wave of Discontent," *National Journal* 32 (September 9, 2000): 2792.

23. Richard E. Cohen and David Baumann, "Exit Strategies," *National Journal* 32 (September 9, 2000): 2774. Cohen and Baumann also provide a helpful overview of the 106th Congress.

24. Richard E. Cohen and Eliza Newlin Carney, "A Do-Little Congress?" *National Journal* 31 (February 13, 1999): 394.

3. What the American Public Wants Congress to Be

John R. Hibbing and James T. Smith

Congress is designed to be a permeable institution. If it is doing its job, public opinion should be able to enter and affect the policy actions taken by Congress. This reflection of public views in congressional policy decisions is called representation, and Congress is specially designed to facilitate it. Large collections of formally equal officials who are subject to frequent elections and incredibly open operating procedures, and who are all directly responsible for acting in the interests of specific groups of constituents, should generate policy representation if any institutional structure can. Indeed, if Congress were not representative why would we have it? A smaller, more hierarchical body is far better at getting things done, but "getting things done" is not the only goal of government. After all, the cry of the revolution was not "no taxation unless it is enacted by an efficient, hierarchical body"; it was "no taxation without representation."

The question of whether or not Congress is successful in fulfilling its constitutional mission to provide policy representation is one that has occupied observers for quite some time. Although liberals tend to think Congress is too conservative and conservatives tend to think it is too liberal, for the most part the people prefer centrist policies and believe Congress provides centrist policies. Certainly, on some issues, such as gun control, campaign finance reform, and limiting legislative terms, policy is severely out of step with majority public sentiment, but issues of constitutionality hamper the ability of Congress to act in all three of these areas; moreover, these policy inconsistencies seem to be more the exception than the rule. In general, Congress addresses the issues the public believes to be important and acts on those issues in the moderate ways the public prefers (see Chapter 4).

But public opinion can also affect Congress in a manner quite different from influence on specific policy decisions. The public's opinion of Congress itself can serve as an important institutional constraint on it. If the public strongly disapproves of Congress, sitting members may decide against seeking reelection and prospective candidates may decide against running for a seat in the first place. If members are sensitive to the public's opinion of them and of Congress, they may be reluctant to address new policy initiatives, especially any that are mildly controversial. And solid evidence even suggests that negative views of Congress render people less likely to comply with the laws it passes.[1]

Given these important consequences of public attitudes toward Congress, it is imperative that we understand the factors that lead the public to regard the institution favorably or unfavorably. In this chapter we employ data and arguments from a variety of sources in order to explicate the reasons people feel as they do toward the American Congress. Our presentation is divided into five main parts. In the first, we look at variations in the public's opinion of Congress since the mid-1970s, asking why attitudes seem to be more favorable at some times than others. In the second, we briefly compare attitudes toward Congress with attitudes toward other institutions, especially political institutions. In the third, we look at public opinion of the many different parts of Congress. In the fourth, we determine the kinds of people who seem most willing to proffer negative evaluations of Congress. These sections are tied together by the hope that determining the situations under which a favorable (or unfavorable) judgment of Congress is returned will permit a clearer view of the reasons the public feels as it does. We then conclude with a summary of our theory of public support for the political system, for political institutions, and especially for the Congress.

Why People Like Congress More Sometimes than Others

Maybe the public simply detests Congress and that is all that needs to be said on the matter. Perhaps it is erroneous to think that Congress under any circumstances could be even remotely popular. As tempting as it may be to jump to this conclusion and as much as popular press coverage encourages such inclinations, the situation is actually much more complex than that. Survey data from across the decades reveal a surprising amount of variation, as is apparent in Figure 3-1, which presents the percentage of people approving of Congress from 1975 through the third quarter of 1999, according to various Gallup polls.

The last quarter of the twentieth century began with Congress (and the rest of the political system) struggling to pull itself out of a trying period. In fact, although soundings were taken much less frequently prior to 1975, the data that are available demonstrate that the mid-to-late 1960s was a period of relative popularity for Congress and for all of government. But starting about 1968 and continuing into the first half of the 1970s, the public's approval of political institutions and, indeed, societal institutions generally declined precipitously.[2] Thus, the opening data points in the figure, coming on the heels of the Watergate scandal and other societal frustrations, reflect a disillusioned people, and barely one out of four American adults approved of Congress.

After these initial low ratings, the rest of the figure suggests three phases of congressional approval: high, low, and high again. By 1985 Watergate and perhaps the economic difficulties of the late 1970s and early 1980s were distant memories and the Reagan "feel-good" period had arrived. Well over half of the American public approved of the job Congress was doing in the latter 1980s. But by 1992 approval levels had reverted to 1970s levels or worse, with sometimes just one in five adults approving of Congress. Just before the 1994 midterm election, Congress's popularity bottomed out with a whopping 75 percent of the population *disapproving* of the job Congress was doing.

This high level of dissatisfaction with Congress continued well into the mid-1990s even though by then the economy had long been booming. In fact, it was not until very late 1997 that approval levels turned around. By January

Figure 3-1 Approval of Congress, 1975–1999

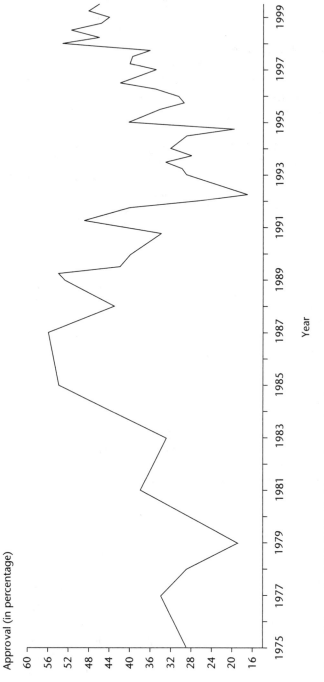

Source: Gallup polls, 1975–1988; *Washington Post*, various issues, 1989–1999.

Note: Data were available on a yearly basis between 1975 and 1988, with the exceptions of 1976, 1980, 1982, 1984, and 1986. Between 1989 and 1999 data were available on a quarterly basis, with the exceptions of the following quarters: 1989/4, 1990/2, 1990/3, 1991/1, 1991/3, 1992/3, 1992/4, 1994/2, 1995/2, 1996/4, and 1999/4.

1998 more people approved of Congress than disapproved, a situation that had not been seen since the late 1980s. Approval levels then stayed high until impeachment proceedings were commenced in the House against President Bill Clinton. In August 1998 Congress was enjoying 55 percent public approval, but as soon as impeachment of the president became the dominant congressional issue these marks began to drop, although perhaps not as much as might have been expected. By early 1999 approval was down more than 10 points to 44 percent. And then, as the painful national episode faded, approval of Congress improved slightly, to the upper 40s by the end of 1999. The divisive period reduced public approval of Congress but never threatened to return approval to the low levels of the late 1970s or early 1990s.

Taken as a whole, the pattern is not an easy one to explain. Societal conditions seem to affect the public's approval of Congress, but the relationship is not as powerful as is usually anticipated. Economic conditions, for example, are sometimes strong when approval of Congress is weak (the mid-1990s, for example), and vice versa. The authors of the most systematic effort to account for the ups and downs of public approval discovered that economic conditions have far less of an impact on congressional than on presidential approval.[3] A broader analysis of attitudes toward various parts of government, including Congress, notes that "it is by no means clear that economic performance has actually played a decisive role in generating [the] decline in trust."[4] And Katharine Seelye may have put it best: "Most Americans still deeply distrust the federal government despite the end of the cold war, the robust economy and the highest level of satisfaction in their own lives in 30 years."[5]

If societal conditions such as the health of the economy explain only a small portion of changes in the public's attitudes toward Congress (and the entire polity), then what accounts for the rest? One obvious possibility is that people are more influenced by congressional actions than by societal conditions. Rather than holding Congress accountable for society generally, approval of the job Congress is doing may actually depend, sensibly enough, on perceptions of the job Congress is doing. Perhaps not surprisingly, evidence presented in previous research finds support for this possibility, but the particular congressional actions that warm the hearts of most Americans are not the actions that may have been expected. Passage of particular policy proposals traditionally has done little to enhance approval of Congress. In fact, when Congress is engaged in meaningful debate, when it is being newsworthy by passing important legislation and by checking presidential power, people are *least* happy with the institution.[6] One writer correctly observes that "the less people hear from Congress, the higher Congress' ratings soar."[7]

This surprising finding suggests that conflict in the political arena is not something the American public likes to see, largely because the public commonly believes that consensus is wide in the United States and so conflict in the political arena is unnecessary. Many people may prefer divided government but this does not mean they like to see open conflict between Congress and the president and between the parties in Congress.[8] The more that parties and institutions are at odds, the more the people believe the interests of ordinary Americans are being neglected. For most people, the model for how government should work is the balanced budget agreement that dominated the news in the second half of 1997. Here was a case in which the major institutions of government, even though they were controlled by different parties, quietly cooperated in addressing a problem consistently rated as "the most important problem" by the public. People were spared the usual partisan hyperbole and gamesmanship and a reasonable solution was produced (even if the roaring economy made the task of politicians infinitely less difficult). It is probably not a coincidence that approval of Congress went up shortly thereafter, when it became increasingly apparent that the deficit really was trending downward at a brisk rate.

People do not want an activist, contentious, marketplace-of-ideas Congress, and they are unable to fathom why earnest problem-solving cannot be the norm rather than the exception. Citizens are more likely to approve of Congress when it is being still and not rocking the boat. For much of the public, conflict is a sign that elected officials are out of touch with ordinary, centrist Americans and that they are too much "in touch" with nefarious special interests. The leaders of Congress have recognized the public's inclinations and have been known to trim the sails of the legislative agenda when they are concerned about public perceptions of the institution. Thus, Congress may go into "hibernation" when an election is approaching and approval ratings are high.[9]

Why People Like Other Components of the Political System More than Congress

So, public approval of Congress varies and does so in predictable, if in some respect counterintuitive, ways. If conditions (especially economic) are favorable and Congress is not caught in the unforgivable acts of openly debating tough policy issues, serving as a counterweight to presidential initiatives, representing diverse views, and pursuing activist legislative agendas, Congress is likely to be approved of by more than half of the American public. Still, it is unlikely that even under these conditions Congress will be nearly as popular as just about any other feature of government in the United States. Despite ups and downs over time, relative to other institutions and levels of government, Congress is consistently liked the least. This conclusion is apparent in Figure 3-2.

These results come from a Gallup survey administered in early 1998 to a random national sample of 1,266 adults in the United States.[10] Respondents were asked whether or not they approved of six different aspects of government, including the "overall political system." As may be recalled from Figure 3-1, this particular (pre-impeachment) time period was one in which Congress was relatively popular, so we see that a respectable 52 percent of the respondents approved of Congress. Compared with other components of the political system, however, approval of Congress fares much worse. Specifically, Congress is the least-liked

Figure 3-2 Approval of the Federal Government and Its Parts, 1998

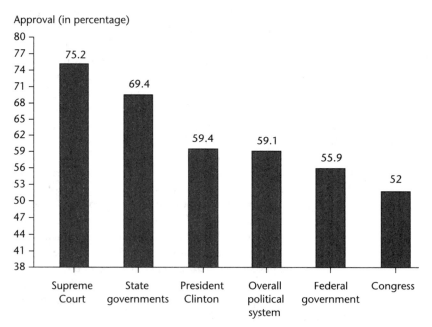

Approval (in percentage)

Source: 1998 Gallup Survey on Preferences for Government Processes; see John R. Hibbing and Elizabeth Theiss-Morse, *Stealth Democracy: Americans' Beliefs about How Government Should Work* (forthcoming).

part of the political system. Even the federal government is more popular (56 percent approval). The overall political system is at 59 percent approval, which is about the same approval level accorded President Clinton at that time (it may be recalled that a few months later, with impeachment proceedings in full swing, his popularity, unlike Congress's, went up several percentage points). Levels of approval for state government are quite a bit higher than for the federal government (69 to 56 percent), and the Supreme Court is easily the most popular political body, with better than three out of four Americans approving of it.

Lest it be thought that the spring of 1998 was unusual, we present Figure 3-3. According to those data (taken from the Harris poll's annual "confidence" battery), the Supreme Court is always the most popular institution and that Congress is almost always the least popular. Even through the Watergate scandal, the public expressed more confidence in the presidency than in Congress, although confidence in Jimmy Carter late in his term did momentarily dip below confidence in Congress. Thus, the relative popularity of governmental institutions is quite consistent over time and may be growing even more distinct. Notice that in the late 1990s the gap between confidence in Congress and confidence in the Supreme Court reached unprecedented proportions (nearly 30 percentage points).

Figure 3-3 Confidence in Political Institutions, 1966–2000

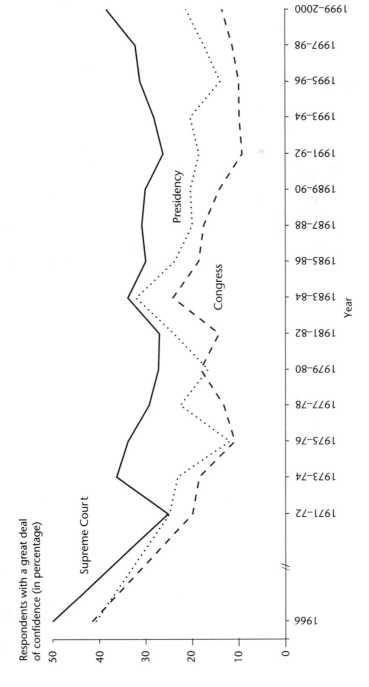

Respondents with a great deal
of confidence (in percentage)

Supreme Court

Presidency

Congress

Year

Source: Harris polls, various years.

Note: Data for the years between 1966 and 1971 were unavailable.

The variations in approval displayed in Figure 3-2 are not easy to explain. The two most popular referents are two of the most different. State government, we might speculate, is relatively popular because it is perceived to be close to the people. But if this is what people like, why is the Supreme Court even more popular than state government? Of all the elements of government, the Supreme Court is undoubtedly the most detached from the people: just nine justices, all with life terms and no real representational role and who seem to delight in being distant and insular. What is it about the Supreme Court that makes it so much more popular than Congress?

The answer offered in the previous section—that people are put off by political conflict—fits equally well with the results in this section. Compared with Congress, the Supreme Court has developed an amazing capacity to cloak its conflict. If open warfare occurs among the justices, it is hidden behind curtains and a vow of secrecy; and if conflict occurs between the Court and another political institution, it is not typically the stuff of front-page news stories. Thus, the Supreme Court is popular for all the reasons Congress is not; particularly, its ability to keep the people from seeing what is going on inside. Contrary to common interpretations, political popularity is not enhanced by openness, by democratic accountability, and by representation of diverse popular views. Rather, it is often enhanced by processes that move to some kind of resolution without a lot of fuss and blather, even if some measure of accountability is sacrificed in the process. Congress is relatively unpopular with the public precisely because it is so public.

Why People Like Certain Parts of Congress More than Others

Further information on the reasons people feel as they do about Congress can be obtained by paying careful attention to the aspects of Congress they do and do not like. Congress, of course, is an amazingly multifaceted institution. It is not just organized into many different parts but it is organized along many different lines: parties, committees, caucuses, delegations, leadership structures, staffs, and two separate houses all play important roles in congressional organization, and it is quite likely that, just as the people like some components of the political system more than others, they also like some components of Congress more than others.

Love Our Member but Hate Our Congress?

One of the most oft-repeated points about congressional popularity is that people "hate Congress but love their own member of Congress."[11] Survey research consistently provides support for this observation. According to polling conducted by the National Election Studies at the University of Michigan in 1980, 88 percent of the people approved of their own member of the House but only 41 percent approved of Congress itself. By 1998 this gap had diminished a

Figure 3-4 Evaluations of Congressional Referents, 1992

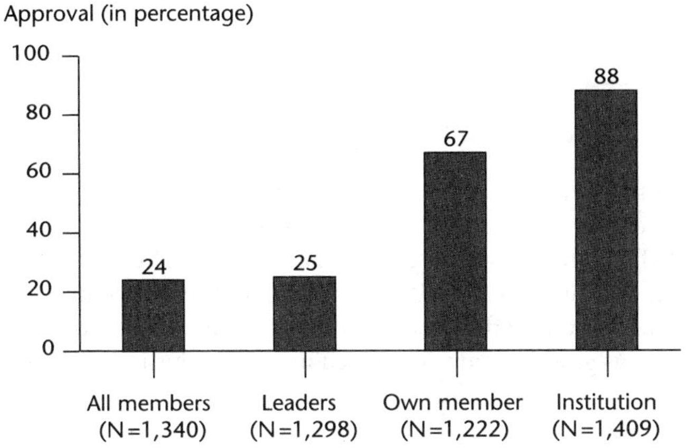

Approval (in percentage)

Source: Perceptions of Congress Survey, 1992, conducted by the Bureau of Sociological Research at the University of Nebraska; see John R. Hibbing and Elizabeth Theiss-Morse, *Congress as Public Enemy* (New York: Cambridge University Press, 1995).

little but was still quite large, with 82 percent approving of their own member and 51 percent approving of Congress. People clearly distinguish between their own member and a generic "Congress."

This conclusion may be only part of the story, however. When people are asked to evaluate "Congress," what comes to their mind? Most of them probably envision a tumultuous collection of 535 members, and they often do not approve of this facet of Congress. But when the public actually thinks of Congress less as a collection of inevitably flawed human beings and more as an important institutional component of the nation's governance, reactions are likely to change noticeably. This speculation is supported by the results obtained from a 1992 survey and that are presented in Figure 3-4.

In the battery of questions used to compile this figure, respondents were asked whether or not they approved of four different congressional referents. The first was "all members of Congress." The second was "the leaders of Congress." The third was "their own member of Congress." And the fourth was "Congress as an institution of government, no matter who is in office."[12] The different reactions evoked by these various referents are noteworthy. Dissatisfaction is certainly generated by mention of "all members" and of "congressional leaders." Only one in four Americans approved of these groups at the time the survey was taken. Approval levels of the respondent's "own member" were, as previous research has consistently demonstrated, much higher, with two of three responding favorably. But people were even more approving of Congress "as an institution," with a remarkable 88 percent approving. Although it is not tremendously surprising that people would respond positively to a question that weeds human foibles out of the mix, it is still worth noting that people do not really disapprove of Congress; rather, they disapprove of the membership of Congress, their own member excepted of course.

Political Parties in Congress

In light of the fact that people are put off by conflict in the governmental process, it will come as no surprise that they view the political parties with disfavor. People believe that parties argue because of selfish reasons rather than a desire to better the entire country. Parties are believed to be a central reason there is so much conflict and ineffectiveness in government. The following exchange occurred in a focus group session conducted in 1992 and is indicative of the public's stance.

> Bob: I think that there has to be major communication between . . . the Democrats and Republicans and the Senate and the House, you know, everybody. Just have to say, "There's a problem. We won't leave this room until it's fixed."
> Lisa: They never could do that.
> Barb: Take them all to Camp David.
> Lisa: No, they don't deserve anything that good. They need to be put in small spaces in the summertime that is not air conditioned, and say, "Get on the ball and do something!" And they'd do it.[13]

Although people do not think highly of parties in Congress generally, perhaps they are more favorable to their own party and any dissatisfaction stems from reaction to the "other" party. For the most part, this expectation is unfounded. Democrats tend to be more pleased with Congress when there is a Democratic majority (as was the case for most of the second half of the twentieth century) and Republicans are more pleased when there is a Republican majority (as has been the case since 1994), but for many people party control is either unknown or irrelevant. Approval of Congress is influenced by partisanship, but not heavily.

After the Republican takeover of Congress in late 1994, many polling organizations began asking new questions. Rather than just asking people to evaluate the job of Congress (see Figure 3-1), they asked people to evaluate the job "the Republicans in Congress are doing," and, separately, the job "the Democrats in Congress are doing." By asking distinct questions about the two major parties, it has become possible to determine if evaluations of them move together or move in more of a zero-sum fashion. In turn, it has become possible to draw inferences about the manner in which people view the parties' role in Congress. If one party's demise in the eyes of the public is accompanied by the other party's rise, it would suggest that people credit (and blame) just one party, with the other party becoming an automatic counterbalance to the touchstone party (presumably the majority party). But if evaluations of the two parties in Congress move together—that is, if high approval of the Democratic Party in Congress is typically accompanied by relatively high approval of the Republican Party—it suggests a more institutionalized Congress in which the two parties, however much they seem to disagree with each other, share a common fate.

THE DATA USED to create Figure 3-5 come from various issues of the Harris polls and therefore follow the Harris practice of asking respondents not just if they approve or disapprove but to evaluate performance as either excellent, pretty good, only fair, or poor. "Excellent" and "pretty good" responses are then collapsed into positive verdicts, whereas "only fair" and "poor" responses are collapsed into negative verdicts. The figure plots positive reactions from December 1994 until the end of 1999 and there is some support for both the "teeter-totter" and "joined at the hip" views.[14]

When it formally assumed power in 1995 for the first time in forty years, the Republican Party in Congress was riding high with 42 percent approval ratings compared with only 31 percent for the Democratic Party in Congress. But within the next year, this situation changed markedly and by March 1996 the Democratic Party in Congress was more popular than the Republican Party in Congress, thanks largely to a rapid drop of positive ratings to 31 percent for the Republicans. During the first-year adjustment to the Republican majority and its pointed legislative agenda, the fate of the two congressional parties was not strongly related. But by the start of 1997, that situation had changed dramatically, as both parties enjoyed substantial increases in the percentage of positive evaluations. From that time on, fluctuations in these evaluations generally moved together. In other words, the Democratic Party in Congress is unlikely to receive more favorable evaluations just because the public is down on the Republican Party in Congress. The more typical pattern is for evaluations of the two parties to rise and fall together.

We have already noted that the time between late 1994 and early 1995 is an understandable exception to the joint party responsibility pattern. In fact, the differential evaluation of the Republican and Democratic Parties probably allowed the Republicans to make the gains they did in the elections of 1994.[15] This Republican advantage then diminished as the situation reverted to what we predict to be the normal pattern of the minority party being the more popular but moving in the same general direction as the majority party. But the size of the gap between approval of the majority and minority parties is not a constant and, as might be expected, the clearest example of a change in the size of the gap is provided by the events surrounding presidential impeachment. Beginning in the spring of 1998, the gap, which traditionally is 3 to 6 percentage points, grew to 8, then 10, and topped out at 14 points in November 1998. By the end of 1999, well after impeachment proceedings and trials had faded, approval of the Democratic Party in Congress was still running 10 points higher than approval of the

Figure 3-5 Evaluations of the Parties in Congress, 1994–1999

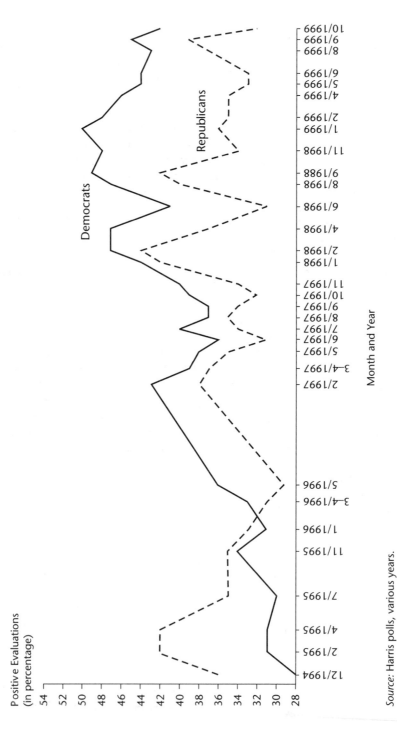

Positive Evaluations
(in percentage)

Month and Year

Source: Harris polls, various years.

Note: Questions were posed at uneven intervals, only during the months listed on the horizontal axis.

Republican Party. Whether this larger gap will persist is difficult to say. We think it probably will not.

Interest Groups

Political parties may not be viewed very favorably by the American public but they are not viewed nearly as unfavorably as interest groups or, as they are usually called by the people, "special interests." Whereas parties have an institutionalized place in the organization of Congress, it may seem that interest groups are not actually a part of Congress and thus not appropriate for this section. Although this is technically true, the American public sees an intimate and unseemly connection between Congress and special interest groups. In the 1998 Gallup survey mentioned earlier, respondents were asked whether they agreed or disagreed with the following statement: "interest groups should be banned from contacting members of Congress." This proposal clearly violates first amendment rights to "petition" the Congress, but an amazing 45 percent of all respondents agreed with it, thus suggesting the extent to which interest groups are viewed with suspicion. In another item from the same survey, 69 percent of all respondents felt special interests had "too much power," far higher than any other aspect of the political system.

Focus group comments concerning interest groups and their allegedly undeserved influence are no less favorable.

> Maria: They [politicians] think about who's in power, who's the dominant group. And they do the laws according to who's going to benefit from it. And they forget about the people down here, you know. . . . It doesn't work for the benefit of all the people, which it should.
>
> Robert: I think interest groups have too much control of what our elected officials say in our government. And Congresspeople are basically just like, well this guy gave me ten million dollars so no matter what I think, I've got to vote this way. They're bought, you know, bought by the interest group.
>
> Sally: I don't like the way they [members of Congress] seem so easily influenced by lobbyists. I don't. . . . there should be a better way that money and influential groups that have a lot of money shouldn't be, shouldn't be able to influence the decisions . . . so easily.

The basis for this intense suspicion toward interest groups is easier to understand if we recall earlier references to the tendency of people to believe that real Americans are generally in agreement and thus to believe that noisy special interests must be a part of something else and must want to benefit only themselves and not the country as a whole. If this is people's perception, it is not surprising that they would see interest groups and the connection they have with members of Congress as the root of all that is evil in the political system.

Staffs and Other Features of the Institutionalized Congress

Because people tend to think members of Congress are acting to benefit themselves rather than ordinary Americans, they tend to be skeptical of the perquisites associated with the office and there is an accompanying public desire to reduce the level of those perquisites. Thus, proposals to reduce the salary of members of Congress, to reduce the staff assistance of members of Congress, and to shorten the length of stay permitted members of Congress (term limits) are wildly popular with the American public. Typically, about 75 percent of the adult population wants to lower congressional salaries and limit terms of service. Questions measuring public support for congressional staff reductions are asked less frequently but, when they are, receive endorsement from almost as many people as term limits and salary cuts.

Lest it be thought that people's enthusiasm for these reforms is driven by an overestimation of the actual salary, staff support, and mean length of service in Congress, results obtained from a survey in late 1992 found that people do misperceive the salary and staff available to members of Congress, but they tend to underestimate, not overestimate these benefits. On average, respondents guessed that members of Congress had 7.5 personal staffers, when at the time of the survey representatives averaged 17.4; and they underestimated the congressional salary by about $30,000. Finally, respondents also underestimated the typical length of career in Congress, guessing (on average) eight years when the real answer was eleven. Thus, providing the public with accurate information on salary, staff, and service would not put out the flames of public unrest with Congress but would actually fan those flames.[16]

It is difficult, but not impossible, to find aspects of Congress the public likes. Most people view the institution of Congress and their own member in favorable terms, but offsetting these positive feelings are strong negative feelings toward political parties, special interests, and the membership of Congress.[17] Moreover, the public does not seem to like the activities in which Congress is typically engaged. Fifty-six percent of respondents in the 1998 Gallup survey said they believed that compromise was just "selling out on principles." Eighty-four percent agreed that "elected officials would help more if they stopped talking and took action." And 69 percent expressed the belief that "the current system does not represent the interests of all Americans." If debate and compromise are viewed negatively and if it is believed that Congress is not representing the interests of the people, it is no wonder that the overall reactions to the body are often negative.

Why Do Some People Like Congress More than Others

It is easy to lose sight of the fact that many people do approve of Congress — over 50 percent, in fact, in the last years of the 1990s. Just as Congress is more popular at some times than at others, so too is Congress looked upon more favorably by some people than by others. Identification of the kinds of individuals most likely to either approve or disapprove of Congress should allow us to say more about why Congress generates the kind of public reaction that it does. Thus, first, we compute the mean score of various demographic groups on our standard question regarding approval of Congress. Respondents were asked if they strongly approved, approved, disapproved, or strongly disapproved of "the way Congress has been handling its job lately."[18] "Strongly approve" responses were coded 4; "approve," 3; "disapprove," 2; and "strongly disapprove," 1. A group's mean score of 2.5 indicates that approving and disapproving answers were perfectly balanced. The larger the number, the more approving the group. We computed mean approval scores for several demographic groups and report them in Table 3-1.

For example, there has been much talk lately about "angry, white males." Is it the case, then, that males and whites are less approving of Congress? Table 3-1 suggests there is little difference between males and females and between whites and nonwhites in attitudes toward Congress. The anticipated patterns are in evidence, but barely. Males are a little less approving of Congress than females (2.42 to 2.50) and whites are a little less approving than nonwhites (2.45 to 2.50), but differences of 0.08 and 0.05 on a 4-point scale are quite modest. The findings for most of the other demographic variables are similar. More education, perhaps surprisingly, does not bring much improvement in attitudes toward Congress. The pattern across income levels is not consistent. The youngest age bracket (eighteen to twenty-five) is the most approving of Congress, but after that there is no apparent pattern. And those who scored well on a four-question political knowledge test were not any more approving of Congress than their less-informed compatriots.[19]

Once we move to the area of simple political attitudes and identifications, relationships are only marginally more visible. With regard to party identification, even though Republicans controlled both houses of Congress at the time the survey was administered (1998), respondents identifying with the Democratic Party were more approving (but only slightly) than Republicans (2.57 to 2.53). The only real difference is produced by "independents." They are more negative toward Congress than either Democrats or Republicans (2.32) and, in fact, are the most negative of virtually any group. With regard to political ideology, the pattern is the opposite of the one that might have been expected on the basis of party identification. Whereas partisan independents are the least supportive of Congress, ideological moderates are the most supportive (2.54), and whereas Democrats are the most supportive of Congress, ideological liberals are the least (2.35). Conservatives, like their closest partisan equivalent, Republicans, are in the middle (2.47). Independents may dislike Congress, but this should not be taken to mean that moderates do.

But the more important point is that the differences across all these standard demographic groups are surprisingly modest. If one attempts to describe the type of individual who is most likely to disapprove of Congress, it is clear that basing a description on people's age, gender, skin color, income, education, polit-

Table 3-1 Approval of Congress by Various Demographic Groups, 1998

	Mean Approval (1–4)	N
Gender		
Male	2.42	590
Female	2.50	620
Race		
White	2.45	1,008
Other	2.50	203
Age		
Less than 26	2.57	196
26–39	2.47	362
40–54	2.40	325
55–69	2.41	204
More than 70	2.49	123
Education		
Less than high school	2.43	144
High school	2.44	465
More than high school	2.47	312
4-year college	2.51	165
More than college degree	2.50	92
Income		
Less than $10,000	2.60	70
$10–20,000	2.50	115
$20–30,000	2.36	147
$30–40,000	2.49	199
$40–50,000	2.43	226
$60–100,000	2.53	167
More than $100,000	2.31	63
Political knowledge (answers correct)		
0	2.40	90
1	2.55	270
2	2.45	485
3	2.42	349
4	2.46	18
Party identification		
Democrat	2.57	377
Independent	2.32	327
Republican	2.53	298
Ideology		
Liberal	2.35	275
Moderate	2.54	342
Conservative	2.47	569

Source: Computed by the authors from a 1998 Gallup Survey; see John R. Hibbing and Elizabeth Theiss-Morse, *Stealth Democracy: Americans' Beliefs about How Government Should Work* (forthcoming).

ical knowledge, and even party identification and ideology will not be particularly helpful. To the extent that there are predictable patterns in who likes and dislikes Congress, we must look beyond demographics toward more specific political attitudes and preferences.

One reasonable expectation is that those who are satisfied with the policies government produces, other things being equal, will be more likely to approve of one of the most important shapers of those policies, the United States Congress.[20] The specific survey item we employ asked if respondents strongly agreed, agreed, disagreed, or strongly disagreed with the statement that they were "generally satisfied with the public policies the government has produced lately." But one of the themes that has surfaced throughout this chapter is that people's attitudes toward Congress are influenced by more than just the policies produced; they also seem to be influenced by people's attitudes toward certain processes of making policy.

For example, as alluded to earlier, two central activities in Congress are debate and compromise. Congress is designed to give voice to an incredible variety of opinions from across the country and then to negotiate some type of brokered solution from this welter of preferences, so debate and compromise occupy much of the time of members of Congress. But, as indicated by the survey results referred to above, some ordinary people are not particularly tolerant of debate and compromise. In light of this fact, one obvious expectation is that those people who are less persuaded of the importance of debate and the necessity of compromise will also be disapproving of an institution as heavily invested in debate and compromise as Congress. The item we selected to measure people's perception of the necessity of compromise reads as follows: "the American people disagree with each other so much that politicians need to compromise in order to get anything done." The hypothesis is that the more strongly people agree with this statement, the less likely they will be to approve of Congress. To measure people's attitudes toward debate, we used this item: "Elected officials would help the country more if they would stop talking and just take action on important problems." We expect that the more strongly people agree with this statement, the less likely they will be to approve of Congress.

To test these hypotheses, we use regression analysis. Although the numbers generated by this technique seem confusing at first glance, a major advantage of regression is that it is possible to "control" for the other variables included. If we relied only on results such as those presented in Table 3-1, we would not know, say, if young people (eighteen to twenty-five years old) were more favorable toward Congress because they tend to be ideological moderates or if ideological moderates tend to be more favorable toward Congress because many young people tend to be in the ideological middle. Thus, in Table 3-2 we present the results obtained when approval of Congress is regressed on all the variables in Table 3-1 plus the one policy and two procedural variables just described.

The top portion of the table indicates that most of the conclusions implied in Table 3-1 hold up in a more complete, multivariate specification. Age, gender,

Table 3-2   Causes of Approval of Congress, 1998

Independent Variable	Regression Coefficient	Standard Error	Significance Level
Age	−0.01	0.02	.63
Gender	0.05	0.04	.24
Nonwhite	0.01	0.06	.87
Education	0.01	0.01	.16
Income	0.00	0.01	.47
Party identification	0.01	0.01	.38
Political knowledge	−0.08	0.03	.00[a]
Ideology	0.08	0.03	.00[a]
Like recent policies	0.34	0.04	.00[a]
See little value in debate	−0.10	0.03	.00[a]
See little need for compromise	−0.11	0.03	.00[a]
Constant	2.16	0.20	.00[a]

Source: Computed by the authors from a 1998 Gallup Survey; see John R. Hibbing and Elizabeth Theiss-Morse, *Stealth Democracy: Americans' Beliefs about How Government Should Work* (forthcoming).

R^2 = .15

Adj. R^2 = .14

F = 12.63 (*p* < .00)

N = 795

[a] = significant at (.01)

race, education, income, and party identification exert minimal or no effect on approval of Congress.[21] This leaves only two variables from Table 3-1 with significant coefficients. Other things being equal, conservatives are more likely to approve of Congress (which had a Republican majority at the time of the survey) than are liberals and, more surprisingly, the more political knowledge a person possesses the *less* likely that person is to approve of Congress. Although observers might have expected that political knowledge would lead to an understanding of the challenges of governing and, therefore, a more approving attitude toward institutions such as Congress, this is not the case. In fact, more knowledge seems to lead to higher expectations of government and, inevitably, disappointment with the actual performance of government. Knowledge of government does not equal an appreciation of the difficulties of arriving at a decision in the face of tremendously divided public opinion on most issues. This seems to be why variables tapping education and political knowledge tend to be either insignificant or in the unexpected direction. This is true of the findings we report here as well as the findings reported in much previous work.[22]

Certainly, people are more likely to approve of an institution if they are pleased with the policies it helps to produce. This is apparent to some extent in the results for ideology and even more directly in the coefficient for "like recent policies." In fact, this is the most powerful variable in the equation. People who like recent governmental policies are substantially more likely to approve of Congress, although with a question such as this there is always the danger that many people who approve of Congress are merely projecting desirable traits (such as agreeable policy choices) to it. In any event, approval is undeniably connected to policy satisfaction.

What may be more surprising for some readers (but perfectly consistent with our expectations) is that even when controlling for the influence of policy satisfaction, people's attitudes toward the desirability of debate and the need for compromise are important predictors of attitudes toward Congress. These general attitudes toward abstract activities are unlikely to be the product of the kind of reverse causation described in the previous paragraph. Although a favorable attitude toward Congress may lead people to like recent policies, it is less likely to lead them to have positive attitudes toward compromise and debate. But these attitudes toward compromise and debate certainly are related to approval of Congress. The more that people believe "the country would be helped if elected officials would stop talking" the less likely they are to approve of Congress. And the more that people believe "compromise is unnecessary because of Americans' level of agreement with each other" the less likely they are to approve of Congress. These two relationships are strong and statistically significant.

This means that if more people realized the extent of policy disagreement in American society and the resultant need to discuss our differences and to reach a mutual accord by being willing to compromise with those holding divergent views, Congress would then be a more popular institution. But when people view all debate as bickering and see compromise as selling out, they naturally are less likely to approve of an institution that spends much of its time bickering and selling out. Even if people were given the exact policies they want, the results in Table 3-2 suggest that some of them would still be unhappy with Congress, assuming Congress continued to rely, as any representative institution in a divided society must, on open presentation of diverse opinions, discussion of those opinions, and brokered solutions.

Summary

When is Congress unpopular? Not surprisingly, when negative economic and other societal conditions exist, but also when Congress is particularly active and newsworthy in proposing and debating important legislative matters and balancing presidential power. Why is Congress less popular than other parts of government? Because more than those other parts, Congress is charged with giving voice to tremendously varied interests from across the country and then, in full public view, coming to a single policy decision in the face of that diversity. Which parts of Congress are particularly unpopular? Any part that can be seen as serving an interest narrower than the entire country whether that interest belongs to a political party intent on winning an election, a special interest intent on securing a benefit for that particular group, or members of Congress (other than one's own member) intent on getting reelected so they can continue to lead the high life at the expense of hard-working American taxpayers. What kind of person is most likely to disapprove of Congress? Not surprisingly, someone who dislikes recent policy actions, but also someone who dislikes debate and who believes there is little need for politicians to compromise.

Taken together, these findings make it difficult to deny that the processes by which decisions are made matter. People are not consumed solely by the desire to obtain a certain policy outcome. Indeed, on an amazing number of issues, most people have weak or, more likely, nonexistent policy preferences. But even when people do not have a pre-existing preference on a policy issue, government action can still affect attitudes. In fact, it is precisely when people see governing officials spending copious amounts of time arguing about what the people regard to be trifling issues that they become most disgusted with government. Moreover, whether or not people have a pre-existing stake in a particular policy outcome, they have a standing preference that all policies result from a process designed to benefit the general welfare of all Americans rather than the specific welfare of fractious, overly influential, individual interests. The public unquestionably errs by assuming there is a reasonably consensual general will in as heterogeneous a country as the United States, but the fact remains that congressional popularity is damaged when the institution is perceived to act on the basis of narrow, selfish interests. And because virtually every congressional action is perceived by the people in precisely these terms, the most popular Congress is usually the most inert Congress.

Notes

The authors gratefully acknowledge the assistance of Elizabeth Theiss-Morse. Some of the data for this chapter were gathered thanks to a grant from the National Science Foundation (SES 97-09934).

1. On choosing to retire, see Sean Theriault, "Moving Up or Moving Out: Career Ceilings and Congressional Retirement," *Legislative Studies Quarterly* 23 (August 1998): 419–34; on deciding against running for Congress in the first place, see Linda L. Fowler and Robert D. McClure, *Political Ambition: Who Decides to Run for Congress* (New Haven: Yale University Press, 1989); on avoiding controversial issues, see David Hess, "Congress Hibernating till Fall," *Houston Chronicle*, March 19, 1998, A8; and on not complying with the law, see Tom Tyler, *Why People Obey the Law* (New Haven: Yale University Press, 1990).
2. See Seymour Martin Lipset and William Schneider, *The Confidence Gap* (Baltimore: Johns Hopkins University Press, 1987).
3. Robert H. Durr, John B. Gilmour, and Christina Wolbrecht, "Explaining Congressional Approval," *American Journal of Political Science* 41 (January 1997): 195.
4. See Robert Z. Lawrence, "Is It Really the Economy, Stupid?" in *Why People Don't Trust Government*, ed. Joseph S. Nye Jr., Philip D. Zelikow, and David C. King (Cambridge: Harvard University Press, 1997), 111.

5. Katharine Q. Seelye, "Americans Take a Dim View of the Government, Survey Finds," *New York Times,* 10 March 1998, A15.
6. See John R. Hibbing and Elizabeth Theiss-Morse, *Congress as Public Enemy* (Cambridge: Cambridge University Press, 1995); Durr, Gilmour, and Wolbrecht, "Explaining Congressional Approval."
7. Hess, "Congress Hibernating till Fall."
8. On the public's preference for divided government, see Morris Fiorina, *Divided Government,* 2d ed. (Boston: Allyn and Bacon, 1996).
9. Hess, "Congress Hibernating till Fall."
10. For more details, see John R. Hibbing and Elizabeth Theiss-Morse, *Stealth Democracy: Americans' Beliefs about How Government Should Work* (forthcoming).
11. Richard F. Fenno Jr., "If, as Ralph Nader Says, Congress Is 'The Broken Branch,' How Come We Love Our Congressmen So Much?" in *Congress in Change: Evolution and Reform,* ed. Norman J. Ornstein (New York: Praeger, 1975).
12. For more information, see Hibbing and Theiss-Morse, *Congress as Public Enemy,* 42–46.
13. Ibid., 97.
14. It would be instructive to have this information extending back before the 1994 elections and resulting switch in majority party, but these questions were not asked before December 1994.
15. John R. Hibbing and Eric Tiritilli, "Public Disapproval of Congress Can Be Dangerous to Majority Party Candidates," in *Change and Continuity in House Elections,* ed. David W. Brady, John Cogan, and Morris P. Fiorina (Stanford, Calif.: Stanford University Press, 2000).
16. Hibbing and Theiss-Morse, *Congress as Public Enemy,* 72–74. The national survey was commissioned by John Hibbing and Elizabeth Theiss-Morse and funded by the National Science Foundation. It was conducted by the Bureau of Sociological Research at the University of Nebraska.
17. We wish we had questions on committees, but the only one available comes from the 1998 Gallup survey and merely asks whether or not respondents agree that "Congress needs to have committees to get its work done." Better than 70 percent agreed that it did.
18. This national survey was commissioned by John Hibbing and Elizabeth Theiss-Morse and was funded by the National Science Foundation. It was conducted in 1998 by Gallup.
19. Only the bivariate relationships for age and gender are significant at the 0.05 level.
20. In fact, respondents view Congress as a more important shaper of policy than the president. See Hibbing and Theiss-Morse, *Congress as Public Enemy,* 51–53.
21. A separate code for "independent" would have shown a small but statistically significant negative effect.
22. See Roger H. Davidson, David M. Kovenock, and Michael K. O'Leary, *Congress in Crisis: Politics and Congressional Reform* (Belmont, Calif.: Wadsworth, 1968). For an extended discussion of the relationship between high expectations of Congress and subsequent evaluations, see Samuel C. Patterson and David C. Kimball, "Living up to Expectations: Public Attitudes toward Congress," *Journal of Politics* 59 (August 1997): 701–28.

Part II
Elections and Constituencies

4. Voters, Candidates, and Issues in Congressional Elections

Robert S. Erikson and Gerald C. Wright

Elections for the U.S. House of Representatives fascinate observers of American politics almost as much as presidential elections do. Unlike Senate elections, which come at staggered six-year intervals, House elections provide a regular bienniel measure of the electoral pulse of the nation. Interest in House elections centers on the partisan balance of seats, and on the collective motivations of the electorate that underlie this verdict.

Another source of fascination with House elections is their large number. Every two years the composition of the new U.S. House is the result of 435 separate contests for 435 separate seats. In part, these outcomes are determined by national electoral forces. But also, to a large extent, they are determined by the candidates in these contests and the conduct of their individual campaigns.

In this chapter we first examine the national forces determining House elections and their influence on the partisan division of votes and seats. Next, we look at the role of candidates in individual House contests. Finally, we compare elections for the House with elections for the Senate.

The National Verdict in House Elections

The Founders designed the House of Representatives to be the popular branch of government. Elections for the House were expected to reflect the ebb and flow of public preferences. Even though the Senate has also become responsive to public opinion, analysts and journalists continue to pay particular attention to the House elections as indicators of what the public wants and what the future directions of U.S. public policy will be.

Until quite recently, a question about the House of Representatives' partisan makeup would be framed as a question about the precise size of the Democrats' majority. For forty years—from the elections of 1954 to 1994—the Democrats controlled the House. Then, remarkably, in 1994 the electorate gave the Republicans the majority, surprising virtually all observers. Since the watershed 1994 elections, the national campaign for the House of Representatives has been transformed from a tug of war over the majority (Democrat) seat margin to a high stakes battle for control of the institution itself. In 1996, 1998, and 2000 the Republicans retained their newly won control, albeit with shrinking margins. For the foreseeable future the House elections will be a battleground, with party control of the institution a matter of contention and doubt from one election to the next.

Over the second half of the twentieth century, the party division of House seats varied from 67 percent Democratic and 33 percent Republican, after the 1964 election, to 53 percent Republican and 47 percent Democratic, after the historic 1994 contests—a range of 91 seats (out of 435) between each party's high and low marks. As Figure 4-1 shows, the partisan seat division follows closely (but imprecisely) from partisan division of the national vote. The party that gained seats in a particular election gained on average seven new seats (about 1.5 percent of the total) for each added percentage point of the major-party vote. This ratio of seat percentage gained or lost per vote percentage gained (1.5) is called the swing ratio.

The exact swing ratio varies from one election to the next, depending on how the vote shifts are concentrated among the districts. For example, if one party gains most of its votes in districts where the other party had previously won by a large margin, its added votes may not allow it to win any additional seats. If the party gains the same number of votes in districts where the opposition party barely squeaked by in the last election, it gains many more seats for the same number of votes.[1]

The Democratic run of party control that lasted for forty years was based on a stable but small Democratic majority of the congressional vote. In the twenty House elections between 1954 and 1992, the national division of the major-party vote varied only within the narrow range of 51–59 percent Democratic. Thus, a swing of only eight votes in a hundred separated the elections that most favored the Democrats from those that most favored the Republicans. Even when the electoral landscape changed dramatically with the 1994 Republican landslide, the swing was due to a small minority of voters. Between 1992 and 1994, the national major-party vote shifted only six percentage points.

To summarize, changes in the party composition of congressional seats typically are a function of a small fraction of the electorate switching its congressional vote from one party to the other. We next discuss the causes of these small changes in the partisan tide. Relevant explanatory variables include the electorate's party identification, the electorate's ideological mood, and reactions to the performance of the current presidential administration.

The Partisan Base of the Congressional Vote

Most voters in the United States identify with one of the two dominant political parties—the Republicans or the Democrats. This identification

Figure 4-1 Democratic House Seats and Vote Share, 1952–1998

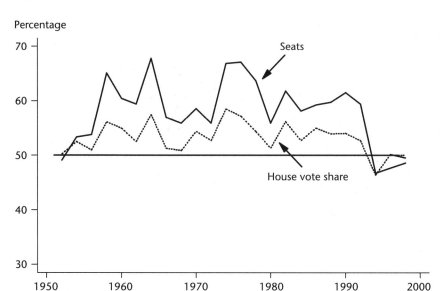

Source: Compiled by the authors.

amounts to a standing decision to vote for their favored party—unless the current campaign gives them reason to temporarily defect. Most votes are partisan votes (Republicans voting Republican and Democrats voting Democratic), and voters rarely change their partisanship. This provides a certain stability to the national congressional vote over time. The national division of party identification—sometimes called "macropartisanship"—is not a constant, however; small changes in macropartisanship reflect small changes in the electorate's collective standing decision, and these small changes have electoral consequences. Macro-level changes in partisanship typically represent shifting evaluations of the parties' relative competence in governing, as in areas such as economic performance.

The national verdict in House elections closely follows the national division of party identification. Most Democrats vote Democratic; most Republicans vote Republican; and Independents usually split their vote about evenly between the two parties. The outcome of this process is the "normal vote."[2] Figure 4-2 illustrates the normal vote for Democrats, tracking macropartisanship and the House seat division over time.[3]

The figure illustrates how the Democrats were able to control the House of Representatives for forty years. The Democrats were the dominant party in terms

Figure 4-2 Partisanship and House Seat Shares, 1952–1998

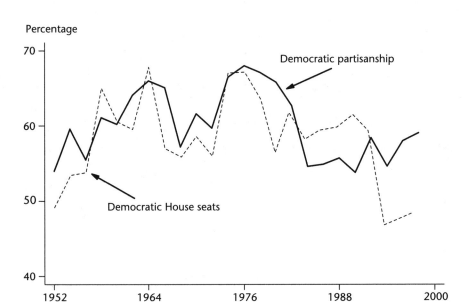

Percentage

Source: Compiled by the authors.

Note: Partisanship is the average percentage of respondents identifying themselves as Democratic in third quarter Gallup national polls (the quarter just before the election).

of party identification; thus more people voted Democratic than Republican. The Democrats' loss of their competitive advantage in partisanship in the late 1980s and early 1990s eventually caught up to them in 1994, with the Republican takeover.

Policy Mood

Partisanship is not the only force that shapes long‑term voting patterns. In addition, the national verdict depends on the nation's collective preference for more liberalism or more conservatism in its national policies — the nation's policy (or ideological) "mood." James Stimson has measured the nation's policy mood on an annual basis, using a sophisticated composite of available public opinion polls.[4] The national electoral verdict for the House — as in elections for the presidency and for the Senate — is significantly related to the nation's ideological mood. When the public wants more government activism from Congress, it gives the Democratic Party more votes. The nation's most liberal mood, according to Stimson's index, was in the early 1960s, which was also a time of Democratic congressional dominance. The most conservative times were around 1952, at the start of Stimson's series, and around 1980, when Reagan was elected president, accompanied by considerable Republican gains in Congress.[5]

Presidential Election Years

In presidential election years, the short-term forces behind the presidential election and the House elections work in the same partisan direction, so that the party that performs better than the "normal vote" in the presidential election will also perform better than normal in the congressional elections. Whether this happens because the House vote and the presidential vote are independently influenced by the same national issues, or because some people choose their congressional vote to mirror their presidential vote, is not clear. The phenomenon is known as the coattail effect, as if a number of candidates of the party that wins the presidency are swept into office on the president's coattails.

Democratic coattails were at their strongest in 1964, when Lyndon Johnson's landslide victory was accompanied by an overwhelming 295–140 Democratic majority in the House. Republican coattails were particularly strong in 1980, when Ronald Reagan won the presidency. In some elections, presidential coattails appear to be virtually nonexistent. For instance, Clinton's reelection in 1996 carried so few Democratic House candidates to victory that the Democrats were unable to regain control of Congress.

The size of the coattail effect is decidedly irregular. One statistical estimate for post–World War II elections puts it at +.31 congressional votes nationally for each additional vote gained by the party at the presidential level.[6] Put another way, every added percentage point of the vote gained beyond the normal vote by a presidential candidate also adds almost one-third of a percentage point to the totals of congressional candidates of the presidential candidate's party. Before World War II, presidential coattails appeared stronger than they are today; the national presidential vote and the national congressional vote moved more closely in lockstep. One consequence of the weakening of the coattail effect is the increased frequency with which control of the government is divided, with one party controlling the presidency and the other party controlling at least one house of Congress.

The Midterm Loss

One phenomenon that has regularly governed House elections has been the midterm loss — in which the party that controls the presidency suffers a net loss of seats in Congress in midterm elections. Until 1998, only once in the twentieth century (1934) did the presidential party gain seats in the midterm elections. We must try to account for the astounding regularity of midterm loss.

Every rule has its exceptions, and the 1990s was an era of exceptional congressional elections. The 1994 election ended four decades of Democratic rule. The 1996 election showed that coattails are not guaranteed to the winner of the presidential elections. And the 1998 election broke the long-standing rule that the party controlling the presidency loses congressional seats in midterm elections. Despite the Monica Lewinsky affair and Clinton's pending impeachment battle, the Democrats gained seats in 1998. What happened? Was 1998 somehow the exception that proves the rule?

There are two leading explanations for the midterm loss: the "withdrawn coattails" argument and the "ideological balancing" argument. The withdrawn coattails argument is as follows: In presidential years the congressional vote for the party of the winning presidential candidate is inflated beyond the normal vote by the winning candidate's coattails. At the next midterm the congressional vote reverts to the normal vote. The result is an electoral decline for the president's party. This argument has its plausibility.[7] Over the fourteen midterm elections from 1946 through 1998, on average the presidential party suffered a decline of 1 percent of its seats in Congress for every 1 percent of its margin of victory in the prior presidential election. In other words, the stronger the coattail effect in the preceding election, the greater the decline in seats. The withdrawn coattails argument can explain the elections of 1996. Clinton had virtually no coattails in 1996; therefore with no coattails withdrawn in 1998 the Democratic congressional vote did not decline.

According to the ideological balancing argument, parts of the electorate vote against the president's party at midterm as an ideological hedge. Moderate voters, seeing themselves as occupying an ideological position between those of the Democrats and Republicans, have an incentive to balance the president's ideology with a congressional vote for the "out" party. This tendency works to encourage a divided government, in which one party controls the presidency and the other at least one house of Congress.[8] Whereas the withdrawn coattails argument explains midterm loss in terms of the circumstances in the prior election, the ideological balancing argument explains the loss in terms of the circumstances at midterm itself.

As does the withdrawn coattails argument, the ideological balancing argument has its plausibility. On average over the fourteen midterm elections in 1946–1998, which are equally divided between Republican and Democratic presidencies, each party has enjoyed an increase of about thirty-five more House seats in elections when it did *not* control the presidency. In other words, a party would achieve the highest level of success at midterm if it had lost the prior presidential election. The ideological balancing argument can also explain the absence of presidential coattails in 1996, when when party control of the House was at stake. A potent partisan argument of the 1996 Republican congressional campaigns was that moderate voters should vote Republican for Congress to block Clinton, whose reelection seemed certain. Clinton thus had no coattails, according to this argument, because of ideological balancing in anticipation of

Clinton's election. Thus in 1998 there were no coattails to be withdrawn, and the 1998 election became the exception to the rule of a midterm loss for the presidential party.

Electoral Change as a Search for Policy Direction

Every two years the electorate collectively chooses a new Congress, with a new partisan makeup. Does Congress's party composition reflect the electorate's policy preferences? The popular view, often propounded by pundits at election time, is that partisan tides reflect the electorate's changing ideological mood—as if Democratic gains signify a demand for more liberalism, and Republican gains a demand for more conservatism. For example, the major Democratic gains associated with Johnson's landslide victory in 1964 were interpreted at the time as a mandate for a new liberal policy agenda. Reagan's surprise win in 1980 and the accompanying Republican gains in Congress were similarly attributed to a switch to a conservative mood. More recently, the Republican takeover of Congress in 1994 was widely proclaimed by the victors and the media as indicating a sharp rejection of the liberalism of President Clinton and the Democratic Party. In each case, Congress responded with legislation that matched the purported public cries for change.

It would be dangerous to read every turn in partisan electoral fortunes as a demand for a corresponding change in policy direction. Many variables apart from ideological demands affect the national verdict, from the personal appeal of the presidential candidates to the degree of the nation's prosperity at the moment to variables that are beyond our ability to measure. Still, among the conflicting signals from congressional election outcomes, the electorate's collective preference for more liberalism or more conservatism is an important part of the mix. The electorate was relatively liberal at the time of Lyndon Johnson's Great Society and conservative when the Reagan revolution began; similarly, it was liberal when it elected Clinton and a Democratic Congress in 1992 but conservative in 1994. The electorate chooses the partisan makeup of Congress based in part on its preferred degree of policy liberalism, adjusting also for the expected ideological pressure from the occupant of the White House.

Election outcomes matter because the candidates who run under different party banners stand for very different policy agendas. We begin by showing how the parties differ on some representative issues, drawing on a survey of candidates in the 1998 election by Project Vote Smart.[9] Among other questions, the survey asked House candidates whether they wanted changes in a number of spending programs. In Figure 4-3 we plot the average responses of Democratic and Republican candidates to a set of questions about what changes they would like to see in different policy programs. They were given the following options, with the scores we used to construct the figure in parentheses: "greatly increase" (+2), "slightly increase" (+1), "maintain status" (0), "slightly decrease" (−1), "greatly decrease" (−2) or "eliminate" (−3). The direction of the bar indicates whether

Figure 4-3 Spending Preferences for Democratic and
Republican Congressional Candidates, 1998

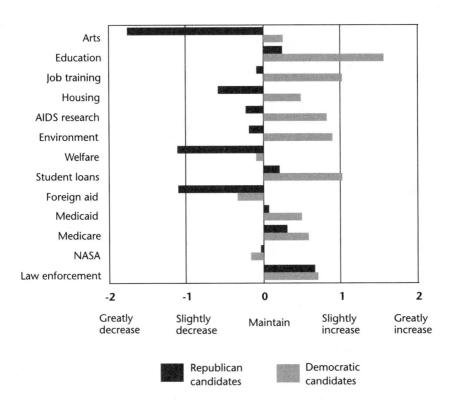

Source: Compiled by the authors from the 1998 Project Vote Smart congressional survey.

Note: Candidates were asked their preferences for spending for each program, from greatly decrease to greatly increase. The bars represent the average response for each party's candidates.

they wanted an increase or decrease; a bar extending to the left of the vertical line indicates that more party members wanted to decrease than to increase the program, and a bar extending to the right indicates an overall preference for increases in spending. The length of the bars in the figure indicates by how much party members wanted to increase or decrease the program.

We see that Republican candidates were strongly opposed to funding for the arts, and their Democratic counterparts had a slight preference for increases in spending. There are other areas in which the preferences were quite clear: Republicans would cut funding for job training, housing, and AIDS research,

Figure 4-4 Party Differences among House Candidates on Selected Issues, 1998

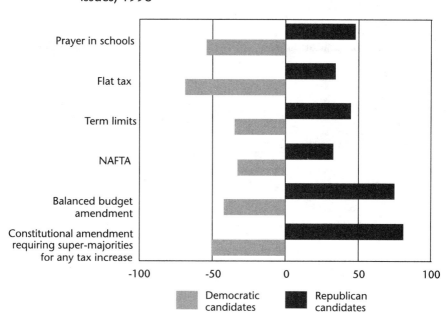

Source: Data are from the 1998 Project Vote Smart National Political Awareness Test given to all congressional candidates.

Note: Bars represent the percentage favoring minus the percentage opposing each policy.

and Democrats preferred more spending for these programs. By contrast, for several other programs the parties agreed on the direction of spending changes but differed as to how much should be spent. For example, Republicans tended to favor moderate increases in education spending, and Democrats were overwhelmingly in favor of increases. Both parties agree on welfare cuts, following the reforms in 1996, but Republicans called for substantially larger cuts. Republicans wanted a slight increase in money for student loans, Democrats wanted larger increases, and so on for most of the policy areas. Only in the area of law enforcement was there essentially no difference between parties in spending preferences; both parties called for increases of about the same magnitude.

Party difference also extended to areas other than spending. Figure 4-4 displays the differences in party responses to six different policy proposals. In each case candidates were asked whether they favored, opposed, or were undecided on the proposals. The bars indicate the percentage of candidates of each party favoring a program minus the percentage opposed. For example, when asked whether

Figure 4-5 Distributions of Candidate Ideology by Party, 1998

Candidate Ideology (in percentages)

Candidate Ideology (in percentages)

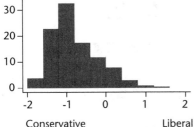

Republican Candidates

Conservative   Liberal

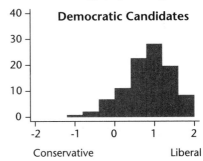

Democratic Candidates

Conservative   Liberal

Source: Compiled by the authors.

Note: The scores are our candidate ideology index, derived from the Project Vote Smart 1998 congressional National Political Awareness Test, www.vote-smart.org.

they supported a constitutional amendment that would permit religious expression and voluntary prayer in public places, including schools, 64 percent of the Republican candidates favored the amendment and 15 percent opposed it, for an overall score of 64−15 = 49. In contrast, only 16 percent of the Democratic candidates favored this amendment and fully 70 percent opposed it, for a score of 16−70 = −54.

Other policy proposals showed very clear party differences: Republicans in 1998 favored a flat tax system, in which everyone would pay the same percentage of their income in taxes, rather than the progressive tax system we have now, in which people with higher incomes pay a higher percentage. Democrats opposed the flat tax. Republicans favored term limits for members of Congress, a balanced budget amendment to the Constitution, and a constitutional amendment requiring super-majorities in both houses of Congress to raise taxes. Democrats opposed all of these conservative proposals.

Finally, notice that the party differences were weaker on the North American Free Trade Agreement (NAFTA) than on the other issues. Applying ideological principles, many staunch conservatives oppose free trade legislation such as NAFTA, whereas many liberals support it. Indeed President Clinton's enthusiastic backing was a key to NAFTA's success in Congress. Complicating matters, NAFTA was supported by American businesses hoping to profit from lower tariffs on their manufactured goods in trade with Canada and Mexico, whereas it was opposed by many in the labor movement who fear the export of jobs to countries such as Mexico where labor is cheaper. In the end, Clinton won passage of NAFTA with more support from Republicans than from Democrats, many of whom were concerned about their labor constituencies.

The accumulated Democratic and Republican differences over specific issues are reflected in their overall ideological tendencies. To examine these differences we developed an index of candidate ideology, which measures the general policy liberalism or conservatism of House candidates, based on responses to the Project Vote Smart survey. The index includes responses from a wide array of policy areas, from taxing and spending preferences to affirmative action and foreign policy. (See the appendix to this chapter.) The index ranges from approximately -2 to $+2$, with high scores indicating greater liberalism.

Figure 4-5 shows the distributions of the scores of the two parties' candidates for the House in 1998. Republicans cluster on the conservative side, Democrats on the liberal side. Although the parties have become more polarized in recent years—largely as a result of the dwindling presence of southern conservative Democrats—we do see variation. Within each of the parties some candidates clearly hold views that are some distance from their party's norm. As we discuss in the next section, these exceptions play a significant role in the dynamics of congressional representation.

The Role of Candidates in House Contests

Voters in congressional elections vote not only on the basis of national issues and the parties' policy positions but also on the basis of what they learn about their local candidates. At first glance, it would seem that most voters have insufficient information about the candidates to vote on anything more than a partisan basis. Consider some evidence from surveys: only about one-half of voters can name their U.S. representative, and only slightly fewer claim to have "read or heard" something about him or her. The content of the information they have heard is generally a vague sentiment such as "he is a good man" or "she knows the job" and rarely touches on policy issues or roll-call voting. Only by the generous test of recognition of the representative's name does the electorate score well. More than 90 percent claim to recognize their representative's name when supplied with it. Candidates for open seats are even less visible than incumbent candidates, and challengers trying to defeat incumbent representatives are the least visible of all. Typically only about 20 percent of the voting electorate can recall the challenger's name or anything else about him or her. Only about half will claim to recognize the challenger's name when supplied with it.[10]

Although voters generally are not well informed about their district's House candidates, it does not follow that the candidates themselves have little impact on election outcomes. Movement by a few voters within a constituency can create a major surge for or against a candidate. This movement, the "personal" vote, results from the constituency's reaction to the specific candidates, as opposed to the "partisan" vote, which results from the constituency's partisanship. The personal vote is about as important as the partisan vote in deciding elections.

The Success of House Incumbents

One prominent fact about House elections is the success rate of incumbents. Averaged over many election years, more than 95 percent of incumbent candidates have been reelected. In 1998 incumbents enjoyed a 99 percent reelection rate. Even in 1994, the year of the "Republican revolution," 93 percent of incumbent candidates were returned to Congress.[11] Why do incumbents do so well at the ballot box? Several factors contribute to their electoral success.

To guide our discussion of incumbency, Figure 4-6 graphs the relationship between the 1998 House vote of each district on the vertical axis, as the percentage voting Democratic, and the 1996 presidential vote on the horizontal axis, as the percentage voting for Clinton. The district-level vote for Clinton is a useful indicator of underlying district partisanship and ideology. Had the district vote for the House in 1998 always matched Clinton's vote in 1996, all the districts would fall on the diagonal line. Figure 4-6 is divided into three panels on the basis of incumbency. The middle panel presents the data for the baseline of 1998 open seats (with no incumbent running). Without an incumbent in the race, the vote followed closely from district partisanship as reflected in the Clinton vote. The top and bottom panels show the data for districts where Democratic and Republican incumbents, respectively, seek reelection. Inspection of Figure 4-6 shows most incumbents winning sufficient votes for reelection in 1998, often running ahead of their party's 1996 presidential ticket.

District partisanship. The most obvious explanation for why incumbents so often win reelection is district partisanship. Most districts are either dominantly Republican or dominantly Democratic (as measured in Figure 4-6 by the presidential vote). Most House seats, therefore, are nearly guaranteed for the candidate of the locally favored party.

We see the importance of district partisanship from the following statistics. In 1996 President Clinton averaged 55 percent of the major-party vote in the 435 congressional districts. Twenty-one percent of districts were highly competitive, by the standard that the Clinton vote was within three percentage points of the average—between 52.0 and 58.0 percent. The two parties divided these districts evenly in the 1998 congressional election. In the other 79 percent of districts, the Clinton vote was not within three percentage points of the average and therefore considered at least reasonably safe for the district's dominant party. Eighty-eight percent of these seats were won by the dominant party in 1998.

Electoral selection. One simple but sometimes overlooked reason that incumbents usually win is that (in competitive districts) incumbency status must be earned at the ballot box. Apart from district partisanship and partisan trends, elections are won on the basis of which party can field the stronger candidate. Strong candidates tend to win and retain their strength in subsequent contests as

Figure 4-6 The Incumbency Advantage in the House, 1998

Democratic House Vote in 1998

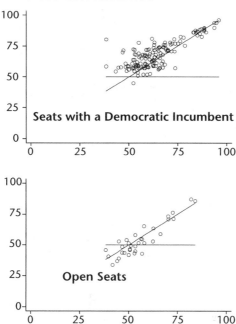

Seats with a Democratic Incumbent

Open Seats

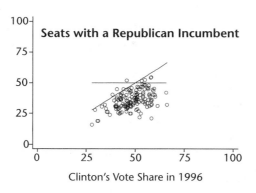

Seats with a Republican Incumbent

Clinton's Vote Share in 1996

Source: Compiled by the authors.

Note: Dots above the diagonal line indicate that the district House vote for the Democratic candidate in 1998 exceeded the vote for Clinton in that district in 1996. Dots below the diagonal line indicate that the Democratic House candidate in 1998 ran behind Clinton's percentage in 1996. Dots above the horizontal line at 50 percent indicate a Democratic victory; dots below this line a Republican victory.

Table 4-1   Incumbents Facing Quality Challengers in the 1998
House Elections

1998 Electoral Margin	Democratic Incumbents	Republican Incumbents
Safe: won by 60% or more	12% (91)	10% (88)
Competitive: won by less than 60%	42% (60)	44% (68)

Source: Data on candidate experience (quality) supplied by Gary Jacobson.

Note: Figures represent the percentages of incumbents running for reelection who faced experienced challengers. The numbers of incumbents are in parentheses. Experienced challengers are defined as those who have been previously elected to political office. The challenger is far more likely to be experienced when the election is competitive.

incumbents. They survive until they falter or lose to even stronger candidates. Retirement of a successful incumbent starts the process again.

Weak challengers. Incumbents augment their electoral success with their ability to draw weak challengers. Candidates and their supporters behave strategically, so they are reluctant to expend funds and political reputations against formidable foes.[12] Strong challengers conserve their political resources for races in which they have a chance of winning, either because the incumbent is vulnerable, short-term national forces favor the party, or they have a shot at an open seat.

The tendency for potential challengers to behave strategically affects the quality of the challengers facing incumbents in safe and competitive districts. In 1998, as in other years, incumbents with safe margins were the least likely to face experienced challengers (see Table 4-1). Experienced and otherwise strong candidates are scared off by strong incumbents. In their place we find weak challengers, which works to hand even larger victories to the incumbent.

Strategic retirements. One reason why incumbents rarely lose is the practice of "strategic retirement." When incumbents are threatened by an imminent loss, they will more frequently retire rather than face the verdict of the voters. On average, incumbents retire with about the same frequency as their objective probability of defeat. For instance, House members facing a 60 percent chance of losing will retire about 60 percent of the time. Strategic retirement is one reason why there were not more incumbents defeated in 1992 following the House check-bouncing scandal. Rather than face risky reelection battles, about one third of the House members with overdrafts at the House bank chose to quit.[13]

The incumbency advantage. Finally, there is the incumbency advantage—the electoral benefits that accrue to the incumbent by virtue of being the incumbent. More precisely, incumbents have opportunities to strengthen their electoral position by virtue of the service they perform in the House. Most members exploit these resources, although some do so more energetically than others.

Several means can be used to measure the incumbency advantage. Arguably the best is the sophomore surge, or the percentage of the vote that candidates gain between their first election (as a non-incumbent) and their first reelection attempt (as an incumbent). Averaged across elections and adjusted for the national partisan trend, the sophomore surge is a simple and accurate measure of the typical vote share gained from incumbency.

The value of incumbency has increased substantially in recent decades. The sophomore surge was only about two percentage points in the 1950s, when partisanship was the dominant consideration in congressional elections. By the 1970s the sophomore surge had reached about 7 percentage points, and it remains at this level today.[14]

This increase in the incumbency advantage coincides with two important trends. One is the loosening of voters' party ties, along with an increase in the numbers of independent voters, which means that forces other than party loyalty can have more of an influence. The other trend is that members of Congress have increasingly turned their offices into reelection machines.[15] In the mid-1960s Congress changed its rules to bestow on its members several increases in the resources of office, or "perks." These perks included free mailing privileges (the frank), increased travel allowances for members to visit their districts, and increased staff for handling constituents' growing concern with the federal bureaucracy.[16] These new rules give incumbents more of an opportunity to become well thought of by their constituents, often for reasons that have nothing to do with policymaking considerations at all.

A seven-point incumbency advantage may not seem sufficient to ensure success for most incumbents. But the incumbency advantage is not a simple seven points across-the-board for all incumbents; the seven-point advantage is instead an average. Some incumbents work harder than others to please their constituents. Members trying to stay elected in districts with adverse partisanship have the greatest incentive to expand their incumbency advantage. Meanwhile, members from very safe districts have little incentive to attract additional voters, because their seats should be safe as long as their district votes close to its partisan predisposition. We would expect such incumbents to earn little or no incumbency advantage at all.

Referring back to Figure 4-6, one can see this logic at work. Incumbents in 1998 from very safe districts earned about the same vote margin as their party's presidential ticket — no more and no less. Meanwhile incumbents in competitive districts received far more votes than the presidential ticket of their party. Few such incumbents would survive electorally without the incumbency advantage. If they could earn no more votes than their party's presidential ticket, they would be out of office.

The incumbency advantage as an investment. Because incumbents almost always win, it might seem that incumbents can ignore constituency concerns. But this impression would be quite mistaken. A central source of the incumbency advantage lies in incumbents' ability to read the interests of their districts and provide constituents with what they want. Incumbents are well aware that their long-term electoral security depends on satisfying their constituencies. Even though House members know that they are unlikely to lose the next election, they also understand that their chances are roughly one in three that they will eventually lose. After all, roughly one in three got to Congress in the first place by defeating a sitting incumbent.[17]

If House members were to ignore their districts, we would see no incumbency advantage and, instead, rapid turnover. House members do not receive their incumbency advantage automatically; they must earn it with hard work. Part of the work is constituency service and bringing home the "pork" in the form of government construction projects, local government contracts, and the like. But there is also an important policy component to the incumbent's investment. One way House members earn the incumbency advantage is by representing their districts' policy interests. Often these interests can be expressed as a summary ideological preference. As we shall see in the next section, House members add to their vote margins by representing the policy interests of their constituencies.

Candidates, Issues, and the Vote

In this section we explore how House members hold onto their seats by offering ideological representation. As we have seen, the typical constituency will be given a choice between a relatively conservative Republican and a relatively liberal Democrat. The process works as follows. Voters make their selections based in part on which candidate's views are closest to their own. This gives the candidates an incentive to move to the constituency's center—toward the position of the district's median voter.[18] The strength of this incentive is proportional to the attentiveness of the electorate to the member's ideological behavior and the extent to which non-ideological factors have worked to ensure that a contest will be close.

If ideological proximity were all that the voters cared about, candidates would always converge toward the center, because to fail to do so would be to lose. But voters are only partially attentive and responsive to ideological appeals, which limits the electoral gains that can be achieved by moderation. Moving to the center will gain candidates the support of some but not all voters who are ideologically closer to them than to their opponents. As a result, candidates strike a balance between the electoral security that can be gained from adopting the position of the constituency's median voter, on the one hand, and the ideological satisfaction that comes from adopting their favored, more "extreme" ideological positions and those of their core supporters, on the other.[19]

Figure 4-7 shows candidate ideological positions as a function of both party and district partisanship. We measured candidate ideology using Project Vote Smart data, as described above. For open seat races we included only cases where Project Vote Smart successfully surveyed both major-party candidates. For races with an incumbent we omitted cases where the challenger failed to respond to the Project Vote Smart questionnaire. For cases in which the challenger respond-

Figure 4-7 Republican and Democratic 1998 Candidate Ideology
(by District Presidential Vote in 1996)

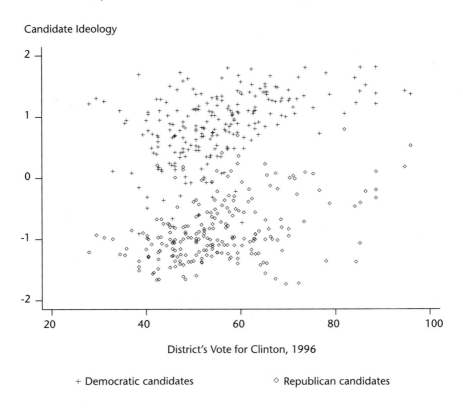

Candidate Ideology

District's Vote for Clinton, 1996

+ Democratic candidates   ◇ Republican candidates

Note: Candidate ideology is measured using the 1998 Project Vote Smart congressional National Political Awareness Test. High scores are liberal, and low scores are conservative.

ed but the incumbent did not, we estimated the incumbent's ideology by projecting from observed roll calls using Keith Poole and Howard Rosenthal's DW-NOMINATE scores.[20] Ideology scores are scaled so that high scores are liberal and low scores are conservative. Throughout this section, all demonstrations are based solely on the districts where ideological positions could be scored for both the Republican and the Democratic candidate.

Although some Republican candidates score to the left of some Democrats, Republican candidates rarely score more liberal than the Democratic opponent within their own constituency. Indeed, among the 228 districts in our 1998 data set, the Republican scores more conservative in every single instance. The candidate's party affiliations clearly provide voters with the basis of an ideological choice.

Table 4-2   Regression of 1998 Democratic Vote on 1998 Candidate Ideology,
1996 District Presidential Vote, and 1998 Candidate Spending, for
Incumbent Races

Independent Variable	Regression Coefficient	t-ratio	Beta	
Democratic incumbents				
Incumbent ideology	−3.02[a]	−2.3	−0.20	
Challenger ideology	−0.26	−0.2	−0.01	*Adj. R^2* = .684
Presidential vote	0.47[b]	5.0	0.52	
Log (Democrat spending) −				
Log (Republican spending)	3.67[b]	8.2	0.57	
Constant	33.31			N = 85
Republican incumbents				
Incumbent ideology	−3.56[b]	−3.7	−0.28	
Challenger ideology	−0.38[b]	−0.4	−0.03	*Adj. R^2* = .568
Presidential vote	0.55[b]	7.5	0.58	
Log (Democrat spending) −				
Log (Republican spending)	2.41[b]	7.3	0.49	
Constant	12.04			N = 101

Source: Compiled by the authors.

Note: Candidate ideology scores are based on Project Vote Smart data (Dimension 1) or (if the incumbent Project Vote Smart data are missing) equivalently scaled incumbent DW-NOMINATE scores. The presidential vote is the Democratic percentage of the two-party vote in 1996. The candidates' relative spending advantage is measured as the Democrat minus Republican difference in logged dollars spent (minus 5,000).

[a] Significant at .05.

[b] Significant at .001.

Figure 4-7 also shows that the ideological variation within parties is a function of constituency. The more liberal and Democratic the district (as measured by the district's vote for Clinton), the more liberal the two parties' candidates. Their responsiveness to constituency preferences indicates that congressional candidates believe that constituencies vote on the basis of ideological proximity to the candidates. Next we examine the evidence regarding whether this belief is correct.

Table 4-2 examines the effect of candidates' ideology on their vote share, controlling for their district's presidential vote in 1996 and the relative spending levels of the candidates. It presents regression equations for 1998 incumbent candidates, separately for seats held by Democrats and Republicans. We ignored open seats due to a dearth of cases. Since our hypothesis was that moderation (conservatism) wins votes for Democrats and that moderation (liberalism) wins votes for Republicans, we expected the signs of the ideology variables to be negative.

In a pattern consistent with other election years, Table 4-2 shows that incumbent ideology is a significant predictor of the vote share for both Democrats and Republicans, and that challenger ideology shows a small but decidedly non-significant effect (although with the expected positive or negative value).[21] Candidate ideology evidently matters for incumbents, although the exact position of their challengers is not discernibly relevant. This is consistent with evidence from voter surveys, which consistently show that challengers are considerably less visible to voters than are incumbents.

We can visualize the estimated effects of incumbent ideology in the following way. The coefficients are −3.0 for Democrats and −3.6 for Republicans, for an average of −3.3. For each party the observed ideological range was about 3 units between the most liberal and most conservative member on the candidate ideology scale. A 3.3 movement per unit multiplied by 3 units comes to a value of 9.9, suggesting that a range of 10 percentage points of the two-party vote is in play as a function of ideological positioning. For instance, the most conservative Republican member could gain 10 percentage points by adopting the position of the least conservative Republican member. Similarly, the most liberal Democratic member could gain 10 points by adopting the position of the least liberal Democratic member.[22]

We show the same process visually in Figure 4-8. This figure displays the relationship between the 1996 presidential vote (the marker for district partisanship) and the 1998 congressional vote for incumbents with distinctive ideological positions. Within each party, we separate the most moderate from the most extreme.

For Democrats, we separated the most liberal incumbents, or those who scored at least one standard deviation more liberal than the party mean (L's in the top panel), from the moderates who scored at least one standard deviation more conservative than the party mean (M's in the top panel). Two things should be noted. First, whereas the liberals represented safe seats, the moderates represented competitive seats in which the vote for Clinton in 1996 was approximately 50 percent. This is evidence that politicians moderate according to electoral need. Second, whereas the liberals ran about even with Clinton in their districts, the moderates all exceeded Clinton's 1996 margin by a considerable amount. One can readily project from this figure that the moderate Democrats depicted would have been in considerable electoral trouble had they assumed liberal ideological postures in their more moderate and competitive districts.

The pattern for Republicans mirrored that of the Democrats, although it was not quite as distinct. We separated the most conservative incumbents, or those at least one standard deviation to the right of the party mean (C's in the bottom panel), from the moderates who were at least one standard deviation to the right of the party mean (the M's in the bottom panel). The more conservative Republicans tended to represent the districts more strongly opposed to Clinton. And, although most Republicans of all ideological stripes received a higher vote share in 1998 than did their party in the 1996 presidential election (that is, most led Dole), this advantage was stronger for the moderates than for the conservatives. One could readily project that if the moderates from competitive districts had run as extreme conservatives, many would have lost in 1998.[23]

Robert S. Erikson and Gerald C. Wright

Figure 4-8 Ideology and the House Vote, 1998

Democratic Vote Share (in percentage)

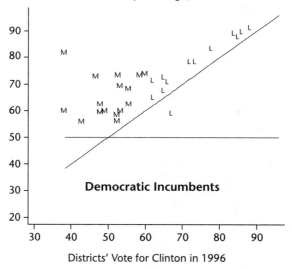

Districts' Vote for Clinton in 1996

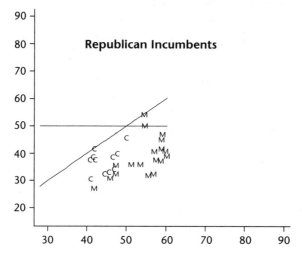

Source: Compiled by the authors.

Note: C denotes conservative Republicans, M denotes both moderate Democrats and moderate Republicans, and L denotes liberal Democrats. The diagonal line indicates where equal vote percentages for the Democratic House candidate in 1998 and Clinton in 1996 would be plotted. The horizontal line indicates 50 percent of the House vote. Districts above the horizontal line were won by the Democratic candidate, and those below it were won by the Republican.

Congressional Elections and Representation

The political parties and the candidates themselves provide mechanisms with which constituencies can electorally determine the policy positions of their representatives in Congress. First, consider the role of political parties. Democratic and Republican candidates for Congress are sufficiently divergent from one another on the liberal–conservative spectrum to provide their constituencies with a clear choice. Liberal districts generally vote Democratic and elect liberals, and conservative districts generally vote Republican and elect conservatives.

Second, not only the parties' general reputations but also the precise ideological positions of the candidates matter to the voters. Candidates for Congress often deviate from their party's ideological orthodoxy. By moving toward a more moderate position, one that is closer to a constituency's prevailing views, the candidate enhances his or her electoral chances, and by doing so enhances the representation of constituency views.

As Figure 4-9 shows, the net result is a clear pattern whereby the most liberal districts elect the most liberal members and the most conservative districts elect the most conservative members. The vertical axis of the figure represents the member's ideology; the horizontal axis represents constituency liberalism as measured by presidential voting. Representatives' ideological positions and constituency opinion (proxied by the presidential vote) correlate at a substantial rate of +.77. Very liberal districts almost always elect Democrats; very conservative districts almost always elect Republicans. In the battleground districts in the middle, candidate ideology can be the decisive factor. Although we find no evidence that the ideology of non-incumbent candidates matters, once they become incumbents their electoral survival often depends on their ability to satisfy the ideological preferences of their constituencies.

Although we have observed strong evidence that members effectively represent their constituents, we cannot be sure about the prevalence of a residual ideological bias. We can compare ideology scores of congressional candidates on the one hand with the presidential voting of constituencies on the other. Both may reflect ideological positioning, but they are not calibrated on a common scale. It could be the case, for instance, that members of Congress are systematically more liberal (or systematically more conservative) than their constituencies, despite the evidence of district-level representation.

Similarly, we can ask whether the House as a whole is too liberal, too conservative, or just right in terms of the net taste of the American electorate. A Congress that is off-center from the people ideologically would be a Congress out of equilibrium. To restore equilibrium, Congress would either realize that it is not representative and change its policymaking, or the people would elect a Congress more ideologically compatible with their views. Another possibility would be a system in equilibrium due to forces beyond public opinion. For instance, the persistent influence of money on politics could permanently skew congressional policymaking away from the trajectory preferred by public opinion.

Figure 4-9 Winner's Ideology by District Presidential Vote

Winner's Ideological Liberalism, 1998

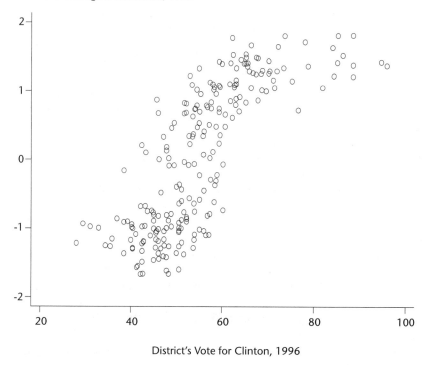

District's Vote for Clinton, 1996

Source: Winner's ideology is calculated from the Project Vote Smart survey and roll call data.

Note: Higher scores for winner's ideology indicate greater liberalism, and higher district vote percentages for Clinton indicate greater constituency liberalism.

One way to estimate the ideological match between Congress and the public is to compare voters' ideological ratings of their recently elected representative with their personal ideological preferences. Relevant data from several elections, available from the National Election Studies, are displayed in Table 4-3. For several Congresses, approximately the same percentage of voters see themselves as more liberal than the member they just elected as see themselves as more conservative. This balance indicates that, at least perceptually, Congress has not been too liberal or conservative for the electorate. In most years when the public has been surveyed, slightly more people have seen their member as too liberal than as too conservative. However, statistics show that people with lower levels of education, who may have more difficulty evaluating the parties in abstract ideologi-

Table 4-3 Voter's Perceptions of the Ideology of Their House Representatives

Percentage who see their representative as	1978	1980	1982	1986	1990	1994	1998
More conservative than themselves	27%	33%	31%	37%	37%	34%	36%
Similar to themselves	26	26	27	24	21	26	20
More liberal than themselves	47	41	42	40	42	41	43

cal terms, tend to vote Democratic. Even though they may be silent on the exact ideological position of their representative, we can presume that they still know their political interests.

House–Senate Differences in Electoral Representation

The Framers of the Constitution intended the Senate to be an elite chamber, isolated from the popular demands on the House. Regardless of how well or poorly this intention has been realized, there are fundamental constitutional differences between the two chambers. The most remarkable difference has been eliminated. Before 1913 and ratification of the Seventeenth Amendment, state legislatures selected their state's senators. Today, voters elect their senators directly. Because senators have six-year terms, they are relatively free from the never-ending campaigns carried on by representatives. And, for the most part, the constituencies senators represent are larger and much more diverse than those of representatives.

Election Results and the Senate

In terms of national election results, the party composition of the Senate reflects the same forces that determine the party composition of the House. The division between Democrats and Republicans in the Senate is influenced by presidential coattails in presidential years and the bounce to the out party at midterm. The Senate's partisan division responds more sluggishly to national trends, however, because only one-third of the senators are up for reelection in any election year.

As a general rule, Senate elections are more competitive than House elections. Senate races with no incumbent are almost always sharply contested by both parties, and an incumbent senator who seeks reelection has a considerably greater chance of defeat than does an incumbent House member who seeks reelection. Incumbent senators are reelected at a rate of about 78 percent, in comparison to 95 percent for House incumbents. One reason that Senate races are more closely contested is that the statewide Senate constituencies are rarely dominated by one political party, as the smaller House districts are. Another major factor is that Senate races attract strong challengers. A senator is far more likely than a House member to face a politically seasoned and well-financed election opponent. Finally, senators seem unable to obtain the strong incumbency advantage that House members enjoy, averaging no better than a few percentage points as their average sophomore surge. (Evidently, senatorial challengers find it easier to generate visibility for their campaigns than do challengers to House incumbents.) Senators perform well electorally, compared with nonincumbent candidates of their party, partly because they had to be good candidates to be elected the first time.

Although reelection to the Senate is more difficult than reelection to the House, senators need to run only once every six years. The appropriate comparison of electoral security is a comparison of survival rates over the same period of time. Measured over six years, House members seeking reelection have a survival rate of approximately 78 percent—about the same as the reelection rate for senators.[24]

Therefore, the six-year term for senators almost exactly offsets the greater incumbency advantage of the House. Senators run less often but at higher risk. The long-run survival rates for the two houses would appear to be roughly equal.

Is the Senate any less responsive to popular opinion than the House? Six-year terms would seem to provide senators with ample freedom from electoral concerns, except for the final run up to election. Moreover, when senators decide to be attentive to their electorates, their diverse constituencies make full representation difficult.

As are House members, senators are sensitive to constituency opinion, with each party's most conservative senators found in conservative states, and most liberal members found in liberal states. In terms of partisan politics, the states are competitive enough that each party has a chance at a Senate seat. As a result, many states send both a Republican and a Democrat to the Senate, a pattern that baffles some observers. In a pattern similar to that of the House, senators from states in which the other party dominates often are ideologically atypical for their party.[25]

State Populations and the Senate

Although states vary considerably in population, each has two senators. California's 31 million people get the same number of senators as Alaska's 600,000. To some extent, this constitutionally designed "malapportionment" favors political conservatism. Indeed, state population correlates rather strongly (+.34) with our measure of citizen liberalism, based on pooled CBS News/*New York Times* surveys.[26] Small, politically conservative states enjoy an extra margin of representation in the Senate.

During the Reagan years, when the Republicans enjoyed a six-year Senate majority, the Senate was the more conservative chamber. One is tempted to attribute this senatorial conservatism to the Senate's overrepresentation of small states. However, in the immediate aftermath of the Republican takeover of both houses of Congress in 1994, the Senate was the more moderate of the two chambers. The greater responsiveness of the House to national forces in that year brought in a crew of conservative freshmen legislators that, coupled with vigorous conservative leadership, put the House distinctly in the lead of the Republican revolution launched by the 1994 election.

The Six-Year Term

Because the next election for representatives is never more than two years away, electoral considerations are always important for members of the House. For senators, the six-year term can provide some leeway. Voters — so it sometimes seems — are electorally myopic, forgetting what senators do early in their terms and remembering only what they do close to the election.

Whether or not this view of the electorate is valid, there is a good deal of evidence that senatorial roll call voting responds to the six-year cycle.[27] In the year or two before they must run again, incumbents move away from their party's extreme. Democrats inch in a conservative direction, and Republicans edge over to the left. The purpose in each instance is to appeal to moderate voters.

Because senators moderate their ideological positions as reelection approaches, they presumably have good reason to do so: senators must believe that moderation enhances their chances of electoral success. Earlier we saw evidence that House members with moderate ideological positions are more likely to be reelected. Is the same true for senators?

Candidates' policy positions affect their election chances. For the Senate, candidates do better if they avoid their party's ideological extremes. Gerald Wright and Michael Berkman estimated the effect of candidates' issue positions by comparing different pairings of ideological positions while statistically controlling for the effects of several constituency characteristics and attitudes.[28] They estimated that whether a Senate candidate represents the party's moderate wing or more extremist wing creates a difference ranging from five to eight percentage points. This effect is similar to that observed for House elections. The evidence suggests that the same electoral connection leading to representation exists in the Senate as in the House, with the added twists of the larger, more heterogeneous constituencies and the latitude of the six-year Senate term.

Conclusion

Along with presidential elections, congressional elections provide citizens with their main opportunity to influence the direction of national policy. When elections bring about significant changes in the party composition of Congress, we can be fairly confident of two things. The first is that the new Congress will have a different ideological cast. Democratic and Republican candidates for House and Senate stand for quite different things. Therefore, electing more

Democrats or more Republicans increases the likelihood of policy movement in the ideological direction of the advantaged party. Ironically, the second is that such changes do not always stem from the electorate's desire for new policy directions. The Republican takeover in 1994 did coincide with an increase in conservative Republican sentiments in the mass electorate. Other, less substantial changes, however, have stemmed from factors such as presidential coattails or the usual slump the presidential party experiences at midterm.

We see the electorate's influence on policy direction most clearly in the relationship between constituencies and their elected representatives. In terms of ideological direction, individual House and Senate members respond to their constituencies. In turn, ideological direction matters when constituencies decide which candidates they will elect and which they will not.

The average voter knows little about his or her representative and only a bit more about his or her senators. House challengers are almost invisible, and only a portion of the electorate has even a modest amount of information about senatorial challengers. Nevertheless, the electorates that candidates and parties face are smart and discerning, and they reward faithful representation. Candidates, generally desirous of attaining and staying in office, heed their electorate's wishes and work to give them what they want. Elections bring about much higher levels of policy representation than most observers would expect based on the low levels of citizen awareness.

Appendix 4-A: The Project Vote Smart Factor Scores

Project Vote Smart attempts to provide objective and useful information about candidates for American voters. One of its main activities is the administration of their National Political Awareness Tests (NPATs), which are comprehensive questionnaires in which candidates for the presidency, Congress, and state legislatures are asked to indicate the policy positions that they support. The 1998 congressional NPAT scored more than two hundred policy items, covering eighteen policy areas. Our ideology scores for congressional candidates are based on fifteen of these. We first did factor analyses of the items in individual policy areas, including abortion; how to spend the current budget surplus; general preferences for government spending of different programs; anti-drug policy; and policy preferences on affirmative action, education, the environment, foreign affairs, gun control, health, crime, immigration, social security, welfare, and taxes. Where respondents failed to express any preferences within a battery of items we created a new dummy variable, in which they were given a "1" and everyone else was given a "0." These missing data indicators were then included in the next step in which we did a factor analysis of the individual policy scales together. Our measure of ideology is the scores derived from the first factor, which absorbed the vast majority of the variance among the individual scales.

Notes

1. The swing ratio is inversely related to the size of the incumbency advantage, discussed below. The more incumbents can protect themselves with a strong incumbency advantage, the less the seat swing depends on the national division of the vote. The classic discussion of this point is David Mayhew, "Congressional Elections: The Case of the Vanishing Marginals," *Polity* 6 (Spring 1973): 295–318.

2. Until recently, the "normal vote" was thought of as essentially a constant 53–47 or 54–46 Democratic advantage. On the origin of the "normal vote" concept, see Philip E. Converse, "The Concept of the Normal Vote," in *Elections and the Political Order*, ed. by Angus Campbell, Philip E. Converse, Warren E. Miller, and Donald E. Stokes (New York: Wiley, 1966), 9–39.

3. Macropartisanship is measured here as the Democratic percentage of Republican and Democratic identifiers in the third quarter of the election year. The correlation between macropartisanship and the vote is +.58.

4. James A. Stimson, *Public Opinion in America*, 2d ed. (Boulder, Col.: Westview, 1999).

5. See Stimson, *Public Opinion in America;* Robert S. Erikson, Michael B. MacKuen, and James A. Stimson, *The Macro Polity* (New York: Cambridge University Press, 2001, forthcoming). The electorate's mood is not the same as its macropartisanship and the two should not be confused with each other. In fact, if anything the sign of the over-time correlation between mood and macropartisanship is negative rather than positive. (When Democratic identification is high, policy preferences tend toward conservativism.) In part, mood is driven by the nation's economy—inflation worries trigger desires for conservatism or less government, unemployment worries stimulate demand for liberalism or more government. Mood is also a function of past policies. For instance, when a pent-up demand for more liberalism goes unmet, the electorate gets even more liberal; the more liberal policies the government produces, the demand eases and the public becomes more conservative.

6. John A. Ferejohn and Randall L. Calvert, "Presidential Coattails in Historical Perspective," *American Journal of Political Science* 28 (February 1984).

7. Angus Campbell, "Surge and Decline: A Study of Electoral Change," in *Elections and the Political Order*, 40–62. See also James A. Campbell, "The Presidential Surge and Its Midterm Decline in Congressional Elections," *Journal of Politics* 53 (1991): 477–87.

8. Alberto Alesina and Howard Rosenthal, *Partisan Politics, Divided Government, and the Economy* (New York: Cambridge University Press, 1995), and Morris Fiorina, *Divided Government* (New York: Allyn and Bacon, 1995).

9. Project Vote Smart is a national nonpartisan organization focused on providing citizens with information about the political system, issues, candidates, and elected officials. Information about Project Vote Smart and access to much of the data it collects can be found at www.vote-smart.org.

10. The limits to the public's knowledge of congressional candidates have been known for some time. See Donald E. Stokes and Warren E. Miller, "Party Government and the Salience of Congress," in *Elections and the Political Order;* and Thomas E. Mann, *Unsafe at Any Margin: Interpreting Congressional Elections* (Washington: American Enterprise Institute, 1978). For a discussion incorporating recent data on voter information, see Michael X. Delli Carpini and Scott Keeter, *What Americans Know about Politics and Why It Matters* (New Haven: Yale University Press, 1996).

11. The balance of incumbents' success in 1994 decidedly favored the Republicans, who reelected all their incumbent candidates, compared to the Democrats, who, while losing their majority status, still managed to reelect 84 percent of their incumbents.

12. Gary C. Jacobson and Samuel Kernell, *Strategy and Choice in Congressional Elections*, 2d ed. (New Haven: Yale University Press, 1983).

13. Susan A. Banducci and Jeffrey A. Karp, "Electoral Consequences of Scandal and Reapportionment in the 1992 House Elections," *American Politics Quarterly* 23 (January 1994): 3–26; Gary C. Jacobson and Michael A. Dimock, "Checking Out: The Effects of Bank Overdrafts on the 1992 House Elections," *American Journal of Political Science* 28 (February 1994); Timothy Groseclose and Keith Krehbiel, "Golden Parachutes, Rubber Checks, and Strategic Retirements from the 102d House," *American Journal of Political Science* 38 (February 1994): 75–99.

14. Robert S. Erikson, "Estimating the Incumbency Advantage in Congressional Elections" (paper presented at the annual meeting of the Political Methodology Society, St. Louis, July 1990); and Andrew Gelman and Gary King, "Measuring the Incumbency Advantage without Bias," *American Journal of Political Science* 34 (1990): 1142–64. For earlier estimates see Robert S. Erikson, "Malapportionment, Gerrymandering, and Party Fortunes in Congressional Elections," *American Political Science Review* 66 (December 1972): 1234–45; and Mayhew, "Congressional Elections: The Case of the Vanishing Marginals."

15. David Mayhew, *Congress: The Electoral Connection* (New Haven: Yale University Press, 1974).

16. Morris Fiorina, *Congress: Keystone of the Washington Establishment,* 2d ed. (New Haven: Yale University Press, 1989).

17. Robert S. Erikson, "Is There Such a Thing as a Safe Seat?" *Polity* 9 (1976): 623–32.

18. Anthony Downs, *An Economic Theory of Democracy* (New York: Harper and Row, 1957), chap. 8, is the classic source on ideological moderation.

19. Gerald C. Wright, "Policy Voting in the U.S. Senate: Who Is Represented?" *Legislative Studies Quarterly* 14 (November 1989): 465–86.

20. Keith T. Poole and Howard Rosenthal, *Congress: A Political-Economic History of Roll Call Voting* (New York: Oxford University Press, 1997).

21. See our analysis of the 1974, 1978, 1982, 1990, and 1994 congressional elections in the fourth, fifth, and sixth editions of *Congress Reconsidered,* ed. by Lawrence C. Dodd and Bruce I. Oppenheimer (Washington, D.C.: CQ Press, 1989, 1993, 1997).

22. These results are comparable with our findings in other elections. In addition to the items cited in the previous footnote, see Robert S. Erikson, "The Electoral Impact of Congressional Roll Call Voting," *American Political Science Review* 65 (December 1971): 1018–32; Gerald C. Wright, "Candidates' Policy Positions and Voting in U.S. House Elections," *Legislative Studies Quarterly* 3 (August 1978): 445–64; Robert S. Erikson and Gerald C. Wright, "Policy Representation of Constituency Interests," *Political Behavior* 1 (Summer 1980): 91–106; Robert S. Erikson and Gerald C. Wright, "Representation of Constituency Ideology in Congress," in *Continuity and Change in Congressional Elections,* ed. by David Brady and John Cogan (Stanford, Calif.: Stanford University Press, forthcoming).

23. To see the electoral advantage from ideological moderation, consider the following. Although the 1996 presidential vote was more Republican in the districts held by our "conservative" Republican incumbents than in those held by our "moderates," the "moderates" on average had safer electoral margins in 1998. Moderation generated safer seats than those held by conservative Republicans from more Republican districts.

24. Amihai Glazer and Bernard Grofman, "Two Plus Two Plus Two Equals Six: Tenure of Office of Senators and Representatives, 1953–1983," *Legislative Studies Quarterly* 12 (November 1987): 555–63.

25. Robert S. Erikson, "Roll Calls, Reputations, and Representation in the U.S. Senate," *Legislative Studies Quarterly* 15 (November 1990): 623–42.

26. Robert S. Erikson, Gerald C. Wright, and John P. McIver, *Statehouse Democracy* (New York: Cambridge University Press, 1993), chap. 2. For a detailed examination of asymmetries of state size and senatorial representation, see Frances E. Lee and Bruce

I. Oppenheimer, *Sizing Up the Senate: The Unequal Consequences of Equal Representation* (Chicago: University of Chicago Press, 1999).

27. Richard F. Fenno Jr., *The United States Senate: A Bicameral Perspective* (Washington, D.C.: American Enterprise Institute, 1982); Martin Thomas, "Electoral Proximity and Senatorial Roll Call Voting," *American Journal of Political Science* 29 (February 1984): 96–111; Gerald C. Wright, "Representation and the Electoral Cycle in the U.S. Senate" (paper delivered at the annual meeting of the Midwest Political Science Association, Chicago, April 15–17, 1993).

28. Gerald C. Wright and Michael B. Berkman, "Candidates and Policy in U.S. Senatorial Elections," *American Political Science Review* 80 (June 1986): 576–90.

5. The Money Maze:
Financing Congressional Elections

Paul S. Herrnson

In 1974 Congress enacted the Federal Election Campaign Act (FECA). This law, passed in response to the public outcry following the Watergate scandal, sought to revamp the financing of congressional and presidential election campaigns. In the process of establishing new contribution, expenditure, and disclosure requirements, the new law created a maze of regulations that drastically changed the flow of money in federal elections. No longer could wealthy individuals, business groups, or labor unions contribute unlimited amounts of personal or treasury funds directly to federal campaigns. Political parties were prohibited from donating money collected from these sources or in unlimited amounts to federal candidates. Instead, individuals, interest groups, and parties wishing to participate in the financing of federal elections could make only limited contributions that originated as donations from citizens. As a result of the FECA, these groups' participation in the financing of congressional campaigns would depend less on their ability to invest large amounts of their own funds and more on their ability to collect contributions from large numbers of individual donors and strategically distribute those funds to candidates.

Although the 1974 reforms have had a major impact on the financing of federal elections, they have been weakened over the course of time. Court rulings, administrative pronouncements, and congressional amendments, oversight, and appropriations have altered the contours of the regulatory regime in which campaign money flows. More important, these decisions have enabled individuals and organizations that wish to have an effect on federal elections to spend so-called soft money, which is raised and spent outside the FECA's regulatory regime, as well as "hard money" within it.[1] In this chapter I discuss the development of the campaign finance system established by the FECA and its amendments, identify how the system has been eroded, and analyze the flow of money within the system and outside of it during the 1998 congressional elections.

Early Campaign Finance Law

A host of laws governed federal elections prior to the passage of the FECA of 1974.[2] The first law regulating money in federal campaigns was part of a naval appropriations act that was passed on March 2, 1867. The legislation was intended to stop naval officers from pressuring shipyard workers to donate part of their salaries to politicians. Later legislation prohibited all federal civil servants from making or soliciting contributions on behalf of federal candidates or political parties; prohibited national banks, corporations, public utilities, and labor unions from donating money to federal candidates; required federal candidates to disclose their campaign finances; and sought to limit spending in federal campaigns.

One of the major weaknesses of these laws was that they were laced with loopholes, enabling candidates, parties, individuals, and interest groups easily to evade them without technically breaking them. For example, candidates evaded federal contribution and expenditure limits by establishing several campaign committees, each of which could collect and spend the full amount allowed by law in a coordinated campaign effort. Individuals evaded the contribution limits by giving the legal maximum to each campaign committee in their own names and those of family members, including children who were too young to vote. Political parties and interest groups got around the law by creating campaign committees to carry out activities in support of their candidates. Some labor and business leaders responded by holding fund-raising dinners and creating the forerunners to the modern political action committee (PAC) for the purpose of collecting and redistributing contributions.[3]

Another set of shortcomings in the laws was that they lacked adequate mechanisms for disclosure and enforcement. As a result, some candidates, parties, interest groups, and individual contributors became so brazen that they rode roughshod over the law. Recognizing that the clerk of the House of Representatives and the secretary of the Senate, who were charged with enforcing the law, had neither the staff nor the political motivation to do so, some candidates and donors did not even bother to search for loopholes. Instead, they hid their contributions by making them under others' names or exchanged suitcases full of illegal donations privately behind closed doors. Candidates were emboldened by the fact that their campaign treasurers, not themselves, were held accountable for their campaign's finances.[4]

Despite the existence of so many statutes, the financing of federal campaigns was in a very sorry state throughout this period. In 1923 the political commentator Frank Kent wrote: "The fact is . . . that nowhere in the country has there been devised any legal method of effectively limiting the amount of money that may be spent in political fights. No law has been enacted through which politicians cannot drive a four-horse team."[5] Roughly twenty years later Charles Michelson, publicity director of the Democratic National Committee, explained that donors and candidates devised elaborate ruses to avoid the law. He complained that a result of such avoidance "was to make constructive criminals of all the officials of the two great parties."[6]

The criticisms and complaints of politicians, reformers, and those who helped to pay for elections did little to inspire the enactment of new campaign finance laws. Numerous commissions were created, bills introduced, and proclamations made, but ideological disagreements over the proper role of money in politics, political leaders' desire to gain partisan advantage, and the self-interest of individual members of the House and Senate prevented reformers from passing new legislation regulating the flow of campaign money.[7] It was not until 1971, when Congress passed the first Federal Election Campaign Act and the Revenue

Act, that it succeeded in taking a few concrete steps to influence the flow of money in federal elections.

The Federal Election Campaign Act of 1971 established new contribution and spending limits for candidates and created new disclosure requirements, but it repealed existing limits on individual, political party, and interest group contributions. It also created a special fund to finance future presidential elections. The Revenue Act allowed taxpayers to claim a modest tax credit or deduction on their federal income taxes for political contributions. It also created a check-off to allow taxpayers to designate $1 of their federal taxes to a campaign fund to be used to publicly finance presidential elections. The tax incentives, which were abolished in 1986, did not significantly affect the number of individuals making campaign contributions, but the tax check-off enjoyed modest success.[8]

The Federal Election Campaign Act of 1974 and Its Amendments

The public furor that followed the Watergate scandal led to the passage of the FECA of 1974. The investigation following the break-in at Democratic Party headquarters in the Watergate hotel revealed that President Nixon's Committee to Re-Elect the President accepted illegal contributions, gave ambassadorships and other major appointments to large donors, granted political favors to businesses that made large campaign contributions, and used a slush fund to finance the Watergate break-in and other illegal activities. The scandal created a groundswell of support for campaign finance reform.

The FECA of 1974 is often regarded as an amendment to its 1971 predecessor, but it replaced much of the 1971 law. The new FECA had several objectives, including reducing candidates' and parties' dependence on large contributions; increasing candidates' and parties' incentives to raise large sums of money in small donations; diminishing the political influence of businesses, unions, and other interest groups; decreasing the costs of running for federal office; bringing transparency to the financing of elections, and eliminating corruption. Political reformers sought to accomplish these objectives in several ways. First, they created contribution limits for candidates, individuals, parties, and interest groups and prohibited contributions from corporations, unions, trade associations, and other groups. This resulted in a campaign finance system funded solely with money that originated as limited contributions from individual donors. Second, they instituted spending limits for all federal campaigns and created opportunities for candidates for presidential nominations to finance their campaigns with a mix of private and federal funds and for general election candidates for the presidency to finance their campaigns entirely with public money. Third, they enacted rigorous reporting requirements for all federal campaign finance activity. Finally, they created the Federal Election Commission (FEC), an independent regulatory agency entrusted with administering and enforcing the law.

Shortly after the law was enacted it was challenged in court. In January 1976 the Supreme Court ruled in *Buckley v. Valeo* that provisions of the law limiting candidates' contributions to their own campaigns, imposing spending limits on candidates' campaign committees, and prohibiting others from spending independently of a campaign were in violation of constitutionally protected free speech rights. The Court also ruled that the method used to appoint members to the FEC was unconstitutional. Congress responded by amending the FECA in 1976, eliminating those aspects of the law that were found in violation of the Constitution.[9] A third set of amendments to the FECA was passed in 1979 to simplify reporting requirements, change some aspects of the law's enforcement, and make it possible for state and local parties to have a larger role in federal elections.

The FECA of 1974, its amendments, and associated court rulings and regulatory decisions constitute the most comprehensive federal campaign finance regulatory regime in American history. The law severely restricts the contributions that can be made to or accepted by congressional candidates (see Box 5-1). It also includes provisions for independent expenditures, which consist of political advertisements that are made to expressly help or harm a candidate. These expenditures must be made without the knowledge or consent of the candidate they are intended to help. Originally, only individuals and PACs were allowed to make independent expenditures. However, in 1986 the Supreme Court ruled that nonprofit ideological organizations could make independent expenditures, and in 1996 it deemed that political parties could also make them.[10]

A final major provision of the law allows state and local party committees to carry out grassroots campaign activities without their efforts counting toward federal contribution and spending limits. The 1979 FECA freed state and local parties to use nonfederal soft money to conduct grassroots campaign activities, such as voter registration and mobilization drives in connection with federal elections. The law also included provisions permitting state and local parties to use soft money to distribute bumper stickers, yard signs, slate cards, and other paraphernalia that make reference to federal candidates and are associated with volunteer efforts.

Learning to Navigate inside and outside the FECA's Regulatory Maze

Following enactment of the 1974 FECA and each of its amendments, donors and recipients of political contributions needed to learn how to navigate the law in order to avoid breaking it. In addition to discerning what was permissible within the narrow confines of the statutes and the regulatory language written for them, some individuals, candidates, and groups challenged aspects of the law to test their constitutionality and to determine whether the FEC or the Department of Justice would prosecute violators. Some of the bolder participants in the campaign finance system were interested in learning about the timeliness of that prosecution and the nature of penalties that would be meted out to those

---

Box 5-1   Contribution Limits in Congressional Elections

- Individuals can contribute a maximum of $1,000 per candidate in each stage of an election (primary, runoff, and general).

- Political action committees can contribute a maximum of $5,000 per congressional candidate in each stage of the election.

- Party congressional campaign committees can contribute a maximum of $5,000 per House candidate in each stage of the election. They can spend a maximum of $10,000 (adjusted for inflation) in coordinated expenditures on behalf of a House general election candidate. In 1998 this amounted to $32,550.

- Party senatorial campaign committees can contribute a maximum of $17,500 to Senate candidates (including in the primary). They can spend a maximum of 2 cents per voter (adjusted for inflation) in coordinated expenditures on behalf of a general election candidate. In 1998 the limits ranged from $65,100 per committee in the smallest states to $1,517,937 in California.

- National party committees can contribute a maximum of $5,000 per House candidate in each stage of the election, make a portion of another party committee's contributions in Senate elections, and make a portion of another party committee's coordinated expenditures in House or Senate elections.

- State and local party committees can contribute a combined maximum of $5,000 per candidate in each stage of a House or Senate election. They can each spend a combined maximum of $10,000 (adjusted for inflation) in coordinated expenditures on behalf of a House general election candidate and a combined maximum of 2 cents per voter (adjusted for inflation) in coordinated expenditures on behalf of a Senate general election candidate.

Note: The coordinated expenditure limit for party congressional campaign committees in at-large House races was originally set at $20,000 and reached $65,100 in 1998. State and local party committees also are subject to a separate, inflation-adjusted $20,000 limit in these races. Occasionally the congressional campaign committees contribute to Senate candidates, the senatorial campaign committees contribute to House candidates, and state party committees contribute to candidates running for offices outside their states.

---

convicted of violating the law. These efforts, some of which are discussed below, are consistent with those of other individuals and groups whose activities are subject to regulation. They helped to complicate the regulatory maze that provides contours of the contemporary campaign finance system.[11]

Interest Groups

Business interests were among the first groups to adapt to the law. Although labor unions and a small number of independent ideological groups had since the 1930s been sponsoring organizations that were forerunners of the modern PAC, businesses had yet to organize political action committees. In 1975 the Sun Oil Company requested that the FEC evaluate the legality of its plans to create a PAC and carry out other political activities. The commission's response, often referred to as the SUN PAC Decision, determined that Sun Oil could use its treasury to establish, administer, and solicit funds for use in federal elections as long as those funds were kept in a separate, segregated account.[12] The ruling maintained that SUN PAC funds had to be collected from the corporation's stockholders and employees on a voluntary basis. It allowed the company to direct the spending of those funds.

The SUN PAC Decision demonstrated to corporations, trade associations, and cooperatives that they could effectively participate in the financing of congressional elections by creating PACs. The number of PACs skyrocketed from just over 600 in 1974 to almost 4,600 in 1998. Most of the growth took place in the business sector. The number of corporate PACs increased from 89 to 1,821 during this period. PACs representing trade associations, corporations without stock, and cooperatives grew to number 921, 133, and 45, respectively. Labor PACs, by contrast, grew from 201 to only 353 because the centralization of the labor movement into a relatively small number of unions limited the possibilities for creating new labor PACs. Nonconnected PACs, that is, those with no sponsoring organization, had grown to 1,213 by 1998.

Trends in PAC spending roughly parallel the growth in the number of PACs. In 1974 PACs spent about $12.5 million; by 1998 PAC contributions had reached in excess of $219 million, of which 95 percent was spent in congressional races. Corporate PACs made 35 percent of all PAC contributions, trade PACs donated 28 percent, and PACs sponsored by cooperatives and corporations without stock accounted for 3 percent. Unions, by contrast, made 21 percent, and nonconnected PACs, including leadership PACs sponsored by politicians, accounted for the remaining 13 percent.

As PACs began to mature as organizations and learn the ins and outs of the campaign finance system, their managers became skilled at spending their money in ways that would help them better achieve their goals. At first most PACs followed election-oriented strategies (also known as ideological strategies) to try to influence election outcomes and the composition of Congress. PACs spent most of their funds in close contests. Business-oriented PACs made most of their contributions to Republicans in tight contests, labor PACs contributed mainly to those Republicans' opponents, and nonconnected PACs contributed to candidates in close races who shared their position on a major issue or broad ideology. During the 1980s, most business PACs learned that their best strategy for influencing legislation was to largely ignore considerations of electoral competitiveness and contribute most of their money to party leaders, committee chairs, ranking members, policy entrepreneurs, and other incumbents. These contributions could be used to gain access to powerful incumbents, an important first step to most lobbying strategies.[13] Most nonconnected PACs continued to follow election-oriented strategies that focused their money on close races, including those waged by challengers and open-seat candidates, enabling the PACs to influence the outcomes of those elections and the composition of Congress. Many labor PACs developed what are commonly referred to as mixed strategies. The election-oriented element consists of distributing campaign contributions to Democrats in close races; the access-oriented part consists of contributing to incumbents, mainly Democrats, who are in a position to influence labor issues.

PACs also learned to make strategic adjustments in response to major changes in the political environment. Following the Republican takeover of Congress in 1994 access-oriented PACs, including most corporate and trade committees, shifted the vast bulk of their contributions from Democrats to Republicans. Democratic leaders, ranking members, policy entrepreneurs, and other Democrats in positions to influence the policymaking process continued to raise money from these organizations, but the business PAC fund-raising of other members of their party suffered relative to their Republican counterparts. Some of the PACs that used election-oriented and mixed strategies also responded to the new realities on Capitol Hill, including a few labor PACs that increased their support of Republican incumbents.[14]

Other signs of increasing sophistication among PACs is that some began to develop tactics that enabled them to increase the value of the resources they delivered to their preferred candidates without violating the FECA. In addition to making cash contributions to candidates, some began to distribute "in-kind" contributions of campaign services. The staff of some PACs provided polling, media, or research services to candidates. Other PACs took advantage of economies of scale by purchasing campaign services from political consultants and distributing them to candidates at discounted rates. Giving a candidate campaign services in lieu of cash contributions enabled these PACs to make a donation that was worth more than its reported dollar value and to have an enduring effect on the conduct of the campaign.

Some PACs also learned to make independent expenditures attacking or promoting a specific candidate. The PACs who chose to make these expenditures had to learn not only to identify close contests—where they had the biggest potential to influence an election—but also to determine what kinds of expenditures would be most helpful in producing their desired outcome. This is no simple task when a PAC manager is prohibited from discussing campaign strategy with a member of a candidate's campaign organization. PAC managers had to learn to assess the dynamics of individual election districts and campaigns in order to spend their funds effectively and to prevent their expenditures from generating a backlash that could harm their favored candidates.

A small group of PACs also learned to extend their influence by affecting the contributions of other donors. So-called "lead PACs" collect information about the competitiveness and issue positions of individual candidates and distribute this information to like-minded PACs and individuals in order to influence their contribution decisions.[15] Other PACs extend their influence by bundling individual contributions. One type of bundling occurs when a PAC director or some other interest group leader hosts a fund-raising event for a candidate. Another type of bundling takes place when an interest group leader sells tickets to a fund-raising event. Perhaps the most highly publicized type of bundling occurs when a PAC collects checks from its members and mails them to a candidate in one envelope. The goal of all these bundling efforts is to help a candidate raise money in a way that brings recognition to the individuals' and the group's contributions to the campaign.

A very important way in which interest groups learned to participate in congressional elections was by finding out what election-related activities they could legally conduct outside of the confines of federal law. These include rallies, speeches, intra-organizational communications, and voter mobilization drives that do not involve monetary contributions to candidates. Chambers of Commerce, the American Federation of Labor-Congress of Industrial Organizations (AFL-CIO), the Christian Coalition, and numerous other business, labor, trade association, and ideological groups carry out these activities.

Many groups responded to the constraints the FECA places on campaign finance the same way they responded to limits that the Internal Revenue Service (IRS) code places on group participation in politics more generally: they formed separate organizations to conduct different activities. For example, the League of Conservation Voters (LCV) formed the League of Conservation Voters Education Fund, a tax-exempt 501(c)(3) organization under the IRS code, to distribute information about environmental issues, including the environmental voting records of members of Congress. This part of the LCV publishes the *Green Guide,* which details legislators' views on environmental issues. The LCV formed the League of Conservation Voters, Inc., a 501(c)(4) organization to participate more actively in politics. This part of the LCV issues the *National Environmental Scorecard,* a report card that rates the environmental voting records of members of Congress and endorses candidates. It also publishes the "Dirty Dozen," which lists the twelve congressional candidates who have the worst environmental voting records, and the "Earth List," which includes the ten members who have the most pro-environment voting records. The League of Conservation Voters Political Action Committee is the part of the organization that is most extensively involved in congressional elections. It gives campaign contributions of cash and campaign services directly to candidates and makes independent expenditures intended to affect the outcomes of congressional elections. Finally, the LCV has encouraged the formation of environmental organizations at the state level. Some of these groups, including the California League of Conservation Voters, have formed their own separate PACs, which participate in congressional elections.[16] As the case of the LCV demonstrates, interest groups have learned to navigate effectively the mazes of federal and state laws that regulate their political activity.

Soft money has become a major vehicle for interest groups to participate more fully in congressional elections since the passage of the FECA. Some groups contribute hundreds of thousands and even millions of dollars in soft money to the parties' nonfederal accounts with the understanding that these funds will be used, in part, to help the parties' House and Senate candidates. A few groups have received soft money contributions from the national party organizations. For example, Americans for Tax Reform, an antitax group with ties to the former Republican National Committee chair Haley Barbour, received $4.6 million from the Republican National Committee during the 1996 elections. The Rainbow Coalition and the A. Philip Randolph Institute each received a few hundred thousand dollars from the Democratic National Committee. The parties donated these funds to help the groups energize their constituents, who form important parts of the parties' electoral coalitions.[17]

The final, and most visible, use of interest group soft money is issue advocacy advertising. Interest groups spend soft money on television, radio, and direct-mail ads to set a campaign agenda that revolves around their issues, to help or harm a candidate without *explicitly* advocating or opposing the candidate's election, or to mobilize their supporters. Despite the fact that these ads often tell voters to send a candidate "a message" rather than call on them to "vote for" or "vote against" the candidate, their electoral intentions are clear. Interest group issue advocacy advertising first had a major presence in 1996, when groups spent an estimated $65 million to $80 million on issue ads to influence the outcomes of the presidential election and many competitive congressional contests.[18]

Party Organizations

Parties have developed many strategies and tactics for increasing their influence under the FECA. First, and foremost, the parties' congressional and senatorial campaign committees have learned to target party resources in ways that enable them to pursue seat maximization goals. This includes identifying which races are the most likely to be competitive and determining how the candidates in those races can best be supported. Parties consider the competitiveness of the district and whether the seat is incumbent-occupied or open. For incumbents, poll results and the quality of the challenger are criteria used to determine if substantial party assistance is warranted. For nonincumbents, the candidate's political experience, his or her visibility, and the professionalism of the campaign organization the candidate has assembled are also used to speculate about the candidate's election prospects. Candidates in close races typically receive the lion's share of party support.[19]

Some of the parties' strategic learning involved adjusting to different political environments. National political and economic conditions can have a significant effect on midterm elections. Members of the president's party often bear the brunt of public dissatisfaction when the president is unpopular or the economy sours.[20] During elections held under these conditions the congressional campaign committee of the president's party generally uses a defensive strategy that involves devoting extra resources to incumbents. The other party's congressional campaign committee usually takes advantage of the situation by using an aggressive strategy that involves distributing more resources to competitive challengers and open-seat contestants. When conditions favor the president's party, its congressional campaign committee invests more in nonincumbents, and the other party's congressional campaign committee is more prone to support marginal legislators.[21]

Parties have learned to use creative approaches to deliver hard money where it will have its biggest impact. In situations where a state party committee does not have sufficient funds to make the maximum legal contributions or coordinated expenditures in a close election, the party's congressional, senatorial, or national campaign committee may make an agency agreement enabling it to assume the state party's donations or expenditures.[22] When a state party committee possesses more hard money than it can legally spend in all the close congressional races taking place within its borders, it may swap some of its hard money for an even greater amount of soft money that it can use in conjunction with state elections or for grassroots campaign efforts that will benefit the entire party ticket. This enables the national party organization that receives the hard money to deploy it to other congressional races.[23]

Crossover spending is another arrangement that enables party committees to work within the FECA's contribution limits without violating them. Some crossover expenditures occur when a party in one state makes a contribution to help a candidate running in another state. Others occur when one of the senatorial campaign committees contributes to a House candidate or one of the congressional campaign committees contributes to a Senate candidate.[24]

Parties, like PACs, also distribute campaign services to increase the amount of assistance they can give to candidates. For example, parties increase the value of the surveys they commission by holding poll results for several days before providing them to a candidate so that they can use a depreciation option to minimize the value of the contribution.[25] A second approach is to claim the poll is being used to formulate both the organization's and the candidate's election strategies. This enables a group to split the costs of the poll evenly with a candidate so that the candidate can get immediate full access to the entire poll for only half price. A third approach is to provide a candidate with advice based on the poll without actually giving the candidate the results. Sometimes the poll results are released in order to manipulate the informational environment in which PACs and large individual donors make campaign contributions. A major aspect of the parties' fund-raising assistance involves channeling money toward their most competitive nonincumbents and incumbents who hold marginal seats.[26]

Following the Supreme Court's ruling in 1996 parties learned how to make independent expenditures. The parties' senatorial campaign committees have made most of these. Because the law requires independent expenditures to be made without the knowledge or consent of a candidate or members of the candidate's campaign committee, these organizations had to go to significant lengths to give the appearance of divorcing their independent expenditures from their other operations. The Republicans accomplished this by assigning some personnel to an independent expenditure group located in offices away from its head-quarters building. Although the Democrats did not create a separate headquar-ters for the purposes of making independent expenditures, they too claim to have established a firewall between party officials who directly assist a particular can-didate's campaign and those involved in making independent expenditures. Of course, it is only natural to suspect that some communication about an individ-ual campaign occurs among regular party aides, party staff who make indepen-dent expenditures, and political consultants who are employed by the intended beneficiary of those expenditures. After all, many of the party aides who are assigned the task of making independent expenditures once worked with other senatorial campaign committee staff, possess an extensive knowledge of party strategy, and have personal and professional relationships with the constellation of party aides and political consultants who orbit around a party.[27]

Parties, like interest groups, use soft money to influence congressional elec-tions in a variety of ways, including mobilizing voters, trying to set a national polit-ical agenda, creating a campaign agenda in individual races, and influencing a can-didate's election prospects without explicitly advocating that contestant's election or defeat.[28] A comparison of party issue advocacy ads with candidate ads shows that the issue ads focus more on the opponent, are more attack oriented, use more emo-tionally loaded words, and provide more negative audio and visual backdrops.[29] Most of the party soft money that is not directly spent for the preceding purposes flows from the parties' national, congressional, and senatorial campaign committees to state party committees. The top-down flow of soft money enables the national parties to affect state and local party strategy significantly.[30]

Party Leaders

Shortly after the enactment of the FECA, party leaders in and out of Con-gress who were in a position to raise large sums also began to help other con-gressional candidates fill their campaign coffers. Some used traditional approach-es, such as hosting fund-raising events, providing candidates with portions of their donor lists, or personally soliciting contributions for needy candidates from national networks of PAC and individual donors who had supported their own reelection bids. Other members of Congress devised new ways to raise and spend money to help congressional candidates. Those who faced little opposition in their bids for reelection transferred up to $1,000 per candidate (per each stage of the election) from their own campaign accounts to fellow members and some competitive nonincumbents.[31] Others formed PACs, sometimes called member or leadership PACs. Still others chose to contribute large sums to party commit-tees, usually their party's congressional and senatorial campaign committee.

Each method of giving has advantages. Member-to-member contributions allow the donor to select the recipient of the contribution and require little effort because the donor does not have to establish a PAC. They are also a simple way for retiring members to distribute excess campaign funds. The leadership PAC approach has the same advantages as member-to-member giving and it enables the member to contribute up to $5,000 to a candidate in each phase of the campaign. Its major disadvantage is that it requires a member to establish a PAC. Both of these options enable members to use excess campaign funds to advance their party's interests as well as their own. That is, members can distribute funds to candidates in close races to help their party increase its number of congressional seats or they can make donations to colleagues in the House or the Senate to build support for their policy preferences, a congressional leadership race, or some other quid pro quo.

The final option, contributing money to a party committee, gives donors the least control over who receives their funds, depriving members of the ability to plant seeds for later favors. It has the advantage, however, of allowing donors to avoid having to choose among colleagues and other candidates. Moreover, the leadership of both parties expects members of their caucuses to make contributions to their congressional and senatorial campaign committees. In fact, they refer to these contributions as dues and have created different levels of giving for party leaders, committee leaders, senior members, and first-term legislators. Some members of Congress give much more than their expected level or play a major role in helping their party raise both hard or soft money. The rise of member-to-member contributions, leadership PACs, and member-to-party-to-candidate donations has fueled a massive redistribution of wealth among congressional candidates.[32]

Individuals

Individuals, the original source of all campaign funds in federal elections, also have learned to increase their influence within the confines of the law. Some created PACs, bundled contributions, hosted fund-raising events, and used fund-raising techniques commonly associated with political organizations. Others have expressed their candidate preferences when contributing to existing PACs and parties. Unless the donors explicitly earmark their contributions for specific candidates, which is exceedingly rare, these organizations are not bound to pass their contributions to specific candidates. Nevertheless, most organizations consider their donors' preferences when distributing campaign funds. Finally, some individuals with spouses, children, and the wherewithal to make large contributions have given them under the names of family members. FEC reports disclose that a significant number of infants, young children, and children who are not old enough to vote make large contributions to congressional candidates.

Candidates

Candidates probably did the most learning of any participants in congressional elections after the FECA was enacted. The fund-raising restrictions imposed by the law combined with the professionalization of congressional campaigns and candidates' fears of losing to encourage congressional campaigners to retool their fund-raising operations. Candidates, particularly incumbents, who had been accustomed to relying on relatively few contributions from sources and in amounts that became prohibited under the FECA, had to learn to collect large numbers of smaller donations. Congressional candidates had long understood that campaigning for votes involves communicating with and mobilizing a large electoral coalition in their election district. They learned that the new campaign finance rules would require them to wage a more organized and sophisticated campaign for resources that would involve building a large coalition of financial supporters consisting of individuals, parties, and PACs, including many located outside their geographical election district.[33]

The campaign for resources usually begins prior to the campaign for votes. It almost always involves capitalizing on the candidates' personal and professional ties and tapping into national donor networks based on issues, ideology, party affiliation, occupation, gender, race, ethnicity, or religion.[34] It also requires packaging the candidate's assets in ways that groups of prospective donors will find attractive and reaching out to those individuals using cost-effective means, including direct mail, telemarketing, events, and the Internet. The vast majority of campaigns hire paid staff or professional consultants to help them with fund-raising.[35]

When members of Congress passed the FECA, they were well aware that they would possess tremendous advantages over challengers in the campaign for resources. Incumbents are typically more visible, popular, and politically experienced than their opponents. Reelection rates of above 90 percent for representatives and above 75 percent for senators give them an air of invincibility that helps them attract contributions, votes, and media support. Many incumbents successfully adapted to the new finance regime by creating permanent professional fund-raising operations.

Incumbents learned to capitalize on the influence that comes with officeholding when raising money from PACs and individuals who are interested in gaining political access. This includes the multitude of interest group representatives who are affected by legislation that an incumbent is in a position to influence. Incumbents often ask group leaders to serve on their finance committees, help organize events, and personally solicit contributions for their campaigns. Party leaders, committee and subcommittee chairs and ranking members, members of powerful committees, and policy entrepreneurs have big advantages in fund-raising over others. Incumbents who are involved in competitive races are also able to raise money from donors who want to influence the composition of Congress. Some incumbents help their parties raise money with the understanding that they will receive party support should they need it.[36]

Challengers have the greatest need to spend campaign funds and the most difficulty raising them. Visibility, political experience, and the other factors that function as assets for incumbents are liabilities for most challengers. Challengers tend to rely more on campaign volunteers for fund-raising than do incumbents. Nevertheless, like most incumbents, strong challengers have learned to organize finance committees to help them raise money. Most challengers first focus on raising funds in their districts and then seek to raise money from donors nationwide. Challengers ask supporters of local interest groups to help them raise money from their groups' national PAC and individual big donors. Challengers who have political experience, assemble professional campaigns, and are involved in hotly contested races usually attract more campaign funds from individuals, parties, and PACs than do those who are involved in one-sided contests.[37]

Candidates for open seats lack the fund-raising advantages of incumbents and the liabilities of challengers. Their fund-raising operations tend to be just as professional as those used by incumbents, but like challengers, open-seat candidates need to inform potential donors about their political experience, campaign organization, and the competitiveness of the race.[38] The unpredictability surrounding the outcomes of their races puts open-seat contests among the most expensive and financially competitive.

Spending within the Confines of the Law

The flow of money in the 1998 congressional elections reflects the adaptations that candidates, interest groups, parties, party leaders, and individuals have made to the campaign finance system. These sources spent approximately $780.1 million in those contests. Roughly 70 percent took the form of hard money spent within the confines of the FECA's regulatory system.[39] The rest occurred outside that system in the form of soft money.

PACs contributed $203.6 million to Democrats and Republicans competing in the 1998 congressional elections (see Table 5-1). Corporate and trade association PACs contributed the most, followed by labor PACs and nonconnected PACs. The distribution of PAC funds to candidates competing in major-party contested general elections show that most business-oriented groups pursued access-oriented strategies. Corporate and trade association PACs distributed in excess of 80 percent of their House contributions to incumbents, making roughly half of their contributions to incumbents who won by vote margins of more than 20 percent (see Table 5-2). They made approximately 73 percent of their Senate contributions to incumbents (Table 5-3).

Labor PACs pursued mixed strategies. The ideological component of their strategy was visible through their support of Democrats, who received 94 percent of the PACs' House contributions and 90 percent of their Senate contributions. The access component of their strategy was visible through their support for incumbents, including those involved in lopsided races. Labor PACs made 63 percent of their House contributions to Democratic incumbents, including 36 percent to incumbents whose victory margins were greater than or equal to 20 percent of the vote. Their contributing patterns for Senate candidates were similar, although labor was slightly more supportive of Senate than House incumbents in close races.

Nonconnected PACs, which had followed ideological strategies in previous elections, adopted mixed strategies in 1998. They made 58 percent of their

Table 5-1 PAC Contributions in the 1998 Congressional Elections (in thousands)

	House		Senate		
	Democrats	Republicans	Democrats	Republicans	Total
Corporate	$16,047	$33,794	$6,910	$13,963	$70,714
Trade, member- ship, and health	17,385	28,332,	4,640	7,892	58,249
Cooperative	851	945	233	185	2,214
Corporations without stock	1,258	1,576	485	591	3,910
Labor	33,022	3,115	5,425	606	42,168
Leadership	2,600	5,996	375	1,741	10,712
Nonconnected	4,843	5,745	2,673	2,334	15,595
All PACs	$76,006	$79,503	$20,741	$27,312	$203,562

Source: Compiled from Federal Election Commission data; originally printed and discussed in Paul S. Herrnson, *Congressional Elections: Campaigning at Home and in Washington,* 3d ed. (Washington, D.C.: CQ Press, 2000), 134.

Note: Figures are for PAC contributions to all major-party candidates, including candidates in primaries, runoffs, and uncontested races.

House contributions to candidates in competitive contests, and distributed 70 percent of those contributions to incumbents, including 38 percent that was given to incumbents in uncompetitive contests. The Senate contributions of nonconnected PACs showed similar patterns, except the PACs were more supportive of Senate than House incumbents. It is premature to conclude that the increased support for safe incumbents represents a one-time deviation from established giving patterns that is due to the specific factors surrounding the 1998 contests—an unusually unpredictable political environment and a close battle for majority control over Congress. It is possible that some ideologically motivated PACs have changed strategies because they believe that they need to contribute to incumbents to guarantee that their priority issues are discussed on the floor of the House and the Senate.[40]

In addition to cash contributions, some PACs gave contributions of in-kind services or bundled the contributions of others in 1998. The National Committee for an Effective Congress, for example, provided Democratic candidates in marginal districts with targeting data and advice on how to communicate with and mobilize Democratic voters. The Realtors PAC, the American Medical Association's PAC, and the AFL-CIO's PAC provided many incumbents with polls. The National Federation of Independent Business's PAC hosted campaign training schools and produced media advertisements for many candidates it supported, most of whom were Republicans.[41] EMILY's List (whose name stands for Early Money Is Like Yeast), which supports pro-choice women Democratic candidates, made $222,851 in cash contributions, $10,870 in in-kind donations consisting of campaign services, and $115,050 in independent expenditures. This

Table 5-2   The Allocation of PAC Contributions to House Candidates
                 in the 1998 Elections

	Corporate	Trade, Membership, and Health	Labor	Leadership	Non-connected
Democrats					
Incumbents					
Competitive	13%	15%	27%	9%	16%
Uncompetitive	18	18	36	7	18
Challengers					
Competitive	1	2	13	6	6
Uncompetitive	—	—	4	1	1
Open-seat candidates					
Competitive	1	3	10	6	6
Uncompetitive	—	1	3	1	1
Republicans					
Incumbents					
Competitive	21%	19%	2%	21%	16%
Uncompetitive	35	30	6	8	20
Challengers					
Competitive	3	4	—	20	7
Uncompetitive	1	1	—	3	2
Open-seat candidates					
Competitive	6	6	—	17	7
Uncompetitive	1	1	—	2	1
Total House contributions (in thousands)	$13,923	$37,943	$32,454	$8,221	$8,992

Source: Compiled from Federal Election Commission data; originally printed and discussed in Paul S. Herrnson, *Congressional Elections: Campaigning at Home and in Washington,* 3d ed. (Washington, D.C.: CQ Press, 2000), 135.

Notes: Figures are for major-party candidates in contested general elections. Dashes = less than 0.5 percent. Competitive elections were decided by vote margins of 20 percent or less. Uncompetitive elections were decided by margins greater than 20 percent.

activity pales next to the almost $2.3 million in individual contributions it bundled for House candidates and the $3.4 million it bundled for Senate contenders.[42] WISH List (Women in the Senate and House), the GOP counterpart to EMILY's List, contributed $88,287 to pro-choice Republican women candidates, including $14,453 in in-kind contributions, and it bundled $207,780 on their behalf.[43]

   In 1998, PACs also spent $9.3 million in independent expenditures to explicitly advocate the election or defeat of individual congressional candidates without those candidates' knowledge or consent. Trade associations accounted for 98 percent of these expenditures, and the vast majority of them were made in

Table 5-3 The Allocation of PAC Contributions to Senate Candidates in the 1998 Elections

	Corporate	Trade, Membership, and Health	Labor	Leadership	Non-connected
Democrats					
Incumbents					
Competitive	8%	10%	31%	25%	7%
Uncompetitive	19	19	29	18	3
Challengers					
Competitive	1	1	12	3	3
Uncompetitive	—	—	2	1	1
Open-seat candidates					
Competitive	3	5	12	4	3
Uncompetitive	2	2	4	2	1
Republicans					
Incumbents					
Competitive	19%	18%	1%	13%	19%
Uncompetitive	27	25	8	20	21
Challengers					
Competitive	11	10	—	7	22
Uncompetitive	—	1	—	—	5
Open-seat candidates					
Competitive	7	6	—	5	11
Uncompetitive	2	2	—	1	4
Total Senate contributions (in thousands)	$20,646	$12,394	$5,827	$4,954	$2,103

Source: Compiled from Federal Election Commission data; originally printed and discussed in Paul S. Herrnson, *Congressional Elections: Campaigning at Home and in Washington,* 3d ed. (Washington, D.C.: CQ Press, 2000), 136.

Notes: Figures are for major-party candidates in contested general elections. Dashes = less than 0.5 percent. Competitive elections were decided by vote margins of 20 percent or less. Uncompetitive elections were decided by margins greater than 20 percent.

closely contested races. Eighty-two percent of all independent expenditures made by PACs in 1998 were negative, calling for the defeat of specific candidates; only 18 percent were positive.

The two major parties contributed $33.5 million in cash, in-kind contributions, and coordinated expenditures to House and Senate candidates in the 1998 elections. Most of this money was spent to help competitive candidates in two-party contested elections. The Democrats distributed 82 percent of the approximately $5.2 million in contributions and coordinated expenditures they made in House races to candidates whose races were decided by 20 percent or less of the two-party vote (see Table 5-4). They distributed 57 percent of their funds to

Table 5-4   The Allocation of Party Money in the 1998 Congressional Elections

	House		Senate	
	Democrats	Republicans	Democrats	Republicans
Incumbents				
Competitive	31%	22%	52%	42%
Uncompetitive	12	7	—	5
Challengers				
Competitive	30	38	33	35
Uncompetitive	6	12	1	5
Open-seat candidates				
Competitive	21	21	8	12
Uncompetitive	—	—	5	—
Total (in thousands)	$5,161	$7,098	$9,652	$9,189

Source: Compiled from Federal Election Commission data; originally printed and discussed in Paul S. Herrnson, *Congressional Elections: Campaigning at Home and in Washington,* 3d ed. (Washington, D.C.: CQ Press, 2000), 96.

Notes: Figures are for major-party candidates in contested general elections. Dashes = less than 0.5 percent. Competitive elections were decided by vote margins of 20 percent or less. Uncompetitive elections were decided by margins greater than 20 percent.

nonincumbents, reflecting the Democrats modified defensive strategy. The Democrats adopted this strategy for several reasons. Because a member of their party occupied the White House and the president's party has lost House seats in every midterm election since 1938, the Democrats anticipated that some of their incumbents would need extra support in order to be reelected. This historical lesson was reinforced by the results of the 1994 midterm elections, in which the Democrats lost fifty-two House seats, eight Senate seats, and control of both chambers of Congress. Finally, two highly publicized scandals—one concerning Democratic fund-raising in the 1996 elections and the other concerning President Bill Clinton's liaison with White House intern Monica Lewinsky—heightened Democratic incumbents' insecurities. Democrats believed the scandals would drive down Clinton's popularity, and they recognized that the president's party usually suffers more losses when the president is unpopular.[44] It was not until late in the election, when it appeared that the president's popularity would hold firm and the public was becoming increasingly disenchanted with the Republicans' attacks on the president, that some of the pressure to distribute large sums to House incumbents abated and more effort was made to help challengers and open-seat contestants.[45]

The Republicans hoped to capitalize on the same conditions that caused House Democrats to experience so much anxiety early in the election season. Indeed, in July 1998, House Speaker Newt Gingrich, R-Ga., predicted that his party would gain up to forty House seats.[46] Most other GOP leaders were not quite so optimistic, but many predicted their party would gain between ten and twenty House seats.[47] It was not until late in the election season, when the Republicans began to observe the public's less-than-favorable response to their attacks on President Clinton, that GOP members began to fear that their attacks could backfire. Their response to the 1998 political environment led them to distribute their contributions and coordinated expenditures consistent with a modified aggressive strategy, allocating 81 percent of the approximately $7.1 million to candidates in close contests. It distributed 71 percent of these funds to nonincumbents.

Both parties also delivered substantial amounts in Senate races. Because there are fewer of them than House races, it is easier for the parties to target their Senate contributions and coordinated expenditures to candidates in close contests. In 1998 the Democrats targeted all but 6 percent of their funds to candidates in races that were ultimately decided by margins of 20 percent or less of the two-party vote. Because of the political environment, and Democratic senators' electoral insecurities, they distributed over half of these funds to incumbents. The Republicans delivered all but 10 percent of their funds to GOP candidates in close contests, delivering more funds to nonincumbents than incumbents.

In addition to their direct contributions and coordinated expenditures, party organizations made almost $1.8 million in independent expenditures in 1998. The Democrats spent $650,342 to help reelect the first-term California senator Barbara Boxer and to assist Scotty Baesler, the unsuccessful Kentucky open-seat Senate candidate. They spent $800,000 to call for the defeat of Baesler's opponent, Jim Bunning, and to harm the prospects of Mark Neumann, who failed in his bid to replace the Wisconsin senator Russell Feingold. The Republicans spent $302,392, most of which was used in an unsuccessful attempt to try to help reelect Sen. Lauch Faircloth of North Carolina.[48] Party independent spending had decreased significantly since 1996, as both parties saved their hard money for other purposes.[49]

Party leaders also distributed a significant amount of funds in the 1998 elections. Members of Congress, congressional retirees, and members' leadership PACs contributed roughly $16 million to House and Senate candidates. The distribution of funds was similar to the allocation of money by formal party committees, except that the politicians distributed more of their contributions to incumbents, particularly safe incumbents. This reflects the fact that members of Congress are interested in both maximizing the number of seats under their party's control and increasing their influence with their colleagues.[50]

Individuals contributed roughly $422.8 million in the 1998 congressional elections, including $353.9 million to general election candidates in two-party contested races. Many of their contributions appear to have been access oriented. Individuals made 64 percent of their House contributions to incumbents, including 37 percent to incumbents in one-sided contests. Other contributions appear to have been aimed at influencing election outcomes. Individuals gave 55 percent of their contributions to candidates in close races, including 28 percent that they contributed to competitive nonincumbents. Republicans, who controlled the House, enjoyed a slight edge in individual fund-raising, collecting 56 percent of the total.

Individual contributions to Senate candidates were in some ways more equally distributed. Incumbents raised half of them, challengers 38 percent, and open-seat candidates about 12 percent. Democrats and Republicans raised roughly equal amounts. Individuals made 71 percent of all their contributions to candidates in close contests.

The combined effect of the fund-raising decisions of donors and the fund-raising efforts of candidates is a campaign finance system that drastically favors incumbents. The typical House incumbent in a 1998 two-party contested race raised $818,000 in cash, in-kind contributions, and party coordinated expenditures. This is roughly three times more than the typical challenger raised and slightly more than was raised by the typical open-seat candidate. Senate incumbents in contested races raised about $5 million in 1998, on average, roughly $1.8 million more than their opponents. Senate candidates for open-seat contests raised an average of $2.9 million.[51]

Spending outside the Law

The efforts of interest groups, parties, and candidates resulted in record sums of soft money being spent during the 1998 elections. It is impossible to pinpoint the exact amount of soft money expended because much of it was not reported to the FEC. Nevertheless, some estimates are possible. It is safe to assume that parties spent in excess of the $75 million that the national parties reported transferring to state and local party committees and candidates. Interest groups are estimated to have spent between $170 million and $200 million on issue advocacy efforts, which do not include the organizing and voter mobilization efforts of labor unions, business associations, religious groups, and ideological organizations.[52] Individual expenditures are perhaps the most difficult to estimate, but the fact that individuals contributed more than $50 million to the national parties suggests that wealthy citizens found ways to make their voices heard by spending soft money.

The AFL-CIO carried out the most extensive soft money effort in 1998, investing between $18 million and $19 million on a ground war that included 9.5 million pieces of direct mail, 5.5 million telephone calls, and 300 professional organizers who worked to turn out the vote for Democratic candidates. It also invested $5 million on television and radio issue advocacy ads.[53] The National Federation of Independent Business and a coalition of business groups it helped organize, named the Coalition—Americans Working for Real Change, spent an estimated $1.3 million on televised issue ads in 1998.[54] U.S. Term Limits spent $11.6 million on various forms of issue advocacy.[55] EMILY's List also spent roughly $3 million on about 8 million pieces of mail and more than 2 million telephone calls to 3.4 million women in twenty-six states.[56] Other ideological groups, such as the League of Conservation Voters and the Christian Coalition, also spent millions of dollars on issue advocacy, grassroots organizing, and voter mobilization. The vast majority of this spending took place in order to influence close elections.[57]

In addition to these direct campaign efforts, organized groups contributed at least $133.9 million in soft money to national party organizations during the 1998 election cycle. They donated $48.6 million to the Democrats and $85.2 million to the Republicans.[58] These included contributions in excess of $1 million each from Phillip Morris, the Communications Workers of American, Amway Corporation, and seven other groups, and contributions of more than $100,000 from a total of 457 corporations, labor unions, and trade associations.[59] Because the FEC does not require state and local parties to report the soft money contributions they collect, information about these contributions, which probably amount to millions of dollars, are unavailable.

Party organizations in Washington raised roughly $224.4 million in soft money and transferred almost $75.3 million to state and local party committees and candidates in 1998, in many cases in exchange for hard money that they could directly spend in congressional races. GOP national organizations raised $38.8 million more in soft money than their Democratic counterparts. Most party soft money was used to influence the most competitive House and Senate elections. The centerpiece of the House Republicans' issue advocacy effort, "Operation Breakout," was a centrally coordinated series of advertisements targeted at fifty-eight House contests in thirty-six states. The first wave of ads, disseminated in early October, were generic spots in which a narrator asks, "So what has the Republican Congress done?" and answers "How about a $500 per-child tax credit? . . . Or health insurance that goes with you when you get a better job? . . . Republicans like [a candidate's name is recited] are reaching out to find solutions to the problems families face. Call Congressman [the candidate's name is repeated]. Tell him to keep working for our families."[60] The second wave, disseminated in mid-October, consisted of ads that drew unflattering contrasts between Democratic and Republican House contestants on issues such as abortion, crime, and taxes.[61]

The final and most controversial wave of ads ran from late October to just a few days before the election. It consisted mainly of three generic thirty-second spots attacking President Clinton that were broadcast in thirty-two, mostly southern, districts. The first ad featured a narrator stating, "In every election, there is a big question to think about. This year the question is: Should we make the Democrats more powerful? Should we reward the Democratic plans for big government? More big spending? . . . And should we reward not telling the truth? This is the question of this election. Reward Bill Clinton. Or, vote Republican." The second ad consisted of footage of Clinton's infamous denial of his having an affair with Lewinsky. In the final ad, designed to influence suburban voters, one woman told another, "For seven months, he lied to us." Another thirty-two House districts, mostly in the suburbs, were saturated with milder, customized, spots that contrasted Republican challengers with their Democratic opponents.[62]

Neither the GOP's issue advocacy effort in the Senate nor the Democrats' issue advocacy effort in either chamber was as generic or nationally focused as Operation Breakout. Instead, the parties aired ads that were customized to the specific needs of particular congressional candidates. The parties sought to set individual campaign agendas on issues that worked to their candidate's advantage, allowing the candidate's campaign to develop those issues further in its own communications and attacking the candidate's opponent late in the campaign.[63]

Although the soft money efforts of private citizens were not as visible as those of interest groups or parties, individuals did play a significant role in the soft money activities conducted in connection with the 1998 congressional elections. Individuals contributed almost $52.4 million to the national party organizations, donating $25.5 million to the Democrats and $26.5 million to the Republicans. The top individual donors in 1998 were Bernard Schwartz, chief executive officer of Loral Space and Communications Corporation, who contributed $1 million to the Democrats, and Carl Lindner, head of American Financial Corporation, who donated $250,000 to the Democrats and $710,000 to the Republicans.[64] As was the case with interest group soft money contributions to state and local parties, figures for individual contributions to these organizations are unavailable.

Congressional candidates did not spend soft money on their own elections in 1998, but many had a hand in raising soft money for parties and interest groups that spent soft money to help the campaigns of their benefactors and others who shared their views. Speaker of the House Gingrich; Senate Majority Leader Trent Lott, R-Miss.; House Minority Leader Richard Gephardt, D-Mo.; and Senate Minority Leader Tom Daschle, D-S.D., played a major role in helping their parties raise money. Other congressional and party leaders with fund-raising clout, including President Clinton, also played an important role in party and interest group soft money fund-raising. According to Joe Hansen, national field director of the Democratic Senatorial Campaign Committee, his organization encouraged Senate candidates to work with state party committees to raise soft money and to consider the communications and voter mobilization efforts of those organizations when formulating their own campaign strategies.[65]

Conclusion

The Federal Election Campaign Act of 1974 and its amendments were designed to overcome some of the weaknesses of earlier laws. It created a maze of contribution and spending limits, disclosure requirements, and an independent agency charged with enforcing the law. This regulatory regime forced those who wanted to participate fully in the financing of congressional elections to devise new strategies for raising and spending money. As they learned to navigate the law, many individuals and groups identified some of its weaknesses. Some sought to exploit small cracks in the law, whereas others directly challenged some of its provisions.

The more than two decades of searching for loopholes, identifying weaknesses, and directly challenging the FECA have led to the development of two congressional campaign finance systems. The first system consists of funds that originated as individual contributions of limited amounts. These funds flow in and out of the campaign treasuries of congressional candidates and the federal accounts of political parties and interest group PACs. They are spent largely in accordance with the FECA's intent. The second campaign finance system consists of soft money that is raised and spent outside of the confines of the law but is used to influence congressional elections. Some of these expenditures, particularly those used to help finance local grassroots activities, are consistent with the FECA's goals. Others, most notably issue advocacy ads that closely resemble candidate campaign ads, are not.

The erosion of the FECA has prevented it from fully achieving its sponsors' primary objectives. First, although the law originally encouraged candidates and parties to become less dependent on large contributions and to rely more on small donors, the growth in activities that are conducted using soft money has resulted in the parties becoming heavily dependent on wealthy individuals and organizations for large portions of their funds. Similarly, candidates who have come to expect soft money to play a large role in their elections now help parties and other organizations to raise it. These candidates may be prohibited from directly accepting large soft money contributions, but their efforts to help others raise it demonstrate that they depend, at least in part, on election activities financed with soft money. Second, the rise of PACs and soft money undermined the ability of the reforms to accomplish another major objective: a reduction in the influence of businesses, unions, and other organized interests in elections. Third, the rise of soft money also means that huge sums of money that are now spent to influence federal elections are hidden from public scrutiny, which the FECA was supposed to prevent. Fourth, the successes of individuals and groups in challenging the law, and the failure of the FEC and the Justice Department to effectively prosecute those who have flagrantly violated it, show that the FECA has not eliminated corruption in the financing of elections, even though it may have reduced it. Many contemporary reformers also argue that the emergence of the second—soft money—campaign finance system in and of itself is evidence that campaign finance is almost as corrupt as it was before the FECA was enacted. Finally, the professionalization of campaign politics and the rising costs of television, radio, and direct mail have greatly increased the costs of running for federal office, contrary to the reformers' goals.

The contemporary state of affairs in the realm of campaign finance resembles that of other regulated areas of public life in that many of those who are regulated learn to navigate within and around the law. It also demonstrates that continued vigilance, an occasional tinkering with existing statutes, and even a rare overhaul of the law may be required for a regulatory regime to continue to have its intended effects. Where the campaign finance system differs from most other areas of regulatory politics is that those who are most directly affected by the law are the same individuals who are entrusted with occasionally reforming it. As a result, members of Congress, each of whom knows which aspects of the law work to their individual advantage, have been unable to agree on how to reform the regulations governing the financing of congressional elections despite their ability to reform many other regulatory regimes.

Failure to take appropriate action to shore up the nation's campaign finance laws, or other laws that are so directly tied to the conduct of elections, can be harmful to the political system. The state of congressional campaign finance at the dawn of the new millennium is not far removed from that identified by nineteenth- and twentieth-century researchers, who described how a relatively few wealthy individuals and groups financed federal elections, often by skirting the law. The current state of affairs is also open to many of the same criticisms that were made by pre-FECA era reformers. In 1873 Edward G. Ryan, who was soon to be appointed chief justice of the Wisconsin Supreme Court, asked, "The question will arise . . . which shall rule—wealth or man; which shall lead—money or intellect; who shall fill public station—educated and patriotic free men, or the feudal serfs of corporate capital?"[66] This question is always worth pondering in a capitalist democracy, especially one that allows wealthy individuals and groups to spend unlimited amounts of unreported money to influence the outcomes of elections.

Notes

I wish to thank Robert Biersack and Clyde Wilcox for their helpful comments and suggestions.

1. The term *soft money* was coined by Elizabeth Drew in *Politics and Money: The New Road to Corruption* (New York: Macmillan, 1983), esp. 15. See also Robert Biersack, "The Nationalization of Party Finance," in *The State of the Parties*, 108–124; and Anthony Corrado, Thomas E. Mann, Daniel R. Ortiz, Trevor Potter, and Frank J. Sorauf, eds., *Campaign Finance Reform: A Sourcebook* (Washington, D.C.: Brookings Institution, 1997), 165–224.
2. See Herbert E. Alexander, *Financing Politics* (Washington, D.C.: CQ Press, 1984), 23–31.
3. George Thayer, *Who Shakes the Money Tree? American Campaign Finance Practices from 1789 to the Present* (New York: Simon and Schuster, 1973), 73.
4. Ibid., 62.
5. Ibid., 63.
6. Ibid., 72.
7. One bill, introduced by Sen. Russell Long, D-La., was attached as a rider to a bill unconcerned with campaign finance. It became law on the last day of the Eighty-ninth Congress. However, early in the Ninetieth Congress members voted to make its provisions inoperative, thereby preventing its provisions from going into effect without having to repeal the legislation. See Alexander, *Financing Politics*, 31–35.

8. David B. Magleby and Candice J. Nelson, *The Money Chase: Congressional Campaign Finance Reform* (Washington, D.C.: Brookings Institution, 1990), 186; Anthony Corrado, *Paying for Presidents: Public Financing in National Elections* (New York: Twentieth Century Fund, 1993), 33–36.
9. *Buckley v. Valeo,* 424 U.S. 1 (1976).
10. *Federal Election Commission v. Massachusetts Citizens for Life, Inc.,* 479 U.S. 238 (1986) and *Colorado Republican Federal Campaign Committee v. Federal Election Commission,* 116 S. Ct. 2309 (1996).
11. Frank J. Sorauf, *Inside Campaign Finance* (New Haven: Yale University Press, 1992), 27–28.
12. Federal Election Commission, Advisory Opinion 1975–23.
13. Laura Langbein, "Money and Access: Some Empirical Evidence," *Journal of Politics* 48 (1986): 1052–1062; Richard Hall and Frank Wayman, "Buying Tie: Moneyed Interest and the Mobilization of Bias in Congressional Committees," *American Political Science Review* 84 (1990): 797–820.
14. Paul S. Herrnson, "Money and Motives: Spending in House Elections," in *Congress Reconsidered,* ed. Lawrence C. Dodd and Bruce I. Oppenheimer, 6th ed. (Washington, D.C.: CQ Press, 1997), 122–124; Thomas J. Rudolph, "Corporate and Labor PAC Contributions in House Elections: Measuring the Effects of Majority Party Status," *Journal of Politics* 61 (1999): 195–206; Gary W. Cox and Eric Mager, "How Much Is Majority Status in the U.S. Congress Worth?" *American Journal of Political Science* 93 (1999): 299–309.
15. On lead PACs, see Robert Biersack, Paul S. Herrnson, and Clyde Wilcox, "Lead PACs," in *Risky Business? PAC Decisionmaking in Congressional Election,* ed. Robert Biersack, Paul S. Herrnson, and Clyde Wilcox (Armonk, N.Y.: M. E. Sharpe, 1994), 17–18.
16. Philip A. Mundo, "League of Conservation Voters," in *After the Revolution: PACs, Lobbies, and the Republican Congress,* ed. Robert Biersack, Paul S. Herrnson, and Clyde Wilcox (Boston: Allyn and Bacon, 1999), 118–33.
17. Paul S. Herrnson, *Congressional Elections: Campaigning at Home and in Washington,* 2d ed. (Washington, D.C.: CQ Press, 1998), 95.
18. Figures compiled from Deborah Beck, Paul Taylor, Jeffry Stanger, and Douglas Rivlin, "Issue Advertising during the 1996 Campaign" (Philadelphia: Annenberg Public Policy Center, 1997), http://appcpenn.org/appc/reports/rep16.pdf.
19. Paul S. Herrnson, *Congressional Elections: Campaigning at Home and in Washington,* 3d ed. (Washington, D.C.: CQ Press, 2000), 92–97.
20. Gerald Kramer, "Short-Term Fluctuations in U.S. Voting Behavior," *American Political Science Review* 65 (1971): 131–43; Gary C. Jacobson and Samuel Kernell, *Strategy and Choice in Congressional Elections* (New Haven: Yale University Press, 1983), chap. 6; Gary C. Jacobson, "Does the Economy Matter in Midterm Elections?" *American Journal of Political Science* 34 (1990): 400–404.
21. Jacobson and Kernell, *Strategy and Choice in Congressional Elections,* 39–43, 76–84.
22. Paul S. Herrnson, *Party Campaigning in the 1980s* (Cambridge: Harvard University Press, 1988), 43–44.
23. Diana Dwyre, "Spinning Straw into Gold: Soft Money and U.S. House Elections," *Legislative Studies Quarterly* 21 (1996): 411.
24. Paul S. Herrnson, "National Party Organizations and the Postreform Congress," in *The Postreform Congress,* ed. Roger H. Davidson (New York: St. Martin's Press, 1992), 59–60.
25. The allocable costs of the polls vary by their type, size, and when they are released to candidates. General Services Administration, *Title 11_Federal Elections,* sec. 2, U.S.C. 106.4, pp. 77–78.
26. Herrnson, *Congressional Elections,* 3d ed., 102–3, 107–8.

27. Herrnson, *Congressional Elections*, 2d ed., 97–98; Robin Kolodny and Angela Logan, "Political Consultants and the Extension of Party Goals," *PS: Political Science and Politics* 31 (1998): 155–59.

28. See, for example, Anthony Corrado, Thomas E. Mann, Daniel R. Ortiz, Trevor Potter, and Frank J. Sorauf, eds., *Campaign Finance Reform: A Sourcebook* (Washington, D.C.: Brookings Institution, 1997).

29. Paul S. Herrnson and Diana Dwyre, "Party Issue Advocacy in Congressional Elections," in *The State of the Parties*, ed. John C. Green and Daniel M. Shea, 3d ed. (Lanham, Md.: University Press of America, 1999), 86–104.

30. John F. Bibby, "The New Party Machine: Information Technology in State Political Parties," in Green and. Shea, *The State of the Parties*, 69–85.

31. Clyde Wilcox, "Share the Wealth: Contributions by Congressional Incumbents to the Campaigns of Other Candidates," *American Politics Quarterly* 17 (1989): 386–408.

32. Herrnson, *Congressional Elections*, 3d ed., 98–100.

33. Ibid., 150, 156–160.

34. Ibid.; Clifford W. Brown, Lynda W. Powell, and Clyde Wilcox, *Serious Money: Fundraising and Contributing in Presidential Nomination Campaigns* (New York: Cambridge University Press, 1995), 68–113.

35. Herrnson, *Congressional Elections*, 3d ed., 75.

36. Ibid. See also Sorauf, *Inside Campaign Finance*, 60–66, and the sources in note 14.

37. Herrnson, *Congressional Elections*, 3d ed., 75, 164–68.

38. Ibid., 75, 171–73; Paul S. Herrnson, "Campaign Professionalism and Fundraising in Congressional Elections," *Journal of Politics* 54 (August 1992): 859–70.

39. The figure for hard money includes all candidate disbursements, party coordinated expenditures, party independent expenditures, and PAC independent expenditures. The figure for soft money is estimated to be $350 million and includes issue advocacy advertising.

40. Herrnson, *Congressional Elections*, 3d ed., 137.

41. Ibid., 138.

42. Stephanie Kahn, communications director, EMILY's List, interview, August 9, 1999; http://www.emilyslist.org/el-about/index.html, cited in Herrnson, *Congressional Elections*, 3d ed., 138–39.

43. Figures obtained from the Federal Election Commission and WISH List.

44. Gerald Kramer, "Short-Term Fluctuations in U.S. Voting Behavior," *American Political Science Review* 65 (1971): 131–43; Gary C. Jacobson, "Does the Economy Matter in Midterm Elections?" *American Journal of Political Science* 34 (1990): 400–404. For another interpretation see Robert S. Erikson, "Economic Conditions and the Vote: A Review of the Macro Level Evidence," *American Journal of Political Science* 34 (1990): 373–99.

45. Herrnson, *Congressional Elections*, 3d ed., 95–96.

46. Jim VandeHei, "Speaker Predicts Republicans Could Gain Up to 40 Seats in Fall,"*Roll Call*, July 16, 1998.

47. Scott Douglas, deputy political director, National Republican Campaign Committee (NRCC), interview, October 10, 1998; John Mercurio, "Linder, Frost Both See Gains," *Roll Call*, July 30, 1998.

48. Both parties spent lesser sums on a few other candidates.

49. National party organizations are required to adhere to a hard money/soft money ratio when spending soft money in individual states. In 1998 they spent less hard money on independent expenditures so that they could spend more total money, including soft money, on issue advocacy.

50. Herrnson, *Congressional Elections*, 3d ed., 98–99.

51. Ibid., 155–56, 164–65, 171, 177–78.

52. Figures compiled from Jeffrey D. Stanger and Douglas G. Rivlin, "Issue Advocacy Advertising During the 1997–1998 Election Cycle" (Philadelphia: Annenberg Public Policy Center, 1998), http://appcpenn.org/ and http://appcpenn.org/issueads/profiles.
53. Aaron Bernstein and Richard S. Dunham, "Laboring Mightily to Avert a Nightmare in November," *Business Week,* October 19, 1998; Donald Lambro, "AFL-CIO's Election Day Effort Paid Off Big for Democrats," *Washington Times,* November 5, 1998.
54. Jill Lawrence and Jim Drinkard, "Getting Out the Vote, *USA Today,* October 29, 1998.
55. Staise Rumenap, field representative director, U.S. Term Limits, interview, August 12, 1999.
56. Kahn interview; http://www.emilyslist.org/el-about/index.html.
57. Herrnson, *Congressional Elections,* 3d ed., 138, 142–48.
58. Figures obtained from the Center for Responsive Politics.
59. Center for Responsive Politics, "Top Soft Money Donors: 1998 Election Cycle," December 6, 1998, http://www.opensecrets.org/parties/.
60. Ed Brookover, political director, NRCC, interview, July 14, 1999; Linder, NRCC, "Operation Breakout"; Rachel Van Dongen, "Making their Case a Coast-to-Coast Offensive," *Roll Call,* October 8, 1998.
61. Brookover interview; Thomas B. Edsall, "GOP Spends Millions in Key House Races in Ohio Valley," *Washington Post,* October 31, 1998.
62. Brookover interview; "Clinton Scandal Takes Center Stage in Last Days," *Roll Call,* October 29, 1998.
63. Herrnson, *Congressional Elections,* 3d ed., 114.
64. Figures obtained from the Center for Responsive Politics.
65. Herrnson, *Congressional Elections,* 101–2.
66. Edward G. Ryan, speech to the graduating class of the Law School, University of Wisconsin–Madison, June 17, 1873, *Speeches and Arguments of Chief Justice Ryan While at the Wisconsin Bar* (Madison, Wis., 1909).

6. The Gender Gap in the House of Representatives

Rosalyn Cooperman and Bruce I. Oppenheimer

Since the election of Ronald Reagan in 1980, scholars and journalists have reported on the "gender gap" in the electorate, or the gender-based differential in the vote share of the Democratic and Republican candidates in presidential elections. In the 2000 presidential election campaign much attention was given to the efforts of the Republican Party to close the gender gap and increase its support among women voters, for example in the emphasis the Bush campaign placed on education. Although important, this focus on the gender gap in the electorate provides a picture of gender differences in partisan politics that is incomplete. For over a decade a gender gap has also existed between the two parties' success in recruiting and electing women candidates to the House of Representatives. By comparison, the gender gap in the number of women representatives has received little attention.

The emergence of a gender gap in the House is a more recent development than the emergence of a gender gap in the electorate. Indeed, until the late 1980s the number of women in each party who ran for and were elected to the House was relatively the same. Since 1988, however, women Democrats have substantially outnumbered women Republicans as candidates to and members of the House. In this chapter we explore the development of the gender gap in the House and examine some explanations for it. In particular, we look at the changing number of women who run as Democratic and Republican candidates for the House, the types of races in which they run, the partisan composition of the districts in which they compete, and their success rate as compared to their male counterparts. We then examine the growth in the number of women elected to the House and assess whether they have followed through on these gains by moving into positions of influence as party leaders and committee chairs, or whether a gender gap exists in positions of influence as well. Finally, we evaluate the prospects for women candidates in the 2000 elections and discuss whether the gender gap in the House is likely to diminish in the future. This chapter will focus on the gender gap within the House, but many of the same trends also exist in the Senate.

The Development and Growth of the Gender Gap in the House of Representatives

Many see the gender gap in the House, or the gap between the number of Democratic and Republican women members, as beginning after the "Year of the Woman" elections of 1992.[1] However, there is evidence to suggest that it emerged earlier. As the data in Table 6-1 reveal, until 1990 there was relative parity between the parties in terms of the number of women House members.

Table 6-1   Women in the House of Representatives by Party, 97th–106th
Congresses (1981–2001)

Congress		Number of Women Democrats (percentage of party membership)		Number of Women Republicans (percentage of party membership)	
97th	(1981–83)	10	(4.1%)	9	(4.7%)
98th	(1983–85)	13	(4.9%)	9	(5.4%)
99th	(1985–87)	13	(5.1%)	9	(4.9%)
100th	(1987–89)	12	(4.7%)	11	(6.2%)
101st	(1989–91)	14	(5.4%)	11	(6.3%)
102d	(1991–93)	19	(7.1%)	9	(5.4%)
103d	(1993–95)	36	(14%)	12	(6.8%)
104th	(1995–97)	31	(15.2%)	17	(7.4%)
105th	(1997–99)	35	(16.9%)	16	(7%)
106th	(1999–2001)	39	(18.4%)	17	(7.7%)

Source: Norman J. Ornstein, Thomas E. Mann, and Michael J. Malbin, *Vital Statistics on Congress, 1999–2000* (Washington, D.C.: AEI Press, 2000).

The number of Democratic and Republican women elected to the House in the 1980s was quite small, hovering just above double digits. The Republican Party had a higher percentage of women House members in four of the six Congresses from 1981 to 1991 (the 97th–102d Congresses). During this period, women accounted for between 4.1 and 7.1 percent of the Democratic House membership and between 4.7 and 6.3 percent of the Republican House membership. Women Democrats represented a smaller percentage of their party's membership but nonetheless outnumbered their Republican counterparts, because Democrats held substantial majorities in the House during most of the 1980s. From the 97th to 102d Congresses, the number of women Republican members remained constant while the number of women Democratic members increased unevenly, and women's percentage of the Democratic Party membership increased as well. Thus even before the "Year of the Woman," women Democrats had begun to increase their numbers in the House while the number of women Republicans remained essentially the same.

After the 1992 elections the gap between women Democrats and Republicans in the House became much more pronounced. Women Democrats outnumbered women Republicans three to one in the 103d Congress, posting a net gain of seventeen members from the previous Congress for a total of thirty-six Democratic women members. Women Republicans also increased their numbers between the 102d and 103d Congresses but by a much smaller margin, adding a net of three members. Subsequently the increase in the number of women Democratic House members has slowed, but it continues to outpace the increase in Republican women. The historic 1994 elections increased the number of women Republican members but only by a very modest amount. Despite the election of seventy-four Republican freshmen, only seven of them were women, and the net

Table 6-2   Women Candidates by Party and Seat Status, 1982–1998

Election Year	Party	Incumbents Seeking Reelection	Open Seat Candidates	Challengers	Total
1982	Democrat	8	6	12	26
	Republican	8	6	14	28
1984	Democrat	10	2	17	29
	Republican	9	2	24	35
1986	Democrat	9	2	16	27
	Republican	9	3	22	34
1988	Democrat	11	4	16	31
	Republican	11	0	15	26
1990	Democrat	15	7	17	39
	Republican	9	1	20	30
1992	Democrat	17	26	27	70
	Republican	9	13	14	36
1994	Democrat	36	10	26	72
	Republican	11	5	24	40
1996	Democrat	27	9	41	77
	Republican	14	5	23	42
1998	Democrat	34	12	29	75
	Republican	16	4	26	46
Total	Democrat	167 (37%)	78 (18%)	201 (45%)	446
	Republican	96 (31%)	39 (12%)	182 (57%)	317
		263	117	383	763

Source: For data through 1994, Jody Newman, *Perception and Reality: A Study Comparing the Success of Men and Women Candidates* (Washington, D.C.: National Women's Political Caucus, 1994). For 1996 and 1998 data, Center for American Women in Politics.

gain in Republican women members was only five. There has been no net gain in Republican women since then. In the 106th Congress there were more than twice as many women Democratic House members as women Republican members. Nearly one in five of Democratic House members were women, and fewer than one in every thirteen House Republicans were women.

How might we explain why the gender gap in the House arose in the 1990s? There are several possibilities. The logical place to start is by looking at the changing number of women candidates for the House.[2] After all, a party cannot elect women if women do not win party primaries. Thus, the explanation for the gender gap in the House may lie simply in the fact that the Democrats ran more women for the House beginning in the 1990s than did the Republicans. Alternatively, Democratic women candidates may be running for more winnable seats, such as in open seat contests or in more partisan friendly districts, than Republican women. The Democrats may also be providing more resources to women

candidates. Or maybe a combination of all of the above explains the House gender gap. Let us examine data that bear on each of these potential explanations.

A comparison of the total number of women candidates by party from 1982
to 1998 (in the "Total" column of Table 6-2) offers a partial explanation for the
gender gap in the House. During this time period, almost all of the growth in the
number of women Democratic candidates occurred after 1988, when their numbers more than doubled, from thirty-one in 1988 to seventy-five in 1998.
Republicans had smaller gains in their number of women candidates, which
increased from twenty-six to forty-six. (In fact, if 1984 or 1986 is used as the
base year for the Republican Party, there was almost no increase in its number of
women House candidates until 1994.) Since 1988 Democratic women candidates have outnumbered their Republican counterparts. Thus, one explanation
for the House gender gap is that the Republicans have run fewer women for the
House in the 1990s than have the Democrats.

Second, as we examine the types of House races in which women have run
(also in Table 6-2), we find that Democratic women are more likely to run in
contests where their chances of winning are higher (as incumbents or in open
seat contests). From 1982 to 1998, women Democrats accounted for 63 percent
of incumbent women candidates (167 of 263) and two-thirds of women candidates in open seat contests (78 of 117). But there was near parity in the number
of women running as challengers (52 percent were Democrats and 48 percent
Republicans). Parity in this category is less important because challengers stand
little chance of defeating incumbents. Running the percentages the other way
(asking what percentage of each party's women candidates run in the different
types of races), we also see that women Democrats are more likely to run as
incumbents or for open seats, whereas women Republicans are more likely to run
as challengers. Fifty-five percent of Democratic women candidates and 43 percent of Republican women candidates ran either as incumbents or in open seats.
Fifty-seven percent of Republican women candidates ran as challengers, but
only 45 percent of women Democrats challenged incumbents.

The number of winners by seat status provides compelling evidence that
Democrats appear to give their female candidates a greater chance to win. From
1982 to 1998, 95 percent of women House incumbents were reelected, and 45
percent of women candidates for open seat House contests were elected.[3] However, fewer than 5 percent of challengers defeated incumbents during this same
time period. Women Democrats and Republicans were not given equal chances
at winning. With a higher percentage of candidates running as incumbents or in
open seat contests, Democratic women were poised to take advantage of more
favorable election rates. In contrast, women Republican candidates were more
frequently relegated to "hopeless races" in which the chances of unseating an
incumbent were small.[4]

The difference in the frequency with which the two parties ran women in
open seat contests in the 1980s, as opposed to the 1990s, is one of the main causes of the gender gap. An increasing number of women incumbents would be the

Table 6-3 Women Candidates as a Percentage of Total Party Candidates, 1982–1998

Seat Status and Party	1982–1988	Women as a Percentage of Total Party Candidates	1990–1998	Women as a Percentage of Total Party Candidates
Incumbents				
Women Democrats (total Democrats)	38 (944)	4.0%	129 (1040)	12.4%
Women Republicans (total Republicans)	37 (644)	5.7	59 (876)	6.7
Open Seats				
Women Democrats (total Democrats)	14 (156)	9.0	64 (256)	25.0
Women Republicans (total Republicans)	11 (156)	7.1	28 (256)	10.9
Challengers				
Women Democrats (total Democrats)	61 (578)	10.6	140 (744)	18.8
Women Republicans (total Republicans)	75 (736)	10.2	107 (923)	11.6

Source: Compiled by the authors using data from the Center for American Women in Politics, National Women's Political Caucus, and the *CQ Weekly* (various issues).

result of a party having women candidates elected in the first place, which usually means that the candidate won an open seat contest rather than defeated an incumbent.[5] As the data in Table 6-3 demonstrate, the change in the frequency with which the two parties ran women in open seats is marked.

Table 6-3 aggregates the number of women candidates as a percentage of total party candidates into decades (1982–1988 and 1990–1998). During both election periods, Democratic women constituted a higher percentage of their party's candidates for open seats than did Republican women, and they outnumbered the Republican women candidates as well. Differences in the percentage of women candidates were less pronounced in the 1980s (9 percent versus 7.1 percent), because so few women of either party ran in open seat contests. In the 1990s the number of women Democrats who ran in open seat contests grew substantially, to such an extent that women Democrats accounted for one quarter of their party's candidates for open seats. Women Republicans, on the other hand, accounted for roughly 11 percent of their party's candidates for open seats in the 1990s. Between the 1980s and 1990s, the percentage of women Democratic candidates for open seats as a percentage of the total party candidates nearly tripled, from 9 to 25 percent, whereas their Republican counterparts saw a much smaller increase, from 7.1 to 10.9 percent.

Why the significant difference between the parties in terms of the number of women candidates for open seats? In short, Democratic and Republican women candidates did not take equal advantage of the numerous open seats in the 1992 and 1994 elections. In 1992, redistricting and incumbency retirements created ninety-one open seats. Twenty-six women Democrats and thirteen women Republicans ran as candidates in these races. Women Democrats accounted for close to 30 percent of their party's candidates for these seats, whereas Republican women accounted for only 14 percent of their party's candidates. The rate of success among the women candidates from each party was unequal as well. More than 70 percent of women Democratic candidates who ran in open seat races were successful, but only three of the thirteen Republican women candidates for open seats won their races. Thus, in the 1992 House elections the success of women Democrats was twofold. An unprecedented number of women Democrats won nominations as candidates in open seat contests, and the vast majority of these candidates were able to win their races.

Whereas Democratic women took particular advantage of open seats in 1992, a favorable election year for their party, Republican women were not nearly as successful at sharing in their party's gains in the elections of 1994. In a context far more favorable to their party than 1992 had been, Republican women ran in only half as many open seat contests as did Democratic women. Only five Republican women ran for open seats, and women accounted for less than 10 percent of their party's total candidates in this category. (By contrast, women accounted for close to 20 percent of the Democratic candidates for open seats in 1994.)

In previous years the case might have been made that the paucity of women Republican candidates in open seat contests simply reflected women's inability to win primary elections and was not necessarily a result of the candidate recruitment efforts of the Republican Party leadership. But in 1994 Newt Gingrich, Ga., assumed an active role in recruiting and raising funds for Republican House candidates in his efforts to build a House Republican majority. Many of the candidates he recruited had no previous officeholding experience. So the often-used excuse that there were too few women with enough previous political experience to make them strong House candidates seems invalid. Accordingly, it is surprising how small a role women candidates played in the Republican takeover of the House. Only five of the fifty-two Republican open seat candidates were women. Ironically, the same number of women Republicans won open seats (three) in 1994 as in 1992.

Even when the political climate was more favorable for their party, women Republicans were given few opportunities to increase their numbers in the House by running as candidates in open seat races. On the other hand, more women Democrats have run as candidates in open seat races in the elections since 1994 and won these races. These wins, in turn, boosted the number of women Democratic incumbent candidates as a percentage of total party candidates. By 1998 the number of open seats had sharply declined again, diminishing the opportu-

Table 6-4 District Partisanship Averages, 1982–1998

Candidate	District Partisanship Averages, All Races, 1982–1990	District Partisanship Averages, Open Seat Races, 1982–1990	District Partisanship Averages, All Races, 1992–1998	District Partisanship Averages, Open Seat Races, 1992–1998
Female Democrat	43.76 (n = 147)	44.81 (n = 21)	56.00 (n = 284)	56.90 (n = 57)
Male Democrat	43.45 (n = 1656)	41.90 (n = 161)	54.55 (n = 1251)	54.12 (n = 170)
Female Republican	46.98 (n = 152)	48.00 (n = 12)	58.17 (n = 160)	56.68 (n = 27)
Male Republican	43.15 (n = 1651)	41.81 (n = 166)	54.43 (n = 1375)	54.52 (n = 199)

Note: Averages do not include races where incumbents ran unopposed. District partisanship is determined by the average of the percentage of the two-party vote received in the congressional district by the Democratic presidential candidates during either the 1984 and 1988 elections or the 1992 and 1996 elections.

Source: Data compiled by the authors.

nities for making substantial increases in female representation in the House. Thus, there was little that the Republicans could do at this time to close the gender gap in the House, even if doing so had become a party priority. Whereas Democratic women took advantage of open seat opportunities in the early 1990s, especially when partisan electoral forces were favorable to their party, the story for Republicans is one of missed opportunities.

There may be a third reason for the gender gap in the House, in addition to the Democrats having nominated more women for the House, and having nominated them more frequently to run in open seat contests. Our analysis of open seat contests in 1992 and 1994 suggests that there also were differences in the partisan composition of the districts in which women candidates of the two parties ran. If women Democratic candidates have run in more partisan friendly districts, then that advantage would help to explain why women Democrats have had greater success in winning elections and thereby provide an additional explanation for the House gender gap.

Table 6-4 presents the average district partisanship by party and gender for all House races and open seat contests from two election periods, 1982–1990 and 1992–1998.[6] District partisanship is determined by the average of the two-party vote received in congressional districts by the Democratic presidential candidate during the 1984 and 1988 elections, for the first time period, or the 1992 and 1996 elections, for the second time period. The higher the percentages for a category in Table 6-4, the more favorable it is for Democrats and unfavorable for

Republicans. District partisanship averages will be lower in the first election period (less Democratic), 1982–1990, when the Republican presidential candidates won, than in the second election period, 1992–1998, when Bill Clinton, a Democrat, was elected.

The first comparison one should make in Table 6-4 is between the partisanship of those districts in which men and women of the same party ran. Comparing women Democratic candidates to male Democrats, we find that the women consistently ran in more partisan friendly districts than did the men. This is true for both time periods and is true for open seat contests as well as for all the contests together. The largest advantage that Democratic women held over their male counterparts was in open seat contests during 1992–1998, when they ran in districts that were nearly 3 percent more Democratic. The district partisanship averages in the "all races" category for male and female Democratic candidates was nearly the same in the first election period and a point and a half higher for Democratic women in the second election period. By contrast, Republican women on average consistently ran in districts that were less favorable to Republicans in their partisan composition than the districts in which Republican men ran. In fact, in three of the four groupings, Republican women candidates actually ran in districts more favorable to Democrats than those of any of the other party-gender candidate groups. Only in the open seat contests in 1998 do Democratic women exceed them in terms of how partisan friendly the districts are on average for Democratic candidates.

Democratic women candidates run for the House under much different circumstances than their Republican counterparts. Women Democrats constitute a higher percentage of their party's candidates, are more likely to run as incumbents or for open seats, and run in districts that are more partisan friendly. Meanwhile, women Republican candidates remain a small percentage of their party's candidates, are more likely to run as challengers, and are more likely to run as candidates in districts that are less partisan friendly.

Party Performance and Recruitment of Women House Candidates

The findings detailed above help to explain, not only the gender gap in the House, but also the strategic behavior of women candidates for the House and their respective parties. After all, the more favorable treatment and better success rate of Democratic women candidates may help to encourage potential Democratic women candidates to run for the House. Their better success rate may also persuade party leaders that running women candidates is a way to win seats. Conversely, potential Republican women candidates, knowing how few women get Republican House nominations, especially in open seat races and Republican-leaning districts, may decide to run for other offices or to remain on the sidelines. And Republican Party leaders will find little reason to be encouraged to recruit women candidates when it appears on the surface that

Table 6-5 Votes Received by Democrats in Contested House Elections, 1982–1998

	Female Democrat Male Republican	Male Democrat Male Republican	Female Democrat Female Republican	Male Democrat Female Republican
Open seat races (1982–1990)	51.95%	51.58%	53.54%	52.57%
Democratic incumbent vs. Republican challenger (1982–1990)	64.33	63.96	65.92	64.95
Republican incumbent vs. Democratic challenger (1982–1990)	39.57	39.20	41.16	40.19
Open seat races (1992–1998)	51.75	50.10	54.04	53.00
Democratic incumbent vs. Republican challenger (1992–1998)	61.58	59.93	63.87	62.83
Republican incumbent vs. Democratic challenger (1992–1998)	41.92	40.27	44.21	43.17

Note: Does not include races where incumbents ran unopposed. The percentage of the Democratic vote received in contested House elections was calculated after controlling for factors such as incumbency status, candidate spending, and district partisanship.

they do not run as well as male Republicans. Thus, another explanation for the difference in the number of women Democratic and Republican candidates may lie in party performance. The Republican Party may be running fewer women House candidates because it seems that women are not performing as well as men.

Could it be that for Democrats there is an electoral advantage in running women candidates for the House, whereas for Republicans there is an electoral disadvantage? Cooperman's ongoing work on this question provides some insights. She analyzes the House contests from 1982–1998, controlling for the gender of the candidates, incumbency status (open seat races versus races with an incumbent), district partisanship, and candidate spending.[7] Table 6-5 lists the percentage of the Democratic vote received by candidates in two election periods: 1982–1990 and 1992–1998. The elections are divided into three different categories of races: open seat races, races with a Democratic incumbent, and races with a Democratic challenger (against a Republican incumbent). The vote percentages received by the Democratic Party in the four different candidate match-ups indicate that when the opponent is a Republican male, Democrats tend to receive a higher vote share with women candidates. For example, in open seat races during the first election period (1982–1990) where the opponent is a male Republican, Democrats received 51.95 percent of the vote with women candidates and 51.58 percent of the vote with male candidates. Democratic women candidates for open seats did even better against male Republicans (51.75 percent) than did male Democrats against male Republicans (50.10 percent) during the 1992–1998 elections. Similar findings hold in races with Democratic incumbents and in races where Democrats are challengers. In every instance women Democrats received on average a higher percentage of the two-party vote than did male Democrats. These differences, which represent averages, admittedly are relatively small. But when House majorities are small, as they were after the 1998 election, parties will pursue any possible advantage to get an additional percentage point or two of the national vote.

If the vote share results provide Democrats with an incentive to run women candidates, then Republicans may have an electoral disincentive to run women candidates. In open seat races for both election periods, the Democratic Party vote share was highest when Democrats ran against Republican women.[8] When women Republicans ran against male Democrats, the Democratic Party vote share increased compared to its share against male Republicans. This is especially true in the second election period (1992–1998), when Democratic Party House candidates ran consistently about three percentage points higher against female Republicans than against male Republicans. These results held for open seat contests, for contests in which Democrats were incumbents, and for contests in which Democrats were challengers.

Whereas the vote share the Democrats received when they ran women candidates, as compared to male candidates, improved modestly in 1992–1998, Republicans have fared consistently worse in both time periods with women candidates than with men. Although an advantage of a percentage point or so for Democratic women may provide only a slight incentive for party leaders to recruit them as candidates, the three-point disadvantage faced by Republican women will certainly undercut efforts to recruit them as candidates.

We have seen that the Democrats, especially in the 1990s, have run more women and run them in more favorable circumstances than have Republicans. But even controlling for those advantages, Cooperman finds that women Democrats are an electoral plus for their party, whereas women Republicans remain underperforming vote-getters. The data suggest that Republican Party leaders lack a compelling reason to aggressively recruit women candidates, if they base their decisions on vote share. The precise reasons why the Republican Party fails to reap the same benefit as the Democrats do when running women candidates, or why Republican women do not, at least, run on a par with Republican males, are uncertain. One cause may be the differential ability of Democratic as opposed to Republican women candidates to attract the votes of women independents and women crossover voters from the other party, but that remains a question for ongoing research.[9]

The House Gender Gap in Positions of Influence

Now that more women are getting elected to the House, it is important to ask whether women members are gaining more clout in the operations and policy outputs of the institution.[10] Have they moved into positions of influence as party leaders and committee chairs? Do Democrats and Republicans differ in their willingness to integrate women members into positions of power? The change in majority party status that occurred after the 1994 elections provides an opportunity to compare party efforts in this regard. Finally, it is also important to consider how the gender gap in the House has affected the ability of women members to cover committees.

In this section we examine three areas of committee representation—coverage, assignment to exclusive committees, and seniority—in order to assess the changing influence of women in the House. Specifically, we examine how successful women House members have been in establishing a presence on committees, in achieving representation on more prestigious committees such as the Appropriations, Rules, and Ways and Means Committees, and in establishing sufficient committee seniority to compete for committee and subcommittee chairs.[11]

Coverage on committees is a critical way in which women members can establish a presence within their party. When a small number of women serve in the House, representation on committees will be thin, because there are not enough women for a woman to be assigned to each committee. Problems with coverage were evident for women of both parties during the 1980s. A few committees had no female representation from either party, and many committees had representation from women of only one party. In the 100th Congress, women Democrats were not represented on more than one third (38 percent) of all standing House committees, including the Education and Labor Committee and the Agriculture Committee. Representation on committees was even more thin among Republican women. Nearly one half of all standing committees had no women Republican members. In addition, representation by Republican women on the exclusive Appropriations, Rules, and Ways and Means Committees was virtually nonexistent, with only one woman Republican, Virginia Smith, Neb., assigned to any of the three (Appropriations).

The number of women in the House had more than doubled after the 1992 elections, and women's coverage on committees in consequence improved. Because women's gains were primarily among the majority Democrats, it was in the majority party that the committee coverage changed. The number of committees with no Democratic women members dropped from eight in the 100th Congress to only one in the 103d Congress.[12] In fact, women Democrats had attained a membership size that enabled an average of four women to serve on each committee. Despite this gain in overall committee membership, women Democrats remained underrepresented on exclusive committees, accounting for only 10 percent of combined total membership on the Appropriations, Rules, and Ways and Means Committees.

Having enjoyed no real gain in numbers from 1987 to 1993, women Republicans saw minimal change in their coverage on committees. In addition to being outnumbered by their male colleagues, they also came to be outnumbered by women Democrats. Republican women in the 103d Congress still had no representation on six of the twenty-one standing committees, including the Energy and Commerce Committee and the Judiciary Committee, which have jurisdiction over issues of particular concern to women. One of the few positives for Republican women in the 103d Congress was their slight overrepresentation (7.5 percent) on exclusive committees. However, this percentage represents, in real numbers, only three Republican women serving on these committees.

The gender gap in the House took on a greater significance following the 1994 election, when the Republican Party won the majority and thereby obtained a much greater influence in the chamber's operation and policy output. The majority party controls the agenda, is responsible for the scheduling, chairs every committee and subcommittee, and possesses a majority of members at nearly every decision-making point. Accordingly, when the Republican Party won control of the House, the influence of women House members necessarily suffered. The total number of women members of Congress did not change between the 103d and 104th Congresses, but the total number of women members in each party did. Women Republicans increased their numbers by five, bringing their total number to seventeen, and the number of women Democrats decreased by five, to thirty-one. As previously noted, in spite of their increased numbers, women Republicans declined as a percentage of their party's House membership.

Some of the patterns of female representation on committees that existed during the period of Democratic control remained largely in effect. As compared to their percentage of total party membership, women Democrats continued to be slightly underrepresented on exclusive committees (9.3 percent), and women Republicans continued to remain without representation on several standing committees. With only seventeen members in the majority party, the influence of women was spread thinner than it had been in the 103d, when Republicans were in the minority. Again, key committees, including the Commerce Committee, with twenty-five Republican members, and the Judiciary Committee, with twenty Republican members, did not have a single Republican woman member. Moreover, the important Appropriations Committee had just a single woman among its Republicans, Barbara Vucanovich, Nev., who has since retired. For women Democrats, the relegation to minority party status meant a loss of representation on the prestigious Rules Committee, as Louise Slaughter, N.Y., was bumped from the committee when the majority–minority party ratio changed.[13]

Female representation on House committees in the 106th Congress has been marked more by continuity than change since the Republican takeover. With sixteen women Republicans in the House, committee coverage continues to be problematic. There are no women Republican members on three standing committees, including the Budget Committee. Five standing committees — Agriculture, Education and the Workforce, International Relations, Judiciary, and Veterans' Affairs—have only one Republican woman member. Three women Republicans serve on the Appropriations Committee; however, they are among the most junior members. Thin coverage on committees further limits the ability of Republican women to influence legislation as it is being written. The influence of women Democrats and Republicans in the House remains limited, but for different reasons. Women Democrats have begun to attain a critical mass in membership size, yet they remain in the minority party. In contrast, women Republicans are in the majority party but are too few in number (and seniority) to wield much clout collectively. Adequately covering the committees, let alone attaining influence on them, will continue to be a challenge for Republican women unless and until they can increase their membership size. The ability of Democratic women to gain influence remains limited as well. As long as Democrats retain their minority party status in the House, women Democrats cannot take full advantage of the increased clout that accompanies increased membership size.

The success of women members in increasing their sphere of influence can also be assessed by examining how frequently women in the majority party were selected as committee or subcommittee chairs, or how frequently women in the minority obtained positions as ranking minority committee members. In the 103d Congress there were no women committee chairs and only one ranking minority member, Jan Meyers, Kan.[14] Four Democratic women received subcommittee chair assignments, including Pat Schroeder, Col., on an Armed Services subcommittee, and Cardiss Collins, Ill., on an Energy and Commerce subcommittee—subcommittees for two relatively prestigious committees.

The shift in majority party status in the 104th Congress, and the attendant turnover in committee and subcommittee chairs, produced some important leadership opportunities for Republican women. One of the most noticeable changes the House Republicans made was that the Speaker assumed a more active role in appointing committee chairs and showed a willingness to violate seniority in doing so. Although in most cases the senior Republicans became committee chairs when their party gained control of the House, Republican leaders did afford themselves a certain amount of flexibility. In the 104th Congress, two Republican women were appointed committee chairs—with Jan Meyers named as chair of the Small Business Committee,[15] and Nancy Johnson, Conn., named chair of the Standards of Official Conduct Committee.[16]

Meyers retired after the 104th Congress and membership of the ethics committee rotated, so that Johnson was no longer chair. No Republican women chaired full committees in either the 105th or the 106th Congresses. The number of Republican women serving as subcommittee chairs increased from seven in the 104th Congress to eight in the 105th Congress. In the 106th Congress, four women Republicans served as subcommittee chairs. These included the three most senior Republican women in the House—Nancy Johnson, Marge Roukema, N.J., and Constance Morella, Md.—who were appointed subcommittee chairs on the Ways and Means, Banking and Financial Services, and Science

Committees, respectively. The three-term limit on committee chairs, imposed by the Republicans during the 104th Congress, ensures that committee chairs will become available in the 107th Congress, but the chairs may not necessarily be awarded to women. Since Republicans remain in control of the House, Roukema is in line to serve as chair of the Financial Institutions and Consumer Credit Committee, but she may be challenged for that position.

The Republican Party may have done a slightly better job of appointing women to committee and subcommittee chairs in the House than did the Democrats immediately prior to the Republican takeover. Although the Democrats did choose committee and subcommittee chairs in elections, they were very reluctant to violate seniority in doing so. The large influx of women Democrats occurred in 1993, the last year in which the Democrats appointed any new chairs. Only those with considerable seniority or those who served on committees with high turnover obtained positions as subcommittee chairs, and the women Democrats thus did not obtain positions of influence proportionate with their numbers. Despite their small numbers, Republican women have fared marginally better. In part this is a result of the huge influx of new members, especially in the Republican Party, in the past four elections. Nearly two-thirds of all House Republicans were first elected to the House in the 1990s. Thus the seniority system was not as much of an impediment for junior Republican members desiring leadership positions.

The House Gender Gap in the Twenty-First Century

The prospects for women candidates in the 2000 elections are mixed. There have been no large increases in the number of women Republicans or Democrats running for the House. Eighty women Democrats and forty-two women Republicans won party primaries. Nearly one-half (46 percent, or thirty-seven of eighty) of Democratic women candidates are incumbents, and just more than one-third (35 percent, or fifteen of forty-two) of Republican women candidates are incumbents. In open seat contests, women Democrats again outnumber their Republican counterparts by more than two to one (eleven to five).[17] In the thirty-five open seat races in the 2000 elections, women Democrats constituted 31 percent of their party's candidates, and women Republicans constituted only 14 percent of their party's candidates. Thus, at least in terms of the number of women candidates for open seats, the efforts of the Democrats continue to outpace those of the Republicans.

Although Republicans have retained control of the House, the sphere of influence of women Republican members will remain essentially the same. Having increased their membership size by one, women will likely continue to have thin coverage of committees, and the number of women subcommittee chairs will likely remain small. Despite an increase in the number of women House candidates in the 2000 elections, the gender gap between the parties in the House will likely persist. Trends in party recruitment of women candidates suggest that Democrats will run more women in the races to fill the numerous open seats that will become available in 2002 through redistricting. If this occurs, the gender gap in the House may become more pronounced. This outcome would especially hurt Republican women, whose sphere of influence within the party remains limited at best.

Notes

1. See Clyde Wilcox, "Why Was 1992 the 'Year of the Woman'? Explaining Women's Gains in 1992," and Carole Chaney and Barbara Sinclair, "Women and the 1992 House Elections," both in *The Year of the Woman: Myths and Realities,* ed. by Elizabeth Adell Cook, Sue Thomas, and Clyde Wilcox (Boulder, Col.: Westview Press, 1994).
2. See Sue Thomas and Clyde Wilcox, *Women and Elective Office* (New York: Oxford University Press, 1998); Richard Fox, *Gender Dynamics and Congressional Elections* (Thousand Oaks, Calif.: Sage Publications, 1997); Kim Fridkin Kahn, *The Political Consequences of Being a Woman* (New York: Columbia University Press, 1996); Irwin Gertzog, *Congressional Women: Their Recruitment, Integration, and Behavior,* 2d ed. (Westport, Conn.: Praeger, 1995); Barbara Burrell, *A Woman's Place Is in the House: Campaigning for Congress in the Feminist Era* (Ann Arbor: University of Michigan Press, 1994); Susan Carroll *Women as Candidates in American Politics,* 2d ed. (Bloomington, Ind.: Indiana University Press, 1994); Robert Darcy et al., *Women, Elections, and Representation,* 2d ed. (Lincoln, Neb.: University of Nebraska Press, 1994).
3. "Women Winners for U.S. House Seats: 1976–1998," Center for American Women in Politics, National Information Bank on Women in Public Office, Eagleton Institute of Politics, Rutgers University, October 1998.
4. Irwin Gertzog and Michele Simard, "Women and 'Hopeless' Congressional Candidacies: Nomination Frequency, 1916–1978," *American Politics Quarterly* 9 (October 1981): 449–66.
5. Ronald Keith Gaddie and Charles S. Bullock III, *Elections to Open Seats in the U.S. House: Where the Action Is* (Lanham, Md.: Rowman and Littlefield, forthcoming).
6. Because voting districts were redrawn prior to the 1992 election, we use 1990/1992 as the dividing point for the analysis rather than 1988/1990 as in the earlier analysis in this chapter. We could not place 1990 House elections in the later era because we do not have the presidential vote by district for the 1992 and 1996 elections for the congressional districts as they existed in 1990.
7. Rosalyn Cooperman, "Women of the House: the Changing Nature of Gender and Political Candidacy in U.S. House Elections" (Ph.D. diss., Vanderbilt University, in progress).
8. Vote share was highest when women Democrats ran against women Republicans. However, very few such candidate-match-ups occurred.
9. See Kathleen Dolan, "Voting for Women in 'The Year of the Woman,'" *American Journal of Political Science* 42 (January 1998): 272–94; Monika McDermott, "Voting Cues in Low-Information Elections: Candidate Gender as a Social Information Variable in Contemporary United States Elections," *American Journal of Political Science* 41 (January 1997): 270–83. Also, the failure of Republican women candidates to attract the votes of women independents and women crossover voters from the other party may be akin to the problem that black Republican candidates have in attracting votes from black voters who are Democrats.
10. Laura Arnold, "Women, Committees, and Power in the Senate," *Legislative Studies Quarterly* (forthcoming); Karen Foerstel and Herbert Foerstel, *Climbing the Hill: Gen-*

der Conflict in Congress (Westport, Conn.: Praeger, 1996); Sally Friedman, "House Committee Assignments of Women and Minority Newcomers, 1965–1994," *Legislative Studies Quarterly* 21 (February 1996): 73–81.

11. Rosalyn Cooperman and Bruce Oppenheimer, "Another Gender Gap: The Representation and Influence of Women House Members" (paper presented at the Women in Congress Symposium, Northern Arizona University, Flagstaff, Ariz., 20 September 1997).

12. The only committee without a Democratic woman representative was the District of Columbia Committee. However, the elected delegate from the District of Columbia, Eleanor Holmes Norton, did serve on the committee.

13. In the 105th Congress, David Bonior, Mich., gave up his seat on the Rules Committee, enabling Slaughter to regain hers.

14. Meyers was the ranking minority member on the Small Business Committee.

15. The Small Business Committee, a committee with a Republican constituency, was not abolished in 1994, although other committees with Democratic constituencies, namely the Post Office and Civil Service, District of Columbia, and Merchant Marine and Fisheries Committees, were. Another possible reason that the Small Business Committee was not abolished in 1994 is that Meyers was the likely choice to serve as the committee's chair.

16. Of course, membership on the ethics committee rotates and is not often a sought-after position. Johnson's service as chair during the committee's handling of the ethics charges against then-Speaker Gingrich nearly cost her reelection to the House in 1996.

17. "Women Candidates in 2000—Congressional and Statewide Office," Center for American Women in Politics, National Information Bank on Women in Public Office, Eagleton Institute of Politics, Rutgers University, November 2000.

7. *Keystone* Reconsidered

Morris P. Fiorina

At the 1999 meeting of the Midwest Political Science Association a panel of congressional scholars conducted a retrospective on my book *Congress—Keystone of the Washington Establishment*, first published in 1977.[1] This chapter is an expansion of my remarks at that panel. Compared with the congressional literature of the time, *Keystone* was distinctive in two respects. First, it applied a rational actor analysis to Congress, an institution studied mostly in institutional or behavioral terms up to that time. Second, in contrast to much of the scholarly literature on Congress, the book was critical, arguing that the unbridled pursuit of constituency benefits had made members of Congress more electorally secure but at the cost of efficient and effective policies and the faithful representation of national preferences.

I begin with some personal remarks about the social and intellectual context that generated such a book. These serve to emphasize that the research agenda is a collective enterprise. I then consider the changes in congressional elections in the intervening years and the relationship of these changes to the research agenda today.[2] I conclude with some general thoughts about Congress and American democracy as we enter a new century.

The Context

It was my good fortune to enter the profession at the young end of a cohort of terrific scholars of congressional elections and representation: Herbert Asher, David Brady, Charles Bullock, Lawrence Dodd, Robert Erikson, John Ferejohn, Gary Jacobson, Samuel Kernell, Warren Kostroski, Thomas Mann, Bruce Oppenheimer, Norman Ornstein, David Rohde, Jim Stimson, Herbert Weisberg, Gerald Wright, and others. Although we hailed from different graduate programs and our research emphases varied, we were not purely political behavior scholars in the Michigan mold, nor were we purely "Congress jocks" in the mold of the scholars who participated in the American Political Science Association's Study of Congress project in the 1950s and 1960s. All were deeply interested in broader questions of representation, and our interest in elections and the Congress reflected that larger concern. Most of us also had an interest in the internal operations of Congress, but we believed that elections and their anticipation significantly shaped those operations.

These scholars had something else in common: skepticism that the existing empirical depiction of Congress's electoral environment was accurate. The literature told us that most members had safe seats and had little to fear from unaware constituents and overrated interest groups.[3] Supposedly, members were free agents whose behavior was shaped more by internal expectations and norms than by electoral or interest group pressures.[4] Looking back, I am not sure just why so many of us found this picture unsatisfying, but we did. Probably our dissatisfaction reflected the divisions evident in Congress in the late 1960s, divisions that seemed clearly related to the demands of aroused constituents and groups. At any rate, this cohort of scholars formed a self-conscious research community in the best sense. We regularly engaged each other at meetings and conventions, and although many political science departments rationed long-distance phone privileges and first-class postage in those days, we managed to circulate and critique our work widely and quickly in the B.E. (before e-mail) era.

Junior scholars live in fear of being "scooped," a fear generally discounted by their senior colleagues. In 1974 I was a junior member of the community, eagerly awaiting publication of my first book to put me on the scholarly map. *Representatives, Roll Calls, and Constituencies* would be the first sustained effort to apply rational choice analysis to legislative behavior. Tenure—if not fame—would be assured. Unfortunately for me, David Mayhew had the same general idea at the same time, but he executed it much more ambitiously, not to mention far more readably. When my book was published it was largely overlooked amid the buzz over the slightly earlier publication of Mayhew's path-breaking work. I considered applying to law school, but my wife nixed that suggestion. So, I decided to start over with another idea I'd been pondering since graduate school—retrospective voting.

It was not to be. Early in 1975 my colleague at Caltech, John Ferejohn, asked whether I'd seen Mayhew's latest article. "No," I replied, "what's he writing on now—retrospective voting?"[5] Ferejohn proceeded to explain Mayhew's vanishing marginals analysis, taking care to point out that it undermined another of the intended contributions of *Representatives, Roll Calls, and Constituencies*—the grounding of electoral competition in the homogeneity or heterogeneity of legislative districts.[6] Since the demographic composition of districts was unlikely to change significantly in the short term, if electoral competition had dramatically lessened during the 1960s, my argument was wrong.

Redistricting was the obvious suspect. There had been a great deal of it in the aftermath of *Wesberry v. Sanders* (1964), which extended "one person, one vote" to congressional districts. Conceivably, congressional districts had become significantly more homogeneous as a result. I waited with anticipation as Ferejohn studied the effect of redistricting on the vanishing marginals, only to be disappointed by his negative conclusions. In the ensuing months I kibitzed his investigation of other possibilities. Ultimately he concluded that voters had changed—they were cuing less on party and more on incumbency. By this point I was thoroughly intrigued by the phenomenon and dissatisfied with the preliminary answers, so I put retrospective voting on the shelf and decided to do what Richard Fenno had been urging his students to do for years—go out into the field and "soak and poke." I did so in the summer of 1975, and the result was *Keystone* two years later.

For this retrospective I listened to the ten hours of tape recordings I made following the interviews in Districts A and B.[7] Listening reminded me that I was frustrated for most of the first week in District A. There, local observers informed me that the new representative had made this previously marginal district safe. Although time might prove them right, the question was why? No one could tell me, or at least tell me in terms that made sense. They only offered general comments to the effect that he was being a "better congressman." That might be true for this particular district, of course, but from a social science standpoint it was an explanation without "legs," unlikely to provide a general explanation of the vanishing marginals across the country. Why would a plethora of "better congressmen" suddenly have appeared on the scene in the late 1960s? It was not until the last interview in District A that earlier comments clicked into place. Implicitly, I had been searching for some sort of policy-based reason for the change. But a young Democratic state representative doing quite nicely in a Republican area set me straight with this argument quoted in the book:

> You've got to understand. The little guy just can't get through the bureaucracy. He can't get anything done. They —— him over all the time. What a state representative can do is to protect the little guy and help the little guy. That's what you do to get reelected. That's the job of the elected official today.

Policy-shmalicy—it's all about license plates! I realized that I had been hearing comments like this all week. A number of interviewees on the Republican side reported that the district's agricultural sector was under siege by fanatical inspectors from the Occupational Safety and Health Administration (OSHA) and the member was fighting for constituents' rights. Others observed that having come out of the educational establishment the new member was working closely with Parent-Teacher Associations (PTAs) and schools to take advantage of opportunities provided by federal programs. Constituents viewed him as a "better congressman" because he and his (greatly enlarged) staff were working closely with them on problems that touched their everyday lives. It's not about policy, stupid, it's about implementation.

Interviews in District B the next week confirmed what I'd learned in District A. The representative from District B simply had found the magic formula some years earlier. Satisfied that I understood at least part of the cause of the vanishing marginals, I headed home, drafted a brief article for the *American Political Science Review*, then tried to go back to retrospective voting.

Again, it was not to be. I taught both undergraduate and graduate seminars on Congress during the academic year 1975–1976, while the presidential campaign was heating up. During the spring primaries Americans were warned repeatedly about a Washington Establishment. Jimmy Carter was not a member, to be sure, in contrast to all those Democratic senators he was running against, but even career congressman and accidental president Gerald Ford denied membership.[8] The bureaucrats were out of control, it was said. The judiciary had become a law unto itself. The Washington Establishment was running the government, not the people. I told my students this was at best half the story—members of Congress rarely were named in these indictments, but it was *their* agencies that were trying to implement *their* statutes. Moreover, judges were trying to interpret and oversee the process Congress had structured. In a sense Congress was getting away with a great frame-up—everyone else was taking the blame for their transgressions. Colleagues encouraged me to make this bolder argument in print.

Originally I titled the manuscript, *Is There a Washington Establishment?*, arguing that yes there was, but it's not whom you might think. Being a financially strapped junior professor I first sent the manuscript off to a large number of trade publishers, all of whom rejected it. Thankfully, Marian Ash at Yale University Press felt differently, although she vetoed the wishy-washy title, so the manuscript became *Congress—Keystone of the Washington Establishment*. There were a few stinging reviews, and I had to spend quite a bit of time and energy defending the argument, but twenty-three years and 70,000 copies later, I can say that the pain was worth it.

The Hunt for the Incumbency Advantage

The research community went after the incumbency advantage like hounds after prey. Several of our number described and dissected the vote advantage itself. When exactly had it occurred? Did it increase linearly with seniority or happen all at once as a "sophomore surge." Knowing more about its specifics, they then tried to evaluate the hypothesized causal mechanisms. Was it something incumbents had done, or were the changes rooted in challengers and their behavior, or neither? As systematic campaign finance data became available, some of us began to pursue that subject. In the midst of this exploding interest in congressional elections a newly reconstituted American National Election Studies (ANES) decided to bring these elections under its aegis, and in the next decade ANES data enabled scholars to paint a far richer and more nuanced portrait of voting in congressional elections than had existed in the 1960s.

The outpouring of work led some journal editors to complain about the number of submissions dealing with incumbency in one way or another, and a few scholars suggested that the subfield had overinvested in studying the subject.[9] But editors and referees have it in their power to push resources in other directions, so I doubt that any harm was done. On the contrary, although the jumping-off point was a relatively narrow question (What underlies the incumbency advantage and why did it increase?), the literature pursued larger questions as scholars examined the implications of the incumbency advantage for swing ratios, presidential coattails, midterm seat swings, party strength in the legislature, the separation of the presidential and congressional electoral arenas, and other important questions of representation and governance. We became increasingly aware of the incentives created by electoral institutions, comparing behavior in the United States with that in other single member simple plurality systems.[10] Before this literature developed, Americanists tended to take our electoral system for granted. Now we understand that it is an important variable.

The Era of Incumbency and Insulation

By the late 1980s the research community had painted a detailed portrait of what I have called "the era of incumbency and insulation."[11] After World War II an array of social, economic, and technological changes began to undermine the state and local party organizations. And in the 1960s new issues and an assortment of crises buffeted citizen allegiances to the political parties. The result was the growth of candidate-centered politics, wherein candidates personalized campaigns and elections, running not as members of long-lived teams, but as individuals who would behave independently in office. Members of Congress were particularly adept at developing electoral techniques that enabled them to personalize their supporting coalitions. Increasingly, they were able to avoid association with their party's presidents and presidential candidates, their national party's image, and larger questions of national policy. Instead, they were able to win on the basis of their personal characteristics, their personal policy positions, their record of service to the district, and their great resource advantages that enabled them to discourage strong challengers and beat those whom they could not discourage. Defeat was a rarity, a result of scandal, political miscalculation, or just plain laziness. Some particulars of this portrait did not rest on as solid empirical ground as others, and we continued to argue over details, but few of us doubted that we had a good general picture. In 1984 Ronald Reagan won the presidency in a landslide, but his coattails were of little help to congressional Republicans. The midterm swing in 1986 was trivial, incumbent reelection rates reached a record high, and the Gelman-King unbiased estimate soared to a record 13 percent.[12] The 1986 reelection record fell in 1988 when 98 percent of all incumbents who ran won. Seemingly the era of incumbency and insulation was at its apogee.

Increasingly I have come to believe that professional consensus on a subject means that it is about to change—or it already has done so but the change has gone noticed. Here was another example. Notification that things had changed came with thunderous emphasis in 1994.

All Politics Is Not as Local as Before

"All politics is local," the famous aphorism of Speaker of the House Tip O'Neill, was the mantra of our generation of congressional scholars. Everyone recognized that it was overstated, of course, but it was a pretty good way of summing up the era of incumbency and insulation. Little did we know that the fit of the aphorism to empirical reality was growing worse even at the apparent height of the power of incumbency. In 1994 the Republicans gained fifty-three seats in the House and eight in the Senate to take control of Congress for the first time since the elections of 1952. The House swing was the largest since 1948, an election well before the era of incumbency, which arrived in the late 1960s, and forecasting models developed during the 1970s and 1980s were far off the mark. To my knowledge no one in the research community saw this upheaval coming (at least they didn't rush to publish their prediction). In the weeks before the elections most of us confidently told journalists that Newt Gingrich was just blowing smoke — Republicans had talked about nationalizing the elections before, but no one knew how to do it with incumbency so strong. We had discounted similar pronouncements for nearly two decades and had been right; this time we were wrong.

After the elections the Hoover Institution held a conference attended by many of those who had painted the 1970s and 1980s portrait of congressional elections, joined by a younger generation that included many of their students. Several of the conference papers reported that indications of increased nationalization of the congressional electoral arena were clearly evident in the record but simply had not been appreciated until 1994. In Figures 7-1 and 7-2 I have graphed coefficients from regressing the current district House vote on the past House and presidential vote in the district.[13] The past presidential vote is treated as an indicator of national forces, and the past House vote as an indicator of local forces — crude, but temporally comparable measures often used in this literature. The picture is similar whether one looks at on-year or off-year elections, whether one includes uncontested elections or excludes them, and whether the South is included or omitted.

Consistent with the portrait in the literature the presidential and House arenas separated in the late 1950s and maintained a good deal of separation until the mid-1970s, a development that probably encouraged candidate-centered politics and reinforced it as well.[14] But — importantly — the national component of the vote began to recover after the traumas of the 1960s, whereas the local component began to drop back from its high. By the mid-point of Reagan's first term the two components had reached statistical parity. Thus, at the time the incumbency literature was in full flower, the phenomena that had generated it were in decline! Probably the principal reason the research community did not notice these developments is that the elections of the late 1980s arrested these trends, showing significant drops in the national component and seemingly validating the prevailing picture. In retrospect, however, they were the last hurrahs of the old era — the national coefficient for 1994 actually is lower than a simple extrapolation of the trend from 1966 to 1982.

Gary Jacobson also reported indications of increased nationalization of House elections.[15] For one thing, Republican seat gains in the 1990s came disproportionately in districts where Republican presidential candidates ran well — in the South of course, but outside the South too. For another thing, the standard deviation of the vote swing fell, indicating that House returns in the 1990s were moving together to a greater extent than in earlier postwar elections. Other researchers have

Figure 7-1 Decomposition of Midterm House Elections (Contested and Uncontested Seats)

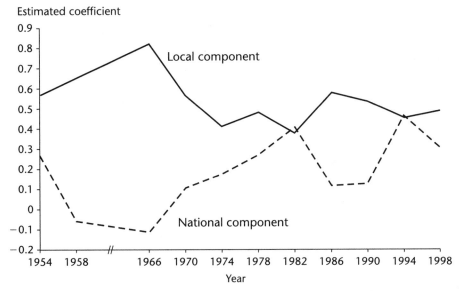

Estimated coefficient

Local component

National component

Year

Source: David Brady, John Cogan, and Morris Fiorina, *Continuity and Change in House Elections* (Stanford: Stanford University Press, forthcoming).

Note: No calculation for 1962 is possible because the past presidential vote in the newly redrawn congressional districts is unavailable. (Congressional Quarterly provided estimates for 1982.)

noted that levels of House-president ticket-splitting have dropped in recent elections, both measured at the individual level or in the aggregate.

Of course, the important changes evident in the 1994 returns should not lead us to overlook the continuities that are equally evident. Most obviously, in a terrible year for incumbents 90 percent of those who ran won. To be sure, there was a major partisan asymmetry, as all thirty-three of the losing incumbents were Democrats. But even for Democrats the Gelman-King measure registered a larger advantage than in 1990, when no one had any inkling that important changes were in progress. The advantages of incumbency were overcome in many cases, but by no means did they disappear.

Nor did the standard techniques by which incumbents in previous decades had built their advantage. After winning control, congressional Republicans acted more or less in the manner of a responsible party for the better part of 1995, leading some to wonder whether the entire literature on Congress needed revision. But after the politically disastrous government shutdowns in the winter of 1995–1996 electorally apprehensive Republicans rediscovered tried-and-true formulas, such as putting daylight between themselves and Speaker Gingrich and emphasizing the services rendered for their districts.

Figure 7-2 Decomposition of Presidential-Year House Elections
          Contested and Uncontested Seats)

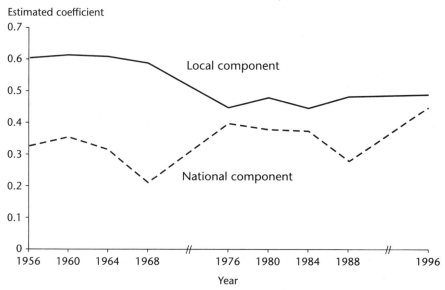

Source: David Brady, John Cogan, and Morris Fiorina, *Continuity and Change in House Elections* (Stanford: Stanford University Press, forthcoming).

Note: No calculations for 1972 and 1992 are possible, because the past presidential vote in the newly redrawn congressional districts is unavailable.

After the Republican majority survived the 1996 elections, Transportation Committee chair Bud Shuster, R - Pa., demonstrated the continued strong appeal of pork barrel politics as he rolled the Republican leadership. And at the end of the session the leadership itself capitulated in the face of electoral realities and negotiated an omnibus appropriations bill that has been called the largest pork barrel bill in history. In the wake of this return to more traditional congressional politics the 1998 election outcomes were something of a throwback to 1986 and 1988. Of 401 incumbents who sought reelection, only five lost, for a new success record of 98.5 percent. Incumbents registered 8.0 on the Gelman - King scale.

The changes of the 1990s are not inconsequential. On the contrary, these changes are real. Even in 1998 there were continued indications of increased nationalization. The standard deviation of the vote swing dropped to an even lower level than it had in 1994. And extension of the analysis reported in Figure 7 - 1 results in a smaller national coefficient in the 1998 regression than in the 1994 regression, but one larger than that for any midterms except 1994 and 1982. Indisputably, the elections of the mid - to late 1990s *were* more nationalized than they had been since the 1960s. The old equilibrium of incumbency and insulation was disrupted. But such important consequences have followed from relatively small changes in the electoral arena.

Finally, it is worth pointing out that not all the contributors to the incumbency literature would have been surprised by the electoral transformation in the 1990s. Indeed, taking a more national and party-centered orientation, one of the editors of this book foreshadowed the Republican revolution, arguing that the electoral entrenchment of the majority party would lead to policy failure, if not crisis, and eventual electoral retribution.[16] Although he didn't predict when the revolution would occur, on the morning after the 1994 elections one could understand Larry Dodd feeling quite satisfied with the outcome (professionally, at least!). Other scholars had not been sufficiently bold to predict an eventual reaction, but at least they had noted that individual responsiveness of incumbents went along with the lack of institutional responsiveness and accountability that was politically damaging to the collective Congress.[17]

Why the Change?

Why has the personal electoral insulation that characterized the preceding era of congressional elections eroded? I think that there are at least three reasons, although these thoughts are more impressionistic than I would like.

The first reason is that the activities that produced the earlier insulation became routinized and in consequence probably less worthy of voter appreciation, or even notice. In the late 1960s a member of Congress who established multiple district offices and came home every two weeks stood out from the crowd. By the late 1980s such a member was just doing what everyone else did, maybe even a little less. There have been numerous attempts using various techniques to measure the magnitude of the incumbency advantage over time. All tend to show a similar pattern—a sudden surge in the incumbency advantage in the elections of the late 1960s from the level typical of the early postwar period. Fluctuation or more gradual increases characterize the elections of 1972–1988, then the magnitude of the estimate recedes.[18] The era of greatest change occurred at the same time as the greatest change in member resources and behavior.

Several analysts have attempted to determine what factors produced the growth in the incumbency advantage. The major possible factors are incumbent resources and behavior, campaign funds, and the ability to scare off strong challengers. My personal belief is that attempts to answer this question are hindered by the fact that the nature of the incumbency advantage may have shifted over time. From approximately the mid-1960s through the 1970s, I believe, it was based primarily on member resources and activities. But as increases in member resources leveled off (Figures 7-3 and 7-4) and a high level of constituency attentiveness became a universal expectation, they declined in importance. During the 1980s elections became much more expensive, incumbents were able to raise far more money than challengers, and the nature of the incumbency advantage increasingly came to reflect those facts. Then, as alternative means of recruiting and financing challengers developed in the 1990s, elections became more national and the incumbency advantage declined.

Figure 7-3 Personal Staffs of Representatives and Senators

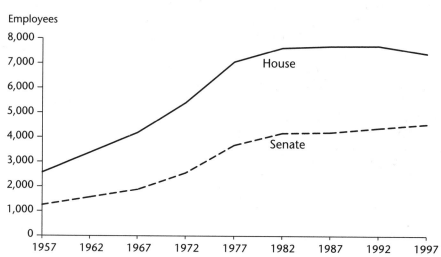

Source: Norman J. Ornstein, Thomas E. Mann, and Michael J. Malbin, eds., *Vital Statistics on Congress, 1999–2000* (Washington, D.C.: American Enterprise Institute, 2000), 131.

That brings us to the second reason for the electoral changes evident in the 1990s. Incumbents were able to maintain a huge advantage on campaign fund-raising in the 1980s and consequently deter strong challengers and defeat weaker ones (see Figure 7-5). That advantage eroded in the 1980s. Why? An anecdote from the *Keystone* interviews suggests an answer.

In listening to the tapes I was struck by the fact that in ten hours of recordings there is only one reference to money in a campaign context.[19] And that lone reference is extremely revealing. In District A I spent an enjoyable evening with a defeated Democratic candidate and his campaign manager. The candidate had run relatively poorly for a challenger in this marginal district, although he still managed a bit more than 45 percent of the vote. As we spoke it became apparent that the man, a lawyer, was a complete amateur politically speaking, so I naturally asked how he had become the Democratic candidate. He told me that he had become increasingly outraged over American involvement in Vietnam and, finally, he felt compelled to try to do something about it. A practical man, he had pondered the alternatives and decided that running for Congress seemed like a reasonable place to start.

The prospective candidate learned that the local Democratic organization—the most important in the district—was headed by a "boss," who called the shots. "So I called him up, and he took the call while he was shaving," the candidate recalled. "I introduced myself and told him that I wanted to run for

Figure 7-4 Mail Franked by Representatives and Senators, 1955–1993

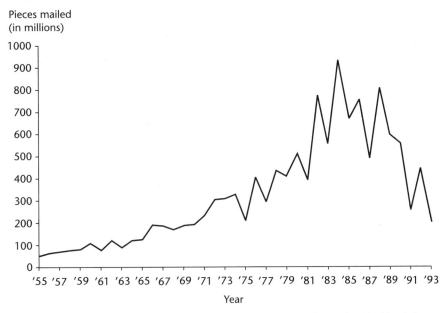

Source: Norman J. Ornstein, Thomas E. Mann, and Michael J. Malbin, eds., *Vital Statistics on Congress, 1999–2000* (Washington, D.C.: American Enterprise Institute, 2000), 165.

Congress on the Democratic ticket, and he asked, 'Just why in the hell should we give you the nomination?' " And the prospective candidate replied, "I'll put $15,000 of my own money into the race." According to the candidate, the "boss" suddenly became very supportive of his candidacy.

Now, even allowing for some exaggeration and the fact that his personal contribution was nearly $50,000 in current dollars, can anyone imagine the Democratic Congressional Campaign Committee today standing by while an amateur walks away with the nomination in a marginal district? Can anyone imagine one of today's major cause groups standing by while a candidate motivated by their cause fights alone for a winnable district? For that matter, can anyone imagine making a serious run for the House today on a $50,000 budget? I think that what did not happen in this marginal district in the 1970s that would surely happen now is an important part of the explanation for the increased nationalization of elections in the 1990s.

Beginning in the late 1970s the national party organizations began a resurgence, first on the Republican side and then later on the Democratic side. To be sure, today's parties are different from those of yesteryear. Rather than patronage-based local organizations headed by "bosses," they are national campaign organizations, with a heavier dose of ideological motivation than previously. These parties became increasingly active at the local level, first identifying and

Figure 7-5 House Incumbent Campaign Spending Advantage

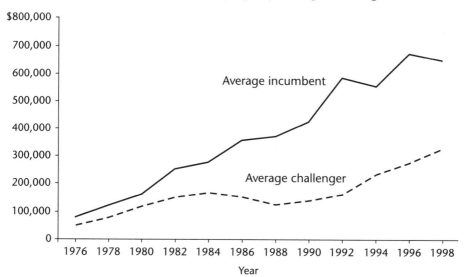

Source: Norman J. Ornstein, Thomas E. Mann, and Michael J. Malbin, eds., *Vital Statistics on Congress. 1999–2000* (Washington, D.C.: American Enterprise Institute, 200), 81.

encouraging strong candidates, then training them and supporting them. With this increasing involvement (some called it "interference" when it first began), came an increasing orientation toward the national parties by the candidates they recruited and supported.

The rise of issue advocacy by the parties reinforces these developments. One of the standard contemporary techniques is to associate your candidate with a popular party leader or party issue and link the other candidate to an unpopular party leader or issue (morphing advertisements are a familiar example). The very concept of a popular or unpopular party leader other than the president also is a recent notion. Morphing House candidates into the visages of Gerald Ford, John McCormack, Hugh Scott, and Mike Mansfield would not have struck 1970 campaign professionals as a particularly effective campaign technique. But when party leaders are Jim Wright and Dick Gephardt, Newt Gingrich, Tom DeLay, and Trent Lott, the technique makes a lot more sense.[20] The implications of such developments for nationalization hardly could be more transparent. Incumbents today do not find it as easy to separate themselves from party leaders, party images, and party performance as did incumbents of twenty years ago.

Along the same lines, I noted in the second edition of *Keystone* that interest groups and political action committees (PACs) that collected and disbursed money nationally could strengthen the hand of interests not tied to specific districts. In retrospect, this was an understatement. So long as interest group spending consisted largely of hard money contributions to individual campaigns, the existing equilibrium was not seriously threatened. But with the rise of independent expenditure campaigns the picture shifts. As abortion, environmental, health care, and other groups increasingly engage in independent issue advocacy, candidates lose control of the agenda. Twenty years ago most of us agreed with congressional scholar Glenn Parker's pithy observation that "the information people have about House incumbents comes from House incumbents." Today, that is less true as incumbents see an assortment of advertisements about them, produced by opposing party and hostile groups, running on their district TV screens. Even if *both* candidates would prefer that an issue not arise in their contest, they may have little say in the matter.

The third reason I think that congressional elections have changed is even more impressionistic than the preceding two. Put quite simply, I believe that today's candidates have deeper policy commitments than their counterparts of a generation ago. In the pre-incumbency days of party-dominated elections, the professional literature told us that the parties were approximately Downsian, motivated to win elections because of the value their members attached to jobs, contracts, and other tangible benefits of officeholding. These parties chose candidates on the basis of qualities like electability, and if that was not an issue, on the basis of such qualities as loyalty to the organization, length of service, local or ethnic claims, and so forth.

That does not seem to be the case today. The new chair of the California Republican Party illustrates the difference. When asked about his priorities he replied that "killing our babies is the issue of the century . . . cutting taxes or any other issue pales in comparison."[21] Fifty years ago the reply likely would have been more along the lines of "to elect as many Republicans as possible."

As traditional patronage-based organizations withered, a wide variety of groups stepped into the space left unoccupied. Increasingly such groups generate candidates and take an important role in organizing and funding campaigns. But the reason for belonging to such groups is commitment to group goals, and that is also a prerequisite for gaining group support. James Sundquist remarked on the increased policy commitment of new members as early as the 1970s, as did Burdett Loomis.[22] It seems likely that members increasingly motivated by policy goals would be more likely to establish records rich in policy content, to emphasize issues as part of their personal political image, and to attract the notice of groups and individuals with similar policy commitments. If all politics still were local, they would not find the job nearly as interesting.

In sum, the rising nationalization of congressional elections probably has many different sources, including diminishing returns from established election strategies, the innovative and increasingly aggressive behavior of reconstituted parties and a host of new interest groups, and the changing motivations and behavior of members themselves. These broad claims are only hypotheses, of course, although there is impressionistic evidence consistent with each.

A New Party Era?

Shortly before the publication of *Keystone,* David Mayhew wrote, "The fact is that no theoretical treatment of the United States Congress that posits parties as analytic units will go very far."[23] Here we see once again an instance of a firm political science conclusion serving as a leading indicator of change. Mayhew was not alone in his thinking. Parties played no role in the arguments presented in *Keystone*, not even in the second edition, in which I was admittedly a little slow to pick up on developments in that arena. At the retrospective panel, David Rohde, a leading scholar of the study of party behavior in Congress, asked what I would say about parties now if there were to be a third edition.

Part of the answer lies in the preceding hypothesis that active party committees and visible party leaders are part of the explanation of the increased nationalization of congressional elections. Although I have written in broad outline, I will say no more on that subject here. Instead, I will shift direction somewhat, and offer some observations about the research agenda today, an agenda dominated by discussions of and arguments about the extent and nature of party influence in Congress today.

Keith Krehbiel has stimulated an important and productive debate in the congressional subfield with a series of recent articles. He first pointed out that commonly used indicators of party influence such as measures of cohesion and unity are highly ambiguous; they can just as easily reflect similarity of legislator preferences as party discipline. Krehbiel then argued that there are conceptual ambiguities in discussions of party strength, party influence, and so forth. Most recently he has contended that, empirically, congressional data are more consistent with preference-based models than with party discipline models.[24] Given the widespread belief in the resurgence of congressional parties during the 1980s and 1990s, Krehbiel's arguments have provoked equally widespread reaction from scholars such as Rohde, John Aldrich, Gary Cox, Mat McCubbins, and Barbara Sinclair. How one conceptualizes and measures party influence are perhaps the leading questions on the congressional research agenda today.

Interestingly, the questions on today's agenda bear more than a passing resemblance to those of a half century ago. In 1951 Julius Turner published his ambitious roll-call study *Party and Constituency: Pressures on Congress,* "an attempt to evaluate the relative significance of party and constituency pressures on voting behavior in the U.S. House of Representatives over a period of four decades."[25] Turner interpreted his data to show a significant amount of party pressure but concluded that constituency pressures helped to explain differences in party loyalty among members of Congress from different types of districts. Importantly, he emphasized that party and constituency did not necessarily conflict, and he concluded, "when constituency pressure permits, the individual representative will vote party. When party and constituency conflict, choices must be made."[26]

Turner's point about the compatibility of constituency and party was neglected by some succeeding researchers who ran the proverbial "horse race" between a dummy variable for party and census measures of aggregate constituency characteristics, concluding that, after controlling for party, constituency characteristics typically had no independent impact. After some years Malcolm

Jewell, Aage Clausen, and others made an argument similar to the one Krehbiel made thirty years later—that correlations between legislative behavior and party membership did not provide much of a basis for inferring anything about the strength of party influence in relation to constituency.[27] Once that point was widely recognized, researchers developed new means of studying the importance of constituency, and they became more sensitive to the alternative possibilities inherent in the data.

Much the same thing appears to be happening today. Krehbiel's critique has stimulated researchers to innovate, in order to find new ways of demonstrating party effects on roll-call voting. Recent examples include articles by James Snyder and Tim Groseclose, Gregory Hager and Jeffery Talbert, and David Brady, Judith Goldstein, and Daniel Kessler.[28] Thus, the near-universal belief that "parties matter" now rests on a firmer footing than a decade ago, although there is plenty of room for further work on the subject.

But *how* do parties matter? This question seems to me to be confused in much of the debate provoked by Krehbiel. The debate is fraught with ambiguity and shifting definitions of party effects and party influence. Again, there is a parallel with Turner's analysis of fifty years ago. Turner's concept of party influence was expansive—to say the least:

> In the legislative process party influence is a compound of many ingredients. Direct pressure from the leadership is one of these, and the one most likely to be perceived; but pressures from constituents, legislative colleagues, interest groups, and even personal opinions—though less likely to be seen as partisan—often produce partisan patterns of cleavage. Party influence that is exerted through informal groups within the legislature or that arises out of 'the recruitment by parties of candidates with certain viewpoints and background characteristics' is less readily perceived but no less significant.[29]

Some of the confusion in the successor literature no doubt arose from Turner's willingness to consider anything that produced a partisan cleavage to be an instance of party "pressure," exactly the tendency that Krehbiel objected to some four decades later.

In the present debate the poles are party versus preference, not party versus constituency, but I think it would be valuable to bring constituency back into the picture. The notion of preference held by advocates of preference-based theories is that of "induced preference," also called "revealed" or "public" preference. We measure such preferences by observing member votes then conduct analyses to see whether party membership exerts any independent effect over and above preferences. The problem is that induced preferences are themselves an amalgam of personal ideology, constituency preferences, interest group pressures, and party pressures, an obvious point not yet fully appreciated even after nearly three decades of argument.[30]

If observed behavior, such as roll-call voting, shows a strong relationship with the party affiliation of the representative, at least three possible mechanisms may underlie the correlation. The first is pure selection. For example, if all candidates belonged to one of two types, liberals, who join the Democratic Party, or conservatives, who join the Republicans, then there would be a strong relationship between voting and party, but it would be epiphenomenal—party labels simply would be shorthand for the personal ideologies of the members. Some have interpreted this as Krehbiel's null hypothesis, although in fact his null hypothesis is agnostic about the source of the revealed preferences. This case also illustrates one of Krehbiel's "paradoxes," that parties appear strongest when there is the least need for strong parties—there would be perfect party unity even in the absence of any kind of party influence. It is likely that much of what we casually refer to as "party effects" are of this kind—Rohde and others of the party resurgence school, for example, see increasing homogenization of intraparty preferences as a precondition for increasing party strength.[31]

A second mechanism underlying a strong relationship between party and legislative behavior is party influence in the strict sense that the term *pressure* connotes. Party leaders within the Congress, the caucus, or perhaps the administration overtly attempt to influence members either by promising carrots such as committee assignments, district projects, support for pet bills, and consideration of specific amendments or by threatening sticks such as withholding the same sorts of prizes, or some mixture of the two. The literature contains examples of such behavior to be sure, but there are also examples that suggest its limitations. For example, at the height of Newt Gingrich's power in the 104th Congress, dissident junior Republicans on the Agriculture Committee torpedoed "Freedom to Farm," an important piece of party legislation. Gingrich threatened sanctions, but after an outcry he was forced to back down.[32] When most political scientists speak of party *influence* in Congress, they are thinking of party in this strong sense—the ability of party leaders to persuade or coerce members into behaving differently from the way they would behave in the absence of party pressure. Clearly there is a huge inferential leap from a correlation between party and behavior to the conclusion that active (or anticipated) party influence in this strong sense is the underlying cause. More detailed analyses that document the actions and effects of party leaders are necessary. An exemplar of such research is a recent article by Aldrich and Rohde in which—among other things—they explicitly link the activities of party leaders to changes in member behavior and the achievement of nonmedian outcomes in the House.[33]

There is yet a third path for parties to exert influence that has been largely ignored in the current discussion. That path lies in the electoral arena rather than in the institution. It has become increasingly clear that the classic median voter model of party competition is a poor description of the realities of congressional elections. At least since the work of Fenno we have understood that a congressional district—a legal entity—is seldom the undifferentiated mass that the spatial models assume. Rather, a district contains numerous constituencies, and Democrats and Republicans will build on different ones to form winning coalitions. Moreover, incumbents of different parties can be drawn even farther from the median by distinct primary constituencies. Numerous models rationalize the taking of such noncentrist positions by candidates.[34]

Thus, when moderate House Republicans announced that they would vote to impeach President Clinton in the winter of 1998, it was widely interpreted as party pressure, since most such incumbents had indicated that they personally favored censure rather than impeachment. The media clearly favored this interpretation, and certainly there was enough bluster within Congress to suggest that it was operating. But it is also very plausible, and consistent with my observations of a few of these members, that they were making a calculation of the following sort: "If I do not vote for impeachment, I will antagonize the hard-core partisans in my district. That certainly may hurt me in the primary, and even if I get by that, it will hurt me in the general election." If this sort of thinking is at work, the induced preference of the member can be a reflection of party-in-the-electorate.

Note that this third path is partly consistent with the arguments of the party skeptics on the one hand and the party resurgence theorists on the other, but it also is partly inconsistent with both sets of arguments. Krehbiel may be correct in doubting that party discipline is being exerted within the institution, and that, instead, members are voting their induced preferences. But if those preferences are induced by party in the district, then that is a kind of party effect, although not the one he has argued against. Similarly, Aldrich, Rohde, Sinclair, and others may be quite correct that parties matter, but the way in which they matter may not be as much through the institutional paths that their arguments often presume. Instead, the paths that produce party cleavages may lie primarily in the way candidates are recruited and elected in their districts.

The truth, of course, is probably somewhere in between, and that is a question that future research will resolve. My point is simply that this lively and important discussion of the role of the congressional parties could benefit from more explicit consideration of the concerns that animated the literature of the 1970s and 1980s — electoral concerns. I think it would be a valuable contribution if the party skeptics were to develop models that are more explicitly grounded in the electoral arena; beginning the exercise with induced preferences abstracts away too much that is of interest and importance. For their part, party resurgence theorists would do well to think harder about different paths of party influence, and to evaluate the state of the evidence consistent with each. Given the data, the statistical and modeling techniques, and the talent available to the subfield today, it would be disappointing if in 2050 someone were to note in the 22d edition of *Congress Reconsidered* that the field was hotly debating another version of a question that first arose more than fifty years earlier!

Congress at the Beginning of the Twenty-first Century

In the early 1970s the attitude of congressional scholars toward Congress was generally positive. My recollection is that these positive scholarly attitudes reflected an appreciation for the values that the legislative branch exemplified, particularly representation and responsiveness. Critics—and there were many outside the fraternity of congressional scholars—who valued efficiency and programmatic coherence more highly were viewed with some suspicion as narrow policy wonks or presidential loyalists who failed to appreciate the complexities of the democratic process in a large heterogeneous country. When it was really necessary Congress would behave responsibly and coherently. It was Congress, after all, that stepped in and stopped the abuses summarized by "Watergate" that were the inevitable accompaniment of the development of the imperial presidency.

To a younger generation coming along, however, there was somewhat less to admire. New problems such as rampant inflation and the energy crisis illustrated all too well the problems with the weak and outmoded organization of Congress, as well as the deeper problem—that unconstrained representation of the parts of this country left the whole of the nation inadequately represented. *Keystone* reflected my belief that distributive politics was out of hand, with consequences not sufficiently understood or appreciated.

Today I am much less concerned about distributive politics and its consequences. For one thing distributive politics has declined in importance. The subgovernments that fostered distributive politics were overrun and dismantled by scores of new interest groups opposed to their activities, not to mention journalists hungry for critical stories. In addition, the hostility of the administrations of Ronald Reagan and George Bush to traditional grant programs and to government regulation (along with twenty years of budget deficits that squeezed their funding) slowed the growth of government in these areas. Deficit politics brought its own set of problems, of course, but by their very nature these called for a more coordinated response by the national parties and national institutions. Compared with the Congresses of the pre-reform era, the Congresses of the post-reform era are more efficiently organized, and along with the nationalization of elections discussed earlier in this chapter, they have constrained distributive tendencies and increased the amount of collective responsibility that exists.

My concern today is less with a Washington Establishment dominated by Congress than a political class that is out of touch with and out of step with the mass of Americans. Many members of Congress are part of this class, but in the era of the permanent campaign they are joined by others—groups, activists, contributors—whom we used to lump together under the rubric of the congressional "environment." Today, the Congress is far less insulated, and the boundary between the environment and the institution has grown very fuzzy. Indeed, members today spend more time in and with the environment than they do in and with the institution.

The Washington Establishment of the 1970s permitted national problems to fester because of unwillingness to harm constituency interests, and indeed used such problems to advance constituency interests. The political class today allows national problems to fester because its members insist on having the entire loaf, not just a portion, because they would rather have an election issue than have incremental progress, and because parties that have only shallow roots in the population at large are increasingly dependent on specific constituencies whose interests are not shared by the general population. These are serious charges that I am developing more fully in another context. For now three related examples will suffice to illustrate the argument.

First, consider the abortion issue. The country has just witnessed a primary campaign in which Bill Bradley charged Al Gore with being insufficiently pro-life because years earlier as a Tennessee congressman, Gore had expressed the personal belief that a fetus was not merely a clump of tissue. On the other side, John McCain was attacked as pro-choice because he would permit abortion in the cases of rape, incest, and birth defects. Analysts of public opinion are well aware that about 80 percent of the population share the conditional views expressed by McCain and a younger Gore rather than the unconditional views of the "wing-nuts" of the two parties. Americans believe that this is a difficult issue, that rights collide, and that trade-offs are inevitable. Consequently, polls show that clear majorities are willing to live with various restrictions such as those permitted by the *Casey* decision in 1992.

The politics of the issue are another matter. The 20 percent who hold more extreme views than the mass of Americans dominate the debate within the parties. The volunteers and resources provided by the pro-choice and pro-life activists are especially important in the primaries, and their high activity levels make them important components of each party's base. But since both viewpoints are decidedly minority viewpoints, we have stalemate even though most Americans could agree to compromise and move on, and courts determine policies when the elected branches cannot act. Too much of contemporary politics is like this — defined by groups whose preferences and goals do not reflect those of the citizenry in general.

Second, consider issues like reform of social security and Medicare. In the present climate of budgetary surplus for the foreseeable future, it should be relatively easy to make some modest reforms and innovations to put these programs on a firmer footing for the next generation. I do not think that one must be overcome by nostalgia to imagine that Everett Dirksen, Mike Mansfield, John McCormack, and Gerald Ford would have found some common ground and acted. Many of today's leaders, however, would rather have issues to use in the upcoming election than accomplishments to point to. In some part it is their own reluctance to compromise, and in some part it is the extreme activists to whom they are responsible. But opportunities for progress are rejected rather than grasped.

Third, consider some of the constituency groups with which the parties are most closely associated, such as the teachers' unions for the Democrats and the religious right for the Republicans. As the parties have ceased to represent broad societal interests such as "the working man," and "the middle class," they have become increasingly dependent on smaller, intensely self-interested or self-righteous groups that many Americans view as detracting from the good of the nation. The state of the educational system in the urban areas threatens to destroy the traditional American ideal of success in life through merit and hard work, but today's Democratic Party is nearly helpless to propose anything that might seriously disrupt union control of public education. And, as mentioned above, its constituency groups make it difficult for today's Republican Party to strike reasonable compromises on contentious social issues, thus contributing to the harsh tone of contemporary politics and the public disaffection with it.

Examples of these problems abound in Congress, but Congress did not create them. It is the processes of political participation and nonparticipation, recruitment, fund-raising, and campaigning that created them. Today, as it did twenty-five years ago, Congress reflects what is going on in the larger electoral environment. Those concerned with the operation of Congress today and its contribution to American democracy in the twenty-first century should pay close attention to that environment.

Notes

1. Originally scheduled for the 1997 meeting of the Southern Political Science Association, the panel was cancelled when fog grounded the flights of several participants. Rescheduled for the 1999 meeting of the Midwest Political Science Association, the panel was organized and chaired by Lawrence Dodd and included David Brady, John Hibbing, and David Rohde. David Mayhew and Timothy Prinz also prepared comments for the cancelled 1997 panel. I am grateful to these scholars for their comments, many of which have informed this chapter. The editors of the present volume graciously invited me to expand on my remarks at the 1999 meeting for this 2000 edition of *Congress Reconsidered*—coincidentally first published in the same year as *Keystone*. Thanks also to Sam Abrams for excellent research assistance.
2. This chapter does not revisit topics and questions treated in the second (1989) edition. Written in the aftermath of two incumbency-dominated elections (1986, 1988), that discussion was more one of additions and refinements, which I will allow to stand as written. Changes evident in the 1990s are more consequential for the original argument and the literature in which it is embedded.
3. Donald Stokes and Warren Miller, "Party Government and the Saliency of Congress," *Public Opinion Quarterly* 26 (1962): 531–46; Raymond Bauer, Ithiel deSola Poole, and Lewis Dexter, *American Business and Public Policy* (New York: Atherton, 1968).
4. As in such classic works as Donald Matthews, *U.S. Senators and Their World* (Chapel Hill: University of North Carolina Press, 1960), and Richard Fenno, "The House Appropriations Committee as a Political System: The Problem of Integration, *American Political Science Review* 56 (1962): 310–24.
5. In 1989 or 1990 I circulated an e-mail to Harvard University graduate students indicating my intention to offer a seminar on divided government. One e-mailed back asking whether we'd be reading Mayhew's new manuscript. It was déjà vu all over again!
6. "Congressional Elections: The Case of the Vanishing Marginals," *Polity* 3 (1974): 295–317.
7. Nowadays many scholars tape interviews verbatim. Way back then, Fenno still advocated recording or transcribing one's recollection of the interview after conducting it. Being a novice at this sort of research I followed his advice, putting everything on tape that I could remember after the interview.
8. Recall that Sens. Birch Bayh, Fred Harris, Hubert Humphrey, and Henry Jackson, along with Rep. Morris Udall, all sought the presidency in 1976.

9. R. Douglas Arnold, "Overtilled and Undertilled Fields in American Politics," *Political Science Quarterly* 97 (1982): 91–103.

10. Bruce Cain, John Ferejohn, and Morris Fiorina, *The Personal Vote* (Cambridge: Harvard University Press, 1987).

11. "Epilogue: The Era of Incumbency and Insulation," in *Continuity and Change in House Elections,* ed. David Brady, John Cogan, and Morris Fiorina (Stanford, Calif.: Stanford University Press, in press).

12. Andrew Gelman and Gary King, "Estimating Incumbency Advantage without Bias," *American Journal of Political Science,* 34 (1990): 1142–64.

13. The equations control for incumbency and national tides. Essentially, they are Gelman-King equations augmented with the previous presidential vote in the district. The desirable qualities of the equations are unaffected by addition of this variable. For details see David Brady, Robert D'Onofrio, and Morris Fiorina, "The Nationalization of Electoral Forces Revisited," in Brady, Cogan, and Fiorina, *Continuity and Change in House Elections.*

14. One naturally wonders what these coefficients might have looked like before the arenas separated in the Eisenhower administration. Although we presume that the elections from the mid-1950s to 1970 are the exception, not the norm, we are currently compiling the presidential vote by district for whole county congressional districts, which should enable us to provide an approximate answer to the question.

15. Gary Jacobson, "Reversal of Fortune: The Transformation of U.S. House Elections in the 1990s," in Brady, Cogan, and Fiorina, *Continuity and Change in House Elections.*

16. Lawrence Dodd, "The Cycles of Legislative Change: Building a Dynamic Theory," in *Political Science: The Science of Politics,* ed. Herbert Weisberg (New York: Agathon Press, 1986), 82–104.

17. I was something of a broken record on this point. See, among other essays, Morris Fiorina, "The Decline of Collective Responsibility in American Politics," *Daedalus* 109 (1980): 25–45. Gary Jacobson also made this argument regularly in the concluding chapter of the successive editions of his textbook. See, for example, *The Politics of Congressional Elections* (New York: HarperCollins, 1992).

18. Gelman and King, "Estimating Incumbency Advantage without Bias," fig. 3; Steven Levitt and Catherine Wolfram, "Decomposing the Sources of Incumbency Advantage in the U.S. House," *Legislative Studies Quarterly* 22 (1997): fig. 1; John Alford and David Brady, "Personal and Partisan Advantage in U.S. Congressional Elections, 1846–1986, in *Congress Reconsidered,* ed. Lawrence Dodd and Bruce Oppenheimer, 4th ed. (Washington, DC: CQ Press, 1989), fig. 6-3.

19. There are various references to money in the context of political corruption and local payoffs. One of those interviewed in District B began serving a prison sentence a few months after we spoke.

20. My recollection is that Tip O'Neill was the first congressional leader to be the subject of an attack ad, by the Reagan campaign in 1984.

21. Quoted in Carla Marinucci, "GOP to Play Musical Chairs over Abortion," *San Francisco Chronicle,* May 15, 2000, A1.

22. James Sundquist, *The Decline and Resurgence of Congress* (Washington, D.C.: Brookings Institution, 1981), 371; Burdett Loomis, *The New American Politician* (New York: Basic Books, 1988).

23. David Mayhew, *Congress: The Electoral Connection* (New Haven: Yale University Press, 1974), 27.

24. Keith Krehbiel, "Where's the Party?" *British Journal of Political Science* 23 (1993): 235–66; Krehbiel, "Paradoxes of Parties in Congress," *Legislative Studies Quarterly* 24 (1999): 31–64; Krehbiel, "Party Discipline and Measures of Partisanship," *American Journal of Political Science* 44 (2000): 212–27.

25. Julius Turner, *Party and Constituency: Pressures on Congress,* (Baltimore: Johns Hopkins University Press, 1951), 1. Most scholars today are familiar with Edward Schneier's revised edition, published by Hopkins in 1970.

26. Turner and Schneier, *Party and Constituency: Pressures on Congress,* rev. ed., 237.

27. For quotations and citations see my *Representatives, Roll Calls, and Constituencies* (Lexington, Mass.: D. C. Heath, 1974), chap. 1. In a close parallel to Krehbiel's work a generation later, one analysis in this period showed that a simple formal model based entirely on constituency preferences could generate the statistical finding of party dominance typically found in the literature. See my "Constituency Influence: A Generalized Model and Its Implications for Statistical Studies of Roll-Call Behavior," *Political Methodology* 2 (1975): 249–66.

28. James Snyder and Tim Groseclose, "Estimating Party Influence in Congressional Roll-Call Voting," *American Journal of Political Science* 44 (2000): 193–211; Gregory Hager and Jeffery Talbert, "Look for the Party Label: Party Influences on Voting in the U.S. House," *Legislative Studies Quarterly* 25 (2000): 75–99; David Brady, Judith Goldstein, and Daniel Kessler, "Does Party Matter in Senators' Voting Behavior: An Historical Test Using Tariff Votes over Three Institutional Periods" (forthcoming).

29. Turner and Schneier, *Party and Constituency: Pressures on Congress,* rev. ed., 1–2.

30. The most complete statement of the argument is by John Jackson and John Kingdon, "Ideology, Interest Groups Scores, and Legislative Votes, *American Journal of Political Science* 36 (1992): 805–23.

31. David Rohde, *Parties and Leaders in the Post-Reform House* (Chicago: University of Chicago Press), esp. chap. 3.

32. David Hosansky, "House Torn on Agriculture: Senate Makes Progress," *Congressional Quarterly Weekly Report,* September 30, 1995, 2980–84.

33. John Aldrich and David Rohde, "The Consequences of Party Organization in the House: The Role of the Majority and Minority Parties in Conditional Party Government," in *Polarized Politics,* ed. Jon Bond and Richard Fleisher (Washington, D.C.: CQ Press, 2000), 31–72.

34. Morris Fiorina, "Whatever Happened to the Median Voter?" (paper presented at the annual meeting of the Midwest Political Science Association, Chicago, April 1999).

Part III
Committee Politics and Institutional Change

8. The Evolution of the
Committee System in Congress

David T. Canon and Charles Stewart III

The earliest sessions of the Federal Congress were extraordinary, both for the historian and the social scientist. Students of history are well aware of the challenges that faced the fledgling nation as it cast around for a set of stable governing institutions. The work of the Constitutional Convention of 1787 was incomplete: there remained a national judiciary to be created and a set of individual liberties to be further delineated. The fragile union also faced monumental policy issues. How would revenues be raised? How would the economy be organized, and with what assistance from the central government? How would the new nation, surrounded by ambitious European colonial powers on land and sea, defend its borders and develop a coherent foreign policy? Even more mundane questions, such as the location of the nation's capital, generated great political heat.

The resolution of these constitutional and policy questions was left to the newly established Federal Congress. Legislative assemblies were well-known to Americans by 1789, so the early organization of Congress was not undertaken entirely *de novo*. Still, a *popular* assembly such as the House, encompassing such a diversity of interests, was unprecedented, and the role of the Senate was not yet defined. Even less certain was *how* these new institutions were to conduct their business. Hence, to the earliest occupants of legislative office came the daunting task of creating the legislative institutions necessary to do the work of a young nation, with only a few patterns to follow. The political challenges did not get any easier in the next several decades, with debates over westward expansion and slavery, and ultimately a bloody civil war. The goal of this chapter is to show how congressional committees very quickly emerged as the primary legislative institutions for debating and establishing the nation's policies.

The early Federal period has long fascinated students of American history. It has held less fascination for modern political scientists, however. Most recent work has focused on the structure of policy divisions and the rise of the earliest glimmerings of political parties.[1] The *organization* of the earliest Congresses has been attended to only occasionally, with Joseph Cooper's study of the early House committee system still the standard in the field after three decades and

George Lee Robinson's research on Senate committees retaining that status after nearly a half-century.[2]

Modern advances in the theories of legislative organization provide a new opportunity to reconsider the early organizational structure of Congress. The reason is simple. Theoretical advances in political science that have constituted the neo-institutional approach to Congress have concerned the optimal organization of legislatures, conditional on the goals of legislators. The stylized facts and theoretical insights that have emerged from this line of work have mostly focused on the "textbook Congress" period of the mid twentieth century.[3] This textbook Congress changes only incrementally, and even the most expansive of reforms are guided by a general understanding of how legislatures work in the United States gained from centuries of practical experience.

The earliest members of Congress did not have this wealth of experience. Although they did not function in the state of nature, they stood about as close as a nation can to unfettered institutional design. That should make this earlier period ripe for study by modern social scientists armed with several decades of statistical and theoretical training. What has stood in the way (other than the general American aversion to history) has been a paucity of good data with which to study early congressional organization systematically. Data about modern Congresses are richer than data about historical Congresses. Still, barriers to the study of the historical Congress have begun to fall as data become available, facilitating new, systematic study of early congressional organization.

This chapter rests on new data, drawn from study of the early organization of House and Senate committees. We sketch a portrait of the committee system during the first ninety years of the republic, reporting basic contours such as the number and timing of committee appointments, the life span of committees, member specialization on select committees, and the establishment of standing committees as the center of legislative activity. The findings in this chapter challenge some of the conventional wisdom about these early committees, although the chapter at times illustrates the lasting endurance of other aspects of that wisdom. Party advantage was evident in the early history of House and Senate committees, despite the disdain with which parties were held by many of the Founders.[4] Select committees played an important role in the early history of Congress, despite the Jeffersonian preference that policymaking authority reside in the full chamber.

We also correct the common view of the early institutional Senate as a sleepy, personality-driven chamber uninterested in policymaking or legislating. This characterization of the upper chamber simply does not bear up to careful scrutiny. True, the Senate was slower than the House in establishing a complex internal organization, being content with following the House's lead at the beginning. But even before George Washington had finished his second term, the Senate committee system had become as complex as that of the House. The Senate was also slower to begin accumulating standing committees, but once it did, it did so with a flourish. Even though the chamber was cut off from direct electoral contact with voters, partisanship infected the committee system of the Senate, as well as that of the House, very early.

The remainder of this chapter is organized as follows. The first section reviews the important literature in the field, surveying general questions of committee organization inherited from historical research. The second section outlines the propositions we will test in this chapter. The third section introduces the data used in this chapter: information on House and Senate committee appointments made during the first forty-five Congresses (1789–1879).[5] In the fourth section we turn our attention to several specific propositions about the early committee system, and in the final section we offer some conclusions.

Conventional Wisdom on the Evolution of the Congressional Committee System

The classic works on the operation of the first Congresses portray an institution struggling to find its legs.[6] The simplest tasks, such as deciding how to handle a petition from a constituent, had no routinized procedures or consistent precedents to facilitate their dispensation. Should such a petition be handled by the entire chamber (or the Committee of the Whole), or referred to the relevant cabinet secretary, or to some subset of the House or Senate? If the latter, should the committee be relatively permanent and have the power to handle similar problems that arose later in the term (a standing committee), or have relatively limited powers and be terminated after dealing with the discrete issue (a select committee), or something in between (what often is referred to as a "semi-standing" committee)? The answers to these questions evolved over the first twenty Congresses. The task of legislative scholars has been to describe and explain the contours of that evolution.

Prior Research on the Early House Committee System

The institutional position of committees evolved through three distinct phases in the first forty years of our nation's history: the early years of institutional flux in the first six Congresses (1789–1801, with Treasury Secretary Alexander Hamilton at the center of most key debates), the Jeffersonian period (the Seventh–Eleventh Congresses, 1801–1811), and the Clay era (the Twelfth–Twentieth Congresses, 1811–1829). Since the Twenty-first Congress (or a bit earlier according to some authors), standing committees have occupied a central place in the legislative process in the House.

The first six Congresses were dominated by the Federalists. Even when the Republicans controlled a majority of the seats in the Fourth Congress (1795–1797), they were too disorganized to advance their own legislative agenda.[7] The defining feature of these early, formative years, according to the conventional wisdom, was a legislative process dominated by the executive branch, primarily by Hamilton. Political scientist Ralph V. Harlow quotes the diaries of

Senator William Maclay, R-Pa., who observed, "It really seems as if a listlessness or spirit of laziness pervaded the House of Representatives. Anything which comes from a Secretary is adopted almost without any examination. . . . Mr. Hamilton is all-powerful and fails at nothing he attempts. . . . Everything, even to the naming of a committee, is prearranged by Hamilton and his group of speculators."[8] Harlow also notes that Hamilton actually attended some committee meetings "to guard against the danger of a slip at any stage."[9]

Despite the Federalists' domination of the legislative process, Jeffersonian principles, Cooper argues, guided the first twenty years of committee formation. Jeffersonians, in accordance with the general principles of strict democracy, equality, and accountability, viewed committees with suspicion.[10] According to Jeffersonian principles, committees did not have the power to report a bill unless that power was explicitly granted; committee members should be favorably disposed to the principles established in the Committee of the Whole; and membership on important committees should be broadly representative, in that membership of important committees should have representation from each region, or in the extreme case from each state. The Federalists did not share these views. However, they did not attempt to establish a strong committee system in these early years, because they saw the executive branch as the more appropriate vehicle for promoting a policy agenda. Thus Jeffersonian principles, the common wisdom holds, dominated the committee system of the first ten Congresses.

According to Cooper, Jeffersonian thinking about congressional committees started to lose its hold in the Eleventh Congress (1809–1811). Gamm and Shepsle point to the Twelfth Congress as the period when standing committees ascended at the expense of the Committee of the Whole and the select committees. House Speaker Henry Clay, in his effort to secure support for war with Britain, stacked the semi-standing committees with War Hawks and for the first time insulated key committee appointments from presidential influence.[11] As part of this evolution, more standing committees were appointed, more powers were granted, and more legislation flowed through the standing committees. By 1815 all standing committees and select committees appointed to review the president's annual message to Congress were granted the power to present their reports in the form of bills. Previously committees could not report a bill unless explicitly granted the power to do so by the Committee of the Whole. In the Seventeenth Congress (1821–1823) four important standing committees were appointed, and by the Eighteenth Congress (1823–1825) 89 percent of all legislation was referred to standing committees, compared to only 47 percent a decade before.[12] The system of standing committees emerged very quickly from the Jeffersonian system that preceded it.

Prior Research on the Early Senate Committee System

The Senate committee system should be considered within the context of the principles that motivated the creation of the Senate during the founding period: equal representation of the states, insulation from the public, and an elitism that would balance the rough and populist House. James Madison forcefully states the case for the check provided by the Senate in *Federalist Paper* no. 62: "The necessity of a senate is not less indicated by the propensity of all single and numerous assemblies to yield to the impulse of sudden and violent passions, and to be seduced by factious leaders into intemperate and pernicious resolutions."[13]

On the other hand, Anti-Federalists were concerned that the Senate would be *too* removed from the people. Elbridge Gerry said, "A Senate chosen for six years will, in most instances, be an appointment for life, as the influence of such a body over the minds of the people will be coequal to the extensive powers with which they are vested, and they will not only forget, but be forgotten by their constituents—a branch of the Supreme Legislature thus set beyond all responsibility is totally repugnant to every principle of a free government."[14] Both views contain political hyperbole. The House was not filled with rabble-rousers, nor was the Senate completely removed from the people.

Within this general context, several issues emerged that influenced the evolution of the committee system in the Senate: the role of states and sectional interests; relations between the House and the Senate; the development of legislative expertise through specialization on committees; individualism; and political parties.

One major issue did not have much impact on the Senate committee system—the equal representation of states. As a practical matter, it was impossible to provide equal representation of states on committees, because half of the Senate would thus have to serve on each committee. Most of the early select and standing committees had three or five members, but one committee in the first Congress, the select committee on Salaries for the President and Vice President, had senators from each of the eleven states which had elected senators. When standing committees were established in the Senate in 1816, other considerations such as the abilities and previous experience of the senator, sectionalism, and party were more important than state equality.[15]

The institutional design of the Framers provided for enormous differences between the House and the Senate. Political scientist Lauros McConachie argued that "the House was made to stand for organization, the Senate for individualism; the House for nationality, the Senate for historic Statehood; the House for the American's coming emancipation from physical environment, the Senate for the lingering necessities imposed thereby."[16] Despite these differences, the development of the committee system in the House and Senate progressed on very similar tracks, with both chambers conducting most business in select committees and on the floor and moving quickly, with the House leading the way, to standing committees as the workhorses of the institution. Though he does not fully develop this point, McConachie provides a possible explanation for the parallel development of committees in the House and Senate: the career path that led from the House to the Senate. "Though few men have gone as members from the upper to the lower body, a continuous procession of legislators, educated under the strict and intricate government of the House and importing its ideas of procedure, has entered the Senate's doors."[17]

Specialization on committees, as it allowed for the development of policy expertise, is consistent both with the Founders' vision of an elite institution made up of refined and erudite leaders and with modern theories concerning the informational advantages the committee system provides.[18] Before standing committees were established, it was more difficult for members to specialize, because there were literally hundreds of select committees in a given Congress. However, some senators did specialize. William Maclay, Anti-Admin.–Pa., served on many private claims committees, Robert Morris, Pro-Admin.–Pa., on commerce and shipping committees, Oliver Ellsworth, Pro-Admin.–Conn., on committees considering judicial matters, and Morris, Ellsworth, Rufus King, Pro-Admin.–N.Y., and George Cabot, Pro-Admin.–Mass., on foreign affairs committees.[19] George Haynes points out that five powerful Federalists served on all the select committees concerning treaties and concludes, "Thus, long before there was any standing Committee on Foreign Relations, this small group was accorded almost as much concentration and continuity of responsibility as in later years gave to the committee of that name dominance in the Senate."[20]

Elaine Swift provides evidence that there were "committee leaders" who served on a disproportionate share of select committees (four to five times as many, on average, as the "rank and file" members), but she sees this evidence as undermining the notion of specialization, because of the number of committees on which the early leaders served.[21] However, when one examines the *types* of committees on which they served, patterns of specialization are evident, especially among some of the committee leaders. Although specialization was by no means a universal norm, early distinctions can be made between "work horses" and "show horses."

One important indication that specialization on Senate select committees occurred was the emergence of "semi-standing" select committees, consistent with the practice described above for the House. Rule 14, which allowed this practice, was adopted in the Senate on March 26, 1806. Robinson cites this occasion as "marking the first step in a tortoise-like advancement of the Senate toward a system of standing committees, for one of the first requirements of a standing committee is that it have control of a definite division of the labor of the parent body."[22] The tendency toward specialization and the creation of semi-standing select committees runs counter to another aspect of the conventional wisdom concerning the early committee system in the Senate: that select committees were "technical aids to the chamber" or the "fingers of the Senate."[23]

The modern literature emphasizes the Senate's individualism, especially in comparison to the majoritarian nature of the House.[24] Although these tendencies sometimes are exaggerated, there is no doubt that the Senate's individualism contributed to its slow institutional development in comparison to the House. Even when the Senate embraced standing committees, McConachie claims, the individual senator was still "the real legislative unit."[25] McConachie further argued that the "individual or a minority can absolutely overawe the committee" through use of unlimited debate and amendments.[26]

Testable Propositions on the Evolution of the Committee System

This brief review of the historical literature reveals fertile ground for systematic examination of important questions about the evolution of the committee system. We suggest several testable propositions: the *state representation hypothesis*, the *distributive hypothesis*, and the *"fingers of the chamber"* hypothesis. The first hypothesis only applies to the House, and we will also only test the distributive hypothesis for the House, because the House is the chamber that was expected to be closer to the people. We will test the "fingers of the chamber" hypothesis for both the House and the Senate.

The state representation hypothesis: Small states were overrepresented on committees in comparison to larger states, due to the principle of state representation, whereby every state was represented on important committees. Equal representation of states on all committees will be pursued as much as possible.[27]

This hypothesis is derived from the Jeffersonian principle of strict democracy.[28] Recognizing the impossibility of dealing with all matters in the Committee of the Whole, Jeffersonians were forced to embrace select and standing committees. The principle of state representation offered some consolation to Jeffersonians, who believed it was the best method for ensuring equal representation and reproducing miniature committees of the whole. This principle was impossible to enforce in its absolute form; from the very first Congress it was evident that committees representing every state would be almost as unwieldy as the Committee of the Whole. However, the principle manifested itself in other important ways, such as in trying to achieve regional balance, and continues to do so today.[29]

The distributive hypothesis: Select committees on private claims were made up of members favorably biased toward the claim. This bias was manifested in the disproportionate representation of members from the claimant's state and region.

As noted above, Jeffersonian principles held that *all* committees should be composed of members who were favorably predisposed to principles established by the Committee of the Whole. This sentiment is most clearly stated in the famous "nursemaid" quote from *Jefferson's Manual,* Section XXVI:

> Those who take exceptions to some particulars in the bill are to be of the committee, but none who speak directly against the body of the bill; for he that would totally destroy will not amend it; or as it is said, the child is not to be put to a nurse that cares not for it. It is therefore a constant rule "that no man is to be employed in any matter who has declared himself against it." And when any member who is against the bill hears himself named of its committee he ought to ask to be excused.

This principle quickly became obsolete as parties solidified their hold on Congress. However, the strong norm of assigning people to select committees who were favorably predisposed to the petition or claim before the committee survived well into the partisan era. McConachie notes, "It was early discerned that a private claim against government also stood much better chances if it could escape to a select committee from the regular standing committee, which was overburdened, and which had rules of decision rather sifting in their nature."[30] This bias toward stacking the claims committees reveals a penchant for credit claiming and delivering the pork that is often not attributed to the early Congresses.[31]

The "fingers of the chamber" hypothesis: Select committees in the first twelve Congresses exerted no independent influence on the legislative process. Rather, they were simply "fingers of the chamber" (House or Senate), carrying out the commands of the Committee of the Whole.

The "fingers of the chamber" hypothesis is perhaps the most firmly established of all the hypotheses concerning the early congressional committees, and it is the one that is most clearly attached to Jeffersonian principles. As noted above, Jeffersonians saw committees as a "positive evil, chiefly because they were not authorized by the Constitution."[32]

When the Republicans gained power in the Seventh Congress (1801–1803), they began to see committees as a viable alternative to the executive-dominated Federalist politics that they deeply abhorred. Even then, they kept committees on a relatively short leash. Harlow argues that all committees in the early years were "simply fingers of the House, and nothing more, convenient organs for putting business in shape for consideration by the committee of the whole. . . . [T]he only part played by committees was to assist the House in getting ready for actual work. . . . The House established the principles, while the committees worked out the details, acting only under specific orders in each instance."[33] McConachie also notes that powers of committees were severely restricted well into the 1820s.[34]

All three of these hypotheses are supported in the current literature by anecdotes and analysis of the historical documents, such as the congressional debates and personal papers of members of Congress. There have been no systematic tests of these central ideas based on the complete record of the evolution of the committee system in the first forty-five Congresses. Before turning to the tests of these hypotheses, we will briefly discuss the nature of the data set and provide an overview of the evolution of the committee system in Congress, from a system that relied almost exclusively on bill-specific select committees to a system of standing committees that in many ways resembles today's Congress.

The Contours of the Committee System

The data in this chapter were drawn from the House and Senate *Journal*, supplemented by the various compilations of congressional debates that were published during these Congresses (*Annals of Congress*, *Congressional Globe*, and *Congressional Record*). For much of this exercise it was necessary to read page by page through the *Journals*, since the indexing was often so poor and incomplete. The payoff to this strategy is evident in the number of select committees we were able to discover. Although Stubbs found only 1 select committee in the Senate before the Fourteenth Congress, we found 2,252.[35] We found 2,122 select committees over this same period in the House, although Stubbs recorded only a few hundred. The data set attempts, as closely as humanly possible, to record the comings and goings of all committee members — not only those appointed at the beginning of a Congress but those appointed during the course of a Congress as well. The result is the documentation of 12,443 standing and 9,838 select committee assignments in the Senate and 14,939 standing and 15,193 select committee assignments in the House from 1789 to 1879.

As noted above, the House established standing committees before the Senate. The House had five standing committees by 1795 and nine by 1808, but the Senate did not establish its first (minor) standing committee until 1807. Still, most of the House and Senate's business flowed through select committees until 1816. The Senate caught up in a hurry at the start of the second session of the Fourteenth Congress, when it created twelve standing committees in place of the customary select committees that were used to review elements of the president's annual message. Despite its slow start, the Senate beat the House by a decade in formally switching over to a standing committee system.

In the appendix to this chapter we report when each House and Senate standing committee in the first forty-five Congresses was created. As that accounting shows, some standing committees were preceded by regularly appointed select committees. These select committees can be considered "semi-standing" committees in those Congresses. Both the House and Senate had semi-standing committees in the early 1800s, but the practice was less common in the Senate.

Congress did not just consider the weighty matters of war and peace — there were claims to be adjudged, public lands to be surveyed, territories to be organized and admitted as states, and revenues to be raised and spent. The need to attend to these more mundane activities was the provenance of select committees before the Fourteenth Congress. Hundreds of select committees were appointed during each Congress. Figure 8-1 shows the number of select committees appointed during each Congress through the Forty-fifth (from 1789 to 1879). The Senate and House patterns share some similarities but differ in important respects. Both chambers relied heavily on select committees until they adopted standing committees in the 1810s and 1820s. In the Senate the number of select committees marched ever upward until the Fourteenth Congress, peaking at 250 select committees, while the number of House select committees trended downward during the earliest period (after hitting a peak of 261 in the Third Congress). The first drop in the number of House select committees was in the Fourth Congress, coinciding with the creation of four standing committees, most importantly the Claims Committee. The second drop occurred during the 1810s and may have reflected Henry Clay's desire to redirect business away from select committees toward the standing committees following the War of

Figure 8-1   House and Senate Select Committees Appointed Each
Congress, 1st–45th Congresses (1789–1879)

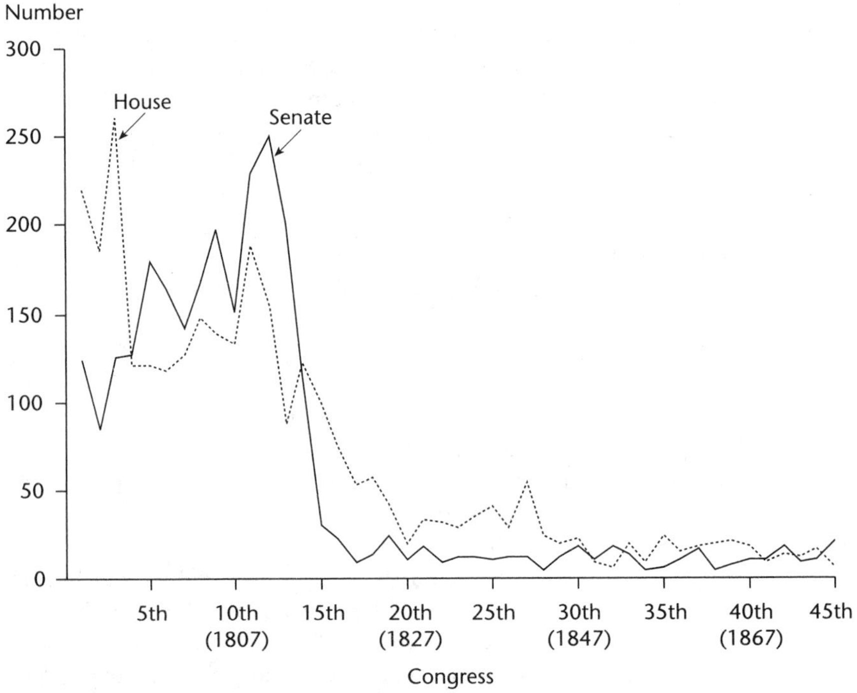

Source: Compiled by the authors.

1812.[36] The House's more gradual phasing out of select committees corresponds
with its slower transition to standing committees, which did not end until the
Twenty-third Congress (1823–1825). In the Senate, the sudden creation of a
standing committee system brought the number of select committees crashing to
the ground in the Fourteenth and Fifteenth Congresses. From that point on, the
number in the Senate never rose above twenty-nine again and was more typically in the eight-to-twelve range. The number of select committees in the
House did not fall to the low levels of the Senate until the Thirty-first Congress
(1849–1851), and even then the number in the House hovered at a slightly higher level than in the Senate for most of the nineteenth century.

   This comparison of the pace with which the Senate and House evolved
from a select to standing committee system is simply descriptive. The explanation for the difference remains an historical puzzle. These data illustrate this puzzle quite clearly, however: the Senate, supposedly the less hierarchical and internally differentiated of the two chambers, abandoned its reliance on ad hoc select
committees earlier and more quickly than the House.

The description of the evolution from select to standing committees will not be complete without a consideration of the semi-standing committees, which represent a hybrid between standing and select committees. Rather than being terminated after considering the specific business before them, these variants of select committees were often reappointed to consider new (but related) pieces of business. This was not the dominant practice in the House or Senate before the Fourteenth Congress. True, some select committees saw repeat business, but this was the exception. In the Senate the greatest number of duplicate select committees occurred in the Ninth Congress (1805–1807), when 73 duplicates were appointed in addition to 124 one-shot select committees. Yet the Ninth Congress was an anomaly. Most other Congresses before the Fourteenth saw only about 15 percent of their select committees reappointed later on to consider more legislation. In the House about 5 percent of select committees were this hybrid type. On the whole, select committee memberships churned pretty thoroughly before the Fourteenth Congress. The most important contribution that semi-standing committees made to the evolution of the congressional committee system was their role as precursors to the standing committees.

Another crucial aspect of the early evolution of the committee system was the change in the relationship between the committees and the floor. The early legislative theories that guided the organizational development of the Senate and House had a narrow vision about the propriety of relying on committees to do the work of legislatures. Committees were not appointed with expansive mandates but were charged with the rather narrow task of drafting legislation whose principles were already agreed on. Our data allow us to test this observation systematically, since we know which committees were appointed to consider broad topics (often prompted by constituent petitions) and which were appointed to draft (or otherwise review) a particular bill and report back to the floor. Furthermore, we can document the degree to which the legislative agenda of the Senate was driven by the House's workload, since many Senate select committees were created to consider legislation passed by the House.

Statistics about how often committees were appointed to consider specific bills (rather than general subject areas) are summarized in Figure 8-2. The solid line reports the percentage of Senate select committees created in reference to a specific bill, whether it be initiated in the Senate or House. For almost the entire period leading up to the Fourteenth Congress (1815–1817), the lion's share of Senate select committees were created for this purpose. The dotted line in Figure 8-2 reports the percentage of Senate select committees created to consider *House-passed* bills. In the first two Congresses — when the Senate was supposedly dependent on the House to take the lead in legislating — most of the bill-specific Senate select committees attended to legislation initiated in the Senate. Then, for roughly the entire decade of the 1790s, most Senate select committees considered and reported back House bills. As tensions with Great Britain rose, the fraction of work spent by Senate select committees on specific legislation (wherever initiated) declined. The dashed line represents the percentage of

Figure 8-2   Senate and House Select Committees Created to Consider a
Specific Bill, 1st–14th Congresses (in percentages)

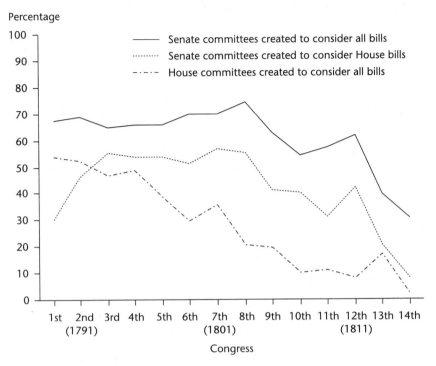

Source: Compiled by the authors.

House committees created to consider specific bills. The proportion of such
select committees in the House is substantially lower than in the Senate throughout these early Congresses. Said another way, select committees in the Senate
were wedded to particular pieces of legislation for a much longer time than in the
House, which was quicker in granting its select committees greater latitude in
considering legislation.

   To this point we have not said anything about the subjects that the select
committees were appointed to consider. In research elsewhere reported, we have
classified each select committee appointed in the House and Senate through the
Twentieth Congress according to the subject matter of legislation referred to it,
using subject names that closely corresponded to the names of standing committees that were eventually appointed.[37] The legislative business of the select committees contained a regular diet of claims, judicial business, taxing, and spending
matters. The Louisiana Purchase and the expansion of the western frontier produced a surge of committees pertaining to the public lands—committees both to
consider the distribution of federally owned lands and to organize the West into

territories. The earliest days of Congress saw a flurry of activity concerning the organization of Congress and the executive branch. After the Second Congress this sort of business never disappeared entirely, but it did significantly abate. Finally, the great surge in the total number of select committees in the Senate coincided with the Congresses immediately before and during the War of 1812. The war led not only to an explosion in the number of select committees devoted to naval and military affairs (especially in the years preceding the war) but also to an increase in the number of committees investigating commercial relations and claims.

Once the Senate switched to a committee system that was dominated by standing committees, the remaining mix of *select* committees changed significantly, because it was rare for a select committee to be appointed when there was already a standing committee that sufficed. On this score, the Senate appears to have taken the jurisdictional boundaries of its select committees more seriously than did the House. House members were often willing—even eager—to circumvent standing committees once they were established.[38] In the Senate the primary use of select committees after the rise of standing committees was to consider internal matters, governmental organization, roads, and public lands.

Further insight into the evolution of the committee system in Congress can be gained by examining it from the perspective of individual senators and representatives.

Members of Congress did not make careers out of congressional service in the nineteenth century as they have done in the twentieth. One of the trappings of twentieth century careerism has been the development of stable membership cores within committees—from Congress to Congress, committee rosters simply do not change much. For instance, at the beginning of the 105th Congress (1997), 62 percent of House and 72 percent of Senate committee assignments were unchanged from the end of the 104th Congress. Among returning members of Congress, this stability was even higher: 73 percent of returning House members kept their committee assignments, as did 80 percent of returning senators. How stable were committee rosters in the period we are interested in?

One hint that turnover should have been higher in the nineteenth century can be found in one of the chambers' rules: committee appointments expired at the end of each session. This did not change until the Forty-fifth Congress in the Senate and the Thirty-fifth in the House. On top of turnover because of electoral change between Congresses, the opportunity the chambers were given to remake their committees once or twice a Congress led to considerable churning among the committee membership.

Leaving aside intra-Congress committee turnover—which could be as high as 20 percent following a session break—inter-Congress turnover in committee membership in the nineteenth century was considerable. Figure 8-3 documents raw standing committee membership turnover at the beginning of each

Figure 8-3   Raw Membership Turnover in House and Senate Standing
               Committee Assignments, 1st–45th Congresses

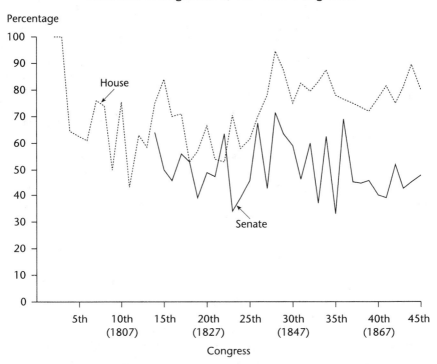

Source: Compiled by the authors.

Note: Figures represent raw membership turnover, uncorrected for electoral turnover.

Congress up to 1879. Throughout the century, the fraction of Senate standing
committee assignments that were new at the beginning of each Congress fluctu-
ated around 50 percent. In the House, turnover was considerably higher — about
65 percent of committee appointments were new assignments before the 1830s,
and around 80 percent thereafter.

Of course, some of the committee turnover was due to *chamber* turnover —
in the nineteenth century only an average of 72 percent of senators and 44 percent of representatives even returned from one Congress to the next. Thus, Figure 8-4 shows committee assignment turnover after we have removed members
who did not return from the previous Congress. Here, we see largely the same
story as before, only with lower turnover levels. Among returning senators,
roughly one-third received new committee assignments each Congress. The net
House turnover pattern changed significantly in the 1830s, rising from about 50
percent each Congress to around 70 percent.

Figure 8-4   Net Membership Turnover in House and Senate Standing
                 Committee Assignments, 1st–45th Congresses

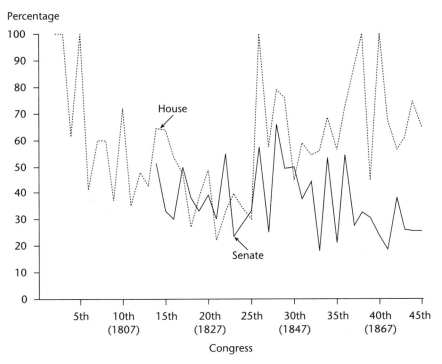

Source: Compiled by the authors.

Note: Figures represent net membership turnover and do not reflect turnover caused by electoral change.

Four Analytical Themes in
Congressional Committee Development

In this section we return to the hypotheses that we presented in the previous section: the state representation, distributive, and "fingers of the chamber" hypotheses.

The State Representation Hypothesis

The state representation hypothesis holds that committee assignments should be distributed as equally as possible among the states, irrespective of each state's population. (As noted above, given that the Senate treats states in this fashion by institutional design, this hypothesis will only be tested for the House.)[39] With appointments being thus distributed in the House, we should observe two

Table 8-1   House Committees Appointed with More Than One Member
from a Single State, 1st–45th Congresses, 1789–1879

	Congress (Years)					
	1st–6th (1789–1801)	7th–11th (1801–11)	12th–20th (1811–29)	21st–35th (1829–59)	36th–45th (1859–79)	Total (1st–45th)
Standing Committees	4.4% (45)	4.8% (84)	29.2% (343)	44.2% (978)	35.6% (447)	36.7% (1,897)
Select Committees	12.2% (981)	7.3% (715)	39.6% (675)	23.9% (360)	20.0% (115)	19.2% (2,886)

Source: Compiled by the authors.

Note: The unit of observation is the separate appointment of each committee. During this period committees were appointed for a single session only.

things. First, a single state should rarely have had more than one member on any committee. Second, members from small states should, on average, have served on more committees than members of the House from large states.

Table 8-1 reports how often a single state had more than one member appointed to any committee. From the First to Forty-fifth Congresses, 1,897 separate standing committees were appointed. In only 36.7 percent of these cases, at least one state had more than one member on the committee. Alone, this would hardly confirm the state representation hypothesis. However, in the first eleven Congresses, when the Jeffersonian impulse is supposed to have been strong, less than 5 percent of standing committees had multiple state representation. Yet from the Clay years forward multiple representation by a single state on committees was common. The same general pattern holds for select committees.[40]

The Distributive Hypothesis

The distributive hypothesis refers to the reputed practice of stacking select committees that handled local petitions and claims with sympathetic representatives. To test this claim, we identified all the House select committees in the first thirty-five Congresses in which the claimant was clearly from a given state (n = 596). Determining whether the committees were stacked in favor of the claim could be done by matching the claimant's state with the states of the committee members, assuming that a member from the claimant's state or region was more likely to be sympathetic to the claim.

The simple descriptive data provide strong evidence for the distributive hypothesis. Of the 596 committees, 18.8 percent had chairs from the same state as the claimant, whereas only 10 percent would have been expected by chance (difference significant at .001; t = 3.42); an additional 50.8 percent were from the same region (defined as any state that shared a border with the claimant's state). Thus nearly 70 percent of the claims committee chairs identified here were from the same state or region as the claimant. When all committee members are considered (rather than just chairs), 44.6 percent were from the same state or region.

The average committee had 1.1 members from the claimant's state, whereas .35 members would have been expected by chance (difference significant at the .00001 level; t = 17.5).[41]

The "Fingers of the Chamber" Hypothesis

The hypothesis that select committees were "fingers of the chamber," or tightly controlled agents of the chamber, is the most difficult aspect of the conventional wisdom to test. This hypothesis holds that select committees were on a short leash, acting simply as the agents of the floor majority. Standing committees, with fixed jurisdictions and greater latitude about whether and when to report back, had greater autonomy. The ideal test of this hypothesis would include data on the preferences of the Committee of the Whole, the mandate given to the committee, the preferences of the members of the committee, and an accurate measure of the relative position of the final outcome. The task is analogous to the attempts by Keith Krehbiel and others to test the "preference outlier hypothesis" in the modern context.[42] To what extent were committees agents of the entire body, and to what extent were they independent actors? The strategies used to test the outlier hypothesis in modern times are either not readily available for the early Congresses or are inappropriate. Using general measures of ideology would not allow one to make inferences about the positions of many committee members, because the subject content of most select committees was so subject-specific. New committees were typically appointed for each topic addressed in the Committee of the Whole. For example, general ideology scores, such as NOMINATE scores,[43] are unlikely to tell us much about the preferences of the members of, for example, the Select Committee on the Survey of the Western Boundary of New York that was established in the First Congress.

Therefore, more creative, available measures must be used. One strategy to determine the length of the select committees' leashes is to use the life spans of select committees as an indicator of the latitude they were allowed. If select committees were used simply to put into language ideas embodied in an already-worked-out floor majority, then select committees should have reported back within just a few days of being created. If not, then they may have taken weeks to report back, perhaps not reporting back at all. In a related vein, some committees were appointed with specific instructions to consider a bill, implying a gatekeeping function not typically attributed to select committees. Such committees were more likely to be operating under a clear mandate and should have reported back sooner.

Before the Fourteenth Congress (1815–1817), the typical select committee in the Senate had a life span of a month or less; rarely did committees last over a month (a committee life span is defined as the length in days between a committee's appointment and its reporting back to the parent chamber). This is in sharp contrast with the House, whose committees had longer lives, particularly in the earliest Congresses. This House–Senate difference is illustrated in Figure 8-5,

Figure 8-5   Average Life Spans of House and Senate Select
Committees, 1st–45th Congresses (1789–1879)

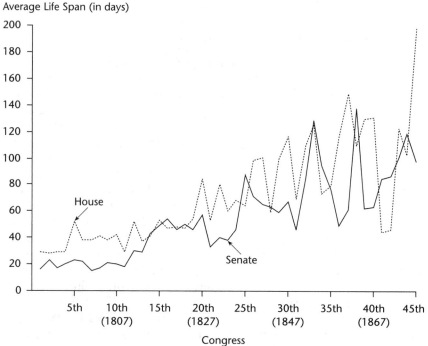

Source: Compiled by the authors.

which reports the average life spans of House and Senate select committees.
Before the War of 1812, Senate committees lasted about two-thirds as long as
their House counterparts.

Did committees appointed to consider specific bills ("bring-in-the-bill"
committees) report back sooner than other committees? Throughout the period,
"bring-in-the-bill" committees in the House did their work within an average
of 30.1 days, compared to 52.9 days for all other committees.[44] Furthermore, very
few of the bill-specific committees exerted gatekeeping power over their subjects
by failing to report back to the floor. Only 6.5 percent of these committees
expired with the end of the session, compared to 23.8 percent of the distributive
committees, 26.1 percent of the semi-standing committees, and 21.6 percent of
the other select committees. The pattern in the Senate is similar. A regression
analysis that controls for the time remaining in the session, the type of select
committee, and whether a bill originated in the House shows that "bring-in-
the-bill" committees reported back to the floor three weeks earlier than committees created with more nebulous assignments.

Did select committees operate as "fingers of the chamber"? On the whole they did, especially in the Senate. Most committees reported back quickly, and those that were delegated the task of drafting or responding to specific pieces of legislation reported back the quickest of all. Furthermore, relatively little legislation died in committees. Over the first fourteen Congresses, only 14 percent of all Senate select committees never reported back to the Senate before they expired with the session's adjournment. In the House, 18.8 percent of the 2,645 select committees in the first thirty-five Congresses did not report back to the House. However, the conventional wisdom does not tell the entire story. Effectively vetoing nearly a fifth of the items coming from the House is more substantial gatekeeping power than select committees were previously believed to have held. Furthermore, the semi-standing committees, which were the most important of the select committees, were more likely to continue to exist at the end of the session and had substantially longer lives than the other select committees. The semi-standing committees in the House worked for an average of 97.1 days, compared to 45.4 days for all other select committees.[45] This suggests that the most important select committees were doing something more than simply crossing the "t"s and dotting the "i"s.[46]

Conclusion

While this chapter should be viewed as the first step in a larger project on the development of the committee system in Congress, we can now offer general conclusions that help inform four areas of theoretical interest: theories of institutional change, the relationship between rules and outcomes, links to areas of current institutional practices and change, and the extent to which the principles of the Founders are evident in the first ninety years of the Senate's history.

Recent research by Elaine Swift has argued that the major institutional transformation undergone by the Senate in the 1810s constituted a "reconstitutive" change, which was abrupt in onset and lasting in effects.[47] We do not have sufficient data to scrutinize her wider argument, but with respect to the committee system, our tentative conclusion is that the transformation of the Senate committee system was more gradual than her argument suggests. The standing committee system created in the Fourteenth Congress constituted a reform evolution, not an abrupt dawning of a new day. More generally, the earliest development of committees in both chambers resembled a bather gradually testing the waters, rather than one suddenly taking the plunge. This contrasts with the modern era. Members of Congress can now rely on two centuries of experience in deciding how to alter the committee system and thus can entertain more far-reaching reforms of the committee system, considering them in light of past experience. Although the gradual evolution of the committee system is still the most common source of institutional change, abrupt reforms are now more likely than in the earliest days of the republic.

Scholars writing in the field of congressional politics have recently made important strides in understanding the institutional development of Congress.

Controversy exists in the literature over which theoretical approach is more powerful in accounting for the most salient features of committee organization.[48] Our conclusion is that each has important applications to the early historical evolution of the committee system. The informational theory of legislative organization is clearly relevant to the earliest development of the committee system. New problems that confronted Congress were met with the establishment of new committees, standing and select. Members of both chambers with significant professional or governmental experience were called to committee service more often than inexperienced members, indicating a preference for their expertise and relevant informational advantages. And even though the Jeffersonian theory of legislation led the earliest members to distrust committees, the real informational advantages that committees brought could not be overlooked. This led to an early domination of policymaking by committees and an early domination of committees by experienced members.

Modern committees do more than just inform the chamber about the pros and cons of legislation, and the same was true of the early committees. Much of the committee system in both chambers was focused on adjudicating the claims of constituents that were filed against the federal government; in those settings the committees were crafted to give the constituents the upper hand. Finally, the partisan domination of the committee system was slow in coming, undoubtedly because pure partisanship itself took nearly a century to entrench itself as the most important organizing principle in the two chambers.

This research also points to other areas of change and continuity in the evolution of the committee system across historical periods. Some aspects of the institutional context within which committees operate have clearly changed since the nineteenth century. For example, as the data in Figures 8-3 and 8-4 show, raw committee turnover was much higher in the nineteenth century than in today's careerist institution. Indeed, committee membership is more stable in today's Congress than the overall membership of the entire Congress in the mid nineteenth century. On the other hand, the place of the committee system within the congressional policymaking process has been remarkably stable since the earliest years of our nation's history. Since the early nineteenth century, members of Congress have tinkered with the structure of the committee system as a means of achieving their various policy, partisan, and institutional goals. The evolution from select to semi-standing to standing committees was the example chronicled here. The most recent manifestation of this institutional tinkering was the institutional reforms associated with the "Contract with America" in 1995. Many of these reforms were aimed at House committees: the Republicans abolished three standing committees, placed six-year term limits on committee chairs, cut committee staff by a third, and abolished proxy voting in committees. Thus members of Congress continue to look to the committee system as a vehicle for achieving their goals.

This chapter also demonstrates how the committee system reflects enduring constitutional principles, such as the equal representation of states. We show that this principle was observed in the early patterns of select committee assignments in the House by giving a disproportionate share of assignments to smaller states. Recently, Frances Lee and Bruce Oppenheimer have shown that the Founders' intention to provide equal representation to the states through the institution of the Senate produces a small-state bias in the allocation of many formula-grant programs.[49] It is noteworthy that the small-state bias we find in select committee assignments occurred in the House, the institution that was supposed to tilt toward the interests of the larger states.

Finally, predictions made by the Founders about the role of the House and Senate in legislating appear to have been partially met through the committee system in the first ninety years of the institution's history. At least in the earliest Congresses, the Senate tended to follow the lead of the House in legislating, as indicated by the number of select committees appointed to consider House-passed legislation and the speed with which select committees reported back to the chambers. Furthermore, the popularly elected House showed great responsiveness to petitioners of the government. However, nearly a fifth of the select committees in the House did not follow the Jeffersonian ideal of limited independent discretion over policy. Rather than simply serving as "fingers of the House," these committees exercised some independent gatekeeping authority.

This research represents only the beginning of a rich line of work, as we attempt to plumb the depths of early congressional organization more precisely. Understanding the earliest Congresses is more than an antiquarian enterprise. In a modern world where new democracies are forming new institutions, it is instructive to understand how one of the world's oldest democracies created its institutions. And, in a nation where reformers are continually harkening back to a simpler, less corrupt, more politically pure epoch, it is important to understand precisely just how that era operated, and how high-minded its politicians really were.

Appendix 8-A Creation of House Standing Committees, 1st–45th Congresses (1789–1879)

Committee	Congress created as standing committee (session in parentheses)	Congress first appointed as select committee (session in parentheses)
Elections	1st (1)	—
Claims	3d (2)	—
Commerce and Manufactures[a]	4th (1)	—
Revisal and Unfinished Business	4th (1)	1st (1)
Ways and Means	4th (1)	1st (1)
Accounts	8th (1)	—
Public Lands	9th (1)	—
District of Columbia	10th (1)	—
Post Office and Post Roads	10th (2)	1st (1)
Judiciary	13th (1)	12th (1)[b]

Appendix 8-A   *continued*

Committee	Congress created as standing committee (session in parentheses)	Congress first appointed as select committee (session in parentheses)
Pensions and Revolutionary Claims[c]	13th (2)	—
Public Expenditures	13th (2)	—
Private Land Claims	14th (1)	—
Expenditures in the Depts. of State, Treasury, War, Navy, Post Office, and in Public Buildings (six separate committees)	14th (1)	—
Agriculture	16th (1)	—
Foreign Affairs	17th (1)	10th (2)
Indian Affairs	17th (1)	1st (1)
Military Affairs	17th (1)	1st (2)
Naval Affairs	17th (1)	4th (1)
Military Pensions	19th (1)	—
Territories	19th (1)	—
Invalid Pensions	21st (2)	—
Roads and Canals	22d (1)	14th (1)[d]
Militia	24th (1)	1st (1)
Mileage	25th (1)	—
Patents	25th (1)	10th (2)[e]
Public Buildings and Grounds	25th (1)	15th (1)[f]
Engraving	28th (1)	—
Rules[g]	31st (1)	—
Library	36th (1)	—
Pacific Railroad	36th (1)	33d (1)
Printing	36th (1)	26th (1)
Expenditures in the Interior Department	37th (1)	—
Appropriations	39th (1)	—
Banking and Currency	39th (1)	—
Mines and Mining	39th (1)	—
Education and Labor	40th (1)	—
Freedman's Bureau	40th (1)	39th (1)
Revisal of the Laws	40th (2)	40th (1)
Railways and Canals	41st (1)	—
Mississippi Levees	42d (1)	—
War Claims	43d (1)	—
Expenditures in the Justice Department	43d (1)	—

[a] Separate committees on Commerce and Manufactures were created in the Sixteenth Congress, First Session.

[b] The Select Committee on Alterations in the Judicial System in the Twelfth Congress is listed as the first Congress with an immediate predecessor to the standing committee. However, there were nine other select committees on the judiciary that were appointed in the Second through Seventh Congresses.

[c] The name of the Committee on Pensions and Revolutionary Claims was changed to the Committee on Revolutionary Claims in the Nineteenth Congress, First Session.

[d] There were also two select committees on Roads and Canals in the Tenth and Eleventh Congresses.

[e] There were also five additional select committees on the topic of patents between the Seventh and Fourteenth Congresses.

[f] There were also three additional select committees on Public Buildings and Grounds from the Fifth to Seventh Congresses.

[g] The Rules Committee was designated as a standing committee in the First Session of the Thirty-first Congress, but the rules change was never codified. The House again elevated Rules to standing status in the Forty-sixth Congress.

Appendix 8-B Creation of Senate Standing Committees, 1st–45th Congresses (1789–1879)

Committee	Congress created as standing committee (session in parentheses)	Congress first appointed as select committee (session in parentheses)
Audit and Control of the Contingent Expenses of the Senate	10th (1)	—
Claims	14th (2)	—
Commerce and Manufactures[a]	14th (2)	13th (3)
District of Columbia	14th (2)	—
Finance	14th (2)	—
Foreign Relations	14th (2)	11th (2)
Judiciary	14th (2)	—
Military Affairs[b]	14th (2)	12th (2)
Militia[b]	14th (2)	13th (2)
Naval Affairs	14th (2)	12th (1)
Pensions	14th (2)	—
Post Office and Post Roads	14th (2)	—
Public Lands	14th (2)	—
Indian Affairs	16th (1)	15th (2)
Roads and Canals	16th (1)	14th (1)
Engrossed Bills	17th (1)	—
Commerce[a]	19th (1)	—
Manufactures[a]	19th (1)	—
Agriculture	19th (1)	—
Private Land Claims	19th (2)	—
Revolutionary Claims	22d (2)	—
Patents	25th (1)	—
Public Buildings[c]	26th (1)	16th (1)
Printing	27th (2)	—
Retrenchment	27th (2)	—
Territories	28th (1)	—
Pacific Railroad[d]	38th (1)	33d (2)
Mines and Mining	39th (special)	—
Appropriations	40th (1)	—
Education[e]	40th (3)	—

Appendix 8-B   *continued*

Committee	Congress created as standing committee (session in parentheses)	Congress first appointed as select committee (session in parentheses)
Revision of the Laws	40th (3)	—
Privileges and Elections	42d (special)	—
Investigations and Retrenchment	42d (1)	—
Civil Service and Retrenchment	43d (1)	—
Rules	43d (2)	—
Enrolled Bills[f]	44th (1)	1st (1)
Library	44th (2)	10th (1)

[a] The Committee on Commerce and Manufactures was split in two in the Nineteenth Congress, with the Committee on Commerce considered the successor committee.

[b] The committee on the Militia was abolished in the Thirty-fifth Congress, and the Military Affairs Committee was renamed as the Committee on Military Affairs and the Militia. This committee's name was changed back to the Committee on Military Affairs in the Fortieth Congress.

[c] The name of the Committee on Public Buildings was changed to Public Buildings and Grounds in the Thirty-fifth Congress.

[d] The name of the Committee on the Pacific Railroad was changed to the Committee on Railroads in the Forty-third Congress.

[e] The name of the Committee on Education was changed to the Committee on Education and Labor in the Forty-first Congress.

[f] The Committee on Enrolled Bills was a joint committee created in the First Congress. The committee became established as separate standing committees of the chambers in the Forty-fourth Congress.

Notes

The committee data used in this chapter were collected under the supervision of David Canon (Univ. of Wisconsin), Garrison Nelson (Univ. of Vermont), and Charles Stewart III (MIT). Cecelia Brown, Judy Cheng, Greg Flemming, Mike Genrich, Donald Gordon, Jeff Hoffner, David Kessler, Brian Kroeger, Hartley Kuhn, and Robert D'Onofrio assisted in the research. This research was made possible, in part, by NSF grants SES 91-12345 and SBR 93-10057 (the "Congressional Historical Relational Database Project," Elaine Swift, principal P.I.).

1. John H. Aldrich, *Why Parties: The Origin and Transformation of Party Politics in America* (Chicago: University of Chicago Press, 1995).
2. Joseph Cooper, "Jeffersonian Attitudes toward Executive Leadership and Committee Development in the House of Representatives, 1789–1829," *Western Political Quarterly* 19 (1965): 45–63; Cooper, *Origins of the Standing Committees and Development of the Modern House* (Houston: Rice University, 1971); George Lee Robinson, "The Development of the Senate Committee System" (Ph.D. diss., New York University, 1954). Also see George B. Galloway, *History of the United States House of Representatives* (Washington, D.C.: Government Printing Office, 1961), chap. 6, for a quick summary of the development of the committee system from 1789 to the modern era.

Other works in early congressional organization include Gerald Gamm and Kenneth Shepsle, "Emergence of Legislative Institutions: Standing Committees in the House and Senate, 1810–1825," *Legislative Studies Quarterly* 14 (1989): 39–66; Thomas W. Skladony, "The House Goes to Work: Select and Standing Committees in the U.S. House of Representatives, 1789–1828," *Congress and the Presidency* 12 (1985): 165–87; Nobel E. Cunningham, *The Process of Government under Jefferson* (Princeton: Princeton University Press, 1978); Ralph Volney Harlow, *The History of Legislative Methods in the Period before 1825* (New Haven: Yale University Press, 1917); James Sterling Young, *The Washington Community, 1800–1828* (New York: Columbia University Press), 132–35; and Elaine E. Swift, *The Making of an American Senate: Reconstitutive Change in Congress: 1787–1841*(Ann Arbor: University of Michigan Press, 1997).

3. Kenneth Shepsle, "The Changing Textbook Congress," in *Can the Government Govern?* ed. by John E. Chubb and Paul E. Peterson (Washington: Brookings Institution, 1989).

4. The role of parties in the evolution of the committee system is an important topic that we will discuss only briefly in this chapter, having addressed this topic elsewhere. See Charles Stewart III, David Canon, Greg Flemming, and Brian Kroeger, "Taking Care of Business: The Evolution of the House Committee System before the Civil War" (paper presented at the annual meeting of the American Political Science Association, Chicago, 1995); David T. Canon and Charles Stewart III, "The Development of the Senate Committee System, 1789–1879" (paper presented at the annual meeting of the American Political Science Association, Boston, 1998).

5. We end our analysis with the Forty-fifth Congress for the simple reason that the Senate's rules were changed in that Congress so that committees no longer expired at the adjournment of a session and were from that point forward appointed for an entire Congress. The House made this change in the Thirty-fifth Congress.

6. Harlow, *The History of Legislative Methods in the Period before 1825;* Joseph Cooper, *Congress and Its Committees: A Historical Approach to the Role of Committees in the Legislative Process* (New York: Garland Publishers, 1988); Lauros G. McConachie, *Congressional Committees: A Study of the Origins and Development of Our National and Local Legislative Methods* (New York: Burt Franklin Reprints, 1898, reprinted 1973); Joseph Charles, *The Origins of the American Party System* (New York: Harper and Brothers, 1956); William Nisbet Chambers, *Political Parties in the New Nation: The American Experience, 1776–1809* (New York: Oxford University Press, 1963).

7. Harlow, *The History of Legislative Methods in the Period before 1825*, 154–55.

8. Quoted in ibid., 140–41.

9. Ibid., 142.

10. Cooper, *Congress and Its Committees.*

11. Gamm and Shepsle, "Emergence of Legislative Institutions," 48–49.

12. Ibid., 51.

13. *The Federalist Papers,* ed. by Roy P. Fairfield (Baltimore: Johns Hopkins University Press, 1981), 184.

14. Quoted in Richard Allan Baker, *The Senate of the United States: A Bicentennial History* (Malabar, Fla.: Robert E. Krieger Publishing, 1988), 123.

15. On the characteristics of the senators see John Quincy Adams, *Memoirs of John Quincy Adams,* 12 vols. (Freeport, N.Y.: Books for Libraries Press, 1969, originally published in 1874), vol. 1, 329; on sectionalism see McConachie, *Congressional Committees,* 267, and Robert C. Byrd, *The Senate, 1789–1989: Addresses on the History of the United States Senate,* 4 vols., ed. by Mary Sharon Hall (Washington, D.C.: Government Printing Office, 1988), vol. 2, 211; on the role of parties see *Memoirs of John Quincy Adams,* vol. 1, 384–85.

16. McConachie, *Congressional Committees*, 261.

17. Ibid., 259–60.

18. Keith Krehbiel, *Information and Legislative Organization* (Ann Arbor: University of Michigan Press, 1991).

19. Byrd, *The Senate, 1789–1989*, 210.

20. George H. Haynes, *The Senate of the United States: Its History and Practice* (Boston: Houghton Mifflin, 1938), 272.

21. Swift, *The Making of an American Senate*, 138–39.

22. Robinson, "The Development of the Senate Committee System," 28.

23. Byrd, *The Senate, 1789–1989*, 218.

24. Samuel C. Patterson, "Party Leadership in the U.S. Senate." *Legislative Studies Quarterly* 14 (1989): 393–413; Barbara Sinclair, *The Transformation of the U.S. Senate* (Baltimore: Johns Hopkins University Press, 1989); Steven S. Smith and Marcus Flathman, "Managing the Senate Floor: Complex Unanimous Consent Agreements Since the 1950s," *Legislative Studies Quarterly* 14 (1989): 349–74; Sarah A. Binder and Steven S. Smith, *Politics or Principle: Filibustering in the United States Senate* (Washington, D.C.: Brookings Institution, 1997).

25. McConachie, *Congressional Committees*, 306.

26. Ibid., 309.

27. Frances E. Lee and Bruce I. Oppenheimer, *Sizing Up the Senate: The Unequal Consequences of Equal Representation* (Chicago: University of Chicago Press, 1999).

28. Ibid., 44; Cooper, *Congress and Its Committees*, 32.

29. McConachie, *Congressional Committees*, 46.

30. Ibid., 148.

31. Swift, *The Making of an American Senate*.

32. Harlow, *The History of Legislative Methods in the Period before 1825*, 213.

33. Ibid., 222–23.

34. McConachie, *Congressional Committees*, 80.

35. Walter Stubbs, *Congressional Committees, 1789–1982: A Checklist* (Westport, Conn.: Greenwood Press, 1985).

36. Gamm and Shepsle, "Emergence of Legislative Institutions"; Jeffrey Jenkins and Charles Stewart III, "Order from Chaos: The Transformation of the Committee System in the House, 1810–1822" (paper presented at the annual meeting of the American Political Science Association, Washington, D.C., 1997).

37. Canon and Stewart, "The Development of the Senate Committee System, 1789–1879"; Stewart et al., "Taking Care of Business: The Evolution of the House Committee System before the Civil War."

38. See also Jenkins and Stewart, "Committee Assignments as Side Payments: The Interplay of Leadership and Committee Development in the Era of Good Feelings" (paper presented at the annual meeting of the Midwest Political Science Association, Chicago, 1998).

39. Empirically, both senators from a single state served on only 6 percent of Senate committees during this period; see David T. Canon and Martin Sweet, "Informational and Demand-Side Theories of Congressional Committees: Evidence from the Senate, 1789–1993" (paper presented at the annual meeting of the American Political Science Association, Boston, 1998), for an analysis of same-state committee assignments in the Senate.

40. Stewart et al., "Taking Care of Business: The Evolution of the House Committee System before the Civil War," examine the state equality hypotheses in a more sophisticated manner, employing a multiple regression framework.

41. If the analysis is limited to claims that came from states (rather than the District of Columbia, territories, or foreign countries), the number of committees is reduced to 469, but the relationships outlined above are even stronger.

42. Krehbiel, *Information and Legislative Organization.*
43. See Keith T. Poole and Howard Rosenthal, *Congress: A Political-Economic History of Roll Call Voting* (New York: Oxford University Press, 1997).
44. The difference-of-means test of this difference yields a *t* score of 7.48 (p < .0001).
45. The difference-of-means test yields a *t* score of 8.04 (p < .0001).
46. One other minor amendment to the conventional wisdom is that the "bring-in-the-bill" committees actually had slightly shorter lives under the period of Jeffersonian rule than under the Federalists. The conventional view predicts the opposite, because select committees in the Jeffersonian period would have been expected to be on a shorter leash than those in the Federalist era. In a regression to predict the length of service of committees, a dummy variable for the Jeffersonian era has a coefficient of 0.91 (s.e. = .046, t = 19.8). While a one-day difference in the length of a committee's life is not substantively significant, it is theoretically significant because the conventional wisdom predicted a negative and statistically significant coefficient.
47. Swift, *The Making of an American Senate.*
48. The most direct introductions to these three theories to committees are Keith Krehbiel, *Information and Legislative Organization* (information theory); Barry R. Weingast and William Marshall, "The Industrial Organization of Congress, *Journal of Political Economy* 96 (1988): 132–63 (distributive theory); and Gary W. Cox and Mathew D. McCubbins, *Legislative Leviathan: Party Government in the House* (Berkeley: University of California Press, 1993) (partisan theory).
49. Lee and Oppenheimer, *Sizing Up the Senate: The Unequal Consequences of Equal Representation.*

9. Committee Theories Reconsidered

Tim Groseclose and David C. King

The daily drama of congressional lawmaking plays out in committees. Committees are center stage, and party leaders or presidents rarely eclipse their policymaking powers. Congressional committees, numbering nineteen in the House of Representatives and seventeen in the Senate, have proved remarkably resilient in the face of ongoing pressures for reform, even though they are not constitutionally protected. Committees periodically come under attack from party leaders, caucuses, bureaucracies, interest groups, and journalists. Scholars, too, often lament committees and call for any number of reforms, such as defining their boundaries more clearly and restricting their influence over legislation. A year rarely passes without somber calls for major changes, yet somehow committees and the committee systems of the two houses persist decade after decade. The spotlight never wavers; they are always center stage. Why is this the case, and how resilient can we assume that committees really are?

Political scientists have offered four general explanations for why committees exist, and in this chapter we clarify those theories. Then we compare them in order to determine which theory—or combination of theories—seems best to explain the presence and persistence of congressional committees.

Ask a member of Congress why committees exist, and you could receive a dozen different reasons. Political scientists have just four, and we introduce them in the first part of this chapter. Committees exist, we are told, for harnessing the *informational* advantage of members who specialize in policy areas, and committees make it easier for members to trade favors and secure *distributive benefits* for their districts. To some extent, committees are also creations of *political parties* and allow the parties to maintain some control over policies. Finally, committees may exist to maximize the power of one of the chambers in a *bicameral rivalry* for money and power.

In the second part of the chapter, we evaluate these theories by looking at how committees actually operate, and we examine whether one or more of the theories could have predicted specific elements of the committee system (such as the existence of discharge petitions). Other scholars, most notably David Mayhew and Forrest Maltzman, have used this approach.[1] This chapter, though, examines far more aspects of how committees work and also looks at how the four important theories compare to one another in their ability to predict specific aspects of the committee system. For instance, which theories—if any—imply that the House and Senate will have separate, not joint, committees? Which—if any—imply the existence of discharge petitions? And so on.

Does any theory about why committees exist seem consistently right when we look how the committee system really operates? We answer this question by the end of the second part, and we devote the final part of the chapter to a discussion of our findings. One benefit of the chapter is that it presents committee rules and procedures in a systematic way, but we think the greater payoff comes in the third part, because an analysis of the spotty successes and failures of the four theories can suggest why committees persist and why they remain so powerful.

Committee Theories

Informational Theory

We begin with the informational theory, which is most closely associated with Tom Gilligan and Keith Krehbiel.[2] This theory assumes that a committee is better informed about the consequences of a policy than the full membership of the House or Senate. (We will refer to the full membership as the "floor.") When the committee reports a bill, this sends important information to the floor. The floor, which may amend the bill, tries to use this information to ensure a policy outcome that is as close as possible to its most preferred position. If this position differs from the committee's most preferred position, the committee will want to exaggerate or distort the information in order to cause the floor to write the bill that the committee wants. But the floor recognizes the committee's incentives to exaggerate, so it discounts the information the committee provides accordingly. Gilligan and Krehbiel show in a formal model that the greater the differences between floor and committee preferences, the less information the committee will be able to transmit successfully. However, when the committee's wishes are the same as the floor's, the committee has no reason to exaggerate, and consequently the floor learns all the information the committee possesses.

One prediction of this theory is that, if the floor has some control over the membership of the committee, the committee should not be a *preference outlier*.[3] That is, the preferences of the median member of the floor should not differ greatly from the preferences of the median member of the committee. The theory is more complicated than that, though. If the information is costly, the floor may have to set up special incentives for the committee to gather it. One of the incentives may be special institutional rights such as a closed rule for the bills that it reports. However, as its goal is always to maximize the preference of the median member of the floor, the floor is very reluctant to give up power to a committee. As Krehbiel explains, "The subservient nature of committees in informational theories cannot be overemphasized. Committees are exclusively instruments of the legislature that perform for the legislature."[4]

Distributive Benefits Theory

The informational theory sees Congress choosing bills from a one-dimensional policy space, but distributive benefits theory posits a policy space that is multi-dimensional. Congress's problem is similar to that of a collection of minority special interests trying to divide a pie. Because the division is not a zero-sum game, the process is more closely analogous to dividing up a pie that contains slices of many different flavors. All members want as large a slice as possible, but the members have different preferences for different flavors. One set of members may prefer a large agriculture slice, another a large urban-benefits slice, another an import-restrictions slice, and so on.

Each special interest is a minority, so to obtain the special benefits desired, it must form a coalition with other interests. The art of politics is the art of coalition formation, and few members of Congress forget that old saw, "No permanent friends; no permanent enemies; just permanent interests."

A variety of problems can occur in forming temporary coalitions to pass bills. Most troubling, one group (or a collection of like-minded members) can renege on an agreement with other groups. For instance, suppose group A wants a particular regulation, while group B wants some public works projects. Neither group composes a majority on its own, but together they do compose a majority. How can they muster a majority on the floor of the legislature? Write an omnibus bill that contains the policies that each wants, and they both benefit.[5] That is the nature of a logroll.

The logrolling solution is not as simple as it seems. Once the public works projects are built, nothing prevents group B from withdrawing its support of the regulation that A desired. In fact, since the regulation does not benefit group B, group B has an incentive to vote for future legislation that rescinds it. Although this would mean reneging on the agreement with A, B does not care, since its public works projects have already been built. Even worse for the process of coalition-building, A anticipates this and realizes that it should not make the agreement in the first place. The incentive to renege is a major impediment to such logrolls between coalitions of minorities in Congress.

According to distributive benefits theory, a specialized version of the committee system comes to the rescue. Suppose that group A dominates the committee overseeing the regulation. If it makes the agreement with group B, and afterward someone tries to rescind the regulation, A can simply exercise its gatekeeping power in committee. That is, it can refuse to introduce the bill that rescinds the regulation. Because of this power, A is now happy to join the logroll with B. The committee system thus provides a way for the two groups to enforce the prior agreement. Furthermore, group B actually prefers that its hands be tied from canceling the original agreement—otherwise the agreement is not possible. Moreover, it does not mind if group A dominates the committee that oversees the regulation.

One important implication of distributive benefits theory, then, is that committees will be unrepresentative of the chamber. They will be preference outliers. (This contrasts with the informational theory, which implies that if the committee's preferences differ too much from the floor's, the floor cannot trust the information that the committee reports.) However, the theory also implies, as scholars often overlook, that committees should have gatekeeping power, which means committees can block legislation from moving forward. This is an important implication. For instance, it allows us immediately to reject the distributional theory as an explanation of other institutional bodies such as subcommittees, task forces, and caucuses, since these bodies do not have gatekeeping power.

Majority-Party Cartel Theory

Scholars have long noted—and sometimes lamented—the apparent weakness of political party discipline in Congress.[6] With a few exceptions, the scholarship on party discipline has had little to say about how parties affect committee rules and procedures.[7] Majority-party cartel theory, associated with Gary Cox and Mathew McCubbins, is the great exception. A majority party, they argue, excludes the minority party from the lawmaking process, and party members cooperate to achieve a party's collective goals.[8]

If the majority party is a legislative cartel, how much power—if any— should it give to the committees? What is the form of this power? Does it involve negative power, positive power, or both? That is, will the committee only be able to prevent legislation it does not prefer, or will it also be able to enact legislation that it does prefer, possibly over the wishes of the party or floor? Three elements of the theory are crucial.

First, committees are part of a reward system for the majority party, and the most loyal party members are rewarded by being more likely to get the committee assignments they request. If a seat on a committee can be viewed as such a reward, then committees must possess power. Otherwise, the seats would be hollow rewards.

Second, preferences of the majority-party members of a committee typically are not much different from the median preference of the entire majority party. Cox and McCubbins interpret this as evidence that the majority caucus holds the committee in close check. Again, this implies committees have power. Otherwise, the majority party would not care about the preferences of committees. This also implies that the majority party members on the committee collude among themselves and exclude the minority members. Otherwise, the relevant statistic would be the median of the *whole* committee.[9]

Third, the majority-party cartel theory implies an important sequence for considering bills in Congress. For example, imagine that the Democrats are the majority party, the House is considering a minimum-wage bill, and the status quo is a minimum wage of $5.00 an hour. Suppose the median member of the House prefers $6.00 an hour, but the median House *Democrat* prefers $6.50. Utilizing the majority-party cartel approach, Democratic leaders could implement $6.50 as follows:

1. The relevant committee (with Democrats constituting a majority) writes a bill raising the minimum wage to $6.50 an hour.
2. The Rules Committee (with Democrats again constituting a majority) introduces a resolution that disallows amendments to the bill.

3. The House floor votes for the resolution to restrict amendments. Although the moderate members of the Democratic party would prefer to join a coalition of Republicans and defeat the resolution (since unlimited amendments would allow the median of the House to adopt its most-preferred policy of $6.00), party leaders apply pressure to prevent this outcome.

4. Once the vote on the rule passes, the party can go on auto-pilot for the vote on final passage, and leaders do not need to apply any further pressure. Since the final vote is an up-or-down decision between $5.00 and $6.50, even moderate Democrats prefer to vote for a $6.50 minimum wage.

The first and third steps may be especially difficult for the party leaders. However, the first step can be accomplished in either of two ways. One is to stack the committee so the median prefers $6.50, thus making the committee a preference outlier. However, a more likely route is for caucus leaders to pressure moderates into writing the $6.50 bill, despite their preferences. The third step, to persuade a majority of the chamber to vote for the restrictive rule, also can be accomplished through party pressure.

The strategy allows the party to achieve its policy goal. Meanwhile, it allows its members to vote their sincere preferences on the substantive issue, the final vote, but vote the party line on committee and procedural issues. Given constituency pressures, and given that constituents may be less watchful on such committee and procedural matters, the strategy may be easier for party leaders than applying pressure only on the final vote.

Bicameral Rivalry Theory

Students of American history will recall the debates of the Founders over two proposed legislative systems — James Madison's bicameral "Virginia plan," in which seats in both chambers were determined by population, and the rival, unicameral "New Jersey plan." The Founders settled on a compromise that combined the interests of large and small states, opting for a bicameral legislature with one chamber responsive to small states and the other reflecting the large states.

Interbranch rivalry has often been mentioned as an important force in the development of the twentieth-century committee system, particularly in the reorganizations of the early 1920s, and there has been a recent flurry of scholarship about how the great compromise has influenced today's committee system.[10] What can bicameralism teach us about committees?

Daniel Diermeier and Roger Myerson propose a model that seems almost too simple (and perhaps too cynical) to be true yet captures important features of modern legislatures. They imagine two competing lobbyists paying bribes to pass a bill. Because of the competition between the lobbyists, legislators receive excess "rents," which means they get more rewards than they would if there were only one lobbyist. Understanding this, legislators set up hurdles that maximize "rents." These hurdles can take various forms, including a committee that can veto legislation, a chair who can refuse to hold the necessary hearings for a bill, a Speaker or a Rules Committee that can kill a bill through scheduling, or a rule that requires a super-majority to pass a bill (such as the cloture rule in the Senate). All of these hurdles make it more difficult for outside interests to maneuver a bill through the legislature. We have seen legislative leaders keep bills from a final vote until after a crucial fundraiser, and in the quiet of their offices they will admit to us that their reason for doing so is to extract more money from lobbyists.

There is a fine line between setting up too many and too few hurdles. If passing a bill proves too costly, measured against the potential rewards, then lobbyists will not "pay to play," and legislators will not be rewarded. This institution-design problem is a balancing act. The legislature wants neither too many nor too few hurdles.

According to the bicameral rivalry theory, the more veto points in the constitutional structure of the government, the more hurdles a legislative chamber will want to create within its own chamber. In a parliamentary system with few veto points, the chamber creates few, if any, internal hurdles. However, in a system such as the United States', with numerous veto points, the two legislative chambers create many internal hurdles. Under Diermeier and Myerson's way of handling the uncertainty about lobbyists' willingness to pay, each chamber in a system with such a structure will want to have one more internal hurdle than the other chamber, so each chamber will create an infinite number of hurdles. Of course, there are practical considerations against this result. Furthermore, we suspect that under different parameterizations of lobbyists' willingness to pay, the equilibrium would be finite, but still large.

The bicameral rivalry theory, with its stark assumptions and scant consideration of real-world concerns of legislators, seems to be little more than an intellectual exercise. On second glance, however, it offers several insights.

- First, it offers an explanation for why committees typically have at most only negative power—that is, why committees can only veto legislation and cannot unilaterally implement legislation against the wishes of the chamber.
- Second, it sheds light on the multiple veto points within Congress. Some scholars argue that it is not just committees that can keep the gates; this can also be done by committee chairs, the House Rules committee, individual senators bucking unanimous consent agreements, and others.
- Third, it helps explain a regularity between the constitutional structure of a country and the power of committees within the country's legislature. Unicameral parliamentary systems usually do not have committees, or at least not committees strong enough to veto legislation.[11] Meanwhile, multi-chamber and division-of-powers systems usually have strong committees.

Reconsidering Implications of Committee Theories

We turn now to our data (committee institutions) for testing these theories. All of our findings are summarized in a table that shows the institutional rules in its rows and the theories in its columns (see Table 9-1). When the way things actually work corresponds to a theory's prediction, we put a plus mark in the cell. Presumably, the more plus marks, the better a theory performs.

As an illustration of our approach, consider the seniority system in the House of Representatives. With rare exceptions, the seniority system specifies that the committee member of the majority party with the longest continuous service on the committee becomes chair. Subtle components are often overlooked. The norm rewards not seniority per se but within-committee seniority specifically. Total service in the chamber rarely matters. Furthermore, House and Senate committees require prospective chairs to be members of the majority party, which contrasts with the rules in some state legislatures. Also, the House and Senate seniority systems refer specifically to full committees; a similar rule does not necessarily hold for subcommittee chairs or party leadership posts. Theories of committee institutions that purport to explain seniority systems would, ideally, illuminate these multiple subtleties.

The Seniority System

Several details of the seniority system are especially relevant in deciding which theory—or combination of theories—works best:

- The seniority system exists.
- Seniority in the House (though not the Senate) refers to continuous, not total, service.
- House seniority refers to committee, not chamber, service.
- Seniority does not transfer when a member switches chambers.
- There is no similar seniority system for subcommittees.
- Seniority is party specific.
- Seniority is not binding; that is, committee chairs are still subject to a caucus vote.
- Caucus slates are still subject to a vote in the whole chamber.

Chamber versus committee seniority, continuous versus total service. The first three details noted above—that seniority exists, that it refers to continuous service, and that it refers to committee service—support the informational theory very well. Seniority "pulls members toward greater legislative specialization: members settle into the committee slots, cultivate expertise in a distinct policy field, and spend their time managing legislation and conducting oversight in that field."[12] To the extent that longevity within a committee leads to greater expertise, committee-specific seniority—as opposed to chamber seniority—rewards

Table 9-1 Committee Institutions and Their Agreement with the Theories

Committee Institution	Theory			
	Informational Theory	Distributive Benefits Theory	Majority-Party Cartel Theory	Bicameral Rivalry Theory
The House and Senate have separate, not joint, committees.	− Information could be provided by one joint committee. Why form separate committees?	− Logrolls could be protected by one joint committee. Why form separate committees?	? The theory only applies to the House. Also, a party in one chamber might not want to help the reelection chances of the party in the other chamber.	+ A joint committee could not function as a proper within-chamber hurdle.
The minority party receives committee seats.	+ Otherwise committees would necessarily be unrepresentative of the floor.	+ Otherwise minority party members intensely interested in an issue could not self-select to the appropriate committee.	− If the majority party acts as a cartel to control committees, why give seats to the minority?	?/+ Theory has no parties. But if intrachamber cooperation depends on equitable division of power, the minority receives seats.
The minority party receives proportionate seats.	+	− If, for example, the Democrats are the highest demanders for the Education Committee, why not let them have more than their proportional share of seats?	−	?/+
A seniority system exists.	+ *Direct support:* Ensures committee members will be more experienced. *Indirect support:* Disincentive for transferring, thus encouraging specialization.	+ Makes seat a property right. Most intense interests can't be kicked off, and they eventually become chair.	− Takes power away from caucus and party leaders.	?/+ Theory only specifies how a chamber will maximize resources, not how it will divide them. But equitable division may explain this.

Table 9-1 *continued*

Committee Institution	Informational Theory	Distributive Benefits Theory	Majority–Party Cartel Theory	Bicameral Rivalry Theory
			Theory	
Seniority is calculated by service in the committee, not in the chamber.	+	+	? Given that there is a seniority system, it's not clear which would be worse for the caucus, a system based on committee service or chamber service.	?/+
Subcommittees do not have a seniority system.	− Contradicts the theory for the opposite reason a committee seniority system supports the theory.	− Contradicts the theory for the opposite reason a committee seniority system supports the theory.	The alternative is no better for caucus. Republicans: chair of parent committee appoints. Democrats: seniority in parent committee is the rule.	?/− Contradicts the theory for the opposite reason a committee seniority system supports the theory.
Committee seniority does not transfer across chambers.	− Expertise should have the same value in the Senate as in the House.	+/− Members might not represent the same interests in the Senate as they did in the House. But if they do, why not let them keep their seniority?	? Theory doesn't seem to imply that seniority should exist, much less transfer between chambers.	+ The chambers do not cooperate, so there is no reason they should honor seniority from the other chamber.
Committee chairs are subject to votes of the caucus.	− Opposite reason why seniority supports the theory.	− Contradicts the theory for the opposite reason the seniority system supports the theory.	+ Unquestionably gives more power to the caucus.	?/− Theory has no parties. Contradicts the theory for the opposite reason the seniority system supports the theory.

+ The institution supports the theory.

− The institution contradicts the theory.

? It is uncertain whether the institution supports or contradicts the theory.

Table 9-1 *continued*

		Theory		
Committee Institution	Informational Theory	Distributive Benefits Theory	Majority–Party Cartel Theory	Bicameral Rivalry Theory
But the floor must ratify the vote of the caucus.	+ More power to the floor median.	+ Protects seniority from intrusions by caucus. (But why must self-selection pass hurdle of a majority vote?)	− Takes power away from the caucus.	?/+ Takes power from caucus. Ensures more equitable division of resources.
Committees have limited gatekeeping powers.	−/+ Less power to the floor median.	+ Exactly what the theory predicts. Committees must have gatekeeping power to protect previous logrolls.	−/? Why should committees be able to withhold legislation, possibly against the will of the majority party? However, if the committee is controlled by the majority party, gatekeeping power is irrelevant.	+ Exactly what the theory predicts. A committee must have gatekeeping power (but not positive power) to bring extra resources to the chamber.
The rule for a bill must be approved by the floor.	+ Power to give a closed rule remains with floor.	? Existence of a rule for a bill is not consistent with the theory. Therefore, it is not clear why the floor must approve.	− Restricts the Speaker's scheduling power.	+ The Rules Committee does not need positive power but only gatekeeping power.
Discharge petitions exist.	+/− The floor retains power.	− Restricts gatekeeping power, hence the ability of a committee to enforce logrolls.	? Disallows committees from thwarting the wishes of the caucus. But it also upsets the scheduling power of the Speaker.	− Negates a hurdle that committees create.

Table 9-1 *continued*

Committee Institution	Theory			
	Informational Theory	*Distributive Benefits Theory*	*Majority-Party Cartel Theory*	*Bicameral Rivalry Theory*
But discharge petitions are costly.	−/+ Opposite of the above reason.	+ Opposite of the above reason.	? Opposite of the above reasons.	+ Opposite of the above reason.
Closed rules exist.	+ If the information is very costly and the committee has similar preferences as the floor, then the floor prefers to grant a closed rule.	− Committee only needs gatekeeping power.	+ Enhances the Speaker's scheduling power.	− Committee only needs gatekeeping power.
But open—and modified open—rules are the norm.	+/− Power remains with the floor. But what if above conditions are frequently satisfied? Then closed rule should be the norm.	+	− Restricts the Speaker's scheduling power.	+
Subcommittees exist, but they do not have formal gatekeeping power; nor do they receive closed rules when they report bills to the committee.	+ Without positive or negative power, information seems to be the only possible purpose of a subcommittee.	− How can a subcommittee protect a logroll without gatekeeping power?	? It is unclear how subcommittees help the majority caucus.	− The subcommittee cannot form a legislative hurdle without gatekeeping power.

+ The institution supports the theory.

− The institution contradicts the theory.

? It is uncertain whether the institution supports or contradicts the theory.

expertise. Furthermore, if it depends on continuous service, it rewards specialization, since it discourages members from transferring to different committees during their career in Congress. Legislators come to treat service on a committee as a long-term investment, and the more senior they become, the less likely they are to leave the committee.

The presence of a seniority system is also consistent with the distributive benefits theory. Committee service is a property right. Without it, a majority of the chamber could decide to oust the most intensely interested members from a committee. But if this is possible, the members would not be able to protect prior logrolls. This, in turn, would cause the logrolling process to unravel. Also, since the most intensely interested members would presumably stay with a committee the longest, the seniority system helps ensure that they become chairs.

In contrast to a strong-party system, the seniority system is a norm that takes away power from the party caucus. Accordingly, it is hard to imagine the current seniority system supporting the party government theory. Some historical lessons support this claim. After the Civil War, strong House Speakers, "struggling to control the unruly chamber, sometimes ignored seniority to appoint loyal lieutenants to major committees."[13] Speaker Newt Gingrich, R-Ga., took similar action in bypassing three senior Republicans for committee chairs in January 1995. However, the era of strong Speakers did not last. When Speaker Joseph G. Cannon, R-Ill. (1903–1911), asserted party prerogatives over seniority by passing "over senior members for assignments and behaved arbitrarily in other ways, the House revolted, divesting the Speaker of committee assignment power."[14] Indeed, generations of political scientists have argued that the seniority system represents a check on the powers of party leaders.[15] Similarly, Gingrich's strong hand as party leader was short lived. Witness his reluctance to admonish—much less remove—James Leach from his Banking Committee chair after the Iowa Republican led a small revolt against the Speaker in early 1997.

The existence of the seniority system neither directly supports nor contradicts the bicameral rivalry theory. The same is true for the fact that seniority refers to committee, not chamber, service. However, when one adds equity considerations to the theory—that the chamber not only maximizes its power and resources but also seeks to allocate them equitably among its members, to maintain cooperation—then these two facts seem to support the theory. They are a mechanism for members to "get in line" to receive power and benefits, and they reward members who have patiently waited and cooperated in the system that maximizes chamber power, instead of their own.

Seniority is nontransferable between chambers. In computing seniority on a committee, neither chamber recognizes the service of a member in the other chamber. When Jon Kyl, R-Ariz., won a Senate seat in 1994, he had served for eight years on the House Armed Services Committee. Had he received a seat on the Senate Armed Services Committee, he would have entered at the bottom rung of the committee.[16]

This rule seems inconsistent with the informational theory. If the expertise of a member was valuable while he or she was in the House, why not in the Senate? Meanwhile, it is consistent with the bicameral rivalry theory, which assumes that the chambers will not cooperate on matters such as seniority. Under one interpretation, it also supports the distributive benefits theory. When a member, for instance, switches from the House to the Senate, he or she usually does not continue to represent the same interests from his or her House constituency. It is more important for the House district's new representative to fill in the committee seats of the former representative. In fact, there is a weak norm in the House for new members to do just that — they often are granted the first shots at filling in committee seats of the members they replace.

Finally, it is questionable how the party government theory relates to the seniority system. Which would be less consistent with the theory: seniority transferring across chambers, or not transferring? That seniority does not transfer across chambers underscores the myriad of possible, alternative forms of the seniority system that Congress does not choose. A member's age, for example, does not matter for a member's seniority. It is not even considered as a tie-breaker when two members have the same committee or chamber seniority. Also, the House and Senate do not count service in other legislatures in computing committee seniority. For instance, Tip O'Neill thought that his experience as Speaker of the Massachusetts Legislature helped him land a seat on the House Rules Committee when he entered Congress, but on the committee his Massachusetts past mattered not a whit in granting him extra seniority.[17]

Subcommittee seniority. There is no explicit seniority system within subcommittees, with the exception of House Appropriations subcommittees. Before the 1995 Republican rules changes, House subcommittee slots were allocated through a bidding process that explicitly followed full-committee seniority—a pattern still used in the Senate.[18] Today, however, House Republican committee chairs are authorized—without sanction from committee caucuses—to name subcommittee chairs and assign members to subcommittees.[19] In choosing subcommittee chairs, subcommittee seniority does not explicitly come into play. And in the Senate subcommittee bidding process, the critical factor is committee-level seniority, not prior service on any particular subcommittee.

In general, for the same reasons that the committee seniority system would support a theory, the absence of a subcommittee seniority system fails to support the same theory. The party government theory is an exception. Although the seniority system does not support this theory, its substitute for subcommittees does not support it either. The Republican norm for choosing subcommittee chairs is to allow the chair of the full committee to appoint the subcommittee chair. The Democratic norm is to allocate subcommittee chairs according to *committee* seniority. Both systems reallocate power that would otherwise be held by the caucus. Therefore they do not support the party government theory.

Parties and seniority. The seniority system for selecting committee chairs only applies to the most senior member *of the majority party.* This aspect of the system seems inconsistent with information theory. If the most senior and expert member belongs to the minority party, why cannot he or she become chair? For similar reasons, this aspect does not support the distributive benefits theory. Also, because it works against the notion of spreading power equitably (it excludes minority members), it is inconsistent with the bicameral rivalry theory. Of course, this aspect of the seniority system supports the party government theory very well indeed.

Caucus ratification and floor ratification. The seniority system is not a hard and fast rule. Rather, it is a norm that members follow when electing chairs of committees through their party caucuses. The caucus votes are then perfunctorily ratified on the floor. Occasionally, caucuses violate the seniority norm, such as in January 1975 when a bloc of first-term Democrats voted en masse to oust three committee chairs: Eddie Herbert, D-La., of the Armed Services Committee, W.R. Poage, D-Texas, of the Agriculture Committee, and Wright Patman, D-Texas, of the Banking Committee. In 1984 Les Aspin rose to be Armed Services chair despite being seventh in seniority among committee Democrats. And in the aftermath of the 1994 Republican revolution, House Republicans—with the careful orchestration of Speaker Newt Gingrich—violated committee seniority three times when selecting chairs.

The rules allowing caucuses to vote on committee chairs lend strong support to the party government theory and contradict the other three theories. Indeed, it is curious that the caucus is given this power. For instance, why not instead let the whole chamber vote on each chair separately, similar to a vote for the Speaker? Or if not the whole chamber, why not let the committee itself vote on its chair? This seemingly is the rule that would be most consistent with the informational and distributive benefits theories. After all, the committee members have the most expertise and the most intense interest. Why not let them choose their own chair? Finally, why not let the majority-party members of the committee choose the chair? In fact, this rule seems more consistent with the party government theory than the actual practice of allowing the entire caucus to choose.

Caucus slates subject to chamber vote. The last word on selection of committee chairs remains with the whole chamber, not the caucuses. Each caucus forms its slate of committee members and chairs. These slates are bundled, and they must pass an up-or-down vote by the whole chamber. These votes are almost always along strict party lines, but it is possible for members to defect from caucus positions, as seven Republicans did when they did not vote for Newt Gingrich as Speaker on the House floor in early 1997.

By rule, the final authority resides with the chamber. In practice, however, it is not clear how much power this actually affords the chamber. First, the vote is up - or - down. Thus, the caucuses have agenda - setting power, and their only constraint is that a majority of the chamber must approve the proposal. On the other hand, it is not clear what a nay vote means. If the floor rejects the slate, no one believes that the result will be no committees. Rather, in practice, the floor would instruct the caucuses to rewrite their slates, and the floor would vote again on the new slates. This would continue until the floor finally okays the slates. Unlike as in the standard political science voting model, there is a *series* of up - or - down votes rather than a single vote.[20] As a consequence, the agenda - setters in this situation have less power than they would with a single up - or - down vote, and the floor median has more power.

Although the party government theory is supported by the fact that caucuses nominate committee chairs, to the extent that the floor ratification takes away some of this power, floor ratification is evidence against the party government theory. Further, the opposite occurs with the other three theories. They are supported by the institution of floor ratification.

Minority Members Receive Committee Slots

It is not written in stone that members of the minority party have to be given seats on committees, yet they are, and this fact is consistent with the informational theory. If, instead, a committee were composed solely of majority - party members, it would be almost impossible for the committee median to have the same preferences as the floor median. And it would be almost impossible for the committee to provide an informative signal to the median of the chamber floor. This institutional fact is also consistent with the distributive benefits theory. If, for instance, the minority party is more pro - agriculture or more pro - defense than the majority party, then the theory implies that minority members will receive seats on these committees.

The practice of assigning minority party members to committees, however, is not consistent with the majority party cartel theory. It conjures a quip attributed to Thomas "Czar" Reed, R - Maine. "When asked in 1890 about the rights of the minority party, legend tells it that Speaker Thomas Reed retorted that the only right of the minority party was 'to draw its paycheck.' "[21] Even Czar Reed allowed Democrats to sit on committees. Why not simply deny seats to the minority? The recent House Republican majority, begot by the 1994 elections, effectively did just that on important legislation during the first 100 days of the 104th Congress. Speaker Newt Gingrich thought the committee system antiquated, cumbersome, and not sufficiently responsive to a centralized party voice—such as his own. Instead, for important legislation, he created task forces that would mark up bills and then introduce them to the rest of the House.[22]

This caused a stir among Congress scholars, if not among the wider public. Democrats grumbled about being excluded from the new system, and the grumbles reached a roar when one of Gingrich's task forces began drafting a plan to overhaul Medicare. Democrats reacted by holding renegade hearings on the Capitol steps. The hearings met with great fanfare from the press and some discontent from voters. More importantly, some moderate Republicans began to lose their stomach. Once they threatened to join the Democrats to end Gingrich's task-force system, Gingrich relented. He and fellow Republican leaders expressed a metaphoric "oops," and the experiment ended.

The Republican system of task forces looked very much like the committee system that the majority party cartel theory would predict. The Speaker largely appointed the members, and the majority party held the seats almost exclusively. The Republicans' bold experiment and the results that followed offer some insights into why congressional committees *do* include minority party members. If they did not, the minority would revolt. More important, the moderate wing of the majority party might join the revolt. Since these members prefer to be deal-makers and conciliators between the extremes of the chamber rather than an excluded voice within a strong majority, the threat is credible. Consequently, the majority party has little choice but to include the minority.

Minority Members Receive Proportional Representation on Committees

Representation on committees is proportional by party, based in general on the proportion of seats that each party holds in the entire chamber. So while the House in the 104th Congress was composed of 228 Republicans, 206 Democrats, and 1 independent (a 52.5 percent Republican majority), Republicans held 54.0 percent of the seats on the Agriculture Committee, 53.6 percent on the Banking Committee, 54.9 percent on the Commerce Committee, and so on. Some committees are exceptions, such as the House Rules Committee (which was 69.2 percent Republican) and the House Oversight Committee (which was 66.7 percent Republican), but the general thrust is toward proportional representation. This is by no means inevitable in U.S. legislatures. For instance, committees in early Congresses often did not follow the norm.[23] Also, although many state legislatures mandate proportional representation (and it is even required by statute in Kansas), there are notable exceptions. For example, minority parties in Alabama, Alaska, Arkansas, Georgia, Louisiana, and Texas are afforded no guarantee of committee representation at all.[24]

Proportional representation on committees seems to be evidence against the party government theory, which predicts that minority members should receive *less* than their proportionate share. It is also inconsistent with the distributive benefits theory, which predicts that minority members could sometimes receive *more* than their proportional share. Consider the House Armed Services Committee when Republicans were in the minority. Even though Republicans were generally the highest demanders, this did not give them any extra seats. Certainly, proportional representation on committees is consistent with the informational theory, since proportional representation makes it more likely that committee preferences will be representative of the whole chamber.

Finally, since the bicameral rivalry theory does not incorporate the party, or even ideological preferences, of the members, it is difficult to construct an implication of the theory for the party-ratio norm. However, one interpretation yields a prediction. The theory assumes that members cooperate in maximizing the total resources or power that the members of the chamber accrue. Presumably, the chamber will distribute such power and resources in an equitable way; otherwise members would not necessarily continue to cooperate. Once such an equitable-division assumption is added to the theory, the party-ratio norm—which grants the *most* equitable division of power within the committee—is consistent with the theory.

Separate versus Joint Committees

Most congressional committees are separate, not joint. That is, each chamber of Congress has its own committee on agriculture, armed services, appropriations, veterans' affairs, and so on. Of course, Congress does have joint committees. There are four: the Joint Economic Committee, the Joint Committee on the Library of Congress, the Joint Committee on Printing, and the Joint Committee on Taxation. But these committees are not powerhouses, meeting infrequently and very rarely "marking up" legislation of any kind. This pattern is by and large found in the states as well. However, of the forty-nine bicameral states, three—Connecticut, Maine, and Massachusetts—consistently utilize joint committees.[25] As a practical matter it would be *possible* for Congress and other state legislatures to adopt joint committees as the norm.

Party leadership committees—such as the House Republican Committee on Committees, the House Republican Steering and Policy Committee, and the House Republican Campaign Committee—are also separate.[26] For these committees especially, one might expect the parties to coordinate through joint committees, yet they remain separate—even to the point of competing with each other for dollars from the same contributors through mass mailings.

What does the predominance of separate committees imply about the four theories? It does not provide support for the informational theory. If the sole purpose of committees is to gather information, they could do this just as well if they were joint across the chambers. In fact, if information gathering were costly, why would Congress duplicate this process with two committees? The same is true for the distributive benefits theory. If committees exist to protect previous logroll agreements, one joint committee with veto power could do this just as well as two. Similarly, if the sole purpose of committees is to aid the majority party, why create two different committees in each house? For example, if it is possible for the Senate Democrats to take action that could harm the reelection chances of House Democrats, then the parties would presumably coordinate across chambers and accordingly form joint committees. Perhaps worse, the fact that *caucus* committees, such as steering and policy and committee on committees, also are separate across chambers is troubling for the party cartel theory.

In contrast, the institution of joint committees is consistent with the bicameral rivalry theory. If committees exist to create hurdles for interest groups in ways that bring more power and resources to each chamber, then it would make little sense to have joint committees.

Gatekeeping Power

Several institutions that involve gatekeeping power are relevant to the four theories. Consider:

- Committees seem to have de facto gatekeeping power;
- yet they have no de jure gatekeeping power, since the floor can extract legislation with a discharge petition;
- the chairs of committees and subcommittees do not have gatekeeping power, and neither do subcommittees as a whole.

Gatekeeping power and the discharge petition. According to conventional wisdom, committees have gatekeeping power. That is, if a majority of the committee does not prefer that bill become law, the committee can refuse to report it. This prevents the floor from considering it, which effectively gives the committee a veto.

However — in the Rules Manuals, at least — specific authorization of gatekeeping power for committees is hard to find. In the House, any bill that a committee refuses to report can be extracted with a discharge petition. In the Senate, extracting a bill is even easier (though formal discharge petitions are extremely rare). Because the Senate rules are more lax on the germaneness of amendments, if a committee refuses to release a bill, any member can introduce it as an amendment to another bill — effectively extracting it from committee.

Nevertheless, the conventional wisdom is that, de facto, gatekeeping power does exist for committees. Some scattered facts and anecdotes are usually offered to support this idea.

- Approximately 87 percent of all bills that are referred to committees do not reach the floor. In the 102d Congress, for example, 10,238 bills and joint resolutions were introduced in the House and Senate. Only 1,201 made it to the floor, and just 667 passed both chambers.[27]
- Perhaps because it is so cumbersome, the discharge petition is rarely used in practice. As Randall Ripley notes, between 1923 and 1975 only 396 petitions were filed. Of these, only 25 obtained the required 218 signatures.[28]

No wonder Woodrow Wilson called committees "dim dungeons of silence."[29] More colloquial, the phrase "die in committee" has become a part of common parlance, and a famous Saturday morning cartoon ("I'm Just a Bill") features bills literally dying in committee.

Even if committees do possess de facto gatekeeping power, the above facts severely overstate its extent. Although 87 percent of bill do not reach the floor, this figure neglects bills introduced under duplicate labels. Some bills that appear to die in committee really do not; they are just considered under a different label. Some of these reach the floor as amendments to another bill, yet they are record-ed as part of the 87 percent that do not. More importantly, many of the bills that never reach the floor would have been voted down if the floor had considered them. That the committee never sent them to the floor may have been just a means to save the floor the trouble of a nay vote. If so, this is not properly called gatekeeping. For a committee to have true gatekeeping power it must be able to prevent a bill from becoming law, *despite the floor's preferences for the bill.*

The evidence showing how infrequently the discharge petition is used ignores the threat value of the discharge. As Speaker James Beauchamp "Champ" Clark, D-Mo., explained in 1910,

> I predict that if this [discharge] rule is adopted we will never have very many occasions to put it into operation, because it will be held in terrorem over the committees of this House, and they will report out the bills desired by the membership of the House, which is the great desideratum. . . . Therefore the bad practice of smothering bills in committee will cease and there will be little necessity of using this rule.[30]

Consistent with Speaker Clark's prediction, there have been cases where a com-mittee sent a bill to the floor, not because its members favored it, but to prevent the embarrassment of having the bill discharged from the committee. Krehbiel and Oleszek report cases of a committee reporting a bill because it was clear that a discharge petition either had reached or would soon reach 218 signatures.[31]

These two considerations—the infrequency of successful discharge peti-tions and the frequency with which bills do not reach the floor—tell us little about what we would really like to know: How often does a committee kill a bill, *despite the support of a majority on the floor?* We offer no precise answer. However, because discharge petitions are costly, we are confident that (in the House) the answer is at least "sometimes"—though possibly very rarely. Of course, any costs at all imply a weak form of gatekeeping.

Some evidence that there are at least small costs is the fact that the House could make the discharge petition a less cumbersome procedure but does not. For instance, instead of requiring members to trek to the office of the House Clerk to sign a petition, the House could allow members simply to request a vote to extract a bill. Other possibilities would still require signatures but require a fewer number. In fact, in 1924 the House required only 150 signatures, and from 1931–1935 it required only 145 signatures.[32]

How do the theories stack up in their ability to predict gatekeeping institu-tions? First, on the surface the gatekeeping power of committees seems at odds with the informational theory. Why would the floor give up power so that the committee can have a veto? Next, it does not support the party government theory. Why would the caucus want to give up such power to the floor? Under another interpretation, the party government theory might not make any prediction. If the caucus indeed controls the majority-party members of the committee, gatekeeping power is irrelevant. The caucus would not care whether the committee has or does not have gatekeeping power. Yet another interpretation shows a questionable relationship between gatekeeping power and the party-government theory, according to which committee assignments are rewards for members who have been loyal to the party. If the committee did not have gatekeeping power, along with other power, such rewards would not be as valuable.

Gatekeeping power is largely consistent with the distributive benefits and bicameral rivalry theories. Each of these theories predicts gatekeeping power for committees and no other power. Of course, for opposite reasons, the existence of the discharge petition works against these two theories. Further, the absence of gatekeeping power for Senate committees is troubling for the bicameral rivalry theory. Meanwhile, it is not as troubling for the distributive benefits theory. This theory requires only one body to protect logrolls. It does not need a duplicate body in the Senate to achieve this.

Gatekeeping powers of committee and subcommittee chairs. According to conventional wisdom, chairs of committees and subcommittees also have gatekeeping power. However, as with committees, de jure their powers are very limited. Every tool that can block the gatekeeping power of a committee—such as the discharge petition—can also block the gatekeeping power of the *chair* of a committee or subcommittee. Other less-costly tools further limit the gatekeeping power of chairs. The chair can be overruled by any majority within a committee or subcommittee. Indeed, some have argued that a chair's power lies in his or her ability to anticipate what a majority of the committee wants, to avoid being visibly defeated in committee. Votes alone cannot upset committee gatekeeping power—the more cumbersome procedure involving signatures recorded with the House Clerk is also required. However, as with chairs, votes alone—namely those of a majority of the committee—can destroy their gatekeeping power.

For example, one of the myths surrounding the legend of Judge Smith, D-Va., is that he alone was able to thwart the liberal agenda of President Kennedy. However, without the support of Republicans and William Colmer, D-Miss. (the only other southern Democrat on the committee), Smith would be remembered as just another Rules chair, not as the legend he has become to students of congressional procedures.

Our view is not widely shared among congressional scholars, many of whom regard committee and subcommittee chairs as gatekeepers of the highest order. However, we suspect the conventional view has fallen prey to a missing-variable problem. The preferences of a chair are likely to be highly correlated with the preferences of a majority of his or her panel. Therefore, when he or she refuses a hearing or a mark-up, a majority of the committee or subcommittee is likely to favor that decision as well. If one does not control for the preferences of the majority of the committee, one never knows if the chair is exercising true gate-keeping power (at the expense of the preferences of the majority) or simply doing what the majority of the panel wants.

Subcommittees and gatekeeping power. Similarly, subcommittees do not have gatekeeping power. As with chairs of committees, any mechanism, such as the discharge petition, that works against committee gatekeeping power also works against subcommittee gatekeeping power. There are other measures as well: a majority vote in the full committee can negate *any* power of the subcommittee, including gatekeeping power. For instance, if the majority of the full committee wants to report a bill but the relevant subcommittee refuses to hold hearings or conduct the mark-up sessions, there are several ways the committee can subvert the subcommittee. It can simply force the subcommittee to report the bill. It can refer the bill to another subcommittee, or it can conduct the mark-up or hearing on its own.

Certainly, subcommittees since the 1970s play a much more central role than they once did, and certainly power in Congress became more decentralized throughout the 1970s and into the 1980s—but subcommittees still do not have nearly as much institutional power as full committees. Their gatekeeping powers are more limited. Further, they do not have very much positive power as well. That is, unlike the relationship of committees to the floor, subcommittees are never given closed rules when they report bills to the full committee. Also, there are no sure-fire safeguards that would prevent the full committee from altering the jurisdictions of subcommittees, and there is no strong seniority system on subcommittees that would prohibit the removal of subcommittee members from their posts.

That subcommittees have little gatekeeping power is consistent with the informational theory. However, at the same time this fact poses a question for the informational theory. Given that the particular form and power for subcommittees supports the informational theory, why don't committees take the same form? That is, why isn't their relation to the floor more like the relation of subcommittees to their parent committee?

The relative weakness of subcommittee gatekeeping powers is not consistent with the bicameral rivalry theory, since subcommittee gatekeeping power is a hurdle that the House and Senate could adopt but choose not to. Neither is it consistent with the distributive benefits theory. Although special interests can protect previous logrolls through *committee* gatekeeping power, what if the interests are so small that they do not compose the majority of a committee? If so, subcommittee gatekeeping power would be needed to protect logrolls they create. Of course, it is an empirical question just how large special interests in Congress are; it could be that they are all large enough to compose the majority of a committee. Finally the institution fails to give power to the subcommittee, reserving more power for the caucus, which seems to support the party government theory. On the other hand, if the majority party dominates subcommittees as they are hypothesized to dominate committees, gatekeeping power is irrelevant and the caucus would not care if the committee had it or not.

Closed versus Open Rules

Rules are said to be "closed" when amendments are not allowed on the floor, meaning that the committee position cannot be changed but can only be voted up or down. This tends to support the informational theory. One of the primary motivations for Gilligan and Krehbiel's original 1987 paper was to show that a rational floor would sometimes grant a closed rule in order to give a committee more incentive to gather information. Often overlooked is that the power is granted conditionally. Unlike gatekeeping power, for instance, closed rules are not given to all committees, nor to all bills that a committee reports. Rather the Rules Committee and the floor decide to grant this power only in special circumstances. We interpret this as further support for the informational theory. Just as the Gilligan-Krehbiel model shows, whether the floor should want to give a closed rule depends on such things as the costs of retrieving information, the status quo, and the preferences of the committee.

The institution is also consistent with the party government theory. Cox and McCubbins show how the scheduling power of a speaker (through his control of the Rules Committee) greatly aids his policy goals. One aspect of the power is the ability to grant closed rules to committees that report bills especially favorable to the Speaker's preferences. Since the Speaker is chosen by the majority caucus and represents its interests, closed rules help to further the goals of the majority caucus.

In contrast, the variance in uses of closed rules is not consistent with either the distributive benefits or bicameral rivalry theories. Both theories imply that committees only need gatekeeping powers to stop legislation. They therefore do not need the positive power of a closed rule.

Discussion

Our brief review of various committee institutions and their relation to the four theories is summarized in Table 9-1 (pp. 198-201). Several patterns are noteworthy. First, although the bicameral rivalry theory makes no prediction for quite a few institutions—thus indicating low power—the predictions it does make are very accurate. This is remarkable for a theory that is probably counter to the intuition of most scholars and observers of Congress. For that matter, we have not heard one single journalist, member of Congress, or other political scientist claim that committees exist because of a rivalry between branches of government. Also remarkable is that the theory was introduced with the attempts to formalize it. That is, Diermeier and Myerson did not simply formalize a received theory fashioned by many political scientists or the conventional wisdom of congressional observers; they introduced the theory themselves. So it is especially note-worthy that the theory is consistent with so many of the committee institutions.

Second, given that the party government theory *is* the formalization of the received wisdom of many pundits and political scientists, it is surprising that it does not make more predictions. There is a surprisingly—to us at least—large number of question marks in its column. The reason, we believe, is that in trying to adapt a party-government model to the U.S. system, scholars often find it hard to refrain from adding retreats and caveats to the theory.[33] Indeed, the very nature of a "*conditional* party government" theory follows in this spirit of caveats and retreats.[34]

Third, the information theory and distributive benefits theory frequently make the same prediction. This is also surprising, given how often the literature treats the two theories as opposites. That the two make so many similar predictions may help explain the glut of preference outlier tests, as this is one of the few areas where the theories differ.

Fourth, no theory consistently gets all plus marks for explaining the way things really work in Congress. Thus, no theory in itself is an accurate descrip-tion of the world of committee institutions. Instead we believe that all four the-ories contribute to an understanding of why committees exist. A variety of rein-forcing mechanisms or historical experiences led to the creation and persistence of each of the institutional facts we described above. Certainly, different aspects of the committee system evolved and solidified at different points in time, when different forms of congressional politics (parties, bicameral rivalry, expertise) were dominant. For instance, when the system is under attack from the parties for not being partisan enough (as was the case when former Speaker Gingrich turned to task forces in the mid-1990s), the important role of committees as information centers becomes a counterbalance, returning the system to status quo. When committees become too focused on handing out goodies to districts, as the House Science Committee did with Department of Energy installations in the late 1980s, then the committee's gatekeeping powers can be temporarily taken away (in that case by the House Appropriations Committee).

At the heart of the four theories are the basic political impulses driving members. Members are rewarded for making laws that rely on the best available information and predictions (information theory). Yet members are also reward-ed for bringing district-specific benefits back home, often at the expense of other members (distributive theory). As coalitions of interest groups themselves, polit-ical parties are the biggest interest groups in politics, and their very survival necessitates institutionalizing and rewarding party discipline (party cartel theo-ry). Finally, members need to amass financial and other rewards to mount reelec-tion bids, and this is easiest when petitioners can be cleverly extorted (bicameral rivalry theory).

Yet, although each theory reflects different motivations of members, and each theory also contributes to our understanding of committees, we caution against a conclusion that the true theory of why committees exist must be a simple weighted average of the four theories. Such a conclusion would be unimaginative and wrong. It would be unimaginative, because it ignores the possibility that a yet-undiscovered fifth (or sixth or seventh) theory will be consistent with all the institutions listed in Table 9-1. One should remember that only a few years ago—before Diermeier and Myerson published their research—it appeared that the number of theories explaining congressional committees was stuck at three. Such a conclusion would be wrong because some aspects of the committee system are inconsistent with all of the four theories. For instance, none of the theories imply that subcommittees should not have a seniority system. Also, none can offer an explanation, both for why committees sometimes have closed rules, and simultaneously for why subcommittees never have closed rules.

Finally, another word of caution involves our list of committee institutions. It is not, and is not intended to be, an exhaustive list of committee institutions. For instance, we do not list, or examine the significance of, the simple fact that subcommittees exist at all. That is, why must bills travel through the two-step process of subcommittee, then committee? Why not instead make each subcommittee a committee unto itself that reports directly to the floor?

Neither do we consider the existence of "exclusive" committees. Virtually all state legislatures—and the U.S. Congress—have a set of committees with "exclusive" memberships. If a legislator is on an exclusive committee, that member is not permitted to serve on any other standing committees. Why is it that some committees are exclusive while others are not? Is this a reflection of the amount of work flowing to the committees? (Apparently not.) Is it correlated with the most popular committees in terms of transfer ratios? (Yes in the House; no in the Senate.) Is the purpose of the institution to limit the patterns of logrolls—especially those involving Appropriations Committee and tax committee members? (Perhaps.)

Also notice that none of the theories explain the sizes of committees. In addition, what about conference committees? What about term limits for chairs? For that matter, why are committees composed of members instead of staff? That is, why don't bodies such as the Congressional Budget Office, the Office of Technology Assessment, and the Congressional Research Service replace committees? Conversely, why don't congressional committees replace such bodies? There are plenty of other institutions; the only constraint on our ability to explain them is the limits of our and other researchers' creativity.

The institutions that surround congressional committees are obviously numerous. Further, they are often not readily apparent to observers. Examples of institutions that many scholars have ignored—or at least failed to recognize the significance of—are that subcommittees do not have gatekeeping power, that the two chambers have separate committees, and that the minority receives a proportionate share of committee seats but no committee chairs. The many institutions are each important. Not only do they shape and constrain members' behavior in creating public policy; they also leave clues for judging and assessing theories of Congress.

Notes

1. David R. Mayhew, *Congress: The Electoral Connection* (New Haven: Yale University Press, 1974); Barry Weingast and William Marshall, "The Industrial Organization of Congress," *Journal of Political Economy* 96 (1988): 132–63; Keith Krehbiel, *Information and Legislative Organization* (Ann Arbor: University of Michigan Press, 1991); Forrest Maltzman, *Competing Principals: Committees, Parties and the Organization of Congress* (Ann Arbor: University of Michigan Press, 1997).

2. Thomas Gilligan and Keith Krehbiel, "Collective Decision-Making and Standing Committees: An Informational Rationale for Restrictive Amendment Procedures," *Journal of Law, Economics and Organization* 3 (1987): 287–335; Gilligan and Krehbiel, "Asymmetric Information and Legislative Rules with a Heterogeneous Committee," *American Journal of Political Science* 33 (1989): 459–90; Krehbiel, *Information and Legislative Organization.*

3. Tim Groseclose, "The Committee Outlier Debate: A Review and a Reexamination of Some of the Evidence," *Public Choice* 80 (1994): 265–73.

4. Krehbiel, *Information and Legislative Organization,* 80.

5. James M. Buchanan and Gordon Tullock, *The Calculus of Consent: Logical Foundations of Constitutional Democracy* (Ann Arbor: University of Michigan Press, 1962); Gordon Tullock, "A Simple Algebraic Logrolling Model," *American Economic Review* 60 (1970): 419–26.

6. Woodrow Wilson, *Congressional Government: A Study in American Politics* (Cambridge: Harvard University Press, 1885); Samuel C. Patterson and Gregory Caldeira, "Party Voting in the United States Congress," *British Journal of Political Science* 17 (1988): 111–31; Joseph Cooper and Garry Young, "Partisanship, Bipartisanship, and Crosspartisanship in Congress since the New Deal," *Congress Reconsidered,* 6th ed., ed. by Lawrence C. Dodd and Bruce I. Oppenheimer (Washington, D.C.: CQ Press, 1997), 246–73.

7. David Brady, *Congressional Voting in a Partisan Era: A Study of the McKinley Houses and a Comparison to the Modern House of Representatives* (Lawrence: University Press of Kansas, 1973); Maltzman, *Competing Principals;* Sarah A. Binder, *Minority Rights, Majority Rule* (New York: Cambridge University Press, 1997).

8. Gary W. Cox and Mathew D. McCubbins, *Legislative Leviathan: Party Government in the House* (Berkeley: University of California Press, 1993); for a critique, see Eric Schickler and Andrew Rich, "Controlling the Floor: Parties as Procedural Coalitions in the House," *American Journal of Political Science* 41 (1997): 1340–75.

9. For a critique and alternative theory, see David C. King and Richard Zeckhauser, "Legislators as Negotiators," in *Negotiating on Behalf of Others,* ed. by Robert H. Mnookin and Lawrence E. Susskind (Thousand Oaks, Calif.: Sage Publications, 1999).

10. Thomas H. Hammond and Gary J. Miller, "The Core of the Constitution," *American Political Science Review* 81 (1987): 1155–74; George Tsebelis and Jeannette Money, *Bicameralism* (New York: Cambridge University Press, 1997); Daniel Diermeier and Roger B. Myerson, "Bicameralism and Its Consequences for the Internal Organization of Legislatures," *The American Economic Review* 89 (December 1999): 1182–96; David P. Baron and John Ferejohn, "The Power to Propose," in *Models of Strategic Choice in Politics,* ed. by Peter C. Ordeshook (Ann Arbor: University of Michigan Press, 1989).

11. Matthew S. Shugart and John M. Carey, *Presidents and Assemblies* (New York: Cambridge University Press, 1992); Malcolm Shaw, "Conclusion," in *Committees in Legislatures: A Comparative Analysis,* ed. by John D. Lees and Malcolm Shaw (Durham: Duke University Press, 1979); Kaare Strøm, "Parliamentary Governments and Legislative Organization," in *Parliaments and Majority Rule in Western Europe,* ed. by Herbert Döring (New York: St. Martin's, 1996).

12. Roger H. Davidson and Walter J. Oleszek, *Congress and Its Members*, 5th ed. (Washington, D.C.: CQ Press, 1996), 135.
13. Ibid.
14. Ibid.
15. James K. Pollock, "Seniority Rule in Congress," *The North American Review* 222 (1925): 235–45; Nelson W. Polsby, Miriam Gallaher, and Barry S. Rundquist, "The Growth of the Seniority System in the U.S. House of Representatives," *American Political Science Review* 63 (1969): 787–807.
16. Some aspects of seniority do transfer between chambers. Chamber seniority (as contrasted with committee seniority) is used in allocating office spaces and (among Senate Republicans only) in offering open committee slots to members. For Senate seniority, all prior public service — elected and non-elected — counts, so a new senator with prior House service would be slightly advantaged when selecting offices and making initial committee assignments.
17. Thomas P. O'Neill, *Man of the House* (New York: Random House, 1987).
18. Richard L. Hall, *Participation in Congress* (New Haven: Yale University Press, 1996), 118.
19. C. Lawrence Evans and Walter J. Oleszek, *Congress under Fire: Reform Politics and the Republican Majority* (Boston: Houghton Mifflin, 1997), 92.
20. Thomas Romer and Howard Rosenthal, "Political Resource Allocation, Controlled Agendas, and the Status Quo," *Public Choice* 33 (1978): 27–43.
21. Binder, *Minority Rights, Majority Rule*, 33.
22. Christopher J. Deering and Steven S. Smith, *Committees in Congress*, 3d ed. (Washington, D.C.: CQ Press, 1997), 191–93.
23. Polsby, Gallaher, and Rundquist, "The Growth of the Seniority System in the U.S. House."
24. *Inside the Legislative Process: A Comprehensive Survey of the American Society of Legislative Clerks and Secretaries* (Denver: National Conference of State Legislatures, 1998), 68.
25. The following states also have joint committees to coordinate finance issues: Arkansas, Colorado, Delaware, South Dakota, Utah, Wisconsin, and Wyoming. Wayne L. Francis, *The Legislative Committee Game: A Comparative Analysis of Fifty States* (Columbus: Ohio State University Press, 1989).
26. Randall B. Ripley, *Majority Party Leadership in Congress* (Boston: Little, Brown, 1969); Barbara Sinclair, *Legislators, Leaders, and Lawmaking: The U.S. House of Representatives in the Postreform Era* (Baltimore: Johns Hopkins University Press, 1995); Samuel C. Patterson, "The Congressional Parties in the United States," Columbus, Ohio: Ohio State University, Department of Political Science, 1995.
27. Walter J. Oleszek, *Congressional Procedures and the Policy Process*, 4th ed. (Washington, D.C.: CQ Press, 1996), 93.
28. Randall B. Ripley, *Congress: Process and Policy*, 3d ed. (New York: Norton, 1983).
29. Wilson, *Congressional Government*, 63.
30. *Congressional Record*, 61st Congress, 2d Session, 8441–42, in David Epstein, "An Informational Rationale for Committee Gatekeeping Power" (New York: Columbia University, Department of Political Science, 1993).
31. Keith Krehbiel, "Why Are Congressional Committees Powerful?" *American Political Science Review* 84 (1987): 149–63; Oleszek, *Congressional Procedures and the Policy Process*.
32. Schickler and Rich, "Controlling the Floor."
33. For instance, Cox and McCubbins suggest that the majority caucus will allow some committees (those with *targeted* externalities) to be free from representing the collective interests of the whole caucus.
34. David Rohde, *Party Leaders in the Postreform House* (Chicago: University of Chicago Press, 1991).

10. Committees, Leaders, and Message Politics

C. Lawrence Evans

Early in 2000, efforts to add a prescription drug benefit to Medicare had emerged as a defining element of the national political agenda. According to public opinion polls, over 75 percent of Americans wanted to create such a benefit. By a wide margin, voters also believed that a Congress controlled by Democrats would do a better job handling the issue than would a Congress controlled by Republicans. Not surprisingly, Democrats incorporated the issue into their party's message for the fall campaign. In both chambers of Congress, Democratic leaders tried to force floor action on prescription drug proposals.

House Speaker Dennis Hastert, R-Ill., and other Republican leaders at first chose not to make the issue a priority. Their party's message early in the year focused on tax reduction, defense readiness, and education reform rather than on the creation of expensive new domestic programs. However, the popular appeal of the prescription drug issue and the prospect that Democrats might be able to force a floor vote on their plan convinced Hastert to change course.[1] Republican strategists did not feel that their party had to win the prescription drug issue outright. Instead, they sought to reduce the Democratic advantage on the matter in public opinion and neutralize it as a partisan campaign issue in the fall. But accomplishing this goal meant that House Republicans would have to counter Democratic prescription drug proposals with legislation of their own.

On Capitol Hill the crucial early work on legislation traditionally has been done in committee, and two House panels share jurisdiction over Medicare—the Committee on Commerce and the Committee on Ways and Means. The two panels often disagree on health issues, and such conflict surfaced in their work on prescription drugs. Faced with similar disputes over policy and turf, former Rep. Newt Gingrich, R-Ga., Hastert's immediate predecessor as Speaker, often appointed a Republican task force to formulate policy. But Gingrich's tendency to downplay or even bypass the committee system had angered senior Republicans. Upon assuming the Speakership in January 1999, Hastert pledged that the committees of the House would resume their long-standing role as policy initiators.

This pledge was easier made than delivered. On a number of major bills, the need to manage and advance the Republican message forced Hastert to become integrally involved in legislative activities traditionally delegated to the committees of jurisdiction. In the case of Medicare prescription drugs, he was concerned that the Commerce and Ways and Means Committees might fail to develop a consensus plan. In January 2000 the Speaker attempted to appoint a Republican prescription drug task force, so that, in his words, "we don't have apples and oranges."[2] A top aide to the Republican leadership described the response:

> Hastert tried to set up a task force for prescription drugs, but [Commerce Chair] Tom Bliley said "no." Hastert's intention was to appoint the [committee] leadership and a representative group of members. Have them draft a proposal, coordinate a proposal, and then the committees would mark it up. Our concern was that, if the committees proceed on their own with separate bills, we might get to June and not have legislation. But Bliley said, "no way." Gingrich would have set up that task force anyway.[3]

In February 2000 the Commerce and Ways and Means panels held separate hearings about the prescription drug issue. Although Hastert pushed for cooperation, the two committees also proceeded independently in drafting legislation.

Meanwhile, via a barrage of speeches, press releases, and media events, Democrats pounded the Republicans for their alleged inaction on prescription drugs. In February Democratic leaders filed two highly publicized discharge petitions aimed at bringing prescription drug legislation to the House floor. A number of House Democrats led van trips for their elderly constituents to Canada and Mexico to dramatize that drug prices are lower in those countries. Some Democrats staged media events with senior citizens and their pets because certain drugs actually cost less when purchased for animals rather than human beings. "Fido does better than granny," quipped Rep. Thomas Allen, D-Maine.[4] In April, Minority Leader Richard Gephardt, Mo., sent his Democratic colleagues a letter urging them to devote the coming congressional recess to highlighting their party's differences with the Republicans on prescription drugs.

A concerned Hastert instructed Republicans on the two panels to come together behind a common plan before the April break. Still, the discussions continued to be hampered by policy disagreements, intense political infighting, and strategic leaks to the media. The Speaker then stepped in and took the lead in the negotiations, meeting in his office with key Republicans from the Commerce and Ways and Means Committees until late in the evening. After weeks of intramural wrangling, Hastert brought the two sides together behind the outline for a Republican prescription drug proposal, which he unveiled at a press conference in mid-April. During the two-week recess that followed, Republican and Democratic members trumpeted their respective proposals and sought to convince constituents that their party would do the most to lower drug prices for the elderly.

The political skirmishing over prescription drugs for Medicare recipients raises important questions about legislating in the contemporary Congress. How does the broader electoral competition between the two parties influence the lawmaking process? To what extent do committees operate independently of party leaders on Capitol Hill? What tactics do leaders use to shape the prefloor legislative process? And what are the consequences for congressional policymaking?

The purpose of this chapter is to address these questions. My thesis is that the balance of power between committees and party leaders is increasingly shaped by the strategic demands of *message politics*. In both chambers the parties develop organized messages, which are composed of issues, themes, and policy symbols that legislators believe will generate a positive response toward their party among voters. By message politics I mean the interrelated set of electoral, communications, and legislative strategies that congressional parties employ to advance their respective messages. Especially in the House, how party leaders interact with the committee system depends on whether an issue is a message priority for one or both parties. In addition, the use of many important procedural features of lawmaking, including the discharge petition in the House and cloture in the Senate, is conditioned by the relevance of the issue under consideration to the majority and minority party messages. The legislative process has thus become increasingly inseparable from the broader partisan-electoral environment. On message issues any remaining distinctions between campaigning and governing have largely disappeared.[5]

Formulating the Message

Shortly before the 2000 elections, a Republican leadership aide argued that "the key to victory in November is for Republicans to be 100 percent focused on delivering our message over and over again until we are blue in the face. Whether it's on the House floor, over the airwaves or back home in the district, we must remain disciplined in our efforts."[6] Message politics, however, is about more than posturing and publicity. Congressional leaders seek to integrate the legislative agenda, party communications and campaign tactics, and the grassroots endeavors of key advocacy groups into a single broad strategy aimed at influencing the policy debate and increasing voter support for their respective parties. Democratic efforts to provide a prescription drug benefit for Medicare recipients, for instance, were intended to publicize and move an initiative that reflected the party's long-term commitment to health care reform. The potential consequences for national policy were profound. Democratic leaders also perceived the issue's usefulness in highlighting policy concerns and themes that would predispose many voters to support their party. It is precisely this linkage between party campaigning and congressional policymaking that makes message politics an important topic for analysis.

Party Message Operations

Over the past fifteen years the formal message operations of the House and Senate have grown more extensive and institutionalized. A turning point appears to have been 1989, the year that Newt Gingrich was selected as House Republican whip and Richard Gephardt became House majority leader.[7] Throughout his remarkable rise to power, Gingrich argued that House Republicans needed to coalesce behind a common policy agenda, and he routinely used televised floor proceedings of the chamber to take his message to the public. After his election as whip, Gingrich spearheaded within the Republican Conference the development of a more aggressive communications operation, which eventually produced the 1994 Contract with America. On the Democratic side of the aisle, Gephardt also was an early practitioner of message politics. Shortly after becoming majority leader, he organized a communications team of like-minded House Democrats and began putting out a "message of the day" for the media and anyone else who would listen.

The intensity of partisan message activities in the House and Senate increased substantially during the 1990s. By the 106th Congress, for instance, the House Republican Conference employed twelve staffers who specialized in party communications; the Speaker's office included another six communications aides.[8] Republican Conference Chair J. C. Watts, Okla., was responsible for orchestrating the message for House Republicans. Along with other Republican leaders, he worked with Senate Republicans, the Republican governors, and the presidential campaign of George W. Bush to develop a coordinated message agenda for the party. Among other activities, they provided rank-and-file Republican members with regular talking points and briefing packets about the phrases and themes to emphasize when speaking to constituents and the media. One notebook, for example, included sample speeches for Republican members on education reform, including four key phrases (safe, parental involvement, child-centered, and equality) that polls and focus groups indicated would resonate for Republicans with the public.[9]

During the 106th Congress, House Democrats ran a similar message operation, under the leadership of Rep. Rosa DeLauro, Conn. The Democratic Caucus employed nine communications specialists and, among other initiatives, sent out a daily email message to all Democratic members proclaiming a theme or policy proposal that they should emphasize in their public statements.[10] Particularly on key party issues such as Medicare prescription drugs, House Democratic leaders attempted to coordinate their message agenda with Senate Democrats and the Clinton White House.

U.S. senators are highly independent, and coordinating activities across different Senate offices has been compared to "pushing a wet noodle." But over time Senate leaders have come to emulate their House counterparts in fully integrating party communications efforts and the legislative agenda.[11] Interestingly, many of the individual members who worked most closely with Gingrich or Gephardt on message tactics in the House were later elected to the Senate, and they brought to the chamber their commitment to message politics. Among these members were Senate Minority Leader Thomas Daschle, D-S.D., Byron Dorgan, D-N.D., and Richard Durbin, D-Ill.—all Gephardt allies during their House years. Shortly after becoming minority leader in 1995, Daschle created a message team patterned on Gephardt's House group, with Dorgan as the initial chair. During the 106th Congress, Durbin led the group, and six of the eight team members were former members of the House. Senate Republicans, in contrast, did not have a single message team for all policy areas and instead organized issue-specific working groups to coordinate legislative and communications strategies on major bills. For instance, Bill Frist, Tenn., chaired the Senate Republican working group on education, while Majority Whip Don Nickles, Okla., led the group on health policy.

In constructing a message agenda for their party, congressional leaders rely on a range of information sources. The leadership offices themselves lack the resources necessary to conduct regular national polls, but the Republican and Democratic National Committees routinely provide their fellow partisans on Capitol Hill with timely polling data. According to a Republican National Committee spokesman, "We constantly focus-group and poll to find out what reaction our messengers and our messages are having with the American people."[12] Polls and focus groups reduce the level of uncertainty among party leaders about voter priorities and preferences, and they thus facilitate efforts to link the legislative agenda to campaign needs.[13]

The process of message formulation should be viewed as poll-influenced, rather than as poll-driven. Legislators also use constituent meetings and the mail to gauge which issues and themes resonate for them with voters. Most important, members base their preferences about message priorities on their own electoral experiences: they know which issues "worked for them" during the last campaign. These impressions are articulated to party leaders via the periodic retreats that congressional Republicans and Democrats conduct, as well as the regular party caucus meetings that occur in Washington when the House and Senate are in session. Leaders occasionally survey their own members about potential issue priorities for the party. In December 1999, for instance, Hastert asked House Republicans to complete a questionnaire about the items they believed should dominate the party's legislative agenda in 2000.[14] In short, the information that party leaders consider during the process of message construction bubbles up from a range of sources, including sophisticated survey data.

Selecting Message Priorities

In important research, Patrick Sellers has argued that two main factors influence which issues party leaders include in their message agendas: (1) the extent to which party members are homogeneous in their preferences on an issue; and (2) whether or not a party "owns" an issue in the eyes of the public.[15]

In choosing their message agenda leaders look for issues on which there is a high degree of preference homogeneity within their party caucus, because serious divisions will make it difficult for rank-and-file members to coalesce behind a single coherent message.[16] If preferences on an issue are relatively homogeneous within both parties, then it becomes a potential message item for both Republicans and Democrats. If preferences within one party are homogeneous, while the rank and file of the other party is divided, then the issue is a potential message item only for the unified caucus. And if preferences on a matter are heterogeneous within both parties, neither will be able to coalesce behind a single position and message. Among the issues that the party rank and file can unite behind, leaders search in particular for issues that can be used to distinguish their party from the opposition, that is, issues for which there is a significant divergence of preferences between the two parties. However, if a policy problem is highly salient and clearly favors one party, the opposing party may try to "inoculate" itself by crafting and publicizing a similar proposal in the same general issue area.

The distribution of preferences within the congressional parties certainly influences the process of message formulation, but leaders also may designate an issue as a message vote in order to increase intraparty loyalty and interparty divergence on it. During Senate consideration of managed health care reform in July 1999, for instance, Republican and Democratic leaders held party defections to a minimum by stressing the need to present a unified partisan front to the media and the public. When the Senate acted on tax reduction the following month, both Lott and Daschle convinced moderate elements within their parties not to offer a compromise proposal on the floor because the issue was so important to the message agendas of their respective parties. Middle ground never formed, and Republicans and Democrats coalesced behind dramatically different positions.[17]

"Issue ownership" is a concept from the work of John Petrocik, who argues that the two parties have each developed reputations with the public for handling certain issue areas better than the opposing party.[18] Figure 10-1 portrays public evaluations of party competence in ten key policy areas during the 1990s. These data are from various NBC News/*Wall Street Journal* polls that asked, "When it comes to dealing with [an issue], which party do you think would do a better job—the Democratic party, the Republican party, both about the same, or neither?" Panel A features the policy areas of crime, defense, foreign policy, and taxes, all of which tilted Republican throughout the decade. In contrast, the issues in Panel B—education, the environment, health care, Social Security—tilted Democratic. Panel C portrays two issues for which the partisan advantage shifted markedly over the decade, the economy and welfare reform.

The concept of issue ownership makes good intuitive sense. We do tend to associate the policy areas in Panel A with the Republican legislative agenda, and the areas in Panel B with the Democratic agenda. But the "ownership" metaphor should not obscure the considerable discretion exercised by congressional leaders in formulating message agendas. A congressional party may include in its message an issue area that advantages the other party if that matter is sufficiently salient. The recent action of House Republicans on prescription drugs for Medicare recipients is one example. Education issues have also polled Democratic in recent years, but the policy area emerged as a top voter priority during the 106th Congress. In response Republicans crafted an extensive education agenda, which they highlighted in their party message.

Public attitudes about the relative competence of the parties can change over time, depending in part on how an issue is framed. Economic management

Figure 10-1 Issue Advantages by Party, 1993–2000

Republican advantage

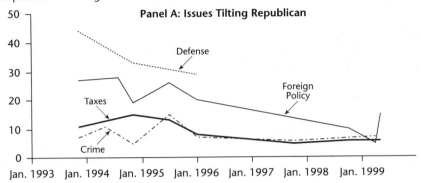

Democratic advantage

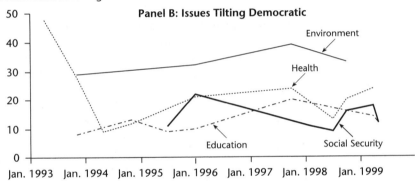

Republican advantage

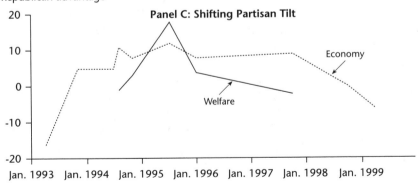

Source: Selected NBC News/*Wall Street Journal Polls, 1993–2000.*

Note: Republican advantage is the percentage responding that Republicans can better handle an issue minus the percentage responding that Democrats can better handle it. *Democratic advantage* is calculated in an analogous fashion. Data are missing for certain issues and years because respondents were not always asked about the same set of issue areas.

is a classic performance issue, and we would expect public attitudes about partisan issue competence to vary, as they did over the time period the figure surveys, depending on consumer confidence and the identity of the party holding the White House. But consider the matter of welfare reform. Although neither party had a significant advantage on welfare issues in fall 1994, by June 1995 the Republicans had opened up a twenty-point lead in the NBC News/*Wall Street Journal* tally. What had happened? For a time, Republican leaders were able to focus the broader welfare debate on criteria and themes that resonated favorably for them with voters. Throughout 1995, Republicans orchestrated an elaborate legislative and communications effort aimed at portraying their welfare reform proposal as a compassionate attempt to help recipients escape the bonds of dependence. The strategy was successful until the partial government shutdown of fall 1995, which fostered a countervailing view among voters that House Republicans were ideologically extreme and excessively confrontational. The Republican advantage on welfare issues dropped to just four percentage points by the end of the year.

Thus both the distribution of preferences within Congress and public attitudes about each party's respective competence influence the process of message formulation. Party leaders also have significant room to maneuver in deciding how to respond to particular scenarios. Issue areas such as welfare, education, health, and crime are sufficiently broad (and interconnected) that specific proposals can be crafted within these categories that evoke favorable images for either party. Consider the items that composed the party message agendas of House Republicans and Democrats during 1999, the first session of the 106th Congress. There are a number of indicators that can be used to relate the two party messages to concrete bills and resolutions, including the priorities and goals announced by party leaders at the beginning of each session, press releases produced by the Republican Conference and Democratic Caucus, and interviews with members and other participants in the process. Particularly useful information can be derived from the one-minute speeches delivered on the House floor at the beginning of a legislative day. Most mornings that the chamber is in session, tag teams of Republicans and Democrats take to the floor and make brief presentations in which they highlight their own party's message and attack the opposing party. Remarked Rep. Roscoe Bartlett, R-Md., "I was asked by someone the other day, 'What is the Republican agenda?' Now, of course, my first reaction was to think clearly this is someone who has never watched the 1-minute speeches."[19] If a bill or issue area was repeatedly discussed by Republican lawmakers during the one-minute speeches in 1999, then that measure can be treated as a message item for the majority party. Likewise, if the Democratic tag teams repeatedly emphasized a piece of legislation, then that measure can be viewed as a message item for the minority.

Table 10-1 lists thirty major bills that received some consideration on the House floor during 1999.[20] Included are the measures that *CQ Weekly* categorized as "major legislation" or upon which key votes, as defined by CQ, occurred,

Table 10-1 Relevance of Major House Bills to Party Messages, 1999

	High relevance for Democrats	Low relevance for Democrats
High relevance for Republicans	***Shared message priorities*** Budget resolution Education block grants Kosovo involvement Labor/HHS appropriations Supplemental appropriations Tax reduction Teacher training Title I (education)	***Majority message priorities*** Education flexibility Defense authorization Defense appropriations Juvenile justice Marriage penalty tax repeal Missile defense spending
Low relevance for Republicans	***Minority message priorities*** Campaign finance reform Gun control Managed health care reform	***Other major bills*** Agriculture appropriations Assisted suicide ban Banking overhaul Bankruptcy reform Census FAA reauthorization Fetal protection Satellite TV rules State Department authorization Steel imports Tax extenders VA/HUD appropriations Y2K liability

Source: Message categorization is based on "one-minute speeches" presented on the House floor during 1999. The list of major bills is from *CQ Weekly,* various issues, supplemented by the four largest appropriations measures.

as well as the four largest appropriations bills in terms of budget authority. I reviewed the one-minute speeches delivered during 1999 for evidence that the party message teams were active on the legislation or issue area, and based on these materials, placed each measure in one of four categories. *Shared message priorities* are bills that were highly relevant to the message agendas of both parties. *Majority message priorities* refers to legislation that was highly relevant to the Republican but not the Democratic message. *Minority message priorities* were highly relevant to the Democratic but not the Republican message. And *other major bills* refers to items of limited relevance to both party message agendas.[21]

Notice that seventeen of the thirty major bills (56.7 percent) can be classified as message items for one or both parties. This high percentage reflects the importance of message politics in the contemporary Congress, especially for significant legislation. As would be expected, defense, foreign policy, taxes, and juvenile crime were prominent on the Republican message agenda, and a major health care initiative was the centerpiece for the Democrats. Both parties were competing for public support on education issues, a traditional Democratic strength. The Democrats had engaged congressional Republicans in a contest over framing the criteria and considerations the public would use to evaluate tax cut proposals. Finally, the small number of minority message priorities in Table 10-1 underscores a central procedural reality of the House. Even with a small and divided majority (just six seats), the Republicans retained significant control over the agenda, and Democrats had to struggle to bring their bills to the floor.

Message Politics and the Legislative Process

Although the operating autonomy of House and Senate committees has declined over the past few decades, the committee stage remains an important arena for policy formulation and initial legislative consideration. Committee assignments are allocated via a process of constrained self-selection, and members tend to serve on panels that consider issues important to their career and policy goals. Committee members also receive sustained exposure to the items within their jurisdictions, which secures for them important strategic and informational advantages relative to other legislators. Thus the standing committee system provides individual members with special advantages on the issues they care about the most, and it also provides the institution as a whole with a source of specialized expertise, which can improve the quality of legislation.[22]

On many issues, however, the committee-based division of labor can impede the ability of rank-and-file legislators to pursue collective (often partisan) goals, and under such conditions members will expect party leaders to assume a more activist role, usually at the expense of the committee system.[23] First, legislators cannot depend on the standing committees to formulate a unified and coherent party message, because message agendas typically cross jurisdictional boundaries and require a degree of centralized coordination. Second, in contrast to committee chairs, party leaders are able to expand the range of feasible bargains and side-payments beyond the jurisdiction of one or two panels, facilitating efforts to broker disagreements between warring factions. Third, majority party members rely on their leadership to prioritize items for floor action, which in turn can require leadership intervention in agenda-setting at the committee stage—for example, to ensure that key measures are ready for floor consideration, or that opposition priorities are buried in committee. Fourth, as in the attempt to provide a prescription drug benefit for Medicare recipients, members rely on party leaders to coordinate the decisions of different panels when legislation has been multiply referred. Finally, because of their enhanced leverage and visibility, individual legislators often depend on party leaders to represent them in the bargaining that occurs across chambers and branches.

House members and senators routinely strike a balance between relying on the traditional strengths of the committee system and using the capacity of party leaders to advance collective partisan or institutional goals. Over the past three decades, the balance has shifted toward increased activism by leaders, especially on the floor.[24] But party leaders also have become more involved in the process when legislation is in committee. For the thirty major bills considered by the House in 1999, for instance, the level of prefloor activism by the Republican leadership can be ranked on a simple five-point scale (1 representing low involvement, and 5 representing high involvement), which takes on the following concrete values:

1. *Routine monitoring.* Leadership keeps track of which items are moving, when bills are ready for floor consideration, and potential points of conflict.
2. *Coordination and consultation.* Directly or through staff, leadership plays a more active role — for example by brokering jurisdictional disputes — but does not significantly influence the committee agenda or participate in substantive deliberations.
3. *Agenda-setting or content.* Leadership influences the pace of committee action, perhaps by making a measure a party priority, *or* participates extensively in substantive deliberations in committee.
4. *Agenda-setting and content.* Leadership influences the pace of committee action *and* participates extensively in substantive deliberations.
5. *Committee circumvention.* The committee markup stage is partially or completely bypassed, and the leadership coordinates preparation of a measure for floor action.

Based on the public record and interviews with leadership staff, I used this index to rate the involvement of the extended House Republican leadership on each of the major bills.[25] Overall, the leadership was highly active on these items (two-thirds were ranked 3 or above), but the modes and level of leadership activism varied significantly, depending on a bill's relevance to the Republican and Democratic message agendas. The message status of a measure determines the political stakes on it for the congressional parties, and thus shapes the choice of strategies by leaders and rank-and-file members throughout the legislative process. For example, the average level of prefloor leadership activism was highest for minority message priorities (4.33) and lowest for the category of other major bills (2.31). The averages for shared message priorities and majority message priorities (3.63 and 3.5, respectively) fell in the middle range. I will now consider each message category (in the order of relative leadership involvement), focusing primarily on the House, and then explore the impact of message politics on legislative strategy in the Senate.[26]

Minority Party Priorities

Minority party priorities are issues that by design tend to evoke favorable public attitudes about the minority party, and perhaps negative images of the majority party as well. The distribution of preferences within the minority party on these issues will be relatively homogeneous, while the absence of the initiative from the majority message suggests significant divisions about policy, or at least pockets of indifference. The majority leadership will work to keep these items off the agenda or to severely limit the scope and duration of congressional action. Compared to their Senate counterparts, majority party leaders in the House have significant control over the decision-making agenda. The House germaneness rule limits the ability of the minority to attach its message priorities to other issues in committee or on the floor, and the Speaker's effective control over the Rules Committee enables the leadership to further constrain the floor amendment process.

However, the political context on minority message priorities—homogeneous preferences within the minority party, a degree of heterogeneity within the majority, and favorable public attitudes about the minority's ability to handle the issue—makes it likely that there will be a cross-partisan coalition of some size in support of these initiatives. If the majority party is large and its internal divisions are not serious, then the leadership will have the leverage necessary to contain minority message priorities. But if the majority party is small and divided—as was the case for House Republicans during the 106th Congress—then the leadership's control over the agenda is endangered. Unless the committee of jurisdiction is stacked with leadership loyalists, it will not be able to manage the legislation for the majority party. Members of the minority party may heighten this pressure by filing a discharge petition to bring their bill directly to the floor. Under such conditions, majority party members will expect their leadership to step in and manage the process. This is exactly what occurred during House consideration of gun control, managed health care, and campaign finance reform measures in the 106th Congress.

Consider the issue of gun control, which was featured in the Democratic agenda but was mostly absent from Republican message activities. Following the April 1999 rampage at Columbine High School in Littleton, Col., House Democrats attempted to secure floor consideration of a proposal for background checks on purchasers at gun shows (some of the weapons used in Littleton had been obtained in this manner). Initially, Hastert worked with Judiciary Chairman Henry Hyde, R-Ill., to draft a consensus Republican proposal on guns, but anti–gun control factions within the Republican Conference revolted. Attention turned instead to the Judiciary Committee, which has jurisdiction over firearms and is also one of the most partisan and polarized panels in Congress. Hastert was concerned that a formal markup featuring gun issues would provide yet another public arena within which Democrats could attack the majority party. As a result, the leadership bypassed the markup stage and brought a streamlined provision affecting gun show sales directly to the floor, where it was defeated by a coalition of Democratic gun control advocates, who favored a stronger measure, and eighty-two Republicans who believed that the proposal went too far.

Similar dynamics were at work on managed health care reform, another minority message priority that was highly popular with voters. The core Democratic constituencies activated by the issue were united behind a proposal called the "Patients' Bill of Rights," but the medical profession and the insurance industry—two traditional Republican constituencies—were sharply divided. Hastert initially charged the Committee on Education and the Workforce with formulating a managed care plan for House Republicans, but the committee included a number of moderate Republicans who joined Democrats on the issue. As a result, the panel was unable to devise a proposal acceptable to the leadership and a majority of the Republican Conference. Faced with a looming political disaster, Hastert bypassed the committee and appointed a Republican task force to consider the issue. This group also failed to produce a consensus package for the party. In the end, the Speaker relented to Democratic pressure and the House adopted a version of the Democratic proposal, with sixty-eight Republicans defecting from the Hastert-backed position.

In the contemporary House, use of the discharge petition is closely associated with minority message priorities. If the requisite 218 signatures can be secured, the discharge procedure provides individual legislators, especially members of the minority, with a mechanism for bringing before the full chamber items not reported from committee. Few bills are formally discharged from committee.[27] But as the number of signers increases, the pressure on the leadership to schedule the targeted bill (or an alternative more acceptable to the majority party) also rises.[28] During the 1990s, the overall number of petitions (per Congress) fell, the percentage of petitions with a large number of signatures increased, and the entire discharge process became more partisan. In the 103d Congress (1993–1995), for instance, twenty-six discharge petitions were filed, and fifteen (57.7 percent) were signed by more than a hundred members.[29] Eight of the petitions (30.8 percent) drew the signatures of more than ten majority party members, indicating a degree of bipartisan support for the discharge effort. In the 106th Congress only eleven discharge petitions were filed, as of November 2000. But ten of these petitions (90.9 percent) received more than a hundred signatures, and none were signed by more than ten majority party members. In contrast to earlier Congresses, the discharge process was primarily used for minority message priorities.[30] Indeed, the list of targeted items reads like a Democratic wish list—campaign finance reform, gun control, managed health care reform, a minimum wage increase, and school modernization. Typically, Democratic leaders would orchestrate a mass signing ceremony on the floor of the House and then hold a press conference in which they publicized their proposal and castigated the Republicans as obstructionists.

In the 106th Congress, the difficult strategic challenges that Republican leaders confronted on minority message priorities led them to also be innovative in the crafting of floor amendment rules. For example, the gun control issue initially surfaced as part of a juvenile justice bill that was central to the Republican message agenda. Conservative Republicans wanted to take a public position in favor of the juvenile crime measure, but they could not cast such a vote if Democrats and moderate Republicans were successful in adding significant firearms restrictions to the bill on the floor. So the leadership devised a new procedure, called a *bifurcated rule*, which effectively relegated the gun issue to a separate bill that was considered in tandem with the juvenile justice measure.[31] As a result, Republicans were able to cast separate votes against the Democratic gun control language and in favor of clamping down on juvenile violence. Republican staff to the Rules Committee jokingly referred to bifurcated rules as *MIRVs*, which stands for "Multiple Independent Reentry Vehicles." Such procedures have been utilized on other minority message priorities in the 106th Congress, including managed health care reform and the minimum wage.

Shared Message Priorities

Shared message priorities are issues featured on the message agendas of both political parties. In consideration of such issues the strategic competition between Republicans and Democrats concerns the terms of the debate, or how an issue will be framed for the media and the public. Preferences within the rank and file of each party are relatively homogeneous (at least on the broad contours of the legislation), and there are significant differences between the two parties. Most likely, the distribution of preferences in the chamber will be reflected in the committees of jurisdiction, and the majority leadership will not need to circumvent the markup stage.

The stakes for the two parties on shared message priorities are high. Centralized coordination is necessary because these issues often cross jurisdictional boundaries or surface in diverse arenas and legislative vehicles. A large portion of the shared message priorities relate to budgetary, spending, and tax matters. The main arena for these decisions is the congressional budget process, which is relatively centralized and leadership-driven.[32] For these reasons, the leadership typically is involved in committee agenda-setting on shared message priorities and actively participates in legislative deliberations during the committee stage.

The framing strategies that party leaders employ come in two main forms: *interpretation* and *linkage*. *Interpretation* refers to the parties' attempts to influence media coverage and public opinion by emphasizing different dimensions or policy images for evaluating an issue.[33] During the 106th Congress, for instance, both party messages touched on education issues, especially congressional efforts to reauthorize the Elementary and Secondary Education Act (ESEA). As mentioned, education traditionally has polled well for Democrats, but the high salience of the issue in the public view (and a growing "comfort level" among congressional Republicans on education policy) convinced the Republican leadership to formulate and publicize an ambitious legislative agenda in the area.[34] To maximize media coverage, House Republican leaders divided the ESEA reauthorization into five different bills, which they moved separately. They also attempted to frame the issue in terms favorable to the Republican Party. Rather than school modernization and national accountability, they emphasized state and local flexibility and reduced red tape. To further blur the Democratic message, Republicans also included more education funding in the budget resolution than Clinton did in his budget submission. The centerpiece of the Republican education agenda, the *Straight A's Bill,* was drafted under the direction of the Republican leadership and first released at a leadership press conference.

Linkage refers to attempts by party leaders to tie—legislatively and politically—a message initiative put forth by the opposition to another issue area in which their own party has the advantage.[35] President Bill Clinton's 1998 State of the Union address contained a classic example of this strategy, which fundamentally altered the political terrain for the Republican tax cut proposals. As Clinton prepared his remarks, it was apparent that the federal government would soon have a sizable budget surplus. Republicans wanted to devote the surplus to tax reduction, whereas Democrats preferred to shore up or expand major domestic policy programs. Clinton's strategy was to link proposals for tax reduction to the solvency of Social Security and Medicare, which are highly popular programs, particularly with key Democratic constituencies. "What should we do with this projected surplus?" Clinton asked the joint session of Congress and the national television audience. "I have a simple four word answer: Save Social Security first."[36] He received a standing ovation. Congressional Democrats quickly embraced Clinton's position as their primary line of defense against the Republican tax message, and polls indicated that it resonated with the public.

The linking of tax reduction to Social Security structured the entire budget and appropriations process during the 106th Congress, especially the first session—even on spending bills that were not viewed as message items by either political party. As part of this process, House Republican leaders became involved in allocative decisions that in previous years were the primary responsibility of Appropriations Committee members.

Early in 1999 the budget process was still operating subject to binding constraints on discretionary spending (the so-called appropriations caps) that had been put in place by the 1997 budget agreement. The consensus view on Capitol Hill was that the caps would have to be lifted to pass the appropriations bills. The previous year, congressional Republicans had been unable to adopt a budget resolution, and the ensuing end-of-the-session logjam of unfinished appropriations measures had allowed Clinton to leverage large spending increases for key Democratic priorities.[37] To avoid a repeat of that process, Hastert pledged to finish all the appropriations bills by August 1999. Republicans also devised a Social Security "lockbox" proposal that purportedly fenced off those portions of the budget surplus that derived from Social Security.

The linking of tax reduction to Social Security in the public debate between the parties created a vexing strategic problem for congressional Republicans. They intended to propose a $792 billion tax cut and make it the centerpiece of their message agenda. For political reasons, the Republicans could not rely on the Social Security trust fund to finance the cut, which in turn meant that they would have to clamp down on discretionary expenditures and support a continuation of the caps. As part of their broader agenda, Republican leaders also were proposing funding hikes for education and defense, placing additional strain on the appropriations process. But unless the party rejected the appropriations caps, passing the year's spending bills by August was highly unlikely, raising the specter of another fall bargaining game in which Clinton would hold most of the cards.

Traditionally, the House and Senate Appropriations Committees operate in a bipartisan fashion, with limited involvement by party leaders in specific decisions about spending.[38] However, the role and operating style of the House Appropriations Committee was significantly altered by the Republican majorities of the 1990s. In 1995, for example, Speaker Newt Gingrich and other Republican leaders added an array of conservative policy "riders" to the year's appropriations bills. These provisions pleased party conservatives, but they drew a succession of presidential vetoes and contributed to the partial government shutdown of December 1995.[39] The number of policy riders declined after that year, but the leadership still intervened regularly in the work of the committee because of pervasive pressures to hold down spending.

The level of prefloor leadership involvement in the appropriations process was particularly extensive during the 106th Congress. Early in 1999, for example, Hastert, Lott, and other Republican leaders met with the chairs of the two Appropriations panels to set overall limits on discretionary expenditures and to discuss how funds should be allocated across the thirteen annual appropriations bills (the 302b allocations). The leadership chose to transfer funds from the larger domestic spending bills (especially Labor/HHS) to smaller, less contentious measures, and to move the narrower bills first. Hastert and Majority Whip Tom DeLay, R-Texas, determined the schedule for the appropriations process, and they were integrally involved in the major allocative decisions on each measure. An aide to Hastert observed that, "on appropriations in general, there were regular meetings with the subcommittee chairmen and the leadership. There was lots of leadership involvement in the numbers, in the texts of the bills."[40] During committee consideration of a supplemental appropriations bill, for instance, Hastert overruled Appropriations Chairman Bill Young, R-Fla., and instructed the panel to offset any spending increases with reductions in other programs. "We didn't have to have offsets," remarked one subcommittee chairman, "however, it wasn't up to me."[41]

In August 1999 congressional Republicans passed their tax reduction proposal, fully expecting a presidential veto. Republican members devoted the three-week August recess to mobilizing public opinion behind the plan. But polls indicated that their efforts were unsuccessful, and in September they shifted their core message away from tax cuts to debt reduction and the need to protect Social Security. As a result, Republican leaders were able to back away from the appropriations caps, which in turn enabled them to reach an agreement with Clinton on the remaining spending bills. The resulting "consensus" between Clinton and congressional Republicans not to spend the Social Security surplus and to focus on debt reduction was a significant policy outcome, and it derived in part from strategic posturing over message by the White House and congressional party leaders.

Majority Message Priorities

Majority message priorities are measures that are highly relevant to the message agenda of the majority party but that, unlike those of the previous category, are of limited direct relevance to the minority message. Minority party leaders may attempt to frame these proposals in a manner that undermines public support for the majority agenda. But the absence of these items from the minority's message suggests that they do not poll well for the party, or that there are serious policy disagreements within the minority rank and file. On proposals to eliminate the so-called "marriage penalty" in the tax code, for instance, the Republican Party is highly united, the public is supportive, and Democrats are divided. As a result, the issue is a natural message priority for the Republican majority, whereas it has only limited message value for the Democrats (mostly as a point of attack).

Depending on the importance of an issue area to the public, the leaders of the minority party may seek to keep majority message priorities off the agenda or to alter the scope of the conflict by linking them to other proposals that are important to the minority (or perhaps divide the majority). Institutional differences between the chambers are critical here. In the House, the majority leadership's control over the agenda dampens the ability of the minority to obstruct or divert legislation. The majority leadership thus will usually be able to control the agenda and ensure that these priority items move expeditiously through committee to the floor.

Consider the so-called Ed-Flex bill, which was a key majority message item during the 106th Congress. Early in 1999 the bicameral Republican leadership moved the measure to the top of the post-impeachment congressional agenda, in order to demonstrate to voters that their party could work with Democrats to pass major legislation. The bill itself was narrowly drawn and supported by a large bipartisan coalition. In both chambers, Democratic leaders sought to broaden the debate to include the minority's education priorities, especially after-school aid and a Clinton administration proposal to hire a hundred thousand new teachers. House Republican leaders primarily relied on chamber rules to contain the Democratic strategy. During committee consideration of the bill, an amendment to add the teacher-hiring proposal was ruled out of order as nongermane. Similarly, the germaneness restriction prevented Democrats from offering the proposal on the floor. The Ed-Flex bill quickly passed the full House by a 330–90 margin.

A similar strategic dynamic was apparent during congressional consideration of legislation to repeal the marriage tax penalty. The item originally was included in the massive Republican tax bill that was vetoed by Clinton in September 1999. In January 2000, the House Republican leadership decided to peel off certain targeted tax reductions, including the marriage tax provision, and move them as freestanding bills. At the direction of Speaker Hastert, the Ways and Means Committee expedited the markup process on the marriage penalty measure (the earliest in a session the panel had ever reported a major tax bill), and the Housed quickly passed the bill on February 10 (timed to coincide with Valentine's Day), with the support of forty-eight Democrats.

Other Major Bills

The fourth category, other major bills, is composed of legislation that is not a message priority for either party. Of the thirty major bills listed in Table 10-1, thirteen (43.3 percent) fell in this quadrant. On average, the leadership was less involved during the prefloor legislative process on these items, but there was considerable variance. On four of the measures (the assisted suicide, bankruptcy reform, fetal protection, and Y2K liability measures), the level of leadership activism did not extend beyond routine monitoring. But on the VA/HUD appropriations bill, Republican leaders were highly involved in the timing and substance of committee work. And on the measure imposing a steel import quota, the leadership essentially instructed Ways and Means Republicans to conduct a perfunctory markup and report the measure without modification, even though a majority of the panel opposed the bill on its merits. In comparison to the message items, the process for the bills in this category more closely approximates the traditional committee process—but with the caveat that the legislative process in general has become more fluid and less committee-centered in recent years.[42]

A common incentive for leaders to assume an activist role on non-message items before they reach the floor is jurisdictional infighting. The House parliamentarians emphasize that the incidence of jurisdictional disputes declined sharply after the Republicans assumed majority status in 1995.[43] For one, the Republicans slashed committee staff allocations, and individual panels are now less likely to have the staff resources necessary to continually search for new turf or obsessively protect existing boundaries.[44] The Republicans also abolished open-ended joint referrals, in which two or more committees share control over entire bills. Instead, the Speaker now designates a primary, or lead, committee of jurisdiction for legislation that has been multiply referred, which has reduced jurisdictional infighting (particularly in the appointment of conference committee delegations).[45] The new Republican committee chairs also were less personally invested in the decades-old turf wars that had cropped up among their Democratic predecessors. Compared to the Democrats when they were the majority party, Republicans members in general were less tolerant of jurisdictional squabbles.

Still, jurisdictional issues did arise during the 106th Congress, often relating to the wide-ranging policy domain of the Committee on Commerce. Typically, the leadership would attempt to mute the intercommittee conflict and manage the process through which competing committee recommendations were merged into a common package before floor action. For a decade or more, disagreements between the Banking and Commerce Committees about policy and turf had helped derail legislative efforts to restructure the financial services industry (the two panels share jurisdiction). Passage of such a measure was a top priority in the 106th Congress, and by most accounts it was the most important enactment of the first session. There were significant differences between the measures reported by the two committees, and Rules Chairman David Dreier, R-Calif., acted for the House Republican leadership in fashioning a single bill for floor action. Hastert was also personally involved on the measure, brokering substantive differences between the Banking and Commerce panels. An intense, if less far-reaching, jurisdictional fight broke out on the satellite television bill, this time involving Commerce and the Committee on the Judiciary. In this case Hastert helped coordinate decision making across the two panels and dampen the ensuing jurisdictional difficulties, which continued through the appointment of the conference committee.

Committees are more likely to operate independently of the leadership on non-message items. By most accounts, the most aggressively independent chairman during the Gingrich and Hastert Speakerships was Rep. Bud Shuster of the Committee on Transportation and Infrastructure. Shuster's committee has jurisdiction over highway construction, aviation, water projects, and other issues that scholars call "distributive policy" and congressional critics label "pork."[46] In his Pennsylvania district, one federally funded road is named "The Bud Shuster Byway."

As chairman, Shuster was remarkably successful at protecting or expanding the programs within his jurisdiction, often in the face of significant leadership opposition. During the 105th Congress, for instance, Shuster and his allies pushed through a unique change in House Rules that restricted the ability of members to use the appropriations process to reduce highway spending beneath the authorized level. Appropriations Chair Bill Young complained that the rule "signifies the triumph of powerful committee members at the expense of all of us, and therefore represents the worst kind of institutional policy."[47] In a June 1999 floor fight, Shuster confronted a coalition of House leaders and committee chairmen (including Majority Whip Tom DeLay and the chairs of the Appropriations, Budget, Rules, and Ways and Means panels) who opposed a Shuster-backed effort to ensure that the aviation trust fund could only be used for aviation purposes. After weeks of careful lobbying, Shuster prevailed by almost seventy votes.

Congressional observers routinely compared Shuster to former Democratic committee barons such as Jack Brooks (Judiciary), John Dingell (Commerce), and Dan Rostenkowski (Ways and Means). But Shuster's prominence was rooted in the size and diversity of his committee membership, as well as in his skills at logrolling and constructing broad bipartisan coalitions in support of committee programs. In the 106th Congress there were seventy-five members on the Transportation and Infrastructure Committee, making it the largest panel in congressional history. Unlike a number of other Republican chairs, Shuster worked closely with his Democratic counterpart, Rep. James Oberstar, Minn. As Shuster put it, "There's no such thing as a Republican or a Democratic bridge, or a Republican or a Democratic airport."[48] Because his issues were not central to the message agenda of either party, rank-and-file members usually were reluctant to support leadership efforts aimed at curbing Shuster's parochialism.

Message Politics in the Senate

In the Senate, message priorities are disproportionately likely to receive abbreviated or pro forma consideration in committee, or to be brought directly to the floor. During the 1999 session, for example, Majority Leader Lott opted to bring the juvenile justice measure, with the accompanying dispute over gun control, to the full chamber without a markup in the Judiciary Committee. Managed health care reform was considered in committee in 1999, but most of the key legislative decisions for Senate Republicans were made by a leadership-appointed task force chaired by Majority Whip Nickles. The Senate is generally less committee-centered than the House. The tactical and procedural consequences of message politics are thus particularly apparent on the Senate floor, where the absence of a general germaneness requirement and the chamber's reliance on unanimous consent provide the minority party with significant leverage over the agenda. Two procedural tactics are especially relevant here—filing for cloture and filling the amendment tree. In the 106th Congress, both tactics were closely associated with just two of the issue quadrants that we have explored—minority message priorities and majority message priorities.

Throughout the 106th Congress the primary strategic challenge for Senate Democrats was to secure floor action for their message priorities, and Majority Leader Lott usually attempted to block such consideration. These interactions had a predictable rhythm. First, Senate Democrats would seek to offer their message priorities as nongermane amendments to other bills—often key Republican message items, such as the proposed Social Security "lockbox" or the juvenile justice bill. Lott would refuse to agree to a unanimous consent agreement (the bill-specific procedural accords that senators use to structure floor action) if it permitted consideration of the Democratic amendments, or he would require that minority party members substantially scale back their amendment demands. Senator Daschle would object to Lott's requests for a streamlined amendment process. Lott would attempt to invoke cloture, because only germane amendments are permitted after cloture. Daschle in turn would mobilize Senate Democrats against the cloture attempt. Since Lott lacked the sixty votes necessary to cut off debate, the cloture motion would fail and bargaining between the parties would continue.

In 1999, thirty-two separate cloture motions were contested (defined here as drawing five or more no votes) and thus merit special scrutiny.[49] Of these contested cloture motions, only six garnered the sixty votes necessary to cut off debate. Ten of the contested motions dealt with Democratic efforts to secure floor consideration on just four minority message priorities—campaign finance reform, gun control, managed health care, and a minimum wage hike. Another nine of the contested cloture motions were attempts by Lott to secure a vote on just two Republican message priorities—four cloture votes on the Ed-Flex bill and five on various versions of the Social Security lockbox. Thus almost 60 percent of all the contested cloture motions in the Senate that year occurred in these two message quadrants, on a mere handful of issues. One more contested cloture motion dealt with a shared message priority (Kosovo involvement), and the remainder were sprinkled across major and nonmajor bills that were not message items for either party. As with the House discharge petition, the Senate cloture procedure is closely associated with message politics.

In a related tactic, Lott occasionally responded to Democratic message amendments by filling in the amendment tree, which delineates the number, form, and order of permissible amendments on the Senate floor.[50] As majority leader, Lott had the right to priority recognition, based on Senate precedents dating back to the 1930s. In at least seven instances in 1999, he used that prerogative to submit enough amendments to effectively preclude other members from offering their own alternatives—that is, he filled in all the available branches on the relevant amendment tree. Every one of these cases related to a majority or minority message priority. For instance, Lott filled the tree on the Y2K bill in order to block Democratic amendments dealing with gun control and the minimum wage. On the Africa Growth Act (a trade measure not included on our list of major bills), he filled the tree to block a minimum wage proposal by Sen. Edward Kennedy, D-Mass. The majority leader also filled the tree on the Ed-Flex legislation, to keep Democrats from offering their own education priorities, particularly Clinton's proposal to hire a hundred thousand new teachers. And on five different occasions, Lott filled the amendment tree during Senate consideration of various versions of the Social Security lockbox. Interestingly, Minority Leader Daschle also filled the amendment tree on campaign finance reform to keep Republicans from offering amendments that might have provided them with a degree of political cover on the issue.

Lott's efforts to keep Democratic legislative priorities off the floor fueled partisan tensions throughout the 106th Congress. In June 1999, for instance, Democrats shut down the Senate floor for a full week until the majority leader agreed to floor action on a managed health care bill. In May 2000 Lott pulled from the floor the major education bill of the year, largely because Democrats intended to use it as a vehicle for gun control amendments. The next week, Daschle blindsided the majority leader with a gun-related amendment to the military construction appropriations bill. An angry Lott orchestrated a procedural change that further restricted the amendment process on spending bills. Daschle countered by temporarily delaying Senate consideration of any appropriations measures that had not been passed by the House ("regular order" is for the House to go first on spending bills). In a May 17 floor statement remarkable for its personal animosity, Daschle chastised the majority leader: "The way the Senate is being run is wrong. No majority leader in history has attempted to constrain Senate debate as aggressively as Senator Lott has chosen to do. . . . He is trying to protect his members so they don't have to vote on tough issues." Lott responded, "I am not going to be threatened and intimidated by the minority in trying to get our work done . . . if you want to shut down everything, then everybody loses in that process."[51] The procedural wrangling between Lott and Daschle was yet another by-product of party competition over message and the legislative agenda.

Conclusion

In the contemporary Congress, party leaders in both chambers develop organized message agendas aimed at advancing the legislative and electoral interests of their respective parties. Message items typically address the major issues of the day, such as health policy, tax reduction, defense spending, and gun control. Most important, the process of legislating on message issues is inseparable from the process of campaigning.

The relevance of a bill or proposal to the majority and minority party message has significant implications for key aspects of legislative strategy. Majority party leaders are more likely to play a major role in committee (and before) on message items, especially minority party initiatives that threaten the majority's control over the decision-making agenda. During the 106th Congress, the internal deliberations of the House Appropriations Committee were fundamentally altered by the broader competition over which party would frame the terms of public debate and understanding on tax policy and the burgeoning budgetary surplus. And important procedural tactics, including the House discharge petition and Senate cloture, are closely associated with message issues.

In this chapter I focused on the 106th Congress, and particularly on the House. The intensity and pervasiveness of party message operations during this period derived in part from narrow partisan majorities on Capitol Hill, the divided partisan control of Congress and the executive branch, and the approach of what many legislators believed would be a watershed election in November 2000. Depending on the political configuration in the 107th Congress, the importance of message politics may decline somewhat. But the links between party campaigning and the legislative agenda predate the 106th Congress, and there is little sign that the intense elite-level partisanship of recent years will decline anytime soon. The specific bills that constitute the majority, minority, and shared message categories, as well as the number of items in each category, may change. But the close ties between the broader partisan-electoral environment and internal legislative strategy should extend beyond the 106th Congress.

What does such a close connection imply for congressional deliberation? The implications are not good, according to some observers. During House consideration of juvenile justice and gun legislation in June 1999, for instance, Rep. David Obey, D-Wis., asserted that, "More and more, the Congress is not passing real legislation, it is passing institutional press releases aimed far more at sending political messages than they are at solving problems." Obey was particularly incensed that the juvenile justice and gun control bills were brought to the floor without full consideration in the relevant committee. "What Congress is able to do best," Obey argued, is "carefully sort out in committee the nuances of critical issues, aided by the expertise that committee members develop in their specialty areas of jurisdiction."[52]

However, the forms of distributive decision making that produced the Bud Shuster Byway usually occur in committee, after extensive bipartisan discussion and careful management by expert lawmakers who know exactly what they are doing. Few congressional observers would single out such distributive logrolling as a model of effective deliberation. Also consider the Senate Republican task force on managed health care reform, which met regularly during the 106th Congress to discuss the details of liability policy, the problems of the uninsured, and other regulatory issues. Assisted by expert staff, the members of the task force spoke extensively with moderate Republicans about their policy concerns and made significant changes in the Republican managed health care proposal to maintain party unity. Was this process less deliberative because it occurred for the most part outside the committee system, with little direct participation by Democratic members?

Most scholarship and popular commentary about congressional deliberation focuses on decision making in committee.[53] In a Congress characterized by intense partisanship, an activist leadership, and a committee system that is high-ly permeable to the broader political environment, we need to rethink how we gauge effective deliberation and perhaps look for it in different institutional venues and arenas. One likely consequence of message politics, though, is height-ened difficulty in brokering legislative compromises, especially across partisan lines. Party campaigning, by its nature, is a zero-sum game. Tactics that increase the margin of public support for one party or candidate necessarily reduce the margin of support for the opposition. Legislative compromise, in contrast, works best in a positive-sum environment in which more than one side can take some-thing away from the table. On message issues, most distinctions between cam-paigning and legislating are more pedagogical than real. As a result, legislative bargaining takes on the zero-sum cast of party campaigning, further complicat-ing the already difficult task of building winning coalitions on Capitol Hill.

Notes

The preparation of this chapter was assisted by many conversations with Dick Fenno, Walter Oleszek, and especially Lee Rawls.

1. In contrast, Senate Republican Leader Trent Lott, R-Miss., chose to downplay the issue.
2. *National Journal's Congress Daily,* online version, January 27, 2000.
3. Not-for-attribution interview conducted by the author and Walter Oleszek in Washington, D.C., on March 10, 2000.

4. Julie Rovner, *National Journal's Congress Daily*, online version, February 24, 2000.
5. The message operations of the congressional parties can be viewed as attempts to promote a favorable partisan "name brand," and thus fully consistent with the analysis of Cox and McCubbins. See Gary Cox and Mathew McCubbins, *Legislative Leviathan: Party Government in the House* (Berkeley: University of California Press, 1993). Richard Fenno has repeatedly emphasized the close relationship between campaign activity and legislative decision making. Consult, for instance, his "Observation, Context, and Sequence in the Study of Politics," *American Political Science Review* 80 (1986): 3–15. Also see W. Lee Rawls, *The Art of Legislation: A Practitioner's Guide* Policy Report of the Thomas Jefferson Program in Public Policy, The College of William and Mary, February 1999.
6. John Bresnahan, "Poll Shows Trouble for House Republicans," *Roll Call*, June 8, 2000, 3.
7. C. Lawrence Evans and Walter J. Oleszek, "Message Politics and Senate Procedure," in *The Myth of Cool Judgement*, ed. by C. Campbell and N. Rae (Boulder, Col.: Rowman and Littlefield, 2000).
8. Daniel Lipinski, "Communicating the Party Record: How Congressional Leaders Transmit Their Messages to the Public" (paper delivered at the annual meeting of the American Political Science Association, Atlanta, September 2–5, 1999).
9. *A Conversation with America 2000*, The Luntz Research Companies, 2000, 141.
10. Daniel Lipinski, "Communicating the Party Record," 7.
11. On the topic of message tactics in the Senate, consult Patrick J. Sellers, "Winning Media Coverage in the U.S. Congress" (paper delivered at the Norman Thomas Conference on Senate Exceptionalism, Vanderbilt University, Nashville, October 21–23, 1999); and Evans and Oleszek, "Message Politics and Senate Procedure."
12. Al Kamen, "In the Loop," *Washington Post*, March 2, 2000, A27.
13. John G. Geer, "Critical Realignments and the Public Opinion Poll," *Journal of Politics* 53 (1991): 434–53.
14. Juliet Eilperin, "For House GOP, a New Prescription," *Washington Post*, April 26, 2000, A1.
15. Sellers, "Winning Media Coverage in the U.S. Congress."
16. In emphasizing intraparty homogeneity, Sellers builds on the concept of conditional party government, which originated with David Rohde and has been refined by Rohde in collaboration with John Aldrich. See David W. Rohde, *Parties and Leaders in the Post-Reform House* (Chicago: University of Chicago Press, 1991); and John H. Aldrich and David W. Rohde, "The Transition to Republican Rule in the House: Implications for Theories of Congressional Politics," *Political Science Quarterly* 112 (1997–98): 541–67.
17. C. Lawrence Evans, "How Senators Decide: An Exploration" (paper delivered at the Norman Thomas Conference on Senate Exceptionalism, Vanderbilt University, Nashville, October 21–23, 1999).
18. John R. Petrocik, "Issue Ownership in Presidential Elections, with a 1980 Case Study," *American Journal of Political Science* 40 (1996): 825–50.
19. *Congressional Record*, June 25, 1999, H4956.
20. The sampling technique is modeled on Barbara Sinclair, *Legislators, Leaders, and Lawmaking* (Baltimore: Johns Hopkins University Press, 1995), chap. 9. I dropped two of the CQ major bills (dealing with electricity deregulation and encryption export controls) because they received only limited consideration during 1999. Although it did not receive CQ major bill status until January 2000, the marriage penalty bill was included in the sample because it was initially considered by the chamber in July 1999, as part of the GOP reconciliation package, and was also viewed as a key Republican message priority throughout the 106th Congress.

21. Evans and Oleszek relate certain of these bills to the message agendas of Senate Republicans and Democrats based on the impressions of leadership staff. Using the one-minute speeches on the House floor is probably a better gauge, because it derives from observable behavior rather than informal perceptions after the fact. For instance, the leadership staff interviewed for Evans and Oleszek's paper rated the juvenile justice bill as a message priority for Senate Democrats as well as Republicans, most likely because it was so closely related to Senate action on gun control. But the one-minute speeches indicate that the Republicans were primarily interested in the juvenile justice item, while the Democratic message emphasized guns. In addition there were differences during the 106th Congress between the message agendas of House and Senate Republicans. The Senate Republicans eventually included managed health care reform in their party message, whereas the more divided House Republican Conference did not emphasize the issue for message purposes. Still, the two measurement strategies produced similar results. See Evans and Oleszek, "Message Politics and Senate Procedure."

22. Christopher J. Deering and Steven S. Smith, *Committees in Congress*, 3d ed. (Washington, D.C.: CQ Press, 1997).

23. On these points, consult Sinclair, *Legislators, Leaders, and Lawmaking*, chap. 9.

24. Ibid., chap. 4.

25. Detailed information about the coding criteria and how each measure was rated can be obtained from the author.

26. These data are primarily used here for illustrative purposes. I am currently collecting similar evidence about message status and leadership involvement on major bills for the House and Senate from the 102d–105th Congresses.

27. Since 1931 only 46 discharge petitions have garnered the necessary 218 signatures. Richard S. Beth, "Discharge Rules in the House: Recent Use in Historical Context," Congressional Research Service Report for Congress, November 15, 1999.

28. On the discharge petition in particular and minority party prerogatives in general, consult Sarah A. Binder, *Minority Rights, Majority Rule* (New York: Cambridge University Press, 1997).

29. Data about discharge petitions are from the records of the Clerk of the House. At the time this chapter was drafted, such information was available through November 2000.

30. One petition was introduced by a Republican member, but it dealt with campaign finance reform, a key minority message priority.

31. Bifurcated rules are not entirely a creation of the 106th Congress. A similar procedure was used in 1996 to structure floor action on a proposed minimum wage hike. The underlying rationale for the rule was the same—to allow the majority Republicans to deal with an extremely popular Democratic message item. Jackie Koszczuk and Julie R. Hirschfeld, "Dreier Steers Gun Bill around Rules Pitfalls," *CQ Weekly*, June 19, 1999, 1425.

32. Allen Schick, *Congress and Money* (Washington, D.C.: Urban Institute, 1980); Sinclair, *Legislators, Leaders, and Lawmaking.*

33. See Richard Smith, "Advocacy, Interpretation, and Influence in the United States Congress," *American Political Science Review* 78 (1984): 44–63.

34. Evans and Oleszek, "Message Politics and Senate Procedure."

35. On linkage tactics generally, see William H. Riker, *The Art of Political Manipulation* (New Haven: Yale University Press, 1986). For an application to media strategies in the Senate consult Sellers, "Winning Media Coverage in the U.S. Congress."

36. *Congressional Quarterly Weekly Report,* January 31, 1998, 251.

37. Based on the public's reaction to the partial government shutdown of 1995, Clinton and congressional leaders from both parties believed that the public would mostly

blame the Republicans if appropriations measures were not enacted, and a continuing resolution became necessary to avoid having to close portions of the federal government. As a result, Clinton built up substantial bargaining leverage as the October deadline for completing the appropriations process neared. By the late 1990s a number of Senate Republican staff were referring to the funding hikes (for Democratic priorities) that congressional Republicans had to swallow during the appropriations end-game as the "Clinton exit fee"—that is, expenditures they had to concede to Clinton to end the appropriations process, adjourn Congress, and get out of town. Many congressional observers believe that Newt Gingrich lost his Speakership over the size of the Clinton exit fee in 1998.

38. Richard F. Fenno Jr., *The Power of the Purse* (Boston: Little, Brown, 1966). For an argument that the Appropriations panels have long served as agents for the majority party, see D. Roderick Kiewiet and Mathew D. McCubbins, *The Logic of Delegation* (Chicago: University of Chicago Press, 1991).

39. C. Lawrence Evans and Walter J. Oleszek, *Congress under Fire* (Boston: Houghton, Mifflin, 1997); John H. Aldrich and David W. Rohde, "The Republican Revolution and the House Appropriations Committee" (paper delivered at the annual meeting of the Southern Political Science Association, Atlanta, 1996).

40. Not-for-attribution interview conducted by the author and Walter Oleszek in Washington, D.C., on March 10, 2000.

41. Lori Nitschke, "GOP Consensus on Budget Blueprint Holds," *CQ Weekly*, March 13, 1999, 603.

42. On these changes, see Barbara Sinclair, *Unorthodox Lawmaking*, 2d ed. (Washington, D.C.: CQ Press, 2000).

43. Not-for-attribution interviews conducted by the author, December 1999 and February 2000.

44. On the nature and consequences of jurisdictional politics during the years of Democratic control, consult David King's prize-winning study, *Turf Wars* (Chicago: University of Chicago Press, 1997).

45. Walter Oleszek, *Congressional Procedures and the Policy Process*, 4th ed. (Washington, D.C.: CQ Press, 1996).

46. David Mayhew, *Congress: The Electoral Connection* (New Haven: Yale University Press, 1974). See also Diana Evans, "Policy and Pork: The Use of Pork Barrel Projects to Build Policy Coalitions in the House of Representatives," *American Journal of Political Science* 38 (1994):894–917; and James T. Murphy, "Political Parties and the Pork-barrel: Party Conflict and Cooperation in House Public Works Committee Decision Making," *American Political Science Review* 68 (1974): 169–85.

47. Jeff Plungis, "Shuster's Use of Budgetary 'Firewalls' Takes Other Chairmen by Surprise," *CQ Weekly*, August 7, 1999, 1917.

48. Philip D. Duncan and Christine C. Lawrence, *Politics in America 1996* (Washington, D.C.: CQ Press, 1995), 1133.

49. A recent history of Senate cloture politics is provided in Barbara Sinclair, "The Sixty-Vote Senate" (paper delivered at the Norman Thomas Conference on Senate Exceptionalism, Vanderbilt University, October 21–23, 1999). See also Sarah A. Binder and Steven S. Smith, *Politics or Principle?* (Washington, D.C.: Brookings Institution, 1997).

50. On the tactic of filling the Senate amendment tree, see Wendy J. Schiller, "Trent Lott's New Regime: Filling the Amendment Tree to Centralize Power in the U.S. Senate" (paper delivered at the annual meeting of the American Political Science Association, Washington, D.C., August, 2000), and various issue briefs and memos by Richard S. Beth of the Congressional Research Service, U.S. Library of Congress.

51. *Congressional Record*, May 17, 2000, S4068.

52. *Congressional Record*, June 18, 1999, H4643

53. Joseph M. Bessette, *The Mild Voice of Reason* (Chicago: University of Chicago Press, 1994). See also Donald R. Wolfensberger, *Congress and the People: Deliberative Democracy on Trial* (Washington, D.C.: Woodrow Wilson Center, 2000); and George E. Connor and Bruce I. Oppenheimer, "Deliberation: An Untimed Value in a Timed Game," in *Congress Reconsidered*, 5th ed., ed. by Lawrence C. Dodd and Bruce I. Oppenheimer (Washington, D.C.: CQ Press, 1993).

Part IV
Congressional Leadership and Party Politics

11. The Dynamics of Party Government in Congress

Steven S. Smith and Gerald Gamm

A remarkable transfer of power took place in the House of Representatives in the last weeks of 1998. Newt Gingrich, R-Ga., who had been touted in 1995 as the most powerful Speaker in almost a century, stepped down from the Speakership and resigned his seat in the House. The Republicans had just lost five seats in the midterm elections of an opposition president's second term, a nearly unprecedented event. In less than four years, Gingrich had fallen from grace with his Republican colleagues. For many of them, the 1998 elections were the last straw. Republican members of the House voted first to replace Gingrich with Rep. Robert L. Livingston, R-La.—but Livingston himself resigned within a matter of weeks, before ever formally assuming the office of Speaker. In December 1998, in the aftermath of these two startling resignations, Republicans chose Rep. Dennis Hastert, R-Ill., someone who was virtually unknown to the public and the media, to be the next Speaker. Hastert instantly proved to be a reserved leader who gladly shared power with other party leaders and committee chairs.

While House Republicans were changing leaders and shifting gears, Senate Republicans made no changes. Senate Majority Leader Trent Lott, R-Miss., had assumed his leadership post in the summer of 1996, when Sen. Robert Dole, R-Kan., relinquished the position to run full-time for president. No discussion of replacing Lott took place in late 1998; in fact, little blame was placed on Lott for the poor showing of congressional Republicans in the November elections. Those elections generated no net change in the size of either of the two Senate parties, which certainly was a disappointment for the Republicans. As in the preceding Congress, the new Senate was made up of fifty-five Republicans and forty-five Democrats. In advance of the elections, many Republicans had hoped for a "filibuster-proof" majority of sixty-plus senators in the 1998 elections, one that could force a vote on legislation that the Democratic minority filibustered. But Lott was seldom mentioned in the postmortem media coverage of the elections. If anything, Lott was placed in a favorable light: he would fill the void created by the change from Gingrich to Hastert as the chief spokesperson of the party.

The events of late 1998 represent a puzzle for political scientists who attempt to analyze the nature of party leadership in Congress. The purpose of this chapter is to outline the standard view of party leadership, to evaluate its strengths and weaknesses, and to suggest some new perspectives on congressional leadership. We draw two conclusions. First, the 1998 developments reflected long-standing differences between the House and Senate in the nature of party leadership that are too often ignored. Second, those developments highlight the importance of distinguishing between the policy and electoral goals of congressional parties, a distinction that is avoided in the standard account.

The Ebb and Flow of Leadership Power

Observers of Congress describe the policymaking process in terms of the degree to which it is centralized or decentralized. When a party leader (of the majority party) controls the agenda and influences how other legislators vote on the legislation considered, power is considered to be highly *centralized*. At the extreme, the central leader dictates outcomes. An alternative is to have agenda control and influence placed in the hands of the many standing committees, or their chairs, so that power appears *decentralized*. In the decentralized pattern, the central party leader bargains rather than commands. He defers to committee chairs, performs the ministerial duty of scheduling, and, as circumstances require, bargains with influential members. Power in Congress often is characterized as shifting back and forth along the centralized-decentralized continuum.

There is a third alternative. Power may remain in the hands of the full chamber. In principle, legislative initiatives can originate on the floor and all members can exercise their votes there. In practice, of course, certain responsibilities are delegated to leaders and committees, but the full membership need not defer to leaders and committees. Thus, a more *collegial* pattern is possible, at least in principle. Indeed, the Senate has retained a more collegial pattern, whereas the larger House delegates more responsibility to leaders and committees.

The most influential account of the ebb and flow of leadership power is an essay written by the political scientists Joseph Cooper and David Brady.[1] In Figure 11-1 we outline the argument. The root source of leaders' power, in this view, rests on election results. The degree of polarization in electoral coalitions of the two congressional parties determines the strength and policy polarization of the congressional parties themselves. Powerful leaders, then, are the product of sharp partisan differences in the electorate, polarized congressional parties, a strong majority party, and the associated formal powers granted to them. If partisan differences weaken in the electorate and in Congress, the formal powers of party leaders will be pared back and policymaking will be more decentralized.

Equally important in the Cooper-Brady argument is what is *not* deemed central to an explanation of centralization: leaders' styles and personalities. Leadership style—assertiveness—is a by-product of party strength and formal powers, but it does not make a strong independent contribution to legislative outcomes. Personality may affect leadership style, but it is less important than party strength and formal powers. Thus, the personal qualities that are so often emphasized in accounts of congressional leadership are of relatively little significance in

Figure 11-1 The Conditional Party Government Thesis

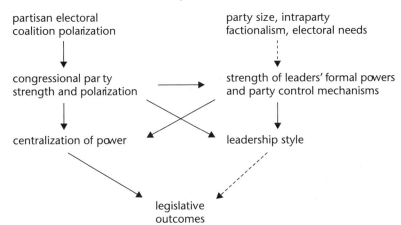

Note: The Cooper-Brady thesis is depicted with solid lines. The conditional party government thesis includes the dashed lines.

the Cooper-Brady explanation of broad historical differences in the centralization of power in the Speaker of the House.

Sophisticated observers of recent Congresses agree with the Cooper-Brady thesis. The term *conditional party government* has been applied by David W. Rohde to capture the idea that assertive majority party leadership occurs only when the parties are polarized—that is, when intraparty cohesiveness is high and interparty differences are great.[2] These observers emphasize how party polarization in the 1980s and 1990s provided a foundation for aggressive strategies by House Speakers, particularly Jim Wright, D-Texas, who served as Speaker from 1987 to 1989, and Newt Gingrich, who served as Speaker from 1995 to 1998.

These accounts of recent House politics differ from the Cooper-Brady argument in one critical respect: they assert that strong majority party leadership makes a difference beyond the effect of party cohesiveness. The majority party benefits from assertive leaders who aggressively employ the resources and procedural tools given to them by their party. Rohde, for example, concludes that "parties are consequential in shaping members' preferences, the character of the issues on the agenda, the nature of legislative alternatives, and ultimate political outcomes, and they will remain important as long as the underlying forces that created this partisan resurgence persist."[3] Rather than being the passive instruments of party members, as the Cooper-Brady argument suggests, these leaders (and rules strengthening these leaders) play an independent role in shaping party behavior. According to Rohde, leaders act to further reinforce party cohesiveness and further enhance the prospects of the achievement of collective policy goals. In this view, the lower dashed arrow in Figure 11-1 represents a significant political influence.

If party leadership has an effect on legislative outcomes independent of the alignment of policy preferences in the membership, then leadership power must have some foundation independent of legislators' policy interests. If only policy interests were at play, legislators would not grant their leaders any power beyond what is required to serve those policy interests. Thus, leadership goals are also driven by the electoral interests of members, and leaders must sometimes pursue strategies that represent trade-offs between the policy and electoral goals of party members.[4] Indeed, assisting the party in making these trade-offs is a strategic challenge that leaders are charged with addressing. Such considerations are represented by the upper dashed arrow in Figure 11-1. This distinction between the electoral and policy interests of congressional parties will prove critical to explaining the election of Hastert as House Speaker.

In this chapter we examine whether the conditional party government thesis—either the Cooper-Brady polarization thesis or the polarization-plus-leadership variation advocated in other recent studies—can adequately account for leadership behavior and party effects. We make two arguments. First, the thesis does not fit the Senate as well as it fits the House. The ability of a Senate minority to obstruct the chamber's business affects the extent to which power can ever be effectively centralized in the Senate, even when the electoral coalitions and congressional parties are polarized. And the absence of a powerful presiding officer further limits the centralization of power in the Senate. Second, we argue, in contrast to Cooper and Brady (but consistent with more recent scholarship), that policy and electoral objectives are not always fully compatible, at least in the short term. Consequently, at any given time the acquired institutional context is partly inherited, partly shaped by electoral challenges, and only partly shaped by short-term policy objectives.

We examine House and Senate party leadership in two eras—the years just before and after 1900 and the years just before 2000. These were eras of high party polarization. In the earlier period the Senate's majority leadership looked similar to the House leadership in its ability to control the chamber, but looks prove deceiving. The "centralized" power of Senate leaders a century ago was grounded in few formal institutions; it could not be transferred, and it could not be reliably employed even by its most powerful practitioners. We argue, in fact, that the century-long effort to equate the Senate's "Aldrichism" with "czar rule" in the House reflects a fundamental misunderstanding of Senate leadership in this era. In the 1990s strong majority party leadership did not emerge at all in the Senate. Meanwhile, in the House, both parties allowed strong central leaders to emerge. But in both eras these strong House leaders were followed by weaker leaders, reflecting the countervailing electoral interests of individual legislators and the party rather than the reintroduction of heterogeneous constituencies and congressional parties.

1890 to 1910

The period from 1890 to 1910 generated the strongest party leaders in the history of the House. A comparable group existed in the Senate in that era, although it lacked the tools necessary to exercise firm control. In both cases scholars have argued that sharp party polarization, rooted in a polarization in electoral constituencies, created centralized policymaking processes. For the House the argument is strongly supported by the evidence, but for the Senate the story is more complicated.

The House of Speakers Thomas Brackett Reed and Joseph Cannon

House Republicans enjoyed the leadership of two aggressive Speakers — Thomas Bracket Reed and Joseph Cannon — when they found themselves in the majority during most of the 1890–1910 period.[5] Speakers appointed all members to standing committees and chairmanships. They chaired the Committee on Rules, which wrote the resolutions that brought major legislation to the floor. During floor sessions, they exercised discretion over the recognition of members to make motions, including motions to bring up legislation. And the Republicans gave their leader a special tool — a vote of the party caucus would bind all party members to support the party's policy position. These tools gave the Speaker important formal controls over the flow of legislation and a set of rewards and sanctions with which to influence the behavior of legislators. Reed and Cannon were known as "czars" of the House.

The conditional party government thesis associates the power of these Republican Speakers with a polarization of the parties. Figure 11-2 characterizes one component of polarization — interparty difference — in the roll-call voting record of the House. The figure is based on statistical estimates of the liberal-conservative position of legislators.[6] In the figure, we indicate the difference between the two parties' median scores. As shown in the figure, the period of strong Speakers in this period corresponds closely to a wide separation of the two parties.

The second component of polarization — intraparty cohesiveness — does not show the same strong relationship to party centralization. This can be shown by using a measure of dispersion (the standard deviation) for the liberal-conservative positions within each party. As Figure 11-3 indicates, both parties in the House demonstrated considerable cohesiveness throughout the late nineteenth century. They showed no greater cohesiveness under the strong Republican Speakers than during other periods. In general, Republicans were somewhat more cohesive than the Democrats, who had long suffered differences between conservative Democrats, who favored the gold standard, and those sympathetic to populism and free silver. The 1890s polarization of the parties, then, appears to have been driven more by their widening differences than from any changes in their internal cohesiveness.

So far the evidence is generally consistent with the conditional party government thesis. But, as the political scientist Eric Schickler observes, a qualification of the thesis is required — the thesis does not explain the adoption of the Reed rules in 1890.[7] Speaker Reed and his fellow Republicans put in place landmark

Figure 11-2   Differences between the Parties in Median Liberal–
Conservative Scores in the House, 1857–1998

Differences between the Parties

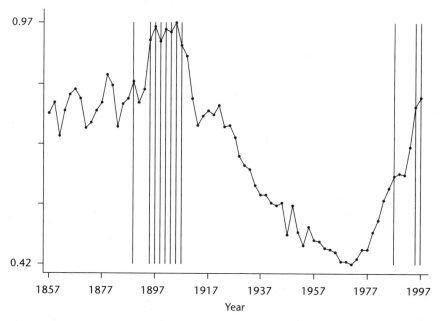

Year

Source: DW-NOMINATE scores are available at http://voteview.uh.edu/dwnomin.htm. See
Keith Poole and Howard Rosenthal, *Congress: A Political-Economic History of Roll Call Voting*
(New York: Oxford University Press, 1997).

Note: Each entry represents the absolute difference between the parties in median DW-
NOMINATE scores. DW-NOMINATE scores represent legislators' placement on a
liberal–conservative scale, based on their roll-call voting record. High values indicate a
large degree of difference between the parties. Scores for an entire session of Congress
are assigned to the first year the Congress met. Vertical rules indicate Congresses led by a
strong Speaker.

rules in 1890 that undercut minority party obstructionism. The parties had distinct policy preferences but were not yet as polarized as they were soon to become
(see Figure 11-2).[8] Even Republicans had noteworthy internal divisions on
important issues, such as currency and tariffs.

A reasonable hypothesis is that the relative sizes of the two parties played a
critical role in the adoption of the Reed rules in 1890. The House parties were
nearly equal in size in 1890—156 Democrats and 173 Republicans—and party
margins had been narrow for some time. This meant that a few absent majority
party members would be a serious problem for their party. By refusing to answer
quorum calls and offering repetitive dilatory motions, a minority party could prevent the House from conducting business. The "Reed rules," as they came to be

Figure 11-3 Dispersions in the Parties' Liberal–Conservative Scores in the House, 1857–1998

Standard Deviation

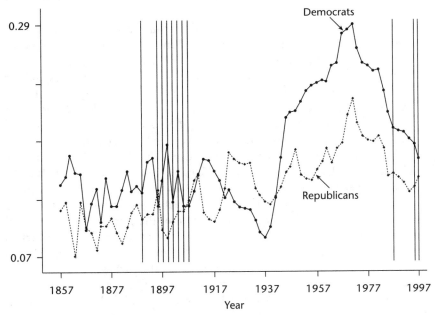

Source: DW-NOMINATE scores are available at http://voteview.uh.edu/dwnomin.htm. See Keith Poole and Howard Rosenthal, *Congress: A Political-Economic History of Roll Call Voting* (New York: Oxford University Press, 1997).

Note: Each entry represents the standard deviation DW-NOMINATE score for the party. High values indicate a large dispersion within the party. Scores for an entire session of Congress are assigned to the first year the Congress met. Vertical rules indicate Congresses led by a strong Speaker.

known, gave the Speaker the power to count members as present if they were in the chamber but not answering to a roll call, reduced the quorum in the Committee of the Whole from a majority of the House to just 100 members, and allowed the Speaker to ignore dilatory motions. Speaker Reed skillfully exploited a partisan debate over contested elections to increase his party's marginal control over the House. He did so not by proposing rules changes in the usual way—offering a resolution at the start of a new Congress—but by making rulings from the chair at opportune moments and asking his fellow Republicans to back him up.

Oddly, immediately after the Democrats gained a majority in the 1890 elections, they dropped the Reed rules.[9] In spite of their interest in preventing minority obstruction, they felt obliged to follow through on campaign promises to restore "democratic" procedures to the House. To be sure, the Democrats were not a unified party and so may not have tolerated a powerful Speaker, as the conditional party thesis suggests, but it does appear that electoral motivations rather than policy considerations led to this precipitous action. Over the next few years, as the Republicans proved obstructionist, the Democrats reestablished some of the Reed rules, often with prodding from Reed himself and other minority Republicans.

Thus, when the Republicans regained a House majority in 1895, their Speaker enjoyed procedural advantages that were not the product of a newly cohesive majority in a polarized House. Rather, they were inherited from previous Republican caucuses that were concerned about election outcomes and the party's reputation—and perhaps concerns about the functionality of the House by members on both sides of the aisle. It is fair to say that Speaker Cannon soon came to use the procedural tools on behalf of a cohesive party in a polarized House, but the tools were the product of a mix of political considerations.

The era of the czars came to an end when divisions within the House Republican Party led to a revolt against Speaker Cannon in 1909–1910. The increasing dispersion depicted in Figure 11-3 during the late 1890s and 1900s gives a hint of what took place. Progressive Republicans from the Midwest and West became unhappy with the policy direction of the eastern establishment of their party, and they resented the strong-arm tactics used by Cannon to try to keep them in line. Moreover, the addition of Progressives to the House Democratic caucus began to reduce the distance between the parties.

Progressive Republicans eventually joined with Democrats to impose new rules that reduced the Speaker's control over the flow of legislation to the floor. In 1909 the consent calendar was created and a procedure allowing committees to call up bills every Wednesday was established. More important, in 1910 the coalition pushed through rules that prevented the Speaker from sitting on the Rules Committee and provided for its election by the House. When the Democrats took over majority control in 1911, they amended the House rules to provide for election of all standing committees.

During most of the rest of the twentieth century, the Speaker was less powerful, and bargaining became the modus operandi of the majority party leadership. In fact, during the middle decades of the century, a conservative coalition of minority party Republicans and southern Democrats held sway on many issues. As shown in Figures 11-2 and 11-3, party polarization declined; the parties became less distant and intraparty cohesiveness declined. Legislative initiative slipped from central party leaders and shifted to committees and their chairs. Many bills were passed with cross-party coalitions, often with little trace of party leader influence.

The Senate of Nelson W. Aldrich and William Boyd Allison

During the 1890–1910 era, Republican leadership in the Senate was centered in a handful of men: Nelson Aldrich, R-R.I., William Allison, R-Iowa, Orville Platt, R-Conn., and John Spooner, R-Wis. A few others—such as

Eugene Hale, R-Maine, and James McMillan, R-Mich.—were considered to be insiders, too. The group functioned as an interlocking directorate of Republican committee and party leaders. With no powerful presiding officer, the Senate parties looked to other means to facilitate collective action.[10] In the mid-1890s, Aldrich and his comrades assumed personal responsibility for leading the Republican cause. Aldrich, in part because of his leading role on the Finance Committee and in part because of his personality and political connections, led the group. Allison chaired the Appropriations Committee and, beginning in 1897, the Republican caucus. The group dominated the Committee on Committees, which made committee assignments for the party, and the Steering Committee, which set a legislative agenda for the party.

The Senate's "Aldrichism" was often equated with the House's "Cannonism" by Progressive politicians and journalists in these years—and by scholars in the century since. On the surface, the Aldrich-Allison team appears to be the Senate counterpart of the House czars, and the conditional party government thesis may fit the Senate equally well. But does it? Our answer has two parts. First, the relation between polarization and centralization is weaker in the Senate than in the House, which is evidenced by the timing of the emergence of a centralized leadership team for Senate Republicans. Second, "Aldrichism" represented much less centralization and control than "Cannonism." Unlike Reed and Cannon, Aldrich possessed no special procedural tools or party office. His leadership was exercised jointly with other senators and, given their positions as committee chairs, reflected the decentralized nature of the Senate chamber. On his own, and even in cooperation with the others, Aldrich showed considerably less ability than the House Speakers of the period to push party legislation through the chamber.

Polarization and Centralization in the Senate. Strong partisanship in the Senate predates the surge in House partisanship in the mid-1890s. In fact, the Senate was remarkably partisan from the end of Reconstruction in the 1870s until the 1910s. In Figure 11-4 we show that the interparty difference on the liberal-conservative scale was large throughout that period. And in Figure 11-5 we show that both Senate parties were internally cohesive during most of the same period.[11] Consequently, it is not possible to associate the period of strong Republican leadership in the Senate with a surge in party polarization. Instead, the Aldrich-Allison leadership emerged long after partisan polarization surfaced in the 1870s, when Democrats regained southern seats in the aftermath of Reconstruction.[12] Thus, the nearly one-to-one correspondence between polarization and centralization emphasized by Cooper and Brady, and others, clearly does not fit the Senate.

Why is correspondence between polarization and centralization far less perfect in the Senate than in the House? The primary reason appears to be the inherited institutional context of the post–Civil War Senate. The essential features of that context were the absence of a presiding officer empowered to act in

Figure 11-4 Differences between the Parties in Median Liberal–
Conservative Scores in the Senate, 1857–1998

Differences between the Parties

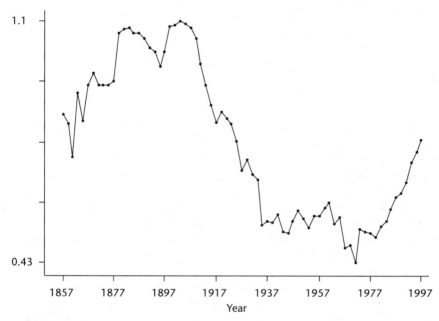

Source: DW-NOMINATE scores are available at http://voteview.uh.edu/dwnomin.htm. See
Keith Poole and Howard Rosenthal, *Congress: A Political-Economic History of Roll Call Voting*
(New York: Oxford University Press, 1997).

Note: Each entry represents the absolute difference between the parties in median DW-
NOMINATE scores. High values represent a large difference between the parties. Scores for
an entire session of Congress are assigned to the first year the Congress met.

the interest of the majority party and the absence of a limit on debate and
amendments.

Unlike in the House, the majority parties in the Senate did not empower the
presiding officer of the Senate. The Constitution provides that the vice president
serve as president of the Senate, and nineteenth-century vice presidents generally served faithfully. But vice presidents need not be of the same party as the
Senate majority, and, even when they were, were not beholden to senators. Senate presidents pro tempore, who were elected in the absence of the vice president,
also proved feeble vessels for majority leadership; nineteenth-century senators
believed that the term of a president pro tempore ended abruptly upon the return
of the vice president, and they also believed that the Senate lacked the constitutional authority to remove a president pro tempore from office under any other
circumstance, including a shift in majority control. Although the Senate experi-

Figure 11-5   Dispersions in the Parties' Liberal–Conservative Scores in the Senate, 1857–1998

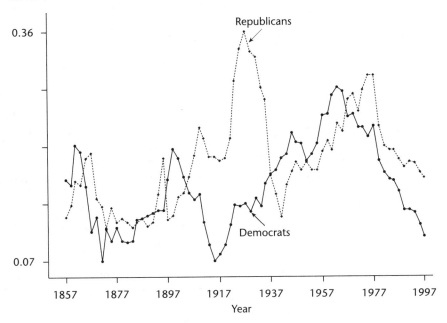

Standard Deviation

Source: DW-NOMINATE scores are available at http://voteview.uh.edu/dwnomin.htm. See Keith Poole and Howard Rosenthal, *Congress: A Political-Economic History of Roll Call Voting* (New York: Oxford University Press, 1997).

Note: Each entry represents the standard deviation DW-NOMINATE score for the party. High values indicate a large dispersion within the party. Scores for an entire session of Congress are assigned to the first year the Congress met.

mented occasionally with the assignment of some powers to its presiding officer, the Senate emerged from the nineteenth century with a presiding officer with very little authority, even over routine floor proceedings.[13] The Senate, therefore, lacked a formal leader who could combine the powers of the presiding officer with the influence of a party leader, as did the Speaker of the House.

Furthermore, unlike the House, where cohesive majorities could impose rules changes, the Senate majority confronted a filibuster of any change in rules that might put a minority at a disadvantage. Until 1917 the Senate had no way to limit debate as long as senators sought recognition to speak. Consequently, in spite of repeated appeals by Senate majority parties for some limit on debate, minority party members regularly killed any hope of such a change.[14] The immediate consequence of this was that Senate majority parties that might have wanted to enhance the formal power of its leadership did not have the ability to do so. Any enhancement of the influence of majority party leadership in the Senate would be limited to innovations within the parties' internal caucuses—proceedings invisible in the official Senate record. The Senate floor, unlike the House floor, was an inhospitable place for establishing majority party prerogatives.

Still, even informal leaders did not emerge until relatively late in the period of partisan polarization in the Senate. The most important innovation—the emergence of an elected majority leader—did not occur until after Aldrich, Allison, and their allies had all died or retired. Yet Aldrich clearly stood at the center of a powerful group of senators. Their leadership was grounded, first, in their control of Senate committees and, second, in the establishment of a regular steering committee in 1892.

Accumulated seniority allowed members of the Aldrich-Allison faction to gain positions of potential influence just as they gained an increment of additional cohesiveness.[15] By virtue of his seniority, Allison became caucus chairman in 1897 and took the unusual step of appointing himself chairman of the Republican Steering Committee, the party's agenda-setting group. He appointed Aldrich, Hale, McMillan, Platt, and Spooner to the committee. He appointed McMillan as chair of the Committee on Committees in 1897, Aldrich in 1899, Platt in 1901, and Hale in 1903, 1905, and 1907. Meanwhile, Allison continued to chair the Appropriations Committee, as he had done for many years when the Republicans were in the majority. Aldrich chaired the Rules Committee in 1897, then became Finance Committee chairman two years later. No new rules facilitated this accumulation of power in a few senators' hands. The seniority rule, which governed committee chairmanships as well as the caucus chairmanship, enabled Allison and Aldrich to coordinate in this fashion.

The only significant structural change in this era was the establishment of the Republican Steering Committee (and, simultaneously, the Democratic Steering Committee) in the winter of 1892–1893. Members of the caucus created the steering committee to pursue policy as well as electoral goals, but it was an election crisis that was the immediate cause of this institutional innovation. Republicans, who had controlled the Senate for a decade, realized in November 1892 that their majority was in serious jeopardy. State elections throughout the country portended an imminent transfer of control to the Democrats. Rather than acquiesce in the result, the Republican caucus established a steering committee, charging it to seek ways to influence the votes being cast for United States senators in doubtful state legislatures.

Once established, these steering committees proved to be durable institutions for both Senate parties. Through the 1890s and 1900s, the steering committees set policy agendas and shaped legislation. Although the Senate party caucuses had often formed committees in the past, the earlier committees had been ad hoc, single-purpose creations, which reported quickly then dissolved. The new steering committees assumed permanence, and Allison and Aldrich understood the importance of these institutions in coordinating decision making in the Senate. By January 1895, within two years of its creation, Allison had become chairman of the Republican Steering Committee. He would not relinquish the position until his death in 1908.

The Nature of Aldrichism. There is considerable testimony that Aldrich had become the dominant force in the Senate by the time Cannon became Speaker of the House in 1903. Was Aldrich, with Allison, comparable to Cannon? At a minimum, a heavy qualification must be placed on the claim. Long before the winter of 1892–1893, party caucuses had become actively engaged in debating legislation, developing and often negotiating policy positions, and fashioning strategies.[16] Polarization of the parties in the 1870s and 1880s was associated with intensified activity in the party caucuses, but without clear leadership on either side of the aisle. In both parties, of course, some senators were more central to party deliberations than others. The Aldrich-Allison team asserted itself at a time when intraparty decision making was shifting decisively from the caucus to the steering committee. But the creation of the steering committee had little to do with the centralization of power in the hands of Aldrich and Allison and much more to do with the severe partisan competition for control of the Senate.[17]

Control over the machinery of the Senate majority party did not translate into control over the chamber as directly or fully for party leaders as it did for the Speaker of the House. In part, this was due to the pivotal place of Populists in the Senate in the 1897–1900 period. But the Republican establishment did not demonstrate the degree of control over committees and policy outcomes that the Speaker of the House did. On an important tariff bill in 1897, at the height of Aldrich's and Allison's power, Republican committee members refused to support the party line and forced significant policy concessions before the bill could be reported from Aldrich's committee. In 1905 another Republican president's top priority, railroad regulation, was derailed by Republican committee members until Democrats provided the votes required to report the bill to the floor. And then a Democrat had to be called upon to manage the bill.[18]

Moreover, majority party leaders' control over the Senate floor agenda was far less perfect than the Speaker's control of the House agenda. In early 1900, for example, Republicans committed themselves to the passage of a gold-standard bill. On this issue, Aldrich was the bill manager and committed himself fully to the effort. In a story entitled "Mr. Aldrich's Clever Move," the *Washington Post* reported how Aldrich took advantage of a nearly empty Senate chamber to secure unanimous consent to have the gold-standard bill considered to the exclusion of all other business until it came to a vote eight days later. "The agreement was secured by Senator Aldrich yesterday afternoon," the *Post* stated, "when there were only eighteen Senators in the chamber, and when Senator Chandler, who is in charge of the Quay case; Senator Pettigrew, who is a persistent opponent of the administration's policy in the Philippines; and Senator Jones, the Democratic leader, were all absent."[19]

When the Senate entered the final days of consideration of the gold-standard bill, the *Post* reported that the chamber's remaining order of business remained unsettled. "After that measure is disposed of there will be a contest for precedence in the interest of several measures. These include the bills for providing forms of government for Hawaii and Puerto Rico, the Nicaragua canal bill, and the resolution for the seating of Senator [Matthew] Quay," according to the *Post*. "Which of these will take precedence remains to be determined. Just now there is some sharp sparring for first place."[20] In 1899–1900 the sparring took place directly among majority party bill managers. The *Post*, which thoroughly covered Aldrich's management of the gold-standard bill, makes it clear that no individual senator coordinated the chamber's agenda. The *Post* described the chaos, noting that "as soon as the Senate had disposed of the financial bill yesterday, Senator [Shelby] Cullom and Senator [William] Chandler sought recognition, the former to press the Hawaiian bill and the latter to suggest consideration of the Quay case."[21] We have found the same general pattern in a review of typical weeks of Senate floor action reported in the *Congressional Record.*

Additional examples illustrate the limitations of Aldrichism. In 1903 a statehood bill and a banking bill, the latter sponsored by Aldrich, died under filibuster and threatened filibuster, respectively. In 1907 a filibuster killed a bill long championed by the Republicans to increase subsidies for American merchant shipping. Democrats, who viewed subsidies for shipping as a gift to the steel industry, easily prevented a vote on the measure. In both years a determined minority was able to thwart the legislative plans of the Aldrich-Allison team and a Republican president.[22]

Even successful attacks upon the institutional bases of power of the Aldrich-Allison group were possible. In 1899, junior and western senators combined to force the adoption of a rule that gave seven committees authority to report appropriations (spending) bills for programs under their jurisdiction. The new rule substantially reduced the jurisdictional reach of Allison's Committee on Appropriations. Both Aldrich and Allison opposed the new rule (as did Democratic leader Arthur Pue Gorman of Maryland), yet many members of the majority party supported the effort to decentralize control over the initiation of spending bills.[23]

Thus the control of the chamber's proceedings by the Aldrich-Allison team was measurably weaker than the control over the proceedings of the House by the Speaker, even when bills of great importance to the faction were involved. In the Senate, control over the party's own committee contingents was weaker. Stealth was sometimes required to get a major bill to the floor. Disputes over the floor agenda among the majority party's bill managers often were not resolved by party leaders. "Aldrichism" was not "Cannonism."[24]

Less intraparty centralization is part of the reason, but so is the fact that intraparty centralization did not extend to chamber centralization. No Senate presiding officer was empowered to enforce an agenda set by party leaders. Floor debate and amendments could not be limited, a situation that continued to generate bargaining power for committee members. And single senators could object to requests for unanimous consent to consider legislation or limit debate, even then important to the majority party, which continued to give every senator a source of leverage. In such a setting, alienating a colleague by imposing penalties on him for noncompliant behavior entailed risks of its own.

In 1913, two years after Aldrich retired, the Democrats gained a Senate majority for the first time since 1895. They established the position of majority leader and elected John Kern, D-Ind., for the position. They used their caucus to impose discipline on votes important to the new Democratic president, Woodrow Wilson. But they discontinued the practice after a few years. When the Republicans regained a Senate majority in 1919, the party represented great regional diversity and lacked a strongly motivated caucus chair and floor leader. As a general rule, the Republican leaders of the 1920s focused on ministerial functions whereas committee chairs took the lead on policy, ushering in the pattern that would last for most of the twentieth century.

From 1990 to 2000

The party polarization of the late 1990s was similar to the polarization of the late 1890s. In both the House and the Senate the central tendencies of the two parties diverged, reaching a peak in the 1995–1998 period after years of widening party differences. Moreover, unlike in the 1890s, when intraparty cohesiveness remained at already high levels, both parties of the 1990s became more cohesive (see Figures 11-3 and 11-5), generating conditions conducive to centralization in policymaking within each house.

The late 1890s and late 1990s exhibit one critical difference. The 1896 elections created unified party control of the House, Senate, and presidency—with Republicans gaining control of the presidency that year, two years after they regained control of the House and Senate—whereas the 1994 elections created divided party control of Congress and the presidency. A reasonable speculation is that this difference would affect which party is credited for good times, influence public perceptions of the legislative program of the congressional majority party, affect who wins and who loses in legislative battles, shape the relation between the policy and electoral interests of the congressional majority party, and condition the value of centralization for the congressional majority party. If these assumptions are sound, the conditional party government thesis requires some elaboration.

The House of Speakers Newt Gingrich and Dennis Hastert

When the House Republicans gained a majority of seats in the 1994 elections, they inherited a decision-making process that already was more centralized than the committee-centered process of the middle decades of the twentieth century. Since the 1970s, the Democratic majority had steadily centralized more agenda-setting responsibility in the Speakership. Speakers Thomas P. "Tip" O'Neill, D-Mass. (1977–1987), James Wright, D-Texas (1987–1989), and Thomas S. Foley, D-Wash. (1989–1995), possessed stronger formal powers than their immediate predecessors. These powers gave the Democratic Speakers greater influence over committee assignments, bill referral, and the Rules Committee. Speaker Wright used these powers to push a legislative agenda more vigorously than any Speaker had done in many decades, at a time when an opposition party president was in the White House. His effort was brought to an end when he resigned from the House after the House Committee on Standards of Official Conduct charged him with several violations of ethics rules.

Oddly, from the point of view of the conditional party government thesis, House majority party Democrats enhanced the formal powers of their central party leader at the lowest point in party polarization in the history of the two parties—in the early 1970s (see Figure 11-2). Sharp intraparty factionalism, more than interparty differences, stimulated liberals to strengthen their central party leader and weaken the powers of full committee chairs, many of whom were conservatives. The Speaker at the time, Carl Albert, D-Okla., neither sought nor fully exploited these powers. Only later did Democratic Speakers begin to draw on these new powers, particularly control of the Rules Committee, and interparty competition clearly stimulated this new aggressiveness. These developments led observers to refer to the "post-reform House" of the 1970s, 1980s, and 1990s, which was much more centralized and party-oriented than the House of the mid-twentieth century.[25]

The post-reform Democratic House set a standard for centralization that the Republican House would rapidly exceed. With his assumption of the Speaker's chair in January 1995, Newt Gingrich quickly, and deservedly, became known as the most assertive Speaker since Cannon. Gingrich had taken the lead in recruiting Republican candidates, in fund-raising for Republicans, and in developing the Contract with America, the Republicans' ten-point policy platform for the 1994 campaign. When the Republicans won a majority, surprising nearly everyone, Gingrich was given much of the credit. He used his standing with his party colleagues to assert centralized direction over the House, going well beyond the standard set by Wright. He hand-picked full committee chairs, who were later endorsed by the party conference, and picked several subcommittee chairs, who were then appointed by committee chairs. He exercised great influence over all important committee assignments and even reviewed the appointments of top committee staff. He directed the content and timing of committee actions on legislation to implement the Contract with America. He limited conference committee delegations to a few top committee leaders and was pro-active in conference negotiations. And he pursued an aggressive strategy to force President Bill Clinton to accept the Republican budget. Standing at the head of a unified party in a polarized House, Gingrich's behavior seemed to confirm the conditional party government thesis.[26]

Gingrich's Speakership ended in political disaster. The seeds of this disaster were planted early, when in 1995 Gingrich led House Republicans as they held spending bills hostage in order to get President Clinton's approval of their budget plan. Clinton won the showdown, persuading a majority of Americans that the Republican majority had "shut down the government"; Republicans eventually agreed to accept the president's compromise legislation and suffered badly in public opinion polls. In the aftermath of this crisis, Gingrich became less aggressive and reduced his public visibility, a strategy that led to criticism from his colleagues. Adding to his troubles was an ethics investigation into the financing of a college course he taught and the campaign fund-raising conducted by organizations he created. By the summer of 1997 he was considered to be so ineffective that several Republican leaders debated a plan to depose him as Speaker. The plan was spoiled when newspaper accounts disclosed it and Gingrich challenged his detractors, but Gingrich never regained his aggressiveness in confronting a now very popular Democratic president.

The last straw came at the end of 1998, when Republicans lost seats in the House; in modern American history, no party had lost seats in the midterm elections of an opposition president's second term in office. Gingrich's greatest strength, election strategy, seemed to have faded. Gingrich was immediately challenged by Bob Livingston, who complained that Gingrich had failed to give voters a reason to vote Republican. Other Republicans seemed to agree; Gingrich announced his retirement, and Livingston quickly gained enough support to become his party's nominee for Speaker. Livingston promised to be a more effective manager than Gingrich had become, but he also promised to give committees greater independence and to be more inclusive in the party's legislative efforts. Livingston went so far as to say that he hoped to model himself after Speaker Tip O'Neill, who managed to combine partisanship, an inclusive strategy of building support within his party, and occasional efforts to attract support from the other party.[27]

Livingston's emergence as a replacement for Gingrich was not inconsistent with the conditional party government thesis. He promised to be a strong Speaker, although not as domineering as Gingrich in 1995. Moreover, the timing of Livingston's challenge and the rationale he offered showed the interdependency of the policy and electoral goals of congressional parties. But there is little evidence that any Republican shifted support away from Gingrich because of legislative battles that he lost or because Gingrich's policy views had somehow fallen out of step with his party. Instead, Gingrich failed to fashion a legislative program that would be attractive to the electorate. Electoral failure, not a change in the policy alignments within the House, was the immediate cause of his downfall.[28]

Livingston did not last long. Soon after Republicans made him their candidate for Speaker, Larry Flynt, publisher of *Hustler* magazine, disclosed that Livingston had had extramarital affairs years earlier. This was a particularly embarrassing disclosure because the House was about to impeach President Clinton for behavior related to his affair with White House intern Monica Lewinsky. Livingston, in fact, announced his retirement from the House during the December 19, 1998, debate on the articles of impeachment. Suddenly, just as Republicans were adopting articles of impeachment that were unpopular with a majority of Americans and just a month before a new Congress, the Republicans were without a leader.

Remarkably, emerging from the rubble was Dennis Hastert, a virtual unknown, even to many Washingtonians, who had not been mentioned at all as a possible replacement for Gingrich just a few weeks earlier. No leader is selected for a single reason, and it would be unrealistic to attribute Hastert's election as Speaker to just one trait. Hastert was a close ally of Tom DeLay, R-Texas, the Republican whip, and was just as conservative as other Republican leaders. But Hastert promised to be even better suited than Livingston to resolving intraparty disputes and reducing partisan tensions. He seemed to have a spotless background and he didn't have any enemies within the party.

Hastert proved to be a Speaker very different from Gingrich—and, it seems reasonable to speculate, very different from the one Livingston would have been. Not only did he follow through on his promise to allow committee chairs more independence and to act with the advice of a much wider range of Republicans, he proved to be nearly invisible in the media. The Republicans' agenda was very small in 1999, because Speaker Hastert preferred to slow action on taxes and other legislation to avoid conflict with an opposition-party president whose poll ratings remained very high.

The shifting of gears in House Republican leadership occurred without a measurable change in party polarization. The policy differences between the two parties did not change greatly with the 1998 elections. The Republicans had experienced an up-tick in intraparty diversity in the previous two Congresses (Figure 11-3), but, by any historical comparison, the House remained highly polarized. The composition of the House had changed only marginally in the 1996 and 1998 elections.

Explaining the new direction of House Republican leadership requires moving beyond policy—and party polarization—to electoral concerns. The strength of public support for the Republican policy program of tax and spending cuts had waned considerably by 1998, and public impatience with the Republican-led impeachment proceedings was growing. Furthermore, public views on a few issues, such as education spending, environmental protection, and health care, appeared to be shifting in the Democrats' direction. Electoral conditions had changed, which generated disagreements among Republicans about how to respond to them. Livingston and, even more, Hastert promised to work with all Republicans to address their concerns and to reduce the partisanship that the public seemed to blame more on the Republicans than the Democrats. Hastert followed through with this approach in 2000 when he produced a ten-point list of "items of agreement between Republicans and Clinton" that he hoped would receive legislative action.[29] The Republicans' legislative strategy was adjusted to their electoral needs.

Moreover, the 1998 elections left Republicans with only a six-vote margin. The slim margin of control meant that the leaders of the still-cohesive party had to worry more about the behavior of a few party members. The balance of policy preferences among Republicans had not changed markedly, but the bargaining power of moderate Republicans had been enhanced by the election outcome. Leaders' legislative sights had to be readjusted accordingly.

The conditional party government thesis has little to say about Hastert's selection and behavior. Without a significant change in the polarization of House parties, but with a substantial change in the electoral circumstances of their party, House Republicans chose a far less assertive leader, one who openly adopted a collegial, bargaining style within his party and who promoted a more committee-centered decision-making process. To be sure, party councils remained active, but centralization weakened considerably in the absence of a substantial change in the underlying alignment of policy preferences.

The Senate of Senators Bob Dole and Trent Lott

Centralization is not a term that any senator would apply to Senate decision-making processes in the late 1990s, in spite of the intensified partisanship of the period. Party activity increased, and party leaders were somewhat more fully engaged in policy making, but bargaining, not command, remained the modus operandi of both parties' floor leaders. The contrast with Gingrich's House could not be sharper.

By 1985, when Bob Dole became Senate majority leader, both parties had rejuvenated their party conferences and generated leadership offices, party committees, and task forces that performed a variety of functions. These forms of party activity and organization had atrophied by the middle of the century. Republicans started regular luncheon meetings in the late 1950s. Democrats did not do so until 1987, after they regained a majority, and even then Democratic Majority Leader Robert Byrd, D-W.Va., did so only under pressure from colleagues. Beginning in the 1980s, each party's leader occasionally appointed task forces to help formulate a party strategy on an important issue. In 1989 Democratic Majority Leader George Mitchell, D-Maine, reinvigorated the party's Policy Committee, which, for the first time had a co-chair who controlled a sizable staff. The policy committee, led by Sen. Tom Daschle, D-S.D., developed and approved an annual legislative agenda. Still, only in exceptional cases did party leaders assume primary responsibility for developing and promoting specific legislation. Thus, by the mid-1990s, and in a manner consistent with the conditional party government thesis, party activity had increased, but the decision-making process remained less centralized than in the House.[30]

Little changed in intraparty decision-making processes after the Republicans gained a majority in the 1994 elections. The new majority Republicans had been led by Bob Dole for ten years by that time. Dole continued his reliance on weekly meetings, sessions with committee chairs, and occasional task forces.

Trent Lott, who took over for Dole when Dole began to run full time for president in 1996, took the approach a step farther. In what one Republican senator called "participatory management," Lott appointed a diverse set of senators to serve in leadership posts and participate in weekly leadership meetings. He also appointed task forces in major policy areas, which would help set the party's agenda but would leave the writing of legislation to committees, several of which were chaired by party moderates. The facilitation of intraparty communication, bargaining, and consensus building—not centralization of power—was the purpose.[31]

Intraparty centralization would have served little purpose for Dole and Lott. Even a cohesive, centrally directed majority party could not force Senate action on legislation if the minority party was reasonably cohesive and chose to filibuster or threaten to filibuster. Moreover, without invoking cloture, the majority leader has difficulty limiting amendments from determined minority party members. On most legislation, in the absence of cloture, unanimous consent is required to limit debate and amendments.

If Senate partisanship does not produce centralized decision making, it does breed obstructionism. In the 1993–1998 period about half of all major legislation was subject to filibusters or threatened filibusters, many times the rate that was typical of previous decades.[32] Many bills on a wide range of subjects—taxes, health care, labor relations, lobbying, and campaign reform, to name a few— were killed by filibuster. For many more, concessions to the minority were required to overcome or avoid a filibuster. Majority party leadership, even House leadership, has been forced to adjust its strategy to the Senate filibuster. In 2000, for example, House Republican leaders agreed to split up a major tax proposal into separate bills in order to avoid a successful Senate filibuster of the entire package, as had happened the previous year.[33]

Senate minorities realize that the filibuster is an all-purpose hostage-taking device. By threatening to block action on bills, the minority can sometimes force the majority to schedule a debate and a vote on other legislation. The strategy is particularly effective if the minority position on the issue is popular with the electorate. Democrats have successfully used this strategy to gain action on measures providing for increases in the minimum wage, gun control, and a patients' bill of rights.

The Senate majority's bills also are subject to nongermane amendments. Thus, however centralized the majority party might be, it cannot prevent a determined minority from gaining floor consideration of its proposals. A majority party can filibuster the minority's proposals, but that only prevents action on other legislation the majority has responsibility for processing. The majority party can try to invoke cloture, which, if accomplished, bars nongermane amendments. And the majority leader, who has the right of first recognition on the Senate floor, can offer amendments of his own, filling the "amendment tree" and preventing other amendments from being offered until his amendments receive action. The minority, of course, can deny cloture. And filling the amendment tree is only a temporary solution; the minority can wait for an opportunity to offer an amendment to that bill or some other bill.[34]

The result is a procedural arms race—one parliamentary maneuver stimulates a counter-move and then other moves. The process seems to intensify partisanship as party members support their leaders' responses to the "unfair" tactics of the other side. As long as the minority party is reasonably cohesive, as it is in a highly polarized Senate, the majority party cannot readily translate its own cohesiveness into significant policy accomplishments. That is precisely what Senate Republicans experienced in the late 1990s.

Conclusion

The comparison of patterns of party leadership in the late nineteenth and late twentieth centuries confirms three related propositions about the sources of centralization in Congress:

- Institutional context influences the degree to which party polarization is translated into the centralization of power within the House and Senate.
- Party polarization appears to be a necessary but not a sufficient condition for centralization.
- Other factors, particularly a party's electoral circumstances and size, influence the creation of leadership powers. These powers are sometimes later used by assertive leaders.

In the House, where inherited rules allow a determined majority to gain action on its policy agenda, party polarization appears to stimulate the centralization of majority party leadership. Polarization was intense in the late nineteenth and late twentieth centuries, and in both cases House Republicans allowed a strong central leader to emerge and direct the decision-making process. However, even in the House, evolving electoral circumstances in the 1990s led to a change in leadership and a significant diminution in the centralization of the decision-making process.

The fairly tight correspondence between polarization and centralization of the House was not duplicated in the Senate. The Senate majority party centralization in the late nineteenth century was delayed and not as complete, and centralization did not appear in the late-twentieth-century Senate. Ironically, truly polarized Senate parties—including a cohesive minority party—may be less conducive to majority party centralization and success than somewhat less polarized parties that make the support of some minority party members for the majority's program feasible. Cross-party coalitions are more important to the Senate than the House for shepherding legislation through a thicket of potential filibusters, nongermane amendments, and other parliamentary maneuvers.

The conditional party government thesis, then, which relies on the observed correlation between party polarization and centralization, can be elaborated to recognize that institutional context, and the forces that shape it, are not entirely a product of the ebb and flow of party polarization. Our hunch is that centralization occurs when the parties are polarized, electoral conditions are favorable to the majority party, *and* the institutional context permits control of legislative outcomes by a centralized majority party. Even in the House, electoral circumstances are not always conducive to centralization when intraparty cohesiveness is strong. In certain circumstances, as when its policy program is not popular, a cohesive majority party may de-emphasize the policy goals shared by its members, and so be in little need of centralized leadership. And in the Senate, inherited rules limit the degree to which the chamber's decision-making process can ever be centralized in the majority party leadership.

Notes

1. Joseph Cooper and David W. Brady, "Institutional Context and Leadership Style: The House from Cannon to Rayburn," *American Political Science Review* 75 (1981): 411–25. The thesis has been extended to the Senate; see David W. Brady, Richard Brody, and David Epstein, "Heterogeneous Parties and Political Organization: The U.S. Senate, 1880–1920," *Legislative Studies Quarterly* 14 (1989): 205–23; David W. Brady and David Epstein, "Intraparty Preferences, Heterogeneity, and the Origins of the Modern Congress: Progressive Reformers in the House and Senate, 1890–1920," *Journal of Law, Economics, and Organization* 13 (1997): 26–49.
2. David W. Rohde, *Parties and Leaders in the Postreform House* (Chicago: University of Chicago Press, 1991).
3. Ibid., 192.
4. See Barbara Sinclair, *Majority Leadership in the U.S. House* (Baltimore: Johns Hopkins University Press, 1983); Barbara Sinclair, *Legislators, Leaders, and Lawmaking: The U.S. House of Representatives in the Postreform Era* (Baltimore: Johns Hopkins University Press, 1995); and Barbara Sinclair, *Unorthodox Lawmaking: New Legislative Processes in the U.S. Congress* (Washington, D.C.: CQ Press, 1997). Others make the same point. See John Aldrich and David W. Rohde, "The Consequences of Party Organization in the House: The Role of the Majority and Minority Parties in Conditional Party Government," in *Polarized Politics: The President and the Congress in a Partisan Era*, ed. Jon Bond and Richard Fleisher (Washington, D.C.: CQ Press, 2000); Stanley Bach and Steven S. Smith, *Managing Uncertainty in the U.S. House of Representatives* (Washington, D.C.: Brookings Institution, 1988); and Steven S. Smith, *Call to Order: Floor Politics in the House and Senate* (Washington, D.C.: Brookings Institution, 1989). For an electoral account of party leadership, see Gary Cox and Mathew McCubbins, *Legislative Leviathan: Party Government in the House* (Berkeley: University of California Press, 1993).
5. On the Speakers of this era, see David W. Brady, *Congressional Voting in a Partisan Era: A Study of the McKinley Houses* (Lawrence: University of Kansas Press, 1973); David W. Brady, Joseph Cooper, and Patricia Hurley, "The Decline of Party in the U.S. House of Representatives, 1887–1968," *Legislative Studies Quarterly* 4 (1979): 381–407; George Brown, *The Leadership of Congress* (Indianapolis: Bobbs-Merrill, 1922); Chang-Wei Chiu, *The Speaker of the House of Representatives Since 1896* (New York: Columbia University Press, 1928); Paul DeWitt Hasbrouk, *Party Government in the House of Representatives* (New York: Macmillan, 1927); Cooper and Brady, "Institutional Context and Leadership Style."
6. DW-NOMINATE scores, a measure of legislators' placement on the liberal-conservative scale, are used. The authors thank Keith Poole for their use. For an excellent discussion of party polarization, see Keith Poole and Howard Rosenthal, *Congress: A Political-Economic History of Roll Call Voting* (New York: Oxford University Press, 1997), 80–85.

7. See Eric Schickler, *Disjointed Pluralism* (Princeton: Princeton University Press, forthcoming), chap. 2. Sundquist emphasizes the factionalism within the Republican Party prior to the realignment of 1896. See James L. Sundquist, *Dynamics of the Party System: Alignment and Realignment of Political Parties in the United States* (Washington, D.C.: Brookings Institution, 1983).

8. For a different perspective and different account of party polarization in the House of the Fifty-first Congress (1889–1891), see Cooper and Brady, "Institutional Context and Leadership Style."

9. Schickler, *Disjointed Pluralism*.

10. See Gerald Gamm and Steven S. Smith, "Last among Equals: The Presiding Officer and the Struggle for Order in the 19th Century Senate" (paper presented at the Robert J. Dole Institute's Conference on Civility and Deliberation in the U.S. Senate, Washington, D.C., July 16, 1999).

11. These observations comport with the historian David Rothman's more detailed account of developments in the Senate, in which cohesive parties date back to the late 1880s. See David J. Rothman, *Politics and Power: The United States Senate, 1869–1901* (Cambridge: Harvard University Press, 1966), 90–108.

12. See Poole and Rosenthal, *Congress: A Political-Economic History of Roll Call Voting*, 82.

13. Gerald Gamm and Steven S. Smith, "Senate Party Leadership in the 1890s" (paper presented at the annual meeting of the Midwest Political Science Association, Chicago, April 2000).

14. On the history of filibusters and filibuster reform, see Franklin Burdette, *Filibustering in the Senate* (Princeton: Princeton University Press, 1940), and Sarah Binder and Steven S. Smith, *Filibustering in the Senate* (Washington, D.C.: Brookings Institution, 1997).

15. Our emphasis is different from that of Brady, Brody, and Epstein, "Heterogeneous Parties and Political Organization," 211–13, who emphasize the committee seniority of northeastern Republicans. What seems more critical is that members of the Aldrich-Allison faction enjoyed such seniority that they held both top party and top committee posts.

16. Rothman, *Politics and Power*, 90–108.

17. Gamm and Smith, "Senate Party Leadership in the 1890s."

18. See Brown, *The Leadership of Congress*, 102, 134–35, and DeAlva Stanwood Alexander, *History and Procedure of the House of Representatives* (Boston: Houghton Mifflin, 1916), 6–7.

19. "Mr. Aldrich's Clever Move," *Washington Post*, February 7, 1900, 4.

20. "Vote on Finance Bill," *Washington Post*, February 12, 1900, 3.

21. "Hawaiian Bill Taken Up," *Washington Post*, February 16, 1900.

22. Burdette, *Filibustering in the Senate*, 69–80.

23. Eric Schickler and John Sides, "Intergenerational Warfare: The Senate Decentralizes Appropriations," *Legislative Studies Quarterly* (forthcoming).

24. Thus, we would qualify the assertion of Brady, Brody, and Epstein in "Heterogeneous Parties and Political Organization," 209, that "in 1900, the U.S. Senate was, in fact, hierarchical, centralized, and heavily partisan. The top leadership controlled committee assignments, set the agenda, and had sanctions to help them enforce party discipline on the floor."

25. Roger Davidson, *The Postreform Congress* (New York: St. Martin's Press, 1992).

26. John Aldrich and David W. Rohde, "The Transition to Republican Rule in the House: Implications for Theories of Congressional Politics," *Political Science Quarterly* 112 (1997–1998): 541–67; Barbara Sinclair, *Unorthodox Lawmaking*, 175–216.

27. Bruce Alpert, "Grab for Top House Job Comes after Plan to Quit," *Times-Picayune*, November 15, 1998, sec. A, p. 18.

28. On the expectations for Livingston, see Richard E. Cohen and David Baumann, "After the Riot," *National Journal,* November 14, 1998, 2700.
29. Many journalistic accounts support this interpretation. See Mary Agnes Carey, "New Strategy, Old Disputes," *CQ Weekly,* January 22, 1999, and Karen Foerstel, "Parties Set Ambitious Agendas in the Shadow of Old Grudges," *CQ Weekly,* January 2, 1999. On the ten-point plan, see Andrew Taylor, "Issues Held Hostage in War between Action, Gridlock," *CQ Weekly,* February 26, 2000, 394–99.
30. On Senate party activity, see Donald Baumer, "Senate Democratic Leadership in the 101st Congress" (paper presented at the annual meeting of the American Political Science Association, San Francisco, September 1990); Samuel Patterson and Thomas Little, "The Organizational Life of Congressional Parties" (paper presented at the annual meeting of the Midwest Political Science Association, Chicago, April 1992); and Steven S. Smith, "Forces of Change in Senate Party Leadership and Organization," in *Congress Reconsidered,* ed. Lawrence C. Dodd and Bruce I. Oppenheimer, 5th ed. (Washington, D.C.: CQ Press, 1993), 259–90.
31. Donna Cassata, "Lott's Task: Balance the Demands of His Chamber and His Party," *Congressional Quarterly Weekly Report,* March 8, 1997.
32. Barbara Sinclair, "Hostile Partners: The President, Congress, and Lawmaking in the Partisan 1990s," in *Polarized Politics: The President and the Congress in a Partisan Era,* ed. Jon Bond and Richard Fleisher (Washington, D.C.: CQ Press, 2000), 145.
33. Lori Nitschke, "GOP Plans an Election Year Push for Tax Cuts Rejected in 1999, *CQ Weekly,* January 8, 2000.
34. Andrew Taylor, "Senate Leaders' Parliamentary Ploys," *CQ Weekly,* February 26, 2000, 399.

12. The Logic of Conditional Party Government: Revisiting the Electoral Connection

John H. Aldrich and David W. Rohde

One of the most influential and enduring books on Congress of the last three decades was David Mayhew's *Congress: The Electoral Connection*.[1] For his purposive theory described in that book, Mayhew assumed that members of Congress were motivated solely by their desire for reelection. Employing this assumption, he seemed able to account not only for most of the behavior of individual representatives but also for much of the institutional structure of the House of Representatives. The House, Mayhew claimed, was organized to facilitate the reelection of its members. One pair of institutional features deemed by Mayhew to be of little importance was the major political parties. Their only purpose was to foster the electoral well-being of individual representatives and otherwise leave them free to pursue their own interests.

The years since publication of *The Electoral Connection* have witnessed a resurgence of partisanship in Congress—in voting, in institutional processes, and in personal conflicts.[2] Party leaders, especially on the majority side, have been granted powers greater than those granted at any time since early in the twentieth century. What do these events mean in light of Mayhew's analysis? Did he misunderstand the motives of members and their consequences, or do the changes over the last thirty years stem from more complex processes that are still consistent with the theory of *The Electoral Connection?* In our previous work we developed a theoretical argument called "conditional party government" (CPG) that we believe accounts for the observed developments. This chapter will focus on the electoral connection from the point of view of CPG—that is, how is it that Congress, beginning with electorally independent members, has ended up with high levels of party loyalty and party conflict and with institutionally strong party leaderships? This chapter will reveal that our theory is, with a few differences, largely consistent with the earlier analysis offered by Mayhew.

The Electoral Connection Revisited

Mayhew began his analysis with an assumption about the motivation of members of Congress: "Specifically, I shall conjure up a vision of United States congressmen as single-minded seekers of reelection, see what kinds of activity that goal implies, and then speculate about how congressmen so motivated are likely to go about building and sustaining legislative institutions and making policy."[3] Mayhew made it clear that he did not think this assumption would provide a complete accounting of congressional behavior, but he also clearly believed the electoral motivation to be sufficient to explain most that was of interest.

In his book, Mayhew explicitly contrasted his perspective with the earlier electoral theory of Anthony Downs.[4] Downs assumed that political parties were the main actors in elections, and for his analysis he conceived of parties as teams whose members were motivated by party victory. Mayhew believed that Downs's conception could apply to the election of executives, but that, for three reasons, it broke down when applied to Congress. First, "the way in which congressional candidates win nominations is not, to say the least, one that fosters party cohesion in Congress. . . . There is no reason to expect large primary electorates to honor party loyalty . . . [and] parties are locally rather than nationally oriented." Second, "the typical American congressman has to mobilize his own resources to win a nomination and then to win election and reelection." And, third, "Congress does not have to sustain a cabinet and hence does not engage the ambitions of its members in cabinet formation in such a fashion as to induce party cohesion." [5] Based on these considerations and others, Mayhew came to one of his central conclusions, which is most important for our analysis: "The fact is that no theoretical treatment of the United States Congress that posits parties as analytic units will go very far. So we are left with individual congressmen, with 535 men and women rather than two parties, as units to be examined in the discussion to come." [6]

In keeping with this conclusion, Mayhew argued in *The Electoral Connection* that parties were shaped by members to serve their electoral needs, not to accomplish policy objectives. "The fact is that enactment of party programs is electorally not very important to members. . . . What is important to each congressman, and vitally so, is that he be free to take positions that serve his advantage. . . . Party leaders are chosen not to be program salesmen or vote mobilizers, but to be brokers, favor-doers, agenda-setters, and protectors of established institutional routines." [7] Indeed, Mayhew noted that it was often vital, because of constituency preferences, for members of the same party to vote in opposite directions. "In regard to these member needs the best service a party can supply to its congressmen is a negative one; it can leave them alone." [8] In support of his perspective, Mayhew pointed out that " 'party voting' in the House, however defined, has been declining since the turn of the century, and has reached a record low in the last decade [1960s]." [9]

In addition to arguing that representatives had little or no personal incentive to support their party programs, Mayhew contended that they were insulated from potential party pressure, principally through the seniority system, by which the senior member of the majority party on each committee became its chair. The chair was protected from losing this desirable post as long as his or her party remained in the majority. "What the congressional seniority system does as a system," Mayhew pointed out, "is to convert turf into property; it assures a congressman that once he initially occupies a piece of turf, no one can push him off it." [10] Thus the committee system existed independent of party leaders and as a competitor with them for power and influence in the House. Members could pursue their electoral interests within the committees and freely choose their positions on the floor. This was particularly true of the three "control committees"—Appropriations, Ways and Means, and Rules. The first two were the most important policy committees in the House, dealing respectively with spending and taxes; the third shaped the chamber's floor agenda and the terms for debate on bills.

In this way, then, Mayhew painted a picture of the House in the early 1970s and presented a theoretical account for what it revealed. Party voting was low, representatives were electorally independent and concerned almost exclusively with being returned to office rather than with enacting policy, and party leaders held fewer powers and were oriented toward serving their peers, with no significant ability to influence either members directly or the committees on which they served. However, in the few years before and in the decade after *The Electoral Connection* was published, Congress changed radically. The next section describes those changes and the theory we offer to explain them.

Congressional Reforms and an Alternative Theory

During the 1970s, in what has become known as "the reform era," the House substantially changed its organization and procedures. Some of the changes involved modifying House rules, but most were accomplished by revising the rules of the Democratic Caucus—the Democratic Party held a majority in the House from 1955 through 1995.[11] Although the reforms had many facets and stemmed from many different motivations, the most important ones for our purpose were explicitly directed at altering the institutional balance between parties and committees that Mayhew had described. The liberal wing of the Democratic Party felt shortchanged by the institutional balance in the House, where a "conservative coalition" of southern Democrats and Republicans dominated many committees, particularly the important ones. The liberals believed their party's majority status should produce policies more to their liking, but they found themselves blocked by the conservatives' institutional advantages, protected by the seniority system and a predominantly one-party electorate who rarely failed to reelect them. Frustrated, the liberal Democrats sought to alter those institutional advantages and tip the balance in their favor.

Working with the two ends of the seesaw, the reformers tried both to increase the powers of the majority party leadership and to decrease the power and autonomy of committee leaders. They began by attempting to enlarge the Democratic leadership's influence over committee assignments. The Democratic members of the Ways and Means Committee had long assigned Democrats to committees, without any direct role for the party leaders. Now assignments would be made by a new party committee (Steering and Policy), which would be dominated by leaders and their appointees. But an exception was made for Democratic members of the Rules Committee. The Speaker was given the power to name those members and to appoint (and remove) the committee's chair. Thus instead of being an independent power center with a strong influence over the agenda, Rules became an arm of the majority leadership, which put control of the agenda firmly in the leadership's hands.[12] The proponents of these changes stated publicly that their intent was to increase the influence of the leadership over the decisions of members by giving party leaders more control over the distribution of desirable posts.

The other reform—weakening the committee leadership and committee independence—involved several steps. One was to terminate the protections of the seniority system. The Democrats adopted caucus rules that provided for automatic secret ballot votes on all committee chairs (and for chairs of the subcommittees on Appropriations). If a chair failed to receive majority support from the caucus, a competitive election for chair could follow. In 1974, after the House welcomed a large number of newly elected liberal Democrats who benefited from the backlash over the Watergate scandal, the caucus voted out three southern committee chairs and replaced them with more mainstream Democrats. The automatic protection of seniority was ended and with it the guarantee of independence that Mayhew had properly noted as its central consequence. From that point on, even though the caucus would rarely reverse seniority, committee leaders had to consider the preferences of the Democratic Caucus when they made decisions and worry whether straying from those preferences could cost them their desired posts.

Reformers also sought to decentralize committee power away from chairs to rank and file members. The reform leaders recognized that they would have an easier time selling the changes if they offered their colleagues opportunities for increased influence over resources and policy. The main vehicle for this effort was a set of caucus rules changes that came to be known as the "Subcommittee Bill of Rights." They restricted committee chairs' control over staff and ended their ability to appoint subcommittee chairs, who were instead selected in order of committee seniority. The "Bill of Rights" also granted subcommittees guaranteed jurisdictions, with the result that all bills had to be referred to subcommittees unless a majority decided otherwise. Thus subcommittee chairs achieved significant independence from the full committee chair in running their panels, and the full committee chairs found their influence diminished.

After the reforms, members of the House began to exhibit significant changes in behavior related to party. Mayhew had cited the decrease in party voting over time, reaching a low point for the century at the end of the 1960s. Shortly thereafter, however, party voting began to rise. The proportion of roll calls on which party majorities voted in opposition increased from 28 percent in 1969–1970 to 42 percent in 1975–1976 to 52 percent in 1987–1988. Average party loyalty on these party votes increased among Democrats from 71 percent in 1969–1970 to 75 percent in 1975–1976 to 86 percent in 1987–1988; the corresponding figures for Republicans were 72 to 76 to 81 percent.[13]

Thus at about the time that *The Electoral Connection* was being published, partisan conflict and party loyalty in voting were beginning to increase, and the majority party had adopted new rules that undermined the independence of members from the party and expanded the powers of the Democratic leadership.

These developments certainly seem contrary to the picture Mayhew presented. Why would partisanship increase? Why would members grant their leaders more influence over them and over valuable institutional resources? Was Mayhew's description of representatives as independent entrepreneurs focused on reelection incorrect? We don't think so. Part of the reason Mayhew's theory did not anticipate the developments just described is that it accepted as stable, implicitly or explicitly, some key features of the electoral context that in fact proved variable. The other part of the reason is that the theory in *The Electoral Connection* simplified a bit too much.

It is a necessary and desirable feature of any theory that it abstract from the full richness of reality by leaving out certain aspects, but sometimes even a very good theory will leave out some features that are necessary to predict and explain events. That is probably the case here. Our theory—conditional party government—seeks to modify the perspective offered by Mayhew with some additional assumptions and a focus on some other aspects of the electoral context, thereby providing an account that is consistent both with the institutional patterns described by Mayhew and with the increased partisanship exhibited shortly thereafter. Our theory also explains the developments in the House after the Republicans took control in the wake of the 1994 elections—developments that occurred after our theoretical argument was initially published. The rest of this chapter will discuss the two theories in general terms, drawing out the logic of CPG in relation to Mayhew's views, and then will consider some evidence that bears on the accuracy of our perspective.

The Electoral Roots of Conditional Party Government

CPG theory begins by accepting the central assumption offered by Mayhew—that is, that representatives are entrepreneurs who focus strongly on electoral success and who are largely *electorally* independent of the party leadership in the House (although this part needs a bit of modification). On the other hand, our theory departs from Mayhew's by focusing on insights offered by the work of Richard Fenno and Morris Fiorina. Most of these additional points are mentioned in *The Electoral Connection*, but because of the nature of the electoral landscape at the time Mayhew wrote, they did not receive the prominence that time soon demonstrated they deserved.

The first embellishment is that CPG adopts a broader perspective on members' goals. We follow Fenno and assume that representatives (and candidates to be representatives) are motivated by the desire to make good public policy, to achieve and wield power within government, and to win elections.[14] Mayhew noted and discussed Fenno's multiple-goals perspective, but he argued that "the electoral goal has an attractive universality to it. It has to be the *proximate* goal of everyone, the goal that must be achieved over and over if other ends are to be entertained." [15] We agree with this statement, but believe that assuming everyone is centrally concerned with winning elections is not the same thing as assuming that everyone is concerned *only* with winning elections.[16] Some members, because they have policy goals, may be willing to take some electoral risks to achieve them. Moreover, some issues offer electoral uncertainty on both sides, making an emphasis on policy ends in such a situation more palatable. In addition, as we will discuss later, the multiple-goals perspective implies that members will sometimes seek to structure situations within the House to achieve simultaneously both policy and electoral goals, something that would not be easily explainable if they were concerned only with reelection. We will consider more of the implications of this assumption shortly.

Another elaboration of Mayhew's perspective revolves around the view of the relationship between representatives and their constituencies, both at the district level and in the aggregate. Here we build on other work by Fenno, who argued that representatives deal not with a single undifferentiated constituency, but rather with a set of concentric constituencies, each smaller and nested within the other.[17] The largest is the geographic constituency—the legal definition of the district. Next comes the reelection constituency, those people who support the member in a general election. Then there is the primary constituency, the representative's strongest supporters who would provide backing in a primary contest, even if the member faced competition from another party member. And finally there is the personal constituency, the representative's closest advisers and confidants. Mayhew made a similar distinction in his analysis, noting that "the congressman must keep in mind that he is serving two electorates rather than one—a November electorate and a primary electorate nested inside it but not a representative sample of it." [18] He also noted that a member might find that the views of the two electorates are sufficiently divergent to make attempts to maintain the support of both difficult. He did not seem to consider the contrast in opinions of the two constituencies to be a generic problem, however.

Another aspect of constituencies also comes into play. Constituencies (and, by extension, the mass parties within them) are composed of voters who vary not only in their issue preferences but also in the intensity with which they hold those preferences. Specifically, the people who care most about issues tend to be more active in politics than those who care less, and they also tend to hold preferences more toward the ends of a given issue spectrum than toward the middle. For example, Gary Jacobson has shown that Democratic and Republican "activists" (people who engage in a number of political activities in addition to simply voting) exhibit substantially greater differences on the liberal–conservative scale than do voters of the two parties.[19] (More evidence on this point is presented below.) Because of the disproportionate tendency of these activists to participate, their comparatively extreme opinions tend to exert a disproportionate influence on the nomination process that chooses candidates. Indeed, activists are often a source of candidates for office, who carry with them the intense policy preferences that got them involved in politics in the first place.[20]

Finally, as noted, Mayhew emphasized that it was often necessary for members of the same party to vote differently because of contrasting constituency preferences. At the time he wrote, such conflicting preferences were often found among northern and southern Democrats. It must have appeared at that time that the North–South divide among Democrats would persist indefinitely—both in the respective constituencies and in the party contingents each region sent to the House—thereby barring any incentive for stronger parties. CPG, however, explicitly recognizes the possibility of variation in the degree of *preference agreement* within parties and the degree of *preference conflict* between them. According to our theory, these characteristics are the most important determinants of whether parties within the legislature will be strong or weak.

The Institutional Consequences of Electoral Forces

We can now bring together the electoral features of our theory and outline their implications for congressional behavior and organization. As just noted, for CPG a primary determinant of the strength of parties within the legislature is how much the members of a party agree on their preferences (preference homogeneity), especially among members of the majority party. If members are independent entrepreneurs concerned about being reelected, they will be reluctant to delegate significant power to party leaders for fear that that power could be used to force them to support policies (or identify with policies) that would make them vulnerable. When a party is quite diverse, the risk that a significant number of members would be put in such a position is considerable. Thus they would presumably not favor a strong leadership. This is the insight and conclusion Mayhew offered, and CPG offers the same conclusion. However, substantial preference diversity within the majority is not a certainty; it can ebb and flow over time. CPG argues that as that diversity shrinks, members will be less worried about leaders choosing positions contrary to theirs and will be more willing to delegate power to leaders.

The amount of preference homogeneity within legislative parties is reinforced by the amount of disagreement over preferences (preference conflict) between them. As conflict increases, the negative consequences of a legislative victory by one party increase for its opponents. If the distribution of opinion is relatively similar within both parties, the policy chosen by the minority party will not be very far from that preferred by the majority, and so a minority victory on a bill will not hurt the majority greatly. But when the respective distributions of opinion are very different, the minority's policy is likely to make the majority very unhappy. In the latter case, members of the majority would have a lot more incentive to empower their leaders to prevent a minority victory on legislation than in the former case.

These two considerations—preference homogeneity and preference conflict—together form the "condition" in the theory of conditional party government. As they increase, the theory predicts that party members will be progressively more willing to create strong powers for leaders and to support the exercise of those powers in specific instances. But when diversity grows within parties, or the differences between parties are reduced, members will be reluctant to grant greater powers to leaders. This is the central prediction of CPG.

By now it may be clear how the various theoretical elements of the electoral process interact to affect the character of parties within the House. If activists who have relatively extreme policy preferences, and for whom such preferences are highly salient, have a disproportionate impact on congressional party primaries, the candidates selected in those primaries and their respective parties are likely to differ more in their policy preferences than if those activists had not played such a role. This effect will be reinforced if the candidates themselves are drawn from the ranks of the activists. Those candidates are more likely to have relatively extreme preferences on policy and are more likely to care about seeing those preferences enacted into legislation.

If the primary constituencies in districts in which a given party has a chance to win general elections vary substantially from one district to another in the distribution of preferences among participating voters, the elected representatives of that party are likely to have quite diverse preferences. This was the situation at the time Mayhew wrote, especially among Democrats, but also to a significant degree among GOP members. In the Democratic camp, southern districts tended to nominate conservative (often *very* conservative) candidates, and northern districts tended to nominate much more liberal ones. This divergence yielded much disagreement among northern and southern Democratic winners, creating the conflicts described in *The Electoral Connection.* If, however, the primary constituencies and party activists across the country become more similar within each party and more different between them, then the candidates chosen by each party would become more similar, and the preferences of the legislative parties would become internally more homogeneous and more polarized between them, *regardless of which party was the most successful in national elections.* The "condition" in CPG would be increasingly well met because of the dynamics of candidate selection. The effect could occur, moreover, even if there were relatively little realignment among the mass of voters, and even if there were no increase in the strength of party identification in the electorate.

In summary, if a party's primary electorates are similar across the country, the policy preferences of the candidates selected within that party will be relatively similar, as will be the preferences of the representatives in the House from that party. Dissimilar primary electorates, on the other hand, will lead to dissimilar party candidates and preference diversity in the House. Furthermore, as the primary electorates of the two parties become more different, the preference differences between the two parties' groups of representatives in the House will become more divergent. The variations in these forces will increase or decrease members' incentives to support strong parties in the House, depending on the degree to which the "condition" in CPG is satisfied. We will now apply these theoretical expectations to developments in the electorate and in the House in the years since Mayhew wrote to see whether our theory can account for the developments that *The Electoral Connection* did not anticipate.

Applications of the Theory and Evidence

This section describes electoral and institutional changes both during the years of the Democratic majority and since the GOP won a majority in the 1994 elections. The events under Republican rule are especially valuable in evaluating our theory, because they occurred after CPG was articulated and so provide a test beyond the data that shaped the theory's development. The events under Democratic rule also are important for two reasons. First, the Democrats held House majorities during the period in which Mayhew was writing. Second, they allow us to take a closer look at how Congress changed from the body observed by Mayhew to that observed in the 1990s.

Voters, Candidates, and Party Images

Surveys conducted by the *New York Times* in 1996 illustrate the variations in policy preferences among activists and voters in the two parties.[21] The paper surveyed a national sample of the electorate and asked the same questions of delegates to the Democratic and Republican national nominating conventions, who represented the opinions of activists (see Table 12-1).

The data show that across a variety of issues the views of the delegates were considerably more polarized than the views of each party's voters. For example, in the most general area 76 percent of Democratic activists think the government should do more to solve the nation's problems compared with only 53 percent of Democratic voters. By contrast, 20 percent of Republican voters agree with this opinion, but only 4 percent of activists do. The full electorate is in between, at 36 percent. Similarly, 81 percent of Democratic delegates believe that affirmative action programs should be continued compared with 59 percent of Democratic voters. Among Republicans, the corresponding percentages are 28 for voters and 9 for delegates. And once again, the electorate balances these two views, with 45 percent agreeing. Overall, the average difference between each group of activists and the full electorate is greater than the average difference between Democratic voters and Republican voters.

Of particular relevance to this discussion is how the differences between the policy views of the two parties' activists changed over time. Although data that correspond precisely to those in Table 12-1 are not available, some studies provide evidence of a pattern. The Jacobson study cited earlier indicates that in terms of average liberal–conservative self-identification, the difference between Democratic and Republican activists increased substantially between the 1970s and the 1990s.[22] Moreover, the increase was much greater than the increase in the corresponding difference between Democratic and Republican voters. Using the same measure, Jacobson also reveals that the difference in average placement on the liberal–conservative continuum between southern and northern electoral constituencies declined over the same period, illustrating a decrease in the diversity of Democratic constituencies. Another relevant result presented by Jacobson is

Table 12-1   Policy Opinions of Voters and Major Party Activists, 1996
(percentage responding favorably)

	Democratic Delegates	Democratic Voters	All Voters	Republican Voters	Republican Delegates
Government should do more to:					
—solve the nation's problems	76%	53%	36%	20%	4%
—regulate the environment and safety practices of businesses	60	66	53	37	4
—promote traditional values	27	41	42	44	56
Abortion should be permitted in all cases	61	30	27	22	11
There should be a nationwide ban on assault weapons	91	80	72	62	34
It is necessary to have laws to protect racial minorities	88	62	51	39	30
Affirmative action programs should be continued	81	59	45	28	9
Children of illegal immigrants should be allowed to attend public school	54	65	60	56	31

Source: New York Times, August 26, 1996, A12.

that from the 1970s to the 1990s the correlation between party identification and ideology of all voters in House elections increased substantially—that is, over time liberals were more likely to identify themselves as Democrats and conservatives as Republicans.[23]

In a related finding on electoral developments, Morris Fiorina, who analyzed the National Election Studies from 1964 to 1998, discovered that among "strong ideologues" (respondents who were at one end or the other of the liberal–conservative spectrum) reported turnout had increased.[24] Meanwhile, turnout had declined slightly among weak ideologues, and even more among moderates. This finding is consistent with the growing electoral influence of those with more extreme policy views. Fiorina also examined the ideology of activists compared with that of all voters. Specifically, he compared the average ideology of Democratic respondents (activists and voters) in districts represented by Democrats in the House and of Republican respondents (activists and voters) in districts represented by Republicans. Paralleling Jacobson's findings, Fiorina discovered that the ideological difference between activists in the two parties increased much more from 1970 to 1998 than did the corresponding difference for voters in the two parties.

These data reveal much about activists and voters, but what about candidates? Our theory expects that the divergence between the two groups of party activists, and between the activists and the whole electorate, will produce divergence in the platforms or positions of the congressional candidates of the two parties. Congressional scholars can use roll call data to measure positions of winners, but good, systematic data are not available to measure the positions of unsuccessful candidates. In a clever and convincing analysis, however, Stephen Ansolabehere, James Snyder, and Charles Stewart were able to exploit responses to a survey administered to all House candidates in the 1996 general election.[25] Conducted by an organization called Project Vote Smart, the survey included over two hundred policy questions on a wide range of topics. The authors used the responses, coupled with roll call data, to measure the (public) positions of both representatives and their opponents in 1996. They also employed the presidential election results in each district as a measure of district political preferences.

One of the authors' principal findings is directly related to this discussion. They say: "One of the starkest facts revealed in our data is that candidates clearly do not converge, either nationally or district-by-district. Nationally, there appear to be two 'pools' of candidates, one Democratic and one Republican, and little overlap between the two." [26] With the exception of only one district, the Republican candidate was always more conservative than the Democrat, and usually substantially so. The average gap between the two parties' candidates was 0.47 on a scale of zero to one. The standard deviations within both parties were less than one-third of this average difference. Thus in 1996 congressional candidates generally presented the voters of America with sharply different policy platforms. This is just the kind of situation that would produce the internally homogeneous legislative parties in the House, divergent from one another, that CPG would expect to lead to support for strong party leadership powers.

Two more findings by Ansolabehere et al. also relate to our analysis. By matching the voting records in consecutive Congresses of representatives who succeeded one another, they were able to extend their comparison of candidate divergence back in time to the 1870s, at least for a subset of districts. They found that, first, divergence generally was the pattern over the whole period. Indeed, in 1,814 races held since 1874, only twice was there evidence that the two party candidates had converged to the same position. They also found, however, that there was variation over time in the tendency of candidates to depart from the national party positions and tailor their positions to district sentiments, but that there was almost no tendency in this direction until 1934. From that point, some Republicans began to exhibit a tendency to respond to district sentiments, but Democrats did not begin to exhibit this behavior to any significant degree until the 1960s. The tendency toward individual candidate responsiveness peaked for both parties between 1970 and 1974 and then declined—precipitously among Republicans. Thus during the 1960s and 1970s congressional candidates of both parties exhibited relatively great propensities to depart from their party's national positions to be responsive to their districts. This is exactly the kind of electoral behavior that could produce less internally homogeneous and less distinctive legislative parties in the House.

The responsiveness of congressional candidates to their districts in the 1960s and 1970s, followed by an increasing degree of responsiveness to their (national) party, is consistent with Mayhew's findings in *The Electoral Connection* for the 1960s and 1970s and with the enhanced partisan influence observed in the decades that followed. This shift occurred for many reasons, but one important source of the shift illustrates the interplay between elections and congressional policy making.[27] Before the civil rights movement in the 1950s and 1960s, the Civil Rights Act of 1964, and the Voting Rights Act of 1965, the South was solidly Democratic. Moreover, it was dominated by a white electorate; its large African American population was effectively disenfranchised. After the enfranchisement of African Americans added a substantially more liberal bloc of voters to the typical southern congressional constituency, the Republican Party slowly began to emerge as a significant competitor to the Democratic Party, and in 1994 it won, for the first time, a majority of southern congressional seats. Conservative voters, once solidly Democratic, were now supporting Republican candidates. Because Democratic candidates in the South found themselves facing a more liberal electoral constituency, formerly conservative Democratic candidates and officeholders either became more liberal in their electoral positioning, retired and were replaced by new, more liberal Democrats, or lost their seats to conservative Republicans.[28] As a result, nationally the southern Democrats were no longer as different from their northern peers, and the influx in the House of conservative southern Republicans moved the Republican Party's congressional delegations further ideologically from the more homogeneous Democratic delegations.

The evidence indicates, then, that the activists in both parties are more extreme in their policy preferences than rank and file voters, and that this propensity has increased since the 1960s and 1970s. Studies also reveal that in 1996 the congressional candidates of the two major parties offered sharply different policy positions to voters in districts across the country, and that the tendency toward divergence was lower in the 1960s and 1970s than before or later. But to complete the picture, what legislative behavior resulted from this electoral activity over time? The most widely used measure of ideological positions in legislative voting is the DW-NOMINATE score derived from scaling techniques developed by Keith Poole and Howard Rosenthal.[29] This measure produces a liberal–conservative scale, with a score for all members of the House of each Congress. The changes in the distribution of voting patterns are illustrated here for two Congresses (Figure 12-1). One is the Ninety-first (1969–1971), the first Congress of the Nixon administration, which sat at a time of deep divisions nationally in the Democratic Party, especially along North–South lines. The other is the 105th Congress (1997–1999), the second consecutive Congress with a Republican majority. In Figure 12-1 the members of each Congress are grouped into deciles — ten groups, each with 10 percent of the representatives — from most liberal (group 1) to most conservative (group 10). The figure reveals that the contrast could not be starker. In the Ninety-first Congress Democrats appear in every one of the deciles, and Republicans appear in all but group 1, the most liberal; both internal

Figure 12-1 DW-NOMINATE Scores (91st and 105th Congresses)

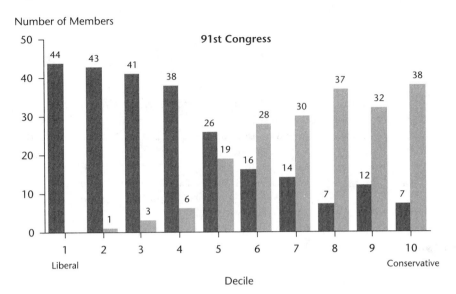

Number of Members

91st Congress

Decile

Liberal · Conservative

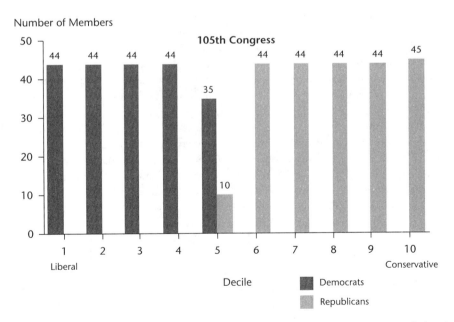

Number of Members

105th Congress

Decile

Liberal · Conservative

Democrats

Republicans

Source: Compiled by the authors from data gathered at http://k7moa.gsia.cmu.edu/ and http://voteview.gsia.cmu.edu/.

homogeneity and party distinctiveness are low. During this period, the influence of the conservative coalition was high and the liberal Democrats began the planning that culminated in the congressional reforms of the 1970s. In the 105th Congress, by contrast, only Republicans appear in the five most conservative deciles, and the four most liberal are made up only of Democrats. The separation of each party from the other is almost the maximum possible.[30]

Given these patterns, CPG theory would expect the members of the two parties in the House at the time Mayhew wrote to be resistant to the creation or exercise of strong party leadership and to tend to their own electoral interests. Indeed, this is precisely the picture presented in *The Electoral Connection*. In the intervening years, however, given the electoral changes and the resulting changes in the distribution of preferences among members of the House, CPG also would predict that the representatives in both parties would be increasingly willing to delegate substantial power to their party leaders and to support the exercise of that power to advance their party's legislative agenda and collective electoral interests. Based on the earlier discussion in this chapter, it should come as no surprise that this is what happened.

Stronger Parties and Electoral Interests

Because a full and systematic discussion of the institutional changes in parties in the House over the last three decades is beyond the scope of this chapter, we will touch here only on a few points that will further illustrate the character of those changes and help to amplify the role of electoral interests in CPG theory. In particular, these points will illustrate the relevance of the assumption that members have multiple goals. They also will illustrate the impact of members' own policy goals (in addition to their electoral self-interest) on their behavior.

As noted, the Democratic reforms of the 1970s had two thrusts: strengthening leaders and undermining committee power and independence. It is difficult to attribute these changes solely to members' reelection goals. How was the reelection interest of House Democrats fostered by removing the protection of the seniority system, a protection Mayhew viewed as an essential feature of their electoral independence? What individual electoral gains resulted from giving Democratic leaders more direct influence over the distribution of valuable committee assignments? If the independence of the Rules Committee, which permitted it to block the floor consideration of bills its members did not like, was valuable to the electoral interests of the membership, why did Democratic members decide to terminate that independence and to vest complete control of the committee in the Democratic Speaker?[31] (Note that Republicans took the same step when they became the majority.)

These decisions were clearly influenced by the policy goals of members. Moreover, it was on the basis of policy interests that these and other reforms were "marketed" to the Democratic membership (as opposed to position taking for outside consumption). The reform leaders—echoing Mayhew's theoretical arguments — complained publicly about the way the seniority system gave committee leaders too much independence on policy matters and promoted the rules changes that would take away that independence. The reformers contended they wanted to give the leadership more influence over committee assignments, because they wanted "members to owe their committee assignments to the leadership." [32] Again, these changes illustrate the policy motives of members and support one of the few direct contrasts between Mayhew's perspective and our theory. CPG expects that some significant part of the membership, at least some notable portion of the time, will seek to achieve policy outcomes and not just be concerned about position taking and credit claiming. We are not arguing, however, that *only* issues matter to members, or even that issues systematically take primacy over electoral interests. Rather, our theory contends that policy interests are relevant to members' decisions in some instances, and that they will particularly pursue these interests or goals if their election prospects are not seriously threatened.

Indeed, evidence from recent Congresses illustrates the interplay in our theory of members' multiple goals. It is clear, for example, that representatives generally will not accept substantial electoral risks, or the loss of election-related resources, to support their party's programs or interests. For example, when the Democrats increased their leadership's powers in the reform era, they also sought to build in controls on the exercise of those powers to reduce the personal risk.[33] Another example is provided by the Republicans. After the Republicans took majority control in 1994, the GOP Conference sought ways to carry out their pledge to cut the costs of running Congress. In one step, they reduced staff funds for committees, but they did not support a reduction of members' personal staff funds, which have (as Mayhew noted) significant electoral benefits. Similarly, the GOP had pledged to cut government pork barrel spending. During the 104th Congress, policy-oriented Republicans on the House Budget Committee sought to force such budget cuts, but they largely failed because of resistance from GOP members of the Appropriations Committee whose personal electoral interests benefited from maintaining the spending.[34] Each of these instances provides support for the perspective, embraced by Mayhew and CPG, that most representatives are independent entrepreneurs who will act to protect their personal electoral interests.

Party Records and Individual Reelection

For members of Congress, two distinct electoral interests may be at issue: their own and that of their party. All members want to be reelected and want to have their own party in the majority.[35] The importance and impact of these motives, however, vary across members. For example, those members who are quite safe electorally can pursue policy goals or seek to foster majority status with little risk to their personal electoral fortunes. Party leaders often are in this situation. Furthermore, the implications of majority status are clearly more salient to party and committee leaders, whose powers and prestige are enormously affected, than they are to rank and file members.[36] Thus party leaders will have strong *personal* incentives to pursue strategies that emphasize the collective party interests.

In doing so, leaders will seek to establish a positive "public record" for the party. Indeed, this effort plays a central role in the partisan theory of Congress articulated by Gary Cox and Mathew McCubbins.[37] The idea is that each party's reputation potentially has electoral effects and so a bad reputation would present an electoral risk both to the party in general (and its chances of achieving or maintaining majority status) and to at least some of its members. Certainly this seems to be a plausible argument in the wake of the Democratic disaster of 1994, and it seems clear that the concept of a party record motivates some aspects of leader behavior and is used by leaders in their dealings with members. In 1995 and 1996 House Speaker Newt Gingrich frequently referred to potential media coverage of the party in trying to persuade the GOP members to stick together. For example, in negotiating with GOP factions on an appropriations bill just before a House recess, Gingrich argued: "We can go home as having the most successful seven months anyone can remember, and have people have a positive view of how we work as a team, or we could lose the bill, with people spending a month saying that we are falling apart." Gingrich added that a public perception of GOP teamwork was "incredibly important in the fall battle with Clinton."[38] About the same time, worries about the congressional party's negative reputation after the government shutdown in 1995–1996 led GOP leaders to make legislative concessions to President Clinton at the end of 1996 so that the party could have some legislative accomplishments to take credit for in the election.

There is evidence as well that the party's image or reputation not only is relevant to short-term voter reactions — that is, in the next election — but also can have more enduring effects on voters' opinions and attachments. In their work on "issue evolution," Edward Carmines and James Stimson argue that changes in the patterns of elite behavior help to redefine the public's images of parties, which can lead in turn to a realignment of voters' party loyalties.[39] They focus on the issue of race — how the national Democratic Party's increasing identification with a liberal position on racial issues in and after the 1960s and the GOP's growing identification with a more conservative position reshaped voter opinion and changed the South from solidly Democratic to tilting Republican. More recent work has revealed a corresponding change in opinion and attachments based on the abortion issue.[40]

It is clear, however, that leaders' appeals linked to the party's record or the party's program do not always sway the membership and therefore do not give leaders a free hand. This situation may arise when the competing interest is the electoral welfare of individual members or when it is the policy interests of a party faction. For example, during the government shutdown in 1995 Gingrich, concerned about the negative public reaction to congressional Republicans, sought to persuade his colleagues to pass a short-term appropriation to reopen the closed government agencies while budget negotiations continued with the

Clinton administration. But by a 12−0 vote his leadership team turned him down, in part reflecting the sentiments of members of the conference who wanted to win over Clinton and balance the budget.[41] Here the top leader, concerned about his party's electoral interests, lost out to the policy interests of members. By contrast, when GOP leaders tried to resist passage of an increase in the minimum wage in 1996, they suffered wholesale defections from more moderate members, who were fearful of voter reactions after a television ad blitz sponsored by the AFL-CIO.[42] Here individual electoral interests dominated.

National Parties in Local Elections

Another illustration of the interplay of policy and electoral interests lies in the national parties' involvement in congressional contests. When Mayhew wrote, he largely dismissed the role of parties in such elections, which was the consensus view of politicians and political scientists. Since then, however, national party organizations have come to play a much more consequential role in congressional elections by providing candidates with campaign funds, offering advice on campaign management, and acting as brokers between candidates and political action committees (PACs).[43] National parties also have become more involved in recruiting candidates. As noted, parties desire majority status in Congress, and the quality of candidates plays a big role in who wins in a district. Contrary to the old saying, however, winning is not the only thing. Who is selected to be the party's candidate also will influence (if the candidate wins) the positions the party takes and the outcomes in the House.

As one might expect, many party leaders—given their strong interest in majority status—tend to search for and support the candidates with the best chance of winning. Other leaders, some rank and file members, and district activists, however, also care about policy and so may seek a candidate who will advocate their desired positions. These competing motives can lead to conflict within a party. For example, in 1998 California held a special election to fill a U.S. House vacancy created by the death of a Democrat; the district had had a long history of representation by a Republican. Because Speaker Newt Gingrich and other House GOP leaders believed that a moderate Republican would have a better chance of winning the district, they endorsed a moderate state legislator. This effort, though, ran into opposition from local conservative activists as well as conservative members of the California GOP House delegation. In the end, the conservatives succeeded in defeating Gingrich's candidate, but their standard bearer lost to the Democratic candidate in the election.[44]

The competition between electoral and policy interests continued into the 2000 elections—not surprising given the narrow majority held by the Republicans in the House. For example, House leaders became involved on both sides of a primary contest between two former GOP representatives seeking the right to try to take back a New Jersey district from the Democrat who had defeated one of them. Republican Speaker Dennis Hastert and the head of the Republican

Congressional Campaign Committee, Tom Davis, backed the more moderate candidate; Majority Leader Dick Armey and Majority Whip Tom DeLay backed the conservative who had been beaten in 1998. Like the California election in 1998, this dispute revolved around ideology versus greater chances of victory. And like the California race in 1998, the Speaker and his allies were most interested in who could win the district and help hold the Republicans' House majority, while the more conservative leaders emphasized ideological considerations. Together, both examples illustrate that the candidate selection process is influenced by policy goals as well as by the desire for electoral victory for the party.

Effects within the House: When *The Electoral Connection* Is Insufficient

As for all alternative theories of political phenomena, the ultimate question is which one better accounts for what happens in the real world. Both Mayhew's theory and CPG try to explain the legislative organization of the House by beginning with the perspective that its members are independent electoral entrepreneurs seeking to protect their chances of reelection. CPG, however, finds members also motivated by their desire to influence policy outcomes, in part for electoral reasons (such as in response to pressures from activists) and in part because of their own policy preferences. Mayhew's theory does not share this view; he maintains that members do not care about policy outcomes and that their activities related to policy are limited to position taking. So then, are there salient aspects of the legislative organization of the House that CPG can account for even though Mayhew's theory does not? This question returns to some aspects of the reform effort of the 1970s described earlier and to later developments along the same lines during the Republican takeover of the House in 1994.

Mayhew cited two features of House organization as particularly important: committee assignments and the seniority system. Here these two features are considered in the context of examining the (relatively few) areas in which Mayhew's theory yields different expectations than ours. Thus we will pursue explicitly the question we asked earlier: Do the developments in the House regarding these features stem solely from the motivations outlined in *The Electoral Connection?* For example, Mayhew argued that committees are central to the electoral interests of members. They are "structural units" that provide important opportunities for claiming credit and taking positions, two of the most important activities for fostering reelection. Thus—as we would expect from Mayhew's theory—both parties until the 1970s had long vested the responsibilities for committee assignments in committees that offered party leaders little opportunity for influencing the allocation of this most valuable commodity.

Yet, as noted earlier, this procedure changed under the Democratic reforms. In 1974, the year a large class of Democrats was elected in the wake of the Watergate scandal, the power to make committee assignments was transferred to the party's Steering and Policy Committee. Where previously the influence of party leaders on assignments was small and indirect, now half of the members of this committee were elected party leaders or members appointed by the Speaker. In 1986 the Republicans also moved in this direction. Previously, GOP assignments had been made by a committee on committees which had one member from each state that had Republicans in the House, plus the elected party leader. Under the arrangement, each committee member had as many votes as there were Republican members from his or her state, and the leader had only one vote. Thus the leadership had little influence and the process was dominated by big states. In 1986 the party adopted a new system, a committee of twenty-one members. As before, the regular members cast multiple votes based on their state delegations, but now the party leader and whip had twelve and six votes, respectively, substantially increasing their influence.[45]

In 1994, immediately after achieving majority status, the Republicans went much further. Prospective Speaker Gingrich personally designed a new assignment committee of twenty-five members with a total of thirty votes. Only two committee members had more than one vote: Gingrich had five and Majority Leader Armey had two.[46] Thus in eight years the Republicans had made the influence of their leadership over assignments progressively stronger, increasing the voting strength of the top two leaders from less than 1 percent to 23 percent of the votes and seeking the second of these increases in their new status as incoming majority party. We cannot attribute either party's shift toward more centralized party leadership over committee assignments solely to the reelectoral incentive of individual entrepreneurs. This increasing control, in the context of increasing intraparty homogeneity and interparty divergence, agrees, however, with CPG theory.

Here we must emphasize again the special case of the Rules Committee. Mayhew underlined the importance of this committee to members, because it controls the flow of legislation to the floor and determines the time and procedures of debate on that legislation. As Mayhew noted, an independent Rules Committee could keep from the floor bills on which the members did not wish to take positions.[47] But, as noted, the Democrats altered this arrangement by granting their party leader power to choose all Democratic members of the Rules Committee, including the chair, and to *remove* them with the agreement of the party caucus. Later, Republicans followed suit, giving their party leader the power to appoint GOP members of the Rules Committee. In 1994 the Republicans confirmed this power under majority status.

Finally, consider again the seniority system. For Mayhew, protection of this system was central to the independence of members from party pressure because of the "property right" to committee membership and the ever-increasing value of membership that the system guaranteed. Yet during the 1970s Democratic members systematically and voluntarily altered the seniority system, abolishing its automatic nature. No longer did members have the certain property right, and chairs served at the sufferance of the party caucus. Furthermore, there is strong evidence that this reform had its desired effect. Research shows that the voting behavior of committee chairs and those close in seniority to the job demonstrated increased party loyalty after the change.[48] For example, the party loyalty score of Jamie Whitten of Mississippi (chairman of Appropriations) went from 39 points below the average for all Democrats in 1975–1976 to two points higher than the average in 1987–1988.[49]

As with committee assignments, the Republicans further altered the seniority arrangements when they took over in 1994. Within a week after the election, Gingrich simply asserted the right to choose the chairs of major committees without any formal alteration of the party or House rules, and even before most of the newly elected members could get to Washington. The GOP members accepted this assertion of authority. On three major committees—Appropriations, Commerce, and Judiciary—Gingrich bypassed more senior members to choose a chair he preferred and who would be responsive to the leadership. In fact, on Appropriations he skipped the four most senior members to choose Robert Livingston of Louisiana. Appropriations was to be a major vehicle for the party to accomplish its policy objectives, so it was particularly important to have the right chair.[50] Indeed, when the new Congress convened, Gingrich compelled Republican members of Appropriations "to sign a 'letter of fidelity.' [It] pledged the members to cut the budget as much as Gingrich wanted."[51] These parties, then, had traveled a long way from the parties of the 1970s in Mayhew's account, which simply left members alone to make their own decisions.

The point of these examples, and the many others that could be taken from the Democratic reform period or the Republican majority, is that members voluntarily adopted rules that removed some of their electoral independence from their parties. They also gave powers to the party leadership that could be used to pressure those same members to do or support what the party wanted. These changes in the House are not explainable within a framework that only recognizes reelection as a motive of members. Such developments are understandable, however, from the perspective of conditional party government, with its emphasis on the interplay of electoral and policy goals for members and on the electoral and institutional effects of the polarization of American politics.

Conclusion

This discussion, or CPG theory more generally, is not intended to constitute a rejection of Mayhew's analysis in *The Electoral Connection*. Rather, it is an extension and elaboration of that analysis. Both theories share the view that representatives are strongly motivated by the desire for reelection and that this desire shapes the organizational structure of the House and of its parties. The main points of difference are CPG's emphasis on the consequences of members' multiple constituencies (particularly the impact of activists), on the variability of preference agreement within and between parties, and on the assumption that representatives maintain and pursue both electoral and policy goals. These amplifications permit us to understand and explain important developments that are not comprehensible based on the reelection motive alone. By combining electoral and policy goals, linked through the electoral connection, the theory of conditional party government provides, we believe, a more complete account of the legislative organization of Congress and the behavior of its members.

But what does the future hold for the theory of conditional party government? That is, will the patterns that our theory describes — internally homogeneous and polarized parties with empowered leaderships — continue to prevail?[52] The future will depend on the degree to which the conditions that produced these patterns persist. Will the electorate continue to be polarized along partisan lines on major issues? Will that polarization continue to be reinforced by the even more extreme polarization among party activists, who dominate the nomination process? And finally, will the personal (and often intense) policy preferences of a significant portion of the congressional membership continue to exacerbate the polarization of the parties? The answer to these questions is probably yes.

By far, the most likely way the electoral roots of CPG can be undermined is if one or more issues emerge that are highly salient to voters and activists and that cut across the parties and divide them just the way race divided the Democrats for so many years. Such a situation would produce the overlapping preference distributions that characterized the parties from the late 1930s until the late 1970s. There does not appear to be an issue on the horizon, however, that would have this effect. Alternatively, polarization between the parties could be reduced by changes in the rules or context that de-emphasize the influence of activists. Failing those developments, the homogeneity and divergence that the parties have exhibited for the last two decades should continue, and in turn so should the willingness of members to empower their party leaders in order to advance their party's policy agenda. These patterns should, moreover, be reinforced as long as the partisan division of the two chambers is close and control in the next election remains seriously in doubt. The electoral roots of conditional party government have been in place for at least twenty years, and its expected consequences in terms of the legislative organization of the House have held, with some variation, throughout that period, including for the "postrevolutionary" 105th and 106th Congresses.[53] We have no reason to expect that these patterns will change in the future.

Notes

1. David R. Mayhew, *Congress: The Electoral Connection* (New Haven: Yale University Press, 1974).
2. See David W. Rohde, *Parties and Leaders in the Postreform House* (Chicago: University of Chicago Press, 1991); and John H. Aldrich, *Why Parties? The Origin and Transformation of Political Parties in America* (Chicago: University of Chicago Press, 1995).
3. Mayhew, *Congress: The Electoral Connection*, 5–6.
4. Anthony Downs, *An Economic Theory of Democracy* (New York: Harper and Row, 1957).
5. Mayhew, *Congress: The Electoral Connection*, 25–27.

6. Ibid., 27.
7. Ibid., 99, 100. Mayhew noted that while *enactment* of a program may not be important, "some [members] may find it important to take positions on programs."
8. Ibid., 99–100.
9. Ibid., 103.
10. Ibid., 95–96.
11. For more detail, see Rohde, *Parties and Leaders,* chap. 2.
12. See Bruce I. Oppenheimer, "The Rules Committee: New Arm of Leadership in a Decentralized House," in *Congress Reconsidered,* ed. Lawrence C. Dodd and Bruce I. Oppenheimer (New York: Praeger, 1977), 96–116.
13. These data are from David W. Rohde, "Electoral Forces, Political Agendas, and Partisanship in the House and Senate," in *The Postreform Congress,* ed. Roger H. Davidson (New York: St. Martin's Press, 1992), 27–47. As that analysis shows, similar increases in party voting and party loyalty were exhibited in the Senate over this period.
14. Richard F. Fenno Jr., *Congressmen in Committees* (Boston: Little, Brown, 1973), chap. 1.
15. Mayhew, *Congress: The Electoral Connection,* 16.
16. Again, we emphasize that for Mayhew this was a theoretical assumption, not an assertion about reality. Our argument is that a more elaborate theoretical assumption about members' goals permits our theory to explain certain institutional arrangements and member behavior that cannot plausibly be explained by the reelection motive alone.
17. Richard F. Fenno Jr., *Home Style: House Members in Their Districts* (Boston: Little, Brown, 1978).
18. Mayhew, *Congress: The Electoral Connection,* 45.
19. Gary C. Jacobson, "Party Polarization in National Politics: The Electoral Connection," in *Polarized Politics: Congress and the President in a Partisan Era,* ed. Jon R. Bond and Richard Fleisher (Washington, D.C.: CQ Press, 2000), 9–30.
20. See Aldrich, *Why Parties?* 180–93.
21. *New York Times,* August 26, 1996, A12.
22. Jacobson, *Party Polarization,* 23. Jacobson's study used the biannual National Election Studies. His measure is based on respondents' average self-placement on a seven-point scale from extremely liberal to extremely conservative.
23. Ibid., 17. In addition, recent work by Larry Bartels shows that over the last twenty-five years there has been a substantial increase in the impact of partisan loyalties on voting behavior in both presidential and congressional elections. See Larry Bartels, "Partisanship and Voting Behavior, 1952–1996," *American Journal of Political Science* 44 (January 2000): 35–50.
24. Morris Fiorina, "Whatever Happened to the Median Voter?" paper presented at the annual meeting of the Midwest Political Science Association, April 1999, Chicago.
25. Stephen Ansolabehere, James Snyder, and Charles Stewart, "Candidate Positioning in U.S. House Elections," manuscript, Massachusetts Institute of Technology, July 1998.
26. Ibid., 14.
27. See Rohde, *Parties and Leaders,* chap. 3, especially 45–58.
28. For more on the building of Republican competition in the South at various levels of office, see John H. Aldrich and John D. Griffin, "Ambition in the South: The Emergence of Republican Electoral Support, 1948–1998," paper delivered at the Twelfth Citadel Symposium on Southern Politics, March 2–3, 2000, The Citadel, Charleston, South Carolina.
29. See Keith Poole and Howard Rosenthal, *Congress: A Political-Economic History of Roll Call Voting* (New York: Oxford University Press, 1997). Although they actually developed several related measures, we use the first dimension DW-Nominate score.
30. Indeed, it appears that the 1950s through the 1970s are the unusual period. The degree of satisfaction of the "condition" in CPG appears to have been uniformly at or

near its typical high point from the late 1800s through about World War II (1940s) in the U.S. House. Then began a period of decreasing satisfaction of the "condition" through about 1970, with an equally consistent return to the usual historical high in the 1990s. Thus it could be that Mayhew just happened to write at the most atypical moment historically. For development of these data and discussion, see John H. Aldrich, Mark Berger, and David W. Rohde, "The Historical Variability in Conditional Party Government, 1877–1986," *Essays on the History of Congress*, ed. David Brady and Mathew D. McCubbins (Stanford, Calif.: Stanford University Press, forthcoming).

31. See Mayhew, *Congress: The Electoral Connection*, 150–51.
32. Quoted in Burton Sheppard, *Rethinking Congressional Reform* (Cambridge, Mass.: Schenkman Books, 1985), 198.
33. See Rohde, *Parties and Leaders*, 26–28.
34. See Gregory L. Bovitz, "Why Did Republican Porkbusters Fail in the 104th Congress? Assessing Competing Theories of How the U.S. House Works," paper presented at the annual meeting of the Midwest Political Science Association, April 27–30, 2000, Chicago; and John H. Aldrich and David W. Rohde, "The Republican Revolution and the House Appropriations Committee," *Journal of Politics* 62 (February 2000): 1–33.
35. For a discussion of the relative advantage of majority status to a party and the asymmetry in power between the majority and minority parties, see John H. Aldrich and David W. Rohde, "The Consequences of Party Organization in the House: The Role of the Majority and Minority Parties in Conditional Party Government," in *Polarized Politics: Congress and the President in a Partisan Era*, ed. Jon R. Bond and Richard Fleisher (Washington, D.C.: CQ Press, 2000), 31–72.
36. The implications of this contrast are more fully explored in Bryan W. Marshall, Brandon C. Prins, and David W. Rohde, "Majority Party Leadership, Strategic Choice, and Committee Power: Appropriations in the House, 1995–98," in *Congress on Display, Congress at Work*, ed. William Bianco (Ann Arbor: University of Michigan Press, 2000).
37. Gary W. Cox and Mathew D. McCubbins, *Legislative Leviathan: Party Government in the House* (Berkeley: University of California Press, 1993), 110–22.
38. Elizabeth Drew, *Showdown: The Struggle between the Gingrich Congress and the Clinton White House* (New York: Simon and Schuster, 1996), 270.
39. Edward G. Carmines and James A. Stimson, *Issue Evolution: Race and the Transformation of American Politics* (Princeton: Princeton University Press, 1989).
40. See Greg D. Adams, "Abortion: Evidence of Issue Evolution," *American Journal of Political Science* 41 (July 1997): 718–37.
41. See David Maraniss and Michael Weisskopf, *"Tell Newt to Shut Up!" Prizewinning Washington Post Journalists Reveal How Reality Gagged the Gingrich Revolution* (New York: Simon and Schuster, 1996), 179–82.
42. See Linda Killian, *The Freshmen: What Happened to the Republican Revolution?* (Boulder, Col.: Westview Press, 1998), 343–45.
43. See Paul Herrnson, *Congressional Elections*, 2d ed. (Washington, D.C.: CQ Press, 1998), especially chap. 4; and Gary C. Jacobson, *The Politics of Congressional Elections* (New York: Longman, 1997).
44. For more details, see Paul R. Abramson, John H. Aldrich, and David W. Rohde, *Change and Continuity in the 1996 and 1998 Elections* (Washington, D.C.: CQ Press, 1999), 263.
45. See Rohde, *Parties and Leaders*, 24, 77, 137.
46. See John H. Aldrich and David W. Rohde, "The Transition to Republican Rule in the House: Implications for Theories of Congressional Politics," *Political Science Quarterly* 112 (winter 1997–1998): 554–55.

47. Mayhew, *Congress: The Electoral Connection,* 150–52.
48. See Sara Brandes Crook and John R. Hibbing, "Congressional Reform and Party Discipline: The Effects of Changes in the Seniority System on Party Loyalty in the House of Representatives," *British Journal of Political Science* 15 (1985): 207–26.
49. Rohde, *Parties and Leaders,* 76.
50. Aldrich and Rohde, "Transition to Republican Rule," 548–50.
51. Thomas Rosentiel, "Why Newt Is No Joke," *Newsweek,* April 10, 1995, 26.
52. This question has been raised by, for example, Lawrence C. Dodd and Bruce I. Oppenheimer, "Congress and the Emerging Order: Conditional Party Government or Constructive Partisanship?" in *Congress Reconsidered,* 6th ed., ed. Lawrence C. Dodd and Bruce I. Oppenheimer (Washington, D.C.: CQ Press, 1997), 390–413.
53. See Marshall et al., "Majority Party Leadership, Strategic Choice, and Committee Power"; and Aldrich and Rohde, "Consequences of Party Organization in the House."

Part V
Congress, the Executive, and Public Policy

13. Congress, the Executive, and the Production of Public Policy: United We Govern?

Sarah A. Binder

We think both parties misread the temper as well as the intelligence of the American electorate if they think it is good politics to stall and delay and eventually come up with nothing.
—New York Times editorial, June 24, 1956

Gridlock is not a modern legislative invention. Although the term is said to have entered the American political lexicon after the 1980 elections, Alexander Hamilton was complaining more than two centuries ago about the deadlock rooted in the design of the Continental Congress. In many ways, gridlock is endemic to our national politics, the natural consequence of separate institutions sharing and competing for power.

But even casual observers of Washington recognize tremendous variation in Congress's performance. To be sure, periods of major lawmaking prowess are the exception, rather than the norm. When they occur, they earn enduring political labels: the New Deal and the Great Society, to name the most obvious two. The Great Society Congress under President Lyndon B. Johnson, for example, enacted landmark health care, environment, civil rights, transportation, and education statutes (to name a few). At other times, gridlock prevails, as it did in 1992, when Congress attempted to cut the capital gains tax and to reform lobbying, campaign finance, banking, parental leave, and voter registration laws (to name a few of its efforts).

What accounts for such uneven performance? Why is Congress sometimes remarkably productive and other times mired in stalemate? For all our attention to the minutiae of Congress, we know little about the dimensions and causes of gridlock. How much do we have? How often do we get it? What drives it up and down? Such questions are particularly pertinent in recent years, given the predominance of divided party control of government, a state of affairs produced by sixteen of the past twenty-three national elections. To what extent is gridlock a function of national elections that divide control of the executive and legislative branches between the two political parties? Or, are more enduring institutional or electoral trends to blame?

In this chapter, I address these questions, using the experience of the last half-century to explore conventional and alternative notions about Congress and the president's capacity to act on issues of major public import. Although divided government may limit the responsiveness of Congress and the president to national problems, I suggest that accounts of legislative stalemate should look beyond the effects of interbranch conflict. Here, I draw special attention to two under-appreciated forces of stalemate within Congress: friction between the House and Senate and the growing polarization of the two major political parties. I conclude by considering potential consequences of gridlock, suggesting some broader political repercussions of gridlock in Washington.

The Concept of Gridlock

Some argue that gridlock is simply a constant of American political life. James Madison bequeathed us a political system designed not to work, a government of sharply limited powers.[1] But surely the framers (dissatisfied with their governing experiment after the Revolution and fearful of rebellious debtors in the states) sought a strong national government that could govern—deliberately and efficiently, albeit insulated from the passions of popular majorities.[2] The result, in this view, was an "intricate balance between limiting government and infusing it with energy."[3] Gridlock may be a frequent consequence of the Constitution, but that doesn't mean the framers preferred it.

Others might object to labeling legislative inaction as "gridlock." If "that government is best which governs least," then policy stability should be applauded, not derided as gridlock. But views about gridlock tend to vary with one's political circumstance. The former Senate majority leader Robert Dole, R-Kan., put it best: "If you're against something, you'd better hope there's a little gridlock."[4] Legislative action, after all, can produce either liberal or conservative policy change. *Gridlock* might simply be an unfortunate choice of words, a clumsy term for Washington's inability to broach and secure policy compromise (whether liberal or conservative in design). If so, understanding the causes of gridlock should interest scholars and observers of Washington alike, regardless of party or ideology.

A Metric for Gridlock

How do we know whether government is deadlocked, productive, or somewhere in between? The most casual observer of Washington can usually tell the difference between a Congress that produces a lot and a Congress that does little. The slim legislative record of the Democratic 102d Congress in 1991–1993—which provoked charges of gridlock by presidential candidates

Ross Perot and Bill Clinton—is a prime example of gridlock at its extreme. Efforts to enact lobbying and campaign finance reform; to enact parental leave, banking, and voter registration legislation; and to cut the capital gains tax—to name just a few salient issues—all ended in deadlock. Likewise, the most productive Congresses are easily tagged, with the Great Society Congress under Johnson in 1965–1967 the exemplary Congress in this regard. Landmark health care, environment, civil rights, transportation, and education statutes, among many others, were enacted by that Congress—a total of twenty-two major laws, a record met only two other times over the past twenty-six Congresses.

Although we can judge gridlock and productivity at their extremes, political scientists lack a metric that would allow us to compare, more or less systematically, changes in the level of gridlock over time. Typically, scholars assess Congress's output, counting up the number of important laws enacted by each Congress. When output is low, we say that gridlock is high, and vice versa. David Mayhew's well-regarded contribution to these debates, *Divided We Govern*, uses such an approach to evaluate legislative performance over the past half-century.[5] But measuring output without respect to the agenda of salient issues risks misstating the true level of gridlock. A Congress might produce little legislation because it is gridlocked. Or it might be unproductive because it faces a limited agenda. With little on its legislative plate, surely Congress and the president should not be blamed for producing meager results. We can explore the causes of gridlock only if we have some idea of the size of the underlying policy agenda in Washington.

Gridlock is best viewed, then, as the share of salient issues on the nation's agenda left in limbo at the close of each Congress. Just what are the salient issues on the nation's agenda? The editorial page of the *New York Times* (the nation's paper of record) serves admirably as an indicator. We can reconstruct the policy agenda of the past half-century of American politics by identifying all the legislative issues of each Congress discussed by the *Times* (whether in support or in opposition—to take into account the paper's often liberal political perspective). Salient issues are those addressed at least four times in a single Congress.[6]

This measure provides a sense of the size of the policy agenda over time (Table 13-1). As we might expect, the agenda was smallest in the 1950s during the quiescent years of the Eisenhower presidency before jumping sharply in the 1960s under the activist administrations of Presidents John F. Kennedy and Lyndon Johnson. The size of the agenda continued to rise steadily in the 1970s and 1980s, declining only in the 1990s—likely reflecting the tightening of budgets and the concordant dampening of legislative activism.

How successful were Congress and the president in addressing the most salient of these policy issues? Figure 13-1 shows marked variation in the level of gridlock over the past fifty years. Is Congress particularly gridlocked today? Critics of Congress who claim so are partially right. Gridlock has trended upward over the period, with the level of gridlock on average 25 percentage points higher in the 1990s than it was in the 1940s. Gridlock peaked in the early 1990s, when

Table 13-1   Size of the Policy Agenda, 80th–104th
Congresses (1947–1997)

Congress (years)	Number of Issues on the Agenda
80th (1947–1949)	85
81st (1949–1951)	85
82d (1951–1953)	72
83d (1953–1955)	74
84th (1955–1957)	84
85th (1957–1959)	89
86th (1959–1961)	70
87th (1961–1963)	129
88th (1963–1965)	102
89th (1965–1967)	96
90th (1967–1969)	119
91st (1969–1971)	144
92d (1971–1973)	135
93d (1973–1975)	133
94th (1975–1977)	138
95th (1977–1979)	150
96th (1979–1981)	144
97th (1981–1983)	127
98th (1983–1985)	138
99th (1985–1987)	160
100th (1987–1989)	140
101st (1989–1991)	147
102d (1991–1993)	126
103d (1993–1995)	94
104th (1995–1997)	118

Source: Compiled by the author.

President George Bush faced a Democratic Congress. Fully 65 percent of the twenty-three most salient agenda issues remained unresolved when the 102d Congress drew to a close in January 1993. With the arrival of unified government under Bill Clinton and congressional Democrats after the 1992 elections, gridlock still remained at a historic high, with over half of the sixteen most visible issues left in limbo when the 103d Congress adjourned.

But the level of gridlock does not simply trend upward. After its unprecedented highs in the early 1990s, gridlock dropped 14 percentage points in the 104th Congress (1995–1997), reflecting election year compromises on reforming welfare, health care, immigration, and telecommunication laws, as well as increasing the minimum wage. Still, no recent Congress has matched the performance of the Great Society, four years of legislative prowess in which Presidents Kennedy and Johnson and their Democratic Congresses stalemated on just roughly a quarter of the policy agenda (deadlocking on fourteen of the fifty most salient issues across those four years).

Figure 13-1 Level of Policy Gridlock, 1947–1997

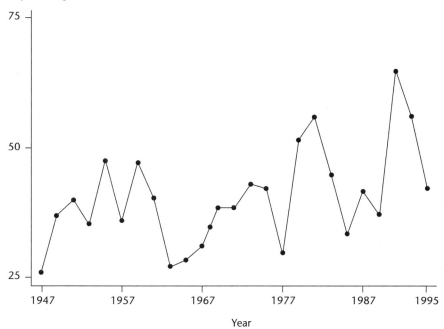

Gridlock Score
(in percentage)

Source: Compiled by the author.

Note: A gridlock score for each Congress was calculated by dividing the number of salient issues that failed in the Congress by the total number of salient issues on the agenda of that Congress. For example, gridlock in the 80th Congress (1947–1949) stood at 26 percent (six failed issues out of twenty-three total agenda issues). Scores for an entire Congress are assigned to the first year the Congress met.

Divided Government and the Production of Public Policy

Split party control of Congress and the presidency is most often indicted as the central cause of deadlock. The indictment is rooted in what might be called political scientists' long-lived love affair with political parties. It is an affair that stretches back to the early twentieth century, to the origins of American political science as a profession. For political scientists Woodrow Wilson, Henry James Ford, Frank Goodnow, and others, political parties were seen as critical instruments for achieving unity of purpose and action in American governance. As Wilson argued,

> The degree of separation now maintained between the executive and legislative branches of our government cannot long be preserved without very

serious inconvenience resulting. . . . What we need is harmonious, consistent, responsible party government, instead of a wide dispersion of function and responsibility; and we can get it only by connecting the President as closely as may be with his party in Congress.[7]

By the mid-1940s, this view of parties had been enshrined as the *doctrine of responsible parties*, a view holding parties as essential to democratic life. Classically stated by E. E. Schattschneider in his 1942 work, *Party Government*, "the political parties created democracy and . . . modern democracy is unthinkable save in terms of the parties."[8] Only parties—by virtue of their goal of assembling majorities to win elections—could claim the authority and legitimacy to rule in a democracy. The obvious alternative, pressure groups, had narrow policy aims and no goal of persuading a majority, and hence no legitimate claim on power.

Arguments about the effects of divided government typically revolve around the importance of political parties for bridging our separated institutions.[9] The logic is straightforward: unified party control of the two branches guarantees an important extra-constitutional link between the legislature and executive, which ensures common interests and shared purpose. Under unified government, shared electoral and policy motivations of the president and congressional majorities give majority party legislative leaders the incentive and capacity to use their tools and resources to pass legislation. In contrast, under divided government, competing policy views and electoral incentives are said to reinforce institutional rivalries between Congress and the president, which makes it difficult to assemble the coherent policy majorities necessary to forge major legislation.[10] Both parties seek policy outcomes that enhance their own electoral reputations, but neither side wants the other to reap electoral benefit from achieving its policy agenda.

If the traditional argument about divided government is correct, stalemate should be higher in periods of split party control and subside under unified government. This expectation is partially borne out. When control of Congress and the presidency has been divided between the parties, 43 percent of the agenda has ended in gridlock; when unified party control has prevailed, only 38 percent of the agenda has been left undone. Still, given the pointed criticism perennially lodged against divided government, the substantive effect of gridlock—a mere 5 percentage points—is relatively small.

A comparison of the 102d (1991–1993) and 103d (1993–1995) Congresses clearly shows the muted effect of unified government. Under divided party control in the 102d Congress, gridlock reached a postwar high of 65 percent: nearly two-thirds of salient policy issues remained in deadlock when Congress adjourned. When the election of Bill Clinton as president in 1992 ushered in unified government for the 103d Congress, expectations were high. Capitol Hill observers anticipated that bills vetoed by President Bush under divided government would be signed into law and that the Democrats would push a heavy agenda of activist policy proposals toward enactment. To some extent, expectations were borne out: voter registration, parental leave, and gun control reforms were enacted into law after being vetoed in the 102d Congress. But unified government failed to ensure enactment of the Democrats' more ambitious policy agenda, including economic stimulus measures and health care and campaign reforms. When Congress adjourned in 1994, the overall level of gridlock had subsided to 56 percent but remained well above the average level of deadlock for the postwar period.

Why is the policy impact of unified government so muted? The experience of the 103d Congress offers a few clues. First, consider what happened to Clinton's proposed package of budget cuts in 1993. The bill passed the House with only Democratic votes. In the Senate, not only Republicans balked but conservative Democrats (including John B. Breaux of Louisiana and David Boren of Oklahoma) also raised objections. As a result, significant tax portions of the package passed by the House were eliminated in the Senate bill. This suggests that the constraint of bicameralism poses a hurdle for major policy change, even in periods of unified control. Even a Congress and president of the same party cannot guarantee that congressional partisans in both chambers will see eye-to-eye on salient policy matters.

Second, consider the fate of Clinton's 1993 economic stimulus package. It passed readily with the support of Democrats in the House. But in the Senate, a Republican filibuster blocked the president's $16 billion package, resulting in a significantly weakened final bill.[11] Proposals for significant health care reform also ran into filibuster-related problems, as they failed to garner sufficient minority party support in the Senate. Because Senate rules require a supermajority, or sixty votes (out of a hundred), to cut off a filibuster and because the majority party rarely has the requisite number of votes from within its party ranks, significant bipartisan support is usually necessary to ensure passage of major legislation. In other words, unified government is not always sufficient for producing significant policy change. Lacking bipartisan support to overcome a filibuster or to overcome a presidential veto, significant policy change is unlikely to occur. Thus, although unified government tends to reduce the level of deadlock, it is not a cure-all for the passage of major policy change.

Electoral Effects beyond Divided Government

Split party control may be the most visible consequence of biennial elections. But elections do more than divide up control of the major branches of government. They also determine the ideological makeup of Congress. At issue is the particular distribution of policy views within the two major parties. The underlying assumption is that American political parties are by nature heterogeneous, failing to maintain a consistent and cohesive ideological position over time. It is an assumption easily maintained by recent empirical analysis.[12]

But even within a context of generally diverse political parties, we can consider two stylized configurations of legislators' policy preferences by party. At times, the policy preferences of the members of the two major parties will be polarized. Under this condition of *partisan polarization,* most legislators' policy views place them at their party's respective end of an underlying ideological spectrum: relatively few legislators occupy the political center. A contrasting configuration of *partisan moderation* finds a greater number of legislators standing close to the ideological center between the two parties. Under this scenario, the members of either one or both of the two parties are spread across the ideological spectrum, with a greater number of legislators overlapping each other ideologically in a common central space.

This distinction is important because it helps to capture one of the most striking electoral trends in recent years: the polarization of the two major parties in Congress. Some have called this the "disappearing political center."[13] If we think of centrists or moderates as legislators who are closer to the ideological midpoint of the two parties than to their own party's center, we can size up the reach of the political center over the past five decades.[14] By this score, roughly one-third of the members of Congress in the 1960s and 1970s were centrists; today, moderates make up less than 10 percent of the House and Senate. Symbolic of the decline of the political center was the death of Sen. John H. Chafee, R-R.I., in October 1999, lauded after his passing by President Clinton as embodying "the decent center which has carried America from triumph to triumph for over 200 years."[15] His passing left only two moderates in the Senate in 1999, as based on their roll-call votes for the year.[16]

Many political scientists are now exploring the causes of polarization.[17] It is also important to consider the *consequences* of polarization. If major policy change is more likely when legislators can forge large, bipartisan coalitions, we might expect the likelihood of gridlock to rise with polarization.[18] The further apart the two parties, the tougher it is to negotiate compromise, partly because fewer legislators are positioned in the center and partly because there is little incentive for others to reach into the middle. As Rep. Barney Frank, D-Mass., observed in the summer of 1999, "Right now, the differences between the two parties are so great, it doesn't make sense for us to compromise. We'll show where we stand, and let the people decide."[19]

The presence of moderate legislators makes bridging party differences easier, because at least a small block of legislators from the two parties share a common centrist electoral constituency. The need to appeal to a similar set of ideological interests at election time would provide an incentive for legislators to try to bridge policy differences between the two parties. When the two parties are clearly polarized, each relying on the support of a different set of constituencies, the parties start with few policy agreements and face little electoral incentive to compromise.

If ideological moderation encourages policy compromise, we should see a negative relationship between the number of moderates and the level of policy gridlock. The greater the number of centrists, the lower the level of gridlock. In contrast, if ideological moderation makes it harder for the majority party to enact an agenda, moderation and gridlock should go hand-in-hand. As the number of centrist legislators rises, gridlock should rise as well. For both the House and the Senate, the expectation that moderation reduces gridlock has been borne out in the period since World War II, although the relationship is stronger for the Senate than for the House.[20]

Viewing the effects of elections more broadly, a national election that produces unified government might also yield a Congress with few ideological moderates. This is precisely what occurred with the 1992 elections, which installed unified Democratic rule in Washington. The elections also returned two political parties with barely any overlap between their members ideologically: moderates claimed less than 13 percent of both chambers in the 103d Congress. Not surprisingly, although gridlock did subside between the 102d and 103d Congresses with the arrival of unified government, it did so only marginally. The boost brought by unified control was dampened by the lack of legislative centrists. With such steep ideological differences between the parties, the Democratic majority could not attract the necessary bipartisan support to enact major changes in public policy.[21]

In what other ways might elections affect policymaking? We might also consider the effect of so-called *electoral mandates* on the prospects for governance. The most prominent such electoral shocks are those associated with critical elections and realignments, sharp changes in the national electoral landscape that either bring a new dominant majority to power or strengthen the electoral position of the existing majority party. Over the course of the nation's electoral history, political scientists normally point to three such major realignments, occurring around the Civil War, the late 1890s, and the New Deal of the 1930s.[22] Each of these realignments was accompanied by major changes in public policy.[23]

For the contemporary period, there is no consensus on whether or not another electoral realignment has occurred.[24] But even electoral shocks short of realignment are likely to affect policy stability. The argument was well stated in a *New York Times* editorial in 1948 at the close of the 80th Congress, the first Republican Congress since before the New Deal:

> The Republicans took control of Congress on the basis of an obvious popular revulsion against some of the policies of the Roosevelt-Truman administrations. There was no landslide but there was a perceptible movement of the political terrain. The new legislators certainly had a mandate to liquidate some war measures, to loosen some New Deal controls, to check some New Deal projects and to effect practicable economics.[25]

The effects of such electoral shocks are likely conditioned by the length of time a new congressional majority was in the minority. The longer a new majority has been out of control of Congress, the more dissatisfied it is likely to be with the status quo, and the greater is its incentive to make changes. There is also a strong electoral incentive for a new majority to prove that it can govern, further increasing the likelihood of altering the policy status quo.[26]

The aftermath of the historic 1994 midterm elections that produced unified Republican rule for the first time in forty years illustrates this trend well. The fervor for conservative policy change after forty years as the minority party surely helped maintain the internal cohesiveness of House Republicans in the 104th Congress (1995–1997). Notably, they passed 95 percent of their campaign agenda (their "Contract with America") after taking control of the House after the elections in 1994.[27] Of course, as discussed below, many of those provisions ultimately ended in deadlock, after encountering opposition from the Senate or the president or both.

Considering the Institutional Context

From the very beginning of the American political nation, elites have recognized the impact of institutions on policy outcomes. By "institutions," I mean the set of constitutional and structural arrangements within which politics takes place. Even before the Constitution had been adopted, Alexander Hamilton warned in the *Federalist Papers* that the institutional arrangements of the Continental Congress were a proven recipe for deadlock. Its supermajority requirements, its voting by state units, and other internal procedures ensured that the policy views of the members of Congress would often be frustrated.[28] The idea that institutions can make it difficult to follow the preferences of a majority, in other words, has a long history in American politics.

Recent work on the politics of gridlock has encouraged scholars to think anew about the relevance of institutions in explaining legislative patterns, including new books by Keith Krehbiel and by David Brady and Craig Volden.[29] The move to incorporate institutional effects is important for several reasons. First, it draws on the insights of an earlier era of political scientists who viewed institutions as paramount in studying American national politics. Second, it highlights the ways in which electoral outcomes alone fail to account for policy outcomes. And third, it forces political scientists to think more extensively about the multiple ways in which institutions can enable or constrain policy change.

In the current thinking about the production of public policy, the critical institutional arrangements are those rules and procedures that directly affect the legislative process. Our interest then is in those institutional features that might help explain why Congress and the executive—even when of the same party—often find themselves unable to enact major policy change. To put it another way, elections are only as decisive as institutional conditions permit. The case of the Republicans' Contract with America is illustrative here. Although the House passed nearly all the provisions of the contract, less than 40 percent of the Contract was eventually enacted into law. Of critical importance to understanding the fate of the Contract is the effect of bicameralism and supermajority rules.

The bicameral character of Congress was crafted, of course, during the Constitutional Convention in the late 1780s. As James Madison argued in *Fed-*

eralist Papers, No. 62, "I will barely remark, that as the improbability of sinister combinations will be *in proportion to the dissimilarity in the genius of the two bodies,* it must be politic to distinguish them from each other by every circumstance which will consist with a due harmony in all proper measures, and with the genuine principles of republican government."[30] Madison's comments leave no doubt that the framers expected bicameralism to affect the legislative process.

Yet, despite the centrality of bicameralism to the Constitution, students of the policy process quite often treat Congress as a unicameral actor.[31] Certainly the traditional focus on divided government implicitly suggests that the legislative process can best be explained as the outcome of interactions between the president and a unicameral Congress.[32] But treating bicameral institutions as if they were unicameral risks overlooking important differences.

Perhaps most fundamental is the idea that the two legislative chambers might not hold the same set of preferred policy outcomes. Even when the same party controls both chambers, elections might distribute policy views unevenly between the two chambers. Given that only one-third of the Senate is up for reelection at one time, electoral trends that influence House members (all of whom are up for reelection every two years) might show limited effect on the Senate. The different constituency bases of House and Senate members also matter here, as House districts are typically far more homogeneous than the states from which they are drawn. A House Republican representing a homogeneous conservative district in southwest Indiana might have little in common with an Indiana senator whose constituency includes more liberal minority groups from the inner cities of the north. The six-year term of senators also might produce some moderation in Senate delegations, given the longer stretch before facing the electorate compared with House delegations.

Ideological differences between the two chambers are important, because they likely affect the ease with which the two chambers reach policy compromise. If the two chambers are ideologically akin to one another—as boll weevil House Democrats and the Senate's Republican median were in the early 1980s—bicameral agreements should be easier to reach. With the House and Senate quite distant, the prospects for bicameral agreement recede. This was certainly the case during the 104th Congress, when moderate Republicans balked at the excesses of the House Republicans' agenda on regulatory reform, crime issues, property rights, and other issues.

Bicameral differences also provide insight into the limits of a party under unified government to achieve its policy goals. Clinton's health care proposals in 1994 are a prime example of the constraints bicameralism places on unified government. Even though Clinton made health care reform a key priority, significant differences between the House and Senate approaches to health care reform emerged during consideration of the issue, helping to block passage of bills in both chambers.[33] Proponents of party government often implicitly assume away bicameral impediments, and as a result overstate the policy impact of unified party control. Given the particular institutional context in which parties work, we should not be surprised to find that unified government cannot always guarantee significant change on important public issues.

Supermajority rules in Congress also pose an institutional constraint on the ability of legislators to forge compromise. Supermajority constraints are particularly important in the Senate, where the filibuster makes simple majorities powerless in the face of a determined minority. "Tit-for-tat" filibustering has compounded the problem, as control of the Senate has passed back and forth between Democrats and Republicans over the past two decades. Republican filibusters stymied much of Clinton's agenda under unified Democratic control in 1993 and 1994. Then, when Republicans regained control of the chamber in 1995, Democrats returned the favor by filibustering conservative initiatives. The effect of the filibuster can be gleaned by comparing a Congress that had no filibusters (the 82d, 1951–1953) with one that had thirty-five (the 102d, 1991–1993). Forty percent of salient issues ended in gridlock in the 82d Congress, compared with 65 percent in the 102d.

Even if a supermajority can be mustered to invoke cloture and kill a filibuster, measures can be significantly watered down by concessions necessary to break the filibuster. A key example is the Republican opposition to Clinton's economic stimulus plan in 1993; the final product bore little resemblance to Clinton's proposal. The Senate can also be held hostage by a minority of one, because any senator can place a "hold" on bills or nominations headed to the floor until the senator's (often unrelated) policy or political demands are met. Angered over recess appointments made by Clinton in 1999, for example, Sen. James M. Inhofe, R-Okla., threatened to block confirmation of all of Clinton's judicial nominations during Clinton's final year in office, placing a blanket "hold" on all such nominations (numbering thirty-five at the start of 2000).[34] By empowering supermajorities in a political system that moves primarily by majority rule, the Senate makes its own contribution to gridlock.

The Impact of the Policy Context

Electoral and institutional factors alone are unlikely to account fully for deadlock. Because different types of policies yield different patterns of politics, the question is whether differences in the broader policy context affect the ease with which legislative compromise is reached.[35] Budgetary slack and broad national trends are key features of the policy environment that can affect policy stability. Recent studies have not reached a uniform conclusion about the effects of these factors, but there is some support for the claims that climates of sunny budgets and a liberal public yield more productive seasons of lawmaking.

The logic underpinning the effect of the budget environment is fairly simple. The greater the surplus relative to outlays, the easier it should be to accomplish legislative goals. Once the budget is in surplus, legislative compromise should be easier—because politicians are no longer caught in a zero-sum game.

Whether a coalition seeks higher spending or lower taxes, ample federal coffers can cover the side-payments necessary to forge a successful coalition. The argument rings true at the extremes. The deficit exceeded outlays by nearly 20 percent during the 102d Congress, when gridlock peaked at over 65 percent. When the surplus exceeded outlays by 20 percent during the 80th Congress (1947–1949), gridlock was a mere 26 percent. Viewed more broadly over the past half-century, the relationship generally holds, with sunnier fiscal times generally associated with lower levels of gridlock.

Excess resources by themselves, however, cannot wipe out gridlock, a finding confirmed by Congress's current predicaments despite the emergent budget surplus. When the government turned the corner in 1999 with a series of budget surpluses—the first since 1969—Democrats characteristically responded with a raft of proposals to expand Medicare coverage and other social programs (as well as targeted tax cuts), whereas Republicans hoisted up a perennial favorite of across-the-board tax cuts (as well as more limited Medicare expansion).[36] Despite the budget surplus, little to no progress was made in 1999 on matters of social security reform, Medicare reform, tax cuts, and other issues high on the parties' priorities.

Prevailing national moods are also said to have a significant influence on both agendas and policy outcomes.[37] Liberal climates of opinion seem to underlie extended periods of activist government. When such waves of citizen support for change through governmental action ebb, government seems to retrench. Arthur M. Schlesinger Jr. and Samuel P. Huntington have called these periods of retrenchment times of "public purpose" or "creedal passion"—times of public engagement that bring an extended phase of legislative accomplishment.[38] Three distinct periods in the twentieth century stand out as exemplary moods: the Progressive era early in the century, the New Deal in the 1930s, and the period from Kennedy through Nixon in the 1960s and early 1970s. In short, moods are ascribed *causal* importance. A public mood emerges, it generates a wave of citizen action, and it smoothes the way for a prolonged period of legislative motion—a raft of ideologically coherent legislative accomplishments.

Getting a grasp on the concept of a mood is difficult. A mood, David Mayhew has observed, "seems to be one of those phenomena that drive political scientists to despair by being at once important and elusive."[39] Their boundaries are fuzzy, their causes unclear, and their effects difficult to peg. They are certainly rooted in mass public opinion and affected by electoral returns, but they are not strictly synonymous with either. John Kingdon, a scholar of public policy, has perhaps said it best:

> The idea goes by different names—the national mood, the climate in the country, changes in public opinion, or broad social movements. But common to all of these labels is the notion that a rather large number of people out in the country are thinking along certain common lines, that this national mood changes from one time to another in discernible ways, and

that these changes in mood or climate have important impacts on policy agendas and policy outcomes.[40]

Casting mood in ideological terms, others have suggested that mood be interpreted as capturing the general direction of American public opinion—"the public's sense of whether the political 'temperature' is too hot or too cold."[41] Intuitively then, moods represent a prevailing consensus of what is appropriate and necessary for the government to do: shared "global attitudes towards the role of government in society."[42]

It makes sense that surges of liberal opinion would lead to higher levels of legislative output. After all, we think of an era as *activist* because of both its ideological tenor and its sheer volume of legislative motion. The question is whether shared public consensus over the role of government also dampens the chances of gridlock. Is general agreement on the aims of government sufficient to overcome other forces that bolster and protect the status quo from change? Much evidence suggests a tight connection between the public mood and legislative performance, with the two generally moving in tandem across the postwar period.[43]

Explaining the Trends

Party control of government is thus only one factor that shapes the production of public policy. Broader electoral and institutional forces are also at play. For social scientists investigating general patterns over time, however, a key question remains. Considering all of these forces together, how well do the trends noted here hold up? That is, once subjected to multivariate controls, what can we conclude about the relative importance of electoral and institutional determinants of policy deadlock? How we answer this question ultimately shapes our evaluation of the constraints and opportunities faced by Congress and the president in pursuing major changes in public policy.

A model of policy gridlock appears in Table 13-2. The dependent variable in the model is the level of gridlock in each Congress between the 82d (1951–1953) and the 104th (1995–1997).[44] The effects of the independent variables can be evaluated by the values in column 1. Coefficient values that are followed by one or more asterisks are statistically significant, meaning that they directly affect the level of gridlock. On balance, the model estimates provide strong evidence that electoral factors are critical in explaining trends in gridlock but display mixed support for the institutional and policy accounts. Most prominently, the coefficient for divided government (0.340) is positive and statistically significant: divided governments are prone to higher levels of gridlock. Party control does appear to affect the broader ability of the political system to address major public problems. In this sense, the party government school that advocates responsible parties is vindicated: deadlock is more likely when the two major parties split control of Congress.

Table 13-2 Determinants of Policy Gridlock, 1951–1996

Hypothesis	Variable	(1) Coefficient (SE)	(2) Change in x (from, to)	(3) Net Change in Predicted Gridlock
Partisan/ electoral	Divided government	0.340* (0.142)	(unified, divided)	+8%
	Percentage of moderates	−0.027* (0.013)	(18.47%, 33.67%)	−10%
	Ideological diversity	6.263* (2.710)	(0.47, 0.55)	+11%
	Time out of majority	−0.177** (0.049)	(0 years, 2 years)	−9%
Institutional	Bicameral distance	2.263** (0.818)	(0.07, 0.30)	+13%
	Severity of filibuster threat	0.035 (0.039)	(0, 7.5)	+6%
Policy	Budgetary situation	−0.006 (0.009)	(−19.02, −2.09)	−2%
	Public mood (lagged)	−0.034* (0.016)	(55.76, 65.20)	−8%
	Constant	−1.509 (1.587)		
	N	22		
	F	4.10**		
	Adjusted R²	0.5413		
	Durbin-Watson d	1.921		
	Breusch-Godfrey LM test (lag 1)	0.0484		
	LM test (lag 2)	1.7842		
	Portmanteau Q	15.3574		

Source: Compiled by the author.

Note: The entries in each cell in column 1 are weighted least squares logit estimates for grouped data (standard errors in parentheses). Time series model diagnostics-based residuals generated by ordinary least squares estimation. Net change in predicted gridlock is calculated as the independent variables change between the values in column 2 (i.e., between 1 standard deviation below and above the mean value for each of the continuous variables and between 0 and 1 for the dichotomous variable). Simulated probabilities are based on the exponential linear predictions generated by the adjust routine in stata 6.0 and are calculated assuming the presence of divided government (all other variables set at their mean values).

$^* p < .05$, $^{**} p < .01$ (one–tailed t–tests).

But interbranch conflict is not the sole factor. Partisan polarization and ideological diversity both contribute to policy stalemate. The effect of party polarization is perhaps the most striking. Despite the faith of responsible party advocates in cohesive political parties, the results here suggest that policy change is less likely as the parties become more polarized and the percentage of moderate legislators shrinks. Clearly there are limits to the power of political parties to break policy deadlock. Indeed, it appears that intense polarization can be counterproductive to fostering policy change. Still, the semblance of a party mandate matters: the longer a new congressional majority has been out of power, the lower is the level of policy gridlock under the new majority.

The substantive effects of these factors can be seen by simulating expected levels of gridlock (column 3), given specified changes in the values of the independent variables (column 2). Using the past half-century as our guide, we can expect divided control of government to increase the level of gridlock by roughly 8 percent. Given on average twenty-five salient issues on the agenda for each Congress, the arrival of unified government should resolve on average only two additional issues. Incremental slips in the share of moderate legislators have similar effects, here increasing deadlock by roughly 10 percent, or an additional two or three issues. Such results confirm the sentiments of many members and observers of Congress who claim that partisan polarization limits the legislative capacity of Congress.[45] The "incredibly shrinking middle"—as Sen. John B. Breaux called it—seems to hamper substantially the ability of Congress and the president to reach agreement on the issues before them.[46]

Turning to institutional factors, the bicameral context matters greatly. Even after controlling for the effects of elections on partisan alignments, when ideological differences between the House and Senate increase, Congress finds it tougher to reach agreement on pressing policy issues, and policy stalemate climbs. Indeed, bicameral differences in fact have the greatest substantive impact on the level of gridlock: as the distance between the House and Senate increases fourfold along the Left-Right spectrum, gridlock increases by 13 percent. This helps explain why students of Congress might have been "overly optimistic" about the prospects for governance under unified government in the 103d Congress (1993–1995).[47] Only twice before in the postwar period had the House and Senate been as far apart ideologically as they were in the 103d, and the last occurrence was twenty years previously. Given the high level of bicameral differences (as well as partisan polarization), it is no wonder seasoned observers concluded at the close of the 103d Congress: "The only good news as this mud fight finally winds down is that it's hard to imagine much worse."[48] Although others have highlighted the constraining effects of supermajority rules to account for "unified gridlock," bicameral constraints clearly help determine the level of stalemate under unified regimes.[49]

Interestingly, the threat of the filibuster shows only marginal effects on policy gridlock.[50] Moderate increases in the severity of the filibuster threat boost gridlock only 6 percent. Still, simulating levels of gridlock across more extreme differences in filibustering activity is instructive. Comparing the Senate in the 1950s that witnessed no filibusters (in the 84th Congress in 1953–1955) with a recent Senate that has experienced quite a few (twenty-two, in the 104th Congress in 1995–1997), the predicted level of gridlock jumps from 42 to 53 percent. Although the impact of supermajority rules is swamped by other sources of variation in the legislative arena, it is premature to reject the hypothesis that Senate supermajority institutions have strong policy and political consequences.

Finally, the policy context exerts some effect on the ability of legislators to produce major public policy. Improved fiscal discipline only marginally affects the incidence of deadlock, with a large fall in the size of the deficit here reducing gridlock a mere 2 percent. Much stronger effects are felt by the prevailing public mood. Using James Stimson's measure of the liberalness of public opinion, we find that public mood clearly matters in shaping legislative performance.[51] A ten-point jump in public preference for activist government lowers gridlock by 8 percent. In sum, the effects of divided government are challenged by alternative sources of variation in American politics.

The Consequences of Gridlock

Arguments about gridlock took an interesting turn in the midst of a budget standoff in 1999 between Clinton and the Republican Congress.[52] Both sides had essentially fought to a draw in a debate over what to do with emerging budget surpluses — whether they should be saved, spent, or devoted to tax cuts. The result, in short, was gridlock. But due to federal budgeting rules, excess revenues flow automatically into reducing the nation's $3.6 trillion debt. As one analyst noted at the time, "Neither party had debt reduction as its priority, but it ended up being the common denominator they could agree on through gridlock."[53] Given the salutary economic benefits of reducing the debt — including lowering interest rates and boosting savings — legislative deadlock was almost uniformly seen as a beneficial outcome.

The idea that gridlock has unintended consequences raises a more fundamental issue. Although students of Congress have recently endeavored to explain the causes of gridlock, its consequences remain unexplored. In fact, we might expect that gridlock has discernible effects. What's more, the effects might not be as rosy as the debt reduction example suggests. Beyond positive economic effects, we might also expect that the level of stalemate has repercussions for legislators' personal fortunes and the institution's reputation more generally.

Consider first the career ambitions of legislators. If, as Richard F. Fenno Jr. argues, the pursuit of good public policy motivates many members of Congress, then high levels of gridlock should reduce the appeal of serving in Congress.[54] As the level of deadlock climbs, so should voluntary departures from the House and Senate. There is strong support for this conjecture, at least based on the record of retirements from the House over the postwar period. Using the level of gridlock as an independent variable to predict the number of retirements in each Congress between 1947 and 1994, legislative deadlock is a significant predictor in accounting for the pattern of House retirements.[55] This result holds up, even after controlling for a host of other variables often said to lead to legislative departures — an aging House membership, the infrequency of pay raises, and electoral disadvantages posed by decennial redistricting.[56]

It is also worthwhile exploring whether legislative performance has demonstrable effects on the institution more generally. Although models of congressional approval tend to concentrate on the effects of economic expectations and legislative scandal, a reasonable proposition is that what Congress accomplishes—or fails to accomplish—also affects public evaluations of Congress. In other words, as the level of deadlock rises, we should expect congressional approval rates to go down. There is some support for this notion, using what limited public approval data exist.[57] Between 1974 and 1994, the percentage of the public expressing approval of Congress ran in tandem with legislative productivity. The better Congress did in addressing salient issues on the agenda, the greater the public's approval of the institution.[58] As gridlock rose, public approval sank.

Whether legislative performance has additional effects—economic, political, electoral, or otherwise—remains to be seen. But the close relationship between gridlock on the one hand and retirements and congressional approval on the other suggests that such consequences of deadlock might only be the tip of the iceberg. If so, enthusiasm for the salutary economic effects of gridlock is likely to wane, as its more negative effects are realized. To be sure, neither party likely saw gridlock in 1999 as a long-term strategy for governing—despite its apparent economic benefits. Both parties remain sufficiently committed to legislative agendas (whether conservative or liberal in design) that neither side will likely pursue gridlock simply for its economic effects. Given the considerable institutional and electoral effects that seem to accompany gridlock, such a strategy would indeed be folly by the political parties. How successful Congress and the executive are in making law ultimately has deep ramifications not only for the state of public policy, but for the character and legitimacy of the two branches as well.

Notes

I thank the Dillon Fund for its generous financial support of this project.

1. James MacGregor Burns, *The Deadlock of Democracy* (Englewood Cliffs, N.J.: Prentice-Hall, 1963), 6; Robert Shogan, *The Fate of the Union* (Boulder, Colo.: Westview Press, 1998), 5.
2. See, among others, Jack A. Rakove, *Original Meanings: Politics and Ideas in the Making of the Constitution* (New York: Knopf, 1996), and Gordon S. Wood, *The Creation of the American Republic, 1776–1787* (New York: Norton, 1969). More recently, see Garry Wills, *A Necessary Evil: A History of American Distrust of Government* (New York: Simon and Schuster, 1999).
3. James A. Morone, *The Democratic Wish: Popular Participation and the Limits of American Government*, rev. ed. (New Haven: Yale University Press, 1998), 336.
4. William Safire, *Safire's New Political Dictionary* (New York: Random House, 1993), 305.
5. See David Mayhew, *Divided We Govern* (New Haven: Yale University Press, 1991).
6. Full explanation of the method used for generating legislative agendas from the *New York Times* appears in the second appendix to Sarah A. Binder, "The Dynamics of Legislative Gridlock, 1947–96," *American Political Science Review* 93 (September 1999): 519–33.
7. "Mr. Cleveland's Cabinet," in *The Public Papers of Woodrow Wilson: College and State*, ed. R. S. Baker and W. E. Dodd (New York: Harper and Brothers, 1925), 1:221–22,

as cited in Austin Ranney, *The Doctrine of Responsible Party Government: Its Origins and Present State* (Urbana: University of Illinois Press, 1954), 32.

8. E. E. Schattschneider, *Party Government* (New York: Holt, Rinehart and Winston, 1942), 1.

9. See James Sundquist, "Needed: A Political Theory for the New Era of Coalition Government in the United States," *Political Science Quarterly* 103 (winter 1988): 613–35; Lloyd Cutler, "Some Reflections about Divided Government," *Presidential Studies Quarterly* 17 (summer 1988): 485–92; Sean Q. Kelly, "Divided We Govern? A Reassessment." *Polity* 25 (spring 1993): 475–84.

10. See Morris Fiorina, *Divided Government*, 2d ed. (Boston: Allyn and Bacon, 1996), chap. 6.

11. A *filibuster* is said to occur when opponents of a measure refuse to end debate in the Senate. Under Senate Rule 22, a three-fifths majority (sixty votes) is required to *invoke cloture* and thus end debate. Lacking a three-fifths majority, it is impossible to cut off debate under Senate rules if any senator or group of senators refuses to end debate. In other words, as long as a coalition can muster forty-one votes, it can block action in the Senate counter to the wishes of a chamber majority (fifty-one votes). Senators can also threaten to filibuster, meaning that they suggest to party leaders that they are likely to filibuster if a particular bill comes to the Senate floor.

12. See, for example, Joseph Cooper and Garry Young, "Partisanship, Bipartisanship, and Crosspartisanship in Congress since the New Deal," in *Congress Reconsidered*, ed. Lawrence C. Dodd and Bruce I. Oppenheimer, 6th ed. (Washington, D.C.: CQ Press, 1997), chap. 11.

13. See Sarah A. Binder, "The Disappearing Political Center," *Brookings Review* 14 (fall 1996): 36–39.

14. Ideological placement of legislators and their respective parties is measured by Keith Poole and Howard Rosenthal in *Congress: A Political-Economic History* (New York: Oxford University Press, 1997), using their first dimension W-NOMINATE scores, which measure legislators' placement along a Left-Right continuum. See extended discussion in Binder, "Dynamics of Legislative Gridlock."

15. The president's remarks appear in Paul Sullivan, "R.I. Senator Dead at 77," *Boston Herald*, October 26, 1999, A2.

16. The remaining moderates were both Republicans: Arlen Specter of Pennsylvania and James M. Jeffords of Vermont. Other senators of the 106th Congress who in earlier years had scored as moderates based on their ideological scores were the Democrat John Breaux of Louisiana, and Olympia J. Snowe and Susan Collins, both Republicans from Maine.

17. See, among others, Jon R. Bond and Richard Fleisher, *Polarized Politics: Congress and the President in a Partisan Era* (Washington, D.C.: CQ Press, 2000).

18. On the connection between the size of coalitions and policy gridlock, see Keith Krehbiel, *Pivotal Politics* (Chicago: University of Chicago Press, 1998), chap. 4.

19. Quoted in Michael Grunwald, "Gephardt's Tireless Quest: Put Democrats Atop House," *Washington Post*, July 12, 1999, A1.

20. The correlation between gridlock on salient issues and the percentage of House moderates (80th–104th Congresses) is −0.22, whereas the correlation between gridlock and Senate moderates is −0.35.

21. The Republicans' strategy of non-cooperation paid royal dividends in the 1994 elections, handing them control of Congress for the first time since 1954.

22. See, among others, Walter Dean Burnham, *Critical Elections and Mainsprings of American Politics* (New York: Norton, 1970); Jerome Clubb, William Flanigan, and Nancy Zingale, *Partisan Realignment*, 2d ed. (Boulder, Colo.: Westview Press, 1990).

23. David W. Brady, *Critical Elections and Congressional Policy Making* (Stanford, Calif.: Stanford University Press, 1988).

24. Debate over the fate of realignment appears in Byron Shafer, ed. *The End of Realignment? Interpreting American Electoral Eras* (Madison: University of Wisconsin Press, 1991).

25. "Eightieth Congress: To Date," *New York Times* editorial, June 20, 1948.

26. But see Richard Fenno, *Learning to Govern* (Washington, D.C.: Brookings Institution Press, 1997); Fenno argues that a new, inexperienced majority also may face the countervailing difficulty of "learning to govern."

27. The fate of the various provisions of the Contract with America are chronicled and tallied in John Bader, *Taking Charge* (Washington, D.C.: Georgetown University Press, 1996).

28. On the impact of structure on policy during the Continental Congress, see Calvin Jillson and Rick K. Wilson, *Congressional Dynamics: Structure, Coordination, and Choice in the First American Congress, 1774–1789* (Stanford, Calif.: Stanford University Press, 1994).

29. See Krehbiel, *Pivotal Politics,* and David Brady and Craig Volden, *Revolving Gridlock* (Boulder, Colo.: Westview Press, 1998).

30. See Gary Wills, ed., *The Federalist Papers* (New York: Bantam Books, 1982), 315 (my emphasis).

31. But see important theoretical and comparative work on the impact of bicameralism, including George Tsebelis and Jeannette Money, *Bicameralism* (New York: Cambridge University Press, 1997); George Tsebelis, "Decision Making in Political Systems: Veto Players in Presidentialism, Parliamentarism, Multicameralism, and Multipartyism," *British Journal of Political Science* 25 (July 1995): 289–325; and Thomas H. Hammond and Gary J. Miller, "The Core of the Constitution," *American Political Science Review* 81 (December 1987): 1155–74.

32. Even scholars diminishing the theoretical importance of divided government often model the legislative process as involving a unicameral legislature. See, for example, Krehbiel, *Pivotal Politics.*

33. The history of the health care debate is retold in Jacob S. Hacker, *The Road to Nowhere* (Princeton, N.J.: Princeton University Press, 1996).

34. See Mark Preston, "Inhofe Will Block All Clinton Judicial Nominations," *Roll Call,* January 10, 2000.

35. On the connection between policy type and politics, see Theodore Lowi, "American Business, Public Policy, Case Studies, and Political Theory," *World Politics* 16 (July 1964): 689–90.

36. On the dueling responses to budget surpluses, see Charles Babington and Eric Pianin, "Clinton and Congress Agree on Budget Goals," *Washington Post,* July 13, 1999, A1.

37. See, in particular, Mayhew's extended discussion in *Divided We Govern,* chap. 6. See also the results presented in John J. Coleman, "Unified Government, Divided Government, and Party Responsiveness," *American Political Science Review* 93 (December 1999): 821–35.

38. Arthur M. Schlesinger Jr., *The Cycles of American History* (Boston: Houghton Mifflin, 1986); Samuel P. Huntington, *American Politics: The Promise of Disharmony* (Cambridge: Harvard University Press, 1981).

39. Mayhew, *Divided We Govern,* 160.

40. John Kingdon, *Agendas, Alternatives, and Public Policies* (Boston: Little, Brown, 1984), 153.

41. See James A. Stimson, Michael B. MacKuen, and Robert S. Erikson, "Dynamic Representation," *American Political Science Review* 89 (September 1995): 548.

42. Ibid., 544.

43. Although the correlation between gridlock and the public mood (lagged by one Congress) is only −0.11, dropping the 102d Congress (which combined a strong liberal

mood and record gridlock) increases the strength of the correlation to −0.32. Support for the hypothesis that a liberal public mood boosts productivity appears in Mayhew, *Divided We Govern,* and Coleman, "Unified Government, Divided Government, and Party Responsiveness."

44. Details on measurement of the independent variables appear in Binder, "Dynamics of Legislative Gridlock."

45. See William S. Cohen, "Why I Am Leaving," *Washington Post,* January 21, 1996, C7; Lloyd Grove, "The So-Long Senators." *Washington Post,* January 26, 1996, F1; and Marilyn Serafini, "Mr. In-Between," *National Journal,* December 16, 1995, 3080–84.

46. Senator Breaux quoted in Serafini, "Mr. In-Between."

47. See James Sundquist, *Back to Gridlock* (Washington, D.C.: Brookings Institution, 1995), 10.

48. "Perhaps the Worst Congress." *Washington Post,* October 7, 1994, A24.

49. On the effects of supermajority rules on unified gridlock, see Brady and Volden, *Revolving Gridlock,* and Krehbiel, *Pivotal Politics.*

50. Filibuster threat is measured as the number of filibusters in each Congress multiplied by the ideological distance in each Congress between the median senator and the "filibuster pivot"— the senator whose ideology places him at the 60th percentile in the Senate (and thus capable of breaking a filibuster via cloture). Before Rule 22 was reformed in 1975, the relevant filibuster pivot was the sixty-seventh senator. For further explanation of the logic of pivots, see Krehbiel, *Pivotal Politics.*

51. See James Stimson, *Public Opinion in America: Moods, Cycles, and Swings* (Boulder, Colo.: Westview Press, 1991).

52. See Richard W. Stevenson, "Standoff on Budget Yields Unexpected Dividend," *New York Times,* October 25, 1999, A1.

53. As cited in ibid.

54. On the goals of members of Congress, see Richard F. Fenno Jr., *Congressmen in Committees* (Boston: Little, Brown, 1973).

55. The equation is Number of retirements = 0.013 (percent gridlock) + 0.068 (mean age of House members) + 0.069 (pay raise) + 0.308 (redistricting year). All variables except the pay raise variable are statistically significant at $p < .05$ (one-tailed test).

56. See Joseph Cooper and William West, "Voluntary Retirement, Incumbency, and the Modem House," *Political Science Quarterly* 96 (summer 1981): 279–300; Michael K. Moore and John R. Hibbing, "Is Serving in Congress Fun Again? Voluntary Retirements from the House since the 1970s," *American Journal of Political Science* 36 (August 1992): 824–28; and Sean Theriault, "Moving Up or Moving Out: Career Ceilings and Congressional Retirement," *Legislative Studies Quarterly* 23 (1999): 419–33.

57. Here, I use a time series on congressional approval kindly provided by Christina Wolbrecht. See Robert H. Durr, John B. Gilmour, and Christina Wolbrecht, "Explaining Congressional Approval," *American Journal of Political Science* 41 (January 1997): 175–207.

58. The Pearson's r correlation between the level of gridlock and the mean level of congressional approval (averaging the eight quarters of each two-year congress) is −0.56 ($p < .05$, one-tailed test).

14. Congress and Foreign Policy at Century's End: Requiem on Cooperation?

I. M. Destler

The fifty years after World War II offered rich variation in the ways Congress engaged in, or disengaged from, American foreign policy. But one pattern recurred throughout. When the president gave high priority to policies that had reasonably strong support in establishment opinion, and faced a showdown vote on these policies, Congress virtually always went along. This was true in administration after administration: for Truman and the Marshall Plan, Kennedy and the nuclear test ban, Nixon and deployment of the antiballistic missile (ABM), Carter and the Panama Canal treaties, Reagan and the sale of AWACS aircraft to Saudi Arabia, Bush and the Persian Gulf War, Clinton and the North American Free Trade Agreement (NAFTA). Key to these victories was the president's success in reaching across partisan lines, to centrists in the other party. Or in cases where the other party housed the main support for the policy, the president was able to retain the support of moderates in his own.

The period since 1995 offers evidence that this pattern may be changing. There were still some congressional votes that fit it — on the chemical weapons convention in 1997, NATO expansion in 1998, and permanent normal trade relations with China in 2000. But Clinton sustained two dramatic rebuffs — in 1997 and 1998, on his request for fast-track authority to pursue international trade negotiations; and in 1999, on the Comprehensive Nuclear Test Ban Treaty. On the first, the president went to the well and failed, despite support from leaders of the other party, and despite the fact that fast-track authority was key to U.S. trade and Latin America policies and had been granted by Congress on six previous occasions. On the second, the Senate failed to give even majority support (two-thirds was needed) to a treaty that was central to multilateral efforts to limit nuclear proliferation. In both of these defeats, particularly the second, deep partisan divisions played an important role.

These two dramatic setbacks — one on international economic policy, one on national security policy — were paralleled by increasingly fractious, ideological executive–congressional conflict over the funding of U.S. foreign policy in general. Claiming that they lacked public support, the Republican Congress slashed funds for the United Nations, the State Department, foreign aid, and UN peacekeeping. It delayed replenishment of the lending resources of the International Monetary Fund (IMF) in the midst of the Asian financial crisis of 1997–1999. And Congress was very negative toward the war over Kosovo, united NATO support notwithstanding. On these matters, Clinton avoided definitive defeat: getting enough money for UN dues before the United States fell far enough behind to lose its vote in the General Assembly, winning belated replenishment of the IMF, and obtaining appropriations if not endorsement for action in Kosovo. But his overall record calls into question Aaron Wildavsky's famous depiction of "the two Presidencies," with the chief executive far stronger on international policy as compared to domestic policy, and Harold Hongju Koh's more recent assertion that "the President (almost) always wins" on foreign affairs.[1]

1945–1995: The Pattern of Cooperation

Executive–congressional conflict on foreign policy is, of course, as old as the American republic. The Framers of our Constitution established a system of "separated institutions sharing powers."[2] The president appoints ambassadors and senior Washington officials, but the Senate must confirm them. The executive conducts diplomatic relations and administers overseas programs, but the legislature sets statutory guidelines and provides (or slashes, or denies) the funds. Congress has the primary authority over trade, with its enumerated power to regulate "commerce with foreign nations." The president's agents negotiate treaties, but they require the "advice and consent" of two-thirds of the Senate for ratification. For other agreements—including those on international trade—the requirement is approval by a majority in both houses. Thus our governing document provides ample leverage to internationally minded actors at both ends of Pennsylvania Avenue, tendering "an invitation to struggle for the privilege of directing American foreign policy."[3] The executive has the advantage of handling the day-to-day action, but the legislature has more than enough authority to take control when and if it asserts that authority.

As recently as in the 1930s Congress did just that, imposing crippling restrictions on the president's capacity to cope with overseas events. The isolationist–internationalist debate polarized elite opinion across the United States until 1941. But Pearl Harbor, followed by victory in World War II, followed by the Cold War, made the internationalists ascendant. Global activism became the norm, with a plethora of new executive-branch agencies and a chastened legislature inclined to acquiesce in presidential leadership.

The half-century that followed victory in World War II featured many ups and downs in the form, extent, and substance of congressional policy engagement. It can usefully be divided into three periods: 1945–1968, when the executive tended to dominate; 1969–1974, when the Vietnam-generated congressional reaction built and crested; and 1975–1994, when ideological polarization coexisted with continuing executive–legislative cooperation on large issues.[4]

1945–1968: Bipartisan Internationalism

In the first quarter-century of the postwar period, Congress provided consistent bipartisan support for major presidential initiatives, although it sometimes dug deep into the details. The United Nations, always popular with the American public, never came close to suffering the fate of Woodrow Wilson's League of Nations, which the Senate repudiated in 1919–1920. The Marshall Plan to save Western Europe was passed by a Republican Congress in the heated election year of 1948. The National Security Acts of 1947 and 1949 created the National Security Council, the Central Intelligence Agency, and the unified Department of Defense. And though President Truman did not seek congressional authorization for engagement in the increasingly unpopular Korean War, Congress tripled the defense budget in his final years to counter the communist threat in Europe as well as in Asia.

There was bitter partisan conflict over the "loss of China," fueling the shameful half-decade of McCarthyism. Nonetheless, by the time President Dwight D. Eisenhower's inauguration in 1953 ended twenty years of Democratic rule, Congress was clearly on record in support of:

- an activist American foreign policy, which was restoring war-torn nations to prosperity and countering Soviet military pressure and political influence;
- full American participation in the United Nations and its specialized agencies;
- a large "peacetime" military, together with a large national security bureaucracy;
- a foreign assistance program costing billions of dollars annually; and
- in a carryover from the 1930s, U.S. leadership in reducing barriers to international trade.

The new president continued all of these elements of U.S. international engagement, and Congress maintained its support. And, with Eisenhower in opposition, Congress failed to pass the proposed Bricker amendment to the U.S. Constitution, which would have restricted the president's treaty-making power.

During this period Congress did not simply enact whatever the president proposed. It insisted, for example, that the Marshall Plan be structured so as to enhance its compatibility with U.S. economic interests and limit the authority of the State Department. It cut presidential budget proposals for foreign assistance and imposed a wide variety of restrictions on its implementation. It insisted that leadership in President Kennedy's trade round be transferred from the State Department to a new White House trade agency. When Kennedy negotiated a ban on nuclear tests in the atmosphere, Senate hawks aligned with the joint chiefs of staff to assure, as a condition of ratification, that a substantial program of underground tests would be maintained.

As this last example suggests, Congress leaned toward the "tough" side, funding weapons that the Pentagon did not want, for example, in sympathy with the late-fifties expert consensus that the Eisenhower defense program was insufficient. Consistent with this orientation, legislators responded overwhelmingly

when presidents sought congressional backing for the use of American troops in
Lebanon, the Taiwan Straits, and the Gulf of Tonkin.

Through most of the sixties, this bipartisan congressional support extended
to the Vietnam War. But as stalemate continued overseas and conflict grew at
home, the Senate became home to growing skepticism, symbolized and reinforced by the transformation of Foreign Relations Committee Chairman J.
William Fulbright, D-Ark., from critic of a "parochial-minded" Congress to
critic of presidential "arrogance of power."[5] His committee held widely watched
hearings in which critics of the war policy held forth, sometimes on national television. By the end of the Johnson administration, congressional criticism of Vietnam was broadening into a general concern about U.S. political-military policies
and a sense that the legislature had delegated authority too freely to the executive.

1969–1974: Congress Writes New Rules

Soon after Richard Nixon took office, legislators who were increasingly
skeptical about Vietnam (and guilty about having abdicated their responsibility)
collided with the new president, who was determined to prosecute the war until
he could negotiate "peace with honor." Nixon avoided binding statutory restrictions on his authority in his first term, but discontent was bipartisan, and criticism spread to include broader defense and political-military instruments—the
ABM treaty, arms sales, covert intelligence activities.

After the peace agreement of January 1973 removed U.S. ground troops
from harm's way, statutory restrictions on U.S. military action were no longer vulnerable to the charge that they threatened American lives. And the Watergate
scandal soon overwhelmed the president's reelection mandate. Congress
responded by terminating all bombing in Indochina that summer and passing,
over Nixon's veto, the War Powers Resolution of 1973 calling for advance con-
sultations and interbranch power-sharing on future deployment of military
forces in hostile overseas situations. By the end of 1974, Congress had imposed
a partial embargo on arms sales to Turkey (in response to that nation's military
operations on Cyprus) and linked the opening of trade with the Soviet Union to
that nation's allowing the emigration of Soviet Jews.

Congress also enacted a range of procedural mechanisms—requiring consultation; providing for congressional vetoes—regulating executive-branch decisions on covert intelligence activities, arms sales, and import relief. Together with
the War Powers Resolution, these measures aimed to alter the interbranch power
balance by pressuring executive officials to listen to Congress before making
important decisions. Their goal was cooperative codetermination of policy, with
Congress as a constructive partner, engaged with the policy take-offs and thereby reducing the number of crash-landings. The new laws did have this effect in
the field of international trade, where the congressional role had an unambigu-
ous constitutional foundation. On political-military matters they also seem to
have constrained the executive branch for a while, particularly in the use of force

overseas. Taken as a whole, the procedural legislation was a noble congressional effort to institutionalize bipartisan, interbranch cooperation on foreign policy.

But the executive branch recurrently challenged the legitimacy of the new laws and in some cases (as in the War Powers Resolution and congressional vetoes) questioned their constitutionality. In its 1983 *Chadha v. United States* decision the Supreme Court sided with the executive, declaring legislative vetoes unconstitutional. Moreover, Congress proved uneven in its readiness to employ the powers it had carved out. By the end of the eighties, the War Powers Resolution had become discredited by the reluctance of Congress, as well as the administration, to enforce its provisions in relation to U.S. military action in the Persian Gulf and Panama. More generally, the procedural mechanisms receded in their impact as the bipartisan, centrist legislators who fashioned them— Sens. John Sherman Cooper, R-Ky., Frank Church, D-Idaho, and Jacob Javits, R-N.Y., and Rep. Dante Fascell, D-Fla., and others—made way for more ideologically minded successors. A new pattern emerged.

1975–1994: Polarized Internationalists

The reaction to Vietnam fueled a counterreaction, which was reinforced by skepticism about the Nixon-Kissinger policy of "detente" with the Soviet Union. Sen. Henry Jackson, D-Wash., worked to toughen U.S. arms control and trade policy with Russia. Sen. Jesse Helms, R-N.C., sought to undermine the administration's Africa policy, and House Republicans challenged the Carter administration's policy on Nicaragua after the Marxist Sandinistas took power in 1979 from long-time dictator Anastasio Somoza. Critics led by former senior State and Defense Department official Paul Nitze organized themselves into the Committee on the Present Danger, which attacked President Jimmy Carter's arms control policies, threatening ratification of the new U.S.–Soviet SALT II treaty (whose negotiation began in the Nixon administration). Coalitions for and against SALT II prepared for the ratification battle of the decade, before the Soviet invasion of Afghanistan in December 1979 rendered the matter moot. Amidst this bitter domestic conflict over U.S.–Soviet relations and arms control, Thomas L. Hughes pointed to the evisceration of the center and its destructive impact on U.S. foreign relations.[6]

When Ronald W. Reagan swept into power it was the left's turn to dissent. Democrats imposed human rights conditions on aid to El Salvador, where Reagan's administration had dramatically drawn the line against leftist rebels. Successive "Boland amendments" first restricted, then banned, U.S. aid to the "contras" seeking to overthrow the Sandinista government of Nicaragua.[7] A "gang of six" representatives and Senators worked, with some success, to condition support of the new MX missile on a more accommodating administration arms control posture.

The polarized political climate was also reflected in one key Senate leadership decision. In 1985–1986 the moderate Richard Lugar, R-Ind., had proved an exceptionally effective Chairman of the Senate Foreign Relations Committee. But Jesse Helms, who had eschewed that role because he had promised his North Carolina constituents not to abandon his chairmanship of the agriculture committee, no longer felt bound by this promise when his party lost its Senate majority, so he challenged Lugar for the ranking minority Foreign Relations Committee position. Motivated by a combination of support for Helms's positions and fear of his power, a solid majority in the Senate Republican caucus backed the challenge—though they knew full-well of Helms's ideological approach and prickliness in the exercise of power.

The waning of the Cold War rendered some of the old issues moot, as a fading Soviet Union made greater concessions on arms control than Reagan's critics (and perhaps also his supporters) ever thought possible. Under George Bush, arms control and Central America were no longer polarizing issues, but China policy became so after the June 1989 repression of student activists at Tienanmen Square. And so, for a brief time, was the Persian Gulf War, with no less than forty-seven Senators (all but two of them Democrats) voting against military action (instead advocating reliance on the severe economic sanctions the world had imposed). For President Bill Clinton, who had attacked Bush for his overemphasis on foreign policy, the first congressional challenge on an international issue was, appropriately, economic—broad opposition to the North American Free Trade Agreement (NAFTA) with Canada and Mexico. The major battles with Congress on national security issues would come in his second term.

IN THE FIRST twenty-five years after World War II, presidents won consistent congressional support for their top foreign policy priorities, particularly those involving the use or threat of force. In the next twenty-five, they did not have it so easy. A period of intense congressional debate and challenge, fueled by opposition to the Vietnam War, was followed by two decades of ideological polarization, substantially but not completely along party lines. Jimmy Carter faced increasing challenges from the right. Ronald Reagan and George Bush encountered resistance from the left. Gerald Ford, during his briefer tenure, was hit from both sides.

Yet direct presidential losses were rare on front-burner issues during the 1969–1994 period.[8] Jimmy Carter was never beaten on an up-or-down vote on an international matter to which he gave priority, winning hard fights on the Panama treaties (by two votes), repeal of the Turkey arms embargo, and a controversial combined arms sales package for Egypt, Israel, and Saudi Arabia. Ronald Reagan won, through personal persuasion, an uphill struggle to avert a congressional veto of the sale of AWACS aircraft to Saudi Arabia in 1981, even though his administration had mishandled the matter egregiously. Two years later, he won endorsement of a dicey (and in the end, unsuccessful) deployment of marines in Lebanon. Bush won a congressional mandate to take the military offensive against Saddam Hussein in January 1991, despite the opposition of Armed Services Committee Chairman Sam Nunn, D-Ga., and an impressive array of recently retired military leaders. He also avoided direct repudiation on

China policies. Despite widespread prognostications of NAFTA's demise, Clinton won House approval in a dramatic uphill battle, with 132 House Republicans joining 102 Democrats in voting "aye."

There were instances of presidents being roundly repudiated on international issues during this period, but one can count them and still have fingers remaining. Nixon sustained two defeats in little over a month, when Congress imposed an unconditional ban on bombing in Indochina and passed the War Powers Resolution of 1973. Reagan saw statutory economic sanctions against South Africa's apartheid regime imposed over his veto in 1985, after the White House refused to compromise. He also had to swallow the second Boland amendment, which banned U.S. aid to "contras" in Nicaragua, and a rejection (later reversed) of his MX missile deployment. Gerald Ford had imposed on him a partial arms embargo against Turkey and a prohibition against covert aid to a faction in Angola's civil war. In almost all other cases where Congress legislated such country-specific policy, however, it provided a "national security waiver" or some other formula for flexibility, which presidents typically exploited. Or the president reluctantly accepted a restriction in exchange for modification of its specifics (as in the Helms-Burton legislation restricting investment in, and trade with, Cuba in 1996) or other congressional action that he needed.

Why were there not more instances of direct repudiation? There are several plausible explanations.

One is that many members of Congress saw presidential credibility as an important asset to U.S. foreign policy. A number gave this reason when they switched sides in 1981 to support Reagan on the sale of AWACS aircraft. Thus, although members might work hard to keep the president from taking a stand with which they disagreed, once he did so they might be reluctant to override him.

Another explanation is an apparent asymmetry of motivation, with the president and his executive branch associates caring more about actual policy outcomes than the typical member of Congress. In 1974 David Mayhew declared members' prime, reelection-promoting activities to be position-taking, advertising, and credit-claiming.[9] Interestingly, none of these activities requires that a member actually win a roll-call vote, much less have a preferred view enacted into law. No doubt there are exceptional individuals who give priority to policy substance—Fulbright, Helms, and Jackson come to mind—and exceptional periods such as the early 1970s, driven by Vietnam. But if one assumes that the typical member often likes to take a politically rewarding position without responsibility for its consequences, it is easier to explain why, for example, House motions to override presidential vetoes of textile quota legislation (which would have breached major U.S. international trade agreements) failed by eight, eleven, and ten votes, respectively, in the 99th, 100th, and 101st Congresses.[10]

One can also gain insight into the rarity of repudiation by looking at the exceptions. Presidents were slapped down either when they took ideologically driven positions lacking broad public support (on Angola, Nicaragua, and South Africa) or at times when the basic thrust of presidential policy was under broad and sustained challenge (as when the Vietnam War led to passage of the War Powers Resolution). When presidents pressed for action with broad backing in establishment opinion (passage of NAFTA, the Panama treaties), they generally won, even when the public was divided and politically potent groups were arrayed on the other side.

Such "against-the-odds" presidential victories required relations of trust across party lines: Truman's Secretary of State Dean Acheson and Senate Foreign Relations Committee Chairman Arthur Vandenberg, R-Mich., were the classic connection. Or to cite Panama and NAFTA again, success in the former depended on Republican leader Howard Baker's working closely with Democratic counterpart Robert Byrd and the Carter White House; success in the latter, on Clinton's willingness to share vote counts with Newt Gingrich. Indeed, although politics never really stopped at the water's edge, the capacity to transcend partisanship was assumed on first-order issues.[11] So was an ability to work closely and constructively with the relevant congressional committees: in these cases Senate Foreign Relations and House Ways and Means.

A different spirit ushered in the last half-decade. In 1994 Newt Gingrich pursued an audacious plan for Republican capture of the House of Representatives. A key element of that strategy was to deny the president any more legislative victories (like NAFTA) that might conceivably redound to the benefit of Democrats. His central victim was the Clinton health care reform plan, but Gingrich also blocked pre-election consideration of the Uruguay Round World Trade Organization (WTO) implementing legislation (which had strong bipartisan backing) by threatening that Republicans would join protectionists in voting against the House rule necessary to bring it up. Thus, for quite marginal partisan advantage, he put in peril a measure consistent with conservative free-trade convictions and backed strongly by the business community.[12]

1995–2000: Toward Partisan Gridlock?

The Gingrich Republicans won that November election, ending forty years of Democratic control of the House of Representatives, and came to town in 1995 determined to bring about fundamental change. Their campaign manifesto, the "Contract with America," focused mainly on domestic issues, but it did include a stand against U.S. participation in UN peacekeeping. Although it would be overly simplistic to describe the new Republican representatives as isolationist, most of them were clearly "non-internationalist." Few had served in the military. Most lacked any involvement in, and commitment to, matters outside U.S. borders (even though the nation as a whole was increasingly affected by globalization). Their number two leader, Dick Armey, R-Texas, exemplified their level of interest in foreign affairs when he declared, "I've been to Europe once. I don't have to go again."[13]

More generally, the new members were militantly partisan and confrontational in their style: pressing for immediate policy change, indisposed to compromise. This reduced their policy effectiveness: as Richard F. Fenno has observed, "Forty consecutive years as the minority party in the House left the Republicans . . . totally without first-hand political experience of two essential sorts: first, experience in *interpreting* electoral victory, and second, experience in *governing* the country."[14] Their inexperience and inflexible style allowed the president to best them in the dramatic budget showdown of 1995. After this defeat they became slightly more pragmatic but also bitterly anti-Clinton. (Their revulsion over his personal traits and frustration over his political skills combined to fuel, in December 1998, the bizarre House impeachment of the president for his statements in the Monica Lewinsky affair, notwithstanding clear public opposition and a November election that had gone badly enough for Republicans to force Gingrich to resign as Speaker.)

The Senate was more moderate, as reflected by its failure to give a majority (let alone the required two-thirds) to either impeachment count. But it changed in a similar way, as reflected when the internationalist Robert Dole was succeeded as Senate majority leader by Trent Lott, R-Miss., a man with a much narrower party and political background.

On some issues, the post-1994 Congress behaved like its predecessors. Lott worked with the Clinton White House in 1997 to secure Senate ratification of the Chemical Weapons Convention, over the vehement opposition of Foreign Relations Committee Chairman Jesse Helms. That same year, the White House managed to negotiate a complex deal with Helms and ranking Foreign Relations Democrat Joseph Biden, D-Del., under which the United States would make good most of its arrears in United Nations dues, on the condition that the United Nations undertake widely supported reforms.[15] In 1998 a well-managed administration campaign won overwhelming Senate approval of the expansion of NATO to include Poland, Hungary, and the Czech Republic.[16] And in May 2000, Clinton and Republican House leaders worked together to win a clear, forty-vote House majority in favor of permanent normal trade relations with the People's Republic of China.

The Republican majority also pushed to expand the military budget. But it exhibited strong resistance to funding non-military forms of U.S. engagement, and readiness to entangle them with ideological amendments. The Helms-Biden deal fell victim to the determination of House Republicans to condition funding for the United Nations on antiabortion restrictions, and to Clinton's equal determination to resist this condition, delaying final action for two years. The same issue blocked for a year action on restoring the IMF's capacity to help countries beset by financial crises. More generally, Republicans pressed sharp cuts in spending for the State Department, foreign assistance, and UN-related appropriations, claiming—incorrectly—that the American public no longer supported these activities after the end of the Cold War.[17] After severe reductions by the 101st Congress in 1995–1996, the U.S. international affairs budget, measured in constant dollars, had declined by 25 percent over seven years, from $25.4 billion in 1991 to an estimated $19.0 billion in 1998.[18] (A contributing factor was the failure of President Clinton to go to bat for these programs as consistently as his predecessors had done.)

The Republican House also opposed the NATO campaign against Yugoslav ethnic cleansing in Kosovo — albeit not very effectively. Its somewhat contradictory behavior stood in sharp contrast with the "rally round the flag" responses of past Congresses to the outset of military conflict. "On April 29 [1999], it voted not to allow ground forces into the Balkans without explicit prior congressional approval. It rejected a measure to require the President to end the conflict; then, in a tie vote, it also failed to signal its approval for the ongoing air campaign."[19] Finally, it voted to double the amount of money in the emergency supplemental appropriation for the war.[20]

The new, partisan spirit was most dramatically reflected in the failure of two major international measures. One was legislation granting the president "fast-track" authority to negotiate new trade agreements. The second was the Comprehensive Nuclear Test Ban Treaty. Both parties contributed fully to both outcomes.

Trade Tangle

After the completion of the Uruguay Round World Trade Organization (WTO) negotiations in 1994, President Clinton lacked fast-track authority to negotiate new international trade agreements and submit them to Congress under expedited voting procedures. None of his predecessors was without that authority for more than seven months since it was first granted Gerald Ford. In principle, the president and Republican congressional leaders both supported such legislation, and at times they worked together to enact it. But most of the time, partisan and ideological priorities prevailed.[21]

Through most of the nineties, trade-liberalizing legislation was opposed by a majority of Democrats (reflecting virulent labor opposition) and a minority of Republicans (some influenced by Buchanan-style populism). Hence its enactment required a coalition of centrists from both parties. In 1993 the Clinton administration and Republican congressional leaders cooperated in building such a coalition, and the result was approval of NAFTA. In 1994 cooperation was more than adequate, except for the pre-election interlude described above. The result was enactment of the most comprehensive trade agreement in history, the GATT-WTO agreement, by strong, bipartisan House and Senate majorities.

Thereafter, partisan priorities prevailed. Initially, it was mainly the Democrats who were at fault. Though the president said that he wanted fast-track legislation in 1995 and 1996, and had in fact made far-reaching summit commitments with Asian and Western Hemisphere leaders that he could not implement without fast-track authority, he submitted no such legislative proposal. Unwilling to reopen the political wounds with labor sustained in the battle over NAFTA, Clinton and his highly political trade negotiator, Mickey Kantor, even rebuffed Republican attempts, initiated by the House Ways and Means Committee, to develop compromise legislation.[22]

After Clinton won reelection, many trade policy specialists expected him to move quickly with a fast-track proposal in 1997. His trade, economic, and foreign policy officials all favored one. The president himself believed in trade liberalization. The Republican congressional leadership was waiting. But the president vacillated. One reason was sharp partisan differences over the substance of the negotiating authority the president would be granted. Most Democrats, including the president, wanted to broaden the agenda to include labor and environmental standards, at least insofar as they related to trade. Republicans were overwhelmingly opposed to thus expanding the president's authority, as was the business community. Neither side took the initiative in seeking compromise. Meanwhile, labor and (to some extent) environmental critics mobilized in opposition. By September, when the president submitted his proposal, most Democrats were locked into opposition. Hence, if the president was to have any chance of winning, he had to lean to the Republican-business side. So in quest of a heavily Republican House majority, Clinton followed conservatives' wishes and largely excluded labor and environmental measures. In the end, after nearly two months of intense lobbying on both sides, vote-counts found a maximum of 21 percent of Democrats in favor (65 percent had backed the Uruguay Round WTO bill three years earlier), and Newt Gingrich could not make up the difference on the Republican side. Clinton asked that the bill be pulled in order to avoid what seemed certain defeat. Gingrich complied.

The next year the Speaker turned partisan on the issue. Though nothing had changed to enhance the bill's prospects, he resurrected it over Clinton's objections in September 1998, in a primarily partisan move designed to squeeze Democrats caught between labor and business constituencies. Gingrich's move drove even ranking Ways and Means trade Democrat Bob Matsui, a stalwart free-trader and a key player in prior House trade battles, into the opposition camp. Whatever the strategy may have done to help Republicans (and the November results suggest it did little), the outcome was a disaster for the trade-liberalization cause. The vote was 243–180 against, with just 29 of 200 Democrats recorded in favor. Public Citizen, the "consumer" lobby, built on the momentum gained by this vote to disrupt the Seattle WTO Ministerial Conference in December 1999.

A compromise on the substance of the legislation, one that would "advance the cause of global labor and environmental standards while authorizing the negotiation of new agreements to reduce barriers to trade," was certainly conceivable.[23] A comprehensive public opinion survey conducted eighteen months later suggested that this is what Americans want: they favor trade expansion and reciprocal reduction of trade barriers, but they also support, by strong margins, the broadening of the agenda to include labor and the environment.[24] But the polarization in Congress was too deep, and the trust needed to strike a compromise was largely absent.

Even more partisan, and at least equally damaging to the international position of the United States, was the Senate's rejection of the Comprehensive Nuclear Test Ban Treaty in October 1999.

Trashing the Test Ban

The Comprehensive Nuclear Test Ban Treaty (CTBT) was the internation-al issue where partisan conflict surfaced in rawest form. The treaty was a center-piece in the administration's policy against proliferation of nuclear weapons, and the president personally signed it in 1996, making the United States the first country to do so. More than 150 other countries followed (though only about one-third had ratified it by fall 1999). In 1997 it was sent to the Senate Foreign Relations Committee, where Chairman Jesse Helms bottled it up, refusing to hold hearings until the administration submitted, and the full Senate voted on (and presumably rejected), two other measures: amendments to the U.S.–Russ-ian ABM Treaty negotiated in 1997 and the Kyoto Protocol on climate change. The CTBT was also viewed with skepticism, however, by former officials in Republican administrations not associated with the far right — former presiden-tial national security assistant Brent Scowcroft and former secretary of state Henry Kissinger, for example.

The United States had not conducted nuclear tests since 1992, and in mid-1999 the administration was pressing India — which had recently become an overt nuclear power — to sign the CTBT. The United States was also preparing for a special international conference on the treaty in early October. To the White House and the State Department, ratification seemed overwhelmingly in the U.S. interest. But Republicans controlled the Senate 55–45; to have any chance at all of winning the 67 votes required, therefore, Clinton would need the sup-port of Republican centrists like Armed Services Committee Chairman John Warner, senior Foreign Relations member Richard Lugar, and rising interna-tionalist Chuck Hagel — and the cooperation, at the very least, of Majority Leader Trent Lott.

Rather than attempt the hard, slogging work of building a bipartisan major-ity, however, the president worked with Senate Democrats in a public campaign to embarrass and put heat on the Senate Republicans, to make the issue a polit-ical if not a legislative winner. In an obviously orchestrated set of events, Clinton appeared in the White House Rose Garden on July 20 and called for Foreign Relations Committee hearings, while on the same day Sen. Byron Dorgan, D-N.D., released a letter urging such hearings signed by all forty-five Senate Democrats. Dorgan also released a poll, conducted jointly by a Democratic and a Republican polling firm, which found 82 percent of Americans (84 percent of Democrats, 80 percent of Republicans) believing that the United States should ratify the CTBT.[25]

Senator Dorgan upped the ante on September 8, telling his colleagues that until Lott allowed consideration of the CTBT, "I intend to plant myself on the floor like a potted plant" and block any routine business. Other Democrats joined in, including ranking Foreign Relations Democrat Joseph Biden, and explained their strategy two weeks later to presidential national security adviser Samuel Berger. Unknown to them, however, hard-line treaty opponent Sen. John Kyl,

R-Ariz., had been working quietly with Helms for months to solidify Republican votes against the CTBT, and he had obtained commitments from many more than the necessary thirty-four. Lott then called the Democrats' bluff. He reversed himself on September 30 and offered to take up the treaty on the Senate floor, with a vote in two weeks. Democrats, thinking they had a shot at persuading enough Republicans to ratify the treaty, quickly agreed.[26] They learned within a week that they had no chance of winning and suddenly became alarmed about the global impact of a Senate rejection. (The Senate had not voted down an important treaty since the Treaty of Versailles in 1920.)

By early October the White House and Minority Leader Tom Daschle, D-S.D., had taken a 180-degree turn and were negotiating with Lott to *avoid* a vote. Sixty-two Senators, including twenty-four Republicans, signed a letter initiated by Warner and Pat Moynihan, D-N.Y., urging that the matter be put off until 2001, and the president made a formal request to Lott that he "postpone consideration." But this would now require either unanimous consent in the Senate or an extraordinary procedural vote. Hard-line Republicans, wanting to sink the treaty once and for all, blocked the first way out. Lott was unwilling to call for, or acquiesce in, the second. So on October 13 the Senate voted 48–51 against ratifying the treaty, with only four Republicans in favor.[27]

"Never before," declared the president, "has a serious treaty involving nuclear weapons been handled in such a reckless and ultimately partisan way."[28] He did not state that his own party bore at least half of the blame. Nor did his national security adviser help matters when he gave an impassioned speech eight days later attacking "the isolationist right in the Congress" for the treaty's defeat.[29] Six months later, Helms confirmed the interbranch deadlock by declaring his advance opposition to any arms agreement Clinton might negotiate with Moscow and vowing to block any Senate action while the president was still in office.[30]

The Broader Growth of Partisanship—and Polarization

Two cases, important though they may be, do not establish that a fundamental change has occurred. Even when one adds to them the fractious and unproductive conflict over spending on international affairs, it is far from proven that there has been a fundamental change in the nature of executive–congressional relations concerning foreign policy. A good share of the causation may lie in the particularly poisonous relationship and lack of trust between President Clinton and many members of Congress, and in Clinton's consequent incapacity to negotiate the centrist compromises that his policy positions, and his political skills, might otherwise produce.

There are, however, three broader, longer-lasting forces at work: the end of the Cold War, centralization of House power in the leadership (and away from the committees), and the ongoing polarization of party politics in the United States. Of the three, the last seems the most important.

There are several reasons that the end of the Cold War might make Congress more ready to repudiate presidents. First and foremost, it has given the United States a margin of security and safety that makes interbranch stalemate and perceived presidential impotence less risky. As a consequence, the national security arena has become less distinguishable from the domestic arena, where rejection of presidential initiatives is fairly common. The end of the Cold War may also have reduced public attention to international issues and led Americans to consider them a lower priority.[31] This, too, would reduce pressure on Congress to accommodate the president when he declared a matter to be of primary interest. However, the end of the Cold War has at the same time drained the ideological fervor out of issues like U.S.–Russian arms control and the fate of Central America (or, today, Cuba). Hence polarization on such issues is less likely to be driven by their perceived substantive importance. On balance, therefore, the Cold War's demise seems a contributor, but a modest one.

A second plausible cause is the weakening of congressional committees, along with the trend toward increasing partisanship in their operations. In prior eras, bipartisan cooperation in the Senate Foreign Relations or Finance Committee, or the House Foreign Affairs or Ways and Means Committee, was an important contributor to constructive interbranch dialogue. The decline of committee power dates at least to the congressional reforms of the seventies, as does their polarization. But both trends were accelerated in 1995 when Newt Gingrich, unconstrained by established baronies and backed by the militant new freshman class, chose the new Republican committee chairs himself, imposed a six-year term limit on their service, and began handling many legislative matters through extra-committee devices such as ad hoc task forces. His departure has put a brake on further centralization of power under the Speaker, but committees remain weak. A frequent consequence has been "party-driven legislation that was hastily brought to the House or Senate floor without a thorough vetting—or any attempts at bipartisan compromise—among the experts at the committee level."[32] In some cases matters may be brought up to advance partisan agendas at the cost of effective policy. It is hard to believe, for example, that Ways and Means Chairman Bill Archer would have marched his trade bill to resounding defeat in September 1998 if he and not Gingrich had controlled the matter—Wilbur Mills and Dan Rostenkowski had insisted on control over whether such a bill went to the floor. In the House of the later 1990s, Archer could not.

The most durable cause of Congress's willingness to challenge the president, however, and one which has contributed to the weakening of committees as well, is the polarization of party politics in the United States. American political leaders have been spending less time seeking a viable consensus in the center, and more time fighting for partisan and ideological advantage.

Our political parties have clearly become more ideological. Drawing on the voluminous data compiled by the American National Election Studies at the University of Michigan, David C. King has demonstrated how polarization has grown, especially since 1980. Americans in general have become somewhat more conservative during this period, and significantly more Republican, but they remain clustered near the political center.[33] But "the parties are becoming more extreme . . . increasingly distant in their policies from what the average voter would like. . . . Strong Republicans have become more conservative, and . . . party activists are drawn almost entirely from their ranks. Likewise, strong Democrats have become more liberal, though the ideological shift has not been as steep."[34]

Congress has reflected, indeed magnified, this trend. The percentage of centrists in Congress "declined from about 25 percent of all members in 1980 to 10 percent in 1996."[35] By 1999 this trend had reached its logical culmination, as reflected in the annual *National Journal* voting survey: perfect polarization! As Richard E. Cohen reports, "In the Senate, for the first time since *National Journal* began compiling vote ratings in 1981, every Democrat had an average score that was to the left of the most liberal Republican." In the junior chamber, *NJ* found that "only two Republicans . . . were in that chamber's more-liberal half on each of the three issue areas. . . . And only two Democrats . . . ranked in the more-conservative half."[36] (One of them left the Democratic Party in January 2000.)

Without specific reference to foreign policy, Cohen draws a plausible conclusion: "The findings help explain why so little got done in Congress last year . . . legislative deal-making became a lost art, as votes were cast to highlight partisan political differences."[37] This conclusion from data-based journalism finds support in data-based political science: in a thoroughgoing analysis of the causes of policy gridlock in Washington, Sarah A. Binder writes:

> The effect of party polarization is perhaps the most striking. Despite the faith of responsible party advocates in *cohesive* political parties, the results here suggest that policy change is *less* likely as the parties become more polarized and the percentage of moderate legislators shrinks. . . . Such results confirm the sentiments of the many members of Congress and observers who claim that partisan polarization limits the legislative capacity of Congress. The "incredibly shrinking middle"—as Senator John Breaux called it—seems to hamper substantially the ability of Congress and the president to reach agreement on the issues before them.[38]

Concluding Thoughts

Five years is a long time to live through but a short time in the sweep of history. Even if one accepts the diagnosis of this essay—that the nature of executive–congressional conflict in this period differed significantly from that in the prior half-century—the change could prove transient. It could prove a peculiar feature of the Clinton-Gingrich era. The new, twenty-first-century president could usher in an era of better feeling and more effective cooperation, though the bitter postelection conflict will make this harder to achieve.

Assuming—as this author does—that such cooperation is desirable, two forces might well make things better. One is the ongoing saneness and balance evident in American public opinion.[39] The American populace remains centrist and pragmatic, capable of striking reasonable balances, impatient with politicians who posture more than produce, and these qualities may somehow become effective in future elections. The second force is the deepening of globalization, which limits the capacity of Americans to march to their own parochial drummers. The vote on permanent normal trade relations with China is a recent example of how internationalist interests can tilt our legislature toward positive-sum, cooperative outcomes.

Among the forces likely to work against improvement are those that have brought us where we are: the dynamics of our electoral process that have produced such polar products. Party activists plus uncompetitive districts produce legislators whose careers are hostage to non-centrist constituents. By its overruling of a recent California law aimed at balancing the influence of activists in party primaries, the U.S. Supreme Court signaled that it judges the right of political parties to make their own rules should prevail over the interest of elected officials in more broadly supported candidates. If no branch of government can constrain it, the nomination-by-parties system will have to grow until it reaches its own natural limits.

Polarization will not always impede the president. In the case of Kosovo, it prevented definitive congressional action either for or against the war, and the administration was able to stay the course until its conclusion. In cases where the executive has the initiative and can move until Congress blocks it, gridlock reduces legislative—not executive—power. But in cases where constructive U.S. foreign policy requires positive action at both ends of Pennsylvania Avenue, polarization may end up reducing the U.S. capacity to cope with the ever-evolving world.

Notes

I am grateful to Josh Pollack for research assistance with the section on the defeat of the Comprehensive Nuclear Test Ban Treaty.

1. Aaron Wildavsky, "The Two Presidencies Thesis," *Transaction* 4 (1966): 7–14; Harold Hongju Koh, "Why the President (Almost) Always Wins in Foreign Affairs: Lessons of the Iran-Contra Affair," *Yale Law Journal* 97 (1988); and *The National Security Constitution: Sharing Power after the Iran-Contra Affair* (New Haven: Yale University Press, 1990).
2. Richard E. Neustadt, *Presidential Power and the Modern Presidents* (New York: The Free Press, 1990), 29.
3. Edward S. Corwin, *The President: Office and Powers,* 4th ed. (New York: New York University Press, 1957), 171.
4. The same party controlled the White House and both houses of Congress in sixteen of the first twenty-five of those years but only six of the next twenty-five.
5. For the evolution of Fulbright's views, compare: "American Foreign Policy in the 20th Century under an 18th Century Constitution," *Columbia Law Quarterly* 47 (fall 1962); "Congress and Foreign Policy," in *Report of the Commission on the Organization*

of the Government for the Conduct of Foreign Policy, appendix L (Washington, D.C.: GPO, June 1975), 58–65; and "The Legislator as Educator," *Foreign Affairs* 57 (spring 1979): 719–32.

6. Thomas L. Hughes, "The Crack-Up," *Foreign Policy,* no. 40, (fall 1980): 33–60. For depiction of the ideological trend as it looked four years later, see I.M. Destler, Leslie H. Gelb, and Anthony Lake, "From Establishment to Professional Elite," in *Our Own Worst Enemy: The Unmaking of American Foreign Policy* (New York: Simon and Schuster, 1984).

7. It was the administration's violation of that ban, through the activities of Lt. Col. Oliver North, among others, that precipitated the "Iran-contra" scandal exposed in November 1986, which was the Reagan administration's greatest crisis.

8. The focus here is on dramatic, highly visible congressional votes on prominent issues. The record on the much larger universe of cases where Congress engages on foreign policy is, of course, a complex mixture of what Ralph G. Carter labels compliance, resistance, rejection, and independence vis-à-vis administration desires. See Carter, "Congressional Foreign Policy Behavior: Persistent Patterns in the Postwar Period," *Presidential Studies Quarterly* 16 (1986): 329–59; and "Congress and Post–Cold War U.S. Foreign Policy," in *After the End: Making U.S. Foreign Policy in the Post–Cold War World,* ed. by James M. Scott (Durham: Duke University Press, 1998), 109–37.

9. David Mayhew, *Congress: The Electoral Connection* (New Haven: Yale University Press, 1974), part I.

10. For a fuller development of this argument as applied to trade policy, where Congress has particular constitutional responsibility, see Destler, "Constituencies, Congress, and U.S. Trade Policy," in *Constituent Interests and U.S. Trade Policies* ed. by Alan V. Deardorff and Robert M. Stern (Ann Arbor: University of Michigan Press, 1998).

11. My essay for an earlier edition of this collection, focusing specifically on sources of interbranch conflict, devoted exactly one paragraph to partisan politics! See "Executive–Congressional Conflict in Foreign Policy: Explaining It, Coping with It," in *Congress Reconsidered,* 3d ed., ed. by Lawrence C. Dodd and Bruce I. Oppenheimer (Washington, D.C.: CQ Press, 1985), 343–64.

12. In an editorial titled "Gutless on GATT," the *Journal of Commerce* denounced Gingrich as "too obsessed with pandering to Mr. Perot and bashing Bill Clinton to uphold his party's historical commitment to free trade" (October 7, 1994). The legislation was approved, by strong House and Senate majorities, in a post-election, "lame duck" session.

13. Quoted in Michael Barone and Grant Ujifusa, *The Almanac of American Politics, 2000* (Washington, D.C.: National Journal Group, 1999), 1583. Armey later modulated this position somewhat.

14. Richard F. Fenno Jr., *Learning to Govern: An Institutional View of the 104th Congress* (Washington, D.C.: Brookings Institution Press, 1997), 3.

15. By UN calculation, U.S. arrears for regular dues and peacekeeping assessments rose from $287 million at the end of 1992 to $1.4 billion four years later. (The administration estimated the debt at $1 billion.) The shortfall generated serious financial problems for the organization and growing international criticism of the United States. The Helms-Biden agreement provided for payment of $819 million over three years—$200 million less than the administration had requested and another $400 billion less than the UN's estimate—on the condition that administrative reforms be undertaken and the U.S. share of the total UN budget be lowered from 25 to 20 percent.

16. Senate approval of the expansion of NATO was facilitated by the favorable inclination of Republican conservatives, but the White House was successful in preventing the inclusion of anti-Russian amendments that many conservatives found appealing.

17. For a comprehensive rebuttal of that argument, see Steven Kull and I.M. Destler, *Misreading the Public: The Myth of a New Isolationism* (Washington, D.C.: Brookings Institution Press, 1999).

18. Larry Nowels, *International Affairs Budget Trends FY 1978–FY 1998,* Congressional Research Service, February 12, 1998, 5. On the overall congressional squeeze on foreign affairs funding, see Robert C. Kaiser, "Foreign Disservice," *Washington Post,* April 16, 2000, B1.

19. Ivo H. Daalder and Michael E. O'Hanlon, *Winning Ugly: NATO's War to Save Kosovo* (Washington, D.C.: Brookings Institution Press, 2000), 161.

20. On this vote, and the anti-internationalism of a substantial portion of congressional Republicans, see James Kitfield, "A Return to Isolationism," *National Journal,* October 9, 1999, 2872–77.

21. This section draws upon the more extensive description and analysis of these events in I.M. Destler, *Renewing Fast-Track Legislation* (Washington, D.C.: Institute for International Economics, Policy Analysis, no. 50, September 1997), esp. part I; and Destler and Peter J. Balint, *The New Politics of American Trade: Trade, Labor, and the Environment,* Institute for International Economics, Policy Analysis no. 58, October 1999, 9–13, 34–42.

22. In a private but now-well-known transition conversation between Kantor and one of his Republican predecessors as U.S. Trade Representative, the Clinton designee was asked: "What will be your top priority as USTR?" "To get Clinton reelected." "I mean, what is your top *trade* priority?" "To get Clinton reelected." This goal was fulfilled.

23. Destler and Balint, *The New Politics of American Trade,* 65.

24. Steven Kull, *Americans on Globalization: A Study of U.S. Public Attitudes,* Program on International Policy Attitudes, Center for International and Security Studies at Maryland, March 28, 2000.

25. Craig Cerniello, "White House, Key Senators Intensify Push for CTBT," *Arms Control Today,* July–August 1999. The poll was conducted in June by the Mellman Group and Wirthlin Worldwide for the Coalition to Reduce Nuclear Dangers. Other surveys showed lesser (but still robust) public support. See Steven Kull, "Comprehensive Test Ban Treaty Draws Strong Public Support, According to Review of Polls," Program on International Policy Attitudes Advisory, October 5, 1999; and Senate Test Ban Vote Little Noticed, Less Understood," a report of an after-the-vote survey by the Pew Research Center on the People and the Press conducted October 15–19. The latter found 47 percent opposed to the Senate vote rejecting the treaty and 26 percent in favor.

26. John M. Broder, "The Tactics: Quietly, Dextrously, Senate Republicans Set a Trap," *New York Times,* October 14, 1999.

27. Eric Schmitt, "Senate Kills Test Ban Treaty in Crushing Loss for Clinton," *New York Times,* October 14, 1999.

28. Dave Boyer, "Senate Rejects Treaty on Nuke Testing," *Washington Times,* October 14, 1999.

29. Samuel R. Berger, "American Power: Hegemony, Isolationism or Engagement," Address to Council on Foreign Relations, October 21, 1999 (available on the White House Web site). The assistant also attacked the "new isolationists" for "devastating cuts to our foreign affairs budget."

30. Helen Dewar and John Lancaster, "Helms Vows to Obstruct Arms Pacts," *Washington Post,* April 27, 2000.

31. Kull and Destler, *Misreading the Public,* 22–24. This is a very different question from whether the end of the Cold War has made Americans less internationalist. It clearly has not (ibid., esp. chap. 2).

32. Richard E. Cohen, "Crackup of the Committees," *National Journal*, July 31, 1999, 2212.

33. When asked to identify their position on the political spectrum, an average of 77 percent of voters in the 1972–1976 period labeled themselves middle of the road, slightly liberal, or slightly conservative, or said they didn't know or hadn't thought about it. In 1990–1994, the average was 75 percent. Comparing the same two periods, the margin of Democrats over Republicans fell from 20 percentage points to 11. (Calculated from tables in David C. King, "The Polarization of American Parties," in *Why People Don't Trust Government*, ed. by Joseph S. Meyer Jr. et al. [Cambridge: Harvard University Press, 1997], 158 and 163.)

34. Ibid., 165, 172.

35. Calculated by Sarah Binder, reported in ibid., 166, 168.

36. Richard E. Cohen, "Going to Extremes: Our Annual Vote Ratings," A Special Supplement to *National Journal*, February 26, 2000, 4. The causes of this polarization are beyond the scope of this essay. One is surely the decennial congressional redistricting process, dominated by the drive for safe seats for incumbents and ethnic groups. To the degree this goal is achieved—and in most election years it seems to be achieved very well—it makes *intra*party politics the primary influence on who is elected, reinforcing the influence of party activists with polar views. Other plausible forces include the rise of television, which may reward confrontational approaches, and activist "cause" groups, which tend to demand 100 percent loyalty to their agendas.

37. Ibid.

38. Sarah Binder, "The Dynamics of Legislative Gridlock, 1947–96," *American Political Science Review* 93 (September 1999): 527–28.

39. The classic study of this point is Benjamin I. Page and Robert Y. Shapiro, *The Rational Public: Fifty Years of Trends in Americans' Policy Preferences* (Chicago: University of Chicago Press, 1992). It is reflected also in Daniel Yankelovich's voluminous writings. Kull and Destler, *Misreading the Public*, finds the Page-Shapiro view vindicated in recent American opinion about international issues. This author draws a contrast between American public opinion and current American politics in "The Reasonable Public and the Polarized Policy Process," draft essay for the *festschrift* in honor of Richard H. Ullman, April 2000 (to be published by the Council on Foreign Relations in conjunction with Rowman and Littlefield).

Part VI
Congress and Political Change

15. The Twentieth-Century Congress

Joseph Cooper

The nineteenth century was the century of Congress. It is no accident that Woodrow Wilson, writing in the early 1880s, saw Congress as the dominant policymaker at the national level and the president as its clerk.[1] In the great majority of instances Congress originated and determined the fate of major legislation without any substantial or decisive involvement by the president. Similarly, Congress easily rivaled and often outmaneuvered the president in its ability to control the personnel and policies of the departments and agencies of the federal establishment. The twentieth century, in contrast, was the century of the president. The New Deal and World War II permanently established the president as the single most powerful figure in both the legislative and administrative processes of government, as well as the elected official charged, in the eyes of the public, with primary responsibility for initiating and securing policies in the public interest.

All this is not to argue that the trends that distinguish the two centuries of constitutional government in the United States from one another were simple and unidirectional, unmarked by ebbs and flows. Nonetheless, in the nineteenth century the march of Congress toward increasing preeminence in both the legislative and administrative processes was a continuing one. On the whole, it was the presidency that was on the defensive. This was true particularly in the latter half of the century. In the late 1860s President Andrew Johnson narrowly escaped an impeachment conviction whose effect would have been to subordinate the presidency to Congress. In the 1870s and 1880s presidents had to overcome repeated congressional attempts to undermine bedrock ingredients of executive authority with respect to their appointment, removal, and veto powers. In the twentieth century, however, the impetus of change reversed in direction and effect. It was Congress, despite instances of assertiveness in periods marked by presidential policy failure, malfeasance, or divided government, that found itself on the defensive. It was Congress that repeatedly had to confront challenges to bedrock elements of its lawmaking, budgetary, and war-making powers.

My goals in this chapter thus extend beyond a purely empirical sketch of how and why Congress changed during the twentieth century. The legacy of the

Table 15-1 Indicators of Party Strength (in percentages)

	1901–1911	1951–1961	1989–1999
Party strength in the House			
Mean party vote	73.8%	49.9%	59.4%
Mean majority party unity	90.9	79.9	88.4
Mean majority party wins	82.4	65.9	84.7
Mean cross-party wins	17.6	34.1	15.3
Mean party rule	73.2	26.1	65.1
Party strength in the Senate			
Mean party vote	73.6%	47.3%	55.2%
Mean majority party unity	86.9	80.2	85.9
Mean majority party wins	88.3	63.2	73.0
Mean cross-party wins	11.7	36.8	27.0
Mean party rule	76.8	10.2	37.8

Key: A *party vote* is one in which majorities of the two parties oppose one another; *majority party unity* is the proportion of the majority party that votes in concert on party votes; *majority party wins* are the proportion of party votes in which a majority of the majority party is on the winning side; *cross-party wins* are the proportion of party votes won by a coalition between defectors in the majority party and minority party opponents; and *majority party rule* is the proportion of party votes in which the majority party musters sufficent votes to win without any minority party assistance.

Sources: Compiled by the author and Garry Young.

nineteenth century to the twentieth was an institutional structure, a pattern of politics, and a civic society that was capable of adapting to and meeting the challenges of the new century while still preserving the essentials of republican government. Whether the legacy of the twentieth to the twenty-first will prove equally successful in the face of the heightened stakes and conditions of modern politics is far from clear. It is this question I ultimately wish to address in this chapter on the basis of an analysis of change in the operation and performance of Congress over the course of the twentieth century.

Patterns of Decision Making

We may start with change in the basic patterns of congressional decision making. In both the House of Representatives and the Senate the story of change is a story of transition from partisan control and independence of presidential leadership at the beginning of the twentieth century to committee dominance and dependence on presidential leadership at mid-century to partisan control and competition with the president at the end of the century. The narrative that follows details the character of this transition in each house and is supplemented by data reported in Tables 15-1 and 15-2. The scores in Table 15-1 document the broad pattern of cyclic variation that marked the majority party's ability to structure voting and control outcomes on the floor from the onset of the

Table 15-2 Indicators of Presidential Leadership

	1897–1901	1949–1952	1993–1994
Presidential news conferences Annual mean	0	40	36
Public activities Annual mean	Few	130	357
	1900	1950	1995
Presidential staff: White House (Budget) Number	13(0)	295(520)	400(542)
	1887–1901	1953–1967	1983–1997
Presidential wins on legislative positions Annual mean (percentage of House-Senate votes)	Few positions	78.0	57.9
Significant bills initiated Annual mean (in percentage)	Few	43.4	17.3
	1969–1970	1981–1982	1995–1996
Veto threats: major measures (in percentage)	14	23	60

Sources: Lyn Ragsdale, *Vital Statistics on the Presidency* (Washington, D.C.: CQ Press, 1996), 167–68, 179, and 257–58; Harold Stanley and Richard Niemi, *Vital Statistics on American Politics, 1999–2000* (Washington, D.C.: CQ Press, 2000), 252–53; George Edwards and Andrew Barrett, "Presidential Agenda Setting in Congress," and Barbara Sinclair, "Hostile Partners," both in *Polarized Politics,* ed. J. Bond and R. Fleisher (Washington, D.C.: CQ Press, 2000), 122 and 145. On 1887–1901 see Gerald Gamm and Renée Smith, "Presidents, Parties, and the Public," in *Speaking to the People,* ed. Richard J. Ellis (Amherst: University of Massachusetts Press, 1998), 87–111; Shirley Warshaw, *The Keys to Power* (New York: Longman, 2000), 143 and 312; and James Bryce, *The American Commonwealth* (New York: Macmillan, 1901), vol. 1.

Note: Public activities include all domestic policy appearances, including speeches and news conferences, but not political appearances. Presidential staff includes White House Office and Bureau of Budget or Office of Management and Budget staff after 1939. Before 1939 it includes White House staff that assist the president in the conduct of public business.

twentieth century to its end. The scores in Table 15-2 testify to the emergence of presidential leadership of the legislative process during the first half of the century and countervailing trends in the second half of the century.

The House of Representatives

The last decade of the nineteenth century witnessed the climax of institutional trends at work in the House during the entire century.[2] The House that emerged in the 1890s was one that contrasted sharply even with Woodrow Wilson's House of the 1880s. It was a House in which the Speaker had become the dominant figure, the standing committees his agents, the minority party bereft of influence over outcomes, and the ordinary member a mere supplicant for the favor of both committee leaders and the Speaker. It was also a House in which Speakers did not think of themselves as lieutenants of the president in designing and passing party legislation, but as his equal, if not superior.

The preeminence of the Speaker in this period rested both on the centralizing effects of the formal rules and high levels of policy agreement within the majority party. Each prompted and reinforced the other. The formal powers of the Speaker provided him with agenda control and with a formidable array of inducements for securing the support of his fellow partisans. The agreements that united the majority party reinforced the beliefs in party responsibility and discipline that characterized the late nineteenth century and served as the glue that bound the party together. The combined effect provided a powerful basis for mobilizing the party majorities required to maintain the formal power the rules accorded the Speaker and to pass party legislation. Nonetheless, the House of the 1890s rested on levels of party agreement that could not be sustained long into the twentieth century. The first turning point came in the years from 1909 to 1911, when a crosspartisan coalition of Democrats and dissident Progressive Republicans successfully attacked the powers of the Speaker. At the end of the process the Speaker had lost the power of appointing the chairs and members of the standing committees as well as his position as head of the Rules Committee. In addition, new procedures were created to enhance the power of the individual member to bring bills to the floor without the consent of the Speaker.

These changes did not immediately diminish the control of party leaders in the House. In the two Congresses that followed the revolt against the Speaker the Democrats took over the House and ruled it as tightly through reliance on the majority leader and the caucus as it had been ruled by the Republicans in the era of *czar rule*. In short, the reforms adopted to make it possible for ad hoc majorities to form and rule fell far short of expectations. The enlarged Rules Committee remained responsive to the wishes of the party leadership, and the newly created Calendar Wednesday and Discharge procedures proved to be ineffective. However, the president's power and involvement in the legislative process expanded substantially. Woodrow Wilson copied and extended the open and activist style of leadership that Theodore Roosevelt had introduced by capitalizing on the president's increasing prominence in national politics and the demise of czar rule. He made the caucus his instrument for passing a set of policy initiatives, which his fellow partisans supported, but which he shaped, advocated before the public, and pressured Congress to adopt.

Still, whatever the immediate failings of reform, the beginnings of a transition to a very different type of House were set in motion. The process of transition was, however, slow and uneven. Although *caucus rule* did not survive beyond 1915, a new and stable form of House did not emerge until two decades had passed. In the interim, levels of party voting and reliance on party mechanisms, such as the caucus or steering committee, increased when party control shifted, but then declined as divisions within the majority party intensified. It was a deep and lasting fissure of this kind that capped the fluctuations in decision-making patterns that followed the demise of czar rule. The catalytic event in the emergence of what is now commonly identified as the *Textbook Congress* was a split in the late 1930s between the northern and southern wings of the Democratic Party, a party that had in the early 1930s taken virtually permanent control of both the House and Senate.

In the Textbook House committees and committee chairs became more independent and powerful than they had been even in the decades that preceded czar rule. Chairmanship positions were transformed into personal property rights because seniority in the years after 1911 became inviolate in order to avoid exacerbating internal party divisions. In addition, chairmen inherited the plenary power over committee agendas, proceedings, and organization they had enjoyed in past periods when they had, not unreasonably, been assumed to be responsible agents of the House and majority party. As for the committees, their power both to block legislation they opposed and to pass legislation they favored became defining features of the legislative process. However, committee dominance did not rest simply on the rules and practices of the House. It rested far more on the fact that southern Democrats in coalition with Republicans controlled most important committees as well as voting on the floor. The loss of control of the Rules Committee to a southern Democratic-Republican coalition meant that party leaders could not easily challenge the ability of committees to bottle up legislation. Similarly, the ability of this coalition both to dominate the major committees and to defeat legislative provisions on the floor meant that the measures committees reported were usually non-controversial or framed to win the support of a majority of southern Democrats. As a consequence, challenges were limited and committees rarely lost on the floor, except in those few cases where a committee had a northern chair and a liberal Democratic majority.

The policy divisions that separated northern and southern Democrats and the fact that southerners constituted nearly half of the party also are key to the role the party leadership now began to play. After 1938 the primary problem that confronted the leadership in securing rules from the Rules Committee and building majorities on the floor was to restrict losses among southern Democrats and to compensate for such losses with Republican votes. Such political needs dictated a very different leadership style from the one that had prevailed in the past—one that relied on personal contacts, not party mechanisms, on bargaining and personal credits, not coercion, on floor voting and strategy, not intervention at the committee stage, and on good relations with the minority, not partisan divisiveness.

Finally, the emergence of the Textbook House was closely accompanied by and connected to the institutionalization of an activist presidential leadership role in the legislative process.[3] Even after Theodore Roosevelt and Woodrow

Wilson had altered expectations regarding the president's role in the legislative process and Congress in 1921 had given the president responsibility for submitting a unified set of annual budget requests, important residues of nineteenth-century attitudes still remained. Republican presidents in the 1920s regarded Wilson's aggressiveness as improper, and Calvin Coolidge openly preferred as much passivity as his fellow partisans in Congress would tolerate. However, Franklin D. Roosevelt and the New Deal relegated nineteenth-century notions of constitutional propriety to oblivion and established the dominance of the model of presidential responsibility and activism, advocated and practiced by Theodore Roosevelt and Woodrow Wilson. Given congressional acceptance of an activist president and the large expansion in the responsibilities of government the New Deal involved, the passage in 1939 of legislation that established an Executive Office of the President, including the previously created Budget Bureau and a newly created White House Office, was a logical, if not, inevitable development. By mid-century other vital and permanent units, such as the National Security Council and the Council of Economic Advisers, had been added, and routinized processes of planning the program and budget initiatives of the president, assessing and controlling all executive branch proposals to Congress, and lobbying Congress on behalf of presidential proposals had been established.

Although the Textbook Congress was so stable as to lead many to assume that its defining features were immutable, in fact, it too was merely the Congress of a particular era. The catalytic event that led to its demise was the election of 1958, which altered the balance between northerners and southerners in the Democratic Party in both houses from one of rough equality to one in which northerners predominated. Again, however, the transition to a new form of House was incremental and uneven. It was not until the Republican Party, led by Richard M. Nixon, took control of the presidency in 1969 that the northern Democrats mounted a sustained and comprehensive effort to transform the distribution of power in the House. Reform occurred largely by resuscitating the Democratic Caucus and using it to enact a series of changes in party procedures during the early and mid-1970s that led everyone to recognize that the type of Congress the phrase *Textbook Congress* was invented to describe had passed from the scene. At the end of the process the power of committee chairs had been circumscribed by subjecting them to nomination by a newly created steering and policy committee, led by the Speaker; by requiring a secret ballot election every Congress by the caucus; and by enacting a set of reforms that guaranteed the existence and power of subcommittees and distributed their chairmanships more widely among Democratic members. In addition, the Speaker was vested with the power of nominating Democratic members of the Rules Committee, and the rules were changed to permit roll-call votes on amendments in committee of the whole.

Given the fact that the main objects of reform were to limit the power of southern committee chairs and to distribute power more widely among Democratic members, many of the direct and associated effects of reform raised new problems to be solved at the same time that they settled old grievances. It was not until the mid-1980s that the current form of House began clearly to emerge. Increased unity in the Democratic Party, as southern Democrats continued to decline in number and became more loyal in their policy views, reversed the descent into the extremely low levels of party voting that characterized the 1970s and sealed the transformation of the committees and their chairs into agents of the northern Democratic majority. Invention and reliance on new procedures, such as multiple referral, restrictive rules, and a streamlined suspension calendar, allowed the leadership to regain control of the agenda and voting on the floor. These changes were prompted both by distaste for the increased uncertainty in outcomes that reform had bred and by a widely perceived need to counter the popularity of President Ronald Reagan with an appealing Democratic Party program. Thus, the return of a partisan House was marked not only by heightened power in the hands of party leaders but also by heightened competition with the president for public approval.

Nonetheless, the partisan House that emerged at the end of the century has taken far less stable form than either of the other two forms of Houses I have identified. The first phase occurred under Democratic control, and although it involved enhanced levels of party voting and a greater role for party leaders and mechanisms, the power of committees and committee chairs remained substantial. The loyalty of chairs to widely shared partisan goals, their roles as advocates of their committees in an age of multiple referral, and the power they retained to assist members in deriving constituency benefits from national programs made them immune from removal by the caucus and, except in a limited number of specific policy areas, more powerful than subcommittee chairs. Similarly, although the party leadership assumed a far more active role at the committee level than in the Textbook House and now had increased leverage over the committees through both formal and party mechanisms, the entrenched positions and expectations of senior Democrats continued to restrict its ability to dictate to the committees. Democratic party leaders thus operated largely as goal setters, overseers, and mediators on behalf of legislation they regarded as necessary for establishing a party record that would promote success at the polls.

The partisan House, created by the Democrats, however, endured for less than a decade. It was succeeded by a Republican House in 1995 that initially was far closer to the House of Speaker Joseph G. Cannon than to the House of Speaker Thomas Foley in its approach to the division of power within the chamber. The first Republican House, the 104th, led by Speaker Newt Gingrich, not only witnessed higher levels of majority party unity than had prevailed in the House since the days of czar rule, it also radically altered the relationship between party leaders and the committees. New mechanisms for appointing committees were created that vested far greater power in the Speaker, and Gingrich, acting largely on his own, departed from seniority in making three key chairmanship appointments. In addition, a variety of new party mechanisms from task forces to working groups to advisory groups to the Speaker were relied upon either to displace the committees as the developers and determiners of legislative and budget proposals or to define their marching orders and hold them to tight timetables.

Nonetheless, the Republican House of the 1990s proved to be much more volatile in its decision-making patterns than its Democratic predecessor. On the one hand, for reasons I will detail later, party voting had become far more ideologically based than in earlier periods of the century and the delineation and merchandising of a partisan policy program a far more important ingredient in member needs and expectations regarding the role of leaders. On the other hand, a skillful opponent held the presidency; the Senate because of the filibuster posed obstacles to party legislation passed by the House; and the majority party margin was not large enough to allow the leadership to have much ability either to overturn presidential vetoes or to ignore accommodating the small minority of moderate Republicans. Yet, despite these constraints, the ability of Speaker Gingrich to sustain the centralization of power he introduced rested on his ability to satisfy the expanded expectations of his members both for realizing their policy objectives and for defining a public record. Under these conditions failure was quite likely, and that indeed is what occurred. Although Gingrich welcomed and intensified the competitive relationship between the president and Congress that had prevailed since the Reagan presidency, he was whipsawed by the difficulty of managing and maneuvering his own party in a political context marked by ideological rigidity, divided government, slim majority margins, and a recalcitrant Senate. Nor in an age of electronic media and plebiscitary politics could he match the rhetorical skills of the incumbent president, Bill Clinton, and his own personal failings only added to the gap.

The result was a steady deterioration in the character and effectiveness of party rule in the Republican House—increased vulnerability to defeat on the floor due to declining majority margins; a retreat in leadership behavior from directing and bypassing committees toward the former Democratic model of setting goals and timetables and serving as a mediator; loss of confidence in Speaker Gingrich after the first session of the 104th House, which forced his resignation at the end of the 105th; and a return, especially in the 106th House of Speaker J. Dennis Hastert, to a less combative leadership style both within the House and with respect to the president. Nonetheless, there was little decline in the basic character of the relationship between the president and Congress. It continued to be one in which Republican Party leaders competed with the president for public approval, both to maintain control of the House and to safeguard the careers of their members.

The Senate

The story of change in Senate decision-making patterns is broadly similar, but parameterized in important and distinctive ways by the nature of the Senate as an institution.[4] The nineteenth-century Senate also ended by centralizing power in the hands of party leaders. But the basis of centralization and the manner of its operation were quite different. Throughout the nineteenth century the Senate resisted both adopting a restrictive set of rules and concentrating floor leadership in the hands of elected party leaders. Rather, the Senate chose to work primarily on the basis of agreement among its members both on the floor and in caucus, and for most of the nineteenth century it relied on committees and committee chairs to serve as its leaders. As a consequence, all individual senators retained great influence over the reference of bills, the access of bills to the floor, and debate and amendment on the floor. Similarly, in the absence until late in the century of party leaders and party steering committees with designated policy roles, the degree to which Senate committees functioned as party instruments depended on the degree of unity in the party and the individuals involved.

Centralization in the hands of party leaders nonetheless occurred in the 1890s. A sizeable increase in partisan agreement on policy issues took place in the Republican Senates as well as Houses in these years and enabled a small set of senators, with close personal relationships, to assume control of the party caucus, the party committee on committees, the recently created party steering committee, and the chairmanships of the most important Senate committees. In short, centralization occurred through the emergence of a small clique of party leaders, whose power rested on the high degree of unity in the Republican Party; generalized commitment, as in the House, to the doctrines of party government, which made caucus decisions difficult to resist; and the leverage that control of committee appointments and powerful Senate committees gave this clique to reward those who cooperated and punish those who did not.

Such a structure of power, however, was far more fragile than in the House. It was anchored simply in party unity and party loyalty, not the formal rules. As a consequence, Nelson Aldrich, perhaps the primary Senate party leader of this era, had less ability to block Theodore Roosevelt's open and active innovations in leading the legislative process than Speaker Cannon. Equally important, oligarchic rule of the Senate based on party did not require any rules revolt to overthrow. It began to wither as the high degree of unity in the majority party began to decline. A small but growing number of Progressives sealed its fate in the very same Congresses that witnessed the revolt against the Speaker.

Once again, however, the decline of party was uneven, although more rapid and pronounced than in the House. As in the House, the initial Senate of the Wilson administration, which the Democrats controlled for the first time in nearly two decades, manifested levels of party voting comparable to those in oligarchically controlled Republican Senates. It is in this Senate that the position of majority leader was formalized, in large part to advance the adoption of Wilson's program initiatives. From this time forth majority leaders, aided by rulings and practice that solidified their right to gain recognition on the floor and extended the reach and effectiveness of unanimous consent agreements, assumed increasing responsibility for managing floor consideration procedurally. Nonetheless, as the role and strength of party declined after Wilson's first term, the balance of power between committee chairs and party leaders again resumed a more traditional form.

In the 1920s the Republicans regained control, but levels of party voting steadily declined. Party leaders deferred to committee chairs on substantive matters and also shared procedural leadership on a more equal basis. Given such patterns and equal representation by state, the Senate, even more than the House, became marked by bloc voting, involving sectional crosspartisan alliances. As in the House, the advent of the New Deal in the 1930s changed the politics of the Senate. Nonetheless, levels of party voting were not strengthened to as high a degree as in the House, and the ability of the Democratic Party to control outcomes rested on the unusually large Senate majorities that the New Deal produced. A more permanent effect was the firm establishment of the Senate majority party leader as an agent of the president, who, as we have noted, had made himself the central figure in determining the policy agenda of the Democratic Party and needed even more help than in the House, where the individual member counted for far less.

The split in the ranks of the Democratic Party in the late 1930s had many of the same consequences in the Senate as in the House, but important differences nonetheless resulted because of the differences in the character and structure of the two bodies. In the Senate the rules conferred scant advantage on the party leadership. An oligarchy, rooted in a stable crosspartisan coalition, could control the operation of the Senate in much the same manner that the party oligarchy had controlled it at the turn of the century—that is, by dominating the party organs that controlled committee appointments and by controlling the leadership positions on important Senate committees.

The Textbook Senate thus was like the Textbook House in the role and power exercised by committees and committee chairs, only more so, given the far weaker position of the party leadership and the stronger hold of seniority, which had become inviolate in the Senate even in the nineteenth century. Return to Democratic rule in the Senate, as in the House, meant southern chairs of most important committees. Equally important, it meant that southerners and their conservative allies from other sections could and would dominate the party committee on committees, while, as in the House, reliance on all other party mechanisms simply disappeared. Power in the Senate thus fell into the hands of a small band of southern chairs, who worked with conservative allies from the West in their party and conservative Republicans to control the key committees and the floor. However, southern power also rested on two other facets of operation. Whereas norms such as apprenticeship, specialization, and reciprocity were strong in the Textbook House, they were even stronger in the Senate. Given the far greater dependence on mutual agreement to transact even ordinary business, these norms were more tightly interwoven into the very fiber of its being and more necessary to impose order in committee and on the floor than in the House. In addition, in the new Senate that emerged in the late 1930s, the increased salience of civil rights issues combined with the difficulty of securing the two-thirds vote required for cloture to transform the filibuster into a hallmark of southern power. It ceased being a weapon that was used sparingly and for a variety of purposes and became a weapon that was used almost entirely by southern Democrats to obstruct action in a specific policy area that was of preeminent importance to their constituents and in which the conservative coalition was subject to breakdown.

As in the case of the House, the catalytic event in beginning a transition to a new type of Senate was the election of 1958, which added a host of liberal northern senators and established their continuing predominance in the Democratic Party. An important sign that the Textbook Senate was in a state of serious deterioration soon appeared—the breaking of the power of the southern filibuster on civil rights legislation in the mid-1960s. Once again, given the lax character of Senate rules, no reform effort was necessary after that event to seal the fate of the Textbook Senate. It could be and was ended by the enhanced numbers of northern Democrats, who within a decade or so took control of both the party mechanisms and the major Senate committees. Still, the transition to the modern Senate was even more volatile than in the House. Absent the structuring that oligarchical control had provided and with the advent of TV and a new and broader set of issues, the Senate soon began to operate in a far more individualized manner, and voting patterns became far more bipartisan.

The emergence of the modern Senate, as in the House, began in the mid-1980s with a substantial strengthening of party voting and the return of Democratic control. Again, what was at work was a sizeable decline in conservative southern Democratic senators and the reappearance of divided government after six years of Republican control. Increased party unity and the need to join House Democrats in competing with the president to win the favor of the American people provided impetus for reinvigorating the strategic role of party leaders on the floor and for transforming them into overseers of the work of committees. Yet, at the same time, the ability of party leaders to meet these expectations was undercut by the consequences of lax rules and the disappearance of the Textbook Senate. As the old norms that promoted order, cooperation, and forbearance among senators eroded, as issues became more nationalized, and as the electronic media expanded in variety and political importance, inclinations toward unrestrained individualism came increasingly to the fore along with heightened partisanship.

Given these developments, obstruction and incivility intensified as the Senate, like the House, became more partisan and more attuned to playing to the public for political advantage. One of the hallmarks of the modern Senate has thus been an explosion in the use of filibusters and holds across all policy areas. As a result, although the cloture rule was strengthened by reducing the number required to sixty and severely restricting opportunities for post-cloture dilatory tactics, both the partisan Democratic Senate that began in the mid-1980s and lasted until 1995 and the partisan Republican Senate that followed it were transformed into bodies in which the ability to garner sixty votes defined the strategy and outcome on all major issues. Another, and related, effect was a growth in the number and complexity of unanimous consent resolutions and their strategic use by the majority leader to ease the arduous path to legislative action.

In sum, during the closing decades of the twentieth century the Senate became more dependent on supermajorities to pass major legislation but less able to mobilize them. Party voting increased substantially and party leaders assumed greater responsibility for leading party forces and managing committee products. Yet these leaders had far less power than responsibility in a Senate that retained its preference for protecting the power of individual members, abandoned many of the traditional norms that restrained the pursuit of personal or partisan advantage, and was divided on partisan grounds on the basis of sharp ideological differences. At the same time, as in the House, the majority margin in the Senate remained less than what was necessary to override a presidential veto. Nonetheless, leaders were expected both to manage the business of the Senate and to do so in a manner that won the favor of the public for their party and all its members—a vexing task under these conditions and one that required even more skillful accommodation both within and between the parties than in the House. Ironically enough, then, to a far greater degree than in the House, the very partisanship that came to define the Senate impeded its ability to function.

Explaining Change

We can conclude that over the course of the twentieth century both the House and Senate traversed a path from party rule to committee rule to party rule once again. Nonetheless, important differences exist in the character of party rule at the beginning and end of the twentieth century with respect to the role of the president, the role of party leaders, and the dynamics of party voting. Assuming that the basic motivations of members are relatively stable, the explanation of these differences is best approached contextually. In explaining the evolution of the twentieth-century Congress, I shall therefore emphasize four external factors that serve as prime vehicles for mediating the impacts of broader social forces and, in so doing, shape the patterns of choice that alter the contours of congressional structures, processes, and goals. They are as follows: expansion in the roles and responsibilities of the federal government, expansion in the roles and responsibilities of the president, change in the character and impacts of the electoral system, and change in the political beliefs and expectations of the American people.[5] Once again my analysis is supplemented by illustrative data. Table 15-3 and 15-4 present a variety of indicators of the breadth and pace of change in societal life over the course of the twentieth century together with salient examples of related changes in patterns of politics and government.

The Internal Distribution of Power

Let us look at the two primary themes that I have interwoven in tracing the evolution of decision-making patterns—the role of party and party leaders as opposed to committees and committee chairs and the role of the president as leg-

Table 15-3 Indicators of Societal Change

	1900	1950	1999
U.S. population (in millions)	76	150.7	272.3
	1929	1950	1997
GNP (in $billions)	104.6	296.1	8,102.9
	1900	1950	1990
Urban population (in percentage)	39.7	64	75.2
	1930	1950	1995
Air passenger miles flown (in billions)	0.09	8	540.4
	1950	1975 (1974)	1995 (1994)
Households with TV (in percentage)	9 (NA)[a]	97 (65)[a]	98 (72)[a]

Sources: Harold Stanley and Richard Niemi, *Vital Statistics on American Politics* (Washington, D.C.: CQ Press, 2000), 166, 173, 355, 387–89; U.S. Bureau of Census, *Historical Statistics of the United States* (Washington, D.C.: Government Printing Office, 1960), 14, 467; U.S. Bureau of Census, *Statistical Abstract of the United States, 1997* (Washington, D.C.: Government Printing Office, 1997), 44, 649.

NA = not applicable.

[a]Parentheses enclose percentage of households identifying television as source of most news.

islative leader. With respect to the first theme, how can we explain the fact that the twentieth century as well as the nineteenth are marked by highly variable levels of party voting, highly variable levels of concentrated power in party leaders, and substantial House and Senate differences in both regards?[6]

As has been suggested earlier, what must be understood from the start are the impacts of variation in the levels of agreement that unite the parties and the institutional differences between the House and Senate. This is not to deny that the purely political interests members share to define a party record that promotes reelection and majority status are also a factor of importance, especially in current patterns of politics. However, without high levels of agreement on the broad direction and substance of policy, the inducements to value a common party record and to yield personal and policy goals to the discretion of party leaders are severely weakened. In short, the shared political interests that contribute to high levels of party voting and concentrated power in the hands of party leaders are themselves highly dependent on shared substantive views and become

Table 15-4 Indicators of Political Change

	1913	1950	1994
Federal social welfare expenditures (in $billions)	0.2	10.5	852.6
	1836–1929	*1930–1959*	*1960–1985*
Founding date of ass'ns headquartered in Washington (in percentage)	216 (28.1)	210 (27.3)	343 (44.6)
	1950	*1974*	*1995*
Number of PACs	NA	608	4,016
	1912	*1960*	*1992*
Pres. primaries: Democratic Party (percentage of delegates)	12 (32.9)	16 (38.4)	40 (88)
	1889–1929	*1945–1960*	*1989–1998*
Treaties vs. executive agreements	382–763	221–3,158	235–2,997
	1947–1948	*1975–1976*	*1995–1996*
Pages of public legislation vs. pages in *Federal Register*	2,236–18,510	4,121–117,293	6,369–137,476

Sources: Harold Stanley and Richard Niemi, *Vital Statistics on American Politics* (Washington, D.C.: CQ Press, 2000), 62, 98, 262, 329, 367; U.S. Bureau of the Census, *Historical Statistics of the United States* (Washington, D.C.: Government Printing Office, 1960), 194; Norman J. Ornstein, Thomas E. Mann, and Michael J. Malbin, *Vital Statistics on Congress* (Washington, D.C.: AEI Press, 2000), 160; and Jack Walker, *Mobilizing Interest Groups in America* (Ann Arbor: University of Michigan Press, 1991), 79. *Federal Register* data for 1947–1948 supplied by James Anderson and Earle Fratus.

NA = not applicable.

devoid of content and effect as the character of and potential for partisan agreement on policy issues declines.

We therefore need not be surprised by the degree and types of variability we find. It takes high levels of agreement on policy matters for the combined effects of shared substantive and political interests to generate high levels of party voting, and very high levels of agreement to generate substantial concentration of power. Similarly, we need not be surprised by House-Senate differences. The Senate is based on a constituency principle that aggregates and represents interests and views in and across the states differently from the House. Equally important, throughout its history the Senate has resisted subjecting individual senators, acting alone or in concert, to the degree of formal control provided in the House. As a result, the potential for party agreement that emerges in the House and Senate varies, and the integrating effects that shared substantive and political interests can have in generating party voting are not as strongly reinforced either by concentrations of organizational power or the character of elections.

Nonetheless, variation in levels of party voting and concentrations of power in the hands of party leaders cannot be explained simply in terms of prevailing levels of substantive agreement and the fixed institutional parameters that define and differentiate the House and Senate. Rather, as indicated above, the impacts of broader contextual factors must be taken into account. This is especially true of the character and impact of the electoral process. The contours of the policy agreements that unite and divide the parties, the degree to which substantive and political interests reinforce one another, and the impacts of institutional parameters are themselves largely determined by broader societal forces whose effects on these outcomes are primarily mediated by and transmitted through the electoral process. This is not to deny importance to the other factors we have identified, for example, the impacts on unity and leadership power of an expanded presidential role. Nonetheless, it remains true that the patterns of politics and modes of campaigning that characterize the electoral process largely determine the strength and compatibility of the shared substantive and political interests on which majority party unity and structure rest. In short, within the constraints set by the fixed, institutional parameters that distinguish the House and Senate, it is change in the character and impact of the electoral process that drives major and persistent patterns of variation in levels of party voting and leadership power in both the House and the Senate.

Change in the character and consequences of the electoral process was substantial during the twentieth century.[7] In the latter part of the nineteenth century state and local party organizations were strong and controlled the choice of candidates as well as the conduct of campaigns; party identification provided an important determinant of voting; sectionalism structured the division of interests and views between the parties; the number of issues that spanned constituencies in a highly salient manner was highly restricted; and pork and patronage were as much a concern as national policy for elected officials and the dominant concern for party activists. In such a context, the careers of members were not primarily focused on congressional service. Rather, members pursued political careers as professional politicians in their states and localities, not as professional legislators in Washington. This, in turn, substantially bolstered adherence to the doctrines of party responsibility and behavior governed by party loyalty. Equally important, the high levels of policy agreement needed for centralizing power in the hands of congressional party leaders were restricted to a small number of national issues, and campaigns were organized and conducted by local party officials and activists on a face-to-face basis with only secondary reliance on the main form of media—local newspapers. Last but not least, party success rested far more on the prior commitments of partisans, both in terms of policy and benefits, than on the skill of congressional leaders in selling a party program to the public.

The twentieth century witnessed profound change in all these regards. In the first half of the century the role of state and local parties declined. Civil service reform and expanding government programs limited the importance of patronage and traditional forms of pork. Reforms, such as the direct primary and the direct election of senators, undermined the primacy of parties in candidate selection in response to mounting public belief that they were instruments of monied interests and corrupt rather than responsible instruments of public will. At the same time, although the strength of party identification remained strong, the correspondence between sectional and economic bases of conflict provided a fragile foundation for party coherence as an increasingly nationalized and industrialized society emerged. The impacts on legislative decision-making patterns were gradual but reinforcing. Members who made careers out of service in Congress became typical, and the personal as opposed to the partisan sources of their advantage as incumbents increased. Concomitantly, although the range of national issues expanded, the forces that promoted party unity and centralization were undermined by the weakening hold of party organizations over elections and new bases of division within the major parties. As a result, members became more resistant to centralization, less inclined to accept the doctrines of party responsibility, and more inclined to see themselves as the best judges of their constituents' interests. Indeed, as noted, the century had hardly gotten started before increased incoherence in the alignments of interests fed into Congress by the electoral party system brought the form of party rule that persisted at the turn of the century to an end and introduced a period of continuing, if irregular, decline in the power of party leaders. Nor did the fact that opportunities for new forms of particularistic benefits expanded as the number of national programs grew strengthen the hands of party leaders. As the period from 1890 to 1910 demonstrates, particularistic politics can coexist with party rule, but it remains a politics that is rooted in nonpartisanship and is incapable of sustaining party rule. Finally, although the New Deal organized the party system more consistently in terms of class, its inner contradictions combined in less than a decade with heightened independence on the part of members to bring the Textbook Congress into existence.

In the second half of the century the decline of the industrial age and the end of the cold war were accompanied by a number of critical changes. Sectional patterns of politics based on race and agriculture disappeared, but the span of national issues grew to involve a far wider set of economic and cultural issues, including many new and highly divisive ones. One result has been to render the patterns of interest that comprise the parties more coherent while at the same time making the electoral process more reflective of and governed by broad policy concerns. However, another has been to increase the stakes of politics and to make partisan divisions more rigid and more rancorous. These changes, in turn, have interacted with changes in the conduct of campaigns that both reflect them and affect their impacts. As the power of state and local party organizations continued to erode, campaigns became increasingly candidate centered, with policy rewards serving as the dominant incentives for activists and party identification substantially declining as a source of support. The result has been increased issue or ideological voting, which, combined with greater coherence in party align-ments, has augmented party voting in Congress. However, given the advent of a host of new technologies, a concomitant result of candidate-centered politics has been to transform campaigns into enterprises in which polling and carefully craft-ed TV ads become the defining activities, and in which the role of interest groups is heightened because of their power over the keys to victory—money and votes.

The overall result has been once again to produce party regimes in the House and Senate, but far more fragile and ineffective ones than at the begin-ning of the twentieth century. Although the increased coherence of partisan alignments has made the power of incumbency far more harmonious with party rule, leaders are faced with followers who are nonetheless more independent, more ideological, and more demanding. As a consequence, thin majority margins in the House can easily undermine the advantages of organizational control, and opportunities for obstruction in the Senate can easily counter high levels of par-tisan support. Yet, the altered circumstances of modern politics require leaders to be held far more responsible for providing their fellow partisans with an appeal-ing record of achievement to run on, and hence they are judged far more than in the past on their public relations skills. Moreover, insofar as party leaders cannot provide such a record, incentives to engage in a rhetorical politics of blaming opponents and to loosen restraints on the distribution of particularistic benefits become difficult to resist.

The Role of the President

The second theme that structures my analysis of decision-making patterns is the heightened role of the president in the lawmaking process. As noted, this aspect of patterning is interwoven with change in the internal division of power. But once again, to be understood, it must be seen in relation to the impacts of the four external factors previously identified. In the latter part of the nineteenth century, practice and belief regarding the president's role in the legislative process and his role in the party system reinforced one another as constraints on his power. In the party system the president's status as national party leader was rivaled by party leaders in Congress, especially those who were also the chieftains of state and local party organizations. In Congress all aspects of leadership were largely in the hands of congressional leaders and open, activist involvement by the president on any comprehensive basis was regarded as neither useful nor legitimate. Thus, when newly elected President Benjamin Harrison asked his friend, Sen. John Sherman, for advice in 1888 on how to conduct himself in office, Sherman responded in a manner that aptly captured the thinking of his age. "The President," he wrote, "should have no policy distinct from that of his party and that is better represented in Congress than the President."[8]

In the twentieth century, however, the role of the president in the legislative process changed so substantially that nineteenth-century practice and norms were erased from public memory. Nonetheless, there are important differences between the first and second halves of the twentieth century. In the first half of the century, economic expansion and the transformation of the country into a world power propelled advances in the roles of both the federal government and the president. As noted earlier, the transformation of the role of the president in Congress and the party system began early in the century when Theodore Roosevelt and Woodrow Wilson began to offer domestic policy programs of their own definition to the country to counter the disruptions that growing industrialization and urbanization created. Equally important, American presidents also began to play a role on the world stage they had never before played, which both increased their prestige at home and their power over foreign policy. These changes, combined with the invention of the presidential press conference, advocacy of concrete policy proposals in campaign addresses, and open attempts to push presidential policy initiatives through Congress, defined a very new kind of activist presidency, and the model was confirmed, extended, and institutionalized by Franklin Roosevelt in leading the nation through the depression and the Second World War.

The dynamics of change thus created a process in which expansions in the roles and responsibilities of government expanded the president's roles and responsibilities and vice versa as presidents took responsibility for solving the nation's problems.[9] The domestic and international forces that amplified the degree to which the policy issues of greatest concern to the public were national in scope worked to the advantage of the president, who was the only nationally elected official as well as the only elected official at the national level who possessed the authority to direct and mobilize the resources of the entire executive establishment. Presidents thus spearheaded the efforts to expand the role and responsibilities of the federal government and directly benefited from such expansion. Over time the power and prestige of the president's rivals in the party system increasingly diminished, and the decline in the power of state and local party organizations sealed their fate. Especially after the New Deal, the president became both the preeminent person in his party and the person the public looked to for leadership in the public interest both domestically and internationally.

These results, in turn, strengthened his position in the legislative process. Increasing presidential power and prestige in the party system and public opinion put the president in a position of being the beneficiary of congressional weakness. The model of legislative leadership created by Wilson and the two Roosevelts was thus more welcomed than resisted by Congress after the demise of centralized party rule. As party strength and leadership power in Congress declined, the lure was that the president possessed leverage that could be used to compensate for the decline in Congress's internal capacity to pass legislation, both partisan and bipartisan. Congress accordingly traded self-direction for presidential resources in energizing action. The price, however, was steep. The president became the definer of party programs and the primary agenda setter, congressional leaders of the same party as the president became his agents, and the president and his staff became active participants in the legislative process, as powerful, if not more powerful, as the most influential legislators. Moreover, as the size and scope of the administrative state grew, institutionalizing the president's role in the legislative process could not be separated from institutionalizing his role in the administrative process, which, in turn, reinforced his power in the legislative process. Nonetheless, the growth of presidential roles and responsibilities was not something Congress could obstruct in either the legislative or administrative processes. Given the president's increasing preeminence in the party system, party weakness in Congress, the emergence of domestic and international conditions that created a far greater need for action than in the nineteenth century, and the sheer growth of government, Congress had little choice but to become an instrument for extending presidential power.

In the second half of the century, the Wilson-Roosevelt activist model of presidential leadership nonetheless declined in power and appeal. With the exception of the 1960s, the period since 1950 has largely been one of divided government, not unified government. Similarly, with the exception of the 1960s and early 1970s, it has also been one in which further expansion in the role and responsibilities of the federal government has been strenuously contested and largely halted. As a consequence, although important features of the activist model have persisted, the legislative role of the president has been redefined in a number of significant regards. In causing this change the halt in any major expansions in the role of government as well as the end of the cold war have had important effects, but primarily in constraining further increases in presidential prestige and leverage. In contrast, changes in the impact of the electoral process have served to reframe the character of the relationship.[10]

Divided government is rooted in the electoral process. Its prevalence after 1950 stems both from the differential manner in which the constituency principles of the House, Senate, and presidency organize and represent opinion and from the growth of candidate-centered politics and a more complex pattern of values and interests across the nation. The combined effect has been to channel partisan alignments into the institutions of government in a more inconsistent manner. Still, it is not simply the absence of unified government that explains the competitive relationship that emerged in the 1980s and 1990s. Dwight D. Eisenhower and Richard M. Nixon also faced Congresses of the opposite party and in domestic policy matters had less conflict with Congress than Harry S. Truman and Jimmy Carter encountered in seeking to lead Congresses of their own party. Yet, all these presidents led in what by mid-century had become the accepted and expected activist mode. In each set of cases, however, the salient factor is that majority party strength, which rests both on unity and size, was weak, especially in the Senate. In Congresses in which government was divided, limited majority party unity, and at times margins as well, led to a cooperative relationship with the president; in Congresses in which government was unified they led to a discordant relationship. In contrast, the only two post-1950 Congresses in which

Figure 15-1   Models of Presidential–Congressional Relations

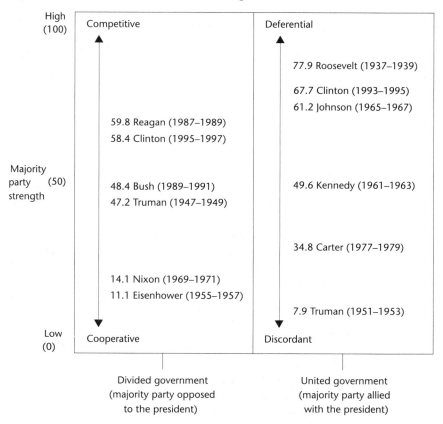

Source: Compiled by the author and Garry Young.

Note: Majority party strength measured in terms of the mean party rule score for the House and Senate.

unified government combined with party strength, Lyndon Johnson's 89th and Bill Clinton's 103d, were also the only Congresses that resembled Franklin Roosevelt's New Deal Congresses before 1938 or Woodrow Wilson's before 1917. They were, in short, Congresses in which the relationship was not only one of activist presidential leadership, but also one marked by a high degree of deference or responsiveness to presidential initiatives. See Figure 15-1, which models the relationships between Congress and the president in terms of both the presence or absence of unified government and the degree of party strength in Congress.

There is thus a second facet of change in the impact of the electoral process that has been critical in reframing congressional-presidential relationships — heightened partisanship. What is distinctive about the 1980s and 1990s is that for the first time divided government occurred at the same time as levels of party unity were increasing and party regimes were emerging in both the House and the Senate. It is this combination that primarily explains the displacement of tight presidential control of the policy agenda and close presidential involvement in shepherding major legislation through the various stages of the legislative process. Rather, in recent decades the president and majority party leaders have competed for public approval in defining preferred agendas, in wrestling to control the features of legislation as it progresses through the legislative process, and in weighing the options of compromise or stalemate in relation to the opportunities for taking credit or assigning blame that they present. The degree to which the internal politics of Congress and member expectations regarding the role of leaders have resulted in an enhanced emphasis on image and message in recent Congresses has thus been a product not only of candidate-centered politics, the nationalization of politics, and new technologies of campaigning but also of divided government marked by policy partisanship.

Assessing the Twentieth-Century Congress

As suggested at the very start of this chapter, any overview limited to the analysis of change is incomplete. The very existence of Congress is premised on the contribution it makes to the success of representative government, and thus the significance of change must also be assessed. Assessment, however, requires standards. The standards I shall rely on are those of the framers of the Constitution, as embodied in the writings of James Madison.[11]

Congress, the President, and the Public

The framers sought to accommodate two primary, but conflicting, concerns. They believed that government should have sufficient power to act effectively, but regarded it as equally essential that it act only in ways that served the general welfare or public interest. They further believed that achieving this aim requires balancing the need for action against the need for consent and that such a balance must be weighted heavily in favor of consent. Finally, they believed that consent should be based on reason and deliberation, not merely the summation of wills, and that a legislature was essential to attain the levels of consent and deliberation necessary for government in the public interest.

The framers therefore established the Congress and vested it with lawmaking power. Clear standards result with respect to Congress's relationship to the president and to the public. The grant of lawmaking power to Congress serves to stipulate that the prime policy decisions of government shall be made in Congress, not by the executive head of government or those under his direction. This, in turn, requires that Congress preserve a substantial degree of autonomy from presidential direction and that it exercise its legislative powers in a manner that preserves its role as the prime policymaker in the political system.

However, Congress's ability to play its designated role is far from guaranteed and, as noted earlier, the dynamics of change in the twentieth century both expanded the power and position of the president in national policymaking and eroded congressional prerogatives the nineteenth century took for granted. Whatever the variation in the internal division of power between party leaders and committee leaders, congressional autonomy declined appreciably as compared with traditional practice. Indeed, even in periods of divided government, the president is now expected to play a role in the legislative process whose activism and assertiveness would shock nineteenth-century sensibilities regarding the separation of powers. The incursions on the scope of congressional control over governmental policymaking were even more severe. This is an aspect of the relationship between the president and Congress that our focus on internal decision making has led us to treat only tangentially thus far, but one that now can be addressed directly.

In part, the decline in Congress's control over governmental actions that affect the daily lives of citizens is due simply to expansion in the role of government. Congress's ability to specify the standards and procedures of administrative action, to exercise oversight over administrative decision making, and to pass on their budgets cannot fully compensate for the breadth of the discretion delegated to the executive branch over the course of the twentieth century. Nor is the situation correctable through committee reforms or procedural innovations, although Congress has tried repeatedly since mid-century to do so. The inescapable truth is that the growth in the role of government necessarily means expansion in the share of government decision-making power vested in the president and bureaucracy.[12]

However, loss of scope or breadth in congressional policy control is also a consequence of the dynamics of expanding presidential power itself. In a context in which the public sees the president as the primary source of leadership in the public interest, presidents easily take expansive views of their responsibilities and inherent powers as chief executive and use their staff resources, their constitutional grants of power, and the discretion delegated to the executive branch to govern on their own. This is true in domestic affairs, especially under conditions of divided government. The second half of the twentieth century was thus marked by expanded reliance on executive orders and recess appointments, increased stonewalling of attempts at congressional oversight, and heightened political control over executive appointments, the budget, and rule making. It is even more true in international affairs where the president has greater authority under the Constitution and his capacity to act quickly confers enormous advantages. As is evidenced by the utter failure of the war powers resolution, increased reliance on executive agreements, and expanded claims of executive prerogative, the assumption of presidents since Truman has been that in defense and foreign policy the proper role of Congress is to stand and cheer, at least until substantial policy failures occur.[13]

Similarly, the twentieth century witnessed serious incursions on the framers' design with respect to Congress's relationship to the public. Here too, the grant of lawmaking power to Congress defines an important standard. In effect, it stipulates that the prime policy decisions are to be made in Congress, not directly by the people. However, the framers chose representative government for reasons that extended beyond their belief that reliance on elections would safeguard popular rule while avoiding the demagoguery, injustice, and civil strife they regarded as endemic in direct democracy. They also chose it because they believed that a separate legislative stage was required for the kind of deliberative decision making they saw as essential for government in the public interest. Such a rationale has clear implications for the behavior of members. It means that elected officials must be responsible as well as responsive. It means as well that to manage the tensions such goals involve, members must engage in a continuing process of interaction with their constituents in which they present and explain themselves in ways that succeed in winning their trust.

In sum, the framers saw representative government as a complex, not simple, standard for ordering the relationship between members and their constituents and believed that satisfying its demands required the presence of a strong balance between independence and responsiveness. Nonetheless, in the twentieth century the strength of this balance substantially declined. In part, the reasons lie in the continuing democratization of public beliefs and expectations. From the time of Andrew Jackson, representative government has increasingly been equated in the public mind with direct and immediate responsiveness to popular will and that will seen as unified or coherent. This trend intensified during the twentieth century. Direct election of the Senate, the direct primary, and a host of internal party reforms were adopted over the course of the century, ostensibly to deny power to party bosses and place it in the hands of the people. In addition, since mid-century the notion of "sunshine" has gained increasing appeal, with the result that requirements for openness in voting and committee proceedings have been introduced to a degree that far exceeds traditional practice. Concomitantly, public understanding and acceptance of the underlying rationale of the framers' design have largely evaporated. Conflict, which the framers saw as a necessary ingredient in the process of consent and deliberation, is usually viewed as mere politics; inaction, which the framers believed should be highly tolerated to guarantee that action would indeed be in the public interest, is seen as obeisance to the rule of special interests. Congress therefore typically suffers in public esteem when it resists presidential initiatives or engages in protracted conflict over the content of legislation. Indeed, although both the presidency and Congress have suffered from the general decline of trust in government that has occurred since mid-century, it is the president that the public now looks to primarily for leadership in the public interest, with the result that trust in Congress almost invariably trails and tends to vary with trust in the presidency.[14]

However, the deterioration of the balance between responsiveness and responsibility the framers intended is also due to the manner in which changes in the conduct of campaigns have combined with changes in decision-making patterns in Congress. The emergence of a partisan-charged, competitive relationship between the president and Congress in conjunction with an increased emphasis on the use of electronic media and polls has greatly expanded the plebiscitary character of politics.[15] These factors heighten the degree to which policy is formulated and decided in Congress with an eye to immediate electoral gain. They advantage the president and intensify the politicization of issues. They encourage the parties to bid for the favor of the public through the distribution of both diffuse and particularistic benefits while increasing the barriers to innovative legislative action that reframes problems and solutions in ways that surmount existing divisions and capitalize on shared goals. Finally, they make electoral politics exceedingly costly, and in so doing heighten the role of money in politics. The result once again is to decrease the autonomy of Congress from the public but, ironically enough, to the detriment of responsiveness, both actual and perceived. What emerges is a politics that emphasizes spin over argument and explanation, rhetoric and symbols over substance, and manipulation over response, while at the same time promoting the belief that government because of the power of campaign contributions responds far more to special interests than to the public.

Congressional Decision Making, Consent, and Action

What, then, can we conclude about the impact of change, both in the internal decision-making patterns of Congress and in the external environment with which it interacts, on the quality of representative government in the United States. In answering this question, we must be careful not to exaggerate the maladies. The declines in congressional power that have occurred in relation to the president have served to restrict Congress's role in the political system, not to destroy it.

Overall, whatever the losses of autonomy Congress has suffered, the manner in which multiple constituency principles channel different patterns of interests and accountability into the House, Senate, and presidency continues to provide a powerful barrier to presidential dominance. Indeed, in the second half of the twentieth century such channeling bolstered autonomy to an even greater degree than in the first half because of its effects in promoting divided government. As a consequence, of the four types of relationships between the president and Congress I have identified in the text and modeled in Figure 15-1—cooperative, discordant, competitive, and deferential—the type that is characterized by deference occurred only infrequently. In general, activist presidential leadership did not often combine with sufficiently high levels of partisan strength in the House and, particularly, the Senate to incline Congress to be highly responsive to presidential desires. This was especially true in the latter half of the century. Only two Congresses qualify as deferential, the 89th and 103d, and even in these cases deference was limited in duration in the 89th and marked by an important exception, health care, in the 103d. The deeper import of Congress's loss of autonomy relative to the nineteenth century thus inheres less in any immediate loss of independence in concrete cases than in the relationship the twentieth century established between legislative action and presidential leadership, which gives Congress's capacity for autonomy a negative cast in the short run and increases the odds that in the long run it will be forced to succumb to presidential desires. Similarly, in arguing that Congress has less impact today on the manner in which the exercise of government discretion affects the daily lives of citizens, I have not meant to argue that Congress does not retain substantial policymaking power. Congress continues to be of great importance in sustaining, reformulating, and extending government authority; in controlling the pace of activity and the distribution of the burden through its appropriations and tax powers; and in providing opportunities for correcting both major and minor abuses in the exercise of executive discretion.

Nonetheless, Congress's role and power in relation to the presidency have declined. Moreover, even within the narrower parameters that now define its capacities for autonomy and policy control, the current character of its ties to the public combine with current decision-making patterns to impair its ability to play the pivotal role the framers assigned it in meeting the system's need for both consent and action. If we look first at consent, the degree to which consent and deliberation conflict, rather than reinforce one another, has intensified. The primary culprits are the increasing tendencies toward partisanship, divided government, and plebiscitary politics, which characterize the second half of the twentieth century. These factors all beget heightened obstruction both to score political points and to defeat majority will. Modern use of the filibuster provides a good illustration. At the same time, they stimulate increased use of leadership power to restrict opportunities for discussion and amendment through mechanisms such as omnibus bills, restrictive rules, and party units that bypass committees. Last, but not least, they promote incivility and rigidity in relations among ordinary members.[16] As a result, not only does the effectiveness of bargaining as a means of resolving conflict decline, so too does the role of deliberation. Both declines are of great consequence for the success of representative government. Given the vital role deliberation plays in reducing the load imposed on bargaining, it typically serves as bargaining's partner, not its adversary, in building agreement. Indeed, if anything, losses in deliberative capability are the more serious. Whereas bargaining usually dilutes policy effects, attention to facts and shared concerns provides a platform both for discovering our common purposes and acting effectively to achieve them.

If we turn now more directly to action, the framers did not and could not provide a substantive standard in terms of which the adequacy of Congress's response to the needs of the nation could be judged. As understood by the framers, the public interest is something to be discovered through the processes of politics. Thus, the only objective standard can be a procedural one—action that attains high levels of consent in the short run and consensus levels of agreement in the long run. Nonetheless, the reality is that prolonged inaction or action that is not effective enough to relieve public distress works over time to the disadvantage of Congress.

Since the New Deal, if not earlier, both objective conditions and public expectations have substantially reduced tolerance for failure to act. However, congressional politics in recent decades have been heavily weighted not only against action, but also against the kind of action that resolves issues in ways that allow the policies adopted to become parts of a broad, moving consensus over time. Thus, the problem of inaction in the modern Congress is not simply one of divided government barring action. The two forms of divided government I have identified are more conducive to action than the discordant form of unified government. Nor is it simply a problem of incremental legislation versus landmark legislation. During the nineteenth and first half of the twentieth centuries the system performed quite satisfactorily, with frequent and continuing instances of incremental legislation, punctuated by isolated instances and brief episodes of landmark legislation.

Rather, the basic problem inheres in the manner in which increasing tendencies toward divided government, partisanship, and plebiscitary politics have combined in recent decades to make the passage of landmark legislation that addresses and attempts to resolve tough problems even rarer than in the past. It is true, of course, that the presence of these factors does not necessarily mean there will be no action. What it does mean is that action will be watered down and tied more closely than in the past to sheerly political determinations of whether cooperation for the purpose of winning favor with the public or intransigence for the purpose of casting blame on opponents best serves to maximize partisan advantage. As a result, the possibilities for action under current patterns of congressional decision making are restricted, not only by the traditional barriers that the separation of powers and bicameral operation impose, but also by their intersection with divided government, heightened partisanship, and plebiscitary politics. Such a politics can produce legislation that addresses and resolves tough problems only haphazardly through fleeting and unstable cross-partisan coalitions within and between the branches, as in the case of welfare reform in the mid-1990s, or difficult to construct and operate special commissions or summits outside the regular processes of government. More typically, it relies on happenstance in which other forces or factors come to its rescue, as in the conflict between the president and Congress in the mid-1990s over eliminating the budget deficit.

Ironically enough, then, we begin the twenty-first century with a politics in which issues and parties are more important, but in which action, whether pro-government or anti-government, is typically so timid that the gap between the outputs produced and the outcomes desired has substantially widened. The most grievous aspects of current patterns of politics, thus, do not derive from heightened partisanship or even divided government, but from the increase in plebiscitary politics. Plebiscitary politics encourages and rewards fearful politicians, not politicians willing to take risks. Yet, especially under conditions of divided government, politicians who are willing to take risks, to offer leadership that cogently addresses issues, rather than limiting themselves to palliatives based on polls or position taking designed for partisan advantage, are all the more critical.

To be sure, the fact that Congress cannot respond definitively at this point in time to pressures either to expand or to retract the roles and responsibilities of the federal government reflects profound disagreement in the public on the proper role of government past the responsibilities established by the New Deal and portions of the Great Society. Nonetheless, as has been noted, the public's willingness to tolerate inaction as the price of representative government is far lower than in the nineteenth century. Congress's representative character thus counts for very little in its favor. Rather, in a context in which special interest contributions to campaigns mount in size and importance, in which the sheer size of government has made the distribution of particularistic benefits in both the legislative and administrative process more prevalent than ever, and in which the public perceives the cant that plebiscitary politics promotes, current patterns of decision making simply nourish dissatisfaction and distrust when they produce inaction or limited action on policy problems the public perceives as major. At the same time, the imaginative and responsible leadership necessary for more far-reaching results that can serve as the basis for a new consensus is undermined by plebiscitary politics. It is exactly these venturesome forms of behavior that plebiscitary politics discourages and stands ready to punish severely.

Future Prospects

This chapter can therefore end in much the same manner as it began. Congress's prospects are far less bright and assured as it enters the twenty-first century than at the start of the twentieth century. Congress rather appears to be caught in an interlocking set of forces that threaten continually to undermine its position in the political system and thus also the quality of representative government in the United States. One negative dynamic involves the interrelationship between expansion in the role of government and expansion in presidential power. A second concerns the interrelationship between the capacity for legislative action and the reduction of congressional autonomy. A third concerns the interrelationship between plebiscitary politics and the subversion of Congress's role in the American political system.

These negative dynamics are not the products of divided government and heightened partisanship, although they absorb and are affected by them. Both were often present in the nineteenth century as well. Such dynamics, rather, reflect more basic forces in modern American politics — the heightened scope and stakes of politics, the preeminence of the president in the party system and national consciousness, the rise of candidate-centered politics, and revolutionary changes in the ease of travel and the immediacy of communication. Still, it is also true that these dynamics are nourished by pathologies of behavior that have been endemic to American politics from its very beginnings — credit seeking, advertising, and position taking at the expense of substance; sacrificing congressional prerogatives for party or policy gain; minimizing political risks by evading responsibility; and exploiting public distrust for personal advantage. At heart, these pathologies all derive from the fact that career, policy, and party concerns can trump institutional and substantive concerns, and the conditions of modern politics have substantially bolstered the incentives for such behavior.

Nonetheless, Congress would not have lasted for more than two centuries if powerful positive dynamics that support its continued existence and power did not also exist. Perhaps the most important is the dedication of the American people to the principles of representative government and their support for Congress as an institution. Thus, no matter how dissatisfied they may be regarding its operation, they remain far from ready to abandon it. A second is the continuing capacity for change institutionalized by elections. The American people thus remain hopeful, despite their cynicism about politics. They can respond to and be mobilized by elected officials who seek to lead and inspire as well as disheartened and frustrated by politicians who pander and dissemble. Third, despite the power of appearance in politics, image is not all controlling. The ability to cloak ugly realities is limited, and the American people are both perceptive in judging the overall state of the nation and repelled by the stratagems of plebiscitary politics.

Given these strengths and the opportunities for redefinition and renewal they provide, distrust is the most threatening of all the consequences of the various negative dynamics and pathologies I have identified. Those who see Congress as the home of self-serving politicians and special interests are not apt to be concerned over whether it loses power or position in the system. What must be understood, however, is that careerism and particularism are not an exclusive product of the defects of Congress. Opportunities for careerism and particularism are endemic in the role of government, grow greater as the role of government expands, and are present in the executive to at least as great a degree. They are thus tendencies to be constrained, not accepted or overgeneralized. As the framers understood, the goal of the American political system is to transcend self-interest, not to indulge it. The defining problem of Congress is thus not its inclination toward self-interested behavior but, rather, its need to discipline such behavior in terms of the purposes we share. Congress is not and has never been a simple client of the executive branch whose members are entirely consumed with the search for particularistic benefits and are ever ready to sell their votes for electoral gain. However, to see it as such without recognizing the full complexity of the motivation and behavior that actually exist is to help transform it into just such a body.[17] The supreme irony of such a result would be to trade congressional autonomy for clientelism and to ignore the dangers of an unchecked executive because cynicism had been substituted for the nuanced realism of the framers and naïveté for their sophistication in institutional design.

Nonetheless, it remains true that the demands of sustaining the system of government intended by the framers are exceedingly high. In the twenty-first century, the expanding embrace of a digital world is destined to reduce the United States to the type of "small" republic the framers feared. Equally important, the institutional safeguards that parties and party allegiance, congressional preeminence, and a limited federal role provided for representative government in the past have disappeared. Last but not least, the problems to be solved in the twenty-first century will place even greater strain on the need to premise action on consent. Inevitably, then, the balance the framers struck in the eighteenth century between reliance on mechanisms that exploit conflicts in self-interest and reliance on responsible leaders and civic virtue will prove even less adequate in the twenty-first century than in the twentieth. In an administrative state threatened by heightening patterns of plebiscitary politics, far more will rest on the quality and dedication of leaders and on the character, understanding, and good judgment of citizens. Although reforms can be helpful, especially in reducing the ways in which the present system of campaign finance nurtures distrust, institutional arrangements cannot save representative government in the United States. What we will need, to an even greater extent than in the past, are leaders who are attentive to substance and willing to take risks on behalf of what they believe, and citizens who understand and are dedicated to the processes and benefits of representative government, despite their costs.

All this is a tall order. It may be that only hollow forms or empty facades of representative government will survive the new century, given the size, complexity, and intimacy of modern politics in America. The transition from republic to imperial rule in ancient Rome provides a chilling model. However, representative government in the United States has never simply been a legacy. It has, rather, always been something every generation has had to win on its own. This is a fact that the present generation can ignore only at its peril. Although the current requirements are exceedingly demanding, the stakes are even higher. Preserving our two-hundred-year experiment in self-government is of inestimable value to us and to all future generations. If we fail to do so, the fault, to borrow from Shakespeare, will lie not in our "stars," but in our understanding and in our character.[18]

Notes

1. Woodrow Wilson, *Congressional Government* (Baltimore: Johns Hopkins University Press, 1981). For analysis of the role of the president in the legislative process over the whole last half of the nineteenth century and Congress's continuing attempts at aggrandizement, see Wilfred Binkley, *President and Congress* (New York: Alfred Knopf, 1947), and Leonard White, *The Republican Era* (New York: Free Press, 1958).

2. For material on the evolution of decision-making patterns over the course of the twentieth century in the House, see Joseph Cooper and David Brady, "Institutional Context and Leadership Style: The House from Cannon to Rayburn," *American Political Science Review* 75 (June 1981): 411–25; Ronald Peters Jr., *The American Speakership* (Baltimore: Johns Hopkins University Press, 1997); Barbara Sinclair, *Legislators, Leaders, and Lawmakers* (Baltimore: Johns Hopkins University Press, 1995); and Nicole Rae and Colton Campbell, eds., *New Majority or Old Majority* (Lanham, Md.: Rowman and Littlefield, 1999).

3. For material on the evolution of the role of the president in the legislative process over the course of the twentieth century, see Binkley, *President and Congress;* White, *The Republican Era;* James Sundquist, *The Decline and Resurgence of Congress* (Washington, D.C.: Brookings Institution, 1981); Charles Jones, *Separate but Equal Branches*

(Chatham, N.J.: Chatham House, 1995); and Richard Ellis, *Speaking to the People: The Rhetorical Presidency in Historical Perspective* (Amherst: University of Massachusetts Press, 1998).

4. For material on the evolution of decision making in the Senate, see David Rothman, *Power and Politics* (New York: Atheneum, 1969); Lindsay Rogers, *The American Senate* (New York: Alfred Knopf, 1926); Donald Matthews, *U.S. Senators and Their World* (Chapel Hill: University of North Carolina Press, 1960); Randall Ripley, *Power in the Senate* (New York: St. Martin's Press, 1969); Barbara Sinclair, *The Transformation of the U.S. Senate* (Baltimore: Johns Hopkins University Press, 1989); and Fred Harris, *Deadlock or Decision* (New York: Oxford University Press, 1993).

5. See Joseph Cooper, "Strengthening the Congress," *Harvard Journal on Legislation* 12 (April 1975): 307–68, and "Organization and Innovation in the House of Representatives," in *The House at Work*, ed. Joseph Cooper and G. Calvin Mackenzie (Austin: University of Texas Press, 1981), 319–55. See also Lyn Ragsdale and John Theis III, "The Institutionalization of the American Presidency," *American Journal of Political Science* 41 (1997): 1303–14.

6. On the analysis of party voting in Congress and its organizational impacts, see Gary Cox and Mathew McCubbins, *Legislative Leviathan* (Berkeley: University of California Press, 1993); Keith Krehbiel, *Pivotal Politics* (Chicago: University of Chicago Press, 1998); Joseph Cooper and Garry Young, "Party and Preference in Congressional Decisionmaking" (paper delivered at the History of Congress Conference, Stanford University, January 1999), rev.; and John Aldrich and David Rohde, "The Consequences of Party Organization in the House," in *Polarized Politics*, ed. Jon Bond and Richard Fleisher (Washington, D.C.: CQ Press, 2000), 31–73.

7. The linkage between change in the character of the electoral process and decision-making patterns in Congress is multifaceted. On change in the role of parties and interest groups in elections generally, see V. O. Key Jr., *Politics, Parties, and Pressure Groups* (New York: Thomas Y. Crowell, 1964); John Aldrich, *Why Parties?* (Chicago: University of Chicago Press, 1995); Samuel Eldersveld and Hanes Walton Jr., *Political Parties in American Society* (New York: Bedford/St. Martin's, 2000); Jack Walker, *Mobilizing Interest Groups in America* (Ann Arbor: University of Michigan Press, 1991); and Allan Cigler and Burdett Loomis, *Interest Group Politics* (Washington, D.C.: CQ Press, 1998). On change in the organizational character of parties, their coalitional makeup, and policy consequences, see Walter Dean Burnham, *Critical Elections and the Mainsprings of American Politics* (New York: W. W. Norton, 1970); James Sundquist, *Dynamics of the Party System* (Washington, D.C.: Brookings Institution, 1973); David Brady, *Critical Elections and Congressional Policy Making* (Palo Alto: Stanford University Press, 1988); and David Rohde, *Parties and Leaders in the Postreform House* (Chicago: University of Chicago Press, 1991). On change in the conduct of campaigns and electoral voting behavior, see Barbara Salamore and Stephen Salamore, *Candidates, Parties, and Campaigns* (Washington, D.C.: CQ Press, 1989); Gary Jacobson, *The Politics of Congressional Elections* (New York: Longman, 1997); and Paul Herrnson, *Congressional Elections* (Washington, D.C.: CQ Press, 1998). On congressional careers see Peter Swenson, "The Influence of Recruitment on the Structure of Power in the U.S. House," *Legislative Studies Quarterly* 7 (February 1982): 7–36, and H. D. Price, *Explorations in the Evolution of Congress* (Berkeley: ICGS Press, 1998).

8. Binkley, *President and Congress,* 147. For an equally classic description of the president's secondary role in the legislative process in the latter part of the nineteenth century, see James Bryce, *The American Commonwealth* (London: Macmillan, 1901), vol. 1, 65 and 209.

9. For material on the expanding role of the federal government and changing citizen expectations and beliefs over the course of the twentieth century, see Ballard Camp-

bell, *The Growth of American Government* (Bloomington: Indiana University Press, 1995), and William Mayer, *The Changing American Mind* (Ann Arbor: University of Michigan Press, 1992). On the expanding responsibilities and powers accorded to the presidency through the 1960s, see Thomas Cronin, *The State of the Presidency* (Boston: Little, Brown, 1975); Sundquist, *The Decline and Resurgence of Congress;* and Cooper, "Strengthening the Congress," 343.

10. For material on the role of the federal government and changing citizen beliefs and expectations in recent decades, see Albert Cantril and Susan Cantril, *Reading Mixed Signals* (Washington, D.C.: Wilson Center Press, 1999). On the character and impacts of the electoral process in recent decades, see Jeffrey Berry, *The New Liberalism* (Washington, D.C.: Brookings Institution, 1999); David Menefee-Libey, *The Triumph of Campaign Centered Politics* (New York: Chatham House, 2000); John Green and Daniel Shea, eds., *The State of the Parties* (Lanham, Md.: Rowman and Littlefield, 2000); and John Aldrich and Richard Niemi, "The Sixth American Party System: Electoral Change, 1952–1992," in *Broken Contract? Changing Relationships between Americans and Their Government,* ed. Stephen Craig (Boulder, Colo.: Westview Press, 1996). On the expansion in the institutional resources of the presidency since the 1970s and the role of the president in recent decades, see Ragsdale and Theis, "The Institutionalization of the American Presidency," 1280–1318, and Shirley Anne Warshaw, *The Keys to Power: Managing the Presidency* (New York: Longman, 2000). On the effects of divided government see Sarah Binder, "The Dynamics of Legislative Gridlock, 1947–1996," *American Political Science Review* 93 (September 1999): 519–34. See also George Edwards III and Andrew Barrett, "Presidential Agenda Setting in Congress," and Barbara Sinclair, "Hostile Partners," in Bond and Fleisher, *Polarized Politics,* 109–54. On the impact of the different constituency bases of national institutions, see John Mark Hansen, "Individuals, Institutions, and Public Preferences over Public Finance," *American Political Science Review* 92 (September 1998): 513–33.

11. On Madisonian standards see *The Federalist Papers,* various editions; Emery Lee, "Representation, Virtue, and Political Jealousy in the Brutus-Publius Debate," *Journal of Politics* 59 (November 1997): 1073–96; and Joseph Bessett, *The Mild Voice of Reason* (Chicago: University of Chicago Press, 1994).

12. This is not to deny that the scope of delegated legislation varied in different periods of the twentieth century. Nor is it to deny that members can design the substantive and procedural features of delegated legislation so as to incline administrative decision making in the policy directions they favor. Nonetheless, the point remains that the complexity of administrative contexts, the contingency of future events, and the flexibility required for effectiveness are simply too great for "deck-stacking" to neutralize the consequences of delegation in expanding the contours of executive discretion. For similar reasons, plus the burdens of the workload, the limits of post-hoc control, and weak political incentives, oversight provides an instrument for controlling executive discretion that is highly variable in its effectiveness. Inevitably, then, delegation confers policy power and the cumulative result over the course of the twentieth century was to create what can fairly be described as an administrative state. On the limits of congressional dominance through "deck-stacking" or oversight, see Terry Moe, "An Assessment of the Theory of Congressional Dominance," *Legislative Studies Quarterly* 12 (1987): 475–520; William West, "Searching for a Theory of Bureaucratic Structure," *Journal of Public Administration Research and Theory* 7 (1997): 591–613; Joel Aberbach, *Keeping a Watchful Eye* (Washington, D.C.: Brookings Institution, 1990); and David Epstein and Sharyn O'Halloran, *Delegating Powers* (Cambridge: Cambridge University Press, 1999), 73. On the limits of committee reform as a means of enhancing congressional control, see Melissa Collie and Joseph

Cooper, "Multiple Referral and the 'New' Committee System," in *Congress Reconsidered*, ed. Lawrence C. Dodd and Bruce I. Oppenheimer, 4th ed. (Washington, D.C.: CQ Press, 1989), 245–72, and David King, *Turf Wars* (Chicago: University of Chicago Press, 1997), 137–49.

13. For broad analysis of the decline in congressional power in relation to the president, see Lawrence C. Dodd, "Congress and the Politics of Renewal," in *Congress Reconsidered*, ed. Lawrence C. Dodd and Bruce I. Oppenheimer, 5th ed. (Washington, D.C.: CQ Press, 1993), 417–46. See also Cooper, "Strengthening the Congress," and Theodore Lowi, *The Personal President* (Ithaca, N.Y.: Cornell University Press, 1985). With reference to specific facets of the relationship between Congress and the president, see Louis Fisher, *Constitutional Conflicts between Congress and the President* (Lawrence: University Press of Kansas, 1997); Gordon Silverstein, *Imbalance of Power* (New York: Oxford University Press, 1997); Barbara Hinckley, *Less than Meets the Eye* (Chicago: University of Chicago Press, 1994); Joseph Cooper and William West, "The Theory and Practice of OMB Review of Agency Rules," *Journal of Politics* 50 (November 1988): 864–95; Kenneth Mayer, "Executive Orders and Presidential Power," *Journal of Politics* 61 (May 1999): 445–66; and Bruce I. Oppenheimer, "Abdicating Congressional Power: The Paradox of Republican Control," in *Congress Reconsidered*, ed. Lawrence C. Dodd and Bruce I. Oppenheimer, 6th ed. (Washington, D.C.: CQ Press, 1997), 371–90.

14. On public expectations and beliefs regarding the character and processes of representative government and the patterns of trust in national political institutions and elected politicians, see James Morone, *The Democratic Wish* (New York: Basic Books, 1990); John Hibbing and Elizabeth Theiss-Morse, *Congress as Public Enemy* (Cambridge: Cambridge University Press, 1995); Joseph Cooper, ed., *Congress and the Decline of Public Trust* (Boulder, Colo.: Westview Press, 1999); and Donald Wolfensberger, *Congress and the People* (Washington, D.C.: Woodrow Wilson Center Press, 2000). On the critical role of trust in relations between representatives and constituents, see Richard Fenno Jr., "U.S. House Members in Their Constituencies," *American Political Science Review* 71 (September 1977): 883–917.

15. On the increased role of the media and the rise of plebiscitary politics, see Stephen Ansolabehere et al., *The Media Game: American Politics in the Television Age* (Boston: Allyn and Bacon, 1993); Timothy Cook, *Governing with the News* (Chicago: University of Chicago Press, 1998); Lowi, *The Personal President;* Jeffrey Cohen, *Presidential Responsiveness and Public Policy-Making* (Ann Arbor: University of Michigan Press, 1999); and Douglas Harris, "The Rise of the Public Speakership," *Political Science Quarterly* 113 (Summer 1998): 193–212.

16. On the role of the filibuster, restrictive rules, omnibus bills, and party task forces in the modern Congress, see Barbara Sinclair, *Unorthodox Lawmaking*, 2d ed. (Washington, D.C.: CQ Press, 2000). On the decline of civility, see Eric Uslaner, *The Decline of Comity in Congress* (Ann Arbor: University of Michigan Press, 1993), and Burdett Loomis, ed., *Esteemed Colleagues: Civility and Deliberation in the U.S. Senate* (Washington, D.C.: Brookings Institution, 2000).

17. The fact that patterns of politics are not fixed but vary in relation to levels of trust and expectation is well grounded, even in rational choice theory. See Fritz Scharpf, *Games Real Actors Play* (Boulder, Colo.: Westview Press, 1997), 72–89. See also Elinor Ostrom, "A Behavioral Approach to the Rational Choice Theory of Collective Action," *American Political Science Review* 92 (March 1998): 1–23.

18. The basic thought, quite appropriately, is from *Julius Caesar*, act 1, scene 2.

16. Congress and the Emerging Order: Assessing the 2000 Elections

Lawrence C. Dodd and Bruce I. Oppenheimer

The 2000 election results reinforce the growing perception that Congress and American politics are entering a new partisan era. Only twice between 1930 and 1994—in 1946 and 1952—had Republicans won simultaneous majorities in the House of Representatives and the Senate. Both times their majority status lasted only two years. By narrow margins in both the House and Senate in 2000, Republicans have won control of Congress for four consecutive elections and appear well-positioned to benefit from reapportionment politics and defend their congressional majorities in the 2002 elections. They sustained their control of Congress, moreover, during one of the closest and most hotly contested presidential elections in American history. The election results for both Congress and the presidency appear to reflect a deep partisan divide in American politics and, along with the partisan character of congressional politics in the mid- to late-1990s, seem to point toward the emergence of a new political order.

In this chapter we discuss factors that could define the new political order and consider how the results of the 2000 elections could shape and alter those factors. In doing so, we focus particularly on whether unified, aggressive partisanship, most visible to the public during the government shutdown of late-1995 and during the impeachment proceedings against President Bill Clinton three years later, is likely to dominate Congress in the future.

John Aldrich and David Rohde, in chapter 12 of this volume and elsewhere, make a compelling case that "conditional party government," characterized by significant conflict between the two congressional parties, was the dominant characteristic of Congress during the 1990s and will likely remain so. By reinstating homogeneous and conservative Republican majorities in both houses, the 2000 elections provide strong reason to suspect that Aldrich and Rohde could well be correct.

Although we agree with Aldrich and Rohde that the 1990s was an extraordinary period of aggressive partisanship, we believe that several factors may alter and constrain conditional party government over the next decade or two. At issue is whether conditional party government is the inherent and dominant model of the new era. The 2000 elections yielded some results that appear to mandate a continuance of conditional party government as described by Aldrich and Rohde. Other aspects of the election suggest that conditional party government may be difficult for the Republicans to sustain. Instead, competing forms of rational behavior may arise and result in more muted, complicated forms of partisanship.

Our purpose in this chapter is to clarify the implications that the 2000 elections have for the creation of a new partisan order in Congress. We first discuss the nature of conditional party government and some alternative models of partisan behavior. We then examine the 2000 election results in detail and discuss four ways in which the results of the election, together with broader contextual factors, might impose constraints on conditional party government. In conclusion, we suggest that a party intent on keeping control of Congress may have to move beyond strict conditional party government and embrace a constructive partisanship that demonstrates its capacity to govern. A failure to govern constructively could hinder the party's ability to solidify control of Congress and the national government despite some considerable advantages that would seem to predict success.

The Creation of Conditional Party Government

Because parties contest elections, organize Congress, and control the distribution of institutional resources, the new era will presumably be shaped by the nature of the partisanship that develops in Congress and American politics. The strongest form of partisanship is traditional party government, in which the parties control nominations and electoral resources, present candidates who promise to adhere to the party agenda, and run issue-oriented, party-dominated campaigns. In a parliamentary system, in which the winning party controls both the legislature and the government ministries, the party implements its agenda and governs by relying on the cohesive loyalty of party members. Party loyalty is reinforced by the rewards and resources controlled by party leaders, particularly the prime minister.[1]

National party government of this sort is seldom if ever possible in the United States, because the nation's regional complexity, size, and social diversity make it unlikely that a large group of citizens and politicians will share homogenous policy preferences across all salient policy issues.[2] State control of election laws, the widespread use of party primaries, and a party organization that is based in states all make it difficult for a national party to prescribe nominations of congressional candidates or ensure agreement among members on a policy agenda. Separation of powers, bicameralism, and the existence of a popularly elected and powerful president further complicate the system, so that party leaders cannot exercise firm control over the government and its resources. And constitutionally prescribed election dates deprive congressional leaders of the ability to encourage cooperation by threatening to call early elections, as parliamentary leaders can. Thus, built into the American system are institutional divisions and constitutional prescriptions that make unified party government across policy domains unlikely at best and short-lived should it ever occur.

Beginning in the 1980s and coming into full flower in the 1990s is a model of party behavior, referred to as conditional party government by Aldrich and Rohde, that is less encompassing than traditional party government in parliamentary systems but considerably more developed than party government has been in the past eighty years in this country.[3] Conditional party government exists when a party pursues the dominant or median position of its members across a broad (though not exhaustive) array of policy areas. Aldrich and Rohde posit that conditional party government emerges when the parties' officeholders are in relatively homogeneous agreement on policy but the two parties hold distinctly separated or polarized positions.[4] Under these conditions of high intraparty agreement and high interparty difference, members (usually in the majority party) will cede substantial authority to their party leaders so that the leaders can facilitate the coordination and cooperation of their members in behalf of the common agenda. The majority party achieves high levels of cohesive party voting, in opposition to the minority party. In the strictest form of conditional party government, the governing majority depends on the votes of the majority party and does not need support from the minority.

As opposed to traditional party government, in which leaders hold the rank and file together to support a comprehensive program, conditional party government allows leaders to act only where the party is already highly united. It is therefore limited in scope to areas of widespread agreement and limited in time to periods of agreement. Moreover, since it is the congressional party caucus that gives its leaders their authority and prerogatives, the caucus can bring a leader down without changing the shape of national government or facing new elections, should leaders pressure them too aggressively or show poor judgment in crafting party strategies. Conditional party government thus is not only a weaker and less encompassing form of partisanship than traditional party government; it also leaves congressional party leaders in a considerably more vulnerable and defenseless position, compared to parliamentary leaders.

In the process of constructing and passing party legislation, leaders use strategies, rewards, and sanctions to encourage members who deviate from the party median in their behavior in committees and on the floor to move back to the median position. Leaders can do so because party members have electoral, policy, and influence goals that conditional party government may serve.[5] In particular, when the electorate is polarized on an issue in a manner that parallels an agenda difference between the legislative parties, conditional party government can serve multiple goals. It builds a base for reelection by enacting policies desired by majorities in members' constituencies and enables members to achieve their personal policy preferences. Conditional party government ensures that the party retains majority status in the legislature when its policy positions reflect the dominant policy concerns of a polarized electorate, and that its members maintain their personal power within the institution.[6]

Because conditional party government can be attempted only when a party has reasonable preference homogeneity, it has not been the norm for American parties over the past century. Rather, the parties have been characterized by internal divisions and preference heterogeneity: the Democratic Party was divided between a conservative southern wing and a liberal northern wing, and the Republican Party was divided between its liberal eastern establishment and more conservative western members. However, as southern conservative voters left the Democratic Party in response to the expansion of civil rights and joined the

Republicans, and as northern liberal Republican voters left their increasingly conservative party to join the national Democratic Party, the social conditions became ripe for conditional party government. In response, from the mid-1970s to the late-1980s, the Democrats, growing more liberal, strengthened their party leaders and organization within Congress, and the Republicans resorted to policy and procedural obstruction, especially in the House, to block liberal policymaking.[7]

Conditional party government blossomed in the 1990s, first in the 103d Congress, when the Democrats tried to use their control of Congress to enact President Clinton's legislative agenda, then in the 104th Congress, when the Republicans attempted to use their control to enact the Contract with America. Its highwater mark may well have come at the end of the 105th Congress, as House Republicans moved with near-unanimity to impeach the Democratic president, Bill Clinton, and during the first session of the 106th Congress, as partisan animosities continued to poison congressional deliberations. It then receded during 2000 as Speaker Hastert led the House to a more conciliatory stance toward President Clinton and helped enact legislation granting normal trade relations with China that the president badly wanted.

At issue for the 107th Congress and thereafter is whether conditional party government will prove to be the dominant pattern in a new partisan order or a transitory phase that is followed by a return to a more muted partisanship. In the sixth edition of *Congress Reconsidered,* Joseph Cooper and Garry Young detailed alternative forms of partisan behavior that could replace conditional party government.[8] These more muted forms of partisan behavior could include a constrained partisanship, in which the majority party votes cohesively and dominates the legislative process, but does so in pursuit of a moderated party agenda that is more centrist than that of the party; crosspartisanship, in which the legislative majority depends on a coalition between a slight majority of one party and a slight majority of the other; or bipartisanship, in which large majorities of both parties support the median position of the legislature.

A number of factors may mitigate against conditional party government and in favor of a moderated partisanship. In particular, voters can send messages in elections that limit a party's mandate, or they can elect a closely divided Congress, which undercuts the ability of leaders to maintain firm control of congressional policymaking by relying solely on their own party. We now will consider whether the 2000 elections may have imposed such constraints on congressional Republicans and limited their opportunity for conditional party government.

The 2000 Congressional Elections

On the surface the 2000 House and Senate elections mirror the presidential election in terms of their closeness. The Republican majorities elected to the 107th Congress will be the slimmest of any party since the 83d Congress. With an edge of only nine seats over the Democrats in the House and a fifty–fifty tie in the Senate, in which the Republicans are likely to be the majority party,[9] the

Republicans may possess numerical majorities. But, as will the new president, they will lack a mandate to govern. The composition of the two houses of Congress, as does the closeness of the popular and electoral college votes for president, attests to the evenness of the division within the American electorate. However, the close partisan divisions in Congress do not reflect a high level of competitiveness for individual congressional seats. Just as most of the states were carried easily by Gore or by Bush, with the most notable exception being Florida, most of the congressional races were not closely contested, especially those for the House. Thus, although the closeness of the partisan divisions in Congress may suggest the need for compromise between the parties, individual members may not have incentives to seek middle-ground positions. They represent districts with distinct liberal Democratic or conservative Republican constituencies.

One reason often cited for the low level of competitiveness in congressional elections is the success rate of incumbents. Whether it is due to incumbents' ability to use their offices for reelection purposes, their fund-raising advantages, or the absence of strong, experienced challengers, the track record of incumbents, especially in House contests, is very good. The 2000 election was no exception. With a strong economy and few issues providing a national partisan swing, incumbents fared very well. Of the 400 House incumbents running in the general election, over 98 percent won reelection. Only six incumbents—two Democrats and four Republicans—were defeated.[10] That rate is comparable to the two previous highs in 1988 and 1998. Also contributing to the low level of competitiveness was the small number, as in 1988 and 1998, of open seats. Incumbents had little incentive to retire, because few feared strong challengers at a time when the electorate viewed conditions in the country so favorably.

The low rate of turnover in House seats, accordingly, came as no surprise. Various estimates throughout the campaign season suggested that 10 percent or fewer of the House races had some chance of being competitive. And the results bear out those predictions. For only 24 of the 435 House seats was the contest truly close, with the winner's margin 6 percent or less of the vote.

To conclude, however, that the low level of competitiveness in House races simply reflects the continued value of incumbency misses an important change that has been occurring in American politics. As John Alford and David Brady argued in an earlier edition of *Congress Reconsidered*, it is important to distinguish between the personal incumbency advantage that accrues because of things like resource advantages and weak challengers and that which accrues from the partisan composition of the incumbent's district and the strength of partisanship in influencing voters' choices.[11] Recent research by Gary Jacobson demonstrates an increasing congruence between the partisan composition of House districts and the party affiliation of the House member representing those districts. Although in the 1970s and 1980s it was not uncommon to find districts voting for one party's presidential candidate and electing the other party's candidate for the House, such districts were far rarer in the 1990s. In addition, Jacobson finds increasing partisan polarization among voters, following the growth in polarization that had occurred among House members and among party activists.[12] Prelimi-nary examination of the data from the 2000 election suggests that the trend Jacobson presented continues. The low level of competitiveness in House races may be more a consequence of the partisan divisions in congressional districts and less a consequence of the personal incumbency advantages of individual members.

Of course, one would be correct in noting that much of the play in the 2000 House elections came in open seat contests, with twelve of the thirty-five open seats switching party. In ten of those twelve races, however, the partisan compo-sition of the districts was competitive.[13]

As in the three previous Congresses, the House in the 107th is largely made up of members who comfortably fit into one of the two polarized and cohesive par-ties. There are perhaps ten to at most twenty moderates in each party. As the size of the majority party has shrunk, those moderates increasingly hold sway in build-ing winning coalitions. But the mainstream of the two parties may prefer gridlock to compromise. After all, almost all represent districts where their reelection bids will be safely backed by either liberal Democrats or conservative Republicans. The collective goals of their parties and leaders, in the case of the Republicans, to main-tain and expand their majority, or, in the case of the Democrats, to return to major-ity status, may not be sufficient to offset their individual preferences.

By comparison, the 2000 Senate elections were far more competitive. Still, only nine of the thirty-four Senate races were decided by 6 percent or less. The outcome of more than half the contests was never in doubt, and many others strongly favored one of the candidates.

In addition, Senate incumbents had a lower rate of reelection than did House incumbents. Only about 80 percent of Senate incumbents who sought reelection were victorious. Given the partisan advantage that Republican candi-dates had in 1994, when this class of senators was last elected, the Democratic gains were hardly surprising. Not only were the Republicans more exposed, hold-ing nineteen of the thirty-four seats at stake in the election; nine of the Repub-lican incumbents had first been elected in the 1994 midterm landslide. Demo-cratic challengers defeated three of those incumbents, all in competitive midwestern states. The sole Democratic incumbent to lose, Charles Robb, Va., had barely survived the 1994 challenge of Oliver North, the controversial candi-date of a deeply divided Republican state party. In addition, five of the thirty-four incumbents chose not to seek another term, a retirement rate nearly twice as high as in the House. Democrats captured the one formerly Republican open seat and won three of four from which Democratic incumbents were retiring.

As in the House, the question remains whether senators will have the incen-tive to compromise in a closely divided chamber. Because more of them (in per-centage terms) represent constituencies that remain party competitive, senators may be more willing than House members to work to find common ground. On the other hand, two-thirds of them know that they will not have to face the vot-ers in 2002. And the cloture rule in the Senate ensures that either party will have enough votes to block narrow majority coalitions.

The regional divisions of the two parties' membership in the House and the Senate continue to be evident in the 107th Congress. (See Tables 16-1 and 16-2.) In the Senate, the base of the Republican Party strength since the 104th Congress has been in the South and the West. Not including the six Democratic senators from Florida, California, and Hawaii (states not typical of their regions), Republican senators in the 107th Congress will outnumber Democrats in the South and West combined by a nearly three-to-one margin. Meanwhile, the Democrats have incrementally increased their Senate seat margins in both the East and the Midwest. In fact, the Democratic margins in those two regions are the same as in the 103d Congress, when the Democrats held a fifty-seven–forty-three majority. The control the Republicans have in the Senate in the 107th Congress rests largely on net gains they made in the 1994 elections in the South and the West, to which they have made small additions.

These regional distinctions in the Senate are particularly important as we look to the 2002 elections. Even more than in 2000, the class of Senate seats to be contested in 2002 is heavily weighted with Republican incumbents. Twenty of the thirty-four seats are in Republican hands. Sixteen of those incumbents, however, come from the South and the West, the strongest regions for Republicans (and only one of those is from a Pacific Coast state). Even if a number of the anticipated retirements occur, creating open seats, Republicans are likely to be favored to hold most of those seats.

In the House the regional picture is somewhat different. In no region is one party as dominant as is the case in the Senate. In the South and in the East, where the Republicans and Democrats respectively have their biggest margins, the minority party still holds 40 percent of the seats. In the population-based House, Democrats fare far better in the West than they do in the Senate, because of the party's strength in California, Washington, and Oregon. Republican dominance is in the low-population Rocky Mountain states. In the Midwest, Republicans have done better in the House than in the Senate, continuing to hold a majority of House seats since the 1994 elections.

The reallocation of House seats among the states and redrawing of district lines, to reflect the 2000 Census results, creates uncertainties about the 2002 House elections. Although some may wish to speculate about the net effects reapportionment and redistricting will have on party fortunes, we believe that it is premature to do so. Even when one party dominates the redistricting process in a state, it may be cross-pressured by those wanting to maximize the party's total number of seats and incumbents wanting to make their districts even safer. There will likely be an increase in the number of open seats, especially compared with 1998 and 2000. A larger number of open seats raises the potential for greater partisan seat swings. And given that 1998 was only the first midterm election since 1934 in which the party of the president made net gains in the midterm elections, the 2002 elections could have consequences for the president's party that far exceed the partisan effects of reapportionment and redistricting.

Table 16-1   Distribution of Senate Seats, 1994–2000, and Seats to be
Contested in 2002 (by Party and Region)

	East	Midwest	South	West	Total
104th Congress*					
Democrats	14	13	10	10	47
Republicans	10	11	16	16	53
105th Congress					
Democrats	14	13	8	10	45
Republicans	10	11	18	16	55
106th Congress					
Democrats	15	12	8	10	45
Republicans	9	12	18	16	55
107th Congress**					
Democrats	16	15	9	10	50
Republicans	8	9	17	16	50
108th (contested seats)					
Democrats	5	6	2	1	14
Republicans	2	2	10	6	20

East = Conn., Del., Maine, Md., Mass., N.H., N.J., N.Y., Pa., R.I., Vt., W.Va. *Midwest* = Ill., Ind., Iowa, Kan., Mich., Minn., Mo., Neb., N.D., Ohio, S.D., Wis. *South* = Ala., Ark., Fla., Ga., Ky., La., Miss., N.C., Okla., S.C., Tenn., Texas, Va. *West* = Alaska, Ariz., Calif., Colo., Hawaii, Idaho, Mont., Nev., N.M., Ore., Utah, Wash., Wyo.

*For the purposes of this table Richard Shelby, Ala., who switched parties shortly after the 1994 election, is counted as a Republican, but Ben Nighthorse Campbell, Colo., who switched parties after the first session began, is counted as a Democrat in calculating the partisan composition of the 104th Congress.

**The totals for the 107th Congress assume that Maria Cantwell, Wash., is the winner of the Washington Senate contest.

An increase in open seats would also create opportunities for increasing the number of women and minority members in the House. With only thirty-five open seats in the 2000 elections, the opportunities to elect more women and minorities were limited. The 107th Congress will have four new Democratic and three new Republican women. Because of retirements, however, the net increase will be only two women Democrats (for a total of forty-one) and one Republican (for a total of eighteen). This continues the incremental growth of women House members, following the marked increase in the 1992 elections. There was not a similar increase in African American or Hispanic representation in the House in either the 2000 election or in the three prior elections. The 2000 election produced no net gains for either group. Since the 103d Congress, the number of African American House members has actually declined by two, and there has been an increase of only two Hispanic Americans. The House in the 107th Con-

Table 16-2 Distribution of House Seats, 1994–2000 (by Party and Region)

	East	Midwest	South	West	Total
104th Congress					
Democrats	54	46	64	40	204
Republicans	45	59	73	53	230
other	1				1
105th Congress					
Democrats	60	50	55	43	208
Republicans	39	55	82	50	226
other	1				1
106th Congress					
Democrats	61	51	55	44	211
Republicans	38	54	82	49	223
other	1				1
107th Congress*					
Democrats	59	48	55	50	212
Republicans	40	57	81	43	221
other	1		1		2

East = Conn., Del., Maine, Md., Mass., N.H., N.J., N.Y., Pa., R.I., Vt., W.Va. *Midwest* = Ill., Ind., Iowa, Kan., Mich., Minn., Mo., Neb., N.D., Ohio, S.D., Wis. *South* = Ala., Ark., Fla., Ga., Ky., La., Miss., N.C., Okla., S.C., Tenn., Texas, Va. *West* = Alaska, Ariz., Calif., Colo., Hawaii, Idaho, Mont., Nev., N.M., Ore., Utah, Wash., Wyo.

*At the time this table was constructed the partisan outcome of two House seats, one in Florida and one in New Jersey, was still in doubt. For the purposes of this table each seat is credited to the party of the incumbent in the respective contest.

gress thus will contain thirty-seven African American members—thirty-six Democrats and one Republican—and nineteen Hispanic members—sixteen Democrats and three Republicans. There are no African American or Hispanic members of the Senate.

In the Senate, where there were proportionately more open seats, women made substantial gains. Pending the final outcome of the Washington Senate contest, there will likely be four new women senators, all Democrats. Kay Bailey Hutchison, Texas, easily won reelection, but she was the only woman Republican candidate running in the thirty-four Senate contests. Accordingly, in both the House and the Senate, the gender gap not only continues to exist but is widening.

The initial picture created by the 2000 elections, thus, would seem to portray a Congress poised for conditional party government. The two congressional parties appear as polarized in demographic, policy, and electoral terms as they have been at any time in contemporary politics. The bitter fight over the presidency in the aftermath of the election seems likely to enflame partisan divisions in the new Congress and reinforce the pressure toward conditional party government. It is thus tempting to expect that conditional party government will dominate the new

Congress, pushing it further toward a long-term era of extreme partisanship. This expectation is reinforced by evidence provided by Jeffrey Stonecash in *Class and Party in American Politics* suggesting that the growth of deep, class-based polarization within the American electorate could sustain such partisan conflict in Congress.[14] On the other hand, despite the partisan bitterness over impeachment in 1998, by the second session of the 106th Congress a surprising degree of moderation and level-headedness had returned to Congress. Although there are several factors pushing Congress toward conditional party government, there are also factors constraining or limiting its consolidation. Let us now address such potential constraints, in light of the 2000 elections, and their implications for Congress.

Constraints on Conditional Party Government

Under what conditions might congressional parties be homogeneous and polarized and yet be restrained from aggressive pursuit of conditional party government? Aldrich and Rohde acknowledge that complicating circumstances can limit members' ability to realize their personal goals through the pursuit of conditional party government and push them toward other strategies of governing, even when the parties are relatively homogeneous and polarized. Here we will discuss four such circumstances and consider how they might undermine the emergence of conditional party government as the dominant mode of partisan behavior in Congress.

Close Seat Distribution between Parties

Our first concern is with how the partisan distribution of seats in Congress can influence whether conditional party government can be created and sustained. It is generally agreed that a governing party with a large majority will likely be unable to maintain internal cohesion or sustain strong leadership coordination of party activities.[15] Such a majority will usually emerge in a landslide party victory that brings in a number of members from outside the party's political base and who therefore deviate in critical ways from the party's dominant policy positions. The result is a heterogeneous and factionalized membership that is not amenable to cohesive and coordinated party government.

When a governing party has a modest majority, the possibility for conditional party government increases. Such a majority may naturally be more homogeneous than a large majority, because it is unlikely to contain deviant members elected in a party landslide. Yet it is not so large that policy victory is always guaranteed. The party may need leaders strong enough to successfully negotiate with small groups of members at committee and floor stages, to craft legislation that reflects the party's median policy concerns, and to overcome the procedural obstacles generated by opponents.

It does not follow, however, that close party seat divisions facilitate conditional party government. As the seats controlled by each party approach an equal number, the modest cushion of votes enjoyed by the governing party disappears, and the party must rely on a narrow majority to govern. Under such circumstances, a governing party may have to construct a near consensual level of membership coordination and vote cohesion, which can be difficult to achieve even in conditions of membership homogeneity and party polarization. The loss of support from just a few party members can defeat bills or force leaders to rely on votes from the other party, undercutting the majority party's claim to full credit for the legislation. Or it can encourage party leaders to forego bringing legislation to floor vote, so that the party fails to address critical policy problems and suffers a loss of public support.

The leaders' fear of losing on critical policy votes in a closely divided legislature, combined with their equally important need to build a viable legislative record, gives increased bargaining leverage to party moderates. The policy positions of moderates are more centrist than those of the party as a whole, but the party cannot win without them. Centrists can bargain for moderated policy positions before they agree to vote with the party. As the party becomes more moderate, it moves away from the median position of party members and toward the median policy preferences of the legislature as a whole. This movement undercuts the party's ability to govern in behalf of its dominant policy orientations and shifts the legislature away from conditional party government, with its strongly partisan voting patterns, and toward more muted and complicated forms of partisanship, such as a more constrained partisanship, cross-party coalitions, or bipartisanship.

Alternatively, a majority party may narrow its policy agenda so markedly that the conditional party government conceptualization applies to an increasingly small fragment of the nation's policy concerns. The party may refuse to allow conflictual policy issues to reach floor vote, thus maintaining an appearance of high cohesion on roll-call votes that masks intraparty division. Continued avoidance of a significant range of policy issues, however, would appear to throw into question whether meaningful conditional party government actually exists, regardless of the cohesiveness the party maintains in roll-call votes on the limited range of issues it addresses. It would appear particularly inappropriate to use the conditional party government label to characterize a party should it avoid addressing central issues on which it campaigned and that are important to much of its support base, such as legislation regulating social morality promised by the Republican Party to the Christian Right. The very purpose of "party government" is to govern in behalf of the party's core constituencies, not to avoid issues dearest to them.

Close party division within a legislature can therefore threaten meaningful conditional party government. It can do so, moreover, even when parties hold distinct policy positions and attain a high degree of homogeneity. This concern is particularly relevant to the 107th Congress (2001–2003), in which there are close seat divisions in both the House and Senate. It could complicate the Republican Party's ability to sustain strong conditional party government. In the

104th Congress (1995–1997), the Republicans enjoyed a relatively modest majority, where an eighteen to twenty seat shift would have been required to move the Republicans to minority status. But over the subsequent three elections their cushion of votes steadily decreased, so that by the 107th Congress their seat margin will be roughly ten seats. This close margin could embolden some less conservative Republicans to push for moderation or to join with Democrats on critical votes, as happened at the end of the 104th Congress on the vote to increase the minimum wage.

The Republicans face a particularly difficult problem in the Senate. As indicated by Barbara Sinclair's discussion in chapter 1, most major legislation must pass the upper chamber by the sixty-vote margin needed for a filibuster-proof majority. With a seemingly even division between Republicans and Democrats in the Senate following the 2000 elections, the Republicans in the 107th Congress would need the support of 20 percent of the Democratic caucus in order to pass key bills. (Moreover, Republican Senate losses in the 2000 election were all among party loyalists — Spencer Abraham, Mich., John Ashcroft, Mo., Slade Gorton, Wash., Rod Grams, Minn., and William Roth, Del., lost their elections, and in addition Connie Mack, Fla., retired — not among moderates such as Lincoln Chafee, R.I., James Jeffords, Vt., and Olympia Snowe, Maine, who were reelected in states carried by Gore.) The realization that Senate legislation will require significant support from Democrats (and Republican moderates) may encourage Republican centrists in both houses to push for moderation in their party's policy positions.

Competitive Seats

The willingness of members to support conditional party government can also depend on how competitive their districts are. When members serve districts whose constituents generally support their party and its policy positions, they are more likely to cooperate with party leaders, occasionally take some controversial stands that constituents might oppose, and vote cohesively with the party's median position. But when members come from competitive districts with a substantial presence of independents or supporters of the opposition party, they may face some significant reelection costs for supporting conditional party government. These members will be inclined to pay close attention to the median position of their constituency, which would lie between the two parties, rather than the median position of their legislative party. Although the median position of their constituency cannot dominate members' voting decisions — because they also need to win primary elections and therefore must please voters of their own party — members who represent competitive districts will have to find ways to moderate their policy behavior in order to appeal to their broader constituency. Such calculations should lead them to deviate from strict adherence to the median position of their party and to push for moderation of the party's policy behavior.

When members from competitive districts try to influence their party to moderate its policies, they have special bargaining leverage. The leaders and most members may want to enact the party's dominant policy position, but all have a collective stake in the reelection of the members from competitive districts. These members could be defeated if they supported the party's dominant policies, or perhaps even if the policies were implemented without their support. (And with very narrow majorities, Republican leaders cannot afford to let moderates "go off the reservation" as easily as they could in previous Congresses.) With their defeat, a party may lose its control of the legislature. For this reason, party leaders and other members must be sensitive to the policy concerns of electorally vulnerable members, particularly if they are numerous or if control rests on a small number of seats. Even party members from safe districts whose constituents whole-heartedly support their party's policies may fear that an aggressive pursuit of party government could lead to the defeat of vulnerable party incumbents, and thus to the party's loss of legislative control. For this reason they may support policy moderation.

A consideration of such individual and collective concerns, taken together, suggests that the Republican Party could face moderating pressures in the 107th Congress and thereafter, particularly in the Senate. In the Senate, where many Republican members come from relatively heterogeneous states with competitive party systems, there is a natural hesitancy to pursue narrow partisan policies as aggressively as have Republicans in the House—the failure of several Senate Republicans to support conviction of President Clinton being a very visible manifestation of this caution. In addition, with a number of Republican senators up for reelection in 2002, individual members may push for party moderation because they want to avoid the sort of bruising partisan conflict that might encourage and fuel a strong Democratic challenge.

Looking to the 2002 elections, most House members should feel relatively safe, based on their victory margins in 2000, but they may be concerned that the party could lose control were the members from competitive Republican seats to lose reelection. The survival of the Republican majority in 2000 depended in part on unexpected successes in midwestern and northeastern districts; to survive in 2002, the new Republican incumbents in those seats may need to take a more moderate position on key legislation than their southern and southwestern colleagues, restraining the conservatism of the party's legislative agenda. These collective considerations may lead House Republicans to moderate their legislative stance, at least through the 2002 elections, particularly if other developments in the economy or national politics point toward off-year seat losses for incumbents or for congressional Republicans. Should the party pick up a substantial number of seats in 2002 as a result of reapportionment and redistricting, then it may become more aggressive in its policymaking. All of these considerations assume that the structure of policy conflict in the nation will remain relatively constant, so that the parties will not suddenly be confronted with divisive internal struggles or external shifts in public opinion.

The Cross-Cutting Structure of Policy Conflict

Conditional party government in Congress is always fragile and tentative, because it can occur only as long as no serious intraparty divisions develop on pressing policy questions. Party members may be willing to give their leaders considerable resources if they can help the party govern effectively in areas of agreement, and if they believe that the leaders will not pressure members in areas where general agreement does not exist. In actual practice, it is virtually impossible for party members to limit leaders' use of power to the areas of general agreement. Skillful leaders understand that they can undermine their hold on power if they use it cavalierly; therefore, members can generally trust the leaders to focus only on the issues on which there is preference homogeneity. If party leaders violate that trust, support for strong leaders and conditional party government may dissipate.

The greatest threat to conditional party government comes from the emergence of salient policy issues that are critical to the party's governing success, and on which party members seriously disagree. In such situations, party leaders may be tempted to use their power to ensure that the governing party remains cohesive and effective, and perhaps they may even feel compelled to do so to demonstrate the party's ability to govern and maintain its national support. If leaders insist on unity in areas of deep intraparty division, they can generate rebellion. This is precisely what occurred in 1910 when progressive Republicans, angered by Speaker Joseph Cannon's use of his leadership power to push conservative policies, joined with Democrats to strip the Speakership of most of its power.[16]

The question facing the congressional Republicans is whether the nation has entered a period in which its policy conflicts will remain polarized along partisan lines for some time, so that Republicans can freely embrace conditional party government, or whether some intense and cross-cutting "wedge" issues will emerge that are central to the governing responsibility of a majority party and also divisive. (Aldrich and Rohde acknowledge the latter possibility but minimize its likelihood.) Perhaps the most critical test the Republicans will face is their ability to sustain a coalition between southern social conservatives, whose concern over segregation and traditional values divided the Democratic Party for decades, and traditional fiscal conservatives, who have long been the backbone of the party.

As Theodore Lowi argues in *The End of the Republican Era*, the move of the southern conservatives to the Republican side has introduced a social conservatism into the party, ranging across issues such as race relations, abortion, school prayer, gay rights, and government assistance for the underprivileged, that is distinctly different from the economic conservatism of most northern and western Republicans.[17] Southern social conservatism envisions a government that uses its power to support traditional moral values but that opposes using government for social goals such as reducing poverty and social betterment. Traditional economic conservatives in the Republican Party want a government that supports capitalist enterprise, limits its regulatory role in economic matters, and restrains its taxation of business. These Republicans are usually social moderates who accept diversity in personal values and lifestyles and support some degree of government action in behalf of minorities, the disadvantaged, and general societal improvement.

The detrimental effects of this intraparty division can be seen at the presidential level, where social conservatives have demanded party platforms and presidential nominees firmly committed to pro-life policies and similar moral positions. As a consequence many traditional Republicans who support more moderate social positions abandoned the party in presidential elections, which contributed to the humiliating defeat of two Republican presidential candidates in the 1990s and the extraordinary closeness of the contest between Texas governor George W. Bush and Vice President Al Gore. In this last instance the Republican candidate downplayed the party's conservative social agenda during the general election with tacit cooperation from the party's right wing, which remained largely invisible during the fall campaign after having provided Bush his margin of victory in critical primary contests with Sen. John McCain of Arizona. Social conservatives are unlikely to remain quiet during a period of unified Republican government, however, particularly if they believe that their efforts were critical to its creation, and they could push legislation that would challenge the survival of conditional party government.

Because congressional majorities are built on a district-by-district basis across the nation, the Republicans have been able to finesse their intraparty division by emphasizing different forms of conservatism in different regions. They have succeeded in submerging these differences because much of their governing effort has focused on opposing or restraining the legislative agenda of the Democratic president. Yet these intraparty differences are real, and they could well rise to the fore in a period of united Republican government. Also of concern is that the social conservatism of many southern Republicans has intensified their economic conservatism. Even in areas of greatest party agreement—fiscal policy and regulatory restraint—the southern and southwestern Republicans tend to emphasize a strong hostility toward government, and northern and western Republicans tend to accept some government involvement in economic and social policy. This division is apparent across a variety of issues: minimum wage increases, environmental protection, education policy, welfare reform, and entitlement control. All of these policy conflicts, moreover, involve issues that will be central to effective governance in the years ahead.

As the Republican Party attempts to solidify its position as the nation's governing congressional party, and particularly should it also control the presidency, its members will have to build a governing record that addresses social, economic, and moral issues on a continuing basis, and they will have to do so despite the fault line dividing southern and non-southern members. While in the minority, or as the new majority congressional party opposing a Democratic president, the Republicans have maintained cohesiveness in opposing the legislation proposed by the Democratic majority or Democratic president. But once established as a seasoned majority party, the Republicans will be increasingly judged by how well they craft and enact a legislative agenda of their own. It can prove much more difficult to maintain cohesion across policy domains in support of specific legislation than it is to maintain cohesion in opposition to legislation. Groups across an ideological spectrum can often find specific reasons to unite and oppose legislation, with different groups focusing on different concerns. But crafting an agreement in support of legislation that reaches across social divides can be quite difficult. Such difficulties can be magnified, as Lyndon Johnson and the Great Society Democrats discovered, should conflicts over foreign policy split the governing party and undercut cooperation among members on its domestic agenda.

The longer Republicans are in power in Congress, the harder it may be to suppress their internal policy differences and the more likely it is that a wedge issue may arise to divide them and tear conditional party government apart. These considerations will be even more important if a Republican president is elected, giving the party clear responsibility for governing the nation and addressing critical problems. Any such policy divisions within the Republican Party could create difficult governing tasks for its party leaders and complicate the continuation of conditional party government.

Distrust of Party Leaders

As House and Senate Republicans enter a period in which their policy unity could come under increased pressure, their success depends on the ability of their leaders to facilitate policy agreement and to defuse disagreements in policy areas where governing failure could hurt the party and the nation. To do so party leaders need strong resources. The question is whether party members will cede to their leaders the formal and informal authority necessary to coordinate and lead the party. In the face of the various policy pressures and personal calculations we have discussed, are members willing to trust their party leaders with power, or will distrust of leaders prevail, limiting their power?

Members may trust party leaders with strong resources when they closely reflect the dominant characteristics of the rank and file. In such cases the rank and file can more easily believe that the leaders understand their concerns and will be attentive to their interests. For this reason, congressional parties often prefer a centrist leader and attempt to construct leadership teams that reflect the parties' regional and ideological diversity. A classic example of such balance was the House Democrats' selection of a Speaker from Texas, Sam Rayburn, and a majority leader from Massachusetts, John McCormack, during the 1950s and 1960s. This balance helped hold the House Democrats together during the early years of the civil rights movement. During much of the 1970s and 1980s the Democrats reversed the pattern but maintained regional balance by choosing a Bostonian, Thomas P. "Tip" O'Neill, as Speaker and a Texan, Jim Wright, as majority leader. In the early 1990s the House Republicans created a similar balance by selecting Bob Michel of Illinois as minority leader and Newt Gingrich of Georgia as minority whip.

In the 107th Congress, one factor supporting trust of party leaders could be the presence of Speaker Dennis Hastert of Illinois in the Republican Party leadership, balancing two southerners, House Majority Leader Dick Armey of Texas and Senate Majority Leader Trent Lott of Mississippi. Prior to Hastert's replacement of Speaker Gingrich of Georgia, the top Republican leaders were all southerners. The dominance of southerners in the leadership may have made it difficult for the party to stay attuned to the sentiments of non-southern Republicans during the early years of Republican control and helped generate misjudgments about how party actions would resonate outside the South. The southern dominance of the House leadership may also have contributed to Gingrich's miscalculations about how the country would react to government shutdowns over the budget impasse and to the impeachment of Clinton, which fueled the defeat of Republicans outside the South in 1996 and 1998. With Hastert at the head of the House Republicans, the party did moderate its governing and policy strategies during the 106th Congress, particularly in the second session, defused potential confrontation with the president, and did well in northern and midwestern districts during the 2000 elections.

A second factor that could affect members' willingness to invest power in their leaders is the generational aging of the congressional party. At the beginning of the 104th Congress Speaker Gingrich was given power to shape committee assignments and the selection of committee chairs, but this came at a time just after his party had spent decades in the minority. Also at this time a majority of Republican members were in their first or second terms, did not yet have extensive seniority, personal resources, or congressional experience, and felt indebted to Gingrich for the role he had played in their recruitment and election. With Gingrich gone from the House, such considerations no longer exist. Rather, as members advance in their careers, they generally develop a vested interest in power positions and discretionary control of personal resources. They become more likely to support a fragmentation of power rather than its centralization. Should the Republicans remain the majority congressional party and return most of their current members over the next four to eight years, the party's growing number of mid-career and senior members may be more concerned with acquiring greater personal influence in Congress and be less prone to support centralized leaders and policy coordination. The aging of congressional Republicans could undercut conditional party government.

Finally, the willingness of party members to maintain strong leadership resources will depend on the performance of the leaders. As discussed in chapter 2, Newt Gingrich fell from power because he had alienated members of his party with his brusque governing style, and because his actions during the government shutdowns of 1995–1996 and the impeachment efforts against President Clinton had raised serious questions about his political judgment. Hastert appears to have realized better than Gingrich the importance of moderation and a less openly combative partisan demeanor. The unexpectedly good showing of House Republicans in the 2000 elections may lead party members to trust Hastert's leadership and rely on his guidance. This could aid effective Republican activism in the House, reinforcing conditional party government in areas where such an approach seems to aid the party fortunes but limiting reliance on conditional party government when cooperation with the opposition appears advantageous. In contrast, the unexpected loss of Senate seats by Republicans could put a spotlight on the judgment and leadership skills of Senate Majority Leader Trent Lott, whose personal demeanor and legislative style are more combative than Hastert's. Senate Republicans, facing the possibility of a number of difficult election contests in 2002, may be less inclined to trust Lott and follow his leadership, further complicating conditional party government in the Senate.

At the beginning of the 107th Congress, the Republican leaders appear to head homogeneous House and Senate parties that are distinctly different in policy preferences from the Democratic minority. The Republican caucuses in both houses thus seem primed for another round of aggressive conditional party government, as in 1995 and 1998. Such aggressive partisanship would likely be reinforced, moreover, by the partisanship that characterized the 2000 presidential elections and the bitterness of the struggle to determine the presidential winner in the weeks following the election. Divisive partisanship is certainly possible. Yet the Republican leaders face constraints on the creation of conditional party government in Congress, including the close partisan divisions in the two chambers, the vulnerability of some members, the underlying policy cleavages within the party, and limits on members' faith in the party leaders. These constraints should be particularly evident in the Senate. They suggest that even if the leaders want to pursue conditional party government, their task may prove difficult unless they are aided by national events or presidential action.

Perhaps most critical, the Republicans face the paradoxical lesson of the 104th and 105th Congresses: aggressive assertion of a legislative party's dominant ideological positions is not always the best way to ensure sustained party control of Congress. It is not always in the party's long-term interest, even when a party is as united and polarized in opposition to the minority party as was the Republican majority in its initial support of the government shutdowns or President Clinton's impeachment. Moderation and a focus on constructing a productive legislative record, and even cooperating with the opposition, may pay significant partisan dividends.

Speaker Hastert's acceptance of this lesson as the 106th Congress progressed may have been the product of a learning process that led him and his colleagues to understand the benefits of pursuing a moderated partisanship and constructive congressional government.[18] In such a pursuit, moreover, the constraints on conditional party government that we have discussed may help him and other party leaders reinforce the need for moderation and legislative productivity to their members. If they can create a productive legislative record, even in the face of the bitterness that enveloped the political parties during the 2000 presidential election and its aftermath, the Republicans may convince citizens that they can be trusted as a majority congressional party and should stay in control of Congress. Ironically, to do so, the Republicans may be required to move away from conditional party government and toward a more moderated and constructive partisanship.

Conclusion

In fairness we should note that Aldrich and Rohde's prediction that a high level of conditional party government will continue may prove correct. After all, many of the reservations we have about the persistence of conditional party government are ones that we expressed in the previous edition of *Congress Reconsidered*, in 1997. And while there has been a certain ebb and flow to conditional party government since then, with it more pervasive early in a Congress and then fading as new elections approach, it has certainly not been displaced by a more muted form of partisanship thus far. Yet we have seen considerable constraining of the Republican issue agenda and clear movement toward the Democratic president and congressional moderates in spending measures enacted by Congress. And even while giving Aldrich and Rohde their due, we also need to note that a conditional party government strategy has not generated the electoral success that Republicans foresaw in the aftermath of the 1994 elections. Not only has backpedaling and a more conciliatory partisanship been necessary as the Republican Congress approached each election; the party's majority in each house has been steadily shrinking as well. The party enters the 107th Congress with a numerical, not a governing, majority. As the party grapples with the constraining factors outlined in the previous section, party leaders and activists may yet be persuaded that alternative models deserve a try. They would then join a long line of legislators who have confronted the limits of party government in America.

Throughout American history, majority parties have succeeded in maintaining congressional control, not by adopting conditional party government, at least on a strict and continuous basis, but by embracing constructive partisanship. Strong, united partisanship within Congress is relatively rare, particularly since the rise of a professionalized Congress and careerist legislators. When it comes into existence it then decays rapidly, as a majority party faces the difficulties of governing a heterogeneous society within a separation-of-powers system. Such a collapse is even more likely when the congressional majority party also controls the presidency, allowing the public to more clearly see which party to hold responsible for policy failures. But a collapse of conditional party government is also possible when a party acts in a visibly aggressive manner, so that the public is clearly aware of its governing role.

Conditional party government is also difficult to maintain in a nation such as the United States because policy conflicts seldom remain polarized in ways that reinforce the distinctiveness of the two parties. In a heterogeneous society such as ours, it is common for cross-cutting conflicts to arise that divide each party internally along some major issues and create overlapping agreement or commonality among factions composed of members from both parties. The cohesiveness of the New Deal Democrats lasted barely six years before concern about executive usurpation of power and fears about national government intervention into southern segregation combined to split them and give rise to a long-term coalition of southern Democrats and Republicans.[19] Likewise, the Great Society coalition of Lyndon Johnson lasted only about eighteen months before preoccupation with the Vietnam War split the party again. The Democrats survived both periods of division, not by trying to impose party government, or even by pursuing conditional party government, but by using a broad range of partisan strategies designed to demonstrate their ability to contribute to effective national governance.

A majority party concerned with maintaining control of Congress must demonstrate the ability to address the cross-cutting policy conflicts of a heterogeneous society and manage the governing complexities created by the bicameralist, separation-of-powers system. To do so, the party's leaders must construct shifting coalitions within and across the majority and minority parties and generate policy results that voters will embrace. Such constructive partisanship sustains a majority party in office and creates a reputation that enables it to compete for control after a loss. A party that learns to engage in constructive partisanship can continue to contest for majority control of Congress even in the presence of the internal divisions and restrictions on leadership power that are normal byproducts of political life in a heterogeneous nation with a separation-of-powers system.

The Democratic Party proved successful in pursuing constructive partisanship and contesting for control of Congress as the presumptive majority party for more than six decades. It did so, moreover, despite facing one of the nation's most severe cleavage issues, the division between the North and the South over segregation and race relations. Ironically, the Democrats lost their preeminent position as the congressional majority in the 1990s, at a point when they became a more homogeneous party characterized by conditional party government. With apparent party unity, strengthened party leaders, and a vigorous young president, they created strong expectations that their united control of government could effectively address the nation's health care problems. They failed because they could not overcome the divisions built into national policymaking by our separation-of-powers system and institutional arrangements—particularly the complex rules and policymaking procedures in the House and Senate, which provide numerous veto points for policy dissidents. The public judged their unified governing effort a failure and delivered them a devastating electoral defeat.

The test facing Republicans in Congress is whether they can learn to engage in constructive partisanship, face inevitable cross-cutting policy conflicts and frustrating constitutional or institutional obstacles, and still find partisan strategies with which to build a productive record of governance. The party must present itself as capable, not just of passing legislation through one house or the other, or of maintaining narrow majorities unable to act decisively, but of contributing forcefully to constructive national governance. The proven ability to participate in governance—that is, to manage the nation's crises and maneuver through prolonged periods of cross-cutting conflict and bitter partisanship while enacting effective public policy—is central to the public's faith in a party and its willingness to entrust the party with a sustained majority in Congress. The 2000 elections have given the Republicans a renewed opportunity to demonstrate such ability and thereby consolidate their hold on power. If they fail at governing during the 107th Congress they could squander this opportunity, which would put their hold on power in question during the 2002 elections. Effective governance, combined with favorable redistricting as a result of reapportionment, could allow them to increase their House and Senate majorities in 2002 and approach the 2004 elections with the real opportunity to become the nation's presumptive majority party.

Notes

1. See the discussion, for example, in Leon Epstein, *Political Parties in Western Democracies* (New York: Praeger, 1967).
2. Pendleton Herring, *The Politics of Democracy* (New York: Norton, 1940).
3. See, in particular, David W. Rohde, *Parties and Leaders in the Postreform House* (Chicago: University of Chicago Press, 1991), and John Aldrich, *Why Parties?* (Chicago: University of Chicago Press, 1995).
4. An early statement of this model is found in John Aldrich and David Rohde, "The Republican Revolution and the House Appropriations Committee" (paper presented at the annual meeting of the Southern Political Science Association, Atlanta, Nov. 7–9, 1996), 1–2.
5. The stress on reelection, policy, and influence goals by Aldrich and Rohde owes a debt to the initial work on member goals by Richard Fenno Jr. in *Congressmen in Committees* (Boston: Little, Brown, 1973).
6. For a particularly strong statement of a party government model, somewhat similar to but more encompassing than Aldrich and Rohde's conceptualization of conditional party government, see Gary Cox and Mathew McCubbins, *The Legislative Leviathan* (Berkeley: University of California Press, 1993). For an argument suggesting that party government may ebb and flow in a cyclical fashion, appearing strong in periods of crisis and realignment but fading as members' careerist ambitions and institutional fragmentation take hold, see Lawrence C. Dodd, "A Theory of Legislative Cycles," in *Political Science: The Science of Politics,* ed. by Herbert Weisberg (New York: Agathon Press, 1986).
7. Rohde provides a superb analysis of this change in *Parties and Leaders in the Postreform House.* We would emphasize, however, that much of the procedural and organizational foundation of this change was laid in the 1970s and before, prior to the southern realignment, by party leaders and reformers seeking mechanisms with which to nurture greater cooperation among party members in the face of considerable intraparty division. For a discussion of the effort during the 1960s and 1970s to bring the House Rules Committee under the increased control of party leaders, see Bruce I. Oppenheimer, "The Rules Committee: New Arm of Leadership in a Decentralized House," in *Congress Reconsidered,* 1st ed., ed. by Dodd and Oppenheimer (New York: Praeger, 1977). For an analysis of policymaking activities by the House Democratic leadership in the 93d Congress (1973–1975), which argues that the conditions for effective party leadership and strengthened party government were emerging by the early- to mid-1970s, see Dodd, "Coalition-Building by Party Leaders: A Case Study

of House Democrats," *Congress and the Presidency* 10 (1983): 145–68. For evidence that committee chairs shifted toward support for the party during the mid- to late-1970s, see Fiona M. Wright, "The Caucus Reelection Requirement and the Transformation of House Committee Chairs, 1959–94," *Legislative Studies Quarterly* 25 (August 2000): 469–80.

8. Joseph Cooper and Garry Young, "Partisanship, Bipartisanship, and Crosspartisanship in Congress since the New Deal," in *Congress Reconsidered*, 6th ed., ed. by Dodd and Oppenheimer (Washington, D.C.: CQ Press, 1997).

9. If Bush is elected president then Cheney, as vice president, would break the Senate tie in favor of the Republicans. Should Gore win, the Republican governor of Connecticut will appoint a Republican to fill the vacancy in the seat formerly held by Lieberman, giving the Republicans a fifty-one–forty-nine majority.

10. As of this writing, two races involving incumbents are too close to call. In both cases, however, recounts are expected. We have credited each seat to the party of the current incumbent.

11. John R. Alford and David W. Brady, "Personal and Partisan Advantages in U.S. Congressional Elections, 1846–1990," in *Congress Reconsidered*, 5th ed., ed. by Dodd and Oppenheimer (Washington, D.C.: CQ Press, 1993).

12. Gary C. Jacobson, "The Electoral Basis of Partisan Polarization in Congress" (paper presented at the 2000 annual meeting of the American Political Science Association, Washington, D.C.).

13. In the other two open seat races in which the district switched party, the switches have more specific explanations. Both are districts where the previous incumbent lost renomination in the primary. The Thirty-first District in California is only classified as a party switch because the previous incumbent joined the House Republican Conference after losing renomination in the Democratic primary.

14. Jeffrey Stonecash, *Class and Party in American Politics* (Boulder, Colo.: Westview Press, 2000).

15. Frank Sorauf, *Party and Representation* (New York: Atherton Press, 1963).

16. Kenneth W. Hechler, *Insurgency: Personalities and Politics in the Taft Era* (New York: Columbia University Press, 1940).

17. Theodore Lowi, *The End of the Republican Era* (Norman: University of Oklahoma Press, 1995).

18. For discussion of the difficulties the Republicans faced in learning such lessons, as a result of their decades out of power in the House, see Richard F. Fenno Jr., *Learning to Govern* (Washington, D.C.: Brookings Institution, 1997), as well as our essay, "Congress and the Emerging Order: Conditional Party Government or Constructive Partisanship?" in *Congress Reconsidered*, 6th ed., 407–10.

19. James T. Patterson, *Congressional Conservatism and the New Deal* (Lexington: University of Kentucky Press, 1967).

17. Re-Envisioning Congress:
Theoretical Perspectives on Congressional Change

Lawrence C. Dodd

The arrival of the twenty-first century has coincided with a time of remarkable change in the U.S. Congress. For much of the twentieth century, from the Great Depression onward, the Democrats served as the majority party in Congress, steering the country toward an activist social agenda and generating a remarkable amount of institutional and policy innovation. The party's core agenda issues such as Social Security were so popular, and Democratic incumbents paid such close attention to constituents' service needs and to interest groups' programmatic concerns, that the party appeared to have a permanent lock on Congress, particularly the House of Representatives. Thus as Congress entered the 1990s most observers expected Democratic control to continue,[1] despite public opinion polls demonstrating widespread unhappiness with Congress as an institution.[2] Instead, the decade witnessed a dramatic Republican assault on the Democrats and on Congress itself, which culminated in the "Republican Revolution" in the 1994 elections.

Once in control of Congress, the Republicans pursued a political and policy struggle of historic proportions with the Democratic president and his congressional party. This struggle included two government shutdowns, the enactment of welfare reform over the objections of most congressional Democrats, and the impeachment of President Clinton. As the struggle went forward, the Republicans maintained control of the House and Senate by slim margins in the 1996 and 1998 elections. The 2000 elections, again generating narrow Republican majorities, extended Republican control into a fourth Congress, the longest such stretch since the 1920s.

How could this have happened? What does it tell us about Congress as an institution? And what might it tell us about America at the dawn of this new century?

This chapter seeks to address these concerns by presenting three theoretical perspectives that, taken together, help us to understand such periods of unexpected change and to clarify the placement and meaning of such changes in contemporary politics. These theories argue that such upheavals, illustrated forcefully by the Republican Revolution, can best be understood not as aberrations in our politics but as the natural long-term outgrowth of three factors: the goals and strategies that politicians bring to congressional politics, the shifting societal contexts that they confront, and the changing ideas about politics with which they experiment as they pursue their goals and address societal problems. To better understand these three theories and their significance for Congress, we will start by considering why the Republican Revolution was so puzzling and how the three theories can help us address that puzzle. Then we will examine the three theories, the sense they make out of contemporary politics, and what they together can tell us about the current state of Congress and the nation.

The Puzzle and Explanatory Strategy

What is so puzzling about the Republican Revolution is that it occurred at all, given the hold on Congress that the Democrats appeared to enjoy, and that it followed the path it did once the Republicans assumed control of Congress. Three aspects of this overall puzzle require particular attention.

First, the Republican victory came at a time when members of Congress possessed more resources than at any other time in history for conducting constituent service, contacting constituents personally, addressing specific programmatic needs, and traveling home to meet with constituents. The incumbent advantage in congressional elections seemed assured, and there appeared little role for national policy agendas or national election forces in congressional elections. Together these factors seemed to tilt Congress decisively toward Democratic control and to make almost inconceivable a serious Republican challenge, short of conditions such as a major economic crisis. Republican takeover of the House of Representatives seemed particularly unlikely because localized constituent service and targeted federal programs appeared to provide a very special incumbent advantage in the relatively small congressional districts that compose the House. Despite these expectations, in 1994 the Republican Party produced one of the most massive vote swings against an incumbent congressional party in American history.[3] The Republicans captured both the House and Senate and even defeated powerful House committee chairs and the Democratic Speaker, Tom Foley. They accomplished all of this, moreover, in a time of good economic conditions. They did so by stressing a common policy agenda and nationalizing the congressional elections.

Second, as they maneuvered for control of Congress in the decade prior to the 1994 election, and during the 1994 campaign itself, the Republicans systematically attacked the legitimacy of Congress as a governing institution. After gaining control of the Congress that they had worked so hard to capture, Republicans then found themselves constrained by the public distrust of Congress they had helped enflame. Unable to put in place a strong leadership structure, instead they found themselves blamed for two government shutdowns, embroiled in factional fights, and subjected to three straight elections in which they lost seats in the House and stumbled precariously in the Senate, barely holding on to control of Congress. Their remarkable surge forward in 1994 thus was followed not by the consolidation of a new Republican era that it seemed to portend but by stalemate.

Third, despite the difficulties the Republicans faced as they sought to govern, their control of Congress did not collapse. They rebounded from the government shutdowns and maintained control of both houses during the 1996,

1998, and 2000 elections, despite a Democratic resurgence. Along the way, the party enacted major new legislation, from reform of welfare laws to trade normalization with China. Congress did not revert to a Democratic majority, which would have indicated that the 104th Congress had been an anomaly. Instead, although both parties struggled in the years following the 1994 elections, the nation's political and policy landscape clearly had changed in qualitative ways.

In response to these developments, the journalistic community presented an interpretation of the Republican Revolution that stressed its uniqueness and attributed it almost entirely to the hard work and brilliance of one man, Representative Newt Gingrich of Georgia.[4] The general image conveyed by the coverage of events of 1994 and thereafter emphasized the overarching role of Gingrich in orienting congressional Republicans toward a systematic assault on the Democrats in the 1980s and early 1990s, in creating a strategy of attacking Congress in order to discredit the governing Democrats, in aggressively using GOPAC to build a Republican base, in building a "farm team" of Republican challengers, and in creating the thematic focus on a Conservative Opportunity Society and on the Contract with America.

The result has been a kind of "great man" theory of revolution that seemed to imply that if only Gingrich had been defeated in 1990, when he had faced an extremely close election, the Democrats would have maintained control of Congress and the New Deal–Great Society hegemony would have gone unchallenged. This perspective further implied that the Republicans faltered midway through the 104th Congress because Gingrich became overwhelmed with hubris; they recovered in the summer of 1996 because he recovered; they struggled thereafter because of his ethical struggles and loss of nerve; and they suffered grievously with his miscalculation in relying on impeachment of Clinton to save the Republican Party. Their rebound in the 106th Congress then could be attributed to Gingrich's sagacity in maneuvering Dennis Hastert, Ill., to the Speakership as he resigned from the House, putting in place a soft-spoken Gingrich ally who could continue the revolution without generating the negative vibes associated with Gingrich himself.

Certainly there is some truth in the emphasis on Gingrich's critical role in the revolution. Individuals do matter in politics and history. A gifted politician may see historical dynamics more clearly than others and act in ways that accentuate them. Yet how can an individual overcome "scientific" truths, such as the argument by congressional scholars that citizens' preoccupation with casework politics, and public disinterest in sweeping policy agendas, had frozen the Republicans out of contention in the House and limited their future in the Senate? And even if Gingrich was remarkably adept at sensing the underlying dynamics of history, what was it that he had sensed? What were the historical dynamics that had suggested opportunities to exploit and strategies to pursue?[5]

In contrast to the great man or personalistic perspective, this chapter argues that developments such as the Republican Revolution reflect broader dynamics at play in institutions and societies, and that it is through our identification of such dynamics that we make systematic sense out of critical events.[6] In the short run there are always advantages — city machines in the late nineteenth century, constituent service in the late twentieth century — that benefit one party or group and appear to contemporary observers to make it impregnable to political challenge. But in the long run there are historical processes at work that erode such advantages and subject legislators, their parties, and Congress to new political circumstances. As we understand these dynamic processes, thinking about Congress not by focusing on short-term and static partisan advantages but by assessing long-term dynamic processes, we gain a general sense of how and why surprising upheavals such as the Republican Revolution occur. We also learn to focus less on great men and more on the underlying dynamics that help generate and constrain great leadership and in the process change the structure of politics.

Our approach will be to understand the historical processes shaping contemporary politics by looking at Congress through the lenses of three theoretical perspectives. First, we will employ a *social choice* or microeconomic perspective, which sees the revolution as a predictable stage in a natural and ongoing cycle of organizational and partisan change in Congress, a cycle generated by the strategic ways in which politicians and parties pursue governing power. Second, we will employ a *social structure* or historical-sociological perspective, which sees the revolution as a product of post-industrial societal tensions and public frustrations that overwhelmed a Congress and governing party still oriented toward industrial-era politics. Third, we will employ a cognitive or *social learning* perspective, which sees the revolution as an experimental phase in the effort of politicians and citizens to discover principles and strategies by which to resolve post-industrial policy problems and legitimize a new governing regime.

In looking at congressional politics through three distinct theoretical lenses, the chapter proposes that we can understand Congress in much the same way as we understand sporting events such as basketball. To some degree we explain which team wins and which loses by focusing on the nature or logic of basketball as a game and the skills, training, personal goals, and team commitment that players bring to it. Invariably, as we do so, we find that one team initially prepares well and works hard to win, but then with success and time it becomes lax and self-indulgent, while another grows strong, leading winners to lose and losers to win. A concentrated focus on the preparation, strategies, and psychology of teams serves us well as we try to explain a basketball game, but few of us rely solely on these "foreground" issues to fully understand teams' successes and failures. We also look at the background context within which games are played: who has the home-court advantage and has best cultivated such advantage; who has the most at stake in a game and may be most willing to take unusual risks or to break normal conventions, as in "talking trash," in order to gain psychological advantage over another team. Finally, as great teams meet on the court, we invariably consider the philosophies of the game held by the different coaches, schools, and regions of the country: which philosophy is better, a strong defense or an aggressive running offense; which philosophy is outmoded and no longer reflects the realities of a new basketball era; which is innovative and in touch with new strategies and understandings?

In explaining college basketball, or some other sport, we consider each of these factors — the foreground game, the background context, and the overarching philosophies — and then we also look across these dimensions, thinking about their interaction. To what extent, for example, can contextual factors like home-court advantage, or a new and innovative basketball philosophy, make a winner out of a sure loser? As we talk about these issues, each of us has our favorite set of arguments or theories that we debate with others. We do so partly to explain who has won, or to predict who will win. But we do so also to understand the essence of the game, to gain perspective on how that essence is changing, and to see how and why the game may change again in the future.

We are following a similar strategy in using a multi-theoretical perspective to understand the congressional game and how it changes. Thus the social choice theory is an argument about the foreground of politics — how partisan teams play the game of congressional politics, and how maneuvering and jockeying for power leads first one party to succeed and then another. The social structure theory is an argument about the background of contemporary politics, about how societal and institutional contexts influence the way citizens feel about congressional politics and thus shape the strategies and opportunities available to parties as they seek power. Finally, the social learning theory is an argument about the ways in which the ideas that politicians bring to the game shape their ability to play effectively, enthuse their fans, and not only generate victory but make their victory worthwhile.

The remainder of this chapter presents these three theories, one by one, and then concludes with a short assessment of what the theories, taken together, tell us about congressional politics as we move into the twenty-first century. In presenting these arguments, I ask the reader not simply to respond to them in terms of partisan or ideological preference but to step back, look beyond which "team" you prefer, and consider the lessons to be learned about Congress and contemporary politics as we bring into clearer focus the dynamic processes that shape the congressional game. With this understanding, let us turn first to our social choice theory and see how far it goes in explaining the broad patterning of the events of the 1990s, and then turn to the social structure and social learning theories, in turn, building a more layered and intertwined understanding as we go.

The Social Choice Theory

We begin with the social choice theory, which is designed to clarify how the political game normally proceeds in the foreground of congressional life, irrespective of historical context.[7] Our concern is with identifying the central goal that drives legislators' behavior, much as the desire to win inspires a basketball team, and with examining how legislators' goal-oriented behavior shapes and alters congressional politics across time. A range of motives exists among legislators, any one of which, separately or in combination with others, could form the basis of a theory of congressional change. These include the reelection motive stressed by Morris Fiorina and David Mayhew,[8] the dual goals of reelection and policy stressed by John Aldrich and David Rohde in chapter 12 of this volume, and the multiple goals of reelection, policymaking, and influence examined by Richard Fenno and Barbara Sinclair.[9] Yet the goal that most universally runs through the discussion of politics, from Machiavelli onward, and that would seem to encompass the other goals, is personal power. Thus it is the concern for governing power around which Anthony Downs builds his classic study of the ways that politicians' goals shape legislative elections and democratic government.[10] It is the concern for personal power that Barry Weingast sees as the basis for reelection activities and norm behavior in Congress.[11] The work of Roger Davidson and Walter Oleszek; C. Lawrence Evans and Oleszek; Glenn Parker; and Raymond Wolfinger and Joan Hollinger provides further evidence that members' concern for personal power or autonomy shapes and constrains party loyalty, resource distribution, and reform on Capitol Hill.[12] Thus the central goal around which we will build our social choice theory of Congress is the quest for personal power.

Our strategy is to specify the logical ways in which legislators' pursuit of power shape the organizational politics of Congress. Microeconomic theorists argue that the pursuit of profit by individuals and firms ultimately leads to national economic cycles of boom and bust. Does the pursuit of power by legislators and their parties likewise lead to predictable patterns of congressional change? Do such patterns provide a plausible explanation of the contemporary upheavals in Congress? To address these questions, we will first lay out our social choice theory. This theory argues that the pursuit of power by members and their parties generates recurring cycles of partisan alternation in Congress. We will then look at how well the theory explains contemporary developments.

Congress and the Quest for Power

The foundation of our social choice theory is that the quest for personal power by individual legislators leads them to seek power positions and resources within Congress that provide influence over national policymaking.[13] In the pursuit of personal power, members organize into partisan teams composed of like-minded members who would use power to serve similar policy objectives. The majority party will control the major power positions within the legislature, such as committee or subcommittee chairs and the Speakership; it will also oversee the organizational resources of the assembly, such as office assignments and staff, and it will largely determine congressional rules and procedures. For these reasons, and in ways discussed more fully by Aldrich and Rohde in chapter 12, the majority's dominance of institutional power and resources gives it the upper hand in policymaking and governance.

Being in the majority provides members with the chance to exercise personal power by becoming committee or party leaders, by skillfully using resources distributed by the party, and by benefiting from rules and procedures that aid majority party policymaking. To attain personal power, members thus must work together to develop political strategies and legislative successes that enable the party and its members to gain public support and consolidate control of the assembly.

The efforts of legislators to gain personal power through service in the majority party involve a special paradox. Members' ability to work together in pursuit of majority party status requires a centralized party leadership that can coordinate their activities. Such coordination helps the party to develop a coherent campaign strategy designed to win a legislative majority, address the central policy problems preoccupying its members and supporters, and demonstrate its effective governing capacities in order to retain power. To ensure effective coordination, a party may want to limit the number of "power positions" and powerful legislators, so that undue resistance to party policy and electoral strategies does not emerge among autonomous power-wielders within the party. Yet the rank-and-file party members will push for the creation of numerous power positions such as committee or subcommittee chairs, and for special resources such as staff, so that they can have real influence on policy. Such influence renders service in the majority a rewarding experience and also allows members to stress significant personal accomplishments in reelection campaigns. Moreover, the majority party itself will need to spread organizational positions and resources somewhat widely in order to draw upon the expertise and energy of members in crafting the details of its policy programs and communicating the programs to constituents. The party also will have incentive to distribute positions and resources widely, so that the resulting incumbent advantage helps the party reelect its members and maintain its hold on power. Doing so, however, carries great risks for the party.

The success of individual members in gaining power positions and resources brings policymaking and electoral benefits to the party but also some considerable detriments. For example, the success of members in gaining extensive staff allotments not only helps them perform constituent service, potentially aiding both their reelection and the party's retention of power, but also can enable them to prepare and push bills that party leaders might find objectionable. Similarly, gaining a committee or subcommittee chair may provide a member special advantage when running for reelection, aiding the party's hold on majority status, but it also gives him or her an opportunity to push constituent interests that could undermine the party's program. As members gain such power positions and resources, and the autonomy such success can bring, their personal policy preferences and distinctive pressures of their constituents may push them away from the party's policy stances, thereby undermining party coordination and limiting the ability of the party to campaign or govern as an effective team.

The pronounced tension between centralized party power and autonomous personal power generates long-term cycles of organizational and partisan change in Congress. These cycles result from the contrasting personal calculus and political strategies of majority and minority party members.[14]

The Cycles of Congressional Change

After cooperating to win majority status and consolidate party control of the legislature, members of the majority party naturally push to divide up significant power resources among themselves so that they can all benefit from the fruits of victory. They will thus support the creation of increasing numbers of formal and informal power positions within the legislature. They will lobby for greater personal resources such as office staff and travel allotments. And they will seek to establish rules within the party caucus and legislative chamber that respect the personal prerogatives of members. In pursuing these various efforts, they in turn fragment the structure of centralized party authority and undermine the majority party's capacity for internal coordination. These developments weaken their party's ability to respond to new policy problems or political circumstances and can thereby undermine public satisfaction with the party's governing success. Yet the decline in enthusiasm for the party itself will appear offset by the growing security of party incumbents who use their increased autonomy and resources to build incumbent advantage in home districts.[15]

In contrast, members of the minority party have far fewer power resources to divide among themselves and significant incentive to support centralized coordination in order to battle with the majority over control of the assembly. Of course, their party may have suffered such a large reduction when it lost control that a rapid return to majority status appears unrealistic. This can constrain minority party members from an immediate focus on cooperation and party loyalty. But as their sojourn in the political wilderness lengthens, minority party members are far more likely than members of the majority to constrain their desire for immediate autonomy and focus on how best to cooperate in gaining majority party status, since that is their only real avenue to meaningful personal power. They will thus increasingly accept some degree of centralized party coordination.

As the minority party challenges the majority, the latter will appear invulnerable owing to the success of its members in winning reelection, but appearances will be deceptive.[16] The fragmented and uncoordinated nature of majority party governance, which helps generate incumbent advantage, also generates festering policy problems in the nation and a growing sense of governing crisis. The electorate, in response, increasingly focuses on assessing the governing capacity of the majority party rather than the personalized benefits received from its members. It is, after all, a party's ability to use institutional power to respond to policy problems and govern effectively that justifies its hold on majority status. Citizens thus will not indefinitely support majority party legislators simply because they ensure the delivery of benefits from programs that address "old problems." Rather, they will consider punishing majority party legislators for current policy failures.[17] This reaction against the majority party will then be assisted by the strategies and actions of the minority.

The out party, sensing the vulnerability of the majority, will use its centralized capacities to coordinate a national election campaign and to focus its candidates on a clear, unified, and coherent party agenda designed to address governing crises and emphasize its capacity to govern. It also will seek to highlight and magnify particular policy problems and perceived crises, even to the point of ensuring policy immobilism that helps to foster such problems. Meanwhile, the majority party will look to the incumbent advantage enjoyed by its members in order to assure itself that the minority party challenge will be fruitless. Its overconfidence will be reinforced by the vested interests that party members have in maintaining the fragmented status quo within Congress, so that they ignore growing public hostility to their party.

Faced with these circumstances, frustrated voters will revolt against the majority party and install the minority in power, doing so in a manner that appears sudden and unexpected but that is in fact a natural consequence of the ways in which members and parties pursue legislative power across time. The old minority party then will have its opportunity to address societal problems and consolidate institutional control. Buoyed by its momentum and the initial loyalty of members, it will almost certainly experience early policy successes. But the underlying issue is whether the new majority party can reform the legislature in ways that reduce the internal fragmentation that the old majority party had built into organizational rules and arrangements. If the new majority party can implement centralizing reforms appropriate to its governing tasks, it may be able to sustain majority status and operate as a powerful congressional party for some time, perhaps several decades, before the power quests of its members erode its centralized structure. If it fails, it may squander its opportunity and allow the opposing party to regain institutional control. Should the minority party itself remain weak and unable to rally, a cross-party coalition of factions may dominate Congress. The resurgent party, or factional coalition, then would face its own challenge in developing a governing structure that could address societal problems and sustain it in power. In time, any successful governing party or coalition would face magnified tensions between its need for centralized power and the desire of its members for autonomy, experience debilitating organizational fragmentation, and confront an unexpected and surprising minority party challenge.

The success of majority party legislators in fragmenting congressional power, combined with the willingness of minority party legislators to accept centralized party guidance, builds long-term cycles of partisan or factional alternation into the organizational life of Congress, according to our social choice theory. How well does this argument account for the upheavals of the 1990s, particularly the coming of the Republican Revolution?

The Revolution as a Cyclical Stage

Seen through the lenses of social choice theory, the Republican Revolution can be explained as a classic product of the recurring cycles of organizational change. The current organizational cycle of Congress began with electoral upheavals of the 1960s and centralizing reforms of the 1970s that solidified liberal Democratic control. The 1980s and early 1990s were a period of fragmentation and growing immobilism, when the popularity of Democratic incumbents as constituent servants masked growing disenchantment with the party's governing capacities. The sudden and surprising defeat of the Democrats in 1994 was a result of the public's long-term unhappiness with the party. This unhappiness came forth in full fury and produced the defeat of the party's most visible and vulnerable incumbents, at a time when the Democrats had proved unable to address the critical governing items that they had promised the nation in the 1992 elections, such as changing the welfare system and implementing national health care, even when joined by a Democratic president. The defeat was unexpected because politicians and political analysts alike had focused on the incumbent advantages the Democrats enjoyed and discounted the public's growing frustration with political gridlock. The defeat was aided by the efforts of the Republicans to pursue a coordinated campaign strategy that used party resources effectively and presented a compelling image of a party prepared to govern cohesively in pursuit of an agenda widely supported by its candidates.

From the perspective of social choice theory, the brilliant electoral strategies of Republican leaders such as Gingrich were a skillful response to the opportunities afforded them by career ambitions, organizational fragmentation, and policy immobilism within the majority Democratic Party, rather than the machinations of a rare political genius. The early organizational innovations and policy successes of the Republican Party were natural consequences of the internal cohesion it had developed in its pursuit of majority status and of members' concerns to act on its governing mandate. Subsequent factional conflict among Republicans resulted, in part, from the natural reemergence of personal ambitions and power pursuits within a majority party, and from frustrations with the realities of governing in a complex policymaking environment.

But the factional conflict was also a consequence of the failure of the party, particularly in the House, to enact reforms that would institutionalize a centralized authority structure. Leaders granted such centralized authority could manage conflict and pursue strategies that would sustain and consolidate the revolution. Rather than decisively strengthening the Speakership, the Republicans enacted limits on service as Speaker that substantially weakened party leadership. Instead, they relied on the personal power of Gingrich, the good will of members, and debts owed him by members and committee chairs. In addition, rather than streamlining the committee system in ways that might make it a more effective policymaking instrument and less a vehicle of member ambitions, for example by strengthening the budget committees and expanding their capacity to constrain and prioritize spending across the federal budget, the Republicans largely kept the old system in place, making changes that were mainly cosmetic and that did little to aid decisive action on their new agenda. The Republicans thus would face a difficult task in consolidating their control, particularly given the electorate's close division between Republicans and Democrats.

The social choice theory of organizational cycles seems to go a long way in accounting for the sudden and surprising nature of the Republicans' defeat of a long-term majority party, yet it also has its limits. Why, at their moment of victory, did the Republicans not follow through and implement real reform, choosing instead to undercut the very centralized leadership that had "brought them to the dance"? Why did they maneuver, moreover, in behalf of constitutional changes such as term limits and budget constraints that would seem to limit their own power as a majority party?[18] Why did the Republicans themselves so rapidly become the object of public scorn? And why did factional problems emerge so rapidly at the highest levels of leadership activity, so that the Republicans' governing capacities were thrown into serious question despite their great electoral victory?

The social choice theory, focused as it is on the general patterning of congressional change irrespective of historical context, cannot satisfactorily account for these distinctive characteristics and problems of the 1994 revolution. To do so, for reasons illustrated powerfully by Steven Smith and Gerald Gamm in chapter 11 and Joseph Cooper in chapter 15, we need to shift our conceptual focus to background factors and examine the social conditions within which it occurred.

The Social Structure Theory

As we shift from the foreground of congressional politics to the background, we will consider how Congress's power struggles and organizational cycles are shaped and altered by the societal conditions within which they occur. In doing so, we will be taking a sociological approach to Congress.

A strong sociological tradition exists in studies of the historical development of Congress. It is exemplified notably by Nelson Polsby's argument that societal modernization generates growing demands on legislatures and induces organizational specialization and institutionalization as they respond, a pattern he demonstrates for the U.S. House of Representatives.[19] We also have insightful sociological analyses of congressional politics during specific eras.[20] Thus James Sterling Young demonstrates how agrarianism, regionalism, and popular suspicion of government generated a passive, factionalized, and constrained early Congress. Woodrow Wilson argues that social changes after the Civil War strengthened the governing role of a centralized party-driven Congress and pushed the nation toward congressional government. Joseph Cooper and David Brady highlight the ways industrialization and growing careerist politics produced a crisis of adaptation in the early-twentieth-century Congress that undermined strong parties and crippled congressional government. And Theodore Lowi charts the ways that advanced industrialization in mid-century helped create a bureaucratized and clientelist politics that he called "interest group liberalism," solidifying committee government and subsystem politics within a weakened Congress.

Our concern is to assess whether changes in social structure during the contemporary period are having an equally profound impact on Congress and its party politics, and whether this shift in context can thereby help us better understand the Republican Revolution. This issue requires us first to identify the fundamental changes occurring in the contemporary era and to consider their potential significance.

The Post-Industrial Transition

Historical sociologists have argued that the most critical change among advanced industrial democracies from the 1950s onward has been the move to a post-industrial society driven by a high-tech economy, dependent on technological innovation, and dominated by service-based employment.[21] The issue facing such nations is whether the policy programs and governing arrangements created to manage industrial-era problems can adapt to this new world.

During the advanced industrial era of the early twentieth century, as the workforce was employed in blue-collar mass-production industry and subject to periods of severe economic dislocations, democracies such as the United States created extensive social service programs. These programs were designed to supplement the health and retirement benefits that blue-collar workers received through union contracts with employers. Governments also created "safety net" programs such as price supports for the industries. Governments created these programs because large numbers of specialized workers, along with stable manufacturing and agricultural sectors, were essential to the industrial production that generated strong national economies. Such nations also created large bureaucracies to implement the programs and generated political processes such as interest group liberalism and subsystem politics that sustained support for the programs. They also solidified class-based party systems that designed and oversaw the operation of the service programs.

According to social structure theory, the move to a post-industrial society introduces policy problems and political pressures that the governing arrangements inherited from the industrial era cannot address.[22] Although the post-industrialist economy creates high-tech jobs that employ a highly educated and specialized workforce, it also erodes the security of citizens as the new post-industrial employment sectors reduce or eliminate the social benefits provided workers by the union contracts of the industrial era. These citizens turn to government, which is already committed to providing safety nets, and expect it to replace and expand the lost benefits.

In addition, the educated citizens of the post-industrial era expect the national government to address a broadening array of quality-of-life issues overlooked in the industrial era—from racial discrimination to gender equality to consumer protection to environmental regulation to quality education, and the list goes on. These "post-materialist" demands put enormous fiscal pressure on the government, pressures not fully offset by growing economic productivity, and also push government into cultural controversies over the values that an activist government should support.

Two political arrangements inherited from the advanced industrial era exacerbate these problems. First, government reliance on expensive and impersonal bureaucracies to implement post-industrial programs further magnifies their cost and accentuates perceptions of cultural insensitivity. Second, electoral rules and interest-group politics entrench pre-existing political parties in power, despite their preoccupation with programmatic positions adopted in the industrial era, inhibiting the rise of new parties that might address the new economic and cultural issues.

Social structure theory suggests that citizens faced with such circumstances will question the legitimacy of their governments. In particular, they will turn against the democratic institutions most responsible for making public policy, and against the traditional parties. Although the severity of public hostility will vary with the boom and bust cycles of national economies, somewhat declining in good times, the public's growing disenchantment with governing institutions eventually should produce a breakdown in democratic government.

This breakdown will occur not because post-industrial citizens are anti-democratic but because the institutional and political arrangements inherited from the industrial era do not provide them with adequate mechanisms with which to generate and legitimate new policy directions and governing regimes. The antiquated structures and procedures of a passing era are instead likely to cripple the capacity of citizens to convey their genuine policy preferences and political loyalties to their elected representatives, leading them to question such democratic procedures. No more vivid illustration of this argument is needed than the crisis over the selection of the new president in the weeks following the 2000 elections. This crisis gives dramatic demonstration of just how debilitated twenty-first-century politics may be when regulated by antiquated procedures, from an eighteenth-century electoral college to nineteenth-century judicial procedures to twentieth-century punch cards, with such procedures throwing the legitimacy of the new president into doubt.

Congress and the Crisis of Legitimation

The social structure argument suggests that disenchantment with the legitimacy of governing institutions should be an integral part of contemporary American politics and that such disenchantment should focus, in particular, on Congress and its two parties.[23] The public would be concerned with Congress because of its powerful role in national policymaking, a role greater than that of national legislatures elsewhere. In addition, as Morris Fiorina argued eloquently in *Congress: Keystone of the Washington Establishment,* the electoral and organizational politics of Congress—including the rise of careerist politicians, the prevalence of constituent service activities, engrained norms of seniority, the limited governing capacity of congressional parties, and the veto power of committees—have made it the institution most constrained by industrial-era clientelist politics, and by safe incumbents who benefit from such politics.[24] These develop-

ments make Congress the national institution most pressured to continue industrial-era policy strategies and reinforce the inclination of citizens to turn their
fury against it.

Most importantly, Congress suffers because it is controlled by parties still
rooted in industrial-era politics. Because the Democratic Party created the service state, and thus is the party most constrained by interest group liberalism and
clientelist politics, public hostility focuses first and foremost on it. This hostility
provides strategic opportunities for short-term Republican challenges. But social
structure theory questions the long-term capacities of the Republican Party, or
any industrial-era party, to solidify public support. Each party will be too
beholden to its own industrial-era clientele groups, too blinded by industrial-era
programmatic positions, and too compromised by the behavior of its own incumbents to address the problems of post-industrialism in innovative ways.

As we look at the contemporary Congress from a critical sociological perspective, we see an institution out of sync with the emerging post-industrial society and prone to a severe crisis of institutional legitimacy. Power struggles and partisan shifts may be proceeding in the foreground according to normal cyclical
patterns predicted by social choice theory. Looking at Congress solely through
social choice lenses, we might conclude that nothing truly serious was occurring on
Capitol Hill, other than the normal alternation of partisan elites that we occasionally expect. But historical sociologists, looking through the lenses of social structure theory, see the Republican Revolution as a more momentous development.

The Revolution as a Product of Post-Industrial Tensions

The Republican Revolution of the past six years, as seen from a critical sociological perspective, has been a consequence of the growing societal tensions
associated with post-industrialism and the legitimation crisis those tensions necessarily generate. In the preceding decades the Democratic Party had held firmly to its orthodox programmatic orientation, the protection and expansion of
Social Security, while otherwise failing to provide innovative leadership. This
failure was demonstrated in soaring deficits and in the continuance of festering
problems with the environment, poverty, crime, and other quality-of-life concerns. With it came the public's growing disillusionment with Congress and its
governing party, and the attendant doubts about their governing legitimacy. As a
party pursuing power and seeking electoral support, the Republicans embraced
the public frustration, gave it public voice, and rode it to power.

The Republican attack began in the 1970s, when President Richard Nixon
chided the "credit card Congress" and wasteful Democrats and impounded funds
that had been enacted by the Democrats in a constitutionally prescribed manner.
Nixon's actions threatened to upend the balance of constitutional power between
Congress and the president, before the courts forced him to retreat. But the concerted assault came to the fore in the 1980s within Congress itself, led by young
Republicans such as Newt Gingrich and Trent Lott. In ways outlined in chapter 2

of this volume, the Republicans highlighted the misdeeds of the Democrats, from Speaker Jim Wright's questionable use of book royalties to members' bounced checks in the House Bank, as a way to underscore the sense of a governing party and Congress that were corrupt and illegitimate at the core. To address the problems, they proposed term limits on members, constitutional constraints on Congress's budgetary power, and strengthening the presidency (the institution Republicans had dominated for most of the previous forty years) by granting presidents the line-item veto. And they also proposed the defeat of the governing Democrats. These tactics and proposals, attacking not just the policy positions of Democrats but the constitutional authority and governing legitimacy of Congress itself, struck a chord with the public, to a large extent reflecting and magnifying rather than creating public opinion. Coming at a time when the Democrats were vulnerable because of their internal fragmentation, the Republican attack swept the majority party from power in dramatic fashion, appearing to shake the foundations of congressional politics and to mandate dramatic change.

Ironically, and as social structure theory would suggest, once in power the Republicans became victims of the legitimation crisis they had helped to fuel. Early on, as they sought to organize Congress, the party's call for term limits on members, which lost momentum once it became the majority party, became transformed into pressure within the party for imposing term limits on the Republican Speaker and committee chairs in the House, as a way of demonstrating to the public the party's sincerity about reform. Thus did their attack on the institution boomerang, limiting their own capacity to put in place a governing structure that would help them pursue broad-scale governmental change.[25] Meanwhile, as discussed by John Hibbing and James Smith in chapter 3, the public continued to be suspicious of Congress and politicians in general. In part this suspicion extended to the Republicans because their earlier investigation of the ethical problems of Democrats (as in the scandal over bounced checks) had also tarnished many of their own colleagues. But the public's wariness of the Republicans had been magnified by the doubts the party had cast on Congress as a governing institution. If Congress was truly as corrupt and outmoded as the Republicans had suggested, it was not clear that they could really improve matters. Citizens thus granted little leeway to the new congressional majority party.

When the Republican Party shut down the government in a budgetary struggle with the president in late 1995, and then proved unable to negotiate with the president because of the weak authority granted to its leadership, the public saw the fiasco as an illustration of the Republicans' own governing incompetence, and the momentum of the revolution stalled. Thereafter, ethical problems associated with Speaker Gingrich, combined with the move of House Republicans to impeach President Clinton despite his public support, deepened citizen disenchantment with Republican governance. It was only the absence of a viable alternative party capable of forcefully moving Congress beyond the Democratic era that kept the Republicans in control.

From a critical sociological perspective, then, the Republican Revolution serves both as a demonstration of the powerful tensions emerging with post-industrialism and as proof of the inability of Congress and the existing congressional parties to address the tensions. This perspective, articulated by Ralph Nader during his 2000 presidential bid, sees the parties and Congress as illegitimate governing instruments destined to lead the nation further astray. Social choice theory then adds the prediction that Republicans' consolidation of their majority will generate renewed pressures toward organizational fragmentation and increased governing problems. The interaction of internal congressional dynamics and external societal tensions seem likely to generate a magnified legitimation crisis, increasing the threat to representative democracy.

These concerns raise serious questions. Is there any model for understanding contemporary politics that might suggest a way to avoid institutional collapse? Is there some ameliorative process at work across the foreground and background of congressional politics that we are simply missing as we look through the lenses of social choice and social structure theories? Moreover, might the Republican Revolution be a part of this process? These questions suggest that we step back and consider whether there is a broader integrative pattern linking these foreground and background worlds, a shift in which might transform the outcome. Let us now look at Congress through the lenses of social learning theory.

The Social Learning Theory

Our goal in turning to social learning theory is to examine how the ideas of citizens and politicians help shape congressional politics and to consider whether new ideas can facilitate the adjustment to a new political era. A cognitive perspective asks that we study Congress by becoming aware of the belief systems and learning processes that characterize society across time and by seeing Congress and its parties as participants in societal learning.

Central to the dominant scholarly conceptions of social learning, particularly as developed by Gregory Bateson and Geoffrey Vickers, is the perception that individuals and groups develop understandings of the world that they share with one another in order to operate effectively.[26] Each generation must develop a realistic understanding of how best to balance personal and collective well-being within its particular historical conditions. Insofar as it does so, its members can compete effectively in pursuit of personal interests at the same time as they address collective social problems and construct viable societies. As the world changes and ideas become outmoded, the ability to accomplish such personal goals and public purposes declines. The solution, from a social learning perspective, is for a new generation to engage in experimental learning of new ideas appropriate to new circumstances. As they discover such ideas and integrate them with orthodox perspectives essential to societal continuity, a more viable social paradigm emerges that can facilitate societal well-being and effective governance.

Our concern here is with what a learning perspective might tell us about the capacity of Congress to respond to post-industrialism and with the role of the Republican Revolution in that process. This requires us first to consider more closely the nature of social learning.

The Process of Social Learning:
Crisis, Experimentation, and Paradigm Shift

All of us have experienced the process of social learning in our lives. As an example, think back to sports as a metaphor for understanding politics. Occasionally we see teams that fail to adjust to new circumstances, such as the adoption of the three-point shot in college basketball, and thus lose regularly. The team's coaching staff understands the school's social culture and recruiting strengths, but the coaches learned the game before the new rules were envisioned, so they are committed to an older, more conservative philosophy of basketball. Frustrated after several losing seasons, anxious fans demand change, and college administrators search for a new coaching staff. The college may have to experiment with several coaching arrangements, introducing new members who embrace a more aggressive basketball philosophy while keeping some existing coaches, before it discovers a staff whose approach effectively balances a respect for the program's historic strengths with new ideas about how best to play the game. Once the school finds such a staff, the players learn new strategies of play, and excited fans learn to appreciate the three-point shot. Such a process of social learning undertaken across several years — by administrators, staff, players, and fans — can rejuvenate support for basketball on a campus.

Social learning theory argues that the significant role that ideas and learning play in our private lives, as illustrated here by basketball, also can be seen in politics.[27] An institution such as Congress may have governing problems, not just because of debilitating power struggles or entrenched interests, but because of outmoded thinking. The ideas or social paradigms that dominate congressional politics may once have worked, but times change. Those who learned about politics in the previous era may be so accustomed to thinking within the old paradigm that they fail to comprehend that society is changing and oppose efforts to experiment with new ideas. A social crisis would then lead groups of citizens to demand action and to support ambitious politicians who are willing to experiment and change.

As with finding a successful coaching staff, it may take time, a series of experimental shifts in leaders and programs, and the creative combination of new ideas and orthodox perspectives to find a viable paradigm. It also may take a new generation of politicians and social activists, drawn to service in Congress because of its great constitutional power, who challenge existing arrangements and push new policy perspectives.[28] As the new generation experiments with innovative ideas and constructs a new approach that appears to work, Congress and the nation experience a paradigm shift that can reshape politics and society as powerfully as a new philosophy of basketball can reshape campus sports.

Extensive change in governing paradigms is necessarily slow, in part because of the difficulty of restructuring politics in the midst of complex structures, anachronistic rules, and entrenched alliances—but also because social learning itself is a slow process. It requires moments of crisis and recognition of problems, both of which can focus attention on the critical issues, and also incremental processes of experimentation and assimilation.[29] The reliance of Congress on popular elections to select its members helps to make it sensitive to social problems and to the occasional upheavals in the public's partisan loyalties, which signal deep societal tensions and crises. The deliberative nature of the committee system and the institution's overall decision-making processes facilitates the informed and methodical reconstruction of paradigmatic understanding in response to crises.

Actual paradigmatic shift comes in phases of innovation followed by assimilative retrenchment, as new ideas break forth amidst crisis and then are integrated into pre-existing understandings. These phases bring with them segmented and partial paradigm shifts: Congress and the nation experiment with some ideas central to a new era, see their value and limits when institutionalized in governing strategies, and move on to new problems and paradigmatic adjustment. This pattern of phased and segmented transformation of paradigms can be seen in the response of Congress and its parties to post-industrialism, with the Republican Revolution being one such phase of experimental learning.

Congress and the Politics of Renewal: Responding to Post-Industrialism

Starting in the 1950s, when the post-industrial transition first began to emerge, we see incremental phases of a paradigm shift across decades of experimentation and assimilation. During the 1950s Congress was still dominated by southern Democrats elected in a segregated political world and was characterized, as it had been since the late 1930s, by a deep resistance to social activism, with the exception of Social Security and occasional increases in the minimum wage. There were few signs of the strong partisan leadership necessary for broad-scale policy innovation. Congressional policymaking depended, instead, on a conservative coalition of southern Democrats and northern Republicans committed to the status quo. Congress truly seemed immune to new ideas, social learning, or a transformative response to post-industrialism.[30] But in fact it did change and respond.

In the 1960s, activated by the influx of a new generation of northern Democratic liberals and presidential leadership from two former members, John Kennedy and Lyndon Johnson, Congress broke its policy immobilism and implemented a broad range of programs designed to address post-materialist policy concerns—including affirmative action for racial and ethnic minorities and women, health care for retired and displaced citizens, environmental and consumer reforms to protect our quality of life, and federal aid to education. This period of expanded activism, highlighted in Sarah Binder's statistical analysis of postwar growth in policy agendas in chapter 13, laid the foundations for a post-materialist paradigm that moved the nation beyond issues of social security and responded broadly to social movements and citizen protests of early post-industrialism.

In the 1970s the Democrats enacted a wide range of reforms, designed to reconstruct their congressional party so as to limit the power of entrenched southern Democrats and ensure the party's sustained commitment to the new agenda. They also joined with reformist Republicans to experiment with new congressional rules and structures that would protect the policymaking authority of Congress in the new era. In doing so they created an innovative new congressional budget process to help Congress maintain fiscal integrity as it pursued its new agenda.

The Reagan Revolution during the 1980s pushed Congress to reassess and reaffirm the extent of its post-materialist commitments and to experiment with new revenue strategies aimed at ending the economic stagnation that had arisen in a time of expanded spending. It also brought a new generation of southern Republicans into Congress and reinforced ideological shifts within the party toward a more socially conservative stance. This growth of Republicanism in the South had begun in response to the Democrats' embrace of civil rights legislation in 1965, which came in the face of the opposition of powerful southern congressional Democrats and led many white southerners to abandon the party.

As Congress entered the 1990s it had in many ways become a new institution, which had responded to post-industrialism in ways that would have seemed inconceivable in the mid-1950s. Although it had not embraced a post-industrial paradigm that addressed the full range of problems posed by the new era, Congress had moved the nation in incremental and segmented phases toward new ideas about what government could do and how it and its parties should implement those ideas. In this process, reformers had shown that the parties were not as entrenched in industrial-era alignments and policy perspectives as social structure theorists had surmised. As additional proof, in the early 1990s, led by a new Democratic president who sought to combine the pursuit of post-materialist programs with fiscal policies that could sustain economic growth, congressional Democrats abandoned a long-term fascination with deficit spending and embraced a commitment to balanced budgets.

Left unaddressed by congressional Democrats was their undue reliance on the federal bureaucracy to implement activist programs. During the 1980s and early 1990s, many state and local governments—Democrat and Republican alike—had experimented with new ideas about how to "reinvent government" and avoid excessive bureaucracy. Bill Clinton and Vice President Al Gore brought this new perspective to the national government in 1993, with the new Democratic administration focused particularly on new "entrepreneurial strategies" for "reinventing government."[31]

These entrepreneurial strategies involved continued government commitment to activist programs such as welfare and public health, but they also utilized the private sector to run some aspects of such programs and implemented incentive systems taken from private industry to redesign the government bureaucracies that would oversee them. They also include devolving to states and localities responsibility for the implementation of key social programs and requiring that citizens take significant responsibility for their own personal well-being.

Congressional Democrats, who had done much to address key post-industrial issues, approached these new ideas cautiously and stymied efforts by the Clinton administration to experiment with them in areas such as health care and welfare. These "old" Democratic reformers, elected in the 1960s and 1970s and now heading key committees and subcommittees, continued to support more traditional, bureaucratized approaches to social policy. They did so, moreover, at a time when citizens were increasingly frustrated by the inability of the government to rein in its bureaucracy. The Democrats' failure to support Clinton's experiments with entrepreneurial reforms provided the congressional Republican Party with a historic opportunity to push new entrepreneurial strategies of its own and become a major player in this next phase of postindustrial experimentation and paradigm shift.[32]

The Revolution as a Phase in Experimental Learning

Characterized by greater generational turnover than the governing Democrats, and thus more distant from New Deal and Great Society ideas about government, the congressional Republican Party had by the early- to mid-1980s come to contain a growing number of new members willing to challenge existing assumptions about government.[33] With backgrounds in private industry and state legislatures, these young Republicans had their own ideas about reinventing government, accepting the need for social programs but often supporting more radical entrepreneurial strategies than had Clinton and Gore.

Although the Republican Party continued to be attached to traditional policies, including support for business and low taxes, these new concerns came to the fore of the party's policy agenda. Most critically, the party balanced its attack on Congress and the congressional Democrats with innovative proposals for policy reform, so that its candidates did not simply oppose existing programs but had constructive strategies to propose for improving them. As congressional Republicans mounted their 1994 campaign, issues such as welfare reform became core elements of the Contract with America and constituted much of what made it innovative, defining the differences between the congressional parties in some distinctly new ways.

Seen through the lenses of social learning theory, what is important about the 1994 election is that it revolved around a choice between the Democrats' bureaucratized approach to social programs and the new entrepreneurial approach of congressional Republicans. The Republican victory can be seen as signaling the electorate's frustration with the congressional Democrats' outmoded perspectives and its willingness to risk experimenting with the Republicans' new direction.

The election thus was not just a stage in the normal, cyclical alternation in parties, nor just a product of post-industrial tensions, though both helped make it possible; it was also a phase in the process of experimental learning whereby the nation was incrementally recrafting its governing regime. It was the opportunity to experiment with new ideas and programmatic strategies—with new philosophies of the game—that impassioned the Republican activists, particularly Newt Gingrich, and constituted their contribution to national governance.

Once in power, the Republicans faced the difficulty of learning to govern after forty years as the minority party while simultaneously pursuing their vision of governmental change.[34] Undermined by a weak leadership structure, by inexperience with the responsibilities of majority party status, and by internal divisions, the Republicans made critical missteps that squandered their opportunity to institute fundamental alterations in national government. Yet when the party sought common ground with the president and various Democrats, as on welfare reform, telecommunications restructuring, and the revamping of agricultural policy, congressional Republicans achieved victories that served to actualize their entrepreneurial agenda. Such accomplishments helped the party to demonstrate the promise of its new paradigmatic shift and to provide citizens with a reason to maintain it in power, despite a concerted Democratic counterattack in the 1996, 1998, and 2000 elections.

The Republican Revolution proceeded in an erratic manner, from the perspective of social learning theory, because reassessment of existing paradigms and experimentation with new ideas is an inherently difficult, lengthy, conflictual, and problematic process. The limits of the Republican Revolution, however, should not divert us from recognizing the contribution it has made.

With the defeat of a long-term governing party and the move to new governing strategies, the Republicans helped break the sense of paralysis that existed in American politics in the early 1990s and helped to focus the nation on vital issues of deep concern to the citizenry. In doing so, they greatly spurred the process of paradigm reassessment and reconstruction, to such an extent that in the 2000 elections congressional Democrats touted welfare reform. Congressional Republicans had moved the public dialogue so far, in fact, that reform of Social Security, long unmentionable in American politics, was an issue in the presidential election.

Most critically, as the congressional Republicans faced the opportunity and responsibilities of governing on a sustained basis, which they had not held, in truth, since the 1920s, they came to see more clearly the strengths and contributions of Congress to national governance, and even came to defend its prerogatives. They asserted the constitutional role of Congress in annual negotiations with the president, and they asserted their right to impeach a president, drawing on powers that a generation earlier they had denounced when used against a Republican president, Richard Nixon. Calls for congressional term limits vanished from party platforms, the push for constraints on congressional authority decreased, and members appeared to increasingly appreciate the balance to the presidency that Congress provided. Although Republicans were still struggling to find a vision of Congress that could mesh with their entrepreneurial policy agenda, the struggle increasingly focused on ways to build on and reinforce its strengths, such as deliberative policymaking in committees, instead of emphasizing its flaws as a justification for reducing its institutional power and constitutional prerogatives. In this sense, the Republican Revolution served to demonstrate just how critical to representative democracy it is for political parties to alternate in power within legislative assemblies, so that they all will appreciate the complexities, strengths, and contributions of representative government and will testify in behalf of such assemblies to their diverse supporters.

With the movement toward new policy perspectives, and the growing appreciation of Republicans for congressional government, the 2000 elections focused less on the adequacy of Congress as a policymaking institution and more on the principles and strategies that should govern the nation's policy response. This shift surely constitutes a further step toward a viable post-industrial paradigm and the relegitimation of Congress as a governing institution.

Conclusion

Congress is a dynamic institution continually being reshaped by cycles of partisan learning and regime change. For a time it may be dominated by one party or factional coalition, by entrenched societal interests and institutional arrangements, and by an overarching philosophy or governing paradigm. But across time governing groups become overconfident of their mastery of electoral and organizational politics, societal change upends the support bases of the entrenched regime, and innovative ideas and experimental learning allow a new generation of partisans to open pathways to policy responsiveness and institutional renewal. The Republican Revolution is a classic instance of these processes at work, as was the rise of liberal Democratic reformers a generation earlier. As Congress and its parties respond to these processes in the contemporary era, they adapt the nation to post-industrialism and incrementally address the issues of governing legitimacy that confront them.

In this watershed year of 2000, enjoying the longest peacetime economic expansion in American history, perhaps we can allow ourselves to consider whether this forty-year process of experimentation and governing innovation within Congress might have contributed to this moment of peace and prosperity. We expect history to have its surprises just around the bend, testing the nation's resolve, creativity, and learning capacities anew. Problems with debilitating ambitions, antiquated procedures, and entrenched interests continue — moderated by waves of reform and change but still capable of inserting themselves destructively into congressional politics and national life. The policy dilemmas raised by post-industrialism are serious and continuing challenges, magnified by a process of globalization whose consequences for our nation we cannot hope to fully foresee or control. The crisis of legitimation that post-industrialism poses for democratic institutions is a persistent threat, and it is reinforced by our policy dilemmas and partisan animosities. In the face of these concerns, we cannot be sure that our policy experiments and institutional adjustments are adequate to the post-industrial challenge.

What we know at this point is that we have adjusted our governing perspectives during these decades and that, despite the bitter partisan battles that have come with the experimentation and shift, and to some extent because of them, our society is as prosperous and productive as ever. We also know one other thing: that Congress, the parties, and the electorate are capable of reassessing governing strategies, experimenting with new ones, learning innovative approaches, and addressing societal problems.

To appreciate this capacity, we must attend to the conceptual lenses through which we examine Congress and craft multiple theoretical perspectives that help us envision it more completely. Such perspectives should enable us to look beyond momentary personalities and short-term stalemate and see the dynamic, historical processes at play in congressional politics. In crafting such lenses, we must bring to the endeavor the common-sense judgment we demonstrate in daily life, taking care to focus on the motives and strategic behavior of participants in the foreground, on the shifting background contexts, and then ultimately on the ideas that participants hold about politics and society.

As we do so, crafting social choice theories to analyze the foreground, social structure theories to interpret the background, and social learning theories to comprehend the role of ideas, we see an overall pattern that no one of our theories could fully illuminate, and that helps us understand how Congress can constructively respond to societal problems. Through these multiple lenses, we see the contest for governing power that ensures partisans will highlight societal problems as they challenge for control of Congress. We see the dynamic societal changes that generate new citizen demands and policy challenges. And we see the coming of a new generation of legislators, social activists, and engaged citizens who push Congress to experiment with fresh ideas, address the pressing policy challenges, and solve societal problems.

Examining the contemporary Congress through these multiple lenses, we see an institution responding to the problems and opportunities of post-industrialism—gradually, incrementally, and partially, but also in sustained and consequential ways. The concerns to which Congress has responded, though perhaps too limited in number and imperfect in their resolution, are significant ones, and they include such seemingly intransigent problems as racial segregation, gender inequality, poverty among the elderly, urban pollution, budget deficits, economic restructuring, and welfare dependency. Although Congress has not tackled these issues alone, and at times it has exacerbated them, it ultimately has contributed to the experimental learning that helped to address them. This capacity of a political institution to contribute to social learning in a sustained and consequential fashion, and in a manner ultimately controlled and shaped by a nation's citizens, is no small accomplishment.

Time will tell whether Congress has helped us learn enough of the right things, and adequately assimilate them with the enduring truths inherited from past generations, to redress the problems of post-industrialism. Insofar as we and Congress have failed in our learning efforts, we should recall that the essence of experimentation is the ability to learn from error and try again. Perhaps that realization will encourage us to confront the remaining problems and to see Congress as a legitimate participant in democratic governance as we approach the challenges of the new century.

Notes

1. William F. Connelly and John J. Pitney Jr., *Congress' Permanent Minority? Republicans in the U.S. House* (Lanham, Md.: Rowman and Littlefield, 1994).
2. Joseph Cooper, ed., *Congress and the Decline of Public Trust* (Boulder, Colo.: Westview, 1999), and John R. Hibbing and Elizabeth Theiss-Morse, *Congress as Public Enemy: Public Attitudes toward American Political Institutions* (Cambridge: Cambridge University Press, 1995).
3. Walter Dean Burnham, "Realignment Lives," in Bert Rockman, ed., *The Clinton Presidency* (Pittsburgh: University of Pittsburgh Press, 1995).
4. For an overview of the Republican Revolution and Gingrich's perceived role in it, see Dan Balz and Ronald Brownstein, *Storming the Gates: Protest Politics and the Republican Revival* (Boston: Little, Brown, 1996).
5. For a revealing look at Gingrich's own take on these matters, see Newt Gingrich and Marianne Gingrich, "Post-Industrial Politics: The Leader as Learner," *The Futurist* (December 1981): 30–32.
6. Walter Dean Burnham, "Pattern Recognition and 'Doing' Political History: Art, Science, or Bootless Enterprise?" and Hugh Heclo, "Ideas, Interests, and Institutions," both in *The Dynamics of American Politics*, ed. by Lawrence C. Dodd and Calvin Jillson (Boulder, Colo.: Westview, 1994).
7. On social choice theory, see William H. Riker, *Liberalism vs. Populism* (San Francisco: W.H. Freeman, 1982), and Kenneth A. Shepsle and Mark S. Bonchek, *Analyzing Politics: Rationality, Behavior, and Institutions* (New York: W.W. Norton, 1997).
8. Morris P. Fiorina, *Representatives, Roll Calls, and Constituencies* (Lexington, Mass.: Lexington Books, 1974); Fiorina, *Congress: Keystone of the Washington Establishment* (New Haven: Yale University Press, 1977); and David R. Mayhew, *Congress: The Electoral Connection* (New Haven: Yale University Press, 1974).
9. Richard F. Fenno Jr., *Congressmen in Committees* (Boston: Little, Brown, 1973), and Barbara Sinclair, *Legislators, Leaders, and Lawmaking: The U.S. House of Representatives in the Postreform Era* (Baltimore: Johns Hopkins University Press, 1995).
10. Anthony Downs, *An Economic Theory of Democracy* (New York: Harper and Row, 1957).
11. Barry R. Weingast, "A Rational Choice Perspective on Congressional Norms," *American Journal of Political Science* 23 (1979): 249.
12. Roger H. Davidson and Walter Oleszek, *Congress against Itself* (Bloomington: Indiana University Press, 1977); C. Lawrence Evans and Walter J. Oleszek, *Congress Under Fire* (Boston: Houghton Mifflin, 1997); Glenn R. Parker, *Institutional Change, Discretion, and the Making of Modern Congress: An Economic Interpretation* (Ann Arbor: University of Michigan Press, 1992); and Raymond E. Wolfinger and Joan Heifetz Hollinger, "Safe Seats, Seniority, and Power in Congress," *American Political Science Review* 80 (1965): 337–49.

13. Dodd, "Congress and the Quest for Power," in *Congress Reconsidered*, 1st ed., ed. by Lawrence C. Dodd and Bruce I. Oppenheimer (New York: Praeger, 1977).

14. Dodd, "The Cycles of Legislative Change," in *Political Science: The Science of Politics*, ed. by Herbert Weisberg (New York: Agathon, 1986).

15. Fiorina, *Congress: Keystone of the Washington Establishment.*

16. Gary Jacobson, "The Marginals Never Vanished," *American Journal of Political Science* 31 (1987): 126–41; and Thomas E. Mann, *Unsafe at Any Margins* (Washington, D.C.: American Enterprise Institute, 1978).

17. This argument reflects the "retrospective voting perspective" developed by Key and Fiorina in their study of presidential elections. See V.O. Key, *The Responsible Electorate* (New York: Vintage, 1966), and Morris Fiorina, *Retrospective Voting in American National Elections* (New Haven: Yale University Press, 1981).

18. For a more extensive discussion of this paradox, see Oppenheimer, "Abdicating Congressional Power," in *Congress Reconsidered*, 6th ed., ed. by Dodd and Oppenheimer (Washington, D.C.: CQ Press, 1997).

19. Nelson Polsby, "The Institutionalization of the U.S. House of Representatives," *American Political Science Review* 62 (1968): 144–68.

20. See James Sterling Young, *The Washington Community, 1800–1828* (New York: Columbia University Press, 1966); Woodrow Wilson, *Congressional Government* (Gloucester, Mass.: Peter Smith, reissued, 1973); Joseph Cooper and David W. Brady, "Toward a Diachronic Analysis of Change," *American Political Science Review* 75 (1981): 988–1006; and Theodore J. Lowi, *The End of Liberalism* (New York: Norton, 1979). Other important historical analyses that reflect the influence of social context include Elaine Swift, *The Making of the American Senate* (Ann Arbor: University of Michigan Press, 1996) and Eric Schickler, *Disjointed Pluralism: Institutional Innovation and the Development of the U.S. Congress* (Princeton: Princeton University Press, forthcoming).

21. For discussion of the "legitimation crisis paradigm" within sociology, see Edward W. Lehman, *The Viable Polity* (Philadelphia: Temple University Press, 1992); for a forceful statement, see Jürgen Habermas, *Legitimation Crisis* (Boston: Beacon, 1973).

22. For a general statement of the powerful influence that antiquated institutions may have on new historical eras, see Karen Oren and Stephen Skowronek, "Beyond the Iconography of Order: Notes for a 'New Institutionalism,' " in *The Dynamics of American Politics.*

23. Dodd, "Congress, the Constitution, and the Crisis of Legitimation," in *Congress Reconsidered*, 2d ed. (Washington, D.C.: CQ Press, 1981).

24. Fiorina, *Congress: Keystone of the Washington Establishment*, 2d ed., 1989.

25. For a discussion of the ways in which term limits on the Speaker, and related factors, helped create a weakened leadership structure, see Ronald M. Peters Jr., "Institutional Context and Leadership Style," in *New Majority or Old Minority?* ed. by Nicol C. Rae and Colton Campbell (Lanham, Md.: Rowman and Littlefield, 1999); see also Dodd and Oppenheimer, "Revolution in the House: Testing the Limits of Party Government," in *Congress Reconsidered*, 6th ed.

26. Gregory Bateson, *Steps to an Ecology of Mind* (New York: Ballantine, 1972); and Geoffrey Vickers, *Value Systems and Social Process* (London: Tavistock, 1968). For a useful application of social learning theory to political science, see Peter Hall, "Policy Paradigms, Social Learning and the State," *Comparative Politics* 25 (1993): 75–96. My application of social learning theory to politics here, following Hall's lead, restates it in the language of philosopher of science Thomas Kuhn. See Thomas Kuhn, *The Structure of Scientific Revolutions* (Chicago: The University of Chicago Press, 1970).

27. For my earlier application of social learning theory to American politics, see Dodd, "Congress, the Presidency, and the American Experience," in *Divided Democracy*, ed.

by James A. Thurber (Washington, D.C.: CQ Press, 1991), and Dodd, "Political Learning and Political Change," in *The Dynamics of American Politics*.

28. Dodd, "A Theory of Congressional Cycles," in *Congress and Policy Change*, ed. by Gerald Wright, Leroy Rieselbach, and Lawrence C. Dodd (New York: Agathon, 1986).

29. John W. Kingdon, *Agendas, Alternatives, and Public Policy* (Boston: Little, Brown, 1984); and David R. Mayhew, *America's Congress* (New Haven: Yale University Press, 2000).

30. See James MacGregor Burns, *The Deadlock of Democracy* (Englewood Cliffs, N.J.: Prentice-Hall, 1963); and Samuel P. Huntington, "Congressional Responses to the Twentieth Century," in *The Congress and America's Future*, ed. by David B. Truman (Englewood Cliffs, N.J.: Prentice-Hall, 1965).

31. On the emergence of this entrepreneurial perspective and its importance for Congress, see Dodd, "Congress and the Politics of Renewal," in *Congress Reconsidered*, 5th ed., ed. by Dodd and Oppenheimer (Washington, D.C.: CQ Press, 1993).

32. See, for supportive analysis, Haynes Johnson and David Broder, *The System* (Boston: Little, Brown, 1996); see also President Clinton's assessment of this period in Joe Klein, "Eight Years: Bill Clinton and the Politics of Persistence," in *The New Yorker*, October 16–23, 2000, 206–9.

33. Michael Berkman, *The State Roots of National Policy* (Pittsburgh: University of Pittsburgh Press, 1991); and Douglas R. Koopman, *Hostile Takeover: The House Republican Party, 1980–1995* (Lanham, Md.: Rowman and Littlefield, 1996).

34. Richard F. Fenno Jr., *Learning to Govern* (Washington, D.C.: Brookings, 1997); and David Price, *The Congressional Experience* (Boulder, Colo.: Westview, 2000), particularly chap. 8.

Suggested Readings

✧ ✧ ✧

Aberbach, Joel D. *Keeping a Watchful Eye*. Washington, D.C.: Brookings, 1990.

Abramowitz, Alan I. "Incumbency, Campaign Spending, and the Decline of Competition in U.S. House Elections." *Journal of Politics* 53 (1991): 34–56.

Abramowitz, Alan I., and Jeffrey A. Segal. *Senate Elections*. Ann Arbor: University of Michigan Press, 1992.

Abramson, Paul, John H. Aldrich, and David W. Rohde. "Progressive Ambition among United States Senators: 1972–1988." *Journal of Politics* 49 (1987): 3–35.

Adler, Scott E., and John S. Lipinski. "Demand - Side Theory and Congressional Committee Composition: A Constituency Characteristics Approach." *American Journal of Political Science* 41 (1997): 895–918.

Aldrich, John H. *Why Parties? The Origin and Transformation of Political Parties in America*. Chicago: University of Chicago Press, 1995.

Aldrich, John H., and David W. Rohde. "The Republican Revolution and the House Appropriations Committee." *Journal of Politics* 62 (February 2000): 1–33.

Alesina, Alberto, and Howard Rosenthal. "Partisan Cycles in Congressional Elections and the Macroeconomy." *American Political Science Review* 83 (1989): 373–98.

Anderson, Thorton. *Creating the Constitution: The Convention of 1787 and the First Congress*. University Park: Pennsylvania State University Press, 1993.

Ansolabehere, Stephen, and Alan Gerber. "The Effects of Filing Fees and Petition Requirements in U.S. House Elections." *Legislative Studies Quarterly* 21 (1996): 249–64.

Arnold, R. Douglas. *Congress and the Bureaucracy*. New Haven: Yale University Press, 1979.

___. *The Logic of Congressional Action*. New Haven: Yale University Press, 1990.

Asher, Herbert B. "The Learning of Legislative Norms." *American Political Science Review* 67 (1973): 499–513.

Bach, Stanley, and Steven S. Smith. *Managing Uncertainty in the House: Adaptation and Innovation in Special Rules*. Washington, D.C.: Brookings, 1988.

Baker, Ross K. *House and Senate*. New York: Norton, 1989.

Bauer, Raymond A., Ithiel de Sola Pool, and Lewis A. Dexter. *American Business and Public Policy*. New York: Atherton, 1963.

Baumgartner, Frank R., and Bryan D. Jones. "Agenda Dynamics and Policy Subsystems." *Journal of Politics* 53 (November 1991): 1044–74.

Baumgartner, Frank R., Bryan D. Jones, and Michael C. MacLeod. "The Evolution of Legislative Jurisdictions." *Journal of Politics*, forthcoming.

Benjamin, Gerald, and Michael Malbin, eds. *Limiting Legislative Terms*. Washington, D.C.: CQ Press, 1992.

Berkman, Michael B. "State Legislators in Congress: Strategic Politicians, Professional Legislatures, and the Party Nexus." *American Journal of Political Science* 38 (1994): 1025–55.

Berkman, Michael B. *The State Roots of National Politics: Congress and the Tax Agenda, 1978–1986*. Pittsburgh: University of Pittsburgh Press, 1993.

Bianco, William T. *Trust: Representatives and Constituents*. Ann Arbor: University of Michigan Press, 1994.

Bibby, John F., and Roger H. Davidson. *On Capitol Hill*. 2d ed. Hinsdale, Ill.: Dryden Press, 1972.

Binder, Sarah A. "The Partisan Basis of Procedural Choice: Allocating Parliamentary Rights in the House, 1789–1900." *American Political Science Review* 90 (1996): 8–20.

___. *Minority Rights, Majority Rule*. New York: Cambridge University Press, 1997.

___. "The Dynamics of Legislative Gridlock, 1947–96." *American Political Science Review* 93 (1999).

Binder, Sarah A., and Steven S. Smith. *Politics or Principle: Filibustering in the United States Senate*. Washington, D.C.: Brookings, 1997.

Bolling, Richard. *House Out of Order*. New York: Dutton, 1965.

___. *Power in the House*. New York: Dutton, 1965.

Bond, Jon R., and Richard Fleisher. *The President in the Legislative Arena*. Chicago: University of Chicago Press, 1990.

___. *Polarized Politics: The President and the Congress in a Partisan Era*. Washington, D.C.: CQ Press, 2000.

Born, Richard. "Changes in the Competitiveness of House Primary Elections, 1956–1976." *American Politics Quarterly* 8 (1980): 495–506.

Bosso, Christopher. *Pesticides and Politics: The Life Cycle of a Public Issue*. Pittsburgh: University of Pittsburgh Press, 1988.

Brady, David W. *Congressional Voting in a Partisan Era: A Study of the McKinley Houses*. Lawrence: University Press of Kansas, 1973.

___. *Critical Elections and Congressional Policy Making*. Stanford, Calif.: Stanford University Press, 1988.

Brady, David W., and Craig Volden. *Revolving Gridlock: Politics and Policy from Carter to Clinton*. Boulder, Col.: Westview, 1998.

Brady, David W., Joseph Cooper, and Patricia A. Hurley. "The Decline of Party in the U.S. House of Representatives, 1887–1968." *Legislative Studies Quarterly* 4 (1979): 381–407.

Bullock, Charles S., III. "House Committee Assignments." In *The Congressional System: Notes and Readings*. 2d ed. Edited by Leroy N. Rieselbach. North Scituate, Mass.: Duxbury Press, 1979.

Burrell, Barbara C. *A Woman's Place Is in the House.* Ann Arbor: University of Michigan Press, 1994.

Cain, Bruce, John Ferejohn, and Morris Fiorina. *The Personal Vote: Constituency Service and Electoral Independence.* Cambridge: Harvard University Press, 1967.

Campbell, James E. *The Presidential Pulse of Congressional Elections.* Lexington, Ky.: University of Kentucky Press, 1993.

Canon, David T. *Actors, Athletes, and Astronauts: Political Amateurs in the United States Congress.* Chicago: University of Chicago Press, 1990.

Canon, David T. *Race, Redistricting, and Representation: The Unintended Consequences of Black Majority Districts.* Chicago: University of Chicago Press, 1999.

Canon, David T., and Kenneth R. Mayer. *The Dysfunctional Congress? The Individual Roots of an Institutional Dilemma.* Boulder, Col.: Westview, 1999.

Canon, David T., Matthew Schousen, and Patrick Sellers. "The Supply Side of Congressional Redistricting: Race and Strategic Politicians, 1972–1992." *Journal of Politics* 58 (1996): 846–62.

Clausen, Aage R. *How Congressmen Decide.* New York: St. Martin's, 1973.

Clem, Alan L., ed. *The Making of Congressmen: Seven Campaigns of 1974.* North Scituate, Mass.: Duxbury Press, 1976.

Collie, Melissa, and Brian E. Roberts. "Trading Places: Choice and Committee Chairs in the U.S. Senate, 1950–1986." *Journal of Politics* 54 (1992): 231–45.

Cook, Elizabeth Adell, Sue Thomas, and Clyde Wilcox, eds. *The Year of the Woman: Myths and Reality.* Boulder, Col.: Westview, 1994.

Cooper, Joseph. *The Origins of the Standing Committees and the Development of the Modern House.* Houston: Rice University Studies, 1971.

Cooper, Joseph, ed. *Congress and the Decline of Public Trust.* Boulder, Col.: Westview, 1999.

Cooper, Joseph, and David W. Brady. "Institutional Context and Leadership Style: The House from Cannon to Rayburn." *American Political Science Review* 75 (1981).

___. "Toward a Diachronic Analysis of Congress." *American Political Science Review* 75 (1981).

Cooper, Joseph, and Garry Young. "Partisanship, Bipartisanship, and Crosspartisanship in Congress since the New Deal." In *Congress Reconsidered.* 6th ed. Edited by Lawrence C. Dodd and Bruce I. Oppenheimer. Washington, D.C.: CQ Press, 1997.

Cooper, Joseph, and G. Calvin Mackenzie. *The House at Work.* Austin: University of Texas Press, 1981.

Cover, Albert D. "Contacting Congressional Constituents: Some Patterns of Perquisite Use." *American Journal of Political Science* 24 (1980): 125–34.

Cover, Albert D., and David R. Mayhew. "Congressional Dynamics and the Decline of Competitive Congressional Elections." In *Congress Reconsidered.*

2d ed. Edited by Lawrence C. Dodd and Bruce I. Oppenheimer. Washington, D.C.: CQ Press, 1981.

Cox, Gary, and Mathew McCubbins. *Parties and Committees in the U.S. House of Representatives.* Berkeley: University of California Press, 1990.

___. *Legislative Leviathan: Party Government in the House.* Berkeley: University of California Press, 1993.

Cox, James, Gregory Hager, and David Lowery. "Regime Change in Presidential and Congressional Budgeting: Role Discontinuity or Role Evolution?" *American Journal of Political Science* 37 (1993): 88–118.

Davidson, Roger H., ed. *The Postreform Congress.* New York: St. Martin's, 1992.

Davidson, Roger H., and Walter J. Oleszek. *Congress against Itself.* Bloomington: Indiana University Press, 1977.

___. *Congress and Its Members.* 5th ed. Washington, D.C.: CQ Press, 1996.

De Boef, Suzanna, and James A. Stimson. "The Dynamic Structure of Congressional Elections." *Journal of Politics* 55 (1993): 630–48.

Deering, Christopher J., and Steven S. Smith. *Committees in Congress.* 3d ed. Washington, D.C.: CQ Press, 1997.

Degregorio, Christine, and Kevin Snider. "Leadership Appeal in the U.S. House of Representatives: Comparing Officeholders and Aides." *Legislative Studies Quarterly* 20 (1995): 491–511.

Destler, I.M. *Renewing Fast-Track Legislation.* Washington, D.C.: Institute for International Economics and Policy Analysis, no. 50, September 1997.

Dexter, Lewis A. *How Organizations Are Represented in Washington.* Indianapolis: Bobbs-Merrill, 1969.

___. *The Sociology and Politics of Congress.* Chicago: Rand McNally, 1969.

Dion, Douglas. *Turning the Legislative Thumbscrew: Minority Rights and Procedural Change in Legislative Politics.* Ann Arbor, Mich.: University of Michigan Press, 1997.

Dion, Douglas, and John Huber. "Procedural Choice and the House Committee on Rules." *Journal of Politics* 58 (1996): 25–53.

Dodd, Lawrence C. "Congress and the Quest for Power." In *Congress Reconsidered.* 1st ed. Edited by Lawrence C. Dodd and Bruce I. Oppenheimer. New York: Praeger, 1977.

___. "Congress, the Constitution, and the Crisis of Legitimation." In *Congress Reconsidered.* 2d ed. Edited by Lawrence C. Dodd and Bruce I. Oppenheimer. Washington, D.C.: CQ Press, 1981.

___. "Coalition-Building by Party Leaders: A Case Study of House Democrats." *Congress and the Presidency Journal* 10 (fall 1983): 145–68.

___. "The Cycles of Legislative Change." In *Political Science: The Science of Politics.* Edited by Herbert F. Weisberg. New York: Agathon Press, 1986.

Dodd, Lawrence C., and Richard L. Schott. *Congress and the Administrative State.* 2d ed. Boulder, Col.: Westview, 1994.

Eckhardt, Bob, and Charles L. Black Jr. *The Titles of Power: Conversations on the American Constitution.* New Haven: Yale University Press, 1976.

Endersby, James W., and Karen M. McCurdy. "Committee Assignments in the U.S. Senate." *Legislative Studies Quarterly* 21 (1996): 219–34.

Epstein, David, and Peter Zemsky. "Money Talks: Deterring Quality Challengers in Congressional Elections." *American Political Science Review* 89 (1995): 295–308.

Erikson, Robert S. "The Advantage of Incumbency in Congressional Elections." *Polity* 3 (1971).

___. "Is There Such a Thing as a Safe Seat?" *Polity* 8 (1976): 623–32.

___. "The Puzzle of Midterm Loss." *Journal of Politics* 50 (1988): 1011–29.

Eulau, Heinz, and Paul Karps. "The Puzzle of Representation." *Legislative Studies Quarterly* 2 (1977): 233–54.

Evans, C. Lawrence. *Leadership in Committee.* Ann Arbor: University of Michigan Press, 1991.

Evans, C. Lawrence, and Walter J. Oleszek. *Congress Under Fire.* Boston: Houghton Mifflin, 1997.

Evans, Diana. "Policy and Pork: The Use of Pork Barrel Projects to Build Policy Coalitions in the House of Representatives." *American Journal of Political Science* 38 (1994): 894–917.

Fenno, Richard F., Jr. *The Power of the Purse.* Boston: Little, Brown, 1966.

___. *Congressmen in Committees.* Boston: Little, Brown, 1973.

___. *Home Style: House Members in Their Districts.* Boston: Little, Brown, 1978.

___. *The United States Senate: A Bicameral Perspective.* Washington, D.C.: American Enterprise Institute, 1982.

___. *Senators on the Campaign Trail: The Politics of Representation.* Norman: University of Oklahoma Press, 1996.

___. *Learning to Govern: An Institutional View of the 104th Congress.* Washington, D.C.: Brookings, 1997.

Ferejohn, John A. *Pork Barrel Politics.* Stanford, Calif.: Stanford University Press, 1974.

Fiorina, Morris P. *Representatives, Roll Calls, and Constituencies.* Lexington, Mass.: Lexington Books, 1974.

___. *Congress: Keystone of the Washington Establishment.* New Haven: Yale University Press, 1977.

___. *Divided Government.* New York: Allyn and Bacon, 1995.

Fiorina, Morris P., David W. Rohde, and Peter Wissel. "Historical Change in House Turnover." In *Congress in Change.* Edited by Norman J. Ornstein. New York: Praeger, 1975.

Fishel, Jeff. *Party and Opposition.* New York: David McKay, 1973.

Fisher, Louis. *The Constitution between Friends: Congress, the President, and the Law.* New York: St. Martin's, 1978.

Flemming, Gregory N. "Presidential Coattails in Open-Seat Elections." *Legislative Studies Quarterly* 20 (1995): 197–211.

Fowler, Linda L. *Candidates, Congress, and American Democracy.* Ann Arbor: University of Michigan Press, 1993.

Fowler, Linda L., and Robert D. McClure. *Political Ambition: Who Decides to Run for Congress?* New Haven: Yale University Press, 1989.

Fox, Harrison W., Jr., and Susan Webb Hammond. *Congressional Staffs: The Invisible Force in American Lawmaking.* New York: Free Press, 1977.

Franklin, Daniel P. *Making Ends Meet.* Washington, D.C.: CQ Press, 1993.

Frantzich, Stephen E. "Computerized Information Technology in the U.S. House of Representatives." *Legislative Studies Quarterly* 4 (1979): 255–80.

Freeman, J. Leiper. *The Political Process.* New York: Random House, 1955.

Friedman, Sally. "House Committee Assignments of Women and Minority Newcomers." *Legislative Studies Quarterly* 21 (1996): 73–82.

Froman, Lewis A., Jr. *The Congressional Process: Strategies, Rules and Procedures.* Boston: Little, Brown, 1967.

Gamm, Gerald, and Kenneth Shepsle. "The Emergence of Legislative Institutions: Standing Committees in the House and Senate, 1810–1825." *Legislative Studies Quarterly* 14 (1989): 39–66.

Gibson, Martha L. "Issues, Coalitions, and Divided Government." *Congress and the Presidency* 22 (1995): 155–66.

Gibson, Martha L. *Conflict amid Consensus in American Trade Policy.* Washington, D.C.: Georgetown University Press, 2000.

Gilmour, John B. *Reconcilable Differences.* Berkeley: University of California Press, 1990.

Gilmour, John B., and Paul Rothstein. "A Dynamic Model of Loss, Retirement, and Tenure in the U.S. House." *Journal of Politics* 58 (1996): 54–68.

Glazer, Amihai, and Bernard Grofman. "Two Plus Two Plus Two Equals Six: Tenure of Office of Senators and Representatives, 1953–1983." *Legislative Studies Quarterly* 12 (1987): 555–63.

Goehlert, Robert U., and John R. Sayre. *The United States Congress: A Bibliography.* New York: Free Press, 1982.

Goodwin, George, Jr. *The Little Legislatures.* Amherst: University of Massachusetts Press, 1970.

Groseclose, Timothy. "The Committee Outlier Debate: A Review and a Reexamination of Some of the Evidence." *Public Choice* 80 (1994): 265–73.

Groseclose, Timothy, and Keith Krehbiel. "Golden Parachutes, Rubber Checks, and Strategic Retirements from the 102nd House." *American Journal of Political Science* 38 (February 1994): 75–99.

Hager, Gregory, and Jeffery Talbert. "Look for the Party Label: Party Influences on Voting in the U.S. House." *Legislative Studies Quarterly* 25 (2000): 75–99.

Hall, Richard L. "Participation and Purpose in Committee Decision Making." *American Political Science Review* 81 (1987): 105–27.

———. *Participation in Congress.* New Haven: Yale University Press, 1993.

Hammond, Susan Webb. *Congressional Caucuses in National Policymaking.* Baltimore: Johns Hopkins University Press, 1997.

Harris, Joseph. *Congressional Control of Administration.* Washington, D.C.: Brookings, 1964.

Hechler, Kenneth W. *Insurgency: Personalities and Politics in the Taft Era.* New York: Columbia University Press, 1940.

Heitshusen, Valerie. "Interest Group Lobbying and U.S. House Decentralization: Linking Information Type to Committee Hearing Appearances." *Political Research Quarterly* 53 (March 2000): 151–76.

Heitshusen, Valerie. "The Allocation of Federal Money to House Committee Members: Distributive Theory and Policy Jurisdictions." *American Politics Research* (formerly *American Politics Quarterly*) 29 (January 2001): 80–98.

Henry, Charles P. "Legitimizing Race in Congressional Politics." *American Politics Quarterly* 5 (1977): 149–76.

Herrnson, Paul S. *Party Campaigning in the 1980s.* Cambridge: Harvard University Press, 1988.

———. *Congressional Elections: Campaigning at Home and in Washington.* Washington, D.C.: CQ Press, 1995.

Hershey, Marjorie R. *The Making of Campaign Strategy.* Lexington, Mass.: Lexington Books, 1974.

Hibbing, John R. *Congressional Careers.* Chapel Hill: University of North Carolina Press, 1991.

Hibbing, John R., and Elizabeth Theiss-Morse. *Congress as Public Enemy: Public Attitudes toward American Political Institutions.* Cambridge: Cambridge University Press, 1995.

Hinckley, Barbara. *The Seniority System in Congress.* Bloomington: Indiana University Press, 1971.

Hoadly, John F. "The Emergence of Political Parties in Congress, 1789–1803." *American Political Science Review* 74 (1980): 757–79.

Holtzman, Abraham. *Legislative Liaison.* Chicago: Rand McNally, 1970.

Huitt, Ralph K., and Robert L. Peabody. *Congress: Two Decades of Analysis.* New York: Harper, 1969.

Huntington, Samuel P. "Congressional Responses to the Twentieth Century." In *The Congress and America's Future.* 2d ed. Edited by David B. Truman. Englewood Cliffs, N.J.: Prentice-Hall, 1973.

Hurley, Patricia, and Kim Quarle Hill. "The Prospects for Issue-Voting in Contemporary Congressional Elections." *American Politics Quarterly* 8 (1980): 425–48.

Jackson, John. *Constituencies and Leaders in Congress.* Cambridge: Harvard University Press, 1974.

Jacobson, Gary C. *Money in Congressional Elections.* New Haven: Yale University Press, 1980.

———. "The Marginals Never Vanished: Incumbency and Competition in Elections to the U.S. House of Representatives, 1952–81." *American Journal of Political Science* 31 (1987): 126–41.

———. *The Electoral Origins of Divided Government.* Boulder, Col.: Westview, 1990.

———. *The Politics of Congressional Elections.* 4th ed. New York: Longman, 1996.

Jacobson, Gary C., and Samuel Kernell. *Strategy and Choice in Congressional Elections*. New Haven: Yale University Press, 1983.

Jewell, Malcolm E. *Senatorial Politics and Foreign Policy*. Lexington: University of Kentucky Press, 1962.

Jewell, Malcolm E., and Samuel C. Patterson. *The Legislative Process in the United States*. 3d ed. New York: Random House, 1977.

Jillson, Calvin, and Rick K. Wilson. *Congressional Dynamics: Structure, Coordination, and Choice in the First American Congress, 1774–1789*. Stanford, Calif.: Stanford University Press, 1994.

Johannes, John R. *Policy Innovation in Congress*. Morristown, N.J.: General Learning Press, 1972.

Jones, Bryan D., Frank R. Baumgartner, and James L. True. "Policy Punctuations: U.S. Budget Authority, 1947–1995." *Journal of Politics* 60 (1998): 1–33.

Jones, Bryan D., Frank R. Baumgartner, and Jeffrey C. Talbert. "The Destruction of Issue Monopolies in Congress." *American Political Science Review* 87 (1993): 657–71.

Jones, Charles O. *The Minority Party in Congress*. Boston: Little, Brown, 1970.

___. "Will Reform Change Congress?" In *Congress Reconsidered*. 1st ed. Edited by Lawrence C. Dodd and Bruce I. Oppenheimer. New York: Praeger, 1977.

Kahn, Kim Fridkin, and Patrick J. Kenney. *The Spectacle of U.S. Senate Campaigns*. Princeton: Princeton University Press, 1999.

Katz, Jonathan, and Brian Sala. "Careerism, Committee Assignments, and the Electoral Connection." *American Political Science Review* 90 (1996): 21–33.

Kazee, Thomas, ed. *Who Runs for Congress? Ambition, Context, and Candidate Emergence*. Washington, D.C.: CQ Press, 1994.

Kelly, Sean Q. "Democratic Leadership in the Modern Senate: The Emerging Roles of the Democratic Policy Committee." *Congress and the Presidency* 22 (1995): 113–40.

Kiewiet, Roderick, and Mathew D. McCubbins. *The Spending Power*. Berkeley: University of California Press, 1991.

Kingdon, John W. *Candidates for Office*. New York: Random House, 1968.

___. *Congressmen's Voting Decisions*. New York: Harper, 1973.

King, David C. *Turf Wars: How Congressional Committees Claim Jurisdiction*. Chicago: University of Chicago Press, 1997.

Krasno, Jonathan S. *Challengers, Competition, and Reelection: Comparing Senate and House Elections*. New Haven: Yale University Press, 1994.

Krehbiel, Keith. "Are Congressional Committees Composed of Preference Outliers?" *American Political Science Review* 84 (1990): 149–64.

___. *Information and Legislative Organization*. Ann Arbor: University of Michigan Press, 1990.

___. *Pivotal Politics: A Theory of U.S. Lawmaking*. Chicago: University of Chicago Press, 1998.

Krehbiel, Keith, Kenneth A. Shepsle, and Barry R. Weingast. "Why Are Congressional Committees Powerful?" *American Political Science Review* 81 (1987): 929–48.

Kuklinski, James H. "District Competitiveness and Legislative Roll Call Behavior: A Reassessment of the Marginality Hypothesis." *American Journal of Political Science* 21 (1977): 627–38.

Lee, Francis E., and Bruce I. Oppenheimer. *Sizing Up the Senate.* Chicago: University of Chicago Press, 1999.

LeLoup, Lance T., and Steven Shull. "Congress versus the Executive: The 'Two Presidencies' Reconsidered." *Social Science Quarterly* 59 (1979): 704–19.

Lindsay, James M. *Congress and the Politics of U.S. Foreign Policy.* Baltimore: Johns Hopkins University Press, 1994.

Loewenberg, Gerhard, and Samuel Patterson. *Comparing Legislatures.* Boston: Little, Brown, 1979.

Longley, Lawrence D., and Walter J. Oleszek. *Bicameral Politics: Conference Committees in Congress.* New Haven: Yale University Press, 1989.

Loomis, Burdett A. *The New American Politician: Ambition, Entrepreneurship, and the Changing Face of Political Life.* New York: Basic Books, 1988.

Lowi, Theodore J. *The End of Liberalism.* New York: Norton, 1969, 1979.

___. *The End of the Republican Era.* Norman: University of Oklahoma Press, 1995.

Maass, Arthur. *Congress and the Common Good.* New York: Basic Books, 1983.

Maisel, Louis S. *From Obscurity to Oblivion: Running in the Congressional Primary.* Knoxville: University of Tennessee Press, 1982.

Maltzman, Forrest. "Meeting Competing Demands: Committee Performance in the Post-Reform House." *American Journal of Political Science* 39 (1995): 653–82.

Manley, John F. *The Politics of Finance.* Boston: Little, Brown, 1970.

Mann, Thomas E. *Unsafe at Any Margin: Interpreting Congressional Elections.* Washington, D.C.: American Enterprise Institute, 1978.

___, ed. *A Question of Balance: The President, the Congress, and Foreign Policy.* Washington, D.C.: Brookings, 1990.

Mann, Thomas E., and Raymond E. Wolfinger. "Candidates and Parties in Congressional Elections." *American Political Science Review* 74 (1980): 616–32.

Matthews, Donald R. *U.S. Senators and Their World.* New York: Vintage Books, 1960.

Mayhew, David R. *Party Loyalty among Congressmen.* Cambridge: Harvard University Press, 1966.

___. *Congress: The Electoral Connection.* New Haven: Yale University Press, 1974.

___. *Divided We Govern.* New Haven: Yale University Press, 1991.

___. *America's Congress: Actions in the Public Sphere, James Madison through Newt Gingrich.* New Haven: Yale University Press, 2000.

McAdams, John C., and John R. Johannes. "Congressmen, Perquisites, and Elections." *Journal of Politics* 50 (1988): 412–39.

Meernik, James. "Presidential Support in Congress: Conflict and Consensus in Foreign and Defense Policy." *Journal of Politics* 55 (1993): 569–87.

Mezey, Michael L. *Congress, the President, and Public Policy.* Boulder, Col.: Westview, 1989.

Moe, Terry M. "An Assessment of the Positive Theory of Congressional Dominance." *Legislative Studies Quarterly* 12 (1987): 475–520.

Mondak, Jeffrey. "Competence, Integrity, and Electoral Success of Congressional Incumbents." *Journal of Politics* 57 (1995): 1043–69.

Nelson, Garrison. "Partisan Patterns of House Leadership Change, 1789–1977." *American Political Science Review* 71 (1977): 918–39.

Niemi, Richard, and Laura Winsky. "The Persistence of Partisan Redistricting Effects in Congressional Elections in the 1970s and 1980s." *Journal of Politics* 54 (1992): 563–72.

Norpoth, Helmut. "Explaining Party Cohesion in Congress: The Case of Shared Party Attributes." *American Political Science Review* 70 (1976): 1157–71.

Ogul, Morris S. *Congress Oversees the Bureaucracy.* Pittsburgh: University of Pittsburgh Press, 1976.

Oleszek, Walter J. *Congressional Procedures and the Policy Process.* 4th ed. Washington, D.C.: CQ Press, 1996.

Oppenheimer, Bruce I. *Oil and the Congressional Process: The Limits of Symbolic Politics.* Lexington, Mass.: Lexington Books, 1974.

———. "The Rules Committee: New Arm of Leadership in a Decentralized House." In *Congress Reconsidered.* 1st ed. Edited by Lawrence C. Dodd and Bruce I. Oppenheimer. New York: Praeger, 1977.

———. "Split-Party Control of Congress, 1981–1986: Exploring Electoral and Apportionment Explanations." *American Journal of Political Science* 33 (1989): 653–69.

———. "The Representational Experience: The Effect of State Population on Senator-Constituency Linkages." *American Journal of Political Science* 40 (1996): 1280–99.

Orfield, Gary. *Congressional Power: Congress and Social Change.* New York: Harcourt, 1975.

Ornstein, Norman J. *Congress in Change: Evolution and Reform.* New York: Praeger, 1975.

Ornstein, Norman J., and Shirley Elder. *Interest Groups, Lobbying, and Policymaking.* Washington, D.C.: CQ Press, 1978.

Ornstein, Norman J., Thomas E. Mann, and Michael J. Malbin. *Vital Statistics on Congress, 1995–1996.* Washington, D.C.: Congressional Quarterly, 1995.

Owens, John E. "Curbing the Fiefdoms: Party-Committee Relations in the Contemporary U.S. House of Representatives." In *The Changing Roles of Parliamentary Committees.* Edited by Lawrence D. Longley and Attila Agh. Appleton, Wis.: Research Committee of Legislative Specialists, 1997.

Parker, Glenn R. *Homeward Bound: Explaining Changes in Congressional Behavior.* Pittsburgh: University of Pittsburgh Press, 1986.

____. *Institutional Change, Discretion and the Making of the Modern Congress.* Ann Arbor: University of Michigan Press, 1992.

Parker, Glenn R., and S.L. Parker. "Factions in Committees: The U.S. House of Representatives." *American Political Science Review* 73 (1979): 85–102.

Patterson, James T. *Congressional Conservatism and the New Deal.* Lexington: University of Kentucky Press, 1967.

Payne, James L. "The Personal Electoral Advantage of House Incumbents, 1936–1976." *American Politics Quarterly* 8 (1980): 465–82.

Peabody, Robert L. *Leadership in Congress: Stability, Succession, and Change.* Boston: Little, Brown, 1976.

Peabody, Robert L., and Nelson W. Polsby, eds. *New Perspectives on the House of Representatives.* 3d ed. Chicago: Rand McNally, 1977.

Peters, Ronald M., Jr. *The American Speakership.* Baltimore: Johns Hopkins University Press, 1990.

Peterson, Mark A. *Legislating Together: The White House and Capitol Hill from Eisenhower to Reagan.* Cambridge: Harvard University Press, 1990.

Polsby, Nelson W. "Institutionalization in the U.S. House of Representatives." *American Political Science Review* 62 (1968): 144–68.

____. *Congress and the Presidency.* 3d ed. Englewood Cliffs, N.J.: Prentice-Hall, 1976.

Polsby, Nelson W., Miriam Gallagher, and Barry Rundquist. "The Growth of the Seniority System in the House of Representatives." *American Political Science Review* 63 (1969): 787–807.

Poole, Keith T., and Howard Rosenthal. *Congress: A Political-Economic History of Roll Call Voting.* New York: Oxford University Press, 1997.

Powell, Lynda W. "Issue Representation in Congress." *Journal of Politics* (1982).

Price, David E. *Who Makes the Laws?* Cambridge, Mass.: Schenkman, 1972.

____. *The Congressional Experience.* Boulder, Col.: Westview, 2000.

Price, H. Douglas. "Congress and the Evolution of Legislative Professionalism." In *Congress in Change.* Edited by Norman J. Ornstein. New York: Praeger, 1975.

Ragsdale, Lyn, and Jerrold G. Rusk. "Candidates, Issues, and Participation in Senate Elections." *Legislative Studies Quarterly* 20 (1995): 305–28.

Ragsdale, Lyn, and Timothy E. Cook. "Representatives' Actions and Challengers' Reactions: Limits to Candidate Connections in the House." *American Journal of Political Science* 31 (1987): 45–81.

Rieselbach, Leroy N. *Congressional Reform: The Changing Modern Congress.* Washington, D.C.: CQ Press, 1994.

____. *Congressional Politics: The Evolving Legislative System.* 2d ed. Boulder, Col.: Westview, 1995.

Ripley, Randall B., and Grace N. Franklin. *Congress, the Bureaucracy, and Public Policy.* 5th ed. Belmont, Calif.: Wadsworth, 1991.

Ripley, Randall B., and James M. Lindsay, eds. *Congress Resurgent: Foreign and Defense Policy on Capitol Hill.* Ann Arbor: University of Michigan Press, 1993.

Rohde, David W. *Parties and Leaders in the Postreform House.* Chicago: University of Chicago Press, 1991.

Rohde, David W., and Kenneth A. Shepsle. "Democratic Committee Assignments in the U.S. House of Representatives." *American Political Science Review* 67 (1973): 889–905.

Rothman, David J. *Politics and Power.* New York: Atheneum, 1969.

Rudder, Catherine E. "Committee Reform and the Revenue Process." In *Congress Reconsidered.* 1st ed. Edited by Lawrence C. Dodd and Bruce I. Oppenheimer. New York: Praeger, 1977.

Saloma, John S., III. *Congress and the New Politics.* Boston: Little, Brown, 1969.

Schick, Allen. *Making Economic Policy in Congress.* Washington, D.C.: American Enterprise Institute, 1983.

Schickler, Eric. "Institutional Change in the House of Representatives, 1867–1998: A Test of Partisan and Ideological Power Balance Models." *American Political Science Review* 94 (2000): 269–88.

Schickler, Eric. *Disjointed Pluralism.* Princeton: Princeton University Press, 2001.

Schickler, Eric, and Andrew Rich. "Party Government in the House Reconsidered: A Response to Cox and McCubbins." *American Journal of Political Science* 41 (1997): 1387–94.

Schiller, Wendy J. "Senators as Political Entrepreneurs: Using Bill Sponsorship to Shape Legislative Agendas." *American Journal of Political Science* 39 (1995): 186–203.

Schiller, Wendy J. *Partners and Rivals: Representation in U.S. Senate Delegations.* Princeton: Princeton University Press, 2000.

Schneider, Jerrold E. *Ideological Coalitions in Congress.* Greenwood, Conn.: Greenwood Press, 1979.

Schwarz, John E., and L. Earl Shaw. *The United States Congress in Comparative Perspective.* Hinsdale, Ill.: Dryden Press, 1976.

Seidman, Harold. *Politics, Position, and Power.* 2d ed. London: Oxford University Press, 1975.

Shepsle, Kenneth A. *The Giant Jigsaw Puzzle.* Chicago: University of Chicago Press, 1978.

———. "The Changing Textbook Congress: Equilibrium in Congressional Institutions and Behavior." In *American Political Institutions and the Problems of Our Time.* Edited by John E. Chubb and Paul E. Peterson. Washington: Brookings, 1990.

Shepsle, Kenneth A., and Barry R. Weingast, eds. *Positive Theories of Congressional Institutions.* Ann Arbor: University of Michigan Press, 1995.

Sinclair, Barbara D. *Majority Leadership in the U.S. House.* Baltimore: Johns Hopkins University Press, 1983.

———. *The Transformation of the U.S. Senate.* Baltimore: Johns Hopkins University Press, 1989.

———. *Legislators, Leaders, and Lawmaking: The U.S. House of Representatives in the Postreform Era.* Baltimore: Johns Hopkins University Press, 1995.

___. *Unorthodox Lawmaking: New Legislative Processes in the U.S. Congress.* Washington, D.C.: CQ Press, 1997.

Smith, Steven S. *Call to Order: Floor Politics in the House and Senate.* Washington, D.C.: Brookings, 1989.

___. *The American Congress.* Boston: Houghton Mifflin, 1995.

Snyder, James, and Tim Groseclose. "Estimating Party Influence in Congressional Roll-Call Voting." *American Journal of Political Science* 44 (2000): 193–211.

Stein, Robert M., and Kenneth N. Bickers. *Perpetuating the Pork: Policy Subsystems and American Democracy.* New York: Cambridge University Press, 1995.

Stimson, James A., Michael B. MacKuen, and Robert S. Erikson. "Dynamic Representation." *American Political Science Review* 89 (1995): 543–65.

Stone, Walter J. "The Dynamics of Constituency: Electoral Control in the House." *American Politics Quarterly* 8 (1980): 399–424.

Strahan, Randall. *New Ways and Means: Reform and Change in a Congressional Committee.* Chapel Hill: University of North Carolina Press, 1990.

Sundquist, James L. *Politics and Policy.* Washington, D.C.: Brookings, 1968.

___. *The Decline and Resurgence of Congress.* Washington, D.C.: Brookings, 1981.

Swain, Carol M. *Black Faces, Black Interests: The Representation of African Americans in Congress.* Cambridge: Harvard University Press, 1993.

Swift, Elaine K. *The Making of an American Senate: Reconstitutive Change in Congress, 1787–1841.* Ann Arbor: University of Michigan Press, 1996.

Talbert, Jeffery, Bryan D. Jones, and Frank R. Baumgartner. "Nonlegislative Hearings and Policy Change in Congress." *American Journal of Political Science* 39 (1995): 383–405.

Thomas, Sue. *How Women Legislate.* New York: Oxford University Press, 1994.

Thurber, James A., ed. *Rivals for Power: Presidential-Congressional Relations.* Washington, D.C.: CQ Press, 1996.

Thurber, James A., and Roger H. Davidson. *Remaking Congress: Change and Stability in the 1990s.* Washington, D.C.: CQ Press, 1995.

Truman, David B. *The Governmental Process.* New York: Knopf, 1951.

Turner, Julius. *Party and Constituency: Pressures on Congress.* Rev. ed. by Edward V. Schneier Jr. Baltimore: Johns Hopkins University Press, 1970.

Unekis, Joseph, and Leroy N. Rieselbach. *Congressional Committee Politics: Continuity and Change.* New York: Praeger, 1984.

Uslaner, Eric M. *The Decline of Comity in Congress.* Ann Arbor: University of Michigan Press, 1993.

Vogler, David J. *The Third House.* Evanston, Ill.: Northwestern University Press, 1971.

___. *The Politics of Congress.* 6th ed. Madison, Wis.: Brown and Benchmark, 1993.

Wahlke, John C., Heinz H. Eulau, W. Buchanan, and L.C. Ferguson. *The Legislative System: Explorations in Legislative Behavior.* New York: Wiley, 1962.

Wayne, S.J. *The Legislative Presidency.* New York: Harper, 1978.

Weingast, Barry. "Floor Behavior in the U.S. Congress: Committee Power under the Open Rule." *American Political Science Review* 83 (1989): 795–815.

Weisberg, Herbert F. "Evaluating Theories of Congressional Roll Call Voting." *American Journal of Political Science* 22 (1978): 554–77.

Weisberg, Herbert F., Eric S. Heberlig, and Lisa M. Campoli. *Classics in Congressional Politics.* New York: Longman, 1999.

Westefield, L.P. "Majority Party Leadership and the Committee System in the House of Representatives." *American Political Science Review* 68 (1974): 1593–1604.

Wildavsky, Aaron. *The Politics of the Budgetary Process.* Boston: Little, Brown, 1964.

Wilson, Rick. "Forward and Backward Agenda Procedures: Committee Experience and Structurally Induced Equilibrium." *Journal of Politics* 48 (1986): 390–409.

Wilson, Woodrow. *Congressional Government.* 1885. Reprint, Gloucester, Mass.: Peter Smith, 1973.

Wolfinger, Raymond E., and Joan Heifetz Hollinger. "Safe Seats, Seniority, and Power in Congress." *American Political Science Review* 59 (1965): 337–49.

Wright, Fiona A. "The Caucus Reelection Requirement and the Transformation of House Committee Chairs, 1959–94." *Legislative Studies Quarterly* 25 (August 2000): 469–80.

Wright, Gerald C., and Michael B. Berkman. "Candidates and Policy in United States Senate Elections." *American Political Science Review* 80 (1986): 567–88.

Wright, Gerald C., Leroy Rieselbach, and Lawrence C. Dodd, eds. *Congress and Policy Change.* New York: Agathon, 1986.

Wright, John. "PACs, Contributions, and Roll Calls: An Organizational Perspective." *American Political Science Review* 75 (1985): 400–14.

Young, Garry. "Committee Gatekeeping and Proposal Power under Single and Multiple Referral." *Journal of Theoretical Politics* 8 (1996): 65–78.

Young, James S. *The Washington Community, 1800–1828.* New York: Columbia University Press, 1966.

Index

✧ ✧ ✧

A. Philip Randolph Institute, 105
Aberbach, Joel, 365n. 12
Abortion politics, 159
Abraham, Spencer, 378
Abrams, Sam, 160n. 1
Abramson, Paul R., 291n. 44
Access-oriented PACs, 103, 110
Accomplishments vs. debate and compromise, 159
Acheson, Dean, 322
Action, congressional, 359–360
Activists
  liberal–conservative differences of, 274, 277–278, 280
  presidents as, 339–340, 342, 353
Adams, Greg D., 291n. 40
Adams, John Quincy, 187n. 15
Advocacy ads, 107, 117–118, 119, 122n. 49, 152
AFL-CIO, PAC of, 111, 116
African Americans, in House, 374–375
Agenda control, Senate, 7–8
Agriculture Committee, House, 136, 206
Albert, Carl, 260
Aldrich, John H., 162n. 33, 186n. 1, 240n. 16, 242n. 39, 266n. 4, 267n. 26, 289n. 2, 290nn. 20, 28, 291nn. 30, 34, 44, 46, 292nn. 50, 53, 364nn. 6, 7, 365n. 10, 387nn. 3, 4, 5, 394
  on conditional party government, 367, 376, 385
  gold standard bill and, 257–258
  on party influence, 154
  on party leaders and member behavior, 156, 157
  Republican Steering Committee and, 256–257
Aldrich, Nelson W., 252, 343
Alesina, Alberto, 93n. 8
Alexander, DeAlva Stanwood, 267n. 18
Alexander, Herbert E., 120nn. 2, 7
Alford, John R., 161n. 18, 371, 388n. 11

Allen, Thomas, 218
Allison, William Boyd, 252, 256
Alpert, Bruce, 267n. 27
Amendments
  germaneness of, 7–8
  majority leader and, 264–265
  Senate message politics and, 236, 237, 242n. 50
  unanimous consent agreements and, 10
American Medical Association, PAC of, 111
American National Election Studies (ANES), 144, 328
American Political Science Association, Study of Congress, 141
Americans for Tax Reform, 105
Amway Corporation, 117
Annals of Congress, 170
Ansolabehere, Stephen, 279, 290nn. 25, 26, 366n. 15
Antiballistic missile deployment, 315
Appropriations Committee, House
  Clinton and, 40–41
  Gingrich and, 288
  government shutdown and, 27
  Hastert and, 38
  policy riders situation, 232
  subcommittee seniority system of, 203
  women on, 135, 136, 137
Appropriations Committee, Senate, 256, 258
Approval of Congress
  vs. other governmental components, 49–52
  variations, 46–49
Archer, Bill, 328
Armey, Dick, 26, 30, 37
  committee assignments and, 287
  on foreign affairs, 322
  New Jersey primary 2000 and, 286
  trust in leadership of, 383
Arnold, Laura, 140n. 10

Arnold, R. Douglas, 161n. 9
Ash, Marian, 144
Ashcroft, John, 378
Asher, Herbert, 141
Aspin, Les, 204
Attack ads, 161n. 20
AWACS aircraft sales to Saudi Arabia, 315

Babington, Charles, 312n. 36
Bach, Stanley, 266n. 4
Bader, John, 312n. 27
Baesler, Scotty, 115
Baker, Howard, 322
Baker, R. S., 310n. 7
Baker, Richard Allan, 187n. 14
Balint, Peter J., 332nn. 21, 23
Balz, Dan, 412n. 4
Banducci, Susan A., 94n. 13
Banking Committee, House, 206,
    234–235
Barbour, Haley, 105
Baron, David P., 215n. 10
Barone, Michael, 331n. 13
Barrett, Andrew, 337, 365n. 10
Bartels, Larry, 290n. 23
Bartlett, Roscoe, 224
Bateson, Gregory, 404, 413n. 2
Bauer, Raymond, 160n. 3
Baumann, David, 44nn. 20, 22, 23,
    268n. 28
Baumer, Donald, 18n. 8, 268n. 30
Bayh, Birch, 160n. 8
Beck, Deborah, 121n. 18
Berger, Mark, 291n. 30
Berger, Samuel R., 326, 332n. 29
Berkman, Michael B., 91, 95nn. 27, 28,
    414n. 33
Bernstein, Aaron, 123n. 53
Berry, Jeffrey, 365n. 10
Bessette, Joseph M., 243n. 53
Beth, Richard S., 18n. 13, 241n. 27
Bibby, John F., 122n. 30
Bicameralism, 299, 302–303, 308, 368
Bicameral rivalry theory of committees,
    191, 195–196, 198–201
    committee chair of majority party and,
        204
    predictions of, 212
    See also Seniority system
Biden, Joseph, 323, 326
Biersack, Robert, 120, 120n. 1, 121nn. 15,
    16

Bifurcated rules, 230, 241n. 31
Binder, Sarah A., 18nn. 1, 7, 188n. 24,
    215n. 7, 216n. 21, 241n. 28, 242n. 49,
    267n. 14, 310n. 6, 311nn. 13, 14,
    313n. 44, 329, 333nn. 35, 38
Binkley, Wilfred, 363nn. 1, 3, 364n. 8
Bipartisanship, 16–17, 316–318, 370
    See also Constructive partisanship
Bliley, Tom, 218
Bloc voting, Senate, 344
Boland amendments, 319, 321
Bonchek, Mark S., 412n. 7
Bond, Jon R., 162n. 33, 266n. 4, 268n. 32,
    290n. 19, 291n. 35, 311n. 17, 337,
    364n. 6, 365n. 10
Bonior, David, 140n. 13
Boren, David, 299
Bovitz, Gregory L., 291n. 32
Boxer, Barbara, 115
Boyer, Dave, 332n. 28
Bradley, Bill, 159
Brady, David W., 43n. 8, 65n. 15, 94n. 22,
    141, 148, 155, 160n. 1, 161nn. 11, 13,
    15, 18, 162n. 28, 215n. 7, 266nn. 1, 5,
    267nn. 8, 15, 24, 291n. 30, 311nn. 23,
    29, 313n. 49, 363n. 2, 364n. 7, 388n. 11,
    399, 413n. 20
    on gridlock politics, 302
    on leadership power, 246
    on personal incumbency advantage, 371
    on Speaker leadership, 29
Breaux, John B., 299, 308, 311n. 16,
    313n. 46, 329
Bresnahan, John, 240n. 6
Broder, David, 414n. 32
Broder, John M., 332n. 26
Brody, Richard, 266n. 1, 267nn. 15, 24
Brookover, Ed, 123nn. 60, 61, 62
Brooks, Jack, 235
Brown, Cecelia, 186
Brown, Clifford W., 122n. 34
Brown, George, 266n. 5, 267n. 18
Brownstein, Ronald, 412n. 4
Bryce, James, 337, 364n. 8
Buchanan, James M., 215n. 5
Buckley v. Valeo (1976), 100, 121n. 9
Budget Committee, House, 136
Budget environment, legislative compro-
    mise and, 304–305, 309
Bullock, Charles S., III, 139n. 5, 141
Bundling individual contributions,
    103–104

Bunning, Jim, 115
Burdette, Franklin, 267nn. 14, 22
Bureaucracies, government, 400–401
Burnham, Walter Dean, 311n. 22,
    364n. 7, 412nn. 3, 6
Burns, James McGregor, 310n. 1, 414n. 30
Burrell, Barbara, 139n. 2
Bush, George, 158, 296, 298, 315,
    320–321
Bush, George W., 381, 388n. 9
Byrd, Robert C., 187n. 15, 188nn. 19, 23,
    263, 322

Cabot, George, 168
Cain, Bruce, 161n. 10
Caldeira, Gregory, 215n. 6
California special House election, in 1998,
    285
Calvert, Randall L., 93n. 6
Campaign financing, 97–123
    candidates and, 108–110
    contribution limits in congressional
        elections, 101
    early law on, 97–99
    FECA and its amendments, 99–100,
        118–120
    individuals and, 98, 99, 108, 119
    interest groups, PACs and, 100–105
    party leaders and, 107–108
    party organizations and, 105–107
    reform measures, 228
    soft money expenditures, 116–118, 119
    spending under FECA, 110–116, 119
Campaign rallies, PACs and, 104
Campbell, Angus, 93nn. 2, 7
Campbell, Ballard, 364n. 9
Campbell, Colton, 240n. 7, 363n. 2,
    413n. 25
Campbell, James A., 93n. 7
Candidate ads, 107
Candidate-centered politics, 146,
    350–351
Candidates
    FECA and, 108–110
    House elections role of, 77–82
    partisan differences of, 278–280
    See also Gender gap; Incumbents
Cannon, Joseph G., 22, 249, 341
    rebellion against, 380
    Reed rules and, 252
    seniority system and, 202

Canon, David T., 172, 186, 187n. 4,
    188nn. 37, 39
Cantril, Albert, 365n. 10
Cantril, Susan, 365n. 10
Careers, legislative
    ambitions, gridlock and, 309, 383
    of House members, 32–34
    from House to Senate, 167–168
    nineteenth century, 176
    twentieth century, 350
Carey, John M., 215n. 11
Carey, Mary Agnes, 268n. 29
Carmines, Edward G., 284, 291n. 39
Carney, Eliza Newlin, 41, 44n. 24
Carroll, Susan, 139n. 2
Carter, Jimmy, 143–144, 315, 319, 320,
    353
Carter, Ralph G., 331n. 8
Cassata, Donna, 268n. 31
Caucuses
    Democratic, 340
    rule of, in House, 249, 338
    slates subject to chamber vote, 204–205
Census 2000, 373
Center for Responsive Politics, 123nn. 58,
    59, 64
Centralized power, 246
    in House, 259–260
    of House Speakers Reed and Cannon,
        249–252
    polarization and, 265
    in Senate, 258–259, 343
    in Senate of Aldrich and Allison,
        253–257
    in Senate of Dole and Lott, 263–265
Centrists, 300
    in Congress, 329
    See also Moderates/moderation
Cerniello, Craig, 332n. 25
Chadha v. United States (1983), 319
Chafee, John H., 300
Chafee, Lincoln, 378
Challengers
    campaign financing, 109–110,
        150–151
    fund-raising under FECA by, 116
    ideological representation and, 85
    quality of, seat maximization goals and,
        105
    weak, 80
    women for House seats, 127
Chambers, William Nisbet, 187n. 6

Chandler, William, 257, 258
Chaney, Carole, 139n. 1
Change, 346–355
    electoral process consequences and,
        349–351
    internal distribution of power and,
        346–349
    political indicators of, 348
    reform programs and, 350
    societal indicators of, 347
Charles, Joseph, 187n. 6
Chemical Weapons Convention, 323
Cheney, Dick, 388n. 9
Cheng, Judy, 186
China, normal trade relations with, 323
Chiu, Chang-Wei, 266n. 5
Christian Coalition, 117
Chubb, John E., 187n. 3
Church, Frank, 319
Cigler, Allan, 364n. 7
Civil Service Committee, 140n. 15
Claims Committee, House, 171
Clark, James Beauchamp, 209
Class and Party in American Politics, 376
Clausen, Aage, 155
Clay, Henry, 165, 166, 171–172
Clinton, Bill
    106th Congress, role in, 38
    1998 State of the Union address, 231
    coattails of, 71
    conditional party government and, 370
    filibusters against, 7
    foreign aid requests of, 315–316, 320,
        323–324
    Gingrich and, 260–261, 331n. 12, 342
    government shutdowns and, 27, 241n. 37
    gridlock and, 295, 296, 309
    Lewinsky scandal effect, 72, 114, 117,
        261–262
    NAFTA and, 76–77, 320, 321
    nuclear test ban treaty and, 326, 327
    policy mood change and, 73
    recess appointments by, 11
    reinventing government, 407–408
    soft money fund-raising by, 118
    unified government under, 298–299,
        354
    See also Impeachment proceedings
Cloture votes, 6, 19n. 13, 311n. 11
    changes in, 345
    message politics and, 236–237
    public debates and, 13

Clubb, Jerome, 311n. 22
Coalition—Americans Working for Real
    Change, 116
Coattail effect, 71
    See also Withdrawn coattails
Cogan, John, 65n. 15, 94n. 22, 148,
    161nn. 11, 13, 15
Cognitive perspective on Republican Rev-
    olution. *See* Social learning theory
Cohen, Richard E., 41, 43n. 7, 44nn. 15,
    19, 23, 24, 268n. 28, 329, 333nn. 32, 36,
    37
Cohen, William S., 313n. 45
Cohesiveness, intraparty
    Reed rules and, 249–252
    Senate, 258–259
Cold War cessation, 327, 328, 350
Coleman, John J., 312n. 37
Collegial power, 246
Collie, Melissa, 365n. 12
Collins, Carlis, 137
Collins, Susan, 311n. 16
Colmer, William, 210
*Colorado Republican Federal Campaign
    Committee v. Federal Election Commission*
    (1996), 121n. 10
Commerce Committee, House
    106th Congress, 38
    Banking Committee disagreements
        with, 234–235
    Gingrich and, 288
    health issues before, 217
    party representation on, 206
    women on, 136
Committee chairs, House
    independence and power of, 339
    Subcommittee Bill of Rights, 272
    term limits for, 32, 36–37, 38, 42
    women as, 137–138
Committee leaders, 168
Committee on the Present Danger, 319
Committee on Rules, House, 249
Committees, evolution of, 163–189
    appointments and turnover, 175–176
    data for, 170–171
    distributive hypothesis, 169–170, 178
    "fingers of the chamber" hypothesis,
        169, 170, 179–181
    historical Congresses, 163–164
    House standing committee creation
        in 1789–1879, 355–357
    prior literature on, 165–169

Senate standing committee creation
   in 1789–1879, 357–358
specialization on, 168
state representation hypothesis, 169,
   177–178, 182–183
testable propositions on, 169–170
See also Committees, theories on
Committees, House
   message politics and, 217–243,
      226–227
   Reorganization Act (1946) and, 32
   weakening of, 327, 328
   women on, 135
   See also Party leaders
Committees, Senate, 344
   message politics and, 226–227
   weakening of, 327, 328
Committees, theories on, 191–216
   bicameral rivalry and, 191, 195–196,
      198–201
   closed vs. open rules, 212
   discussion, 212–214
   distributive benefits, 191, 192–194,
      198–201
   dominance/dependence on president,
      336
   gatekeeping power, 208–212
   informational advantages, 191, 192,
      198–201
   Mayhew's, 270–271, 286
   minority members' proportional repre-
      sentation, 206–207
   minority members' seats, 205–206
   political parties and, 191, 194–195,
      198–201
   seniority system and, 197, 202–205
   separate vs. joint, 207–208
   See also Committees, evolution of
Communications Workers of America,
   117
Comprehensive Nuclear Test Ban Treaty,
   326–327
   See also Nuclear test ban treaty
Compromise. *See* Debate and compromise
Conditional party government, 247,
   269–292
   2000 elections and, 367, 368–370,
      375–376
   candidate partisan differences, 278–280
   close seat distribution between parties
      and, 376–378
   competitive seats and, 378–379

congressional reforms and, 271–273
constraints on, 376–385
effects within House, 286–288
Electoral Connection revisited, 269–271
electoral roots of, 273–275
in heterogenous society, 385–386
historical variability in, 290n. 30
of House majority party Democratic
   power, 1970s, 260
of House Speaker Hastert, 263
of House Speakers Reed and Cannon,
   249–252
institutional consequences of electoral
   forces, 275–276
institutional context and, 265–266
national parties in local elections,
   285–286
party government theory of committees
   and, 213
party image differences, 280–282
party records, individual reelection and,
   283–285
policy conflict structure and, 380–382
of Senate leaders Aldrich and Allison,
   253
stronger parties and electoral interests,
   282–283
trust of policy leaders and, 382–385
voter preferences, 277–278, 290n. 23
Conflict, political, 48–49, 52, 357
   preference conflict, 275
   See also Debate and compromise
Congress: The Electoral Connection (Mayhew), 269–271
   See also Conditional party government
*Congress—Keystone of the Washington
   Establishment* (Fiorina), 141–162, 401
   context for, 141–144
   erosion of electoral insulation, 149–153
   incumbency advantage research,
      144–145
   incumbency and insulation era, 145
   interview recording methods for,
      160n. 7
   party resurgence, 153–157
   politics as local vs. national, 145–149
   twenty-first-century considerations,
      157–160
   and *Congress Reconsidered* essay by
      Cooper and Young, 370
Congressional Globe, 170
Congressional Record, 170

Congressional retirees' PACs, 115
Connelly, William F., Jr., 43n. 3, 412n. 1
Connor, George E., 243n. 53
Consent agreements. *See* Unanimous consent agreements (UCAs)
Consent and deliberation, congressional, 359
Conservative coalition of southern Democrats, House. *See* Southern Democrats
Conservative Opportunity Society, 23–24, 30
Constituencies, concentric, 274
Constituency attentiveness, 149, 151
Constituency preferences, congressional voting and, 270, 275
Constituent meetings, message influence of, 221
Constitution, shared powers system of, 316
Constitutional Convention (1787), 163
Constrained partisanship, 370
Constructive partisanship, 39, 368, 386
Contract with America, 17–18, 24–25, 260, 302
    104th Congress, 26
    conditional party government and, 370
    congressional committee system and, 182
    institutional context of, 302
    as message politics, 220
    non-internationalist view of, 322
    reinventing government and, 408
Control committees, 270–271
Converse, Philip E., 93n. 2
Cook, Elizabeth Adell, 139n. 1
Cook, Timothy, 366n. 15
Coolidge, Calvin, 340
Cooper, Joseph, 43n. 8, 186n. 2, 187nn. 6, 10, 215n. 6, 266nn. 1, 5, 267n. 8, 311n. 12, 313n. 56, 336, 363n. 2, 364nn. 5, 6, 365n. 12, 366nn. 13, 14, 388n. 8, 399, 412n. 2, 413n. 20
    on alternate partisanship types, 370
    on House committee system, 163–164
    on Jeffersonian principles, 166
    on leadership power, 246
    on Speaker leadership, 29
Cooperman, Rosalyn, 133, 134, 139n. 7, 140n. 11
Corporate PACs, 101–102, 110
Corrado, Anthony, 120nn. 1, 8, 122n. 28

Corwin, Edward S., 330n. 3
Cox, Gary W., 43n. 1, 121n. 14, 154, 189n. 48, 194, 212, 215n. 8, 216n. 35, 240n. 5, 266n. 4, 284, 291n. 37, 364n. 6, 387n. 6
Craig, Larry, 13
Craig, Stephen, 365n. 10
Crisp, Charles F., 21
Cronin, Thomas, 365n. 9
Crook, Sara Brandes, 292n. 48
Crossover spending, 106
Crossover voters, 134
Crosspartisanship, 370
Cross-party wins, 336
Cullom, Shelby, 258
Cunningham, Nobel E., 187n. 2
Cutler, Lloyd, 311n. 9
Czar rule era, 249–252, 338

Daadler, Ivo H., 332n. 19
D'Amato, Alfonse, 6
Darcy, Robert, 139n. 2
Daschle, Tom, 263
    message politics and, 220, 222, 236–238
    nuclear test ban treaty and, 327
    as Senate minority leader, 12
    soft money fund-raising by, 118
Davidson, Roger H., 18n. 12, 65n. 22, 121n. 24, 216nn. 12, 13, 14, 267n. 25, 290n. 13, 394, 412n. 12
Davis, Tom, 286
Deardorff, Alan V., 331n. 10
Debate and compromise
    vs. accomplishments, 159
    demographic variations in approval of, 61, 63
    polarization and, 300
    public opinion on, 58
    See also Conflict, political
Decentralized power, 246
Deering, Christopher J., 18n. 11, 43n. 2, 216n. 22, 241n. 22
Deficit politics, 158, 305
DeLauro, Rosa, 220
DeLay, Tom, 26
    appropriations schedule and, 232
    Hastert and, 37, 262
    New Jersey primary 2000 and, 286
    as party leader, 151
Delli Carpini, Michael X., 93n. 10

Democratic National Committee, 98, 105, 221

Democratic Party
106th Congress, 41
2000 elections, 37–38, 370–376
constructive partisanship of, 386
electoral advantage for women candidates of, 133–134
government shutdown and, 27
House candidate ideology, 76
House committee composition and, 135–138
House control by, 21–23, 67–68, 69–70
House election votes by, 69
House gender gap, 125–127
House issues preferences of, 75–77
House reforms of 1970s, 271–272, 282–283, 328
ideological representation by, 85–86
incumbents, 1994 elections, 93n. 11
industrial-era politics of, 402
internal divisions in, 369–370
message politics of, 220
open seat candidates of, 130–131
southern, 22–23, 280, 290n. 28, 339, 340, 341, 344–345
spending preferences of, 74–75
spending under FECA, 113–114, 115
subcommittee chair appointments, 203
teachers' unions and, 159–160
women candidates for House, 127, 128–129

Democratic Senatorial Campaign Committee, 118

Demographic groups, variations in congressional approval by, 58–63
causes of, 61–63

Destler, I. M., 331nn. 6, 10, 332nn. 17, 21, 23, 31, 333n. 39

Dewar, Helen, 332n. 30

Dexter, Louis, 160n. 3

Diermeier, Daniel, 195, 196, 212–213, 215n. 10

Dimock, Michael A., 94n. 13

Dingell, John, 235

Dirksen, Everett, 159

Discharge petitions, 208–210, 229, 241nn. 26, 29, 30

Disclosure, campaign finance, 98

Distributive benefits theory of committees, 191, 192–194, 198–201, 204, 213

Distributive hypothesis, 169–170, 178

Distributive politics, 158

District of Columbia Committee, 140n. 15

Districts, congressional
2000 elections, 371
competitive seats, 378–379
constituencies of, 156–157
elections, national parties and, 285–286
partisan composition of, 78, 84, 131–132, 279
safe, 81, 143
vanishing marginals analysis of, 142

Diversity, of Senate members, 4

Divided government
electoral effects beyond, 299–302
gridlock and, 306, 308
public opinion on, 48–49
public policy and, 297–299
twentieth century, 353–355
unicameral models and, 312n. 32
See also Conditional party government

Divided We Govern (Mayhew), 295

Dodd, Lawrence C., 18nn. 4, 8, 43n. 1, 44n. 21, 94n. 21, 121n. 14, 141, 149, 160n. 1, 161nn. 16, 18, 215n. 6, 243n. 53, 268n. 30, 290n. 12, 292n. 52, 311n. 12, 331n. 11, 366nn. 12, 13, 387nn. 6, 7, 388nn. 11, 18, 412nn. 6, 13, 413nn. 14, 18, 23, 25, 27, 414nn. 28, 31

Dodd, W. E., 310n. 7

Dolan, Kathleen, 139n. 9

Dole, Robert, 7, 245, 263–264, 294, 323

"Do-Little" 106th Congress, 36–41
first session, 36–39
second session, 39–41

D'Onofrio, Robert, 161n. 13, 186

Dorgan, Byron, 220, 326

Döring, Herbert, 215n. 11

Douglas, Scott, 122n. 47

Downs, Anthony, 94n. 18, 270, 289n. 4, 394, 412n. 10

Dreier, David, 235

Drew, Elizabeth, 120n. 1, 291n. 38

Drinkard, Jim, 123n. 54

Duncan, Philip C., 242n. 48

Dunham, Richard S., 123n. 53

Durbin, Richard, 220–221

Durr, Robert H., 64n. 3, 65n. 6, 313n. 57

DW-NOMINATE scores, 83
91st and 105th Congresses, 280–282

Dwyre, Diana, 121n. 23, 122n. 29

Economic management, message politics and, 222, 224
Ed-Flex Bill, 233, 237
Edsall, Thomas B., 123n. 61
Education and the Workforce Committee, House, 136
Edwards, George, III, 337, 365n. 10
Eilperin, Juliet, 240n. 14
Eisenhower, Dwight D., 317, 353
Eldersveld, Samuel, 364n. 7
Election activities, by PACs, 104
Election financing. *See* Campaign financing
Election-oriented strategies, PACs and, 102, 103
Elections, 67–95
  1996 and 1998 House, 30–36
  2000, 35–36, 41–43, 370–376
  candidates' role in, 77–82
  gridlock and, 306
  House–Senate differences, 89–91
  ideological representation, 82–89, 357–358
  institutional consequences of, 275–276
  institutional effects of on public policy, 303
  local, national parties and, 285–286
  Mayhew theory of, 270–271
  midterm losses, 71–73
  partisan base of, 68–73
  policy mood and, 70–71
  presidential elections and, 71
  as public policy direction search, 73–77
  as public policy indicator, 67–68
  representation and, 87–89
  results, party leaders' power and, 246–247
  results, public policy and, 302
  states' law control of, 368
Electoral mandates, 301, 371
Electoral objectives
  leadership powers and, 265
  party leaders' power and, 246–247, 248, 262–263
Electoral rules, post-industrial society and, 401
Electoral system changes, 346
  congressional power distribution and, 349–350
  polarization and, 354–355
Electorate. *See* Voters
Ellis, Richard J., 337, 364n. 3

Ellsworth, Oliver, 168
EMILY's List, 111–112, 116–117
Empirical analysis, 141–142
End of the Republican Era, The (Lowi), 380
Epstein, David, 216n. 30, 266n. 1, 267nn. 15, 24, 365n. 12
Epstein, Leon, 387n. 1
Erikson, Robert S., 74, 93n. 5, 94nn. 14, 17, 21, 22, 25, 26, 122n. 44, 141, 312nn. 41, 42
Evans, C. Lawrence, 19nn. 16, 17, 43n. 5, 216n. 19, 240nn. 7, 11, 17, 241nn. 21, 25, 26, 34, 242nn. 39, 40, 43, 394, 412n. 12
Evans, Diana, 242n. 46
Executive. *See* Presidency
Extended debates, Senate, 8, 9, 12–13, 19n. 15

Faircloth, Lauch, 115
Fairfield, Roy P., 187n. 13
Fascell, Dante, 319
Federal Election Campaign Act (FECA), 97
  erosion of, 118–120
  individuals and, 98, 99, 108, 119
  interest groups and, 100–105
  party leaders and, 107–108
  party organizations and, 105–107
  provisions, 98–99
  soft money and, 104–105, 116–118
  spending under, 110–116
Federal Election Commission (FEC), 99, 102
Federal Election Commission v. Massachusetts Citizens for Life (1986), 121n. 10
Federal government expansion, 346, 350, 355–357
Federalist Papers, 167, 187n. 13, 302, 365n. 11
Federalist Party, 165–166, 170
Feingold, Russell, 115
Fenno, Richard F., Jr., 33, 44n. 12, 65n. 11, 95n. 27, 142, 156, 160nn. 4, 7, 240n. 5, 242n. 38, 290nn. 14, 17, 312n. 26, 313n. 54, 331n. 14, 366n. 14, 387n. 5, 388n. 18, 394, 412n. 9, 414n. 34
  on representative motivation, 273, 309
  on Republican effectiveness as majority party, 323
Ferejohn, John A., 93n. 6, 141, 142, 161n. 10, 215n. 10

Filibusters, 19n. 20, 311n. 11
  1993–1998, 264
  Aldrich-Allison team and, 258
  character of, 6–7
  congressional decision making and, 359
  frequency, 5–6, 344–345
  gridlock and, 308
  legislative outcomes and, 14
  Senate leadership power and, 255–256
  threats of, 10–11, 313n. 50
  "tit-for-tat," 304
  unified government and, 299
  See also Extended debates, Senate
Finance Committee, Senate, 256
Financial services industry restructuring,
  234–235
"Fingers of the chamber" hypothesis, for
  committees, 169, 170, 179–181
Fiorina, Morris P., 65nn. 8, 15, 94n. 16,
  148, 161nn. 10, 11, 13, 15, 17,
  162nn. 27, 34, 290n. 24, 311n. 10, 394,
  401, 412n. 8, 413nn. 15, 17, 24
  on ideologues and turnout, 278
  on representatives' motivation, 273
Fisher, Louis, 366n. 13
Flanigan, William, 311n. 22
Flathman, Marcus, 188n. 24
Fleisher, Richard, 162n. 33, 266n. 4,
  268n. 32, 290n. 19, 291n. 35, 311n. 17,
  337, 364n. 6, 365n. 10
Flemming, Greg, 186, 187n. 4
Floor
  committees and, 173
  House, one-minute speeches, 224–226,
    241n. 21
  ratification, seniority system and, 204
  Senate rules on getting legislation to,
    8–11
Flynt, Larry, 261
Foerstel, Herbert, 140n. 10
Foerstel, Karen, 140n. 10, 268n. 29
Foley, Michael, 18n. 5
Foley, Thomas S., 24–25, 260, 341, 390
Ford, Gerald, 144, 151, 159, 320, 321
Foreign policy, 315–333
  bipartisan internationalism, 316–318
  congressional rules changes, 318–319
  nuclear test ban treaty, 326–327
  partisan gridlock, 322–324
  polarization growth, 327–329
  polarized internationalists, 319–322
  presidential credibility and, 321

  shared powers and, 315–316
  trade agreements, 324–325
Foreign Relations Committee, Senate, 322
Foster, Henry, 7
Fowler, Linda L., 64n. 1
Fox, Richard, 139n. 2
Francis, Wayne L., 216n. 25
Frank, Barney, 300
Friedman, Sally, 140n. 10
Frist, Bill, 221
Fulbright, J. William, 318, 321, 330n. 5
Fund-raising scandal, 1996 elections, 114

Gaddie, Ronald Keith, 139n. 5
Gallaher, Miriam, 216nn. 15, 23
Galloway, George B., 186n. 2
Gamm, Gerald, 166, 187nn. 2, 11, 12,
  188n. 36, 267nn. 10, 13, 17, 337, 399
Gatekeeping power
  of committee and subcommittee chairs,
    210–211
  discharge petition and, 208–210
  subcommittees and, 211–212
Geer, John G., 240n. 13
Gelb, Leslie H., 331n. 6
Gelman, Andrew, 94n. 14, 161nn. 12, 18
Gelman-King measure, 145, 147, 148
Gender differences, variations in congres-
  sional approval by, 59
Gender gap, 125–140
  2000 elections and, 138–139, 374, 375
  candidates and, 127
  development and growth of, 125–132
  district partisan composition and,
    131–132
  for influential positions, 135–138
  open-seat candidates, 129–131
  party performance and recruitment,
    132–134
  seat status, women candidates and,
    127–128
Genrich, Mike, 186
Gephardt, Richard, 37–38, 118, 151, 218,
  219–220
Germaneness, amendment, 7–8, 228
Gerry, Elbridge, 167
Gertzog, Irwin, 139nn. 2, 4
Gilligan, Thomas, 192, 212, 215n. 2
Gilmour, John B., 64n. 3, 65n. 6, 313n. 57
Gingrich, Marianne, 412n. 5
Gingrich, Newt, 260–261, 331n. 12,
  402–403, 412n. 5

Gringrich, Newt (*cont.*)
104th Congress (1995–1996), 26–27, 341–342
105th Congress (1997–1998), 27–29
on 1994 midterm election, 146
1998 campaigns and, 114–115
2000 elections, 42
appropriations schedule, procedures and, 232
California special election and, 285
campaign focus of, 130
committee assignments under, 287
committee chair appointments of, 288, 328
conditional party government of, 247
Conservative Opportunity Society and, 23–25
Contract with America, 17–18
coup attempt against, 28, 43n. 6, 204
Democratic gridlock and, 398
ethics probe, 140n. 16
fall from power, 29–30, 245
Freedom to Farm legislation and, 156
government shutdowns and, 147, 242n. 37, 284–285
message politics of, 219–220
NAFTA and, 322
as party leader, 151
on party reputation, 284
public debates and, 13
Republican Revolution and, 391
seniority system and, 202, 204
soft money fund-raising by, 118
Speakership of, 25–30
task forces of, 205–206, 217
trade agreements and, 325
trust in leadership of, 382, 383
Glazer, Amihai, 94n. 24
Gold-standard bill (1900), 257–258
Goldstein, Judith, 155, 162n. 28
Goodnow, Frank, 297
GOPAC, 24, 391
Gordon, Donald, 186
Gore, Albert, Jr., 38, 159, 381, 388n. 9, 407–408
Gorman, Arthur Pue, 258
Gorton, Slade, 378
Government shutdowns
Clinton and, 241n. 37
Gingrich and, 26–27, 147, 242n. 37, 284–285
Hastert strategy for, 37, 38
party reputations and, 284

Grams, Rod, 378
Grassley, Charles, 7
Great Society Congress, 22, 293, 295, 296, 386
Green, John, 122n. 29, 365n. 10
Gridlock, 293–294
after 2000 elections, 372
consequences of, 309–310
Democratic defeat and, 398
House vs. Senate, 311n. 20
ideological moderation and, 300–301
measures of, 294–296, 297
model of, 306–307
unified government and, 299
Griffin, John D., 290n. 28
Grofman, Bernard, 94n. 24
Groseclose, Timothy, 94n. 13, 155, 162n. 28, 215n. 3
Grove, Lloyd, 313n. 45
Grunwald, Michael, 311n. 19
Gun control legislation, 228

Habermas, Jürgen, 413n. 21
Hacker, Jacob S., 312n. 33
Hagel, Chuck, 326
Hager, Gregory, 155, 162n. 28
Hale, Eugene, 253, 256
Hall, Mary Sharon, 187n. 15
Hall, Peter, 413n. 26
Hall, Richard, 18n. 10, 121n. 13, 216n. 18
Hamilton, Alexander, 165–166, 293, 302
Hammond, Thomas H., 215n. 10, 312n. 31
Hansen, Joe, 118
Hansen, John Mark, 365n. 10
Hard money, 106, 110, 122n. 39, 49
Harlow, Ralph Volney, 165–166, 169, 187nn. 2, 6, 7, 8, 9, 188nn. 32, 33
Harris, Douglas, 366n. 15
Harris, Fred, 160n. 8, 364n. 4
Harris polls, formulation of, 55
Harrison, Benjamin, 351
Hasbrouk, Paul DeWitt, 266n. 5
Hastert, J. Dennis, 29, 245, 262
106th Congress, first session, 36–37, 38
106th Congress, second session, 39–41
2000 elections, 42
financial services industry restructuring and, 234–235
gun control legislation and, 228
impeachment proceedings and, 370

managed health care reform and, 229
marriage tax penalty repeal and,
  233–234
message formulation strategies, 221
New Jersey primary 2000 and, 285–286
prescription drug benefit issue and,
  217–218
presidential activism and, 342
Republican Revolution and, 391
trust in leadership of, 383–384
Hatch, Orrin, 13
Haynes, George H., 168, 188n. 20
Hechler, Kenneth W., 388n. 16
Helcon, Hugh, 412n. 6
Helms, Jesse
  foreign policy and, 319, 320, 321, 323
  hostage taking by, 7
  nuclear test ban treaty and, 326, 327
Herbert, Eddie, 204
Herring, Pendleton, 387n. 2
Herrnson, Paul S., 121nn. 14, 15, 16, 17,
  19, 22, 24, 26, 27, 122nn. 29, 32, 33, 34,
  35, 36, 37, 38, 40, 41, 45, 50, 51,
  123nn. 57, 63, 65, 291n. 43, 364n. 7
Herzke, Allen, 18n. 8
Hess, David, 64n. 1, 65nn. 7, 9
Hibbing, John R., 65nn. 6, 10, 12, 13, 14,
  15, 16, 18, 160n. 1, 292n. 48, 313n. 56,
  366n. 14, 403, 412n. 2
Hickey, Jennifer G., 44n. 13
High-tech economy, 400–401
Hinckley, Barbara, 366n. 13
Hirschfeld, Julie R., 241n. 31
Hispanic Americans, 374–375
Historical-sociological perspective on
  Republican Revolution. See Social struc-
  ture theory
Hoffner, Jeff, 186
Holbrook, William, 7
Hold system, Senate, 10–11, 19n. 15
Hollinger, Joan Heifetz, 394, 412n. 12
Hoover Institution, 146
Hormel, James, 11
Hosansky, David, 162n. 32
Hostage taking, 6–7
House Democrats. See Democratic Party
House of Representatives
  106th Congress, 36–41
  1996 and 1998 elections, 30–36
  2000 elections, 41–43, 370–372
  czar rule era, 249–252, 338
  Democratic control of, 21–23

distributive hypothesis, 169–170
elections for, 67–95
"fingers of the chamber" hypothesis,
  169, 170, 179–180
gender gap in, 125–140
Gingrich as Speaker of, 25–30, 391
junior members vs. careerists in, 32–34
one-minute speeches, 224–226,
  241n. 21
partisan control 1994–2000, 21–44,
  341–342
party leadership in, 247, 343
polarization and centralization in, 265,
  267n. 15
post-reform, 260
power distribution in, 348–349
presidential activism and, 339–340
reapportionment/redistricting and, 33
Reed rules, 249–252
Republican challenge 1994, 23–25
retirements, 1998 elections and, 31
select committees, 172, 173–174
stalemate, fall 2000, 40
standing committees, 171
state representation hypothesis, 169
textbook, 339
twentieth century, 337–342
See also Elections
House Republicans. See Republican Party
Hughes, Thomas L., 319, 331n. 6
Huitt, Ralph, 18n. 3
Humphrey, Hubert, 160n. 8
Huntington, Samuel P., 305, 312n. 38,
  414n. 30
Hurley, Patricia, 266n. 5
Hutchison, Kay Bailey, 375
Hyde, Henry, 228

Ideology
  balancing, 72–73
  bicameralism and, 303
  legislative compromise and, 305–306
  PACs and, 102
  polarization and, 307
  representation and, 82–89
Impeachment proceedings
  Clinton, 28, 35, 36, 38, 48, 157, 323
  competitive seats and, 379
  conditional party government and, 370
  Johnson, 335
  Republican Revolution and, 403
Implementation vs. policymaking, 143

Incumbents
  1994 elections, 93n. 11
  2000 elections, 371, 372
  2002 elections, 373
  access-oriented PACs and, 110
  advantages of, 80–81, 94n. 23,
    144–145, 390
  committee assignments of, 176
  in competitive seats, 378–379
  constituent awareness of, 81–82
  Democratic, scandals and, 114
  district partisanship and, 78
  electoral selection and, 78, 80
  FECA and, 109
  fund-raising under FECA, 116
  House, 78–82
  ideological representation and, 84–85
  information on, 152
  insulation of, 145
  measuring advantages of, 149
  party affiliations and, 151
  personal vs. partisanship, 371–372
  retirement strategies of, 80
  weak challengers and, 80
Independent expenditures
  by PACs, 103, 112–113
  by party organizations, 106–107
Independent voters, 134
Independents, House election votes by, 69
Individualism, Senate, 2–4, 13–14
Individuals
  campaign financing by, 98, 99
  FECA and, 108
  PAC bundling contributions of,
    103–104
  soft money expenditures of, 116, 118
  spending under FECA, 115–116
Induced preferences, 155
Informational theory of committees, 182,
  191, 192, 198–201
  committee chair of majority party and,
    204
  predictions of, 213
  See also Seniority system
Inhofe, James M., 11, 304
In-kind contributions
  by PACs, 103, 111
  by party organizations, 106
Institutional Congress
  public opinion on, 58, 357
  public policy and, 302–303

Institutions, American political
  conditional party government and,
    265–266, 275–276
  public policy and, 302–304, 306
Interest groups
  campaign financing and, 98
  vs. citizenry preferences and goals, 159
  incumbent campaigns and, 109
  independent expenditures by, 151–152
  party politics and, 159–160
  post-industrial society, 401
  public opinion on, 57
  soft money expenditures of, 116
  twentieth-century Congress, 351
Internal Revenue Service, 104
International Relations Committee,
  House, 136
Interpretation, message, 230
Issue advocacy. See Advocacy ads; Message
  politics
Issue evolution, 284
Issue ownership, 222

Jackson, Henry, 160n. 8, 319, 321
Jackson, John, 162n. 30
Jacobson, Gary C., 44n. 11, 93n. 12,
  94n. 13, 121nn. 20, 21, 122n. 44, 141,
  146, 161nn. 15, 17, 290nn. 19, 22, 23,
  291n. 43, 364n. 7, 371–372, 388n. 12,
  413n. 16
  on activists, 274
  on voter party identification and ideolo-
    gy, 277–278
Jacony, Mary, 18n. 8
James, Henry, 297
Javits, Jacob, 319
Jeffersonian principles of congressional
  committees, 165, 166, 169–170, 182,
  183
Jefferson's Manual, 169
Jeffords, James M., 311n. 16, 378
Jenkins, Jeffrey, 188nn. 36, 38
Jewell, Malcolm, 154–155
Jillson, Calvin, 312n. 28, 412n. 6
Johnson, Andrew, 335
Johnson, Haynes, 414n. 32
Johnson, Lyndon B., 22
  coattails of, 71
  congressional criticism of, 318
  gridlock and, 293, 296
  policy conflict and, 382
  policy mood change and, 73
  unified government and, 354
Johnson, Nancy, 137, 140n. 16

Joint committees, 207–208
Jones, Charles, 363n. 3
Journal, House and Senate, 170–171
Judiciary Committee, House, 136, 288

Kahn, Kim Fridkin, 139n. 2
Kahn, Stephanie, 122n. 42, 123n. 56
Kaiser, Robert C., 332n. 18
Kamen, Al, 240n. 12
Kantor, Mickey, 324, 332n. 22
Karp, Jeffrey A., 94n. 13
Kasich, John, 37
Keeter, Scott, 93n. 10
Kelly, Sean Q., 311n. 9
Kennedy, Edward, 13, 237
Kennedy, John F., 22, 210, 296, 315, 317
Kent, Frank, 98
Kern, John, 259
Kernell, Samuel, 44n. 11, 93n. 12,
    121nn. 20, 21, 141
Kessler, Daniel, 155, 162n. 28
Kessler, David, 186
Key, V. O., Jr., 364n. 7, 413n. 17
Keystone. See *Congress—Keystone of the
    Washington Establishment* (Fiorina)
Kiewiet, D. Roderick, 242n. 38
Killian, Linda, 291n. 42
Kimball, David C., 65n. 22
King, David C., 64n. 4, 215n. 9, 242n. 44,
    328, 333nn. 33, 34, 35, 366n. 12
King, Gary, 94n. 14, 161nn. 12, 18
King, Rufus, 168
Kingdon, John W., 162n. 30, 305,
    312n. 40, 414n. 29
Kissinger, Henry, 326
Kitfield, James, 332n. 20
Klein, Joe, 414n. 32
Koh, Harold Hongju, 316, 330n. 1
Kolodny, Robin, 121n. 27
Koopman, Douglas L., 43n. 3, 414n. 33
Kostroski, Warren, 141
Koszczuk, Jackie, 43nn. 6, 9, 241n. 31
Kovenock, David M., 65n. 22
Kramer, Gerald, 121n. 20, 122n. 44
Krehbiel, Keith, 94n. 13, 161n. 24,
    188n. 18, 189nn. 42, 48, 215nn. 1, 2, 4,
    216n. 31, 311n. 18, 312nn. 29, 32,
    313n. 50, 364n. 6
    on discharge petition effects, 209, 212
    on floor and committee preferences,
        192
    on gridlock, 302

null hypothesis of, 156
on party conceptualization and mea-
    sures, 154, 155
preference outlier hypothesis test, 179
Kriz, Margaret, 44n. 22
Kroeger, Brian, 186, 187n. 4
Kuhn, Hartley, 186
Kuhn, Thomas, 413n. 26
Kull, Steven, 332nn. 17, 24, 25, 31,
    333n. 39
Kuntz, Phil, 19n. 14
Kyl, Jon, 202, 326–327

Labor PACs, 102, 103, 110
Lake, Anthony, 331n. 6
Lambro, Donald, 123n. 53
Lancaster, John, 332n. 30
Langbein, Laura, 121n. 13
Lawrence, Christine C., 242n. 48
Lawrence, Jill, 123n. 54
Lawrence, Robert Z., 64n. 4
Leach, James, 202
Lead PACs, 103
Leadership, party politics and. *See* Party
    leaders
Leadership PACs, 107–108, 115
Leadership styles, 246–248
League of Conservation Voters, 104, 117
Lee, Emery, 365n. 11
Lee, Frances E., 94n. 26, 183, 188n. 27,
    189n. 49
Lees, John D., 215n. 11
Legislative vetoes, 319
Legislators, career ambitions, gridlock
    and, 309
Legitimacy of Congress
    Nader's presidential bid and, 404
    post-industrialism and, 410–411
    Republican Revolution, 390, 401–402
Lehman, Edward W., 413n. 21
Levitt, Steven, 161n. 18
Lewinsky scandal, 114, 262, 323
    1998 elections and, 31, 35, 72
    Gingrich reliance on, 28
Lieberman, Joe, 388n. 9
Lindner, Carl, 118, 123n. 60
Linkage, message, 230, 231–232
Lipinski, Daniel, 240n. 8
Lipset, Seymour Martin, 64n. 2
Little, Thomas, 268n. 30
Livingston, Robert L., 28–29, 245,
    261–262, 288

Local elections, national parties and, 285–286
Logan, Anita, 121n. 27
Long Act, 120n. 7
Loomis, Burdett, 18n. 6, 152, 161n. 22, 364n. 7, 366n. 16
Lott, Trent, 7, 239n. 1, 402–403
　106th Congress, 36
　leadership role of, 245
　message politics and, 222, 236–238
　nuclear test ban treaty and, 326, 327
　as party leader, 151
　public debates and, 13
　on recess appointments, 11
　as Senate majority leader, 12–13, 264, 323
　soft money fund-raising by, 118
　trust in leadership of, 383, 384
Louisiana Purchase, select committees and, 174–175
Lowi, Theodore, 312n. 35, 366nn. 13, 15, 380, 388n. 17, 399, 413n. 20
Lugar, Richard, 319–320, 326

Mack, Connie, 378
Mackenzie, G. Calvin, 364n. 5
MacKuen, Michael B., 93n. 5, 312nn. 41, 42
Maclay, William, 166, 168
Macropartisanship, 69, 93n. 3
Madison, James, 167, 195, 294, 302–303, 355
Mager, Eric, 121n. 14
Magleby, David B., 120n. 8
Majority party
　advantages of, 290n. 35
　cartel theory, committees and, 194–195
　close seat distribution between parties and, 377
　congressional change cycles and, 396–397
　electoral mandate of, 301–302, 311n. 21
　heterogenous society and, 385–386
　individual reelection and, 283–285
　leadership of, 247
　message politics and, 226
　message priorities, 225, 233–234
　personal power quest and, 394–395
　preference homogeneity of, 275
　rule of, 336
　Senate, minority party and, 11–13

twentieth century, 353–354
　unity of, 336
　wins for, 336
Malbin, Michael J., 33, 150, 151
Maltzman, Forrest, 191, 215nn. 1, 7
Managed health care reform, 228, 229
Mandates, electoral, 301, 311n. 21, 371
Mann, Thomas E., 33, 93n. 10, 120n. 1, 122n. 28, 141, 150, 151, 413n. 16
Mansfield, Mike, 151, 159
Maraniss, David, 291n. 41
Marinucci, Carla, 161n. 21
Marriage tax penalty repeal, 233–234
Marshall, Bryan W., 291n. 36, 292n. 53
Marshall Plan, 315, 317
Marshall, William, 189n. 48, 215n. 1
Matsui, Bob, 325
Matthews, Donald, 18n. 2, 160n. 4, 364n. 4
Mayer, Kenneth, 366n. 13
Mayer, William, 365n. 9
Mayhew, David R., 19n. 25, 94nn. 14, 15, 142, 153–154, 160nn. 1, 5, 161n. 23, 215n. 1, 242n. 46, 310n. 5, 312nn. 37, 39, 313n. 43, 331n. 9, 394, 412n. 8, 414n. 29
　on candidate/representative motivation, 321
　on committee system, 191
　Congress: The Electoral Connection, 269–271, 272, 275, 289nn. 1, 3, 5, 290nn. 6, 7, 8, 9, 10, 15, 16, 18, 291nn. 30, 31, 292n. 47
　on gridlock, 295
　on policy mood, 305
McCain, John, 13, 17, 159, 381
McCarthyism, foreign policy and, 317
McClure, Robert D., 64n. 1
McConachie, Lauros G., 167–169, 170, 187nn. 6, 15, 188nn. 16, 17, 25, 26, 34
McConnell, Mitch, 7
McCormack, John, 151, 159, 382
McCubbins, Mathew D., 43n. 1, 154, 189n. 48, 215n. 8, 216n. 35, 240n. 5, 242n. 38, 266n. 4, 291nn. 30, 37, 364n. 6, 387n. 6
　on majority caucus preferences, 194
　partisan theory of, 284
　on Speaker's scheduling powers, 212
McDermott, Monika, 139n. 9
McIver, John P., 94n. 26
McMillan, James, 253, 256

Media
  on Gingrich's role in Republican Revo-
    lution, 391
  policy battles in, 12
  Senate process and, 2–3
Medicare reform politics, 159, 217–218
Member PACs, 107–108, 115
Members of Congress
  conditional party government and,
    273–274
  vs. Congress, 52–53
  Fenno's concentric constituencies
    theory for, 274
  Fenno's goals theory for, 273
  Mayhew's goals theory for, 269–270
  resources and activities of, 149–150,
    390
Menefee-Libey, David, 365n. 10
Merchant Marines and Fisheries Committee, 140n. 15
Mercurio, John, 122n. 47
Message politics, 217–243
  issue ownership and, 222
  legislative process and, 226–238
  majority party message priorities, 225,
    233–234
  message formulation for, 219–226
  minority party message priorities, 225,
    227–230
  one-minute House-floor speeches and,
    224–226, 241n. 21
  other major bills, 225, 234–236
  prescription drug benefits and,
    217–218
  Senate, 236–238
  setting priorities for, 221–226
  shared message priorities, 225,
    230–232
Meyer, Joseph S., Jr., 333nn. 33, 34, 35
Meyers, Jan, 137, 140n. 14
Michel, Bob, 24, 382
Michelson, Charles, 98
Microeconomic perspective on Republican
  Revolution. See Social choice theory
Midterm elections
  1994, 24–25, 34, 91, 130, 136,
    145–146, 408–409
  1998, 31, 34–35
  losses in, 71–73
  party organization strategies for,
    105–106
Miller, Gary J., 215n. 10, 312n. 31

Miller, Warren E., 93nn. 2, 10, 160n. 3
Mills, Wilbur, 328
Minority party
  agendas, Senate process and, 7–8
  committee seats for, 205–206
  congressional change cycles and,
    396–397
  message priorities, 227–230
  proportional representation on commit-
    tees, 206–207
  Senate, majority party and, 11–13
Mitchell, George, 263
Mnookin, Robert H., 215n. 9
Moderates/moderation
  aggressive assertion of party ideology
    and, 384–385
  close seat distribution between parties
    and, 377, 378
  gridlock and, 300–301, 308
Moe, Terry, 365n. 12
Money
  in campaigns, 87, 150–151
  in political corruption and local payoffs,
    161n. 19
  See also Hard money; Soft money
Money, Jeannette, 215n. 10, 312n. 31
Monroe, James, 366n. 14
Mood, policy, 70–71, 73, 93n. 5
Moore, Michael K., 313n. 56
Morella, Constance, 137
Morone, James A., 310n. 3
Morris, Robert, 168
Moynihan, Daniel Patrick, 327
Mullins, Brody, 44n. 18
Mundo, Philip A., 121n. 16
Murphy, James T., 242n. 46
Myerson, Roger B., 195, 196, 212–213,
  215n. 10

Nader, Ralph, 404
NAFTA (North American Free Trade
  Agreement), 76–77, 315, 320, 321, 324
National Committee for an Effective
  Congress, 111
National Election Studies, University of
  Michigan, 52–53, 88, 278, 290n. 22
National Federal of Independent Business,
  PAC, 111, 116
National Journal, 38, 329
National Political Awareness Tests
  (NPATs), 92

Nationalization of congressional elections, 146, 151–153, 161n. 13
NATO expansion, 323
Nelson, Candace J., 120n. 8
Nelson, Garrison, 186
Neumann, Mark, 115
Neustadt, Richard E., 330n. 2
New Deal era, 335, 340, 350
    Democratic Party cohesiveness and, 385–386
    Senate politics and, 344
    unified government and, 354
New Jersey primary 2000, 285–286
New York Times, 277, 295, 301
Nickles, Don, 221, 236
Niemi, Richard, 337, 347, 348, 365n. 10
Nitschke, Lori, 242n. 41
Nitze, Paul, 319
Nixon, Richard M., 315, 318, 321, 340, 353, 402
Nominations, filibuster of, 7
Nonconnected PACs, 110–111
Nongermane amendments, 7–8, 12–13, 264
Normal vote, 93n. 2
North American Free Trade Agreement (NAFTA), 76–77, 315, 320, 321, 324
North, Oliver, 331n. 7, 372
Norton, Elizabeth Holmes, 140n. 12
Nowels, Larry, 332n. 18
Nuclear test ban treaty, 315, 325, 326–327
Nunn, Sam, 320
Nye, Joseph S., Jr., 64n. 4

Oberstar, James, 235
Obey, David, 238–239
O'Halloran, Sharyn, 365n. 12
O'Hanlon, Michael E., 332n. 19
O'Leary, Michael K., 65n. 22
Oleszek, Walter J., 19nn. 16, 17, 43n. 5, 209, 216nn. 12, 13, 14, 19, 27, 239n. 3, 240nn. 7, 11, 241nn. 21, 34, 242nn. 39, 40, 45, 394, 412n. 12
Omnibus appropriations bill, 1996, 148
O'Neill, Thomas P. "Tip," 145, 161n. 20, 216n. 17
    Democrats' regional/ideological diversity and, 382
    Gingrich provocation of, 24
    prior service of, 203
    as Speaker, 260, 261

One-minute speeches, House, 224–226, 241n. 21
Open-seat candidates, 110
    2002 elections, 373–375
    fund-raising under FECA by, 116
    party affiliation of women, 129–131
    party-switching in 2000 elections, 372, 388n. 13
Operation Breakout, 117–118
Oppenheimer, Bruce I., 18nn. 4, 8, 43n. 1, 44n. 21, 94nn. 21, 26, 121n. 14, 140n. 11, 141, 161n. 18, 183, 188n. 27, 189nn. 48, 49, 215n. 6, 243n. 53, 268n. 30, 290n. 12, 292n. 52, 311n. 12, 366nn. 12, 13, 387n. 7, 388nn. 11, 18, 412n. 13, 413nn. 18, 25, 414n. 31
Ordeshook, Peter C., 215n. 10
Oren, Karen, 413n. 22
Ornstein, Norman J., 18n. 5, 33, 65n. 11, 141, 150, 151
Ortiz, Daniel R., 120n. 1, 122n. 28
Ostrom, Elinor, 366n. 17
Oversight Committee, House, 206

Page, Benjamin I., 333n. 39
Panama Canal, 315
Paradigm shifts, governing, 405–406
Parker, Glenn R., 152, 394, 412n. 12
Participatory management, 264
Participatory moderation, 300
Particularistic politics, 350
Partisanship
    alternate types of, 370
    Senate, growth of, 3–4
    Senate, legislative outcomes and, 13, 346
    Senate, minority prerogatives and, 7–8
    traditional party government and, 368
    See also Bipartisanship; Polarization
Party and Constituency: Pressures on Congress (Turner), 154
Party Government (Schattschneider), 298
Party government theory, 387n. 6
    of committees, 191, 194–195, 198–201, 213
Party identification, variations in congressional approval by, 59
Party leaders
    campaign financing and, 107–108
    changes in, 44n. 14
    election results and power of, 246–247
    House, 23, 26–27, 327

member behavior and, 156
message politics and, 217–223,
226–227, 241n. 26
non-message legislation and, 234
policy conflict and, 380–382
Senate, 11–13
trust in, 382–385
See also Committees, House
Party organizations
as analytic units, 153–154
campaign financing and, 105–107
committee chair of majority party and,
204
divided government and, 298
gridlock and, 306
hard money/soft money ratio requirements, 122n. 49
influence, conceptualization and measures of, 154–156
leadership committees, 207
messages of, 219–221, 222
national, resurgence of, 151
polarization of, 299–300, 307–308
public evaluation of messages of, 222,
223
soft money expenditures of, 116, 117
spending under FECA, 113–115,
122n. 48
state-based, 368
strong, electoral interests and, 282–283
See also Seniority system
Party organizations, congressional,
245–268
1890 to 1910, 248–259
1990 to 2000, 259–265
House of Speakers Gingrich and
Hastert, 259–263
House of Speakers Reed and Cannon,
249–252
late 1998, 245–246
leadership power shifts, 246–248
public opinion on, 53–57
reelection and, 269–270
reforms in, 271–272
regional divisions in, 373, 374
Senate of Aldrich and Allison,
252–259
Senate of Dole and Lott, 263–265
See also Conditional party government
Party secretaries, Senate, 9–10
Party vote, 336
Patman, Wright, 204

Patterson, James T., 388n. 19
Patterson, Samuel C., 19n. 17, 65n. 22,
188n. 24, 215n. 6, 216n. 26, 268n. 30
Peabody, Robert, 18n. 5
Perks, congressional, 81
Perot, Ross, 295, 331n. 12
Persian Gulf War, 315, 320
Personal power, as goal of politicians, 394
Peters, Ronald M., Jr., 18n. 8, 43n. 4,
363n. 2, 413n. 25
Peterson, Paul E., 187n. 3
Petrocik, John R., 222, 240n. 18
Phillip Morris, 117
Pianin, Eric, 312n. 36
Pitney, John J., Jr., 43n. 3, 412n. 1
Pivot, relevant filibuster, 313n. 50
Platt, Orville, 252, 256
Plebiscitary politics
congressional action and, 359–360
congressional consent and, 359
polls and, 358, 360
Plungis, Jeff, 242n. 47
Poage, W. R., 204
Polarization, 299–300
2000 elections, 367, 371–372, 384
in conditional party government model,
247, 248, 279
congressional decision making and, 359
congressional–presidential relationships
and, 354–355
in Cooper-Brady thesis, 246, 248
foreign policy and, 319–322, 327–329
institutional context and, 265
in Senate of Aldrich and Allison,
253–257
twentieth-century end, 336
Policy
close seat distribution between parties
and, 377
commitments to, 152
conditional party government and,
286–288
conflict structure of, 380–382
context, gridlock and, 304–306, 309
direction search, House elections and,
73–77
implementation vs. making of, 143
indicator, House elections and, 67–68
informational advantage of committees
and, 191
issue ownership and, 222
media battles over, 12

Policy (*cont.*)
　objectives, party leaders' power and, 248
　See also Presidency
Policy mood, 70–71, 73, 93n. 5
Political action committees (PACs)
　access oriented, 103
　challenger campaigns and, 110
　corporate PACs, 101–102
　independent expenditures by, 151–152
　individuals and, 108
　labor PACs, 102, 103, 110
　lead PACs, 103
　leadership/member PACs, 107–108
　precursors, 98
　SUN PAC Decision and, 102
Political change indicators, 348
Political parties. *See* Party organizations
Pollack, Josh, 330
Pollock, James K., 216n. 15
Polls
　allocable costs for, 121n. 25
　message influence of, 221
　party organizations' use of, 106
　plebiscitary politics and, 358, 360
　seat maximization goals and, 105
Polsby, Nelson W., 19n. 24, 216nn. 15, 23, 399, 413n. 19
Poole, Ithiel deSola, 160n. 3
Poole, Keith T., 83, 94n. 20, 189n. 43, 266n. 6, 267n. 12, 280, 290n. 29, 311n. 14
Populists, 256
Pork barrel spending, 82, 148, 283
Post-industrial society, 400–401, 406–408, 411
Post Office Committee, 140n. 15
Potter, Trevor, 120n. 1, 122n. 28
Powell, Lynda W., 122n. 34
Power
　centralized vs. decentralized vs. collegial, 246
　internal distribution of, 346–351
　See also Personal power
Preference-based theories
　party membership and, 155, 162n. 27
　See also Message politics
Preference conflict, 275
Preference homogeneity, 275, 369
Preference outlier, committee as, 192, 193–194
Prescription drug benefit issue, 217
Presidency, 293–313
　divided government and, 297–299

　Executive Office of the, 340
　expansion in roles and responsibilities of, 346, 355–357
　gridlock and, 293–296
　institutional context, 302–304
　leadership indicators, 337
　nineteenth-century independence of, 335–336, 352
　policy context impact and, 304–306
　public policy trends, 306–309
　twentieth-century leadership, 336–337, 338, 346, 351–355
Presidential elections, House elections and, 71
Preston, Mark, 312n. 34
Price, David, 414n. 34
Price, H. D., 364n. 7
Primary elections, 368
Prins, Brandon C., 291n. 36
Prinz, Timothy, 160n. 1
Professionalization of politics, 119
Progressive era, 305, 338, 343
Project Vote Smart, 73, 74, 92, 93n. 9
　House candidates 1996 election survey, 279
　on ideological representation, 82–83, 84
　National Political Awareness Test results, 75
Public Citizen, 325
Public debates, Senate process and, 12–13
Public money for campaigns, 99
Public opinion, 45
　on Congress vs. other governmental components, 49–52
　demographic variations in, 58–63
　gridlock and, 310, 312n. 43
　on institutional Congress, 58, 357
　on interest groups, 57
　on member of Congress vs. Congress, 52–53
　on parts of Congress, 52
　political beliefs/expectations changes, 346
　on political parties in Congress, 53–57
　variations in, 46–49
Public policy. *See* Policy
Public preferences, 155
"Public purpose" eras, 305

Quay, Matthew, 257, 258

Race, party loyalties and, 284
Rae, Nicol C., 240n. 7, 363n. 2, 413n. 25
Ragsdale, Lyn, 337, 364n. 5, 365n. 10
Rainbow Coalition, 105
Rakove, Jack A., 310n. 2
Ranney, Austin, 311n. 7
Rational choice analysis of legislative
  behavior, 142
Rawls, W. Lee, 240n. 5
Rayburn, Sam, 382
Reagan, Ronald W., 3, 145, 315
  1984 attack ads, 161n. 20
  coattails of, 71
  Democratic Party and, 341
  deregulation by, 158
  foreign policy defeats, 321
  foreign policy of, 319, 320
  policy mood change and, 73
  Senate composition under, 89
  Reagan Revolution, 407
Realtors PAC, 111
Reapportionment and redistricting, 33,
  42–43, 373
Reciprocity system, Senate, 2
Reed, Thomas Brackett, 21, 205, 249
Reed rules, 249–252
Reelection, conditional party government
  and, 269–270
Reinventing government, 407–408
Reorganization Act (1946), 32
Reporting requirements, FECA, 99
Representation, 45
  Framers on, 356–357
  House elections and, 87–89
Representatives, Roll Calls, and Constituen-
  cies (Fiorina), 142
Republican National Committee, 105, 221
Republican Party
  1994 midterm elections, 24–25, 130,
    136, 145–146, 322–323
  2000 elections, 41–43, 370–376
  Conservative Opportunity Society and,
    23–25
  constructive partisanship and, 386–387
  electoral advantage for women candi-
    dates of, 133–134
  House election votes by, 69
  ideological representation by, 85–86
  incumbents, 1994 elections, 93n. 11
  industrial-era politics of, 402
  internal divisions in, 369–370
  open seat candidates of, 130–131

Operation Breakout, 117–118
policy conflict and, 380–382
reapportionment politics and, 367
religious right and, 159–160
Senate Steering Committee, 256–257
southern conservatives' influence in,
  380–381
special elections/switched party affiliations and, 44n. 10
spending preferences of, 74–75
spending under FECA, 114–115
See also Republican Revolution
Republican Party, House
  104th Congress (1995–1996), 283
  106th Congress (1999–2000), 36–41
  candidate ideology, 76
  Caucus, 249
  cohesiveness of, 249
  committee assignments by, 287
  committee composition and, 135–138
  electoral mandate of, 1995–1997, 302
  electoral objectives of, 262–263
  gender gap and, 125–127
  government shutdown and, 27
  issues preferences of, 75–77
  legislative accomplishments, 37
  as majority party, 67–68
  message politics of, 220, 232
  policy mood change and, 73
  Reed rules and, 252
  women candidates for, 127, 128–129
  See also Gingrich, Newt
Republican Revolution, 389, 390–393
  governing difficulties and, 390–391
  "great man" theory of, 391–392
  legitimacy of Congress and, 390,
    401–402, 410–411
  member resources and, 390
  social choice theory and, 392, 393–399
  social learning theory, 392, 404–410
  social structure theory, 392, 399–404
Reputation
  of party, 16
  of senators, 15
Responsible parties doctrine, 297–298
Retirements, House, 31, 34, 37, 43, 80
Retirements, Senate, 372
Retrospective voting, 142, 143, 413n. 17
Revealed preferences, 155
Revenue Act, 98–99
Rich, Andrew, 215n. 8, 216n. 32
Rieselbach, Leroy, 414n. 28

Riker, William H., 241n. 35, 412n. 7
Ripley, Randall B., 216nn. 26, 28, 364n. 4
Rivlin, Douglas G., 121n. 18, 122n. 52
Robb, Charles, 372
Robinson, George Lee, 164, 168, 186n. 2,
  188n. 22
Rockman, Bert, 412n. 3
Rogers, Lindsay, 364n. 4
Rohde, David W., 18n. 5, 43n. 1, 141,
  154, 160n. 1, 162nn. 31, 33, 216n. 34,
  240n. 16, 242n. 39, 266nn. 2, 3, 4,
  267n. 26, 289n. 2, 290nn. 11, 13, 27,
  291nn. 30, 33, 34, 35, 36, 44, 46,
  292nn. 49, 50, 53, 364nn. 6, 7, 367,
  387nn. 3, 4, 5, 7, 394
  on conditional party government, 247,
    376, 385
  on party leaders and member behavior,
    156, 157
Roll-call votes, 77, 272
Romer, Thomas, 216n. 20
Roosevelt, Franklin D., 21, 340, 352, 354
Roosevelt, Theodore, 338, 343, 352
Rosenthal, Howard, 83, 93n. 8, 94n. 20,
  189n. 43, 216n. 20, 266n. 6, 267n. 12,
  280, 290n. 29, 311n. 14
Rosentiel, Thomas, 292n. 51
Rostenkowski, Dan, 235, 328
Roth, William, 378
Rothman, David J., 267nn. 11, 16, 364n. 4
Roukema, Marge, 137, 138
Rovner, Julie, 240n. 4
Rudolph, Thomas J., 121n. 14
Rules Committee, House, 260
  majority leadership and, 271–272,
    282–283, 287
  party representation on, 206
  southern Democrat-Republican coali-
    tion on, 339
  Speaker's control of, 337–338, 340
  women on, 135, 136
Rules Committee, Senate, 256
Rumenap, Staise, 123n. 55
Rundquist, Barry S., 216nn. 15, 23
Ryan, Edward G., 120, 123n. 66

Safe districts, 81, 143
Safire, William, 310n. 4
Salaries, congressional, 58
Salaries for the President and Vice Presi-
  dent, Senate Select Committee on, 167
Salmore, Barbara, 364n. 7

Salmore, Stephen, 364n. 7
SALT II treaty, 319
Scharpf, Fritz, 366n. 17
Schattschneider, E. E., 298, 311n. 8
Schick, Allen, 241n. 32
Schickler, Eric, 215n. 8, 216n. 32, 249,
  267nn. 7, 9, 23, 413n. 20
Schlesinger, Arthur M., Jr., 305, 312n. 38
Schmitt, Eric, 332n. 27
Schneider, William, 64n. 2
Schneier, Edward, 162nn. 25, 26, 29
Schroeder, Pat, 137
Schwartz, Bernard, 118
Scott, Hugh, 151
Scott, James M., 331n. 8
Scowcroft, Brent, 326
Seat maximization goals, 105
Seat status, women candidates for House
  seats and, 127–128
Seelye, Katharine Q., 48, 65n. 5
Select committees
  data on, 171
  distributive hypothesis, 169, 178
  "fingers of the chamber" hypothesis,
    170, 179
  of historical Congresses, 164, 168,
    179–180, 183
  House, 171–172
  salaries for the president and vice presi-
    dent, 167
  semi-standing, 168, 173
  Senate, 171, 172, 179–180, 181
Sellers, Patrick J., 18n. 8, 19nn. 17, 18,
  221, 240nn. 11, 15, 16
Semi-standing select committees, 168,
  173
Senate, 1–19
  2000 elections, 370–371, 372–376
  of Aldrich and Allison, 252–259
  bloc voting, 344
  close seat distribution between parties
    in, 378
  committee system, 4–5, 166–169
  competitive seats in, 379
  contemporary legislative process, 4–11
  deal making in, 15–17
  distributive hypothesis, 169–170
  of Dole and Lott, 263–265
  effectiveness, 17–18
  "fingers of the chamber" hypothesis,
    169, 170, 179–180, 181
  vs. House elections, 89–91

individualist, partisan, development of, 2–4
legislative outcomes in, 13–14
majority and minority parties, 11–13
majority leader, 5–11
party leadership in, 247, 343–344
polarization and centralization in, 265, 267n. 24
post–Civil War, 253–255
power distribution in, 348–349
president pro tempore, 254–255
vs. president's foreign policy, 323–324
Rule 14, 168
rules on getting legislation to floor, 8–11
rules' uses, 5–8
select committees, 173, 174
six-year term, 91
standing committees, 171
state size and, 94n. 26
textbook, 344–345
twentieth century, 342–346
See also Elections; Filibusters
Seniority system
caucus ratification and floor ratification, 204
caucus slates subject to chamber vote, 204–205
chamber transferability, 202–203
chamber vs. committee, 197, 202
committee chairmanship and, 339
committee theories and, 197, 202–205
continuous vs. total service and, 197, 202
House, Democratic control and, 22
House restrictions on, 23
House, women and, 135, 137–138
parties and, 204, 270–271, 272, 283, 286, 287–288
Senate, 2, 256
subcommittees and, 203
Sensenbrenner, James, 44n. 14
Separation of powers, 368
Serafini, Marilyn, 313nn. 45, 46
Shafer, Byron, 312n. 24
Shapiro, Robert Y., 333n. 39
Shaw, Malcolm, 215n. 11
Shea, Daniel, 122n. 29, 365n. 10
Sheppard, Burton, 291n. 32
Shepsle, Kenneth A., 166, 187nn. 2, 3, 11, 12, 188n. 36, 412n. 7
Sherman, John, 319, 351

Shogan, Robert, 310n. 1
Shugart, Matthew S., 215n. 11
Shuster, Bud, 148, 235–236, 239
Sides, John, 267n. 23
Silverstein, Gordon, 366n. 13
Simard, Michele, 139n. 4
Simendinger, Alexis, 44n. 16
Sinclair, Barbara, 18nn. 1, 3, 5, 19nn. 13, 17, 21, 22, 43n. 1, 139n. 1, 154, 157, 188n. 24, 216n. 26, 240n. 20, 241nn. 23, 24, 242nn. 42, 49, 266n. 4, 267n. 26, 268n. 32, 337, 363n. 2, 364n. 4, 365n. 10, 366n. 16, 394, 412n. 9
Skladony, Thomas W., 187n. 2
Skowronek, Stephen, 413n. 22
Slaughter, Louise, 136, 140n. 13
Small Business Committee, 140nn. 15, 17
Small states, committee system evolution and, 169, 183
Smith, James, 403
Smith, Renée, 337
Smith, Richard, 241n. 33
Smith, Steven S., 18nn. 1, 7, 8, 11, 43n. 2, 188n. 24, 216n. 22, 241n. 22, 242n. 49, 266n. 4, 267nn. 10, 13, 14, 17, 268n. 30, 399
Smith, Virginia, 135
Snowe, Olympia J., 311n. 16, 378
Snyder, James, 155, 162n. 28, 279, 290nn. 25, 26
Social choice theory, 392, 393–399, 410–411
congressional change cycles and, 396–397
personal power quest and, 394–395
Republican Revolution as cycle of, 397–399
Social learning theory, 392, 404–410, 411
process of, 405–406
Republican Revolution as phase of, 408–410
responding to post-industrialism, 406–408
Social Security reform politics, 159, 231–232, 237
Republican Revolution and, 409
Social structure theory, 392, 399–404, 411
legitimation crisis, 401–402
post-industrial transition, 400–401
Republican Revolution and, 402–404
Societal change indicators, 347

Soft money
estimates of, 122n. 39
expenditures of, 116–118
FECA and, 104–105
party organizations' use of, 107
requirements for national party organizations, 122n. 49
Somoza, Anastasio, 319
Sorauf, Frank J., 120n. 1, 121n. 11, 122n. 28, 388n. 15
Southern Democrats, 22–23
becoming Republicans, 280, 290n. 28, 341, 380–381
House, 339, 340
Senate, 344–345
Speaker of the House
centralized power under, 249, 337–338
organizational context for power of, 29–30
Rules Committee assignments and, 271–272, 340
seniority system and, 202
term limits for, 25–26
See also specific Speakers
Specter, Arlen, 311n. 16
Speeches, PACs and, 104
Spending limits, campaign, 99
Spending, partisan preferences on, 73–75
Spooner, John, 252, 256
Staff, congressional
1957–1999, 150
public opinion on, 58
Standing committees
Clay's use of, 166
data on, 171
House, 171–172, 183–185
House, policymaking expertise and Democratic control, 22
House, women on, 135, 136–137
member expertise specialization and, 168
message politics and, 226
Senate, 164, 167, 171, 172, 185–186
Stanger, Jeffrey D., 121n. 18, 122n. 52
Stanley, Harold, 337, 347, 348
State legislatures, party representation on committees of, 206
State representation hypothesis, 169, 177–178, 179, 182–183
States, election law control by, 368
Steering and Policy Committee, House Democratic, 271, 286–287

Steering Committee, Senate Republican, 256–257
Stern, Robert M., 331n. 10
Stevenson, Richard W., 313nn. 52, 53
Stewart, Charles, III, 172, 186, 187n. 4, 188nn. 36, 37, 38, 40, 279, 290nn. 25, 26
Stimson, James A., 70–71, 93nn. 4, 5, 141, 284, 291n. 39, 312nn. 41, 42, 313n. 51
Stokes, Donald E., 93nn. 2, 10, 160n. 3
Stonecash, Jeffrey, 376, 388n. 14
Strøm, Kaare, 215n. 11
Stubbs, Walter, 171, 188n. 35
Subcommittees
Bill of Rights, 272
gatekeeping power of, 211–212
seniority in, 203
Sullivan, Paul, 311n. 15
Sundquist, James L., 152, 161n. 22, 267n. 7, 311n. 9, 313n. 47, 363n. 3, 364n. 7, 365n. 9
Sun Oil Company, 102
SUN PAC Decision, 102
Supermajorities, Senate, 17–18, 302, 304, 308–309
See also Filibusters
Surveys, message influence of, 221
Susskind, Lawrence E., 215n. 9
Sweet, Martin, 188n. 39
Swenson, Peter, 364n. 7
Swift, Elaine E., 168, 181, 187n. 2, 188nn. 21, 31, 189n. 47, 413n. 20
Swing ratio, 93n. 1

Talbert, Jeffrey, 155, 162n. 28
Talent, James, 44n. 14
Taylor, Andrew, 268nn. 29, 34
Taylor, Paul, 121n. 18
Term limits
public opinion on, 58
Republican Revolution and, 409
by Republicans of committee chairs, 32, 36–37, 38, 42
for Speaker of the House, 25–26
Textbook House, 339, 340, 350
Textbook Senate, 344–345, 350
Thayer, George, 120nn. 2, 4, 5, 6
Theis, John, III, 364n. 5, 365n. 10
Theiss-Morse, Elizabeth, 65nn. 6, 10, 12, 13, 14, 16, 18, 366n. 14, 412n. 2
Theriault, Sean, 313n. 56
Thomas, Martin, 95n. 27

Thomas, Sue, 139nn. 1, 2
Thurber, James A., 413n. 27
Ticket-splitting, changes in, 146–147
Tiritilli, Eric, 65n. 15
Trade agreements, 324–325
Trade PACs, 110, 112–113
Transportation and Infrastructure Committee, House, 235
Truman, David B., 414n. 30
Truman, Harry S., 315, 317, 353
Tsebelis, George, 215n. 10, 312n. 31
Tullock, Gordon, 215n. 5
Turner, Julius, 154, 155, 162nn. 25, 26, 29
Turnout, by ideologues, 278
Twentieth-century Congress, 335–366
    assessment of, 355–363
    candidate-centered politics, 350–351
    change in, 346–355
    Congress, president, and public, 355–358
    congressional decision making, 358–361
    decision-making patterns, 336–346
    electoral system changes and, 346, 349–350
    federal government expansion, 346, 350, 355–357
    future prospects, 361–363
    House of Representatives, 337–342, 347–349
    interest groups, 351
    internal power distribution, 346–351
    president's role in, 351–355
    Senate, 342–346, 347–349
Tyler, Tom, 64n. 1

Udall, Morris, 160n. 8
Ujifusa, Grant, 331n. 13
Ullman, Richard H., 333n. 39
Unanimous consent agreements (UCAs), 8–9, 10–11, 236, 345
Unified government, 298–299
    bicameralism and, 303–304, 308
    gridlock and, 308
    moderates in, 301
United Nations, 317, 323
Unlimited debate. See Extended debates, Senate
Uslaner, Eric, 366n. 16

VandeHei, Jim, 122n. 46
Vandenberg, Arthur, 322

Van Dongen, Rachel, 123n. 60
Vanishing marginals analysis, redistricting and, 142
Velazquez, Nydia, 140n. 17
Veterans Affairs Committee, House, 137
Veto points, congressional, 196, 209–210
Vickers, Geoffrey, 404, 413n. 26
Victor, Kirk, 44n. 17
Vietnam War, 318
Volden, Craig, 302, 312n. 29, 313n. 49
Vote, personal vs. partisan, in House contests, 77
Vote swing
    changes in, 146, 148
    ratio, 93n. 1
Voters
    congressional change cycles and, 397
    gender gap among, 125
    ideological representation and, 83–84, 88–89
    knowledge of candidates/representatives, 77, 92, 93n. 10
    median models of party competition, 156
    mobilization of, 104, 107
    party ties of, 81
    policy/party preferences of, 277–278
    women candidates and, 134
    See also Activists; Constituencies, concentric
Voting Rights Act (1965), 23
Vucanovich, Barbara, 136

Walker, Jack, 364n. 7
Walton, Hanes, Jr., 364n. 7
Warner, John, 326, 327
War of 1812, select committees and, 171–172, 175
War Powers Resolution (1973), 318–319, 321, 322, 356
Warshaw, Shirley Anne, 337, 365n. 10
Washington Establishment, 143–144, 158–159
Washington Post, 257–258
Watergate, FECA and, 99
Watts, J. C., 220
Wayman, Frank, 121n. 13
Ways and Means Committee, House, 135, 217–218, 271, 322
Weingast, Barry R., 189n. 48, 215n. 1, 394, 412n. 11

Weisberg, Herbert, 19n. 17, 141,
161n. 16, 387n. 6, 413n. 14
Weiskopf, Michael, 291n. 41
Welfare reform, message politics and, 224
Wesberry v. Sanders (1964), 142
West, William, 313n. 56, 365n. 12,
366n. 13
White, Leonard, 363nn. 1, 3
Whitten, Jamie, 288
Wilcox, Clyde, 120, 121nn. 15, 16,
122nn. 31, 34, 139nn. 1, 2
Wildavsky, Aaron, 316, 330n. 1
Wills, Garry, 310n. 2, 312n. 30
Wilson, Rick K., 312n. 28
Wilson, Woodrow, 22, 259, 340, 399,
413n. 20
on Congress, 215n. 6, 216n. 29, 335,
363n. 1
on congressional committees, 208
leadership of, 338, 352
League of Nations and, 317
on responsible (political) parties,
297–298
Senate majority leader and, 343
unified government and, 354
WISH List, 112, 122n. 43
Withdrawn coattails, 72
Wolbrecht, Christina, 64n. 3, 65n. 6,
313n. 57

Wolfensberger, Donald R., 243n. 53,
366n. 14
Wolfinger, Raymond E., 394, 412n. 12
Wolfram, Catherine, 161n. 18
Women. *See* Gender gap
Wood, Gordon S., 310n. 2
Workload, committees and, 173
World Trade Organization, 322, 324, 325
World War II, 335
Wright, Fiona M., 388n. 7
Wright, Gerald C., 74, 91, 94nn. 19, 21,
22, 26, 95nn. 27, 28, 141, 414n. 28
Wright, James, 24, 151, 247, 260, 382,
403

Yankelovich, Daniel, 333n. 39
Year of the Woman (1992), 125, 126
Young, Bill, 232, 235
Young, Garry, 215n. 6, 311n. 12, 336,
364n. 6, 370, 388n. 8
Young, James Sterling, 187n. 2, 399,
413n. 20

Zeckhauser, Richard, 215n. 9
Zelikow, Philip D., 64n. 4
Zingale, Nancy, 311n. 22